HANDBOOK
of
AMERICAN
FOLKLORE

Inta Gale Carpenter, *Associate Editor*

Elizabeth Peterson, Angela Maniak, Assistant Editors

With an Introduction by
W. EDSON RICHMOND

HANDBOOK
of
AMERICAN
FOLKLORE

EDITED BY
Richard M. Dorson

INDIANA UNIVERSITY PRESS · *Bloomington*

Library of Congress Cataloging in Publication Data
Main entry under title:

Handbook of American folklore.

Includes bibliographies and indexes.
1. Folklore—United States—Addresses, essays,
lectures. I. Dorson, Richard Mercer, 1916–1981.
GR105.H36   1982   398′.0973   82-47574
                                       AACR2

1 2 3 4 5 87 86 85 84 83

The preparation of this book was supported by a
grant from the Research Materials Program of the National
Endowment for the Humanities (# RT-*0623-76) from 1976 to 1982.

ISBN 0-253-32706-7

Contents

PART III. METHODS OF RESEARCH   359

PART IV. PRESENTATION OF RESEARCH   459

Preface
Richard M. Dorson

Americans have demonstated a keen interest in their record as a civilization. They consult such majestic reference works as the *Dictionary of American Biography*, the *Literary History of the United States*, the *Dictionary of American English on Historical Principles*, *Notable American Women*, and similar compendiums of the nation's annals. The Bicentennial celebration witnessed an outpouring of publications reviewing the two hundred years of the American experience. Yet a large and vital portion of that experience remains largely in the shadows. The guild of historians recognizes and deplores the elitist emphasis among their practitioners and seeks to write history from the bottom up. But their efforts to date have met with little success. What we know about our civilization is largely the high culture, the prominent leaders, the visible achievements.

Folklorists can offer resources and strategies to fill this large gap in our self-knowledge, and to this end the *Handbook of American Folklore* makes its appearance. The folk culture appraised by the *Handbook* stands in one sense opposed to the elite culture. We may contrast sophisticated literature with folk literature, formal religion with folk religion, studio art with folk art, medical science with folk healing, classical music with folk music, documentary history with folk history, and so on in a continuing list of oppositions. Yet the two realms often intersect. In some ways we are all folk: we all participate in traditional rituals, customs, observances, celebrations; we all engage in folkloric modes of expression, such as proverbs, colloquialisms, figures of speech, slurs, curses, jokes, greetings. The folk, we have learned, are not to be equated with the peasants but with the people. Lincoln and Mark Twain, the two most American figures in our politics and our literature, masterfully exploited the vein of home-grown folk humor.

If we would fully comprehend the American experience, then we must include the substantial folk elements in that experience. The collection and study of folklore in the United States have lagged far behind Europe, where folkloristics is a recognized subject in most countries, but at least we show signs of catching up. Four universities in this country now offer the doctorate in folklore—Indiana University, the University of Pennsylvania, the University of Texas, and the University of California at Los Angeles. Over half the fifty states have, in the past few years, appointed state folklorists. Congress established an American Folklife Center in the Library of Congress in 1976. In the Smithsonian Institution a vigorous Folklife Unit sponsors an annual American Folklife Festival on the Mall and other folkloric activities. The American Folklore Society, which seemed on the verge of extinction when I began attending its meetings in the 1940s, now manages six concurrent sessions running four days and nights at its yearly convention. We might glance at one of its programs to gain an idea of the present scope and range of folklore interests.

This typical program contained 106 sessions involving two to six participants in each session. They covered, geographically, North and South American, Asian, African, and European folklore; regionally, folklore of the South, Southwest, Midwest, Northeast, and West; ethnically, folklore of Cajuns, Croatians, Cubans, Czechs, Finns, Germans, Irish, Italians, Jews, Mexicans, Poles, Serbs, and Ukrainians resident in the United States; occupationally, the folklore of cowboys, railroaders, tavernkeepers, policemen. Popular topics, reappearing in half a dozen or more sessions, included Festivals, Folk Speech and Language, Foodways, Games, Humor, Maritime Folklore and Fishing, Religion, Social Struggle, Urban Folklore, and Women, this last theme entering thirteen sessions. Curiously, the old standbys of Witches and Ghosts turned up in only two sessions and Superstitions in just one. The disciplines of history, literature, and psychology especially made their presence felt, and the emerging field of popular culture vied with them. Photography and film were subjects discussed in four sessions during the day and presented in five evening sessions. Films dealt with such matters as death row in a Texas prison, love songs, garlic, Mississippi farmers, a woodcarver, a basketmaker, a tattooer, and Irish folk musicians in Chicago. For the first time in its history the society observed a panel on sign language folklore of the American deaf community. Three sessions dealt with Science Fiction. More sessions grappled with Modern Folklore than with Rural Folklore.

From this panorama of themes one can gain some notion of the many directions in which folklorists today are probing into American life. Folklore specialists are increasingly in demand as consultants and speakers in schools, museums, libraries, county and state parks, and historical societies. The study of folklore now embraces the city as well as the countryside, the office as well as the home, the factory as well as the farm. No segment of human activity and human relationships—prisons, hospitals, sports teams, the armed services, science laboratories, theater companies, fast food restaurants, families, organizations, and so on—falls outside the folklorists' purview. Through folklore we learn much that is otherwise concealed about the human condition. The *Handbook of American Folklore* sets forth the present state of knowledge of this burgeoning subject and points the way to further advances.

1980

Introduction
W. Edson Richmond

It has long been a cliché that there are more definitions of folklore than there are folklorists. For at least a decade after *The Standard Dictionary of Folklore, Mythology and Legend* was published in 1949, it was common for folklorists to initiate articles and books with the statement that The Standard Dictionary included twenty-one different definitions of the word *folklore*, and to note that these definitions were composed by the then most prominent and influential American scholars involved in the field: Stith Thompson, Archer Taylor, MacEdward Leach, Erminie Voegelin, Katharine Luomala, et al. Moreover, many scholars who searched beyond the entry for "folklore" itself found the number of definitions expanded interminably. Thus the concept of folklore in the 1950s and the immediately succeeding decade was nebulous.

The discipline had grown out of a study of medieval literature married, albeit without canonical sanction, to certain anthropological studies. This resulted in a synthesized definition of *folklore*: popular tradition, the French *tradition populaire*, modified by the creative imagination and the more-or-less retentive memory of the folk, though just who the folk were was moot. Such an emphasis on tradition served to maintain the nineteenth-century precept that folklore was a preserved relic and therefore implied that folklore was a vestigial element in culture, an interesting and revealing key to the past, but of little or no significance for modern society.

The word *folklore* is, of course, as abstract a term as are the words *love, liberty,* and *literature.* Its precise meaning lies in the mind of its definer, not in the thing itself, which is both as real and as unreal as any of the concepts mentioned above. The coiner of the word, William Thoms, wrote in an article published in the *Atheneum* in August 1846 that he intended the word to be employed as "the generic term under which are included traditional institutions, beliefs, art, customs, stories, songs, sayings, and the like current among backward peoples or retained by the less cultured classes of more advanced peoples." In brief, in the slightly more than one hundred years between Thoms's creation of the word and the publication of *The Standard Dictionary of Folklore, Mythology and Legend* there was little change in its meaning. Since that time, however, there have been great changes, and the word *folklore* has come to be defined by some as whatever folklorists are interested in. And these things, according to Barre Toelken, are items and events, recurrent forms "of local, dynamic human expression."

In this evolutionary process two fundamental elements of the definition developed by Thoms and his descendants have been severely modified: tradition and a restricted concept of the word *folk*. No longer do folklorists confine their studies solely to those things which are perpetuated orally or by precept; no longer do folklorists concern themselves only with backward classes or the less cultured classes of more advanced peoples. They are, instead, concerned with those things which appear and, most importantly, reappear in varied forms whenever and wherever human beings interact.

In one sense, however, today's folklorists cling to an aspect of tradition: they are concerned, as Toelken says, with "recurrent forms." Folklorists no longer insist that an item that they study have its roots in the past—either the remote or the immediate past—but they do insist that the hallmark of folklore is change, and that for anything to be considered an item of folklore it must exist in more than one form. It must show itself to be a variation on a theme. If, for example, a tale has all of the characteristics of a folktale, it still cannot be called a folktale unless there is more than one text, and these texts must differ in some way from each other. Thus, for an item to be folkloristic it must show some form of continuity; it must be recognizable as itself while at the same time it must reflect the effect of imprecise— imprecise, not necessarily imperfect—transmission. Thus, in one way at least, modern American folklorists are concerned with tradition. They deal with recurrent forms.

On the other hand, today's concept of the folk differs considerably from that of nineteenth-century scholars such as Thoms. No longer do folklorists restrict the concept of folk to "backward classes," whatever they may be. Instead, they are concerned with human interaction on all levels of society, be the participants illiterate, unlettered, or highly educated. Folklorists today are concerned with creations that result from the relationships of human beings within a particular cultural matrix. Folklorists today recognize that the same sort of forces operate in urban, educated societies as in rural, isolated, unlettered societies.

Indeed, it is possible to say that one of the principal forces that binds various members of particular societal groups to each other is their folklore. It is important to note, however, that the primary binding force is something else: the group are dwellers in a particular geographic area, or they are committed to a special way of life—nomadic or static—or occupation—farming, fishing, millworking, teaching, healing, et al.—or they share an interest in a special ritual—religion, fraternal organization—or avocation—model building, collecting, jogging. Out of such interests and situations grows their folklore, which then serves to emphasize the relationship of each individual member of the group to each other. Like the cant of con men, the jargon of educators, and the slang of youth, it is a means of identification. To understand it is a ticket of admission; to use it is a shibboleth.

But to say that folklore is the "items and events, recurrent forms of local dynamic human expression," found in such groups is really not very helpful. One needs to know precisely what these recurrent items and events are. Thus folklorists, who incidentally form the same kind of group as do farmers, physicians, and philologists, are dragged back again and again, often kicking and screaming, to the same kind of genre approach employed by Thoms. The principal differences are that today folklorists no longer insist upon oral tradition as the only method for the transmission of folklore or upon a restricted definition of the word *folk*. Moreover, they often disagree, sometimes vociferously, about how these items, these genres, should be approached.

In general, it is safe to say, however, that folklorists are interested in such genres as tales and songs, in beliefs and customs, in rituals and religions, in proverbs and speech, in jokes and anecdotes, in implements and buildings; in short, they are interested in those things which are produced in such a way that they are pleasing to the group and contribute to their understanding of one another.

In the beginning, folklorists were primarily interested in these things for their own sake. For them the text was the thing. Schooled in the study of literature, they centered their attention upon folktales and ballads and approached these materials in the same way they approached the manuscripts of medieval epics, romances, and chronicles. They concerned themselves with the evolution of texts; they often predicated an original, an *ur-form*, which could be reconstructed by collating all known texts, and though they soon came to realize that such a reconstruction was improbable if not impossible, the construction of such life-histories, even with inevitable omissions and the invention of lost variants, became their *raison d'être*. A basic corollary to this interest in the life-history of texts and the searches for their origins was a concentration on highly structured and substantially complex materials. Folktales and legends were studied at the expense of jokes and anecdotes; ballads were studied at the expense of the more ephemeral lyric folksongs; proverbs were analyzed at the expense of everyday speech; and, for the most part, such modern components of folklore as custom, belief, and material culture were relegated to footnotes.

A case in point is Lowry Charles Wimberly's book *Folklore in the English and Scottish Popular Ballads*. First published in 1928, this book was an expansion of the author's earlier doctoral dissertation, *Death and Burial Lore in the English and Scottish Popular Ballads*, and was intended to show that popular balladry "contains a world of early and primitive thought—this though the ballads represent different cultural strata and derive their sources from medieval literature, from chronicles, from classic sources, and from tradition." In effect, Professor Wimberly's book is an extended footnote to Francis James Child's *The English and Scottish Popular Ballads*, an attempt to substantiate the assumption that ballads were the product of antiquity and of the folk by documenting and explicating the customs, beliefs, and occasionally the references to material items that appear in these texts.

In such an approach, which was not confined to ballads alone, there was an important dichotomy. On the one hand, there were complex texts and artifacts thought to be worthy of preservation (and sometimes reconstruction), and on the other hand, there were those component elements which, if understood correctly, served to prove the folkloric nature of those things of which they were a part. From today's point of view, folklore was thus enveloped in folklore, but the principal interest of American folklorists lay in the major constructs, which were studied for much the same reason as one studied literature. Although it was recognized that the aesthetic of such material differed from that of "sophisticated" literature (exactly how it differed has never been made clear), it was felt that folklore in the sense of tales, legends, ballads, and the like was worthy of study for its own sake. As a result, therefore, the study of folklore gained a foothold in a large number of departments of English literature throughout the United States, with primary attention centered on the traditional, popular ballad, but with an occasional nod given to the folktale.

It is noteworthy, for example, that subsequent to the publication of the first volume of Child's *The English and Scottish Popular Ballads* in 1882 scarcely a single anthology of English literature was published that did not include a sampling of ballads—usually, and we now know inaccurately, placed somewhere late in the section devoted to the literature of the middle ages. It is perhaps also noteworthy that these same anthologies omitted all references to folktales, legends, proverbs, and their ilk, and that most anthologies of American literature did not even include ballads. The emphasis was thus on those things which seemed both old and familiar, upon those things which had the appeal of apparent antiquity and could be approached with the tools and methods already developed for the study of literature. Such an attitude still holds a strong position in the study of folklore in the United States, for a very high proportion of American folklorists are attached to departments of English, but as this *Handbook* demonstrates, the study of folklore has broadened its base, developed its own methodology, and become a discipline in its own right. Though the text may still be the thing, it is looked at in a variety of ways and for a number of very different reasons.

Indeed, the study of texts (or in the case of material folklore, artifacts) is basic to folklore. Texts and artifacts are the concrete manifestation of the lore of the folk. It is clear, however, that texts need not be studied for their own sake alone. They may also be examined and analyzed for the illumination that they throw upon the particular folk groups that perpetuate them. Even before the coining of the word *folklore* and the birth of folkloristics, scholars who dealt with such materials were at least subconsciously aware of this fact. Thus there came slowly to be a *sub rosa* shift from an emphasis on the texts to an emphasis on the folk.

This shift in emphasis was in the air of the times. Just as Alfred Kinsey, the founder of the Institute for Sex Research, shifted his attention during these same years from fruit flies to human beings when he realized that his oblique approach to the study of sexuality was no longer necessary and when he took to heart Francis Bacon's dictum that the proper study of mankind is man, so folklorists shifted their attention from the literary merits of folkloric texts to an analysis of what these texts could tell about mankind in general. Thus, though texts remained the essence of their studies, the purpose for looking at them shifted. They ceased being looked at as remnants of ancient popular literature and attitudes and were instead examined as material revelatory of living, popular attitudes. Texts came to be examined for what they could tell about various societal groups. Moreover, their manner of presentation and their context became as important as the texts themselves.

There were a number of reasons for this shifting focus: the spirit of the times, in which egalitarianism was the mode, the gradual development of the American Folklore Society as a completely independent organization, and the emergence of departments of folklore or their equivalents within the academic systems of the United States and Canada. The first made it possible for incipient folklorists to recognize that they need not concentrate their attention upon "backward peoples . . . or the less cultured classes of more advanced peoples"; the second brought together scholars from what had previously been disparate disciplines into an integrated whole; and the third lent the aura of academic acceptance to a study that had previously been viewed as something fit only for dilettantes and hobbyists.

About the first, it is scarcely necessary to comment. The idea of "backward peoples" became repugnant in America, and it became impossible for American scholars to maintain that there were "less-" or "more-cultured" classes. Thus, having once accepted the principle of equality as an absolute, American folklorists found the way open to look for the same sort of things among the middle and upper classes (never mind the contradiction in logic) and among the urban and suburban as their European colleagues and their academic forefathers had looked for among the peasantry and regionally isolated societies. And having looked, they found. The evolution of the American Folklore Society and the development of the study of folklore in American colleges and universities is, however, worthy of more extended comment.

The American Folklore Society was founded in 1888 with Alcée Fortier as its president *pro tempore*, Francis James Child as its first elected president, and William Wells Newell as the first editor of the *Journal of American Folklore*. Reminiscences of Professors Stith Thompson and Archer Taylor, who were acquainted with scholars who knew both Newell and Child, suggest that these two men effectively represented the folkloric interests of their era. Child, himself a child of the people (his father was a cooper), was a rhetorician, a medievalist, and a generalist in the study of English literature. As incidental to his definitive edition of the English and Scottish popular ballads—and their American variants—he brought together at Harvard, where from 1851 to his death in 1896 he was one of the first professors of English literature and rhetoric, one of the largest collections of folklore in the United States if not in the world. Like Professor Child, William Wells Newell was a student of literature. Though he was an ordained minister, he spent most of his life as a private scholar and made a significant reputation as both a student of the Arthurian legend and as a poet. But unlike Child, Newell was as interested in the burgeoning discipline of cultural anthropology as he was in literature, and he was apparently the catalyst that amalgamated the two disciplines by bringing the principal scholars in each together in the American Folklore Society.

The avowed purpose of the society in its initial proposal, here slightly condensed and paraphrased, was to establish a journal of scientific character designed (1) for the collection of the fast-vanishing remains of folklore in America, namely: (a) relics of old English folklore (ballads, tales, superstitions, dialect, etc.); (b) lore of Negroes in the Southern states of the Union; (c) lore of the Indian tribes of North America (myths, tales, etc.); (d) lore of French Canada, Mexico, etc.; and (2) for the study of the general subject and publication of the results of special studies in this department. Obviously, when this proposal was concocted, students of what William Bascom was to designate as "the verbal arts" were in the ascendant. But anthropologists were soon to exert a significant influence, and the society was to concern itself with living traditions rather than simply with relics.

From its very beginning, the American Folklore Society emphasized the international aspects of folklore. Unlike the folklore societies of many other nations, which centered their attention upon the lore of their own countrymen, the American Folklore Society was conditioned by the concept of America as a melting pot, as a fusion of many cultures and nationalities. As a consequence, most members of the society felt it appropriate to investigate the lore of other nations as well as of their own, for to understand these lores was a necessary foundation for understanding their migrant forms. The result of this was a journal truly international in its content and a society that might more appropriately be called the Society of American Folklorists than the American Folklore Society.

It is important to note, moreover, that the roster of editors of the *Journal of American Folklore* is almost equally balanced between anthropologists and students of literature. Indeed, in the entire history of the *Journal*, only one editor, the late Richard M. Dorson, can be identified primarily as a folklorist, and even he retained a close and important relationship with a department of history throughout his highly productive career. In general, it is also true that in the roster of presidents, secretaries, treasurers, and secretary-treasurers of the society, a balance, which appears to be largely fortuitous, was maintained between anthropologists and students of literature. But it was the editors who determined the content of the *Journal*, and it was the *Journal* that served as a proselytizing device for the society.

It is interesting to compare the contents of the first issue of the *Journal of American Folklore* with the contents of a very recent issue. In the initial issue there was an article about the diffusion of popular tales, another about voodoo worship and child sacrifice, an article concerned with the counting-out games of children, a description of Lenape conversations, a collection of Onandaga tales, and a study of the songs and dances of the Kwakiutl. The issue for April–June 1981 contained the following items: "Quaker Tradition and the Paintings of Edward Hicks: A Strategy for the Study of Folk Art," "Traditional Agricultural Practices in the Arkansas Highlands," "Toward a Kpelle Conceptualization of Music Performance," "Oral Performance: Narrative and Ritual in Tamil Tradition," and "Personal Names in Traditional Ballads: A Proposal for a Ballad Onomasticon." What has changed here during the intervening hundred years is not what is looked at but the manner in which these things are examined. Anthropology married to literature resulted in the birth of a new approach to the lore, although the gestation period was rather extended.

Since, especially in its early years, the membership of the American Folklore Society consisted primarily of faculty members from various universities, the society and the journal reflected their research interests and what they taught in their classes. To a large extent, this is still true, but there has been a change. Although they are few in number, departments devoted solely to folklore have been established in both the United States and Canada. As a consequence, a significant number of scholars have been trained primarily as folklorists even though their eventual employment has traditionally been, and probably will continue to be, in departments of literature and anthropology. The students in these departments of folklore have been able to concentrate, to an extent their predecessors never could, upon folklore as folklore and not upon folklore as an aspect of anthropology or English literature. With the establishment of distinct departments of folklore in some major universities, the discipline was able to show that it had something of value to offer not only to the academic world but also to the sum total of human knowledge.

There can be no doubt that the prime mover of this development was Professor Stith Thompson of Indiana University. Trained by, among others, George Lyman Kittredge of Harvard University, Stith Thompson was first and foremost a student of international literature, but with the unwavering support of Herman B Wells, president of Indiana University, he was able to focus his attention upon the folktale, a *Type-Index of the Folktale*, which grew out of the work of Antti Aarne's studies in Finland, and his own magnum opus, the *Motif-Index of Folk-Literature*. More important, however, than any of these for the world of folklore studies today was his development of a folklore program at Indiana University that became the foundation on which all folklore departments in the United States and Canada were based, most of them originally staffed for the greater part by graduates of the Indiana University program.

In 1942 Professor Thompson was able to establish a series of summer institutes of folklore at Indiana University that attracted students and faculty members from colleges and high schools throughout the United States. The institutes were staffed by the members of the Indiana University faculty involved with folklore and by visiting lecturers and scholars including occasional foreign guests. Nothing unusual in the 1970s and 1980s but a phenomenon in the 1940s, these institutes were the seed whence grew the folklore program at Indiana University. Moreover, in 1950 Professor Thompson was able to expand a regular summer institute into an international seminar attended by the leading folklorists of Europe and a number of their students as well as nearly fifty of the most prominent American folklorists. The results of this conference, described in *Four Symposia on Folklore* (Bloomington, Indiana: Indiana University Press, 1953) were to prove that folklore could be an established academic discipline in North America as well as in Europe and to foster close relationships between American folklorists themselves and with their European colleagues.

The emphasis at Indiana University in its folklore program was placed upon international folklore, especially the folktale and the ballad. Moreover, in its initial phases, it was primarily a graduate program (though it later developed first an undergraduate minor and then an undergraduate major). It drew its faculty from various departments in the humanities and social sciences, especially from English, German, the classics, Spanish, and anthropology. Its students were to go forth to staff incipient programs at the University of Pennsylvania, where MacEdward Leach had already built a firm foundation for the study; at the University of Texas, where Mody C. Boatright, following in the steps of his predecessor, John Lomax, was developing a study of regional folklore; at the University of California at Los Angeles, where Wayland Hand was soon to become the moving force; and, in time, at the Memorial University of Newfoundland, where Herbert Halpert was eventually to establish a major department.

In addition, the Indiana University folklore program was to supply scholars to the University of Kentucky, Western Kentucky State University, the University of Kansas, Kansas State University, the University of New Mexico, the University of Utah, the University of California at Berkeley, the University of Florida, and many other colleges, some of which developed independent departments of folklore and some of which absorbed Indiana folklorists into departments of literature and anthropology.

The acceptance of folklore as an academic discipline in American and Canadian universities did not mean, however, that the discipline immediately gained the status accorded to other humanistic studies. The question "Why study folklore?" often arose and still arises. In answer to this question, it should be noted that how people react not only to world-shaking events but to events of purely local significance or events of solely personal importance is as consequential to the evolution of thought and to the understanding of subsequent events as are the events themselves. What people think has happened, what people say has happened, conditions history. For example, a careful examination of historical "facts" shows that Richard Coeur de Lion was an inept, undiplomatic, and inefficient king of England, while his brother John, oft maligned by historians, his subjects, and their descendants, was actually a highly efficient ruler. But for various reasons, Richard captured the public fancy and lives on in folklore as the defender of the common man, while John, who really established parliamentary democracy in England, lives on in infamy. Thus folklore, in this case the attitudes and traditions of the common people, conditioned popular history and eventually even the attitudes and opinions of historians themselves. Similarly, historians agree that George Washington never really established his attachment to truthfulness by confessing to hacking down a cherry tree, and Lincoln never walked a number of miles to return a penny; yet the myth of American heroes, the folklore of America, has it otherwise. To understand a people, it is necessary to understand their folklore.

What is true of races and nations is true of smaller groups as well. A reader of the manuscript for this *Handbook* questioned the value and significance of studying and analyzing the obscene jokes of various segments of society. Though an oft-repressed and subliminal aspect of our culture, its repertoire of "dirty" jokes, of racist jokes, is certainly far more revealing of popular attitudes than are the pronouncements of politicians. Moreover, since to be called a part of folkore these jokes must be recurrent forms, an analysis of their evolution often discloses the shifting attitudes of a group far more vividly than do studies of political action.

The question about collecting obscene jokes, here briefly and only partially answered, was meant to be critical and was really intended to query the value of collecting any kind of folklore. A number of scholars have answered this question by replying that the study of folklore is, in a sense, the study of history from the bottom up. But this answer creates a dichotomy that is really not valid. The study of folklore is important not because it is concerned with the attitudes, beliefs, customs, legends, songs, tales, proverbs, expressions, and material artifacts of the "common" man, but because it is concerned with those things as they are created, transmitted, and perpetuated by everybody, by all mankind, a group from which the elite are certainly not excluded. Though all people do not have a heritage of some aspects of folklore, people in all walks of life do have a heritage of folklore in general.

As the *Handbook of American Folklore* illustrates, this heritage is vast. Each person is enveloped by it. It conditions everyone's actions and attitudes as a person, as a family member, as a member of a group—bagwoman, fisherman, farmer, lawyer, physician, teacher, philatelist, yachtsman, con man, drug peddler, druggist, et al.—as a resident in a village, city, district, state, nation, and linguistic or cultural enclave, and as one of the human race. In John Donne's words, ". . . no man is an *Iland*, intire of it selfe; every man is a peece of the *Continent*, a part of the *maine.*" And each person identifies with his own particular "part of the maine"— and these parts may be many—by the special characteristics of the folklore in which he or she is a participant.

The *Handbook of American Folklore* is intended to suggest what can be learned about one's folkloristic heritage by showing much of what has been studied in America and by suggesting ways in which folklore can be investigated further. It is both an anthology of scholarly articles about all the major genres with which folklorists are concerned and a guide for future investigations.

Divided into eight major sections, each with its own introduction written by the late Professor Richard M. Dorson, who conceived this volume and saw it nearly to fruition (indeed, no significant changes were made after Professor Dorson's death), the *Handbook* reflects the entire scope of American folklore studies. Under the heading of "Topics of Research," its first five divisions—American Experiences, American Cultural Myths, American Settings, American Entertainments, and

American Forms and Performers—are devoted to exempla, to studies of particular aspects of American folklore, articles of the sort found in scholarly journals. Basically these sections illustrate specifically the results of field—or, occasionally, library—investigations; they are practical exhibits, collections, or explications of collections. The next section, which includes five articles, deals with the various ways in which folklore, once collected, may be interpreted. The next section consists of twelve essays descriptive of various ways in which research may be conducted, practical hints for everything from how to arrange for and conduct an interview to how to select and operate audiovisual devices. And the final section includes twelve articles indicative of the many ways in which folkloristic research may be presented to the scholarly world and to the general public. The reader thus moves logically from what amounts to a definition of American folklore by example, to an analysis of how to interpret such specific materials, to how to go about collecting folklore, and, in conclusion, to a series of discussions of the practical problems involved with the transmission and preservation of the results of research.

The *Handbook of American Folklore* is meant to be read, not simply to be consulted. It is not an encyclopedia or dictionary primarily, though it is possible that students and neophyte folklorists may use it in that way; it is, rather, an introduction to American folklore as it has been studied in America. There are few, if any, references to either European folklore or the study of folklore in Europe, although there are many articles devoted to "ethnic" folklore, by which is meant the perpetuation of traditional materials that originated in areas outside of North America but that evolved in ways peculiar to this continent.

The *Handbook of American Folklore* is, in other words, a guidebook. It is intended to show established scholars, students, and the general public what the discipline of folkloristics is all about. One who reads it from cover to cover will be well prepared to participate in the investigation of folklore, whether it be in a particular geographical area, among a specialized group, or at a particular period in history. In putting this book together, Richard M. Dorson, with the assistance of Inta Gale Carpenter, has made it possible for the study of American folklore to become the vital force necessary for understanding the American people.

HANDBOOK
of
AMERICAN
FOLKLORE

PART I TOPICS OF RESEARCH

American Experiences

Some American experiences that have produced folklore derive from historical circumstances and some from social and institutional structures. The colonial experience, the frontier experience, and the immigrant/ethnic experience have loomed especially large in American history, and each has generated legends, ballads, sayings, folk heroes, folk customs, and other traditions reflecting those chapters. I have discussed these themes in "A Historical Theory for American Folklore," and in the present section, William Piersen, Thomas D. Clark, and Barbara Kirshenblatt-Gimblett supply abundant details on their folkloric implications. Piersen illustrates with hard-won selections from early printed sources the possibilities of recapturing the folk culture of blacks transplanting roots in colonial New England. In a panoramic survey, Clark considers the folktypes and folkways linked to the westward-moving frontier. White Indian fighters and trailblazers, stump politicians, pioneer farmers, circuit-riding preachers, herbal doctors, riverboatmen, railroaders, forty-niners, and cowboys on successive frontiers evolved into folktypes in the popular imagination. Kirshenblatt-Gimblett offers a field guide outline of leading questions for interrogators of immigrants to probe the patterns of their momentous adventure in the New World and record the folk history of the transplantation. She then considers a second body of traditions, the Old World folklore adapted to American life. Finally, she looks at the folklore of ethnic blends and mixes, which results from the convergence of nationality groups in the United States. We see in these essays several ways of examining the folklore content in segments of American history.

The westward movement created a gallery of folk heroes and folktypes who passed from campfire yarns into popular literature into the mass media. They fell into three basic molds: the tall-talking braggart, who first emerged in the canebrakes of Kentucky and Tennessee and enjoyed later incarnations as the riverboatman on the Ohio, Mississippi, and Missouri rivers and as the mountain man in the Far West; the laconic trailblazer, Indian fighter, and scout; and the outlaw or badman who fought the power structure on behalf of the folk. Münchausen figures, who developed their own legends by weaving tall tales about feats of hunting, shooting, fishing, and fighting, sometimes merged with the frontier boaster; Davy Crockett in the canebrakes and Jim Bridger in the Rockies awed tenderfeet with their yarns and also set tales circulating about their comic behavior when confronted with civilization. In sharp contrast was the Daniel Boone–Leatherstocking figure, skilled in woodcraft and Indian lore but little given to talk. Gary Cooper in the film *The Plainsman* exemplifies the type in its western incarnation. This taciturn, quick-draw marksman and horseman never entered cycles of oral legends, but reappeared on all levels of literature, and in films and television, as an immutable folktype, whether woodsman, plainsman, or mountain man. In one ghoulish variation, Liver-Eating Johnson, a solitary trapper in the sierras, ate the livers of Crow Indians in revenge for their killing of his Blackfoot wife. The account of the Liver-Eater does seem to have endured in oral tradition. Buffalo Bill spent more of his years traveling in his Wild West rodeo show than in the West. The public does not distinguish between genuine and pseudo folk heroes, but the folklorist finds it necessary to examine closely the credentials of highly touted frontiersmen.

The experience of two peoples living at first involuntarily under the American flag deserves special attention, since they have contributed magnificently to the storehouse of American folklore. Anthropologists in the nineteenth and twentieth centuries recorded substantial repertoires of Indian tribal narratives, but they never related them to the mainstream culture, nor considered it their mission to do so. Lankford reviews the limited number of theoretical studies that deal with stylistic, thematic, structural, cultural, and cognitive aspects of Indian tales. Only a few folklorists, such as Stith Thompson, Alan Dundes, and Barre Toelken, have explored the interaction of Indian with European, African, and white American tales and anecdotal stuff, and no one has attempted to collect in depth the post-contact narratives growing out of white-Indian relations; these somehow seem out of bounds, falling between two traditions, but should greatly intrigue the American folklorist. Colonial writings of settlers, travelers, and chroniclers are filled with anecdotes about Indians. In later periods such historical events as the removal of the Cherokees on the Trail of Tears, or Custer's Last Stand at the battle of the Little Big Horn, or the ghost-dance religious revival culminating in the Sioux uprising of 1890 have given rise to legend-cycles, which await folkloric analysis. In her suggestive piece complementing Lankford's, Elaine Jahner does connect a traditional tribal tale to the conditions of modern American life.

Afro-Americans have lived within the dominant culture, and under slavery conditions developed creative verbal and musical forms. These are described by Adrienne Seward and Ronald Smith, speaking for a new perspective in folkloristics, the interpretation of Afro-American folklore by black folklorists, who have organized their own exclusive African-American Folklore Association, which publishes annual proceedings. They frankly espouse the position that they can appreciate and interpret black folklore more effectively than white scholars. Their premises, stated by both Seward and Smith, hold to the African origins of Afro-American folklore, folk music, and material culture, a thesis first advanced by white scholars and still supported by almost all of them. Ironically, nineteenth-century racist scholars took for granted the African connection as an obvious link between the low culture of savages and the low culture of slaves. After the publication of Melville Herskovits's *The Myth of the Negro Past* (1935), documenting the history of West African civilizations, white and black scholars stressed African origins and continuing African elements in black folklore as evidence of the rejection of the dominant white society by black people in the

United Sates, even under slavery conditions. The argument becomes translated into a kind of manifesto of black cultural independence. Lawrence Levine supports this argument throughout his extensive study of *Black Culture and Black Consciousness* (1978). I take the position that the African connection steadily diminishes with time and has virtually disappeared in contemporary collections of folktales told by blacks, such as Daryl Dance's *Shuckin' and Jivin'*. The debate can be read in the essays printed in *African Folklore in the New World* (1977), edited by Daniel J. Crowley. I also believe that folklorists should not limit their work to their own ethnic or regional group. A white Episcopal clergyman, Harry M. Hyatt, completed the greatest feat of collecting in Afro-American folklore, the five volumes of *Hoodoo - Conjuration - Witchcraft - Rootwork*, a work, not cited by Levine, that does not lend itself to the interpretation of black folklore as an expression of black pride and defiance. I do feel that black folklore represents the richest single strand of American folk traditions, but, as Dance discovered, the traditions may be self-degrading as well as self-exalting.

Essays in this section consider historical experiences—colonization, the westward movement, immigration—and the special experiences of Native Americans and Afro-Americans, as they have given rise to folk traditions. The Native American experience may be divided into precontact, contact, reservation, and pan-Indian periods. The Afro-American experience may be divided into the periods of the trans-Atlantic crossing in slave ships, slavery, quasi-freedom, and the civil rights movement. Their folklore can be organized to reflect these periods. Lankford has worked out a model for determining precontact strata of Indian tales, and Levine has distinguished between antebellum and postbellum Afro-American folklore.

Are there any other large blocks of American experience that might be added here? The war experience affected Americans deeply during the Revolution, the Civil War, two World Wars, and the war in Viet Nam, and a substantial body of military folklore undoubtedly developed in connection with all these wars, some of which has been collected, especially the GI lore of World War II. But the military experience interrupts rather than accompanies the march of American life, and for most of our history we refused to support a standing army. We might speak of the agricultural experience, during the two and a half centuries when we were primarily a nation of farmers, and of the industrial experience that has shaped our lives for the past century. We could marshal the folklore of farmers and factory workers, but their folklore belongs with traditions of occupations rather than of historical movements. For our purposes, the concept of "experience" requires more specificity than the broad rubrics of agriculture and industrialization can muster. So I believe we have identified the main American experiences productive of legend and lore.

William D. Piersen

Colonizing A New Society

Folklorists interested in the American colonial era have not chosen an easy period for research. They cannot do their own collecting in the field, nor can they scrutinize the field collections of other professionals. Indeed, colonialists are limited to examining a variety of printed materials published long ago by men and women who, for the most part, had no intention of collecting or recording "folklore" at all.

Despite these drawbacks, potential "collectors" should not be discouraged. Colonial folklore is not a rare specialty for dusty scholars of antiquarian interests, nor has it all been pored over many times. No barrier of imposing "definitive" volumes bars the way to would-be researchers; instead, the studies that exist clearly advertise the promise of colonial folklore as a research field. What is now needed is an imaginative consummation of the long-promised union of colonial folklore and history, a romantic endeavor that has not progressed beyond the coy flirtations of a half-dozen scholars.

At first glance the "informants" for the colonial folklorist seem an unlikely lot. Most are printed sources that, by cover at least, appear as out of place in a folklorist's repertoire as several of Boston's *grandes dames* might be at a "down home" church revival. But behind the printed text lies a folk culture that reflects the era of American colonization in a way few documents can match.

Primary materials from the colonial period are constantly surprising in their folkloric content. Cotton Mather's *Magnalia Christi Americana*, for example, sounds like an over-stuffed and pretentious treatise, void of popular tales.[1] But Mather was a man of his age; he did not consider the materials we now call folklore out of place in his scientific and theological speculations. Thus, within the *Magnalia*, readers will find tales of war and witchcraft, passion and humor from out of the colonial oral tradition. The age of colonization relished a good yarn, and in the seventeenth century tales were all the more believable and exciting because the supernatural was, indeed, natural. The Puritan God thundered across the heavens like a modern superhero in final battle with the evil forces threatening the New World, providentially intervening into the affairs of daily life to warn his people and to punish wrongdoers.

The culture of the American colonies was based on face-to-face oral communication—despite growing numbers of books, newspapers, pamphlets, broadsides, and almanacs. In fact, much of what appeared in print derived from or reflected current oral communications. Not surprisingly, then, colonial folklore scholarship exploits this interrelationship between oral and printed sources.

The Salem witchcraft trials have been the most studied and the most romanticized aspect of colonial folklore. George Lyman Kittredge was the first folklorist to examine the role of witchcraft beliefs as they related to the Salem epidemic of 1682. In *Witchcraft in Old and New England* he demonstrates the continuity between witchcraft beliefs in Europe and America and characterizes the Massachusetts disorder as a minor occurrence—small pickings—in the English-speaking world's long tradition of prosecuting witches. Since witchcraft beliefs in themselves were too frequent to explain the excesses of Salem Village, Kittredge was led to anticipate contemporary scholarship by offering a functionalist explanation of the Salem incidents. Through a knowledge of comparative folklore, Kittredge deflated the parochial assumption that Salem symbolized a cancerous marrow of American Puritanism, just as his work punctures a contemporary fascination with the exotic West Indian woman, Tituba, as the dark genius behind the black arts of Salem. Indeed, no work better points out the vital interrelationship between the study of folk belief and the understanding of general American culture in the age of colonization. Nonetheless, modern scholars might usefully update Kittredge's work by carrying the study of witchcraft into more southern areas, and by adding materials from the African, Afro-American, and Native American traditions.

Another study of seventeenth-century America, Richard M. Dorson's *America Begins*, uses folkloristic materials to capture the exuberance, credulity, and coarse strength that energized the colonizing spirit. Few anthologies of early American writings better display that core paradox of American colonization—the image of the New World as both Garden of Eden and Howling Wilderness. Readers acquainted with Dorson's recent work in American folklore may be surprised to find no tale type or motif indexes in this early study and very little folkloristic analysis of the relationship between the printed sources and the oral traditions of the day. Instead, the strength of the collection is in the honesty of its handiwork. Avoiding the hokey, sanitized charm of the popularizers, Dorson's selections are earthy and humorous, violent and bizarre. They reflect the colonial grain unvarnished by the highlightings of filiopietism and stripped of the pasteled hues of "Americana."

Percy G. Adams examines similar materials from early colonial travel accounts in his *Travelers and Travel Liars 1660–1800*.[2] In the best tradition of oral storytelling, early travel writers borrowed themes, images, and sometimes whole stories shamelessly from one another. But Adams's aim is not to see the marvelous exaggerations as part of a long tradition of travelers' tales; instead, he sees their use as part of a plan of "deception for the sake of money, pride, or a point of view." Judging these travelers by twentieth-century standards is helpful in separating fact from fiction, but makes the exaggerations seem squalid and mendacious. Such an approach simply misses the art of travel narrative as it was understood in the colonial era.

The best sources for folklorists interested in the eighteenth century are local histories and local color literature supplemented with travel accounts, journals, diaries, and newspapers. Richard M. Dorson's prospecting study, *Jonathan Draws the Long Bow*, brought back an assortment of gleaming nuggets panned from this stream of New England materials. Over the years colonial oral traditions washed down into the nineteenth-century town histories, permitting the recovery of anecdotes and tales that had traveled through the generations, from smithy and tavern to kitchen fire and back. Indeed, traces of this lore enrich virtually hundreds of local histories, which were every bit as much a point of pride to the villages of early New England as the fast food franchises are to the small towns of our own era.

Jonathan Draws the Long Bow is especially interesting as a study in the technique of collecting folklore from an age long past. Avoiding the hopeless search for the "original" sources, Dorson captures the colorful tales after they have flitted from tongue to tongue and settled on the leaves of printed volumes. Like a taxonomist who displays rare birds for the Smithsonian, Dorson carefully "locates, arranges, and presents" the tales, yarns, and legends. The exhibits speak for themselves, with Dorson offering only a precursory introduction to New England storytelling. Indeed, this book predates the movement toward a more scientific folklore in much the same manner as the static early exhibits of the Smithsonian predate the modern participant museums of our own day. Nonetheless, there is an authenticity to these stories that brings more life to the late colonial New England than all but a few contemporary social histories.

In contrast to Dorson's *Jonathan Draws the Long Bow* is another, more recent examination of colonial and early national materials, Tristram Potter Coffin's *Uncertain Glory*, which fictionally recreates a tale-telling session of the American Revolution to give a twentieth-century, Disneylike animation to the kind of oral traditions Dorson prepared for still-life display.[3] Through this method Coffin demonstrates how Revolutionary folklore, rather than creating a pantheon of heroes for an incipient chauvinism, served the needs of a people hungry for entertainment and diversion. Unfortunately, fictional re-creation of folklore leads away from scientific analysis by overemphasizing its entertainment value. Many professional folklorists would instead recommend Coffin's book for its scholarly treatment of Revolutionary Era ballads, which goes beyond G. Malcolm Laws, Jr.'s *American Balladry From British Broadsides* and clearly adds to our knowledge of the early American song tradition.

Complementary to these studies of folktales and ballads is George Lyman Kittredge's wide-ranging *The Old Farmer And His Almanack*, with its storehouse of handed-down riddles, farming and weather lore, folk cures and customs, signs, taboos, and omens from issues of the celebrated *Farmer's Almanack* between 1792 and 1847. Like long dormant seeds from the tree of colonial folk wisdom, such popular beliefs can be brought to flower; and with a quiver of the nose, a modern student of the colonial era begins to sense the true atmosphere of a basically oral age.

The selections discussed thus far have been chosen to offer a good sense of the themes, content, and approaches of the studies of colonial folklore—a new folklore that mutated slightly away from the Old World stock as it adapted to the greatly expanded possibilities of the American environment. But a consideration of secondary studies, however excellent, can develop only limited insight into the promises and pitfalls of colonial folklore.

A better understanding of colonial folklore requires attention to primary materials. My own work led to an historical examination of Afro-American culture in eighteenth-century New England. At first this search seemed particularly difficult, since the black yankees were, for the most part, examples of history's "inarticulate." But local histories proved that Afro-American lore had penetrated the white folk consciousness and was recorded in much of its original purity and wit. Folklore opened a legitimate and productive way to examine American history "from the bottom up"—if only the kernel of black vision could be separated from the surrounding husk of white tradition.

How, for example, did black New Englanders feel about the Christian impulse that lay at the center of the colonial age? From folk tradition—and folk tradition nearly alone—the beginning of an answer emerges. African immigrants and Afro-Americans often rejected Christianity outright. Cotton Mather misunderstood this rejection, imputing it to the work of the Devil: "Very many of them do with Devilish Rites actually worship *Devils*, or maintain a magical conversation with Devils."[4] But Charles Elliot's family tradition understood the situation better. As he recalled, "One of my Reverend ancestors found his Negro Cuff bowing and mumbling before a rough God, that he had made out of stone. 'What's this Cuff?' he said sharply. Cuff at last answered, 'White man steal nigger; nigger no like white man's God. Cuff make his own God and den he know 'em.' "[5]

The Devil was an important part of yankee Christianity for both the white and black population. Black New Englanders at first feared the power of Satan because he seemed so much like malevolent African spirits. But when Afro-Americans came to understand Christian theology better, the Devil became less fearsome and more of a topic for humor and satire. To the black community it was clear that prideful, slave-owning whites were more vulnerable to the works of "Massa" Devil than humble slaves ever would be—no matter what the white preachers might say. The implications of black uses of the Devil are apparent in the traditional anecdote of old Aaron, who was remembered saying:

> "Now, here is de ring wid old Aaron in de middle, de Lord is wid him here; de devil is on de outside, now keep your distance, Massa devil, and do not dare to come into dis ring." Then with a heavy blow with his cane he would say, "Go your way, Massa devil, and do not come hangin' 'bout here to eat old Aaron up." Some one would banter him by asking how the devil looked, and he would say that he "had a head like a nigger's, only with horns, and eyes that kep' a rollin' like dis (rolling his own), and a mouth dat would eat you up in a minute. He go about to ketch wicked niggers; he ketch white folks too, some o' dem," casting a significant eye on those who were taunting him. "Mistress read about him in de Bible, and Aaron has seen him hisself."[6]

Whites remembered many a good story for the humor, which formed like a white pearl around a core of black irritation. References to the Devil and Hell had become a two-edged sword.

> An old gentleman, at the point of death, called a faithful Negro to him, telling him that he would do him honor before he died. The fellow thanked him, and hoped "Massa would live long." "I intend Cato," said the master, "to allow you to be buried in the family-vault." "Ah! Massa," returns Cato, "me no like dat. Ten pounds would be better to Cato. He no care where he be buried; besides, Massa, suppose we be buried together, and de devil come looking for Massa, in de dark he might take away poor Negro man in mistake."[7]

This brings up a serious problem. Such narratives, taken originally from oral tradition, clearly reflect popular white apprehension of black attitudes, but how do we know such stories are truly a part of black tradition? Through comparative analysis a specific black context may sometimes be discovered, as it can be for the Cato story above;[8] in other instances, a series of similar tales also attributed to black wit provides reinforcing evidence.

> Cuff, a slave of Mr. Torrey was taken up for breaking the Sabbath, tried before Justice Joseph Greenlead . . . , and fined. After he had paid the fine, he asked for a receipt of the justice. The justice asked him for what purpose he wanted a receipt? Cuff answered, "By-and-by you die, and go to the bad place, and after a time Cuff die, and go knock at the good gate, and they say 'What do you want, Cuff?' I say, 'I want to come in'; they say I can't, because I broke the Sabbath at such a time. I say, 'I paid for it.' They will say, 'Where is your receipt?' Now Mr. Judge, I shall have to go away down to the bad place to get a receipt of you, that I mended him, before I can enter the good gate."[9]

Black stories were remembered by white narrators because the humor was too good, the truth of the relationship too revealing, to be forgotten. Consider the story of Devonshire, who had long suffered the sanctimonious preaching of his master.

> On returning from Church (after hearing a discourse from the text, "Dead in trespasses and sins,") he found the barn door open and the "Old Ram" on the hay satisfying the demands of nature (with a ewe). He returned immediately to the house exclaiming, "Massa, Massa, the Old Ram is dead!" Mr. Chauncey followed him to the barn and found as above stated, and then, in a reproving manner said, "Devonshire! how came you to say so?" Devonshire replied quickly, "Dead in trespass and sin, I guess, Massa."[10]

In eighteenth-century Georgia, Henry M. Muhlenberg noted an equally satirical "misunderstanding" of the Christian message: "One Negro," reported Muhlenberg, "said he would rather belong to the Moravian Brethren than to the High Church because the latter was always preaching about work and labor, whereas the former preached faith without works, and he was tired of working."[11] This anecdote, with its play on Christian theology, needs to be treated with caution, since only a tiny minority of the colonial black population were church members. More than likely, the quip is a product of white rather than black humor. However, another anecdote, which turns on the interchange between a trickster minister and his slave in Pawtucket Falls, Massachusetts, has a more likely black provenience. On a fishing outing, Parson Parker planned to have some fun by secretly tying a rat on the line of his slave, but Caesar turned the tables by noting as he pulled in his prize that he appeared to have caught a minister—"it was something with a black coat."[12]

The conditions of slavery were not always remembered in the form of humorous anecdote. For example, in his autobiography, the abolitionist Henry B. Stanton recalled that during the eighteenth century a plaintive dirge was composed to commemorate Miantonomoh, a chief of the Naragansetts, who suffered a cruel death in 1643 after being delivered over to his enemies by white officials.

In my childhood we had a Negro slave whose voice was attuned to the sweetest cadence. Many a time did she lull me to slumber by singing this touching lament. It sank deep into my breast, and moulded my advancing years. Before I reached manhood I resolved that I would become the champion of the oppressed colored races of my country.[13]

This folk lullaby proved to be a weapon sharper than iron, and the course of American history was changed by a nameless slave woman who prepared her young charge well.

These few examples of black folklore indicate the potential for using folklore studies as a new tool to analyze American culture from "the bottom up." Such an approach should prove especially useful in minority and women's studies. Psychohistorians are needed to examine the folk themes and images that appear in the dreams of colonial diarists, and folklorists can play a special role in determining how cultural traditions blended and changed in their New World settings.

For too long our vision of colonial America has been dominated by the culture of the literate few. The insights of oral tradition must be sifted and weighed against our present elitist understanding. Similarly, it is time for folklorists to develop materials that will humanize the overwhelmingly statistical vision of the new social scientists. Indeed, it may be a new Golden Age for colonial America.

NOTES

1. Cotton Mather, *Magnalia Christi Americana* (London: T. Parkhurst, 1702).

2. Percy G. Adams, *Travelers and Travel Liars 1600-1800* (Berkeley: University of California Press, 1962).

3. Tristram Potter Coffin, *Uncertain Glory* (Detroit: Folklore Associates, 1971).

4. The Mather quotation, like much of the material that follows, is quoted and discussed in William Dillon Piersen, "Afro-American Culture in Eighteenth Century New England: A Comparative Examination" (Ph.D. diss., Indiana University, 1975), p. 189 and passim.

5. Charles Wyllys Elliot, *The New England History, II* (New York: Charles Scribner, 1857), p. 180.

6. Thomas Weston, *The History of Middleboro Massachusetts* (Boston: Houghton, Mifflin & Co., 1906), p. 104.

7. William C. Fowler, *The Historical Status of the Negro in Connecticut* (Albany: Joel Munsell, 1872), pp. 130–31.

8. See, for example, the similar tale told by Kentucky slaves, "Narrative of Lewis Clarke," in *Interesting Memoirs and Documents Relating to American Slavery* (London: Chapman Brothers, 1846), p. 91.

9. Benjamin Hobart, *History of the Town of Abington, Plymouth County, Massachusetts* (Boston: T. H. Carter and Son, 1866), p. 255.

10. William C. Fowler, *History of Durham, Connecticut* (Hartford: Wiley, Waterman & Eaton, 1866), p. 164.

11. Henry M. Muhlenberg, *Journals, II* (Philadelphia: The Muhlenberg Press, 1958), p. 638.

12. Samuel A. Drake, *History of Middlesex County, I* (Boston: Estes and Laurial, 1880), p. 408.

13. Henry B. Stanton, *Random Recollections* (New York: Harper and Brothers, 1887), p. 5.

Elaine Jahner

Finding the Way Home: The Interpretation of American Indian Folklore

A folklore fieldworker's unexpected findings often prove more valuable than the anticipated outcome of interviews. An old Mandan Indian woman dramatizing her feelings about white scholars convinced me of the need to find approaches to American Indian oral literature that can highlight its artistic complexity. Interviewing this woman was one of my goals when I first became a folklorist. Everyone knew her to be among the most knowledgeable of the Mandan people, but approaching her directly solely to request traditional stories would have been a mistake. Tribal rules for transmitting lore require that one earn the right to any knowledge through a series of actions. So her grandson, a student of mine, suggested that my having worked with him might entitle me to begin the process of learning from her.

At his request, she agreed to meet me. I found her sitting in a rocking chair reading a book of badly retold Indian legends. She greeted me warmly, then told me she had trouble seeing and asked me to read to her. Here I was, reciting the worst sort of rubbish to a woman who knew more genuine legends than anyone else in her tribe. Occasionally she poked me and pointed out how stupid the book was. Finally having had enough of that nonsense, she looked directly at me and said that what we had just read was an example of how white people misused and misunderstood Indian stories. The Mandan woman went on to state categorically that she would rather let stories die with her than pass them on to anyone who might misinterpret them.

Fortunately, the stories are not such fragile structures that they need the aid of scholars and interpreters to maintain their vitality. Their existence is a protean one, adapting to time and place, and, as my Mandan teacher demonstrated, their meaning does not come easily to a white scholar. Notwithstanding, academically oriented people have a long history of fascinated and often frenzied collection of Indian lore. Falling prey to social evolutionary premises, scholars have gathered the thousands of texts that fill our archives. If the world community is ever to benefit from this particular American cultural resource, academics must abandon outmoded theoretical baggage and vitalize approaches that help us come nearer to an insider's view of meaning. For the texts that we possess are mere skeletons. If we are to reconstruct something of their earlier reality, we need access to the poetic complexity that gave them life and that continues to manifest itself today in other forms. Together, the old and the new tales can bring us to a truer understanding of how the tribal peoples have adapted to change and what kind of role they play in contemporary American culture.

Although American Indians share in much of the surface homogeneity of today's life, they can perceive its meaning in a different light from other ethnic groups because they bring to it perceptions rooted in sharply contrasting historical attitudes. It may seem a strange and circuitous route to go from the media-ruled world of modern America to a detailed analysis of a traditional Lakota tale in order to return to our diversity, but I believe that it is a valid route, especially for the folklorist. A few scholars in our discipline recognize how important it is to begin our study of American Indian texts with micro-analysis at all levels of the text, including linguistic study in the original language.[1] But our goal has not been reached when we are able to demonstrate that certain linguistic devices occur or that a text reflects social structure in a particular way. We must go further and show how tales embody artistic and moral energies that direct the trajectory of change. In the tales we can perceive the people's motivations and sources of psychological renewal, which lead to new ways of living.

In order to make a general appeal for more detailed study of tribal narrative, I want to indicate some of the complexity in one story. There are elements and energies in every good narrative that we have barely acknowledged.[2] A few basic themes in a text are the factors of continuity, and often we have to go to the original languages to discover these vital themes. In order to do the research for this article, I had to move back and forth from the library to informants. A Sioux woman was astounded at how closely the underlying themes of the text corresponded to her personal experiences. Her story now forms the conclusion to my discussion.

The text tells of a woman who leaves a cruel husband and survives the walk back to her own people, thanks to wolves who befriend her. Sioux people of various bands, both men and women, tell the story, but women are especially attracted to it and tend to add emotional details to the heroine's plight. It is easy to find versions of the tale, and I have six; two are in Lakota, one that I recorded in my own fieldwork and one that Ella Deloria published in her volume of Dakota texts.[3] Because Deloria's is the longest and most elaborate of all, I will use it as my exemplary text. This version places considerable emphasis on the woman's acquiring powers of divination while among the wolves, so the theme is not so much about a woman's escape from a bad marrige as it is about the workings of supernatural forces. A Lakota would say, "It is about wolf power."

A first step in understanding the specific tribal meaning of the tale is to learn how Sioux attitudes toward the wolf differ from European ones. Most Sioux bands recognize the wolf as a protector.[4] Many traditions tell about people who get lost and are led back home by wolves. James R. Walker's records of a creation myth include references to the wolf as the animal who led the people from a lower world to the present one.[5] As a protector the wolf helps people glide unseen through dangerous territory and sometimes announces future happenings to them. In pre-reservation times, the Sioux listened to wolf cries to judge the coming of buffalo. One nineteenth-century Lakota text directly links belief in wolves as protectors with the story of the rescued woman. "Long ago, a woman lived with wolves, it is said. Then the wolves took great pity on her. The wolves went scattering away and when it was evening, they came home to the woman with meat, it is said. Therefore they believe the wolf to be *wakan* (sacred or mysterious)."[6] This and many other texts suggest that the wolf is not only the "wilderness-dog" (literal translation of the Lakota term) but also a kind of wilderness-male assuming roles assigned to men in the camp circle. At this level the story can be compared to the dog-husband tale.

Mention of wolves helping lost human beings is commonplace, but Sioux listeners would not be particularly interested in the mere idea of aid. For them the story has at least three intriguing themes that a good narrator can exploit. The major one centers on the kind of power gained as a result of the woman's encounter with the wolves; another is the feminine response to a difficult marriage; and a third is the link between the story and a particular cave in South Dakota. In my example, the first two themes are combined and developed in subtle, elaborate ways, which become evident only when the story is placed in its cultural and literary context. Even a cursory explication of the style can dispel any notion that the tale is primitive or simple.

Quickly and precisely, the first part of the story draws a verbal picture based on images that will be reversed later. The initial scene depicts the heroine's fears. We are told that her husband gave her father many gifts in order to marry her, so we know that she is an attractive, skilled woman whom no husband will easily give up. Her jealous spouse watches her constantly, even going so far as to blacken the soles of her moccasins with soot in order to detect her movements while he is out of the tipi. Because she is always under surveillance, she weeps, causing her eyes to close with swelling.

The stage has been set for the reversals that structure the tale's thematic content. As the woman becomes more and more enclosed in darkness, she is driven to the point where she must begin her journey toward enlightenment. She loses her sight only to regain it after the wolves grant her invisibility. In the Lakota language text, we see some complex word plays that help establish the story's capacity to comment figuratively and literally. Where the text describes her husband checking the moccasin soles for erasures of soot, the word used is *ataŋiŋšni*. The same root word in the very next sentence describes how swelling caused her eyes to "become invisible." *Taŋiŋšni* can imply more than simple invisibility. Another Lakota story in the same collection[7] describes a stranger as *taŋiŋšni*. In this instance the man is visible, but his true nature is unknown. As a result, people do not know rules of proper behavior in his presence, and when they accidentally break a taboo, he causes their destruction. To say that someone is *taŋiŋšni* implies mystery and possible danger. The word appears at crucial points in the story of the woman among the wolves. At first it applies only to her eyes, with limited and literal meaning. Gradually it comes to refer to her entire being and gains its full figurative sense.

After the narrator stresses that something is deeply and terrifyingly wrong with the woman's home life, we learn that one of her husband's maternal relatives also recognizes the danger of the situation and decides to send her back to her own people. To escape, the woman must outwit her husband. The two women plan every detail of the departure, and finally the persecuted wife is on her own in the wilderness.

Fear remains the dominant emotion in the first wilderness scenes. The woman travels by night so that she cannot be seen by possible enemies. As she runs, she weeps, only to hide in bushes as the first light of dawn appears. The story adds detail upon detail to emphasize her total exhaustion and loss of willpower when she meets the wolf, who decides to protect her so that she can be useful to him. The idea of some kind of exchange is clearly present as he grants her the gift of invisibility. Because she has the power to prevent people from seeing her, she is now free to travel by day. But the wolf gives her more than invisibility, and the meaning of his total gift is only gradually revealed in the story.

According to the English text, "from then on something came over her and she lost her eagerness to reach her people." The Lakota text includes the words "*tokeca taŋiŋšni*." A slight difference in pronunciation could change the meaning of the word *tokeca* from "sickness" to "another," so that her mysterious sickness recalls by association something else that is invisible or unknown. The play on sickness and health continues with the use of the word *akisni* to describe the loss of her desire to return home. This word usually means "to cure" or "to get well." She is cured of her desire to get home. She has gained a new power that is both a cure and a departure from normal healthy existence.

The next episode is movingly poetic. First she climbs to the top of a hill, finds some flat rocks, and looks out over the countryside, noticing its great beauty. She finally finds a cave that happens to be the home of wolves; she stays there for an unspecified period of time, and she creates a way of life for herself. While some versions show the wolves providing direct help, they do little in this one to help her attain the tools of culture. The emphasis is on the ingenuity and newly acquired spiritual powers of the woman, who can now make her own decisions and whose knowledge and independence become evident to listeners.

Finally the wolves announce to the woman that her own people will arrive the next day, and she is to rejoin them. Her first thought is to consider her profound contentment or *taŋyéhcis un* among the wolves (the superlative of *taŋyan uŋ*, "well-being" or "culture," the opposite of what she experienced at the beginning of the story).

After she returns to her people, she fulfills her part of the bargain with wilderness life. She feeds the wolves and uses the powers of vision they gave her. According to the text, she now has "transparent eyes." From a state completely without light or well-being, she has so changed that light emanates from within her. Now enclosure helps her to see. When her people need to look beyond present time, they wrap her in a buffalo hide and place a mirror outside it. From within the robe, she is able to see reflections of future events, and the tribe decides that her powers are limitless. All of the transformations are complete. The woman who was trapped inside her husband's tipi can see through anything, including time.

This story clearly belongs to a class of narratives showing how people rise from lowliness to prestige, but its interest and importance today have less to do with this extremely general theme than with the more specific notion that the woman's transformation is dependent on her risking the wilderness. There is a social dimension to this risk. An old song is evidence that the light and darkness theme orchestrated throughout the story was often used in relation to the quality of home life.

> Be not angry, come home, come home.
> Not you, the home is lost, come home.
> . . . .
> Our darkness drove you hence, come home,
> . . . .

It is life for all or none may live.
It's light for all or darkness for all.[8]

This song suggests that culture (which creates a home) is also a source of light to the "eye of the heart."[9] But, as the story narrates so forcefully, social life can be cruelly destructive, and then action is necessary to maintain culture itself. In risking all, the woman helped her people and the wilderness wolves who aided her in transition.

The narrator tells the incident as a true happening that occurred in historical time; the story validates many kinds of belief. We sense their nature and full extent of reference only when we respond to the complex stylistic links that combine notions of culture with light and the needs of the individual as well as the group. When we allow such knowledge to illuminate our reading of the text in English, we can sense something of the force compelling the woman into the wilderness to seek a new life.

Two examples can show how the legend dramatizes motivations that continue to shape the ways in which some members of the Lakota culture respond to contemporary conditions. One day at the laundromat, I met a woman who did not know me very well; she had heard that at noon I was driving to the nearest city, and asked for a ride. I was glad to offer it. She was uncomfortable about the entire visit to the city; her exact purposes were still vague, and her host and hostess for the coming night were almost unknown to her, but she was convinced that the trip was necessary. We were silent for a bit as we drove along. Finally, she began a story. It was her version of the woman among the wolves. Somehow the story comforted her and gave her a sense that our little trip had meaning.

Another example is more dramatic. This time the woman who related the story, an administrator in a major state institution, had an urban background. After a divorce, she felt darkness closing in on her in ways that corresponded to those suggested in the tale. The subjective experience was entirely comparable; so was her response. She felt she had to go back to her own people, so she put her children in a car and began the journey, in spite of the fact that she worried about her job and the children. She also had a sense that, for reasons unknown to her, the journey was extremely dangerous. But "I would have faced death because I felt I had to." In today's equivalent of the wilderness, she encountered powers that she had to face in order to acquire greater independence and strength. Then she could return to her job. She also claims that light had returned to her house.

Aspects of these examples are definitely cross-cultural. Everyone can find travel restorative, but the motivations and the images are culturally based and transmitted through a narrative that engages emotions as well as intellect. The poetic quality of the stories gives them enduring appeal, an appeal and force difficult to glimpse in texts in abbreviated translation. What we need is a poetics of narrative that is culturally and linguistically specific. To achieve such a goal, we require all the tools provided by various theoretical approaches. Our purpose would be entirely humanistic and in line with the folklorist's goals, namely to understand narrative continuity and its impact on human motivation.

The narrative that I have analyzed, in order to highlight thematic elements linked to patterns of imagery in the original Lakota language, fits the folklorist's definition of legend. It can be argued that since legends are, by their very nature, local happenings, they naturally require explication of their historical context, while folktales, with their intertribal plots, do not depend on such regional levels of meaning for their artistic impact. Quite the reverse is true.[10] Because the ties between the folktale and basic cultural themes are less obvious than those of legend, a good narrator relies even more heavily upon indirect reference to carry specific meanings. Each genre requires its own kinds of metaphoric links to other networks of meaning in a culture. Showing how a narrator binds together features of tribally specific meaning is a lengthy process for a form as highly structured as the folktale. As more and more scholars study the process for individual tribes, a critical literature is growing around specific tales.[11]

But what about the texts of varying completeness that were so carefully preserved by linguists, ethnologists, and folklorists during the late nineteenth and early twentieth centuries? Cut off from their performance context, they are like the dry bones of skeletons. They show us only outlines, yet these are precious because they are all we have to tell us how tales were adapted as cultures faced revolutionary change. As we try to understand older tale texts, we must gather every available scrap of cultural and linguistic data, checking the possibilities of various methods—structural, philological, comparative, and psychoanalytic. With the resulting information we will be able to understand how a narrator might have developed certain plots to meet specific demands.

The study of tribal literature requires an information gatherer as attuned to the styles of individual narrators as Richard M. Dorson, as assiduous a hunter of detail as Claude Lévi-Strauss, as sensitive to linguistic context as Dell Hymes, and as concerned with poetic meaning as Dennis Tedlock. Perhaps such combinations of skills come only through team efforts, but if we form such teams we might be able to sense enough of the meaning of cross-cultural analysis to understand some of the folktale skeletons in our archival closets.

NOTES

1. See Dell Hymes, *"In vain I tried to tell you"* (Philadelphia: University of Pennsylvania Press, 1981), and Karl Kroeber, *Traditional American Indian Literatures: Texts and Interpretations* (Lincoln: University of Nebraska Press, 1981).

2. For the purposes of this article I will not discuss any of the fine points of semantic analysis that permit us to demonstrate how basic cultural themes can be orchestrated throughout narrative. I have done that in other theoretical articles. I have described the cognitive and semantic style in a single folktale in "Cognitive Style in Oral Literature," *Language and Style*, forthcoming.

3. Ella Deloria, *Dakota Texts* (New York: G. E. Stechert and Company, 1932).

4. There are many statements of the theme of wolf as protector. Personal-experience stories related to the theme can be found in Frances Densmore, *Teton Sioux Music*, Bureau of American Ethnology 27 (1918): 179-85.

5. Elaine Jahner, *Lakota Myth* (Lincoln: University of Nebraska Press, forthcoming).

6. Elaine Jahner and Raymond DeMallie, *Lakota Belief and Ritual* (Lincoln: University of Nebraska Press, 1980).

7. Deloria, p. 120.

8. Aaron McGaffey Beede, unpublished manuscript, Orin G. Libby Manuscript Collection, University of North Dakota, Grand Forks, North Dakota.

9. Joseph Brown, *The Sacred Pipe* (Norman: University of Oklahoma Press, 1953).

10. Franz Boas recognized the importance of regional stylistic traits, but scholarship since his time has tended to concentrate on the dissemination of plot elements rather than on the specific realization of these elements among a particular tribe. See "The Development of Folktales and Myths," in *Race, Language and Culture* (London: Collier-Macmillan, 1940), p. 397.

11. Jarold Ramsey has used the work of Dell Hymes and Melville Jacobs to add to secondary literature surrounding one Clackamas Chinook tale in "The Wife Who Goes Out Like a Man, Comes Back as a Hero: The Art of Two Oregon Indian Narratives," *PMLA* 92 (1977): 9-18.

George Lankford

The Unfulfilled Promise of North American Indian Folklore

At the conclusion of an excellent survey of North American Indian folklore research, a well-known folklorist made a somber assessment of the field: "No doubt there will always be a few scholars whose area of specialization is American Indian folklore, but the heyday of American Indian studies generally and of American Indian folklore studies in particular seems to be nearly over."[1]

If this prognosis is correct—and the dawn of Indian *self*-study may indicate that it is not—it is certainly not because the field of study has been exhausted. On the contrary, the energy of generations of anthropologists and folklorists was expended largely in collecting texts and data before they vanished under the twin forces of acculturation and extermination. The amount of analytical study is not large, and the synthetic studies are even fewer, yet, as Stith Thompson pointed out, "we are better prepared for a study of the North American Indian tale than for even those of Europe and the Near East."[2]

Reading the collections is a formidable task. Texts and other relevant cultural data are dispersed in ethnographies, travel accounts, and various academic journals. In addition, anthropologists have recorded volumes of folktale texts abstracted from their cultural context and sometimes published them in a series of collections sponsored by various institutions. The best guide to the location of the texts is still Stith Thompson's 1929 classic, *Tales of the North American Indians*. Mastering his apparatus takes some effort, but it is more than repaid in time saved in bibliographic work, at least for the period before 1929.

This great collection of folktales is not complete, of course. In the twentieth century tribes have responded in many creative ways to the challenge of being encysted in technological America. As new cultural systems are being formed, the oral traditions are also changing. Collecting is now a difficult process, for the new self-assertiveness of Native Americans is frequently accompanied by hostility to social scientists of all disciplines. The best hope for future anthropological and folkloristic study of contemporary Native Americans may lie in the work of scholars who are also Native Americans. Ortiz has provided a pilot study of this nature by analyzing the symbolic system of his own Tewa ancestors.[3]

What has been collected already, though, is vast. Instead of encouraging folklorists to seek greener fields, this fact should attract those who have hypotheses to test and those whose questions require large bodies of cross-cultural data. The collected corpus, after all, was never itself conceived as the goal by those who did the work. They saw their fieldwork as an essential first step on the path to solving cultural and historical problems of a general nature. Reacting against global expansiveness of the style of James G. Frazer and the glibness of the nature mythologists, such as Daniel Brinton among the American Indians, they set themselves to the painstaking task of providing enough data to make possible inductive examination of the artistic expressions of Native Americans.

Even though they knew the great work could not be completed in their own lifetimes, they did not back away from the great questions. Waterman analyzed the growing body of data to attack the problem of etiology and showed that explanatory elements were local nonessential additions to migratory legends. Lowie used the North American corpus to discredit the assumptions of the nature mythologists, while Boas documented the ethnographic utility of the study of folk literature and provided the first major cross-cultural index of tales. Through Zuni materials, Benedict demonstrated that cultural elements in tales can be reversed for psychological reasons. As these scholars worked, they noticed patterns and anomalies, and they raised questions still unanswered.

Why, they asked, do Eskimos lack tales that seem to be standard items for most North American tribes, such as Earth-Diver, the Twins, and the Trickster? How can peculiar distributions be explained, such as the legend of the incest between the sun and the moon, found among the Eskimo, Cherokee, and South American tribes? How can anomalies such as the Pawnees' strong astronomical orientation— star-lore that forms an overlay on a more commonly held Caddoan corpus—be understood?

Almost every ethnography and tribal tale collection is prefaced by at least a paragraph describing the local rules for tale-telling. These constraints represent widely distributed beliefs in their own right and as such deserve study. A frequently encountered belief is that certain tales should not be told in the summer, and that the consequence of breaking the taboo is to be bit by snakes. An exhaustive study of such constraints and their meaning remains to be undertaken.

Similarly, analysis of the rules of transmission might explain the longevity and stability of Native American narrative, as well as providing a basis for evaluating the historical trustworthiness of tribal collections. Several of the Plains tribes, for example, used a well-documented "bundle" system. A ritual was concretized in a sacred bundle, and it had its own legend accompanying it. Both bundle and legend were owned by an individual, who demanded verbatim accuracy from his chosen successor. How widespread was such an astounding transmission system, and what were other North American alternatives to it?

Texts as they have been collected vary from dozens of pages to a paragraph in length, and subplots appear and disappear in similar narratives from different tribes. From the beginning, folklorists have debated the utility of devising a code that would reduce texts to similar form for comparative purposes. Thompson's massive *Motif-Index* is one answer to the problem, but there are others. "Motifs" are deliberate attempts to capture in a phrase the uniqueness of an episode's content, but that very uniqueness limits the usefulness of the concept. Dundes has attempted to create a more generalized code in hope of constructing a "grammar" of folktales.[4] His system has not met with acceptance by other scholars, perhaps because the general categories are too abstract to clarify the tale-making process. In recent years Colby and his associates have offered a promising middle road. Inspired by Propp and informed by data-processing procedures, they have produced several tribal studies and a growing vocabulary for coding.[5] As the scope increases, the complexity of the coding system will probably follow suit, demanding participation from many more scholars.

The complexities of tale syntax and the abstract nature of "grammar" make comprehension a long-term goal. Even more concrete problems have been ignored through the years. To date, for example, American Indian scholars have given little attention to the functions, origins, and comparative traits of the specific figures of folktales. A bestiary is badly needed. A folk atlas of ogres in North America might yield surprising results. Full examinations of the origin and nature of such pan-tribal figures as the Thunderbird and the Horned Water Serpent await their authors.

Such research would go a long way toward clarifying the processes governing the spread and absorption of North American religious concepts. Some ethnologists have shown that tales both reflect religious concepts and participate in the spread of them, but the mechanics are poorly known. Lowie, in a model study of this type, compared the folktales and religious practices of the agrarian Hidatsa and their nomadic offspring, the Crow, to illumine the linkage of environment and religious concept.[6] While this work has produced no emulators, Hultkrantz and his students have pursued the same sort of religious-ecological problem in several helpful monographs. The best known is a major analysis of the Orpheus myth in North America.

One of the most striking needs is for explorations of the relationship between verbal art and other cognitive aspects of culture. Visual art forms, which are a legitimate concern of folklorists, have received attention only from anthropologists. Despite particularistic examinations, it is indicative of the neglect of this realm that the classic general text on Native American art is still *Primitive Art*, published in 1928 by Boas. Mammoth efforts at collecting art forms, such as the project to photograph, classify and interpret the engraved shell art dispersed across the nation after the rape of Spiro in the 1930s,[7] if coupled with iconographic techniques developed by Meso-Americanists and a thorough knowledge of the verbal literature, might open new paths to the understanding of prehistoric cognitive systems.

No one has yet completed a model study showing the relationship between how animals are treated in tales and the roles they play in the life of the society. Anthropologists have begun to employ a linguistic approach to reconstruct tribal scientific systems. This new field of ethnoscience will produce biological lore that will be invaluable in interpreting the meaning of animals in tales. The reverse may well be true; analyses of tale collections from this perspective may help produce ethnoscientific data.

One of the few areas of Native American lore that has received significant attention is the enigmatic figure of the trickster. By a curious coincidence, both Radin and Barnouw published studies of the Winnebago/Ojibwa trickster at the same time; moreover, both of them approached the problem from the vantage point of psychoanalytic theory. Toelken wrote a now-classic article on the role of the trickster tales in one teller's repertoire. Ricketts wrestled with the trickster from the perspective of the history of religions, and his study is the only one to attempt a philosophical understanding of the pan-tribal trickster. The rich trickster materials call for more experimental analysis. At present, the Native American contribution to the comparative study of the trickster consists of these few offerings.

Pope provided a tantalizing glimpse of the possibilities of understanding the trickster and other figures through analysis of the syntagmatic structure, and the efforts of Lévi-Strauss to create cognitive models by which folktales may be interpreted continue to inspire new goals for folklorists. Following this lead, Kessel produced an impressive study of a Mandan myth, and Hudson interpreted the function and meaning of an important Southeastern ritual act. These examples are made even more provocative by the hope that refinements in the method may ultimately produce cognitive models that will help interpret all genres of culture expression, including the plastic arts and archaeological manifestations.

All of these areas of study were either implicitly or explicitly called for by the early students. The initial analytic task was the use of historic-geographic techniques to clarify the history and diffusion of verbal and visual art forms. A few such studies were completed, but the task of gathering texts and the shift of interests among folklorists kept the number small.[8] Even so, the compiling of data and the identification of oicotypes was a great contribution, as evidenced by a number of synthetic studies utilizing that data.[9]

A major problem was the lack of historical information. It is only recently that the labors of the archeologists have provided a trustworthy historical framework for Native American life before the Europeans arrived. The lack of such a framework forced most of the early historic-geographic studies to be more geographic than historic, and the conclusions were rendered inadequate. The archaeological record shows that there are several time periods in the Eastern Woodlands that are marked by signs of "super-cultures" of some sort. This historical fact fits the folkloristic fact that few tales are found as isolates, and the suggestion is that certain tale-complexes should be attributable to those prehistoric sharing periods. I have written an essay that attempts to incorporate archeological models within a historical-geographic study. I believe it is possible to assign dates to certain tale-complexes and am currently attempting to produce a volume of "Mississippian myths," those current ca. A.D. 1300. Such projects, undertaken by folklorists, will be useful particularly to archeologists, who now must work from only the material data and the ethnographic present.

Historical studies of this kind are also essential building blocks for constructing even larger models. Stith Thompson briefly opened the question of cultural relationships between North and South America, only to conclude that independent invention was responsible for the similarities.[10] In recent years the debate over the North-South linkage has become respectable among archeologists, and so has the discussion about trans-Pacific contact.[11] Folklore studies have already pointed to Pacific travel of some legends, but most are either single-tale analyses or broad generalized accounts resting on conflicting data.[12] What is needed are many smaller-scale historical studies thorough enough to buttress a transmission model that might span the Pacific.

Another focus of the historical side of folkloristics is the contact between Europeans, Africans, and Native Americans.[13] A major difficulty in analyzing the mixing of cultural traditions is the present inability to distinguish between them.[14] As the ancestral materials become more carefully defined, this problem should vanish, and a better understanding of the relations between groups on the frontier should result. Several studies explore how whites depicted Indians in their folklore, but a definitive examination of how Native Americans portrayed the whites is yet to be written.

The promise of the pioneering North American Indian folklore research still remains to be fulfilled.

NOTES

1. Alan Dundes, "North American Indian Folklore Studies," *Journal de la Société des Américanistes* 56 (1967): 53-79.

2. Stith Thompson, *The Folktale* (New York: Holt, Rinehart and Winston, 1946), p. 299.

3. Alfonso Ortiz, *The Tewa World* (Chicago: The University of Chicago Press, 1969). See also Silvester John Brito, "The Development and Change of the Peyote Ceremony Through Time and Space" (Ph.D. diss., Indiana University, 1975).

4. Alan Dundes, *The Morphology of North American Indian Folktales*, FF Communications, no. 195 (Helsinki, 1964).

5. See especially B. N. Colby, "A Partial Grammar of Eskimo Folktales," *American Anthropologist* 75 (1973): 645-62.

6. Robert Lowie, *Studies in Plains Folklore*, University of California Publications in Archaeology, Anthropology, and Ethnology, no. 49 (Berkeley: University of California, 1942).

7. Philip Phillips and James A. Brown, *Pre-Columbian Shell Engravings from the Craig Mound at Spiro, Oklahoma*, 6 vols., Publications of the Peabody Museum of Archaeology and Ethnology (Cambridge, Mass.: Harvard University, 1977).

8. See, for example, Bert Gerow, "Blood-Clot Boy," (M.A. thesis, Stanford University, 1950); M. L. Sumner, "Lodge-Boy and Thrown-Away: An Analytic Study of an American Indian Folktale" (M.A. thesis, Stanford University, 1951); William Fenton, *Iroquois Eagle Dance*, Bulletin of the Bureau of American Ethnology, no. 156 (Washington, D.C., 1956); Patrick J. Munson, "The Origins and Antiquity of Maize-Beans-Squash Agriculture in Eastern North America: Some Linguistic Implications," *Variation in Anthropology*, ed. D. W. Lathrap and J. Douglas (Urbana: Illinois Archaeological Study, 1973), pp. 107-35.

9. Witness, for example, this series of studies of one tale: Gladys A. Reichard, "Literary Types and the Dissemination of Myths," *Journal of American Folklore* 34 (1921): 269-307; Stith Thompson, "The Star Husband Tale," *Studia Septentrionalia* 4 (1953): 93-163, reprinted in *The Study of Folklore*, ed. Alan Dundes (Englewood Cliffs, N. J.: Prentice-Hall, 1965), pp. 414-74; Alan Dundes, *The Morphology of North American Indian Folktales*, FF Communications, no. 195 (Helsinki, 1964); Claude Lévi-Strauss, "The Structural Study of Myth," in *Structural Anthropology*, ed. Claude Lévi-Strauss (Garden City: Doubleday, 1968), pp. 202-28; Frank W. Young, "A Fifth Analysis of the Star Husband Tale," *Ethnology* 9 (1970): 389-413; George W. Rich, "Rethinking the Star Husbands," *Journal of American Folklore* 84 (1971): 436-41; Guy E. Swanson, "Orpheus and Star Husband: Meaning and the Structure of Myths," *Ethnology* 15 (1976): 115-33; Frank W. Young, "Folktales and Social Structure: A Comparison of Three Analyses of the Star-Husband Tale," *Journal of American Folklore* 91 (1978): 691-99.

10. Stith Thompson, "Analogues and Borrowings in North and South American Indian Tales," in *Languages and Cultures of Western North America*, ed. E. H. Swanson, Jr. (Pocatello: Idaho State University Press, 1970), pp. 277–88.

11. Betty Meggers, "The Transpacific Origin of Mesoamerican Civilization: A Preliminary Review of the Evidence and Its Theoretical Implication," *American Anthropologist* 77 (1975): 1–27.

12. See, for example, Earl Count, "The Earth-Diver and the Rival Twins: A Clue to Time Correlation in North-Eurasiatic and North American Mythology," in *Indian Tribes of Aboriginal America*, ed. Sol Tax, Proceedings of the 29th International Congress of Americanists (1949), pp. 55–62; R. Pettazzoni, "The Chain of Arrows: The Diffusion of a Mythical Motive," *Folk-Lore* 35 (1924): 151–65; Gudmund Hatt, "The Corn Mother in America and in Indonesia," *Anthropos* 46 (1951): 853–914; Douglas Fraser, "The Heraldic Woman: A Study in Diffusion," in *The Many Faces of Primitive Art*, ed. D. Fraser (Englewood Cliffs, N. J.: Prentice-Hall, 1966), pp. 36–99.

13. See Francis Lee Utley, "The Migration of Folktales: Four Channels to the Americas," *Current Anthropology* 15 (1974): 5–27.

14. Alan Dundes, "African Tales Among the North American Indians," *Southern Folklore Quarterly* 29 (1965): 207–19.

Ronald R. Smith

Afro-American Folk Music

Scholars of Afro-American music recognize that we have only recently begun to delve into the complex treasure of black musical traditions in America. In 1963 Harold Courlander remarked, "It may safely be said, I think, that Negro folk music today is the largest body of genuine folk music still alive in the United States, and this alone justifies an effort to see it in the round."[1] While academically oriented research into the origins and nature of black music has a long history, the period since 1960 has seen a renewal of serious interest and an increase in the number of professionals, both black and white, engaged in such work. Although the ebb and flow of interest in Negro life in America has produced many works on religion, folklore, history, art, literature, sociology, and anthropology, few have attempted to integrate these areas with music, dance, and theater. Scholars and lay people alike must keep in mind that a thorough study of Afro-American music requires more than a preoccupation with musical genres and performance practices. Knowledge of the historical and social setting is necessary to an understanding of the forces that have shaped and influenced the people who made music and the institutions in which this music lived and flourished. The context of Afro-American life is very much part of the tradition itself.

PERIODS IN AFRO-AMERICAN HISTORY

The study of Afro-American music in the United States has most often been couched in terms of generalized historical periods roughly paralleling major events in American history. Other studies have concentrated on specific genres that have been strongly identified with black people: blues, gospel, and spirituals. Although these approaches have provided much useful information by documenting many musicians who have long since been forgotten, they have also served to fragment the perception and understanding of the black experience in America. Thus the continuity and meaning of traditions and their effect upon the lives of all Americans have not always been readily evident.

Eileen Southern's standard work on the music of black Americans clearly organizes the material gathered according to major periods and events in American history.[2] Since expressive traditions and behaviors respect no geographical or political boundaries, an organization of history according to external events does not always reflect the nature and development of music and traditions within a community. I do not suggest that there is no influence upon musical traditions or practices by, say, the Civil War, immigration, or the rise of Big Business. I merely suggest that music is more important in the process of sociocultural change than we often imagine. It may in fact act as a catalytic agent or function as the vehicle by which an essential statement is conveyed. The study of Afro-American music and life from such a perspective might cause a major shift in the perception of its role and contribution in America.

The designations sacred vs. secular and traditional vs. popular are in some sense artificial, since it is often the context and not the musical material that is the decisive factor. Because stylistic elements and performance practices continue and change over time, they may be found in many eras and situations. Thus, the periods suggested below concentrate upon certain genres or stylistic elements rather than the termination of a form and the development of a totally new idea.

Colonial Era, 1619–1775

When the first Negro slaves arrived aboard a Dutch man-of-war at Jamestown, Virginia, in 1619, the history of slavery in the New World was already one hundred years old. In Latin America, especially in the Caribbean islands, the process of mixing and developing black musics had begun. Slaves were taken mainly from the west coast of Africa, but historians recognize that some must have come from central Africa and maybe even further eastward. Much of the aesthetic framework and musical practices of current tradition are built upon the African concepts of these early peoples.

Although slaves could not bring musical instruments with them, they did transport songs, dances, compositional techniques, and poetry, as well as extensive knowledge of instrument building. The central place of music in West African communities is well established. Choral singing in the call-response form, drum ensembles with highly complex rhythmic organization, music for work, songs of praise, game songs of children, music for religious events, sung epics, and song-tales were forms through which early slaves expressed themselves.

At first the small numbers of slaves and the lack of a common language hampered the development of a musical style that would represent all groups. The growth of plantations and larger holdings of slaves prepared the way for a homogenization of African traits and musical performance practices. Contact with European harmonic concepts and religious music, especially in the North, allowed talented slaves and later free blacks to make music that was appreciated also by white members of the community. It is well documented in plantation records and handbills that many slaves were instrumental performers. They were highly prized and thus more expensive.

Antebellum Era, 1776–1866

With the advent of the War of Independence and subsequent westward expansion, new areas became open to blacks. Growth in the numbers of free blacks and native-born slaves changed the character of the population. Yet the slave still lived in very much the same world. He had to work in the fields, and he prayed for salvation from the miseries of life. The African heritage was not forgotten, but a shift in emphasis and a lessening of importance of some forms of expression can be noted. Work songs, game songs, choral singing, and music for religious events continued to develop. The white masters' prohibitions against the use of drums, which were feared as communicative devices, only helped the development of percussiveness in singing and other instrumental music. The spiritual is probably the most important and best-known musical form associated with this era in Negro history. Sometimes referred to as "religious song," its text is connected to biblical events and general religious themes. The spiritual is also known for its use as a means of protest and private communication between slaves. Early compilations of spirituals presented a single melodic line and the text. During the late nineteenth and early twentieth centuries, many "concert" versions with piano accompaniments of familiar spirituals were published. The antebellum period is most commonly the point at which researchers begin an investigation of black music. The period between the wars also saw the strengthening of the black church, the rise of secular song, and the conscious assimilation of black music traditions by white performers.

Postbellum, 1867–1919

By the time the Civil War began, it was clear to many Americans that black musical style and performance were distinct from other traditions in the United States. Black performers emphasized religious expression, since slaves were allowed few opportunities for public celebration. In addition, collectors and compilers often ignored secular songs, and thus these appear to have been of lesser importance. Both armies, Union and Confederate, used blacks as musicians. The Union army even bought instruments and hired teachers to instruct the soldiers who had been organized into all-black units. In the camps, however, ex-slaves and slaves who had been pressed into service continued to sing the vast repertoire of songs that were part of their tradition. Added to these were some of the military songs composed during the war. Emancipation was the impetus for much singing of both old and new songs that spoke of the "Great Day."

This era saw the birth of new genres, such as blues and ragtime, early productions of black musical-comedy shows, the invention of a disc-recording method, organization of the NAACP, and the founding of the National Association of Negro Musicians. The older genres continued to flourish, but a greater emphasis was now being placed upon black musical organizations and stage events. The upheaval caused by the war and the displacement of thousands of people, who began a great migration to northern cities such as New York and Chicago, paved the way for the emergence of jazz and the urban ghettos that nurtured black music, poetry, dance, art, and vigorous political activity.

Jazz Age, 1920–30 and after

The history of jazz and its development is a sociological mirror of black people and their adjustment to a new environment and lifestyle.[3] An important part of the story is the interplay of black and white jazzmen. Early black performers important to this development are still remembered: King Oliver, Jelly Roll Morton, Louis Armstrong.

After the rise of jazz, it is difficult to characterize Afro-American music with simple labels. The complex of genres already associated with black tradition continued and became known to a wider audience. The Depression of the 1930s and the end of World War II signaled a greater focus upon urban areas and music that was popular for both black and white patrons. The tempo of change and innovation increased at a rapid rate. Thus the 1940s saw the emergence of a great deal of instrumental music and ensembles: bebop, urban blues, rhythm and blues; the 1950s, hard bop, rock and roll; the 1960s, soul, modern jazz; the 1970s, disco, funk. As early as the 1920s gospel also became an important vehicle for religious expression. It has taken on some of the instrumental ensembles and contemporary harmonic practices of secular musical forms.[4] Also characteristic of the "modern" period is a reemergence of a sense of nationalism and black pride, which has spurred the development of popular musical forms and performance styles that have their antecedents in the sacred music and forms of earlier days.

CHARACTERISTICS OF AFRO-AMERICAN MUSIC

What then are the distinguishing characteristics of Afro-American music? They might be briefly explained under the following categories: general concepts (which affect all performance), rhythm, form and structure, vocal style, and instrumental style.

General Concepts

It is in general performance practices that we find the most tangible evidence of Africa in the music of America. Afro-Americans utilize a musical system that does not always isolate song, dance, and theater. This is not to say there are no distinct forms or compositions for each of these areas, but it suggests that there is an integration of elements so that activities occur within a complex "event." The participation of the audience in the actual performance is also an important part of the musical occasion. Within the musical event, emphasis is placed upon verbal skill and manipulation and coordination of music, movement, and performance in general with the visual effect provided by singers, dancers, musicians, and their instruments. Percussiveness and improvisation are very much a part of musical performance, even when the performer is singing or playing a melodic instrument. These elements permeate the entire tradition and can be found in many guises.

Rhythm

Rhythm is probably the most complex element in Afro-American musical style. The use of flexible time frames, subtle manipulation of multirhythmic contexts, and syncopation lends the music a vitality and energy that is as important in a secular context, such as disco, as it is in the church. Repetition of short rhythmic motifs and extensive use of accentuation within the many instrumental and vocal lines add to the complexity of a composition and give it density and interest.

Form and Structure

The general aesthetic principles mentioned above and the organization of rhythmic patterns aid in the elaboration of musical forms. The percussiveness of consonants and the utilization of word accents that do not always follow normal speech patterns are important elements in textual manipulation within black musical traditions. This type of activity is especially prevalent in gospel, for example, in the pronunciation of the word "Jesus" (Jee'-sus or Jee-sus'). Both syllable elongation and displaced accent have a musical effect. The juxtaposition of opposing accents and the manipulation of meter within an ensemble of three or more musical lines allows performers to construct polyrhythmic textures of great complexity. An emphasis upon duple meter (2/4 and 4/4) and short forms is most characteristic of genres within the tradition. AAB or AAAB forms are very widely utilized in many compositions. In work songs, game songs, and gospel, the use of call-response technique (a solo voice or section answered by the full choir repeating either the solo melody-line or a refrain) is essential to the formal structure of the composition. This type of compositional device is very important throughout the tradition.

Vocal Style

The use of the voice in varied ways is also characteristic of black music. There is extensive application of such devices as falsetto, slurs, moans, shouts, the juxtaposition of extreme registers, and melodic ornamentation. Percussive quali- ties of the text and its melody may also function as a means for variation within a performance. The heavy and dark quality of the "chest" voice in women (lower register) and the "head" voice for men (falsetto) are extensively practiced in both secular and sacred performance.

Instrumental Style

Again percussiveness is part of the stylistic arsenal as well as a technique that allows the performer to imitate the human voice for affective value. It is probably here that most improvisation takes place. Although harmony, in its usual connotation, is important, it too can be utilized percussively and often tends to be very repetitive. The emphasis is then upon the interaction of constituent elements of harmony, melody, rhythm, vocal manipulation, and instrumental variation. What might be termed "development" in European terms often ceases, permitting the progression of the multilined composition in a very different way and with differing goals. The emphasis is not upon the elaboration of longer and longer structural forms with definite parts and relationships, as in a sonata, but upon the manipulation and elaboration of timbre, rhythm, and shorter forms through which individual improvisation might be exercised and developed. There is great aesthetic value placed upon the manner and sincerity of performance in Afro-American tradition.

REPRESENTATIVE MUSICAL GENRES

Because of a dynamic and vigorous musical tradition, some genres that were once more prevalent in Afro-American life are now not as important and have been transformed and absorbed into other forms. Among this group are work songs, field hollers, and vendor street cries, which have been affected by urbanization and changing lifestyles. The stylistic characteristics and performance practices asso- ciated with work songs, for example, are still part of the tradition but find expression in other forms and genres.

Game Songs

As a secular form of musical activity that is the province of children, game songs accompany activities and aid children in the development of various motor skills, coordination, and creativity. Often songs have elaborate rhythmic patterns and include body movements. Games are characteristic of both rural and urban environments.

Field Hollers and Street Cries

Hollers and cries constitute a very individualized form of musical expression. There is no textual or formal unity to the genre, and repetition is greatly utilized. It is identified by function, since the hollers were employed to communicate in the field and to announce things that were happening. Street cries are short melodic phrases uttered by vendors to advertise their wares. Fruits, vegetables, household articles, and other services were often presented to city dwellers in this manner. Particular vendors were often recognized by their distinctive melodic cries.

Work Songs

This category is as varied as the work that was done by hands in the fields, prisons, on railroads, at sea, or in quarries. As in other societies, songs were used to accompany work and served to make heavy, monotonous labor palatable to the workers. The need for coordination and concerted action for heavy jobs made the song caller a key figure and the responsive singing during a job an important activity. Call-response is an important structural device in this genre. Improvisation of texts and the interpolation of personal ideas also characterize this category.

Blues

Probably no other genre has received as much attention as the blues. It is more a textual form (AAB) and a style of performance than anything else. At times a highly personal vehicle for expression, blues often embody the heartache and sadness of the individual who plays and sings the song. In view of the many developments in the genre over the years, a much more extensive discussion would be needed even to outline the types that fall into this category (country, classic, and urban blues).

Spirituals

Spirituals are sacred compositions that typify the relationship to God and slavery as seen by Afro-Americans in the eighteenth century. They are an important window through which to view the collective wisdom and thoughts of a people who lived and grew under an oppressive society. This category has also developed to the point that two major types are recognized: folk spirituals and arranged spirituals (a form of art music).

Gospel

As with all the other types of music found in Afro-America, gospel developed out of the needs and aspirations of people who, now being "free," were again transplanted, this time to northern urban centers. These songs reflect the same concerns and ideas found in other genres and use many of the same musical building blocks but are performed in and for sacred events. Whereas spirituals were usually unaccompanied, gospel is a form that may combine a variety of instruments and voices. It is also characterized by a great deal of improvisation and manipulation of all of the elements previously mentioned. Gospel is for some the symbol of being black in America.

AREAS OF FUTURE RESEARCH

Much research in folklore and ethnomusicology is predicated upon the fact that an investigator from one group studies the expressive behavior of another group.

More and more instances of participants within a group and tradition studying their own behavior are now being published. In the case of Afro-American music this means that black scholars who are trained in research and who still practice their own musical traditions are making in-depth studies of gospel, blues, jazz, and rhythm and blues. For some scholars outside the tradition, this sort of in-group study lacks "objectivity" and thus does not provide a full measure of serious data for analysis and integration into the scholarly literature. For others, it signals an awareness that some aspects of expressive behavior are closed to the outsider and can only be elucidated by knowledgeable participants who speak both the language of the scholar and that of the informants who produce the music. This is indeed a charged issue in some quarters and has important implications for education and funding in folklore and ethnomusicology. I would suggest that the serious study of black music by black scholars does not preclude the study of Afro-American music by outsiders. What it does is to allow for a more complete and dynamic scholarly exchange, which in turn may then truly illuminate the aesthetic that underlies the production, development, and understanding of black music in America.

Applied folklore, the practical utilization of data gathered in organized projects, is not easily accepted by everyone. What is to be used, by whom, and for what purposes are questions that arise immediately. The distrust and fear of exploitation that exist, especially in black communities, make this avenue one that is fraught with special problems but worth careful consideration by folklorists.

Another aspect of musical behavior and its social context that merits even greater research is that of creativity and improvisation in the musical event. The ability to interact dynamically with instrument, voice, form, melody, harmony, and rhythm has always been an important part of the technical equipment of black musicians. Closely related to this topic is the concept of the musical event and its organization, development, constituent elements, and representative genres. Such studies are all the more complicated since they involve the manipulation of large amounts of information and the description and analysis of a multi-channeled and complex activity. Teamwork by a group of investigators, each with some aspect of the event as a special focus, might make this work easier to accomplish.

Finally, urban musics and their development constitute an area of great interest. Although these styles may not be considered "folk" by some scholars, they do embody stylistic features and performance practices indigenous to Afro-Americans. These styles are also important because they have influenced and continue to be an essential part of the musical scene in America, both black and white. Borrowing by the larger society is only now becoming a subject of serious research. Unlike other facets of Afro-American music, urban music is often recorded and accessible to an investigator.

CONCLUSIONS

The history of Afro-American music is marked by the mixing and constant borrowing of musical styles and forms. The process is largely an internal one and has operated for two hundred years. Early writers assumed that slave musicians were merely making imperfect copies of the music and structures that formed part of their masters' music. As we now see, this was not really the case. The aesthetic that permeated West African musics and constituted the basis of slave musical behavior is still very much a part of the contemporary scene.

For the colonial period, records that touch upon Afro-American music are scanty. The music of slaves and their festivals, religious music, and the mixtures of purely African and European styles and performance practices must be documented by means of newspapers, court records, personal journals, travel records, diaries, and reminiscences of visitors to southern plantations. The researcher must be resourceful and sensitive in locating and then interpreting data, because most records from this period are written from a biased viewpoint that neither values nor understands the events being witnessed.

Modern technological advances and contemporary scholarly methodology not only make possible a more reasoned and in-depth view of musical composition and performance in Afro-American communities but also open a channel to the thoughts and feelings that motivate such expressive behavior. Exciting research possibilities beckon in this ever-changing and vibrant part of American life.

RESEARCH CENTERS

Centers and university libraries that contain special collections of materials dealing with the black experience in America are scattered throughout the United States. Although these collections may not have been specifically established for music, they often contain much valuable information and materials for the student of black music. The libraries mentioned below are the most extensive and valuable for a serious researcher. They contain major collections of original documents, manuscripts, recordings, and photographs relating to the history, development, and diversity of Negro life in the Americas.

For regional materials, it is often wise to consult the libraries and collections of institutions such as Fisk University, Tuskegee Institute, Hampton Institute, and Brown University. The major collections available to researchers are: (1) Archive of Folk Culture, Library of Congress, Washington, D.C.; (2) Center for Ethnic Music (Afro-American Collection), Howard University, Washington, D.C.; (3) Archives of Traditional Music, Indiana University, Bloomington; (4) Schomburg Collection, New York Public Library.

NOTES

1. Harold Courlander, *Negro Folk Music* (New York: Columbia University Press, 1963), p. 5.

2. Eileen Southern, *The Music of Black Americans* (New York: W. W. Norton and Co., 1971), pp. 242–43.

3. David Baker, "The Social Role of Jazz," in *Reflections on Afro-American Music*, ed. Dominique-René deLerma (Kent, Ohio: Kent State University Press, 1973), pp. 101–10.

4. See Pearl Williams-Jones, "Afro-American Gospel Music: A Crystallization of the Black Aesthetic," *Ethnomusicology* 19 (1975): 373–85; Horace Boyer, "Contemporary Gospel Music," *The Black Perspective in Music* 7 (1979): 5–58; Mellonee Burnim, "The Black Gospel Music Tradition: Symbol of Ethnicity" (Ph.d. diss., Indiana University, 1980).

Thomas D. Clark

The Westward Movement

From the outset of the Anglo-American advance onto the frontier, from the James River estuary in Virginia and the Massachusetts coast, folklore was a fundamental element in human adaptations to new conditions and lands. First, there were the mysteries of the unexplored "back-country" and its resources. Indian and animal populations offered prizes that at once seduced and frightened timid Europeans who sought a foothold on the new continent. To them the awesome wooded littoral was *terra incognita*, a land that contained both evil and fortune. The invasion of the backwoods, however modest, was in fact the beginning of the American frontier saga.

From the initial association of the Jamestown settlers with the Powhatan Indians onward into this century, the aborigine has been a rich source of American folk history. The Indians' customs, their way of life, their knowledge of natural forces and the environment as well as the location and nature of resources, their adaptations to environmental conditions, and their oral histories all gave the natives stature in the eyes of their white neighbors. European settlers arrived on the North American continent ignorant of its diversified terrain, vast geography, abundant resources, and, most important of all, its environmental influences. Thus any knowledge revealed by the Indians about the land assumed the coloration of profound wisdom. In time the history of the Indian and the American pioneer became so interrelated that it merged into a single piece.

Lore about the Indians gave rise to several important American myths: first, that the Indians knew intimately a wide geographical area; second, that they at all times had an inborn sense of location, which enabled them unerringly to follow trails, interpret natural signs, and sense danger; and third, that they were inured to hardship, pain, and adversity and were capable of great bravery and ferocity. Much factual history sharply revises this view to reveal that Indians reacted much as did white settlers to the human impulses that governed their actions.

The earliest French and English chroniclers began to create the European image of the "noble red man." Together with their artists, they portrayed the North American native clothed in the laurel wreath and toga of classical Rome and Greece. Alongside the noble masculine savage was the noble Indian maiden. Ever since Pocahontas appeared in John Smith's *Generall Historie of Virginia* (1632), the doe-eyed, affectionate Indian maid has remained a standard American character for historians, novelists, and script writers. Among these heroines have been Nancy Ward, Cherokee keeper of the "Black Drink," who helped save the Watauga Fort in eastern Tennessee; Catherine, the Ojibwa girl who warned Major Gladwyn at Detroit of Pontiac's impending attack; and Sacajawea, the Shoshone squaw who accompanied the Lewis and Clark Expedition on part of its journey to the Pacific Coast. The "noble Indian maiden" has been memorialized in both history and literature. Henry W. Longfellow glorified Minnehaha in *The Song of Hiawatha*, and Helen Hunt Jackson's *Ramona* became a beloved personage. James Fenimore Cooper idealized Indians, male and female, in his *Leatherstocking Tales*. In a lesser literary vein, the dime novelists portrayed the "beautiful savage" maiden as a goddess and friend of settlers.

On the other side of the historical coin was the white Indian scout and fighter endowed with the native instinct and wisdom of the savage he tracked. The list of these personalities is almost endless: John Smith, Christopher Gist, Simon Kenton, Daniel Boone, Sam Dale, John Coulter, Kit Carson, Jedediah Smith, Jim Bridger, Thomas Fitzpatrick, and scores of others. Now it is difficult to separate these frontiersmen from their legends, especially in the case of Daniel Boone, who has been sanctified as a folk hero and whose story transcends any restrictions of factual history. In many cases it is almost impossible for either historians or folklorists to write of frontiersmen without injury to the legend.

Every aspect of the westward movement produced its folk characters. As new territories and states were developed in the West, there appeared on the scene a continuous parade of politicians who exemplified in fact and personal acclaim the pioneering experiences of "horny-handed sons of toil." In Tennessee and Kentucky (1775–1815) there were John Sevier and Isaac Shelby, men whose careers spanned the broad spectrum of Indian fighting, farming, and politics. After 1805 in Kentucky, the lawyer-farmer Henry Clay captivated American fancy as a non-military hero for whom fathers named their sons until well after 1850. In the same era, Andrew Jackson of Tennessee rode to political fame as the hero of the Creek War and the Battle of New Orleans. On the angry march away from Natchez in the Mississippi Territory in 1812, his faithful Tennessee Volunteers gave him the rugged frontier soubriquet "Old Hickory," a name worth thousands of frontier votes. William Henry Harrison of the Old Northwest Territory and Indiana, hero of Tippecanoe Creek and the Thames in the War of 1812, was no less successful than Jackson, achieving his political victory under the worshipful nickname "Old Tippecanoe."

Locally, frontier politics produced its lively procession of stump-haranguing "statesmen-demagogues," who associated themselves with the common herd of yeoman sons of the backwoods, spoke in the vernacular, ridiculed opponents with coarse humor, and promised "to turn the rascals out" in support of Old Hickory or Old Tippecanoe or any other national idol. Telling folksy anecdotes and responding to the opposition's jibes with biting repartee were often safer vote-getting devices than a profound discussion of issues. Too often, historians of the American political scene have overlooked the whimsical element of a folklore unrelated to the issues as a decisive ingredient in campaigns and elections. How much, for instance, did the rolling of huge campaign balls from town-to-town, the shouting of nonsensical slogans, the drinking of hard cider, the waving of campaign banners, and the nailing of coon skins to gable ends of houses have to do with electing a president of the United States? There still lingers in American politics a trace of the log-cabin birthplace myth and the mystique of rural birth. The famous "courthouse rings" have ever proved a hardy perennial. These consisted of local officials who exercised power and perpetuated themselves in office by shrewd management and voter manipulation.

The unembellished backwoods political scene was immortalized in George Caleb Bingham's genre paintings, "Stump Speaking" and "County Election," and in the biographies of Henry Clay, Andrew Jackson, William Henry Harrison, Sam Houston, and Abraham Lincoln. It can also be reconstructed from extensive contemporary newspaper coverage or the reminiscences of candidates and managers.

The mudsill of the westward movement was the frontier yeoman, who, seen as an individual, represented the sober aspects of pioneering. But contemporary books, travel literature, and some social histories portrayed him as a type: illiterate, terse of speech, visionary, suspicious of strangers, inhospitable, and a voracious eater. Sweaty and weary, bowed down under the mission of manifest destiny, he was responsive to emotional religious appeals, crude in his social relations, restless and on the move, and sinfully wasteful of natural resources. In actuality the frontiersman exhibited many of these traits plus many stern virtues, and the truth no doubt lies somewhere between the idolatrous later descriptions of the frontier experience and the composite image painted by the omniscient foreign traveler who crossed the Atlantic in the late eighteenth and first half of the nineteenth century to view the American democratic experiment and then published from abroad superficial impressions in travel journals. In more recent years even seminal works by scholars like Frederick Jackson Turner and his disciples have presented the westward movement and the American pioneer in less than full context.[1]

The richest vein of folklore in American frontier history is to be found in the social, economic, and political responses the pioneers made to their challenging environment. On virgin soils the American dream of progress was nurtured and the principles of the Protestant ethic freely applied. The art of boosterism knew no bounds.

Social responses in the westward movement occurred in many areas of life. For example, a folk curative and medical lore developed that supplied specific remedies for most human ills. From the Old World, from the Indian, from immediacy and necessity, from folk knowledge of herbs, crude chemicals, and harsh surgical techniques, and from superstitions, there derived a substantial chapter of folk history. There were herbal resources that had definite curative values. The use of poultices in many instances reduced fevers and pain, and common sense prevailed in the setting of broken and fractured bones and in the cleaning of open wounds.

Another bookshelf of library materials relates to religion on the frontier. Personal memoirs, autobiographies, biographies, scriptural treatises by itinerants, and institutional histories provide a broad spectrum of frontier religious responses and deviations. Ironically, however, many an observant minister, wandering the lonely roads and trails and sharing the crude fare of pioneer families, gained clearer insights into the local folkways and manners than into the spiritual conditions. On the isolated outer fringes of the population movement, the backwoodsmen often made vigorous intellectual responses to everyday issues and challenges based as much on concepts from the scriptures as from secular experiences. Excellent examples of circuit-rider materials are James B. Finley's autobiographical travelogue, the personal observations of the Reverend John Mason Peck, the autobiography of Peter Cartwright, and Timothy Flint's published recollections. Many of these autobiographical travelogues are described in a three-volume work I edited, *Travels in the Old South*. Not infrequently the American backwoodsman equated his own plight with that of the ancients described in the Old Testament.

Fundamentally the westward movement throughout its history involved the basics not so much of classical democracy as of neighborliness and expediency. The nature of the land and environment mitigated against a genuine show of the individualism that more romantic historians attributed to the era. For the rank-and-file frontiersman, the conformist—not the individualist—personified the folk movement across the continent. The husband, the wife, and their brood constituted the ranks of the common man so dear to politician and historian alike. It was this segment of western society who pushed the covered wagon trains west, settled the lonely wind-swept prairies, endured the rigors of life in log cabins, sod houses, and adobe huts, and had the courage to overcome disastrous floods and droughts. The younger generation created new social and political blocs. The sons became farmers, railroad men, streamboat captains and pilots, cattle drovers, mechanics, and even bankers, merchants, and preachers. The daughters became virtuous, long-suffering helpmates, who bore with never-failing patience and faithfulness the vicissitudes of pioneer life. In many respects, the frontier wife symbolized the maternal spirit of American domesticity, or, in beloved political rhetoric, "God, home, and mother."

Fortunately, everyday Americans caught up in the westward movement lost little time feeling sorry for themselves as they moved with the expanding frontier. They were in too big a hurry to gobble up freshly available public lands and take advantage of new opportunities. Incurable optimists, the pioneers developed a keen sense of humor, which enabled them to persevere. They expressed themselves in their more whimsical moments either in grossly exaggerated figures of speech or in belittling and ridiculing terms. The traditions of the western flatboatmen include frequently cited examples of bragging, rowdy stories, and colorful figures of speech. Day after day, these crude farmer-rivermen faced the treacherous currents of the western rivers, the snags, sandbars, swirls, and sudden rain and windstorms, to say nothing of the human hazards of pirates and sharpies waiting around the bends to wreak havoc on crews and boats. It took a lot of rowdy humor and bragging to maintain courage and a belief in their superhuman powers.

There crawled up from the river banks armies of gritty steamboatmen, including such well-known characters as Mike Fink, Mike Stackpole, and "Roaring" Jack Russell. Mark Twain's *Life on the Mississippi* and his lovable classic *Huckleberry Finn* were peopled with such types. In a more sophisticated and slightly more refined period after 1830, there appeared on the rivers the long-fingered riverboat gambler in his checkered vest, the muddle-headed planter and his beautiful daughter, the friendly game, and the lost plantation.

Over a long period of time the western rivers and their boats did more than facilitate commerce and generate statistics. During the years 1830–75 the steamboat contributed substantially to the American folk movement. It hastened the spread of population, the exploitation of the land, and the creation of new states, and it contributed substantially to intersectional intercourse. The more refined and substantial boats gave frontier America its first taste of rapid and luxurious travel. Despite the muddy and treacherous reality of struggling against unruly currents, snags, earthquake tremors, and storms, the riverboats stamped indelibly upon American western history an aura of romance, which endured long after the era of the stern-wheelers, with their elegant salons and spacious texas decks, vanished around the great bend of technical progress.

Frontier Americans created their heroes and characters as they moved westward from one stage to another. In the immigrations of the late eighteenth and first half of the nineteenth century, the "dumb" Dutch and the "greenhorn" Irish became the butt of myriad folk stories, often told in mixtures of broken English and frontier vernacular. The frontier, however, did not have to import characters; it grew a bountiful crop of its own, who made up in cheek and brass what they lacked in sophistication and polish. From the Chesapeake to the San Francisco Bay the greenhorn was as standard a fixture on the American scene as log cabins, cottonwoods, and prairie grass. Among the homegrown greenhorns were the illiterate militiamen, wagon train hangers-on, miners, and, later, cowboy wranglers.

The opening of the trans-Mississippi and Rocky Mountain West produced a bumper crop of heroic frontiersmen. Among them were trail-breakers, mountain men, miners, loggers, cowboys, railroaders, and many others, including highwaymen. The human saga of the frontier would be less colorful without such characters as Manuel Lisa, General William Ashley, John Coulter, Jedediah Smith, James Ohio Pattie, the Sublette Brothers, Kit Carson, and Joseph Redford Walker.

On the heels of trail-breakers and adventurers came the covered wagon settlers and the "Forty-Niners," many of whom kept journals describing their ordeals, wrote memoirs, or contributed reams of material to eastern newspapers. These pilgrims produced one of the most dramatic folk movements in American history; in many respects it was the most colorful human mass movement since the exodus from Egypt. The experiences of this era of the westward movement involved every challenge and emotion imaginable: booming success, excessive hardships, bubbling hopes, frustrated dreams, overwhelming tragedy, and, ultimately, tremendous political, social, and economic accomplishment. Much of the "gold" of the great western rushes can still be mined from the raw ore of contemporary accounts of this vast human transportation to new lands and fresh beginnings in almost every phase of life. Literally hundreds of published contemporary sources give insight into the mores of frontier life.[2]

Changing environmental conditions, geographical influences, and economic demands bore heavily upon the shaping of the frontier folk personality. Beyond the Mississippi old-line frontiersmen were transformed into new folk characters. For instance, no westerner impressed his image upon America more firmly than the cowboy. Back on the old colonial and southern frontiers, there were cattle drovers who moved just a step ahead of the settlement line. Up to the Texas border, these lazy "poor white" grazers were largely footmen who dragged their families along behind their wandering herds across government lands. In the 1840s and on the open plains, the American cowboy mounted a horse caparisoned with a fancy Spanish saddle and trappings and set out across even broader stretches of the public domain. Following the Civil War, cattle and railway frontiers rushed headlong to meet each other. They did not form a junction, however, until the mounted drover, armed with a Colt revolver, lariat, fancy saddle, spurred boots, a broad-brimmed hat, and a boundless taste for hardship, calamity, strong whiskey, and easy-mannered women, had established himself as a permanent folk hero in American history.

There were the quieter heroes on the frontier who made important medical discoveries, invented labor-saving machines and applied them to the conquest of the land, organized towns and cities, railroad companies and banks, established churches and universities, and set up chambers of commerce to proclaim their accomplishments. Earlier the pioneers had brought with them the seeds of a new American civilization, marked by land and environment and by the various experiences of the people who by 1890 had repeatedly started over again, each time moving upward through several stages of a maturing society. In romantic novels, movies, stage productions, and modern television presentations, the more sober pioneers appear on stage as judges, bankers, merchants, doctors, and dependable householders who struggle upward in the midst of a melee of rowdiness and law-breaking. In reality, the line between the rowdies and the "good" citizens was sometimes thin.

No matter how cautious objective historians may try to be in the use of folk materials, they cannot ignore them if they expect to give humanity and color to their writing. In the final analysis of the western movement, there may be no firmer truth than the assertion that it was not cold, objective fact that governed human reactions and decision-making, but what the people believed to be the truth. They cherished their heroes, varnished and unvarnished; they assumed the verities of the democratic form of government; they sanctioned the fundamentals of human rights and placed abiding faith in the limitless promise of the land, in their own capabilities, in progress, and in national supremacy. This ingrained folk-faith enabled frontier families to meet repeated challenges and crises and to develop a sense of triumph. It was a remarkable fact that few or no democratic institutions had their origins on the frontier, but that the basic concept of the fundamental federal system was transported across the continent without undergoing either major revision or disruption.

NOTES

1. See Dixon Ryan Fox, *Sources of Culture in the Middlewest* (New York, 1934); Frederick Jackson Turner, *The Frontier in American History* (New York, 1920); Avery O. Craven, "The Turner Thesis and the South," *Journal of Southern History* 5 (August 1939): 291–314; Richard A. Bartlett, *The New Country, A Social History of the American Frontier 1776–1890* (New York, 1974); Malcolm J. Rohrbough, *The Trans-Appalachian Frontier* (New York, 1978).

2. Among these sources are such informal genre books as William Littell, *Festoons of Fancy* (Louisville, 1814), A. B. Longstreet, *Georgia Scenes* (Charleston, 1843), Joseph G. Baldwin, *Flush Times in Alabama and Mississippi* (New York, 1853), Samuel P. Avery, *The Harp of a Thousand Strings* (New York, 1858), Baynard Rush Hall (Robert Carlton), *The New Purchase* (Princeton, 1916), N. M. Ludlow, *Dramatic Life as I Found It* (St. Louis, 1880), and James B. Finley, *Autobiography of Rev. James B. Finley; or Pioneer Life in the West* (Cincinnati, 1854). More formal and modern sources pertaining to the humorous side of

pioneering are Arthur Palmer Hudson, *Humor in the Old Deep South* (New York, 1936), Walter Blair, *Native American Humor (1800–1900)* (New York, 1937), Mody Boatright, *Folk Laughter on the American Frontier* (Austin, 1943), R. Carlyle Buley, *The Old Northwest, Pioneer Period, 1815–1840*, 2 vols. (Bloomington, 1951), Everett Dick, *The Sod House Frontier, 1854–1890* (New York, 1937), Dixon Wecter, *The Hero in America: A Chronicle of Hero Worshiping* (New York, 1941).

No social historian or folklorist dealing with the westward movement in America can overlook the numerous contemporary travel and descriptive accounts. The quality of these accounts is uneven, but collectively they give a rewarding insight into eighteenth- and nineteenth-century America. Among the classics are François André Michaux, *Travels to the West of the Alleghany Mountains in the States of Ohio, Kentucky, and Tennessee and return to Charleston by way of the Carolina Highlands* (Paris, 1804), Fortescue Cuming, *Sketches of a Tour to the Western Country, Through the States of Ohio and Kentucky . . . in the Winter of 1807, and concluded in 1809* (Pittsburgh, 1810), Timothy Flint, *Recollections of the Last Ten Years* (Boston, 1826), Alexis Charles H. C. de Tocqueville, *De la Democratie in Amerique*, 4 vols. (Paris, 1835–40), James (Viscount) Bryce, *The American Commonwealth*, 2 vols. (New York, 1888), and Albert D. Richardson, *Beyond the Mississippi* (New York, 1867). There are also travel bibliographies: Allan Nevins, *American Social History as Recorded by British Travellers* (New York, 1923), Frank Monaghan, *French Travellers in the United States, 1765–1932* (New York, 1933), and Thomas D. Clark, ed., *Travels in the South*, 6 vols. (Norman, 1948–62).

Barbara Kirshenblatt-Gimblett

Studying Immigrant and Ethnic Folklore

For over twenty thousand years people have migrated to what we know today as the United States. Although migration, culture contact, and awareness of cultural difference have shaped life here from the earliest times, it is only during the last hundred and fifty years that immigration to America reached its maximum size and diversity. With the arrival between 1820 and 1960 of almost fifty million people from all parts of the globe, the United States became "the principal beneficiary of the greatest folk-migration in human history."[1]

FOLKLORE OF THE IMMIGRANT EXPERIENCE

During the period of mass migration (1880–1921), large American cities teemed with new arrivals, some of whom moved to small towns and rural areas. Each one has a story to tell, as do newly arrived immigrants today. There are tales about leaving: when a Jewish immigrant was about to depart, his father told him to write his name on a piece of paper and to throw it into the ocean from the ship, since no one in the New World would know who he was. And there are accounts of the voyage: a Romanian woman obtained the food that sustained her and her young child through the arduous trip by singing folksongs to homesick passengers in exchange for precious oranges. And there are anecdotes about encounters with immigration officials at ports of entry, especially at Ellis Island, where some twelve million steerage passengers were processed: a Jewish man from Russia, hoping to avoid trouble, had decided to abandon his name, Moyshe Stutshevski, and to announce himself as John Smith; when the immigration officer asked for his name, he blurted out in Yiddish, "*Shoyn fargesn*" (Just forgot), and was known thereafter as Shaun Ferguson. The first hours, days, weeks, months, and years were filled with new experiences, many of them traumatic, confusing, or embarrassing. These "first experiences" have given rise to hilarious anecdotes and jokes, in which a greenhorn eats a banana with the skin, or, proud of his knowledge that it is to be peeled, throws away that spongy pith and then eats the skin. Others cannot find a toilet and deposit their wastes in milk bottles, behind fences, and in other unseemly places.

These accounts are but one indication that the immigrant experience, which so often involves culture shock, generates its own culture and folklore. During periods of massive immigration, communities of newcomers are formed and within them immigrant organizations arise—home-town societies, benevolent societies, cultural clubs, social service organizations. The activities of these organizations are worthy of study in their own right. Many of them sponsor choral groups, mandolin orchestras, dance troupes. They hold banquets featuring traditional foods and capped by folk comedians reeling off dialect jokes and other oral lore. Traditional singers may be invited to perform. In addition, immigrant neighborhoods support their own bakers, butchers, dairies, musicians, craftsmen, and other tradition bearers.

In many households and occupational settings, the creative energies of immigrant raconteurs are unleashed by the situation of multilingualism and multiculturalism, in which world views, cultures, and languages clash and undergo massive and rapid change. The protagonists of their stories are often bunglers, sometimes tricksters, who are considered to be without culture because they are between cultures. What they know from the Old Country they cannot use, and what they need in order to make it in America, they do not yet know. These tales are generally preoccupied with culture shock, name changing, linguistic and cultural unintelligibility, social blunders, poverty, and the eccentricities of immigrant characters. Narrators draw from the resources of their Old and New World cultures and languages and mediate between them—they may switch languages, imitate immigrant English, provide mock definitions of terms (in several Jewish jokes, a *mikve* [Yiddish: ritual bath] was glossed as an "overheated swimming pool" and whorehouse as "a place of reclining refreshments"). They also indulge in ethnographic detail in ways that reveal a preoccupation with cultural competence, contact, and change, as well as with the gaps between generations.

One important subject for study, then, is folklore generated during and about the immigrant experience itself. Studies might explore such questions as: does the folklore of immigration take special forms, exploit language in distinctive ways, display a preoccupation with particular themes? In what ways does immigration involve "a visible and striking transformation of the consciousness of the individual . . . a change, not merely in the content of experience, but in the individual's mental and spiritual adjustment to it?"[2] To what extent is immigrant culture a product of such transformations of consciousness and of "fresh contacts" of future generations with the culture of their immigrant forebears and with the culture of others who are American born? What is the role of stories about the immigrant experience in the repertoire of later generations of American-born raconteurs?

Immigrant families are heir to family sagas, often of epic proportions, born of these experiences. These sagas may be elicited as life histories from the foreign born and as family history from their children and grandchildren. The interviewer can prepare a checklist or field guide ahead of time, and toward the end of an interview or at another session, the interviewer can ask the immigrant or other members of his or her family to fill in gaps in the account. Family snapshot albums, home movies, letters, souvenirs, family heirlooms, and documents complement oral accounts and stimulate memories, which surface in such forms as personal narratives, memorates, legends, anecdotes, local character tales, songs, and nicknames. The following field guide[3] suggests general topics that documentation of the immigrant experience might cover, topics around which folklore tends to form. The latter part of the guide will also prove useful for documenting the folklore of ethnicity.

FIELD GUIDE OUTLINE

1. *Life in the Old Country*—home town and community, everyday life, holidays and seasonal patterns.

2. *Historical circumstance in the Old Country*—wars, political conditions.

3. *Contact with the Old Country*—objects brought from home, correspondence with those left behind, visits home, relatives visiting the New World, impact of immigrants on their hometowns and on prospective emigrants.

4. *Conditions leading to decision to leave*—economic, political, personal.

5. *Preparations for departure*—farewells, liquidating assets, clearance for immigration, deciding what to bring.

6. *Voyage*—obtaining ticket, conditions on board.

7. *Arrival*—clearance through immigration officials.

8. *First impressions, encounters, and misadventures in strange environment*—food, lodging, clothing, language, name changing and misunderstandings, school, work, religious and cultural life, immigrant organizations.

9. *The first few years*—work, social life, establishing oneself in business, establishing a family, life in the immigrant community.

10. *Later developments*—dispersal of first area of immigrant settlement, changes in economic status, change of residence, lifestyle, attitudes, language loyalties, relations with compatriots and others, later generations and their life course.

11. *Cultural life*—role of church, immigrant organizations, immigrant entertainments, press, radio, and records; place of music, dance, festivals, and other folklore forms in immigrant life; family get-togethers and community events; formation of family clubs and other organizations.

Interviewers will always find willing subjects for their study of immigrant folklore in the elderly, for whom reminiscence is a life-sustaining activity. Life review has special relevance for foreign-born immigrants, particularly those who live into very advanced years. Such individuals may have moved from a town in Russia to the Lower East Side of New York to a big city in the Midwest, and, upon retiring, to California or Florida. Such a person may be the *only* remaining witness to a life lived in more than one place, in more than one culture, in more than one era. Reminiscence, which is part of the vital process of self-integration at the end of a very long life, can span almost a century in some cases, and can compensate for the partial and restricted experiences of later generations. As Mannheim has explained, "members of any one generation can participate only in a temporally limited section of the historical process, and it is therefore necessary continually to transmit the accumulated cultural heritage."[4] With the rupture in cultural and communal continuity brought about by immigration, reminiscence becomes essential to personal as well as cultural survival, something the elderly know well. As one of Myerhoff's elderly subjects remarked: "If my life goes now, it means nothing. But if my life goes, with my memories, and all that is lost, that is something else to bear."[5]

THE FOLKLORE HERITAGE OF IMMIGRANTS

The culture that immigrants bring with them undergoes change and forms an important subject for study. Dorson has posed these questions:

What happens to the inherited traditions of European and Asiatic folk after they settle in the United States and learn a new language and new ways? How much of the old lore is retained and transmitted to their children? What parts are sloughed off, what intrusions appear, what accommodation is made between Old Country beliefs and the American scene? These are the large questions that confront the assessor of immigrant folk traditions.[6]

Many smaller questions confront the researcher. Which Old World genres are most vulnerable to attrition in the New World context? Will fixed-phrase proverbs or songs in foreign languages undergo and survive translation? Do legends about a revenant in a church or a strange rock formation on the west coast of Ireland lose their relevance across the ocean? Does the hustle and bustle of American life crowd out the long and leisurely wonder tale, eliminate the time and patience for the slow-paced ballad? Do Old World folk beliefs and magical practices come into conflict with American ways and recede? Do regional differences rooted in the Old World disappear in the United States, so that one regional form prevails? For example, in the United States the potato *latke* (Yiddish: pancake) has driven out the buckwheat blini fried in goose fat and, to a lesser extent, the jam-filled fritter as the festive food for Hanukkah (Feast of Lights). Does a prestige form replace local traditions? For example, Italians in Philadelphia have adopted the funeral customs of the *patrone*, rather than of their peasant forebears. What are the channels of transmission and what impact (positive or negative) do mass media, ethnic press, ethnic recordings, and films have on the imported heritage? Are Old World forms retained while their functions change? People may continue to eat kosher food, for instance, but for sentimental rather than religious reasons. Are Old World folklore forms generally shortened and simplified? What conditions are conducive to the maintenance of Old World patterns—isolation in small towns and rural areas or life in the heart of the big city, where large immigrant enclaves can form and support a full array of cultural institutions and activities?

It would be worth examining highly successful examples of persistence in order to understand the processes at work. The Hasidic communities in New York City are excellent cases. A community and its culture are defined as much by what is rejected as by what is accepted, by what is discarded as by what is retained. In this light, "persistence" and "attrition" need not be viewed as passive acts, but as active decision-making that shapes cultural continuities and discontinuities.

The foreign-born elderly are essential to the study of the folklore heritage of immigrant communities, not only because of their vivid, almost century-long memories but also because of the distinctive ways they "recycle" their folklore heritage in the senior citizens' centers and retirement colonies of their last years. Cut off from their natal community and culture, the elderly devise ingenious and highly satisfying ways of "recycling" the culture of their childhood. In a senior citizens' center in California, the elderly draw creatively from the culture of their earlier years. Holidays are rescheduled to accommodate their personal safety—New Year's Eve may be celebrated during the day. Old rituals are adapted and new rituals created to deal with recurring and unique events in their lives; one member specified in his will that his birthday was to be celebrated in the center for a specified number of years after his death, which occurred during his birthday party at the center.[7]

A study of immigrant folklore might explore the relationship of loyalty to Old World traditions to stages in the life cycle. It would appear that in the case of the senior citizens' center studied by Myerhoff, interest in Old World traditions lapsed during the middle years and resurfaced in new ways in the later years of foreign-born immigrants. In other cases, older people of any generation might be expected to know the old ways or to be able to perform certain genres, so that the apparent absence of certain types of folklore in the repertoires of the young and middle-aged may not reflect general attrition or change but rather a life-cycle pattern.

The folklore heritage of immigrant groups can be studied by observation as well as by interviewing. Excellent field guides, designed specifically for particular cultures, are listed by Reishstein.[8] These guides are generally very detailed and specific to the culture in question and can be used to interview immigrants about what they remember of life in the Old Country as well as for observing the practices today. When supplemented by Herskovits's outline for the study of acculturation,[9] these guides provide a useful framework for examining culture change. Good examples of observational studies include *The Two Rosetos* and *Number Our Days*.

THE FOLKLORE OF ETHNICITY

Memories of Old World experiences and the trauma of immigration may fade with the distance from the Old World, the passage of time, migrations within the United States, marriage with members of other communities, and entry into other spheres of American life. With possibly eight great-grandparents born in possibly eight different countries, a fourth-generation child will form and display cultural loyalties in ways that are complex, open to considerable choice, and worthy of study in their own right. Even those whose families show more consistency in terms of national origin have the experience of participating in and identifying with more than one community and more than one cultural sphere.

Just as people can and do acquire more than one language, so too do they acquire various degrees of competence in more than one cultural mode. This multilingual, multicultural competence increases the repertoires and alternatives available to individuals and their various communities. As a result, much *folklore of ethnicity* may also be characterized as syncretic or creolized, and would be productively studied in these terms. Ukrainian country music in Canada is a good example—country-western tunes are performed on the usual complement of instruments, but with the addition of the cymbalom (hammered dulcimer), and are set to Ukrainian lyrics.[10]

We might also view the folklore of ethnicity in terms of *multiple cultural repertoires* and *cultural code-switching*. Italian families who eat an American style *platter* (meat and vegetables) one night and Italian style *gravy* (sauce with pasta) the next on a regular basis may be said to engage in cultural code-switching.[11] Just as bilingual speakers may vary in their attitude toward keeping their languages discrete or allowing interpenetrations and code-switching, so too do the attitudes toward the use of the cultural repertoires vary. An interesting research problem would be to explore how people with multiple codes invoke these codes and alternate among them: when, to what end, and with what meanings and effects?

Indeed, a special feature of the folklore of ethnicity is a heightened awareness of cultural diversity and ambiguity, a well-developed capacity for reflexivity or self-reflection. The presence of cultural alternatives, which is, after all, at the heart of the immigrant/ethnic experience, "brings to consciousness . . . premises or assumptions hitherto in the main covert or implicit."[12] The experience of culture contact throws aspects of each into high relief, creating what may be called the *cultural foregrounding* effect, as one inevitably compares one's own ways with those of others, noting similarities and differences. The issue is not the degree of cultural difference involved, objectively speaking, but the social significance attributed to any similarity or difference, however small.

The notion of cultural foregrounding is helpful as a framework for examining the many forms of ethnic display and ethnic pride, for rethinking "cultural persistence," which has overtones of passivity, in terms of a more active cultivation of tradition, and for thinking about many innovations, especially in the area of popular culture. The interesting research questions become, to what extent, how, and to what effect is folklore used to make cultural comparisons and to mark cultural distinctiveness? How is folklore used to define cultural differences, incongruities, and convergences? What are the nature and content of these "comparisons," of this "marking" or foregrounding?

The following anecdote is an example par excellence of the folklore of ethnicity, defined as cultural foregrounding:

> The president of the United States was going for re-election. And they told him that he was going to lose the Jewish vote and Lyndon Johnson says, "Whadda you mean I'm gonna lose da Jewish vote? Wha?"
>
> They says, "Because you're discriminating."
>
> They says, "Have you ever had a Jewish astronaut?"
>
> LBJ thought about it. He says, "No, we nevah have." Have I told you this? He says, "Well get me a Jewish astronaut," he says, "but don't get me one of these ringers. You go to the *yeshive* [an institution of higher talmudic learning; (in U.S.) Orthodox Jewish all-day school] in New York and you pick up a real genuayne Jewish astronaut."
>
> So they get a guy in New York with the sombrero, and the ten gallon hat with the *peyes* [sidelocks] and the *gartl* [belt; esp. (Jew.) belt worn during prayer] and the *mantl* [coat] and they take him to Cape Kennedy and they give him a crash course on astronauting and he is ready to go up in the cone of the rocket and the commmander comes up and he says,"Astronaut Hymie Berkowits, Astronaut Hymie Berkowits. This is control tower. In honor of your faith we are going to take the count-down in Jewish. Remember?" So he goes, *"Tsen, nayn, akht, sibn,* and holding, *zeks, finf, fir, dray,* and holding, *tsvey, eyns un avek* [ten, nine, eight, seven, and holding, six, five, four, three, and holding, two, one and away]."
>
> And away goes astronaut Hymie Berkowits into the clouds. And he's going for about five minutes and the control tower calls him and says, "Control tower to Astronaut Hymie Berkowits. Control tower to Astronaut Hymie Berkowits. Are you ready to push phase five to start operation twelve?"
>
> "Oy I'll tell you da truth. I got no time."
>
> So this goes on three, four times. Finally the general comes in to the control tower and he calls up and he says, "Astronaut Hymie Berkowits, this is control tower, General speaking. What is this business, we keep calling you and you keep saying you got no time? What's going on there?"
>
> He says, "Vell you see General, it's like dis. I'm going around de vorld very very fast, around and around, from light to dark and from dark to light. In

between putting on de *tfiln* [phylacteries], taking off de *tfiln, minkhe, marev* [the Jewish afternoon prayer, the Jewish evening prayer] I got no time."[13]

Cultural foregrounding is accomplished here through code-switching (standard English, Texas English, astronaut English, immigrant English, Yiddish), the specification of traditional clothing, and the performance of daily rituals. The entire anecdote is designed to exploit the hilarious incongruities of secular American culture, as epitomized by space travel, and immigrant culture, as epitomized by an Orthodox Jewish man. The anecdote also has political implications and suggests ambivalence regarding affirmative action.

In addition to collecting such materials, which present cultural foregrounding so clearly, we can also observe how people display their culture to themselves, as they do in their homes and in their religious and communal organizations, for example. How is cultural foregrounding organized in public and multicultural settings—on the street, at work, in bars, at town festivals, in the mass media? To what is attention drawn and to what effect? What does it mean when peasant costumes are worn only when organized dance troupes perform on a stage or at a festival? Why are old-fashioned foods most likely to turn up at calendar-year, life-cycle, and other family and community celebrations? How do people choose which language to speak about what to whom, and what does their choice signify? (Since so much folklore is verbal, strategies of language choice are central to the study of immigrant and ethnic traditions.) To what extent can the opposite process be discerned—that is, the effort to deemphasize the awareness of cultural distinctiveness?

Seen in terms of these questions, the study of ethnic folklore, which may also be defined as folklore on and about cultural boundaries, requires a shift in perspective. Rather than looking for a bounded and named "group"—the Poles in Chicago or the Czechs in Texas—and studying the traditions of this group, we must look for settings, social occasions, and events in which boundary negotiation is an important activity. Consider, for example, how the Tricentenary was celebrated in Yankee City, the subject of a study by Lloyd Warner:

> The symbols which dominated the historical rituals and pageant were those of the colonial period and the era of the American Revolution. . . . Despite the fact that they already comprised a significant element of the city's population, the ethnic groups were expected to choose themes from the colonial and revolutionary era for the historical pageant. . . . Even in 1976, during the Bicentennial celebration in one of the historic mill buildings in Lowell, Massachusetts, the majority of the participants from the community (who were of different ethnic origins) were wearing revolutionary era costume, though Lowell was founded in 1820 and symbolized the beginning of the new industrial order. Similarly, a recent follow-up study on Yankee City in the 1970s finds that the new owners of the Federalist houses in Newburyport are reconstructing the genealogies of these houses, rather than their own family histories.[14]

These examples suggest that ethnic identification is elective in given situations. We can exercise considerable choice in how we identify ourselves and in how we connect ourselves to the past. How this choice is exercised is a key question for research into the folklore of ethnicity.

CONCLUSION

The three categories of folklore discussed here are really three perspectives that can be applied to *any* generation. Though the "folklore of the immigrant experience" refers specifically to the folklore generated during and about immigration, later generations may continue to narrate their family's immigrant saga. Though "the folklore heritage of immigrants" refers to the traditions of the Old Country, these traditions may continue to be practiced, or at least remembered, by later generations. And since all generations experience cultural boundaries, all of them create "folklore of ethnicity," which we have defined as folklore on and about cultural boundaries. But each generation stands in a different relation to the past and present, and therefore will yield different results when viewed in terms of these three perspectives.

Because of the intense presence of many cultural alternatives and the heightened awareness of cultural difference engendered by them, immigrant and ethnic folklore provide rich opportunities for exploring cultural creativity and innovation, processes that are at work everywhere.[15]

NOTES

1. Maldwyn Allen Jones, *American Immigration* (Chicago: University of Chicago Press, 1960), p. 1.

2. Karl Mannheim, "The Problem of Generations," in *Essays In the Sociology of Knowledge*, ed. Paul Kecskemeti (London: Routledge & Kegan Paul, 1952), p. 293.

3. The guide is based upon Linda Dégh's unpublished "Fieldwork Guide for Collecting Ethnic Culture and Folklore."

4. Mannheim, p. 292.

5. Barbara Myerhoff, *Number Our Days* (New York: Dutton, 1978), p. 74.

6. Richard M. Dorson, *American Folklore* (Chicago: University of Chicago Press, 1959), pp. 135-36.

7. Myerhoff, pp. 195-231.

8. Eleanor Fein Reishstein, "Bibliography on Questionnaires as a Folklife Fieldwork Technique," *Keystone Folklore Quarterly* 13 (1968): 45-69, 121-66, 219-32.

9. Melville J. Herskovits, *Acculturation: The Study of Culture Contact* (New York: Social Science Research Council, 1938; reprinted by Peter Smith, 1958).

10. Robert Klymasz, "Sounds You Never Before Heard," *Ethnomusicology* 16 (1972): 372-80.

11. Janet Theophano, work in progress.

12. F. M. Keesing, "Recreative Behavior and Culture Change," in *Men and Cultures*, ed. Anthony F. C. Wallace (Philadelphia: University of Pennsylvania Press, 1960), pp. 130-33.

13. Barbara Kirshenblatt-Gimblett, "Culture Shock and Creativity: Code-Switching in Immigrant Humor," *Ashkenaz: Essays in Jewish Folklore and Culture* (Philadelphia: University of Pennsylvania Press, forthcoming).

14. Tamara Hareven, "The Search for Generational Memory: Tribal Rites in Industrial Society," *Daedalus* 107 (1978): 147.

15. Barbara Kirshenblatt-Gimblett, "Culture Shock and Narrative Creativity," in *Folklore in the Modern World*, ed. Richard M. Dorson (The Hague: Mouton, 1978), pp. 109–22.

Adrienne Lanier Seward

The Legacy of Early Afro-American Folklore Scholarship

Topsy: "I spect I grow'd. Don't think
nobody never made me." *Uncle Tom's Cabin*

During a few days in May of 1975, a small group of folklorists met in Washington, D.C., for what was later to be referred to as the first meeting of the Association of African and African American Folklorists. That meeting was called to "examine the field of folklore from a black perspective—to evaluate critical concepts and definitions which bear on our lives, to consider some of the problems which black folklorists face in a white dominated discipline, and to move toward the development of theories, agenda, and programs which may help us make the discipline more responsive to the needs of our people." One particular panel ("Concepts and Definitions of Folklore") had been designed specifically to raise questions such as: What is American folklore? What is black folklore? The questions raised by this group of black folklorists for discussion are certainly of the same kind as those being asked by most scholars interested in folklore and black American culture. That they have continued to be asked so persistently over time attests to their significance as questions as well as to a general uneasiness over the various responses proffered thus far. Both are perplexing questions, and their interrelatedness is equally provocative. My concern here, however, is directed toward *attitudes*—particularly those that have helped shape our current understanding of the nature of Afro-American folklore. These attitudes represent part of the legacy of early Afro-American folklore scholarship.

"Spirituals and blues," "Brer Rabbit and Shine" have long been inadquate responses to questions calling for a definition of Afro-American folklore. Neither have more sweeping and less restricting esoteric statements about the "lore of the group," qualified by such terms as traditional, nonelite, or oral, sufficiently served to delineate the area of black folklore study in any holistic way. This definitional dilemma is not limited to the study of Afro-American folklore, but among black folklorists, lore-centered definitions and approaches to Afro-American folklore have far-reaching implications—different from those of other American ethnic groups. General discussions, for example, of Irish-American or Polish-American or Japanese-American folklore implicitly and unquestioningly presume an historically revered and tradition-rich source, which serves as a frame of reference for understanding the culture of the New World group. Such presumptions are less natural and automatic in conventional exchanges treating the folklore and culture of Afro-Americans. When Afro-American folk culture has been examined in terms of its African antecedents, the results have been predictably, if not inherently, controversial. Resistance to so-called Africanist views has rested less, in my opinion, on the overwhelming weight of scholarly evidence than on a conceptual framework influenced by long and deeply held notions about the aberrant nature of black cultural development under slavery in the United States.

Accounting for the "conversion" of the African to an American, Ulrich Phillips commented in 1918 that "the purposes and policies of the masters were fairly uniform, and in consequence the negroes, though with many variants, became largely standardized into the predominant plantation type."[1] What remained of the African slaves' heritage was essentially his "nature," since "the wrench from Africa and the subjugation to the new discipline while uprooting his ancient language and customs had little more effect upon his temperament than upon his complexion."[2] In that same year, the famed sociologist Robert Ezra Park recorded his own impression that "the Negro, when he landed in the United States, left behind him almost everything but his dark complexion and his tropical temperament."[3] Though a number of scholarly researches would surface to offset the positions of Phillips and Park,[4] the continued popularity and buoyancy of their basic thesis hint of a most curious obsession. In 1959, echoing Phillips's notion of a slave personality, his apologist Stanley Elkins shaped the now well-known "Sambo thesis." Fundamental to this theory is the premise of the destruction of the slaves' African past, which "could no longer furnish him guides for conduct, for adjusting to the expectations of a completely new life." In such a situation, Elkins continued, the slave "could look to none but his master" for new standards and cues.[5] Unfortunately, folklorists have not been immune to this way of thinking and have constructed discussions of Afro-American folklore on the same shaky foundation—one that devalues the significance of the Old World experience in informing the new one. Originally published in the same year as Elkins's *Slavery*, Dorson's *American Folklore* introduces its chapter on "The Negro" with the idea that "Torn from his West African culture and denied education, the slave commenced life in America bereft of his own institutions and traditions, and barred from those of his master."[6] Such assumptions as illustrated by these examples have acted to mask the more challenging and complex questions about black cultural development. Consequently, Afro-American folk culture has been seen as self-explanatory and capable of being understood solely within the context of the conventional wisdom about slavery in the antebellum South. In other words, like Topsy, who was not born or made by God, Afro-American culture—"just grew": " 'Never was born,' reiterated the creature, more emphatically; 'never had no father, nor mother, nor nothin. I was raised by a speculator with lots of others. Old Aunt Sue used to take care on us.' "[7]

This narrow conceptual context for the study of Afro-American folklore has come to haunt us and may well be one of the factors limiting the fullest possible theoretical development in this area. It is an attitude that, held consciously or unconsciously, denies the fundamental roots of Afro-American folk tradition, which go deeper than slavery; it is an attitude that fails to recognize that the history of black Americans is also an extension of the history of African peoples.

Unfortunately, an inordinate emphasis has been placed on slavery as the single most important referent for understanding black folk traditions. Failing to look beyond that noxious system's influence on the cultural development of black Americans severely limits fuller, more holistic treatments of black culture and world view. A consequence for folklore study is one that fragments a body of tradition into various genres, linked superficially to a one-dimensional image of a black cultural experience in America. At best then we can identify forms, while the complexities of meaning and aesthetics, as well as theory, continue to elude us. In 1925, for example, folklorist Arthur Huff Fauset woefully noted the injustice done by the focus on pathos and sentimental humor popularized in renderings of Afro-American tales. What he had come to understand was that "the unfortunate thing about American thought is the habit of classifying first and investigating after. As a result this misrepresentation of the temper and spirit of Negro folk lore has become traditional, and for all we know, permanent."[8] Classification has become one of the trademarks of the folklorist, but never have we assumed that it would become an end in itself.

Emphasis on collecting and classifying was guided by the discipline's nineteenth-century character, which was oriented toward recording and preserving traditions thought to be dying rather than exploring them from a point of view reflecting their vital functions and dynamic mutability. This early "Mason jar" approach to folklore study emphasized, of course, the products of the folk experience, many of which were often selectively collected and just as often motivated more by the rewards of humanitarianism and personal discovery than scholarship.[9] These kinds of collections could not have satisfied fully the needs of black intellectuals—particularly scholars like DuBois, Zora Neale Hurston, James Weldon Johnson, Carter G. Woodson, Charles S. Johnson, Sterling Brown, Alain Locke and others—who by the 1920s and thirties were offering credible evidence of the existence of a black culture, with its own functions, values, aesthetic, and tradition. What these men and women knew was that the study of black folklore is the key to understanding the black experience in America, and that folklore is the informing core of that experience. The increasing numbers of rigorously systematic and scholarly collections (of record-breaking numbers, incidentally, within the decade of the twenties) provided needed comparative sources for new interpretations of black cultural life and history, but critical analysis, as Fauset noted, was often misinformed or lacking entirely.

One pivotal area that has continued to capture the attention of black scholars and collectors of Afro-American folklore has been the question of the source of black folk tradition. Among many, the crux of the arguments has rested on the verdict as to whether or not the processes of slavery stripped the African American of all vestiges of a cultural identity, leaving him, *tabula rasa*, to create or imitate, or both. Prior to the 1930s, without the benefit of acculturation theory, most theoretical discussions did not treat the possibility of African retentions seriously at all. Making that point about the controversy over the origins of black music, Richard Waterman comments that for too long the wrong question had been asked: "Did the Negro invent his folk music or did he copy it?" Scientific development of notions about syncretism and reinterpretation permitted, according to Waterman, the formulation of another question: "How did the musical heritage of West Africa change, over generations of contact with alien forms?" Begging this question generated new researches and broadened the scope of theoretical possibilities for the origins of black and American musical elements and styles.[10]

In general, nineteenth-century thinking could not so easily accommodate the notion of an African "musical heritage" or culture, in any commonly understood sense of the terms. Although early observers frequently made allusions to the African character of black folk behaviors, oftentimes "African" was used only as a euphemism for savage or barbaric. This attitude (becoming popular, incidentally, among blacks as well as whites) explains the dubious attention initially paid to black "music." Time and weakened linguistic barriers to communication would contribute to the recognition of a distinct black music. Scholarly notice would be directed toward the songs—particularly the spirituals—elevating the music of black slaves from incoherent moans and wails to the level of "tuneful" distortions or imitations of European hymns. Exceptional sensitivity should be credited to the collectors of *Slave Songs of the United States* (1867), a model example set for early field collections. As a result of *Slave Songs'* publication, interest in the songs increased, though over twenty-five years later Richard Wallaschek, in a skimpy comment, found the spirituals to be not only imitations but overrated ones at that.[11] Later studies by White (1928), Johnson (1930), and Jackson (1943) would continue to reaffirm the theory of imitation with little modification in the basic premise of European origins.[12] Afro-American scholars like Krehbiel[13] and John Wesley Work,[14] on the other hand, consistently rejected the notion of imitation in favor of arguments based on the "originality" of the songs (and their makers) through the processes of reinterpreting and reassembling. An early white observer, Jeanette Murphy, commented in 1899 that the rationale for calling the spirituals "American" folksongs seemed somewhat dubious. Viewing America as a "conglomerate" of peoples, she was of the opinion that a body of folksong "must be considered distinctly belonging to the nationality that imported it." She added, "Why should not the same be true of the genuine negro music? The stock is African, the ideas are African, the patting and dancing are all African."[15] The kind of logic employed by Murphy seems to be one that, to her credit, takes into account a broader performance context than is usually recognized.

Much of the lively debate over the origins of Afro-American folklore has emphasized music. Other collected forms, particularly folk belief and tales, were assumed initially to be of obvious African origin. By 1926, however, Puckett had modified the general position on folk belief by proposing that the effects of acculturation had caused certain areas of black folk belief (maintenance and perpetuation of life) to reflect European influence, while things relating to pleasure seemed more African.[16] Joel Chandler Harris, credited with popularizing and stimulating scholarly interest in Afro-American folktales, fancied an African source for the animal stories.[17] Harris's view, an unsupported one by today's methods, went largely uncontested because of insufficient comparative data. Since these animal tales are not characteristically European, the logic of their African background seemed irrefutable. The stages theory of cultural evolution, which had permeated so much of late nineteenth-century social scientific thought, also lent racist credibility to the assumption of an African (i.e., primitive and uncivilized) source for some of the tales. Interest in Afro-American folktales grew, however, as a result of Harris's first collection in 1880 (*Uncle Remus: His Songs and Sayings*). But the most informed debates over the origin of a majority of the traditional tales would be generated years later,[18] and only after more scholarly collections and indexes had become available to complement the comparative methods of folklorists. But to date, where many of the tales are concerned, some final words from Harris himself ring mockingly: ". . . at the end of investigation and discussion Speculation stands grinning."[19]

Clearly, motif and tale-type comparisons alone will not be the means through which our understanding of the fundamental nature of Afro-American folklore, in general, will be clarified. From the early scholarship we have inherited a number of useful collections and reference materials needed in documenting contemporary studies. By and large, however, the early legacy of analysis and interpretation has been less fruitful. One of its simple, but greatest, shortcomings is the way in which the early studies are weighted by the racial attitudes of their day—attitudes that still enjoy popular appeal. Currently, numbers of trained black folklorists are entering the field with interests that have been directed primarily toward documenting the black folk experience (treating Africa as well as the Diaspora). This seemingly ethnocentric focus is certainly understandable from an historical and political point of view. Quite often one of the reasons for the proclivity among black scholars to concentrate on black American, and tangentially African, subject matter is guided by an urgency to "set the record straight," a record that historically has not fully profited from a black perspective. In perhaps one of the most profoundly perceptive works treating Afro-American culture and thought, *The Souls of Black Folk*, W. E. B. DuBois noted that such a perspective is derived from stepping "within the veil," raised so that "you may view faintly its deeper recesses."[20] I anticipate a kind of revolution in black folklore study because of the number of *trained* black folklorists entering the field who, like Gladys-Marie Fry and William H. Wiggins, can raise higher that veil.

Gladys Fry's dissertation, published in 1975 as *Night Riders in Black Folk History*,[21] explores oral traditional history around the theme of post–Civil War intimidation of southern freedmen. Using folklore sources, Fry draws a direct relationship between actual physical and psychological abuse and black folk belief (the basis for stereotypes ascribing innate traits of superstition and cowardice to black people). Wiggins, too, explores a relatively new area in folklore study—the festival—and unearths for scholarly study "Juneteenth," a national black holiday celebrated since announcements of Lincoln's Emancipation Proclamation.[22] A relatively recent collection of black folklore from Virginia is Daryl Dance's *Shuckin' and Jivin'*.[23] Dance, a newcomer with a degree in English, has collecting skills that make her work as invaluable for comparative purposes as Dorson's conscientiously documented *American Negro Folktales*.[24] Thorough annotation has not been one of the hallmarks of many otherwise important collections. As a consequence, the exhaustive collecting done by great figures in Afro-American folklore study like Zora Neale Hurston[25] and J. Mason Brewer[26] has only been marginally recognized within the discipline. The same, too, can be said of white folklorist Harry M. Hyatt's veritable warehouse of folk belief and practices, an extraordinary collection but unscholarly in its present form.[27]

Reappraisal of issues and contributions to the study of Afro-American folklore has been made easier by editors such as Alan Dundes[28] and Bruce Jackson.[29] Particularly useful for classroom use and in areas where folklore materials are scarce, Dundes's *Mother Wit from the Laughing Barrel* and Jackson's *The Negro and His Folklore in Nineteenth-Century Periodicals* bring together a wide variety of sources either inaccessible or unknown to beginning students. Both works contain extensive headnotes, which summarize positions and provide suggestions for further reading (Jackson also includes a useful appendix). One important difference does exist between these two timely anthologies, a difference other than the time frame being represented. The later collection of articles on Afro-American folklore by Dundes gives prominence to the perspectives of black writers (including late nineteenth-century examples) by reprinting their work. Several of these articles would not likely have been as widely read among folklore students had it not been for their inclusion in *Mother Wit*, a credit to Dundes's broader concerns. Jackson's volume reprints, without explicit rationale, only early works by white authors. Excluding the publication of material by black writers who treat black folk culture leaves a question as to their significance (or very existence) and contributes to a critical weakness in Jackson's collection.[30] One of the most recent successes in interpretation comes from historian Lawrence Levine,[31] who tapped early sources from folklore and history to study the black American world view. Flawed at times by what seems to be Levine's romantic involvement with his material, *Black Culture and Black Consciousness* still stands as the best single analysis, given its comprehensive range, of black American folk culture.

Much of the early scholarship, then, can benefit from a kind of reassessment, reinterpretation, and reaffirmation of critical sources crucial to the theoretical development of Afro-American folklore study. This kind of reevaluation would include all the significant early sources treating Afro-American cultural development. Granted the folklorist is not "a student of a whole culture,"[32] but folkloristics as a manageable unit of culture study, with a focus on a certain aspect of culture, has as a scholarly end an obligation to shed light on the workings of whole cultures. To study, then, the culture or, more narrowly, the folklore of black Americans, demands an insight into and sensitivity toward the life experience and world view of the group.

Finally, as I see it, the Africanisms controversy itself is somewhat artificial. In reality, no folklorist today would deny the existence of retained African elements in Afro-American folklore; the syncretic processes in the development of a black American folk tradition seem intellectually understood and accepted. The debatable issues, particularly in terms of narrative forms, have had to do with, for example, the point of origin for specific tales and tale types.[33] Given the information available to us, the only sound position to take is one that recognizes multiple origins. The idea of multiple *origins*, however, suggests an emphasis on the products—the lore itself—of black folk tradition. This kind of product-centered "debate" does not lend itself to answering other important questions, new questions that folklorists are concerned with relating to, for example, performance contexts. The inadequacy of folklore resources treating Africa also serves to contribute to an already inherited attitude that emphasizes more the significance of borrowed European elements than those retained from an African past. It seems then, that a concept that focuses on the multiple *influences* on Afro-American folk cultural development is, in the long run, more useful. The perpetual search for origins will, of course, go on, because of its intrinsic fascination, but it should not represent the only arena in which discussions of Africanisms take place. What is important and what the new scholarship should be charged to reflect is a more balanced picture of the various influences that have shaped the folklore and world view of black Americans. Our perspectives should be broad enough to recognize that slavery is not the only point of departure for black folklore study. The poet and critic Alvin Aubert summarizes this idea in a poem dedicated to Alex Haley:

> and all the time we stood and walked
> sometimes in glory mostly in fear
> knowing all along we did not spring
> fullgrown from the dust of plantations
> that we came from somewhere.[34]

NOTES

1. Ulrich Bonnell Phillips, *American Negro Slavery* (New York, London: D. Appleton and Company, 1918), p. 291.

2. Ibid., p. 291.

3. Robert Ezra Park, "Education in Its Relation to the Conflict and Fusion of Cultures: With Special Reference to the Problems of the Immigrant, the Negro, and Missions," in *Race and Culture* (Glencoe, Illinois: The Free Press, 1950), p. 267. First published in *Publication of the American Sociological Society* 13 (1918): 38–63. The noted black sociologist E. Franklin Frazier, a student of Park's, also subscribed to the notion that the African heritage had been lost because of what Frazier saw as the destruction of the African family system, "the chief means of cultural transmission"; see *The Negro in the United States* (New York: The Macmillan Company, 1949), p. 20.

4. The best known is the work of Melville J. Herskovits, culminating in the publication of *The Myth of the Negro Past* (New York, London: Harper and Brothers Publishers, 1941).

5. Stanley M. Elkins, *Slavery: A Problem in American Institutional and Intellectual Life*, 3rd rev. ed. (Chicago and London: University of Chicago Press, 1976), pp. 101–102.

6. Richard M. Dorson, *American Folklore* (Chicago and London: University of Chicago Press, 1959), p. 166.

7. Harriet Beecher Stowe, *Uncle Tom's Cabin* (New York: Dodd, Mead and Company, 1952), p. 238.

8. Arthur Huff Fauset, "American Negro Folk Literature," in *The New Negro: An Interpretation*, ed. Alain Locke (New York: Albert and Charles Boni, 1925), p. 241. Though Fauset was primarily addressing himself to popularizers, his remarks reflect some of the attitudes presented by folklorists like Benjamin Botkin, who, in a short discussion of Negro folksong in 1927, commented that "The note of self-pity . . . represents a trait of the Negro, bred in him by centuries of oppression." See his "Self-Portraiture and Social Criticism in Negro Folk Song," *Opportunity* 5 (1927): 39.

9. For an interesting discussion of how abolitionists' motives and musical expertise combined to create the most "sympathetic" and "systematic" of the early collections, see Dena J. Epstein's *Sinful Tunes and Spirituals: Black Music to the Civil War* (Urbana, Chicago, London: University of Illinois Press, 1977), pp. 303–20.

10. Richard A. Waterman, "On Flogging a Dead Horse: Lessons Learned from the Africanisms Controversy," *Ethnomusicology* 7 (1963): 84.

11. Richard Wallaschek, *Primitive Music* (London: Longmans, Green and Co., 1893), p. 60.

12. Newman Ivey White, *American Negro Folk-Song* (Cambridge, Mass.: Harvard University Press, 1928); Guy B. Johnson, *Folk Culture on St. Helena Island, South Carolina* (Chapel Hill: University of North Carolina Press, 1930), Chapter II, p. 63–130; George Pullen Jackson, *White and Negro Spirituals* (New York: J. J. Augustin, 1943).

13. Henry Edward Krehbiel, *Afro-American Folksongs: A Study in Racial and National Music*, reprint (New York: Frederick Ungar Publishing Co., 1962), Chapter II, pp. 11-28.

14. John W. Work, "Negro Folk Song," *Opportunity* 1 (1923): 292–94.

15. Jeanette Murphy, "The Survival of African Music in America," in *The Negro and His Folklore in Nineteenth-Century Periodicals*, ed. Bruce Jackson (Austin and London: University of Texas Press, 1967), p. 328.

16. Newbell Niles Puckett, *Folk Beliefs of the Southern Negro* (Chapel Hill: University of North Carolina Press, 1926), p. 78.

17. Harris grapples with African parallels to his tales in his introduction to *Nights with Uncle Remus* (Boston: James R. Osgood and Company, 1883), pp. ix–xxxvi.

18. See, for example, Daniel J. Crowley, ed., *African Folklore in the New World* (Austin and London: University of Texas Press, 1977); most of the articles in Crowley were previously published in *Research in African Literature* 7 (Fall 1976).

19. Joel Chandler Harris, *Uncle Remus and His Friends* (Boston and New York: Houghton Mifflin Company, 1920), p. vii.

20. W. E. B. DuBois, *The Souls of Black Folk* (Chicago: A. C. McClurg, 1903), p. viii.

21. Gladys-Marie Fry, *Night Riders in Black Folk History* (Knoxville: University of Tennessee Press, 1975).

22. William H. Wiggins, "Free at Last: A Study of Afro-American Emancipation Day Celebrations," 2 vols. (Ph.D. diss., Indiana University, 1974).

23. Daryl Dance, *Shuckin' and Jivin': Folklore from Contemporary Black Americans* (Bloomington: Indiana University Press, 1978).

24. Richard M. Dorson, *American Negro Folktales* (Greenwich, Conn.: Fawcett Publications, Inc., 1956).

25. Zora Neale Hurston, *Mules and Men*, Perennial edition (New York: Harper and Row, 1970).

26. Among Brewer's titles are *The Word on the Brazos: Negro Preacher Tales from the Brazos Bottoms of Texas* (Austin: University of Texas Press, 1953); *Dog Ghosts and Other Texas Negro Folk Tales* (Austin: University of Texas Press, 1958); *Worser Days and Better Times: The Folklore of the North Carolina Negro* (Chicago: Quadrangle Books, 1965); and *American Negro Folklore* (Chicago: Quadrangle Books, 1968).

27. Harry M. Hyatt, *Hoodoo-Conjuration-Witchcraft-Rootwork: Beliefs Accepted by Many Negroes and White Persons These Being Orally Recorded Among Blacks and Whites*, 5 vols. (n. p.: Memoirs of the Alma Egan Hyatt Foundation, 1970–78).

28. Alan Dundes, *Mother Wit from the Laughing Barrel. Readings in the Interpretation of Afro-American Folklore* (Englewood Cliffs, New Jersey: Prentice-Hall, 1973).

29. Bruce Jackson, ed., *The Negro and His Folklore in Nineteenth-Century Periodicals* (Austin: University of Texas Press, 1967).

30. For a criticism of Jackson's work and for a different perspective on views of black folk culture in the nineteenth century, see Melvin Wade's "Through the Rabbit's Eye: Critical Perspectives on African-American Folk Culture of the

Nineteenth Century," in *The Role of Afro-American Folklore in the Teaching of the Arts and the Humanities,* ed. Adrienne Lanier Seward (Bloomington: Indiana University Publications, 1979), pp. 2–57.

31. Lawrence W. Levine, *Black Culture and Black Consciousness: Afro-American Folk Thought from Slavery to Freedom* (New York: Oxford University Press, 1977).

32. Richard M. Dorson, "African and Afro-American Folklore: A Reply to Bascom and Other Misguided Critics," *Journal of American Folklore* 88 (1975): 154.

33. Bascom recently broadened his Africanist position to include mainland United States as a dissemination area of West African tales, in a series of articles in *Research in African Literatures.*

34. Alvin Aubert, "For Alex Haley/author of *Roots*," *Obsidian* 3 (Spring 1977): cover.

American Cultural Myths

Any in-depth consideration of American folklore should attempt to chart connections with the great cultural myths that have captivated the American mind and imagination. We no longer speak of mythology in very precise terms, but in the eighteenth and nineteenth centuries it was regarded as an independent subject matter with its own literature and concepts. Mythology dealt with the pantheons of gods and their orbits of power, and narratives of their adventures in the heavens, on earth, and in the underworld. The cultures of classical times and tribal peoples, but not of industrialized nations, subscribed to mythological systems. Another way of stating the matter is to say that the rise of the monotheistic religions, Judaism, Christianity, and Islam, displaced the older mythologies and relegated them to children's stories about gods and heroes. In this sense we cannot refer to American mythology. A Native American mythology yes, but this system bears no relationship to the mainstream culture.

Yet mythology continues to be used in a metaphorical sense by American cultural and literary historians, and even more frequently one encounters the unit term myth. A set of interconnected myths constitutes a modern mythology, and we may in this wise refer to an American mythology. Unlike the polytheistic systems, this body of myths does not surface in narrative form; it does not invoke supernatural sanctions; and it does not specify a gallery of deities to be worshiped. Still, modern myths resemble tribal myths in concentrating on a special people, in establishing utopian visions of a wondrous life, and in glorifying larger-than-life heroes. Social critics can piece together modern myths from writings and rhetoric on all levels of the culture: novels, legislation, editorials, speeches, sermons, advertisements, movies, histories, textbooks, whatever. The secular myths, like the religious myths, carry a solemn force and exert a heavy pressure on the culture. People denigrate or reject the myths at their peril.

The basic myth of our civilization is America the Land of Opportunity. This vision has been expressed in analogous metaphors, such as The Promised Land, The Earthly Paradise, Manifest Destiny, The Garden of Eden, Land of the Free and Home of the Brave. In the rallying cry of Manifest Destiny, launched in the 1840s, Americans responded to the oratorical assertion that God in his providential design had reserved the most fertile land in the world for the people with the best form of government—the political institutions of democracy—in the world. They were indeed the chosen people, the visible saints of the Bay Colony in the seventeenth century, whose commonwealth would shine as a beacon for all mankind. The narrative of American history chronicled the steady Progress, the evolutionary ascent from wilderness to fabulous civilization, that translated the dream into reality. Heroes and demigods populated this narrative. Some of them were transcendent individuals—Washington, the father of his country, and Lincoln, the savior, who became enshrined in the nation's statuary, place-names, portraiture, legendry. Others were folktypes, the pioneer and trailblazer, the industrious bootblack who works his way up to corporation president, or his counterpart, the farm lad born in a log cabin who becomes president, exemplifying in business and politics the American success story.

A series of American Studies books, beginning with Henry Nash Smith's *Virgin Land* (1950) and followed by Leo Marx's *The Machine in the Garden* (1964), have outlined parts of the basic myth and its component submyths. Smith traced the interplay of the themes of Manifest Destiny, the West as extension of the Promised Land, and the frontier hero who moves from Kentucky's forests to the Rocky Mountains. Marx carried the mythic development a step further by revealing the dissonance and eventual reconciliation between the pastoral and the technological ideals; the Promised Land could encompass industrial as well as agricultural abundance. The classic presentation of the myth—as contrasted to the explication of the myth-complex by Smith and Marx—was rendered by Vernon Louis Parrington in *Main Currents in American Thought* (1927–30), a stirring script with crusaders for the American dream of equal rights and equal opportunities in the land of plenty doing battle against the entrenched forces of power, property, and reaction.

In this section of the *Handbook*, four American Studies scholars single out an American myth for discussion. Although each begins with a separate perception— Washburn with images of the Indian in the forest, Walker with success stories of the poor but honest youth in the city, Marcell with fables of aspiring Americans, Gunn with examples of the Adamic hero—at certain points their readings converge. All see a nobility of character in these figures, a moral innocence that steadies them in their worldly trials and often leads to spiritual and material rewards. But American mythology is two-edged, Janus-faced, as the critics have observed: the Howling Wilderness counterbalances the Edenic Garden; the ignoble savage contends against the noble one; the Hamiltonian exploiters resist the Jeffersonian reformers; the Adamic heroes fail as often as the Horatio Alger heroes triumph. Benjamin Franklin emerges as the archetypal American in the myth, achieving both inner and outer success, and is cited by three of the essayists.

Where does folklore fit into this modern mythology? It fits like a glove at many points. From the first voyages of exploration and settlement, travelers' tales exaggerated the wonders and terrors of the New World. The very longevity or brevity of life in America became the subject of heated debate among European savants. Anecdotes of the powers and the idiocy of Indians filled the pages of colonial chroniclers and set folk stereotypes of Native Americans in the minds of English settlers. Detailed accounts of remarkable providences, which recorded the survival of Puritan saints and the destruction of their enemies, confirmed the belief of New England's first generations that they were God's favorite people. In the expansive years of the nineteenth century, tall-tale folk heroes recited endless wonders of New World abundance: great catches of game and fish, drillings for oil that not only produced oceans of the liquid gold but also champagne and buttermilk, fruits and vegetables that grew as large as houses. Yet folklore also produced its Adamic tragic heroes, loggers and miners and railroad engineers who died on the job and were memorialized in sorrowing ballads. The folk heroes, like the myth heroes, enjoyed an intimate relation with the natural environment and accepted the ethos of limitless individual capacity.

American mythologists and American folklorists can equally benefit from a sharing of each other's preserves. Franklin's proverbs of thrift and industry—"A penny saved is a penny earned"; "Early to bed, early to rise makes a man healthy, wealthy, and wise"—belong to the folklore and underscore the myth.

Wilcomb E. Washburn

The Noble and Ignoble Savage

The treatment and status of the American Indian in the United States have depended more upon the image of the Indian in white eyes than upon any objective reality. So vivid has that image been—whether of a noble or ignoble character—that a major and still unsolved scholarly task is to determine what in fact is imaginary and what is real in the white view of the Indian.

The image of the Indian as dirty, drunken, and ignoble is found most frequently in nineteenth-century writings and continues to this day, fed by examples of despair, disillusionment, and degradation among Indian individuals and groups. An image of the Indian as virtuous, generous, and noble is found more frequently in the earlier literature, though not to the exclusion of the counterimage of the Indian as bestial, savage, and uncultivated. Both images have coexisted throughout the entire period of Indian-white contact, a fact that suggests the power of the perceiver's vision in comparison with the object of that perception.

Like other stereotypes or symbols, the terms "noble" and "ignoble" are vulnerable to ridicule and total rejection. But, as stereotypes tend to capture a portion of the truth and mix it with nontruthful elements, so do the terms "noble" and "ignoble" simplify and conceal other attributes in the process of summarization. But I have asserted, in "The Clash of Morality in the American Forest,"[1] that it is possible to define "noble" and "ignoble" in terms such as generosity and honesty and to measure the conformity of the behavior of an individual or group to the defined standards. Based on the definition and evidence available, I have accepted the historical reality of the concept of the "noble savage" in some specific instances and defended the essential accuracy of the notion as it has appeared in writings against the aspersions of literary scholars. Such scholars have too often attributed favorable views of the Indian to a conscious attempt to attack the corruptions of European society by celebrating an imaginary society governed by ideal but nonexistent virtues. So severe has the skepticism of some writers been that they have dealt with some accounts of native life, such as that provided by the Baron de Lahontan, under the heading of literature rather than history.

Any discussion of the "myth" of the noble or ignoble savage must start, as does the discovery of America itself, with Columbus's voyage of 1492. Columbus found the natives of the West Indies gentle and unoffending and described them in a manner reminiscent of biblical descriptions of the Garden of Eden. Not only were the natives nude—a striking visual and mental shock to the overdressed Europeans—but they seemed to have no concept of *meum* and *tuum*. They gave the Spanish freely of their goods and persons. Their innocence was expressed most tragically in their ignorance of the sharpness of the Spanish swords, on which they accidentally cut themselves.

The story of Spanish conquest that followed Columbus's voyage was graphically portrayed in the writings of Bartolomé de Las Casas and in the pictures of Théodore de Bry. The "black legend" of Spanish cruelty—often asserted to be a "myth" by apologists for Spanish conduct in the New World (who blame the Spanish priest for its creation)—is closely related to the "myth" of the noble or ignoble savage. The debate over the truth of Las Casas's charges stimulated apologists to excuse or justify Spanish cruelty by reference to the allegedly bestial or servile nature of the natives. On the other hand, defenders of the natives were stimulated to condemn and execrate Spanish conduct by emphasizing the innocence and nobility of the victims of Spanish ferocity.

Juan Ginés de Sepúlveda, in his *Democrates alter, de justis belli causis apud Indos*, asserted the justice of Spanish conquest by depicting the Indians as slaves by nature. Las Casas, defending the Indians in his debate with Sepúlveda at Salamanca in 1551–52, asserted that the Indians were as intelligent as Europeans and deserved equal respect for their rights. Las Casas had been instrumental in obtaining a papal bull (Sublimis Deus, June 9, 1537), which asserted that "the Indians are truly men" and which rejected the implication that the natives of the New World were so different in nature from civilized men that they could be deprived of their liberty or possession of their property. Other European observers, though operating from a distance, joined the debate, usually on the anti-Spanish side. Michel de Montaigne was perhaps the most eloquent of these critics, noting in his famous essay "Of coaches" that "as for devoutness, observance of the laws, goodness, liberality, loyalty, and frankness, it served us [Europeans] well not to have as much as they: by their advantage in this they lost, sold, and betrayed themselves."[2]

The debate over the civilization, sophistication, morality, and, ultimately, nobility of the Indians of Mexico has continued over the centuries and is most effectively outlined in Benjamin Keen's *The Aztec Image in Western Thought*.[3] In the late nineteenth century that debate was most clearly etched in the controversy over "Montezuma's Dinner." Lewis Henry Morgan, the pioneer American ethnologist, had concluded that the Spanish accounts of the greatness of Mexican civilization were more the product of fable and romance than of ethnological research. He held up to ridicule Spanish accounts of the splendor of the ritual of Montezuma's dinner reported by Cortes and the early chroniclers (and seized upon by historians like Prescott), claiming that the Spaniards must have misconceived an unpretentious communal meal shared by a nonkingly chief and his nonroyal followers. Morgan's venom and sarcasm were focused directly on Hubert Howe Bancroft's second volume—dealing with the Aztecs—of his *History of the Native Races of the Pacific Coast*, published in 1875–76. Bancroft rejected Morgan's evolutionary scheme of civilization, which placed the Mexicans midway on a scale running from savagery through barbarism to civilization, and accepted the truth of the accounts of the "nobility" of Montezuma's person and court reported by his Spanish conquerors. Morgan, in a forty-page review of Bancroft's volume, entitled

"Montezuma's Dinner," published in the *North American Review* for April 1876, denounced the work as "a crime against ethnological science."[4] Morgan's scornful attitude toward what he deemed the "romantic" school of chroniclers of Mexican civilization was supported by Adolph F. Bandelier. In the hundred years since that time, the approach of Morgan and Bandelier has been refuted and rejected, only to emerge in newer, more subtle evolutionary forms.

As France, England, Portugal, Holland, and Sweden sent explorers, traders, and missionaries to colonize and explore the New World, additional perspectives on the moral worth of the Indian emerged. The French in particular provided the strongest support to the belief in the existence of the noble savage, or, as it was phrased in French, *le bon sauvage* or *la belle sauvage*. France's small colonial population, the orientation of some of her nationals to trading in the interior as *coureurs de bois*, the inclination—officially encouraged—of French colonists to intermarry with the natives, went hand in hand with a generally favorable view of the native Americans. French missionaries—Jesuits for the most part—also praised the character of those they sought to convert. Whether the favorable image of the Indian in French writings can be explained as a *consequence* of the absence of direct economic conflict between the two races is, however, doubtful. The generally less favorable view of the Indian in English writings is sometimes attributed to the opposite situation: the competitive pressure of the larger English population, of both sexes, mostly engaged in farming, for whom the lands of the Indians were a prime need and objective.

Although I would accept the relevance and influence of the economic motive in shaping the European image of the American Indian, any purely economic explanation of the myth of either the "noble" or "ignoble" Indian is deceptive. In the English colonies, to give one example, Thomas Morton of Merry Mount in Massachusetts Bay saw the Indians of that area in the 1620s as noble children of nature, with whom he and his men enthusiastically engaged in the most intimate terms—sexual and otherwise—while linked economically in a trade relationship. Governor Bradford of Plymouth Colony, on the other hand, struggling to maintain an agricultural economy and a strictly religious community, first reproved and ultimately destroyed Morton's outpost while generally denigrating the Indians for their failure to conform to Puritan ideals. In the interpretation of Richard Slotkin, in his *Regeneration through Violence: The Mythology of the American Frontier, 1600-1860*,[5] Puritan antipathy toward the concept of a good and noble Indian was rooted in a fear of being seduced into the attractive life of freedom and sexual license that the natives offered to those compelled to conform to the harsh Puritan creed.

The vast literature of Indian captivities provides one of the largest sources of literary and historical data for the study of the creation and perpetuation of the images of the noble and ignoble Indian. Since the captive was afforded, usually against his will, an intimate glimpse into the heart of the native culture, and was sometimes adopted into that culture as a full-fledged member, there is good reason for giving greater than normal credence to the testimony of captives. Because of the drama of the captivity experience, that experience was always a subject for distortion and misconception, and in the latter stages of the genre—particularly in the late eighteenth and throughout the nineteenth century—imaginary and purely literary "captivity narratives" destroyed the presumption of reality that the earliest captivity narratives, such as Mrs. Mary Rowlandson's famous account of 1682, possessed. The image of the Indian that emerged from seventeenth-century captivity accounts, whether from Captain John Smith's questionable account of his rescue by Pocahontas, daughter of the Emperor Powhatan in Virginia, or from Mrs. Rowlandson's account of her dealings with King Philip and his braves in Massachusetts, was generally favorable, emphasizing the qualities of bravery, generosity, dignity, and respect for the female, even while acknowledging such characteristics as cruelty and ferocity.

With the rise of the "penny dreadfuls" and popular adventure literature in the late nineteenth century, the portrait of the Indian became more often that of a degraded or vindictive foe than of a noble, generous comrade. The white frontiersman or settler was, in such literature, more often the "good guy," the Indian being the "bad guy" who fought the white man, violated the white woman, and stubbornly refused to accept "civilization" as it made its way west in the tide of Manifest Destiny. That movement is graphically portrayed in the chromo-lithograph entitled "American Progress," issued from the offices of George A. Crofutt's *Western World* (New York, 1873).[6]

The image of the "noble Indian" was incorporated in the American school system through such instructional manuals as the McGuffey readers. Dr. William Holmes McGuffey first incorporated the speech of the Mingo chief Logan, at the conclusion of Lord Dunmore's War in 1774, in his *Eclectic Fourth Reader* (Cincinnati, 1838) and continued to reprint it in later editions throughout the nineteenth century. That speech, with its biblical overtones, was recited by many generations of American youngsters:

> I appeal to any white man to say,
> if ever he entered Logan's cabin hungry,
> and he gave him not meat;
> if ever he came cold and naked,
> and he cloathed him not.

After describing the murder of all his relatives by the whites, Logan described the vengeance he took and then concluded: "Who is there to mourn for Logan?—Not one."

Although the authenticity of Logan's speech was doubted by political opponents of Thomas Jefferson, who incorporated the speech in his *Notes on Virginia*, I believe, following Thomas Jefferson, that it is essentially accurate and merits the respect that it has received.[7]

In the twentieth century, movies took the place of "penny dreadfuls" and school readers as the presentation of the two diametrically opposed images of the American Indian. Although there were some sentimental vehicles for Indian heroines like *Ramona* in the early years of the industry, for the most part the only good Indian, until the late 1940s, was often a dead one, though his death was not sought until after he had performed rapid and violent mayhem while mounted on dashing horses (ideal for the new "movies") against a group of valiant ranchers, farmers, or soldiers who were, as usual, carrying "civilization" to the West. In the post–World War II period, beginning with *Broken Arrow* (1950), films in which the Indians were portrayed as noble (and sometimes tragic) heroes, often deceived and abused by scheming white men, began to appear and have continued to provide a good image of the Indian ever since. Often played by whites, more recently the roles of wise, generous, and "noble" Indians have been played by Indians like Chief Dan George. The new movie version of the Indian coincided with and probably reinforced other streams of thought that made the Indian an attractive cult figure among the youth of the tumultuous sixties.

The image of the Indian as guardian of the earth and the first ecologist also emerged in the television advertisements of the 1970s. The Indian, in one such presentation, was dressed to represent a lost past, shedding a tear at the trash that littered the landscape appropriated by his white "successors." While the advertisement suggested a link between the myth of the "vanishing Indian" and the "noble Indian," the concept of the vanishing Indian—a popular concept in the nineteenth century—has been consistent with the existence of either a noble or ignoble Indian.

Sympathy for the apparently vanishing red man (an image that still persists, although the Indian birth rate is about double that of the rest of the American population) has, without doubt, triggered the emotion of nostalgia in the minds of many whites as they see the old order of romance and conflict giving way to a new order of homogenized and sterilized culture. Combined with the emotion of white guilt for the past, and grudging admiration for the reputed virtues of the Indians, there has developed in the past fifty years among whites a positive overall image of the American Indian. The image has resulted in a series of acts of Congress, decisions of the courts, and executive initiatives that have preserved the political autonomy of tribal entities, supported the economic and social underpinnings of Indian communities, and encouraged the development of Indian aspirations even when they run counter to the interests of the other 99.6 percent of the population of the country. The image has been blurred in the past decade by radical Indian elements (who trashed the Bureau of Indian Affairs in Washington in 1972 and shot up the village of Wounded Knee, South Dakota, in 1973), whose actions have caused most champions of the Indians in Congress to beat a hasty retreat from their earlier support of Indian causes.

The power of symbols and the sensitivity of people to them can be illustrated by the furor that arose in the 1970s over the use of the Indian symbol to represent amateur and professional athletic teams. Indian radicals captured headlines by denouncing what they regarded as contemptuous or condescending references to Indians. In January 1972 Russell Means, a leader of the radical American Indian Movement (AIM), filed a lawsuit against the Cleveland Indians' baseball team over its symbol, a caricature of an Indian rendered in a manner that can be called humorous at best and contemptuous at worst. The action reverberated throughout the country, stimulating a series of attacks on teams and organizations represented by some form of an Indian symbol. Perhaps the controversy at Dartmouth College is most revealing of the power of the symbol. Young Indian students, hastily recruited in response to Dartmouth's renewed commitment to Indian education (the college was originally founded as an Indian school) attacked any use of the Indian symbol to represent any college activity, formal or informal. No distinction was made between favorable and unfavorable images. A blue-ribbon committee of the Dartmouth Alumni Council considered the matter and reported to the council in June 1972 recommending that the college discourage as actively as possible any use of the symbol, which, in any event, had never had any official standing. No effort was made to ask Indian graduates of Dartmouth their views and no attempt was made to assess the validity of the student complaints. The issue did not die away, as expected by the committee, but grew more heated. Non-Indian students resented attempts to control their actions at football games. Alumni expressed bewilderment at the hostility toward what they regarded as their well-intentioned efforts to honor Dartmouth's Indian heritage. Indian graduates, who had prominently represented Dartmouth in sports events in the early twentieth century, expressed their support for the symbol. Nevertheless the ban continued as testimony to the coercive power of emotion and ignorance when enlisted in the service of offended sensibilities.

The most perceptive and complete treatment of the contrasting myths of the noble and ignoble Indian is Robert F. Berkhofer, Jr.'s *The White Man's Indian: Images of the American Indian from Columbus to the Present*.[8] Berkhofer, who distinguishes between "native Americans" (to represent the native view of themselves) and "Indians" (to represent the white man's view of the native Americans), presents a detailed and persuasive case for the "Indian," noble or ignoble, as a creation of the white man and one removed both from the native American's perception of himself and from reality. However, Berkhofer concludes that what began as images and stereotypes created by whites and perceived by native Americans as alien have become reality for native Americans. "For Native Americans," Berkhofer writes, "the power of the Whites all too often forced them to be the Indians Whites said they were regardless of their original social and cultural diversity." So, while Berkhofer's running analysis of the misconceptions governing white images and stereotypes of the native American is illuminating, it is also confusing, since he himself concludes that the reality is constantly reshaped by the image even though that image misperceived the original reality.

To sum up, one can give no final answer to the question of the "reality" of the "noble" or "ignoble" Indian. Both concepts exist, and have existed, in the white mind and continue to shape the character of the Indian and to shape white treatment of the Indian. Perhaps this split image demonstrates the difficulty of relating subjective perceptions to objective reality.

NOTES

1. Wilcomb E. Washburn, "The Clash of Morality in the American Forest," in *First Images of America: The Impact of the New World on the Old*, ed. Fredi Chiapelli (Berkeley: University of California Press, 1976), pp. 335–50.

2. Michel de Montaigne, *The Complete Works of Montaigne: Essays, Travel Journal, Letters*, trans. Donald M. Frame (Stanford, Calif.: Stanford University Press, 1957), pp. 693–94.

3. Benjamin Keen, *The Aztec Image in Western Thought* (New Brunswick, N. J.: Rutgers University Press, 1971), p. 391.

4. Ibid.

5. Richard Slotkin, *Regeneration through Violence: The Mythology of the American Frontier, 1600–1860* (Middletown, Conn.: Wesleyan University Press, 1973).

6. Wilcomb E. Washburn, ed., *The Indian and the White Man* (New York: Doubleday/Anchor, 1964), Plate 9 and described in Document 33, pp. 128–30.

7. Wilcomb E. Washburn, "Logan's Speech, 1774," in *An American Primer*, ed. Daniel J. Boorstin (Chicago: University of Chicago Press, 1966), pp. 60-64.

8. Robert F. Berkhofer, Jr., *The White Man's Indian: Images of the American Indian from Columbus to the Present* (New York: Alfred A. Knopf, 1978).

Robert H. Walker

Rags to Riches

In its purest form, "rags to riches" is a late nineteenth-century melodrama. It opens as the hero—we will call him David—learns that the streets of New York City are paved with gold. He may receive this news in Naples or Baden, in an American village, or on a farm anywhere. The one constant factor is the belief that riches lie in a large American city.

David may be orphaned; more likely he supports a widowed mother and a brood of siblings. Honest and impoverished, David's family urges on him the quest for success, both for his own sake and theirs. They sacrifice something to send him on his way; they sacrifice even more in their willingness to support themselves in his absence.

Between late adolescence and young manhood, David arrives in New York too innocent to resist the apparent generosity of that kindly, elaborately dressed gentleman who offers to turn David's meager savings into overnight wealth. Heartrendingly, both man and money disappear. David is homeless, friendless, and penniless in the indifferent metropolis.

Desperation but breeds determination. Our young hero soon finds the welcome that greets diligence everywhere and begins to reap the rewards open to that worker who walks the extra mile unasked, treats his elders with becoming respect, and cultivates those cardinal virtues of temperance and thrift.

Not all New Yorkers are thieves and confidence men. Eventually David finds an employer who trusts him and gives him the chance to display his initiative and imagination. His boss may even regard him as the son he never had.

David's righteous upbringing has fortified him with the strength to resist the snares of temptation, however alluring, and even the easy fellowship of his contemporaries appears aimless to him. He devotes his free time to religious service, altruism, and self-improvement; he goes to the public library or enrolls in night school. By this time he is able to send regular cash enclosures along with his dutiful letters home, thus mitigating his guilt at leaving his family.

Complications will make this biography more suspenseful than it seems in outline, yet it is still an essentially dull tale of work and privation for the sake of survival. David has neither flair nor genius (genius does not equate with success). What has marked our hero for this upward struggle is a disproportionately large measure of self-confidence. He reads, observes, and learns, undistracted by superficial explanations or traditional usages. Sooner or later—perhaps abetted by chance—he discovers a process or a product that significantly alters his own professional setting: a more flexible alloy or a more lasting paint, a system of profit-sharing or a new method of underwriting credit. In the classic tale David's rise will be based on invention related to industrial technology.

With confidence in his own hard-won perceptions, David promotes his innovation into an empire of wealth and power. When he returns to his hometown, he is generous toward those who scoffed at his early misadventures. His family, now augmented by a supportive wife and a rising generation, comes to share the modest comforts that success has brought. But riches bring the responsibility of stewardship. David must avoid the single-minded ambition that would make him an antisocial miser. On the other hand, he must also avoid that indiscriminate charity which, by unduly softening the hard edge of competition, would rob the next generation of the very experience fundamental to David's own rise. A becoming and typical compromise is a gift to a religious school, an act that both thanks a bountiful God and offers an appropriate ladder upward for those who would help themselves.

Familiar though this archetypical tale may be, it by no means represents a fixed stereotype. The success story is not even an American invention. Like so much folklore, it is present both in the Bible (the parable of the talents, for example) and in the myths and biographies from antiquity that show that humble origins are not a final barrier. Yet, as Lyman Abbott writes in a passage so apt that Irvin Wyllie used it as an epigraph:

> The ambition to succeed . . . is emphatically an American ambition; at once the national vice and the national virtue. . . . It gives the individual energy; the nation push. It makes the difference between a people that are a stream and a people that are a pool; between America and China. It makes us at once active and restless; industrious and overworked; generous and greedy.[1]

"Success," the "riches" which are opposed to "rags," has been steadily redefined in America in a way that reflects both the major cultural constants and variables as they have revealed themselves in the colonial and national experience. In its earliest form, the promise of success was an advertisement for immigration. Captain John Smith in *A True Relation*[2] described the New World as made for the ambitious, though they lacked collateral or connections. George Alsop in *A Character of the Province of Maryland*[3] went a step further in commending indentured servitude as a way of entering the colonies in rags but with a fair prospect of riches on the horizon. Yet riches to these men, and to their fellow chroniclers, were not equated with golden palaces or even commercial fleets. Rather, the colonies were depicted as rich in natural abundance (crops and game) and cheap land, in addition to offering a pinch of the exotic (Indians and unfamiliar fauna). To leave Europe was to escape poverty, but the immigrants achieved something closer to comfort than wealth.

Meanwhile, the Puritans of New England were submitting their own definitions. In his memorable sermon delivered on board the *Arabella* in 1630, John Winthrop equated success with the improvement of individual lives "to do more service to the Lord." Cotton Mather, while hardly a representative Puritan, made several important contributions to the rags-to-riches canon. He rediscovered the value of the inspirational biography, that classic form of success literature. In his *Bonifacius*,[4] he set down essays on "doing good," which profoundly influenced Benjamin Franklin, that towering example of the self-made man. In *Theopolis Americana*,[5] he depicted "an HOLY CITY in AMERICA: a *City*, the STREET whereof will be *Pure* GOLD," which could be attained through the avoidance of drunkenness and idolatry and the applications of honest practices. Unlike many of his fellow Puritan divines, he was able to see the attainment of virtue as a process in which individual initiative was balanced against communal well-being.

Among the important ideas circulating during the Colonial Era, the Enlightenment contributed new avenues toward self-realization. The rational mind, unfettered, became the center of the universe. By observation and logic, an individual could understand and—to an extent—control the working society. Benjamin Franklin personified these Enlightenment assumptions in his rise from the status of a poor immigrant (arriving in Philadelphia with those legendary loaves under each arm) to become what some might call the Godfather of his country. So that others might imitate this rags-to-riches saga, Franklin founded an academy, a library, and a discussion group. Through "Poor Richard," he catechized America in the classic self-help virtues, and in his *Autobiography*[6] he provided a manual for attacking imperfections and becoming influential, popular, and prosperous.

As the Enlightenment waned, it was replaced by a new world view that both fortified and opposed the classic story of success. Transcendentalism, popularized from pulpit and platform by William Ellery Channing and Ralph Waldo Emerson, offered a philosophical underpinning for individualism and self-reliance, persuading each person that a conscience was both unique and trustworthy. Know yourself, trust yourself, and go forward—a watchword equally acceptable to Emerson or Andrew Carnegie. Yet the Transcendentalists were producing some disturbing rags-to-riches parables, such as *Walden*,[7] in which a rising pencil factory executive drops out and becomes what Horatio Alger would have called a bum. Henry David Thoreau, striking a vein that reappeared strongly in the next century, equated "rags" with the slavery to time and acquisition that so characterized the classic success story, while finding "riches" in the possession of nothing save a harmony with nature and self.

While hundreds were being inspired by Channing, Emerson, and Thoreau, thousands more were being instilled with precepts much closer to those of Franklin. Schoolchildren learned from William H. McGuffey that they should "Try, Try Again." Thomas Dick opened publishing and educational avenues for the diffusion of knowledge aimed at social uplift. The Englishman Samuel Smiles began inundating America with inspirational biographies of men of achievement, such as the railroad developer George Stephenson. The American people had been supplied with a full library of sermons, essays, speeches, and biographies offering the general and specific elements of self-improvement. They were indeed ready for the fully flowered myth. The poor but virtuous David was ready to slay the rich, devious Goliath of New York.

Before the Gilded Age, rags-to-riches had taken many forms. At first it was a rather mild inducement to escape the squalor of European slums for the comforts of the green and bountiful New World. For the more religious it might be a parable leading toward streets paved with spiritual gold. The Enlightenment added the possibility that anyone could rise to success with the application of self-disciplined rationalism. All major cultural forces stressed education, hard work, thrift, and opportunism. Yet it was not until the late years of the nineteenth century that a combination of circumstances and attitudes brought rags-to-riches into its classic mold.

The concentration on industrial technology required new forms of organization as well as countless physical inventions. The Age of Enterprise vested leadership in the powerful individual—human and corporate. Social Darwinism, as popularly received, stressed human evolution through unrestrained competition and natural selection. The government stood obediently by, offering subsidies instead of taxes, protective tariff instead of social welfare. The churches, benefiting from some spectacular personal gifts, often endorsed a Gospel of Wealth, which allowed God credit for the bestowal of His material blessings, as long as the recipient also accepted a Stewardship of Wealth attuned to holy purposes. The story of David thus responded to the major beliefs of the era.

In its classic mode, rags-to-riches has been perpetuated in many forms. One is the simple success story. It is a part of oral and family history. It is formalized into plays and films. It is versified and sung. Its most celebrated prototype is the narrative exploited with repetitive success by Horatio Alger. Perhaps oddly, the pre-occupation of subliterature with the affirmation of individual success was not reflected in serious literature. To the Fenimore Coopers and Theodore Dreisers, to the Stephen Cranes and Edwin Arlington Robinsons, material success was more a trap than a triumph. Nathanael West wrote a direct parody of Horatio Alger,[8] but he need not have bothered; his predecessors had already done so with a thousand times more subtlety.

Shorter written pieces also project the self-help message in memorable and persistent forms. The most famous examples from the era of Alger were Elbert Hubbard's *Message to Garcia*,[9] dramatizing hard work, devotion, and initiative, and Russell Conwell's hymn to opportunity, *Acres of Diamonds*.[10] Conwell, along with Alger and many other propagators of the faith of self-aggrandizement, were clergymen who reflected the spirit of the age by treating success in a business setting. It was left for the layman Bruce Barton to make the ultimate equation. Writing in the business-dominated 1920s, he retold the story of Jesus of Nazareth, making *The Man Nobody Knows*[11] into a physically powerful outdoorsman who developed the skills of a successful advertising executive.

The dominant form of the success story has always been the individual example in the form of the autobiography or biography. In this mode, Andrew Carnegie was to the Gilded Age what Benjamin Franklin was to the Enlightenment. Like Franklin, Carnegie was eager to have his personal experience used as an example. He told the tale of his arrival in America, poor and friendless, whence he rose to the top by cultivating his inner resources to the fullest. His principal gift to America (public libraries) exemplified self-development. His belief in the value of starting from the bottom was so profound that he fully opposed, in word and deed, the act of inheritance. His advice to young men was, "Put all your eggs in one basket and watch that basket."[12]

Many scholars have asked whether or not the prototypical success narrative corresponds with reality.[13] Judging from analyses of biographical materials, it may well be that successful individuals do not usually come from rural or foreign settings. Their parents may have been alive and supportive. Most of them probably had considerable formal education as well as the advantage of family connections and inheritance. In short, to achieve riches, it is best not to start in rags.

In seeming to debunk the classic rags-to-riches narrative, however, students of successful lives have only reinforced it. Folk wisdom teaches that winners usually start with all the advantages; this assumption gives the rags-to-riches saga its special poignancy. It is a fight against odds that produces drama. Even Carnegie might have agreed that excessive poverty would defeat most people. Goliath, nine times in ten, will crush David. Yet the exceptional individual, through self-confidence, self-denial, and self-discipline, can find in adverse circumstances the kind of schoolhouse that prepares him to catch each opportunity, to look for original solutions. and to seek out rather than avoid competition.

This was exactly the kind of myth useful in a land where talented individuals were more scarce than physical resources, where "opportunity" was advertised for all, and where the social institutions were supposedly designed—in contrast with the Old World—to prevent rather than sustain stratification. If rags-to-riches had not already existed in popular belief, America would have invented it. Yet the social value of the rags-to-riches theme was mixed. Alger's heroes were all white men of Northwest European descent. Insomuch as this myth depended on sympathy for the underdog, it held out hope for women and minority groups, and in its classic form, for the newly arrived migrant to the city whether he came from Warsaw, Poland, or Warsaw, Kentucky.

So many of its spokesmen represented major Protestant denominations that a certain religious focus is evident. As a weapon in the laissez-faire argument, however, it tended to underwrite an un-Christian stress on personal wealth justified by the hope that any ordinary person might one day emulate this success. The turn-of-the-century myth of self-help suggested that individual initiative was better than organized labor, and that private charity was more appropriate than public welfare.

The power of this folk lesson did not end with Carnegie or Barton, but it did undergo an evolution that again questioned the equation of success with material achievement. One new element in this equation was the emergence of psychology. As early as the 1890s, Orison Swett Marden was using self-hypnosis as a means for promoting the traditional competitive drive. But as psychology matured, it was used not just to manipulate oneself and others but to achieve social adjustment. Thus the fierce competition of the classic tale retreated in favor of an attitude that could recognize personal fulfillment in something less than the presidency of U.S. Steel. The Great Depression saw the deflation of business values along with the emergence of a new definition of success much more appropriate in the emerging "other-directed" society, as identified by David Riesman and his collaborators.[14] Dale Carnegie's phenomenally popular *How to Win Friends and Influence People*[15] taught some tricks eminently useful in life's combat zones, but they were recommended equally for the sake of acceptance by family and associates. With the appearance of another best-seller, Rabbi Joshua A. Liebman's *Peace of Mind*,[16] the success story returned to concepts preached by Mather and Thoreau.

In recent years there has been an escalation of the war on material definitions of success, a resurgence of mysticism, a shifting stress away from the strivings and toward the balances of nature. For many contemporary Americans, "riches" may be equated with monastic contemplation or communal harmony. But for even more Americans, there is now and will always be a clear and ineradicable respect for the person who started with nothing, dropped out of school at age ten, and made it all the way on his own.

NOTES

1. Lyman Abbott, *How to Succeed* (New York: Putnam's, 1882), p.v. Quoted at somewhat greater length in Irvin Wyllie, *The Self-Made Man in America* (New Brunswick, New Jersey: Rutgers University Press, 1954), p. xi.

2. John Smith, *A True Relation* (London: J. Tappe, 1608).

3. George Alsop, *A Character of the Province of Maryland* (London: Peter Dring, 1666).

4. Cotton Mather, *Bonifacius* (Boston: S. Gerrish, 1710).

5. Cotton Mather, *Theopolis Americana* (Boston: S. Gerrish, 1710), p. 42.

6. Benjamin Franklin, *Autobiography* (Philadelphia: Lippincott, 1868 [first complete edition; first version published in 1791]).

7. Henry David Thoreau, *Walden* (Boston: Ticknor and Fields, 1854).

8. Nathanael West, *A Cool Million* (New York: Covici, Friede, 1934).

9 Elbert Hubbard, *Message to Garcia* (East Aurora, New York: Roycrofters, 1899).

10. Russell Conwell, *Acres of Diamonds* (Philadelphia: Huber, 1890).

11. Bruce Barton, *The Man Nobody Knows* (Indianapolis: Bobbs-Merrill, 1925).

12. Andrew Carnegie, *Empire of Business* (New York: Doubleday, Doran, 1933 [first published 1902]), pp. 12-13.

13. See the bibliographic clues provided by Wyllie, op. cit., pp. 197-98.

14. David Riesman, with Reuel Denney and Nathan Glaser, *The Lonely Crowd* (New Haven: Yale University Press, 1950).

15. Dale Carnegie, *How to Win Friends and Influence People* (New York: Simon and Schuster, 1936).

16. Joshua A. Liebman, *Peace of Mind* (New York: Simon and Schuster, 1946).

David W. Marcell

Fables of Innocence

A culture's literary expression articulates in more or less explicit terms the culture's sense of itself, its character, its approved range of sanctions, behavior, totems, and taboos. For this reason the task and challenge of the folklorist and the interpreter of literary fables are parallel: both seek to establish the artifact in context, and both seek to establish the meaning of the artifact—whether shard or tool or story—in its essential connection with the process by which it was created and the life it creates for itself in the culture through its usage.

Yet no culture is singular in its sense of itself, and thus the interpreter of literary fables must be careful not to oversimplify. As R. W. B. Lewis pointed out in his now classic study *The American Adam: Innocence, Tragedy, and Tradition in the Nineteenth Century*, cultures express their distinctiveness through "dialogues" over particular issues, themes, or problems that have special meaning or significance for the culture's history or survival.[1] These conversations often include a variety of conflicting opinions, but their special significance for the cultural interpreter lies in the unique patterns they create as they illuminate their subject. These patterns of meaning, repeated over time and elevated into ever more self-conscious narrative and symbolic forms, most dramatically proclaim the culture's literary identity. Importantly, the stories and images of such narratives furnish didactic models for those seeking to learn the culture's mores.

The most pervasive and recurring subject in America's literary mythology deals with a set of normative expectations linking time and fate to human will. These expectations, which outsiders tend to regard as naive and simplistic, are often called American "innocence." While stories that reveal or turn on these ideals take many forms, they basically affirm the characteristically American view that the past is never finally binding on the present, that one can always create a new social or personal order through a disciplined assertion of will and virtue.

As a result of this view, the myths, fables, and gestures through which cultures convey their most fundamental messages in America have assumed a particular cast: they suggest, inexhaustibly it would seem, the possibility of renewal and rebirth, of escape from the past and of venturing onward to new beginnings. Gestures of casting off old mistakes and moving afresh into an unblemished future so constantly present themselves as to seem "characteristically American." A vital part of America's own historical success story, these notions of innocence have become articles of faith for countless believers. As models for the culture's historical sense of itself, they have reflexively conditioned Americans' personal sense of destiny. Consequently, this innocence at once furnishes justification for strenuous personal effort and a familiar, culturally-stylized rationale for any triumph over adversity. For believers in its canons, American innocence in its most familiar guise teaches that in the abyss of every failure lies the prospect of spectacular success. While such expectations encourage believers to view history as open and malleable, they also perpetuate illusions of omniscience and a special exemption from the judgments of time and memory.[2]

Three notable American stories, one each from the eighteenth, the nineteenth, and the twentieth centuries, illustrate the point.

In many ways the *Autobiography* of Benjamin Franklin is the beginning of American literature. Franklin saw himself, as did his contemporaries, as a uniquely representative American, and when he wrote the story of his life it was to explain to the world and to posterity the attributes of this personal and cultural uniqueness. His story, on the surface a rags-to-riches affair in the familiar mold, was at a deeper level an essay on historical and social causation. Pasted together over the years, Franklin's narrative chronicled his rise to fame and fortune from the humblest of beginnings. In a candid, confessional mode, Franklin revealed his strategies, his ambitions, his motives, and his failures. The result is a charming, quasi-mythical fabrication of a human life, which, as his critics are quick to note, left out as much as it included.

From his youth Franklin was an experimentalist, a quizzical, energetic, and self-taught questioner of the world as he found it. His trade as a printer provided him with both a passport to material comfort and an entrée to the world of letters and the lettered, where he found a ready reception to his wit and talent. The world Franklin moved in—eighteenth-century London, Philadelphia, Paris—was a world in social and intellectual ferment, a world much in need of the very talents Franklin possessed in abundance. The *Autobiography* chronicled Franklin's innumerable projects, his tactics for accomplishing social and personal ends, and his philosophy of human psychology. Franklin was, among other things, a manipulative social engineer, and the *Autobiography* sketched for the reader an approach to leadership and success in an emerging democratic culture.

Running through the *Autobiography*, however, is the thread of willed personal change, of individually wrought transmogrification: Franklin begins life as a humble apprentice printer and ends as a distinguished, world-renowed scientist and statesman. He is, in Eric Erikson's phrase, a "protean man," a figure of almost infinite adaptability and resolve. His progression is purposive, deliberate, and self-conscious: it comes as no surprise, then, that Franklin assumed that all human errors (he used the printer's term "errata") could be corrected and forgotten, that one could always, by exercising one's will and determination, make a fresh start and a new life. The malleability of the society in which he lived echoed his assumptions. The result is an autobiographical statement that proclaims history to be a Newtonian, rational series of *quid pro quos*, a mechanical process that can be manipulated and controlled by any individual who exercises virtue, intelligence, and purpose. Franklin's stance toward time is positive, activist, and optimistic. Human ingenuity is adequate to the challenge of living, and success results from opportunities created, seized, and acted upon.

Franklin's book revealed a single life and a particular culture in essential harmony. America needed benevolent, civic-minded philosopher-statesmen, and Franklin, in turn, required an open, developing, achievement-oriented society to reach his goals. His *Autobiography* suited his culture perfectly, and his depiction of his own life and character established an inspiring yet wholly human ideal that others could easily emulate. Franklin zestfully functioned as a social prime mover; if his perspective on himself and his world as reflected in the *Autobiography* seems shallow and naive, it cannot be denied that it helped achieve both personal success and an extraordinary measure of civic accomplishment. It also provided subsequent writers on the American identity with a crucial, early voice in the dialogue of innocence.

Standing in what appears to be stark contrast to the social vision of Franklin is Henry David Thoreau's epochal—and equally fable-like—record of his two-year sojourn in the woods at Walden Pond. The book *Walden*, originally published in 1854, posits a view of human self-sufficiency that rejects categorically the social engagement and striving so central to Franklin's story. By retreating to nature, Thoreau proclaimed the adequacy of the solitary, introspective individual who discovers and affirms his humanity by denying the society of others and putting himself, both physically and spiritually, in direct communion with nature and nature's god. By returning to the woods and opening his senses to the sights and sounds and rhythms of nature, Thoreau discovered the essence of what it meant to be human.

Walden affirmed that the singular person in the right relationship with nature— not with society or history—could discover what true humanity meant. In the woods, Thoreau at once re-created the beginnings of time and culture and history, and offered a trenchant, fundamental criticism of the capitalistic, commercial, and industrial world of the nineteenth century. As Charles Sanford put it, "Thoreau's grand objective is to redeem man out of sinful society."[3] Thoreau's vision stood progress on its head and inverted traditional American notions of achievement: the highest and best forms of humanity were the simplest and the least materialistic. (Thoreau's meticulous rendering of accounts in selling his beans and building his cabin was a deliberate, cheerful spoof of Franklin's ledger mentality; that he began his "experiment" in psychological and cultural independence on the Fourth of July was equally deliberate and symbolic.)

But despite their differences in social values, both Franklin and Thoreau agreed that the shaping of human destiny lay within the single individual's grasp. Franklin consciously created a public self and Thoreau likewise deliberately engineered a private, isolated identity. At bottom both stories unequivocally asserted that will and purpose shape individual character and the meaning of human history. Critics have found it significant that neither Franklin nor Thoreau allowed such considerations as tradition, chance, or death to mitigate this view: as David Noble observed, "The soaring faith of the American romantic affirmed the ability of the average citizen to rise above his personal weaknesses and the traditions and institutions of his European ancestors because, in the United States, every individual was in close contact with nature; the West was a limitless national reservoir of spiritual strength."[4]

Such was not the case with the third voice in our dialogue of innocence, F. Scott Fitzgerald's *The Great Gatsby*. Using materials drawn expressly from the Franklin legend, Fitzgerald fashioned a tale of tragic irony and comedy. At the center of the story, however, is an explicitly American cultural commentary, for the character of the hero, Jay Gatsby, represents what time and the American popular imagination have done to the Franklin archetype.

Where does the fictional identity "Jay Gatsby" that Jimmy Gatz assumes come from? Fitzgerald gives us many clues. At the end of the novel old Mr. Gatz, come east for his son's funeral, proudly shows narrator Nick Carraway a trophy from Jimmy's boyhood: a ragged Hopalong Cassidy book with a crude schedule for daily discipline and a boyish list of "General Resolves" penned inside the back cover. Included on the list are "study electricity" and "needed inventions," "read one improving book or magazine per week," "save $5.00 (crossed out) $3.00 per week." As Mr. Gatz explains, "It just shows you, don't it? Jimmy was bound to get ahead." The ambitious boy who scrawled those clichéd resolves was indeed bound to get ahead, but the traditional means for doing so were far too slow for him, and Fitzgerald deftly sketches Jimmy Gatz's early deviation from the ancient formula in a few lines:

> An instinct toward his future glory had led him, some months before, to the small Lutheran college of St. Olaf's in southern Minnesota. He stayed there two weeks, dismayed at its ferocious indifference to the drums of his own destiny, and despising the janitor's work with which he was to pay his way through.[5]

At the end of two weeks Jimmy drops out of college to return to the lakeside, and thus the twig is bent.

The ragged youth who some months later introduces himself to a degenerate yachtsman as Jay Gatsby has explicitly rejected the Protestant ethic of the Franklin myth in favor of a much more extravagant form of ambition, and the yachtsman, Dan Cody, speeds him on his quest. For Cody, the "pioneer debauchee," is historically the product of the Nevada and the Yukon gold fields, but metaphorically, as his name suggests, he represents the popular, theatrical version of the West of Buffalo Bill and Dangerous Dan Magrew. Dan Cody is veritably a nineteenth-century prototype for Gatsby, a model of romantic decadence and meaningless opulence washed up on the tide of a receding frontier. After five years under Cody's influence, as Fitzgerald tells us, "the vague contour of Jay Gatsby had filled out to the substantiality of a man."

When this "substantiality" meets Daisy Fay, the extravagant dimensions of its composite identity are revealed, for Daisy is the objective correlative for the "fantastic conceits" that have become Jay Gatsby. In the final analysis it is impossible to separate the vapid, translucent Daisy from Gatsby's lurid fantasy, for his dream is actually a narcissistic projection of himself, and so, in his imaginings, is she. This is in some sense the main point of the story, for Daisy is essentially the screen on which Gatsby fatally projects his "incorruptible dream" of romantic self-love. Indeed, his courtship, seduction, and later wooing of her are actually but exercises in the extraordinary power of that self-love. Portentously, Gatsby's early courtship is expressly fraudulent, for it is based on his deceptive representation of himself: his officer's uniform masks his anonymity, and he hastens his seduction lest "the invisible cloak of his uniform . . . slip from his shoulders." When we meet Gatsby five years after he has first won and lost Daisy, it comes as no surprise that he has evolved into a full-fledged criminal, who is using his ill-gotten wealth to concoct a ludicrous, extravagant scenario for regaining her.

As this scenario unfolds, it becomes clear that Fitzgerald is exploring a tragic story that spins out inexorably from the contrivance of the Gatsby fabrication itself, from the cultural accretion that is the "unbroken series of successful gestures" Nick mentions in the novel's beginning. For the artifice of Gatsby is in reality a compounded series of counterfeit but nonetheless characteristically American fact-and-fable identities that dance merrily around each other in a gorgeous, improbable three-ring circus: Jimmy Gatz and Dan Cody, Meyer Wolfsheim and Shoeless Joe Jackson, Buffalo Bill and Horatio Alger, Hopalong Cassidy and old Ben Franklin—all under the baton, in case anyone missed the point, of David Belasco. Gatsby's "vast, vulgar, and meretricious dream" is simply the latest installment in a host of ornate American fantasies that stretch back over time, past the city to the frontier and even beyond. They are the bourgeoisie's aristocratic pretensions, the dreams of nobility that produced the brewer's imitation chateau Gatsby lives in, Tom Buchanan's string of polo ponies, and the yacht Dan Cody pilots on meaningless trips to nowhere. They hark back to America's very beginnings, to the trees that once flowered for Dutch sailors' eyes, "a fresh green breast of the new world," which ordinary men and their extraordinary dreams would one day turn into a valley of ashes. These dreams were at once vague and compelling, and their symbol of Daisy and the green light at the end of the dock merely hinted at their enchantments: "Gatsby believed in the green light, the orgiastic future that year by year recedes before us. It eluded us then, but that's no matter—tomorrow we will run faster, stretch out our arms farther. . . . And one fine morning—." Jimmy Gatz may have paid a high price for "living too long with but a single dream," but he is not alone in having done so.[6]

Franklin, Thoreau, and Fitzgerald present significantly different perspectives on the question of innocence. Yet their voices are all distinctively American and equally instructive. Every culture needs its dreamers, people whose vision is not confined to the past or the present. And every culture supplies its dreamers with a fund of images that give proportion and shape to human aspiration. From such a fund of images we learn to distinguish the heroic from the mundane, and the grotesque from the heroic. We need our Franklins to teach us civic pride and our Thoreaus to remind us to cultivate our inner lives. And we need our Gatsbys too, for they reveal painfully the limits of human possibility. As Americans face the challenges of the last decades of the twentieth century, each fable will contribute a perspective necessary to survival.

NOTES

1. R. W. B. Lewis, *The American Adam: Innocence, Tragedy, and Tradition in the Nineteenth Century* (Chicago: University of Chicago Press, 1955), pp. 3–7.

2. David W. Marcell, "Poor Richard: Nixon and the Problem of Innocence," in *American Character and Culture in a Changing World: Some Twentieth Century*

Perspectives, ed. John A. Hague (Westport, Conn.: Greenwood Press, 1979), pp. 325–26.

3. Charles L. Sanford, *The Quest for Paradise: Europe and the American Moral Imagination* (Urbana: University of Illinois Press, 1961), p. 181.

4. David W. Noble, *The Eternal Adam and the New World Garden: The Central Myth in the American Novel Since 1830* (New York: George Braziller, 1968), pp. 4–5.

5. F. Scott Fitzgerald, *The Great Gatsby* (New York: Charles Scribner's Sons, 1953), p. 100.

6. The above quotations are from Fitzgerald, passim.

Giles Gunn

The Myth
of the American Adam

The myth of the American Adam is curiously one of the most important myths in the American pantheon and yet one of the most elusive. Centered on the heroic figure of Adam before the Fall, it has long been a significant factor in American life and has also furnished support for several other important American myths, most notably the myth of the Chosen People, the myth of the Virgin Land, and the myth of Manifest Destiny. Yet it is nowhere succinctly expressed or definitively elaborated in the American cultural tradition; it is more often encountered as an interpretive thread running through material of somewhat different mythic composition than as a narrative unit standing, so to speak, by itself.

The sources of the myth of the American Adam are to be found in the Book of Genesis, where it is first told how God completed his cosmogonic work with the creation of man. Actually, there is not one creation story in Genesis but two. In the first (Gen. 1:1 ff.), which is presumably the later account, God created the heavens and earth out of a formless void by his Word and then crowned his work with the formation of man in the divine image. In the second Genesis account (Gen. 2:5 ff.), which is much older than the first, creation occurred when God caused a desert to be made fertile by a great flood that arose from the ground. Man was fashioned from the loam and then placed in a garden God had created in Eden for him to cultivate and tend. After God had created the animals and birds and brought them to Adam to name, God formed the woman Eve from one of Adam's ribs to be his companion and consort. In both versions, however, the focus is not solely on explaining the origins of primordial life, but also on accounting for the appearance of evil in the world and dissociating God from responsibility for its presence.

Among a Bible-reading people such as the first Americans, it is not difficult to understand the appeal of these stories. The parallels between the Adamic myth and their own history were vivid and illuminating. The colonists of New England in particular felt that they, too, had been created as a community by God's Word, out of a kind of formless chaos or spiritual void, and that they, too, were called upon to inaugurate a new history. They could see this new history as closely bound up with taking possession of a new land and needed little encouragement to imagine this land, in prospect at least, as a kind of paradisal garden. Furthermore, their mission in this new world could easily be interpreted in Adamic terms as an attempt to recover for mankind, with God's gracious assistance, something of the integrity of man's primordial innocence, of his original purity and simplicity of being.

Despite these parallels between the Adamic myth and the perceptions that America's more religiously minded first settlers had of themselves, the myth of the American Adam did not become culturally consequential until long after the colonial period, and by that time it had lost many of the other elements associated with both biblical versions. In the later American interpretation, which did not achieve clear cultural outline until the early nineteenth century, there is rarely any mention of serpents in the garden or of temptation or disobedience or expulsion and suffering; and the Eve of the second Genesis account, who is no doubt indicative of the androgyny latent in the earliest biblical traditions of primal man, scarcely exists. Instead, the nineteenth-century rendering of the Adamic myth emphasizes the rather isolated figure of Adam himself, a figure of immense possibilities poised on the threshold of a new age, who is also, at least in certain readings, made vulnerable by his own spiritual virtues. Examples abound, from Brockden Brown's Arthur Mervyn and Robert Montgomery Bird's Nathan Slaughter to Ernest Hemingway's Nick Adams, from James Fenimore Cooper's Natty Bumppo to Stephen Crane's Henry Fleming, Theodore Dreiser's Carrie Meeber, J. D. Salinger's Holden Caulfield, and John Updike's Harry "Rabbit" Angstrom.

Unlike his biblical prototype, the American Adam is less the product of God's handiwork than a creature of his own making, at once self-propelled and self-reliant. His most important qualities derive not so much from his place in the hierarchy of being as from his originality, his simplicity, and, above all, his innocence. He constitutes a kind of rare moral phenomenon, not because he is good or bad, but because he represents the possibility of somehow transcending such categories. His chief purpose is to preserve and enhance this state of moral, or spiritual, integrity, and his chief problem is that he must somehow learn to survive in a world not of his own making, a world that can sometimes prove more hostile than accommodating to his own particular form of virtue.

The image of Adam in all his purity of aspiration and boundless optimism is perhaps most classically represented in the pages of Ralph Waldo Emerson's *Nature*, with its strong censure of the present age for being too retrospective, its belief in the goodness and oneness of life, and its conviction that the destiny of all men is to enjoy an original relation with the universe. This viewpoint can also be seen in the pages of Thoreau's *Walden*, where the Concord naturalist takes on the role of a kind of spiritual Chanticleer rousing his neighbors from their moral sleep in the belief that only that day dawns to which we are fully awake. Later in the century, in *Portrait of a Lady*, Henry James's Isabel Archer asserts, in words that could as easily have been uttered by any one of the robber barons of the Gilded Age, that "Nothing that belongs to me is any measure of me; everything's on the contrary a limit, a barrier, and a perfectly arbitrary one." The same image can also be perceived in the assumption so many people shared with William Gilpin, first governor of the Colorado Territory and an ardent proponent of the trans-continental railway, who declared that "the untransacted destiny of the American people is to subdue the continent." But this buoyant, forward-moving, self-generating image of Adam probably achieves definitive expression in Walt Whitman's "Song of Myself," where the poet sets out to take possession of the world as though he were its sole artificer, Man and God in one, installing himself at its center, delegating to himself the right to name its components and define its possibilities, and proceeding at the end to pass judgment on the merits of his creation.

The anti-image of Adam, or at least the more ambiguous image of Adam, did not grow up alongside the positive one but developed more slowly, in fits and starts. What provoked such a development was the realization by writers like Nathaniel Hawthorne, in *The Scarlet Letter* and "My Kinsman, Major Molineux," or John W. DeForest, in *Miss Ravenel's Conversion*, that the moral innocence of the Adamic hero could prove a spiritual liability in a fallen world, and could even become spiritually destructive, as Herman Melville discerned, if innocence became a static condition that cut one off from lived experience and prevented further moral growth. Melville's Captain Ahab is almost the obverse of Emerson's "plain old Adam" when he says, "I feel deadly faint, and bowed, and humped, as though I were Adam staggering beneath the piled centuries since Paradise. . . ." But even without the complicating presence of an alien and often antagonistic world or an iniquitous past, there was still the potentially poignant, dispiriting loneliness of the Adamic condition itself. According to R. W. B. Lewis, the chief historian of the Adamic myth in America, Whitman put his finger on it when he used as his most successful trope for the American Adam a solitary live oak growing in Louisiana, "Uttering joyous leaves all its life without a friend or lover near. . . ." This spectacle struck Whitman as unbearably sad, because, as he put it, "I knew very well I could not."

This ambiguity about the Adamic logic—was the American figure a descendant of the old Adam or the new?—permitted the myth of the American Adam to become the focus of a cultural debate that achieved historical importance by the middle of the nineteenth century and has continued unabated to the present. On the one side were writers such as Emerson, Whitman, and Thoreau, and historians and commentators from Hector St. John de Crevecoeur and George Bancroft to Daniel Boorstin, who saw the myth of the American Adam in essentially positive terms. The Adamic myth gave expression to their sense that America constituted a divinely granted second chance for the human race. The past and the Old World generally were to be left behind or overcome. Members of what Emerson called "the Party of Hope" believed that America's future lay in colonizing the immense interior of the continent, turning the Great Plains into a New World Garden. On the other side of the divide were novelists like Nathaniel Hawthorne, Herman Melville, and, later, Henry James, poets like Emily Dickinson, Edwin Arlington Robinson, and Robert Frost, and historians such as Francis Parkman and Henry Adams, who viewed the Adamic ambition to abolish the past with alarm, and who believed that optimism about the future must be tempered with a realistic assessment of human capabilities and of the nature of life itself.

The debate between these representatives of "the party of Memory," to continue with Emerson's designations, and their hopeful antagonists eventually gave rise to a distinctive American narrative.[1] The essential outlines of that narrative can first be seen in the later tales of James Fenimore Cooper's Leatherstocking series, particularly *The Deerslayer*. Then, with certain variations, they became fixed in such classic American novels and stories as Hawthorne's *The Scarlet Letter*, Melville's *Typee*, *Moby-Dick*, and *Billy Budd*, Mark Twain's "Old Times on the Mississippi" and *The Adventures of Huckleberry Finn*, Henry James's *The*

American, Portrait of a Lady, and *The Golden Bowl,* William Dean Howells's *A Hazard of New Fortunes,* Stephen Crane's *The Red Badge of Courage,* Theodore Dreiser's *Sister Carrie* and *An American Tragedy,* Sherwood Anderson's *Winesburg, Ohio,* Willa Cather's *My Ántonia,* F. Scott Fitzgerald's *The Great Gatsby,* Ernest Hemingway's *In Our Time* and *A Farewell to Arms,* William Faulkner's *Absalom, Absalom!* and "The Bear," Ralph Ellison's *Invisible Man,* Saul Bellow's *The Adventures of Augie March,* Bernard Malamud's *The Assistant,* Flannery O'Conner's collection *A Good Man Is Hard To Find* and "Parker's Back," and Thomas Pynchon's *The Crying of Lot 49.* The distinctive American narrative centers on the Whitmanesque future of "the simple, separate self" bereft of any ancestry, a figure who answers only to some idealized conception of self, even when thrust into a world that falls short of his expectations. The drama of this story then derives from the tension between what the world will do with innocence or purity of being, and, conversely, what innocence or purity of being will do to the world. The more optimistic of American writers, such as Thoreau or Howells or the Henry James of *The Golden Bowl,* dramatize the degree to which the Adamic qualities can be educated under the tutelage of experience, or, like the Melville of *Billy Budd* or F. Scott Fitzgerald, show how the radiance of innocence and hope, even if only momentarily, can somehow transfigure the otherwise drab materials of ordinary existence. The more skeptical and pessimistic of our writers, on the other hand, such as Hawthorne or Stephen Crane or Hemingway, portray the tragic collisions to which innocence is susceptible, or bring out, as Faulkner does in *Absalom, Absalom!,* the process by which innocence can all too quickly give way to spiritual blindness, which in turn leads to moral perversity.

Such discoveries are very often made in the distinctive American narrative not by the Adamic hero himself, but either by the omniscient narrator of the work or, more characteristically, by some character within the tale who becomes progressively more involved in the hero's quest and is drawn deeper into the problem of untangling its conflicting meanings. Thus Melville's Captain Ahab (a kind of innocent outraged who then seeks to avenge the offender) has his Ishmael, Hawthorne's Hollingsworth has his Coverdale, Fitzgerald's Gatsby has his Nick Carraway, Willa Cather's Ántonia Shimerda has her Jim Burden, Faulkner's Thomas Sutpen has his Quentin Compson, Robert Penn Warren's Willie Stark has his Jack Burden—all of whom serve the purpose of conveying such moral and spiritual discoveries as the American Adam's story yields. The myth of the American Adam has thus done more than shape the content and form of many classic novels; it has also determined their particular structure.

The myth of the American Adam and its distinctive narrative bears certain affinities with the classic American success story, with its "Rags to Riches" motif, of which Benjamin Franklin's *Autobiography* may be the classic expression. Both focus on the career of an isolated hero who must learn how to survive and succeed in an often unfriendly world. And both make much of the central figure's self-reliance, which encourages him to define the world in terms of himself rather than himself in terms of the world. But where the Horatio Algers always win, the American Adams frequently lose. In addition, the two sagas place emphasis on different elements. Andrew Carnegie in his *Autobiography* is far less interested either in himself or in the world than in how to make his way in the world. His character is already well formed before he reaches adolescence, and his environment is an open book that simply awaits the skill to read it. But Hawthorne's Hester

Prynne, like Melville's Pierre and Captain Delano, are themselves the riddle they or others must unravel, the puzzle to be solved.

A further difference between the myth of the American Adam and the myth of the self-made man is that the latter produces exemplary tales permeated with a sense of self-congratulation, whereas the former more frequently produces cautionary tales suffused with a sense of wonder and awe. Benjamin Franklin's descendants, like Franklin himself, are secularized pilgrims in search of success, who are surprised, if at all, only by the simplicity and alacrity of their rise. Adamic heroes, on the other hand, tend to inhabit a universe full of portents, mysteries, and marvels, which lend to their chartered odysseys a momentous, if not sacred, aura. What is at stake is not their own fate merely, or even the fate of the institutions and values through which they realize themselves, but the fate of the entire American spiritual experiment.

The influence exerted by the myth of the American Adam on American fiction should not obscure the equally decisive imprint it has left on the history of American poetry. From Emerson and Whitman onwards, as Roy Harvey Pearce has shown,[2] one of the two major strains in American poetry has been dramatically Adamic. With origins going all the way back to the Antinomian Controversy of the 1630s, when Anne Hutchinson risked censure and expulsion from the Massachusetts Bay Colony in behalf of her belief that all men and women can experience through the agency of the Holy Spirit an unmediated relation with the divine, the Adamic strain in American verse has assumed that poetry's chief subject should be the making of poems and that its central affirmation should be the importance of the person of the poet as maker.

> The Adamic poem—to define it as a basic style, a kind of ideal type—is one which portrays the simple, separating inwardness of man as that which at once forms and is formed by the vision of the world in which it has its being. . . . The poem may nominally argue for many things, may have many subjects . . . ; but always it will implicitly argue for one thing—the vital necessity of its own existence and of the ego which creates and informs it. Its essential argument, its basic subject, is the life of poetry itself, as this life makes viable a conception of man as in the end, whatever commitments he has had to make on the way, radically free to know, be, and make himself.[3]

While this poetic mode is, perhaps, most immediately associated with a poem like "Song of Myself" or Emerson's "Merlin," it defines with remarkable exactitude much of the poetry of such moderns as William Carlos Williams, Hart Crane, Theodore Roethke, A. R. Ammons, and preeminently, Wallace Stevens. The Adamic style is perfectly exhibited by the girl who sings beside the sea and somehow beyond it in Stevens's "The Idea of Order at Key West":

> It was her voice that made
> The sky acutest at its vanishing.
> She measured to the hour its solitude.
> She was the single artificer of the world
> In which she sang. And when she sang, the sea,
> Whatever self it had, became the self
> That was her song, for she was the maker.[4]

The Adamic self as artificer can create in either of two ways: one, as William
Carlos Williams suggests in the preface to *Paterson*, is

> To make a start
> out of particulars
> and make them general, rolling
> up the sum, by defective means—[5]

The other is to begin with the unifying, climactic image, as Hart Crane does in his
"Proem," when he addresses the bridge that is to be the subject and symbol of his
epic poem, "The Bridge":

> O Sleepless as the river under thee,
> Vaulting the sea, the prairies' dreaming sod,
> Unto us lowliest sometime sweep, descend
> And of the curveship lend a myth to God.[6]

Either way, there is a resistance to final summaries or certain conclusions. In the
words of A. R. Ammons's "Corson's Inlet," the Adamic poet is always striving,

> to fasten into wider enlarging grasps of disorder, widening
> scope, but enjoying the freedom that
> Scope eludes my grasp, that there is no finality of vision, . . .[7]

Assuming that man is the maker of his own meanings, the Adamic poet construes
these meanings as important chiefly for what they say about the self as maker, and
what they say about the self as maker is that nothing is ever finished; the world is
ever new; the future is more important than the past.

Such faith naturally has its limitations. As many critics have pointed out, it
elevates the idea of Man at the expense of the idea of Men. It deprecates the remedial
value of the Past for the regenerative possibilities of the Future. It discounts the
importance of evil for the sake of idealizing an image of the good. But for all this the
Adamic faith has also kept alive a sense of hope in our culture through recurrent
periods of self-doubt. It has helped defend the democratic notion of the individual
in the face of increasing modern pressures to conform. And not least (especially in
the work of those writers who have viewed it with some irony), this Adamic faith
and the myth by which it has been expressed have led to important discoveries
about human nature—its thirst for experience, its vulnerability, and its innate
optimism—what Stevens defines as belief:

> Again, in the imagination's new beginning,
> In the yes of the realist spoken because he must
> Say yes, spoken because under every no
> Lay a passion for yes that had never been broken.[8]

NOTES

1. R. W. B. Lewis, *The American Adam: Innocence, Tragedy, and Tradition in the Nineteenth Century* (Chicago: University of Chicago Press, 1955), pp. 90 ff.

2. Roy Harvey Pearce, *The Continuity of American Poetry* (Princeton: Princeton University Press, 1961).

3. Ibid., p. 187.

4. Wallace Stevens, "The Idea of Order at Key West," *The Palm at the End of the Mind, Selected Poems and a Play*, ed. Holly Stevens (New York: Vintage Books, 1972), p. 97.

5. William Carlos Williams, "Preface," *Paterson* (New York: New Directions Press, 1963), p. 1.

6. Hart Crane, "To Brooklyn Bridge," in *The Complete Poems and Selected Letters and Prose of Hart Crane* (New York: Anchor Books, 1966), p. 46.

7. A. R. Ammons, "Corson's Inlet," *Corson's Inlet* (Ithaca, New York: Cornell University Press, 1965), p. 8.

8. Stevens, "Esthétique du Mal," *The Palm at the End of the Mind*, pp. 257–58.

American Settings

Where is American folklore to be found? At one time collectors of folklore felt impelled to travel long distances into the hinterland, to Tobacco Road and Death Valley, to ferret out tales and songs and sayings and beliefs. Typical titles spoke of *A Song-Catcher in Southern Mountains* and *Up Cutshin and Down Greasy*, this last work referring to creeks in the Kentucky hills. The whole mood and attitude toward the expression of folklore by those who study the subject have drastically changed, and they now agree that folklore emerges among people everywhere, in the home, at work, in leisure pursuits, in the schools, in cities, towns, and villages—in short, wherever folks gather. The one stipulation is that human beings must congregate and interact. A hermit does not pass on folklore, though he may well give rise to legendary anecdotes in neighboring communities. Nor is a moviehouse a setting for the exchange of folklore, since the audience is passive and quiescent; they have congregated, but they do not interact. Possibly the film may transmit some folk themes to the viewers, but they will need to express them actively to their fellow mortals for the folklore to come alive.

From youth to old age, at work and at play, in school and in church, and in the widening arcs of our orbits, from the local neighborhood to the metropolitan area to the region of the country with which we identify, we encounter folk traditions in various settings. The present section is organized to represent the expanding network of these settings. We begin in the home, with the nuclear family, where the old fairy tales may be read, but are seldom told, yet we now perceive that the household does indeed function as a conveyor belt of small rituals, customs, recipes, momories, heirlooms, sayings, and allusions that in sum constitute a yeasty folkloric brew. Every family, as Kotkin and Zeitlin persuasively contend in the opening article of this section, possesses its own private store of traditions. As I turn my mind inwards on this point, I think of an expression my father was wont to use at the dinner table in our home on Park Avenue in New York, when a festive mood struck him. "Now why don't you speak a little French? Parlez-vous français quaylay." He said this with a half grin, but insistently and almost plaintively, and my two sisters and I groaned, and might or might not make a half-hearted effort to mumble a few French phrases. The *quaylay* was a nonsense word, rhyming with *parlez*, presumably coined by my father, who knew no French. He himself had ceased his education at the eighth grade and gone to work pushing furniture to support his seven younger siblings, children of an immigrant German Jewish couple. A short man, five feet four inches, he had risen to become president of a wholesale furniture company and had sent all his children to private colleges. Proud of their education, he delighted in hearing them converse in French, to him a symbol of status and elegance. So while *quaylay* was an idiosyncratic word in our family lore, it did relate to the widespread American myth of the land of opportunity and upward mobility.

At school and college we inherit vast bodies of folklore, from song parodies to textbook inscriptions to restroom graffiti. Increasingly, the grade school and high school replace the home as the center of activity and social relationships. Then the move to the college campus and dormitory does indeed establish a surrogate home. Opportunities abound for the absorption and relaying of folklore in the midst of high-spirited peer groups. In my case I think, for instance, of the butt-room, so-called, at Exeter, where I attended prep school, and to which, having reached the age of sixteen, we could repair, in basement lounges of our dormitories, to smoke cigarettes. As we smoked we talked, and certain self-assured, worldly-wise youths— who projected a persona of seasoned veterans—held forth on their sexual exploits and imparted advice to the less informed on strategies of sexual conquest. "Never screw a virgin," counseled one young man-about-town, whose father was said to have key Mafia connections; "it's like taking your prick out and banging it against a stone wall," a terrifying image that haunted my adolescent years. In those days much schoolboy talk centered on the problem of dealing with a virgin's maidenhead. Streams of lore cascaded through the walls of the butt-room, not quite all scatological, in the form of epic verses, legends of deviant students and oddball instructors, slurs, taunts, ribaldry, brags, warnings, curses. Even the paperwork folklore of written, typed, and xeroxed items, which Dundes describes below as associated with business offices, found its way into the butt-room, in the form of the Purity Test, a list of sexual transgressions against which each schoolboy checked his record. Had he violated none, he would score 100 percent, but one wise senior stated flatly that the highest possible score was 90 percent, since no one could say no to the first question, "Do you ever play with yourself?"

After school and college we go to work, and the site of every work group becomes a reservoir and channel of folk experiences connected with the job. Whether blue-collar or white-collar, indoors or outdoors, production or sales, professional or service, the occupation breeds its own lore. Some work sites, where the buildings are occupied round the clock, such as hospitals, steel mills, and fire stations, develop especially rich corpora of folklore. In a pioneering ethnographic study of firemen, Robert McCarl labels the fire house a "unique work place/home," in which family life is traded off for the camaraderie of the fire fighters, and he provides thick descriptions, salted with personal narratives, of their traditional behavior and accumulated lore. A hospital in particular beckons the folklorist to undertake a folkloric ethnography, as the work place of nurses, doctors, orderlies, technicians, and staff, the resting place of patients, and the visitation place of relatives and friends, as well as the scene of gripping dramas of life and death. To date very little can be cited on hospital folklore. But the whole field of American industrial-occupational folklore and folklife is only beginning to be addressed. The older outdoor and underground occupations of lumberjacks, cowboys, miners, and railroaders are much better collected.

Some Americans spend a good deal of their time in their church buildings, and those who do are practicing folk religion in good part. Folk elements can be detected in the singing and musical accompaniment, the formulaic chanted sermon, the testimonies of the saved and the cured, and the ritual behavior of the congregation, as William Clements points out in his article on the white folk church. A correlation can be supported between time spent in church and the degree of folkness in the church service and related activities. The limited hour service follows a prescribed, set program. Once when I was attending a black Baptist service in Gary, Indiana, the only white person present, the preacher, who was discoursing on the history of the Afro-American Baptist church as an institution, remarked, "We go to church and stay all day. The church was the only place we could call our own. White folks go for an hour and run home. Isn't that right, professor?" turning to me. True, although with some white churchgoers, such as the Pentecostals and the Mormons, the church occupies a large part of their lives, and contributes to their folklore, as Clements and Wilson demonstrate in their articles.

Shifting to a larger frame of reference, we can indicate cities as a major congregation point of Americans since industry overtook agriculture in the late nineteenth century. Folklorists have until recently shied away from cities, thinking of the hinterland as their primary turf, but revised concepts now make them very city-minded; the denser the population, the thicker the lore. Warshaver in his article on urban folklore lays out a set of guiding principles for the folklorist investigating cityways. We have become conscious that urban—and suburban—behavior follows its own traditional codes, orbits, manners, and styles, which endure and alter, according to a dispatch from the *New York Times* news service of November 1980, as a means of coping with crime in the streets. Affluent males remove their tires; affluent ladies conceal their handbags and jewelry under capes and scarves. Seediness has become a way of urban life. How and where one moves about the city, or to and from the city, where one shops and dines, whom one visits and entertains, all enter into the records of urban folklife.

Americans may live in cities or suburbs, in villages or on farms, but they all belong to a larger regional unit, defined both geographically and culturally. In some of the population the regional consciousness slumbers; elsewhere, it is lively and patriotic. "My region, right or wrong," announces a caption under the cartoon of a rabid regionalist. Lightfoot addresses the question of identifying folk regions and distinguishing between the folklore specific to a given region and general folklore found in many regions. Other articles consider examples of regional folklore expressed in folk speech and local songs. Some folklorists have found the regional approach rewarding, and I myself have applied it in two books dealing with the Upper Peninsula of Michigan and the Calumet Region of northwest Indiana, one heavily rural, the other heavily urban, yet each with a strong sense of identity and a bountiful folklore. How many regions remain to be uncovered, and whether the whole country is subject to regional analysis by the folklorist, remain open questions. Urban consciousness may in some cases block out regional consciousness.

Finally, in our consideration of American settings we must make note of the peripheries of the nation and outlying territories. National boundaries, as contact points between different peoples and cultures, generate a special folklore of cultural friction and political tension. In the case of the boundary with Canada, this folklore is muted, as Klymasz indicates, because the similarities of the two countries are pronounced. In the case of the boundary with Mexico, as Limón illustrates, the cultural differences provoke a strident and one-sided folklore. Looking overseas, Mitchell takes the case of Guam to exemplify the confluence of mainland mores with the Micronesian indigenous folkways.

One thread unites these nineteen articles, the sense of place in the American environment as it affects folklore. None of us can, if we wished to, escape the sense of place, taken in a limited or a broader sense, from the home to the region, and consequently none of us can escape from the tangled webs of folklore that cling to all places.

Amy J. Kotkin and Steven J. Zeitlin

In the Family Tradition

John Jaffe abandoned his family just before Christmas.[1] His daughter Jane was twelve years old and his wife was pregnant. They dreaded the coming holiday. But Mrs. Jaffe and her daughter understood the place of ritual in family life and used it as a cornerstone for rebuilding their family.

In the next year, I don't know whether my mother did this on purpose, but we all sort of concurred in changing everything we had usually done. We had always decorated the house in a certain way. We'd always had a certain kind of Christmas tree—a very tall Christmas tree, maybe because my father is six feet tall. But when it came time to decide what to do, it dawned on all of us at once, I think, that we should buy a short, fat Christmas tree, a Scotch pine, kind of blue. So we bought a tree that was about as wide as it was tall, and we went through all the decorations and threw about half of them out and got a lot of new ones, and we fixed the house differently. . . . It was a good Christmas. It was surprisingly good . . . and we've done it that way ever since.[2]

Jane Jaffe views her family history as having "come in two parts—before my father left us and after he had gone."[3] The change in Christmas rituals symbolized a fundamental shift in the family's life. Ritual is a common denominator of all family folklore, from the most pervasive genres—stories, traditions, and photographs—to family expressions, nicknames, foodways, games, needlework, and the fantasies made up by parents for their children. Considered in context, each genre is closely interwoven with what sociologists have termed family ritual: recurring patterns of expressive leisure time activity.[4]

The stories parents invent for their young, for instance, may be peopled with talking whales, giant rabbits, and anthropomorphized Mack trucks. Yet to understand these imaginative creations, we must grasp the significance of the bedtime ritual, a conscious parental activity designed to quiet the children and lull them to sleep. The plots are often unimportant. We even met one father who put his four-year-old boy, Saul, to bed by recounting his son's own activities that day. "Once there was a little boy named Saul, and he woke up in the morning. . . . "[5]

Similarly, the recipes and needlework passed down in families involve not only preserves and samplers but the patterned activity that surrounds their production. Even family expressions are involved with ritual.

> Someone in my family had three children, one of whom was named Shields. The old man was quite a drunk and often he would beat up on his family when in liquor. One day he started in on Shields, who was by then a grown teenager, and Shields licked the tar out of him. Finally the old man was down and Shields was sitting on his chest. The old man looked up and said ruefully, "Get up Shields, you beat your Daddy."[6]

In the Slemp family, this story has been transformed into a family expression; whenever a child outdoes his parents, someone will say, "Get up Shields, you beat your Daddy." By alluding to this incident at similar moments, the family members transform a shared experience into a verbal ritual appropriate on recurring occasions. Ritual may be the best starting point in the cultural study of the family, just as it has long been recognized as the best one for the study of religion.[7] Each family ritual involves the ceremonial use of leisure, and may be as commonplace as the evening meal, with its ceremonies of cooking, carving, and serving, or as sanctified as a wedding, funeral, or Christmas celebration.

FAMILY STORIES

Storytelling is an important ingredient of holiday celebrations, the evening meal, and other home entertainment rituals. In the following example, storytelling is so formalized that it might be considered a ritual in itself.

> My family is Sicilian and we . . . have a tradition of sitting around a table telling stories. But you can't tell stories except at certain parts of the meal. We have a saying, "When you eat you don't talk." Any of us who [talked] during the first or second course of the meal were always chastised by Grandma and Grandpa. . . . After those courses were over things came out like the artichoke, which was not considered a course exactly, but it was . . . something that followed the meal. Or the chestnuts, or what in Italian families we call the frutte, dolche, cafe—the fruit, the sweets, and the coffee.
>
> My grandfather would eat an artichoke or a chestnut, and all of a sudden he would begin to laugh to himself. Inevitably, someone would say, "Grandpa, why are you laughing?"
>
> That would begin the storytelling time. And he said, "I'm just remembering the time when. . . . " That's how one began to tell stories at dinnertime. It happened the same way almost every night.[8]

What kinds of stories are remembered in families? One informant[9] described them as the "reverse of the horror stories that people tell about vacations. Anytime anybody takes a big vacation that everybody envies—they go to Europe or the South Seas and they come back and you say, 'Well, how was it?' 'God, it was cold,' or 'God, it was crowded,' or 'I got seasick on the ferry. . . . ' " Those, he pointed out, are not the ones that pass into family tradition. He went on to offer an example of a more long-lasting narrative.

The story that's on my mind is on my mind because I just got word that my
great-uncle Jim died. His name was Jim Cobb and this is a story he used to tell
me about looking for work in the Depression. He'd been out of work like
everybody else for months and months and pounded the pavement and wore
out the soles of his shoes—his shoes were threadbare and so forth. And finally
he got hired and the man who hired him, as he told the story, said, "I want you
to know why you got this job, because there were twenty or thirty other
applicants. I hired you because you polished around the soles of your shoes,
you polished around the edges of your shoe soles." And the man said, "I think
that's a sign of somebody who'll take pride in his work." And I polish the soles
of my shoes to this day.[10]

Narratives that describe a character, that pinpoint personality, hold fast in oral
tradition and constitute a "character principle" in family stories. The tales are
often distinguished by a standardized opening and closing, ascribing a particular
attribute to the central character. Lines such as these most often begin, but
occasionally conclude, family narratives: "You know, you always gotta have a
crazy aunt in your family."[11] "The most interesting side of my family is the
Musters. . . . They were one of the biggest hell-raising families in the Ohio
Valley."[12] "He [my grandfather] was a good salesman and a good hustler."[13]

Referring to these stories, family members note how they reveal "so much" about
a relative, how they become "the sum total of things." The narratives are a
distillation of experience, which heightens a family's power to communicate. They
also simplify character, enabling family members to play on the roles and identities
of their kin.[14]

Just as the personalities of particular family members are favorite subjects for
family stories, so too are those events which mark a turning point in the family,
which involve a "transition principle." The stories delving furthest back into a
family's history are often tales of immigration, a pivotal point for most American
families. The narratives tell of the adventures of a patriarch who steps out of the
amorphous flow of European or world history and into the oral history of a
particular family. Hazardous border crossings are a common feature of the
migration saga.

My grandfather was a teacher in Russia and consequently, he was quite
distinguished—had a mustache, spoke High Russian, and didn't have a
Jewish accent or anything like that. Now one day he went out to teach, and two
Russian soldiers attempted to rape my grandmother, who was a redhead of
Dutch extraction, and somebody went and called my grandfather. He came
back and he practically beat the two Russian soldiers to death.

Now, this was unheard of in Russia, and immediately there was a warrant
out for his arrest. And so he had to flee the country.

About the same time, his brother-in-law had been called to service. Jews
never wanted to go into the Russian army, so the two of them decided to leave
the country.

When they reached the border there was a guard with a rifle there, and my
grandfather—who appeared like a Russian—gave all his baggage to my
granduncle and told him, "Now look. I'm going to distract the guard, you

sneak across the border."

So what happened was this. He's busy talking with the guard, and they're talking about the large number of Jews who tried to get across the border. The guard says that if he sees them, he shoots them. My granddad says that that's *absolutely* the right thing to do. And they go on with it. Somehow or other, the guard realizes something is happening, and he sees my uncle, and starts to raise his rifle. So my grandfather grabbed it—"Please, please! You're here all the time, let me have the gun and let me. . . ." The guard gave him the gun and he hit the guard over the head with his own gun, and that's how they crossed the border.[15]

Occasionally, jokes, floating legends, and traditional folktales appear as family stories. It is not uncommon for a grandfather, for instance, who tells a joke about a numbskull to become the numbskull when his grandchildren retell it. One person who helped us record and transcribe family stories had a humorous incident befall her when she tried to retell this bawdy tale.

> My great-grandfather lived in Scotland, and he had a habit of going into a little pub or tavern in the evening and getting a little messed up and then he'd come home. One night he got to talking to this barmaid and she went with him over to the field and they had a little sport and then he passed out. She wanted to tell him how much she had enjoyed it and she couldn't talk to him so she took a blue ribbon from around her hair and tied it on his tool and left his kilt rolled up. My great-grandmother waited for several hours and he didn't come home. So she started toward the tavern in town and found him lying on the hillside with his kilt rolled up and the blue ribbon on his tool. And she said, "I'll not be knowing where you've been or what you've been doing, but I'm proud to see that you won the first prize!"[16]

While transcribing this story from the tape, our staff member, unfamiliar with the word "tool," wrote it as "toe." She then retold the story at a dinner party, where an elegantly dressed woman told her, "Oh, you don't have to say 'toe.' We all know what you mean. We've heard the story before." This experience was an education for our transcriber, but it was also an education for us. We realized that traditional folktales sometimes float into the family context, though for the most part they remain the exception rather than the rule in a family's corpus of folk material. Generally, narratives are traditional within families; between families the *kinds* of content are traditional, not the content itself. Hearing many related stories over time, and having similar experiences, a family will mold their tales and their memories to fit the pattern. But the stories are created anew in each family, and, for the most part, specific plot elements are not borrowed. The story types in family lore most often result from the character and transition principles, and from our experience, the following themes recur in American families: (1) stories of wild antics, (2) poverty and hardship, (3) lost fortunes and career opportunities, (4) notorious deeds, (5) heroic action, (6) courtship and marriage, (7) family migrations, (8) natural disasters and near deaths, (9) supernatural occurrences, and (10) eccentric behavior.

FAMILY PHOTOGRAPHS

The family photographs that crowd albums, drawers, and attic trunks through-out American homes also form an important part of a family's expressive culture. In a sense, a family's collection of photographs can be viewed as the visual equivalent of their narratives, for the most treasured snapshots are often those which illustrate the character and transition principles evidenced in stories.[17] For example, a young woman from New Jersey recalled a photo of her great-uncle Max, who as a young man had briefly joined Buffalo Bill's Wild West Show. Although his cowboy days were short-lived, the only photo of Max that survives in the family shows him dressed in his huge hat and chaps. Max's image fascinated the young woman, who dubbed him "One Gun Blum, The Jewish Cowboy." Though Max Blum spent most of his life as a tailor in Newark, New Jersey, his great-niece, who knew him only through a single photograph, had made him into a cowboy hero. She had developed Max's life into epic proportions and had even started telling her children about her great-uncle's alleged adventures out west.[18] The photograph had become the totality—the summation of his life and character.

The transitions that are so important to family stories are also recorded in photographs, which most often focus on the more formal rites of passage—baptisms, bar mitzvahs, weddings—and other shared time markers, such as Christmases and birthdays. In some instances, photos pinpoint less obvious transitions. The transition in the Jaffe family from a two-parent to a one-parent household was marked not only by the changed Christmas celebration but also with a photograph.

> The first summer after my father left us we went down to the seashore for a vacation. . . . And we went out to eat in one of those places where a person comes around to take your picture at your table and then sells it to you. It's hanging in our upstairs hall now. I looked at it this past Christmas. . . . We looked kind of helpless in the picture. . . . Here was my mother surrounded by all these kids, like what's she going to do. . . . I called my mother out of the bedroom and I said, "Remember that summer? Look at that. Don't we look sort of pathetic?" And she stood there and looked at it, and she said, "Well, we did okay." I think that's the way she feels.[19]

We were curious about this photograph of the "pathetic," "helpless" family. But when we tracked it down, we saw only the standard family vacation picture of people eating well and having a good time (fig. 1). The photograph denied the emotions of the story it evoked. If we analyze the visual "text" alone, we find that it is a recurring photo type.

Just as Americans share notions of the proper structure and content of stories, they also share beliefs about appropriate moments to photograph. In addition to photographs documenting the rites of passage and family celebrations, pictures record families grouped on front porches, in front of their hearths, and around their dining room tables (figs. 2–5). Family members often pose proudly with prized possessions. New cars, bicycles, and backyard pools are standard fare in family photographs, as are idyllic images of children with pets, toys, and snowmen. Family photographs are not a random sample of our past, but a series of idealizations of how we choose to preserve, remember, and be remembered. "Christmas, birthdays—you hate to see the camera come out," Carol Maas told us.

FIG. 1. Though typical in its content, this family photograph recalled a painful transition for members of the Jaffe family. (Folklife Archive, Smithsonian Institution)

"You know it's going to be a picture of the Christmas tree. It's going to be a picture of everyone gathered behind the person . . . you know how it is! Standard family pictures."[20]

Even more than stories, family photographs are embedded in ritual. Looking at photographs, like telling stories, is often part of family celebrations and home entertainment rituals. Similarly, the act of picture taking not only documents family celebrations; it becomes a ritual in its own right. The noted photographer Tod Papageorge remembers: "On Christmas morning my father was a photographer. . . . My sister and I, called to attention, stared ferociously at those awful bulbs, not understanding that even as we sat there, blooming from the ribbons and wrapping paper, we were part of a ceremony; that we were, in fact, its motive."[21]

FAMILY CELEBRATIONS

Holiday traditions also mark transitions and celebrate characters in the family. Seasonal and calendrical changes are the basis of Christmas, Easter, and the New Year. Birthdays, baptisms, bar mitzvahs, weddings, anniversaries, and funerals mark the passages through life at the same time that they focus on a particular figure in the family.

Whereas stories encapsulate experience in a set verbal piece, and photoghraphs on kodachrome, family celebrations capture the past by reenacting it. Oftentimes, American cultural and religious holidays are a symbolic representation of a historical event. Jews partake of the bitter herb on Passover to relive in some way

FIGS. 2, 3. Family meals and holiday celebrations are common scenes in a family's collection of photographs. (Folklife Archive, Smithsonian Institution)

FIGS. 4, 5. Families grouped on front porches and steps are among the most frequently recurring scenes in American family photographs. (Folklife Archive, Smithsonian Institution)

the trials of the Israelites in Egypt. The manger scene on American mantels at Christmas suggests a re-creation of the birth of Christ. In the Dreschler family, the Christmas ritual commemorates an era in the family's history.

> My grandmother and grandfather went to Kansas in a covered wagon. My grandfather took out a section of land, I think that's 640 acres. There are almost no trees in that central section of Kansas. It's the rolling prairie. He planted a big grove of maple trees, and those trees were so sacred to him that he would never cut one, not even for Christmas. So presents were always put at each person's place at the dining room table.
>
> Even later on, when different branches of the family would have Christmas, they still use the table for their presents. . . . We do now have a little tree, but the presents are always on the table. . . . Trees are not for gifts. Trees are sacred in my family.[22]

Family celebrations symbolically re-create not only the original episode but all the subsequent occasions on which it was celebrated. Christmases recall past Christmases. A midwesterner we spoke with found herself spending Yuletide in the Philippines. In a desperate effort to re-create the Christmas she had always known, she turned up the air conditioner, put on a long fleecy robe, fixed some hot chocolate, and pretended it was winter in St. Louis.

Families often traditionalize their experience. A successful picnic or outing is likely to happen again. Families with small children have told us that the young are the true guardians of tradition, insisting that rituals be enacted in precisely the same manner year after year. Celebrations range from the most sanctified occasions to less formal family reunions to one family's "Friday night shoeshine parties," which consisted of no more than television, pizza, and shining shoes, but which will be treasured by the children for as long as they live.

In the family, as in every community, members gather on certain occasions to share in their leisure. The emotional investment of family members often transforms these recurring activities into a set of binding rituals. Bringing together a variety of genres, these rituals represent a nexus in family life. The most common is the evening meal, but camping trips, rides in the car, and reunions are also points at which forms of family folklore may converge. One of our interviewers recalls a family who celebrated each coming weekend with a Friday night poker game. The family's most treasured narratives emanated from that weekly ritual and were repeated each week as similar situations occurred. Family nicknames were also based on this card-playing ritual. Perpetual winners and losers, as well as suspected cheaters, played out their identities and roles at the poker table.[23]

The folklorist working with the family would do well to pay particular attention to the patterned, recurring activities of the kin group. Whether they are the evening snack, birthday dinners, or annual reunions, they form the occasions on which stories are told, nicknames bantered, and photographs taken and eyed. For the family, such rituals represent what the members like about themselves and wish to perpetuate;[24] for the folklorist, they reveal the emotional core of family life.

NOTES

1. All stories used in this article are from the Folklife Archives of the Smithsonian Institution. They were collected between 1974 and 1977 by the authors and other graduate students in folklore at the Smithsonian's annual Festival of American Folklife, where over 2000 taped interviews were conducted with festival-goers. Some background information on the informants is available from the Folklife Program, Smithsonian Institution.

2. Name has been changed upon request. Tape 113-1-75.

3. Tape 113-1-75.

4. James S. Bossard and Eleanor S. Boll, *Ritual in Family Living: A Contemporary Study*, (Philadelphia: University of Pennsylvania Press, 1950), pp. 9, 11, 16, 27. It should also be noted that folklore occasionally embellishes shared household tasks such as cooking or gardening. One of our informants, for example, told us that storytelling was an integral part of the breadbaking activity she shared with her grandmother. Ritual may be employed to make common housekeeping chores more enjoyable.

5. From an informal conversation with Steven Zeitlin, 1977.

6. Mary Slemp, Questionnaire 169-0-74.

7. Bossard and Boll, p. 10.

8. John Giordano, Minnesota Family Folklore Workshop Tape, April 22, 1977.

9. Warren P. Corbett, Jr., Tape 49-3-75.

10. Tape 49-3-75.

11. Kirsten Stromberg, Tape 109-3-76.

12. Juste David Myers, Tape 261-4-74.

13. Myron C. Bretholz, Tape 109-2-76.

14. See Amanda Dargan, "Family Identity and the Social Use of Folklore: A South Carolina Family Tradition" (M.A. thesis, Memorial University of Newfoundland, 1978).

15. Phil Hoose, Tape 122-3-74.

16. Carl Lamar Duff, Tape 123-4-75.

17. All information on photographs for this article is taken from the Folklife Archives of the Smithsonian Institution. In addition to stories, staff members of the Family Folklore Program collected over 200 photograph albums for research and exhibition.

18. Name withheld upon request. Tape 141-4-76.

19. Tape 113-1-75.

20. Audio tape for the film *Harmonize! Folklore in the Lives of Five Families*, by Steven Zeitlin and Paul Wagner, Smithsonian, 1976.

21. Jonathan Green, ed., *The Snapshot* (Millerton, N.Y.: Aperture, 1974), p. 33.

22. Marie Dreschler, Tape 192-6-75.

23. Susan Donahue, Tape 338-1-76.

24. Bossard and Boll, p. 10.

Leonard Roberts

A Family's Repertoire

In the 1940s and 1950s when I did most of my field collecting, it was not the fashion to stay with a family for weeks and even years to record their folklore. Such was the way of anthropologists and archaeologists, who set out on expeditions to study a culture and excavate a cultural site. Or the way of the Irish, who, supported by the government, went out in teams to village homes to listen to a family's repertoire. But a folklorist also needs time, and my own collecting in eastern Kentucky involved me with an extended family—the Couch-Harris family—for two years.

My first intimations of this region's extensive folk traditions came in the early 1950s, when I made an exploring trip to Leslie County with one of my students. On our way to his home, we spent the night with his aunt, who lived on the banks of Cutshin Creek. At dusk, by the evening fire, the aunt, Mrs. York, agreed to record a few of her stories. She began quietly to tell of the "Haunted House." Her tale went on and on, with her daughter clinging to her arms. Later she hummed a few passages and sang the ballad of the "Golden Vanity." Mrs. York just happened to say that she had learned this song while in Pine Mountain Settlement School. The rest of our weekend proved as fruitful, and I continued for many months to ramble into the hills, with Mrs. York's song and tale lingering in my mind.

A year later my own family was living at Pine Mountain Settlement School, where my wife taught and I was a visiting scholar from the University of Kentucky, designated as collector of tales and ballads. With these privileges I was able to ride out to shut-in families with a nurse from the local hospital. On one occasion she set her Jeep toward the head of Cutshin, where, in a new-fashioned log house, we found an ailing woman who was supposed to be a tale-teller. She was Mandy (Couch) Hendrix, oldest daughter of a large family scattered about in three counties. Her several children at home and an orphan living with them gave her away by saying that she could tell the best tales. But to us she owned that she had not told old "lie" stories in nineteen years. She did say that she had a brother Jim, who had "Follered tellin' our mother's old tales and stories. . . . When he would come over here all the children would gather in and he'd start and have them on his knees and all over the floor. He could pleasure the children to death with them ole tales."

As I took down the brother's name and location, I wondered if it was a good lead or a "modesty" protest so commonly used by preachers and singers in the hills. The orphan Bobby then insisted on telling me a story, and all at once I heard the enduring lines and singsong chants of "The Two Gals." Whenever he faltered on the tale, Mandy would correct him and cue him on through the story! The same coaching prevailed when Bobby launched into the familiar tale of "Jack and the Beanstalk." I heard the bald authentic line, "Ah hush, old man, it's just a buzzard flyin' over the house with a bone in its mouth you smell." It seems that Mandy, a delightful talker, had learned all of her mother's stories and had passed them on to the younger members of the family and to her own eight children. She urged her younger brother Jim to keep these tales alive, since she herself, as she put it, had quit telling them when she "became a Christian nineteen years ago."

After this visit, I felt certain that the discovery of an extended family store of traditional lore was possible. But proceeding with the recording proved vexing and uncertain. The members of the family lived in numerous hollows of two or three counties and spread into Virginia. Had they all lived in one valley, or more closely in a small town, the task would have been easier and probably more fruitful. Furthermore, I was not free to spend all my days and years at such arduous collecting. My wife was putting me through school, and in the next two years I had to struggle through my orals and then tackle a dissertation.

Nevertheless, I had to drive across Pine Mountain every month or two to the stores at Harlan and to the university. Bobby's two long *Märchen* urged me, on one of these trips, to find the home of Jim Couch. He lived on a hillside by the road near the bandmill village of Putney. I caught him at home one afternoon, on the porch with two of his brothers, all three smudged from head to foot from a day in the mines. Before many exchanges of conversation, I said, "Jim, I heard from Mandy that you follow telling the family's old stories." "Yep," he replied, "I guess I know about all our mother ever told." Jim was a thin, ruddy-faced, medium-sized man of about fifty. He continued talking while his wife poured bath water back in the kitchen. He said he had told stories at Mandy's house many a time, had told the two Bobby stories frequently, and mentioned "The Little Black Huntchey Hunch," and "Polly, Nancy, and Muncimeg." He eased off his pegleg and explained, "Got mashed up in the mines three years ago." He was ready to bathe and eat supper and went in with the promise that I could stop again to see him.

The next three to six months were a most trying time for me in fieldwork. I was not yet known by any of the family, and they seemed not to be active performers of their lore. My credentials were slowly established when I persevered and explained my purpose—to record their stories and songs. I was born in their mountains and lived at Pine Mountain, where both Jim and his older brother Dave had worked. When I met Dave for the first time I learned that he may have been the last one to keep up banjo playing and singing for occasional gatherings and dancing. He said his dad's old banjo had been unused so long, the strings had broken. I got him a set of strings, and he promised to tune up the banjo and sing some for me in one or two months.

Jim began to emerge in my mind as the leader of the family, but when I dropped in on him he was still only lukewarm toward my project of collecting the family lore. I told him the material was good enough to be published in a book and demonstrated my point by transcribing one of his delightful tales about the use of magic ointment, "The Witch Store-Robber," and publishing it in *Mountain Life and Work.*[1] When I gave him a copy of the magazine, he read it in silent wonder, then rolled the magazine up and thrust it into his front pocket. Without many words of approval or agreement, he began to keep our appointments, and in the course of time he had told the story of his people, where they lived, and their genealogy. He was also aware of the ones who followed telling and singing as well as those who did not perform the family lore.

Most of the Couches at this time lived downriver at Putney, including old man Tom and his children Dave, Jim, Sally, Harrison, and Alex. Amanda lived on Cutshin in Leslie County, and some of their in-laws, the Holbrooks, lived on Big Leatherwood Creek in Perry County. Jim's uncle, John Couch, and cousin, Joe, lived across Big Black Mountain in Appalachia, Virginia. During the years in which I was unable to continue collecting, 1950–52 and 1954–55, Jim moved three times, once into Letcher County with his guitar-playing son, Frank. In the meantime, after finishing a dissertation, I moved to Georgia but luckily found a position the next year at Union College in Knox County, close enough to drive the hundred miles to Putney and resume the Couch sessions.

The family's interest in my collecting project held firm, and Jim was a very prompt letter-writer. Family members recalled tales and songs, and they visited with their father and others to straighten out a song or to untangle a tale. During this intensive time of travel and inquiry, I found I was becoming confused by the family lines and nicknames. Time and again I jotted them down in my notebook, until finally, with Jim's help, I arrived at a working genealogy (fig. 1), which I kept handy at all times.[2]

Anderson Couch, said to be French, settled in North Carolina in the early 1800s. His son John married a Dutch woman, Sally Shepherd, and came to Big Leatherwood, Harlan County, Kentucky. He is supposed to have fought against his mother state in the Civil War. Nothing more was known about him except that he had a son, Tom, born in 1860. Jim's maternal great-grandfather, Pressley Harris, probably of Irish (or Scotch-Irish) background, came to North Carolina in the 1830s. He is said to have married a full-blooded Cherokee by the name of Turner. After his wife had died and his son Lewis had settled on Sang Branch in Kentucky, Pressley came to live with his children. Jim was able to see and hear him in his old age. He talked with a burr and was full of tales and tricks. The one son of his that we know about, Lewis Harris, married and had a daughter, Mary Ann. When she married Tom Couch, she inherited most of Sang Branch and settled there with her extended family around her.

Tom and Mary are the two great performers and teachers of song and story in the family. Tom made his own banjos, and as early as 1915 he won a picking contest at Hyden by playing "The Roving Gambler." He taught all of his children to play and sing. Jim recalls when he was eight or ten and learning to beat the strings while his father noted the tune. I first saw Tom in about 1951, when Jim's son Elmer led me up the point from Jim's place to an old logging road and around the hill to a simple cabin, where Tom lived with his young second wife and two children, born when he was seventy-eight and eighty. Tom was not at home but soon came down through the woods dragging some dry poles for the stove. He shushed the son and daughter and called for chairs from his wife. He was talkative, his face and hands constantly in motion. He had played music all his life and had taught it to them all. His favorite song was a real tearjerker of recent vintage, which he called "A Young Lady in the Bloom of Youth." When I asked him about his wife Mary, he praised

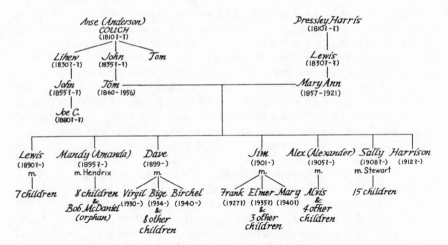

FIG. 1. Short genealogy of the Couches

her as the storyteller. At my suggestion he told "Polly, Nancy, and Muncimeg," with almost too much inflection and gesture. Of course, he was now almost deaf, and, as Jim put it later, "He had no tune." Jim continued to go to him for starts of songs and corrections. Jim also brought him down to one of our sessions, where he put on tape the Civil War song "Hiram Hubbard." As is usual with performers, Tom sang his current favorites and needed to be coaxed back in time to his oldest. At our last session in 1955 Jim had learned from Tom the old English ballads "The Devil and the School Child" and "Lord Bateman." Since Tom knew a number of the Old World *Märchen* and could sing almost any folksong, hymn, or ballad his sons could name, he had a reputation as the most remarkable performer in the mountains.

Tom's first wife, Mary Ann Couch, of Indian-Irish background, was praised by Tom, Jim, and Dave as the most spellbinding storyteller they ever heard. Before she died in 1921, she had passed on a rich body of *Märchen* to Mandy and Jim and a surprising number of animal tales to Dave. She would tell a tale while the family rested at the end of corn rows; she would narrate between banjo numbers in the yard at dusk; she would tell stories at bedtime; and when Tom was late coming in, she would keep the young ones from the supper table with a story. Although she may have been frolicsome like her rowdy grandfather, Pressley, and her father, Lewis, in early years, she became a homebody in later years and would not tell stories for visitors or strangers. In all, she raised seven children.

Dave Couch had damaged his health in the mines and now suffered from black lung and eye troubles. He spent much time in treatment centers, had retired, and, with a few of his eleven children, had been staying alive by gardening and ginseng digging, making as much as $800 a season with "sang." His singing with the banjo turned out to be quite good. With his soft, lonesome expression and steady frailing of the instrument, he performed such numbers as "Barbara Allen," "Mines of Coal Creek," and "Floyd Frazier." His most pleasing tales were "Cat and Rat," "The Fox and the Cat," and "Tailipoe." He was proudest of his role as player for dances in the valleys for many years. Picking had kept him from learning dances and telling tales, because, as he said, not just anybody could pick to suit the dancers.

Jim Couch was the most versatile and lively raconteur of the family. This is not to say that his mother and his oldest sister, Mandy, were not good—from all reports, they were spellbinders. Jim had learned from them and his uncle, John Couch. He grew up when his mother was at her best. But there was a break in the family circle. At eighteen Jim went into World War I and served in France's most bitter battles. When the war was over, he reenlisted and found himself helping to exhume the doughboys for shipment back to the States. He had received the bloodstopping art from his mother and, as he said, he must have saved a thousand lives in battles and in hospitals. He continued his picking and singing for the troops, composing a piece, "Kaiser and the Hindenberger," which caught on by its appearance in an army magazine.

When Jim returned from the devastation of war in about 1922, he had serious adjustments to make. His mother had died, several of the children were married, and his father had taken two or three of the youngest from the area. There was little left. Jim stayed with Mandy and took an interest in the tales she was telling. After he married and tried to settle down, he kept returning to Mandy's. Her children and others gathered as he told the *Märchen* of the "Little Black Huntchey Hunch," "Johnny Conscience," "The One-Eyed Giant," and "Nip, Kink, Curly." He was also full of funny and tall tales, rhymes, riddles, Irishman tales, beliefs, and superstitions.

After Jim and Dave had told slightly different versions of "The One-Eyed Giant," I began to query them about their sources. They thought it had first been told by Basil Holbrook, a neighbor of John's. We went to see Basil and found him in ill health, living in an old log house. He avowed that the story must have been told back in his early days by John. He didn't think he could put it together again. Jim and I chose a good time and went to Appalachia, Virginia, where part of the Couch family had settled after leaving Perry County. John, living alone, had not told a tale in years and immediately directed us to his son, Joe. Joe had been crushed in the mines, was retired, and worked at the bus station. Yes, he could tell some old tales. Aside from many Irishman jokes and big hunting tales, he told "The White Deer," and then went into another version of the One-Eyed Giant tale, calling it "Old Johnny Sore-Nabel." The versions told by Jim and Dave comprised the One-Eyed Giant and the Valley of the Serpents episodes of Sinbad's Third Voyage in the *Arabian Nights*. Joe's version added a detailed summary of "The Old Man of the Sea," of Sinbad's Seventh Voyage. Wondering how these rare appearances from the *Arabian Nights* and the east European tale "Nip, Kink, Curly," told by Jim, got into the rough hills of Kentucky has kept my quest alive.

The repertoires of the family members touched on above show them to be the active carriers of their oral traditions. Jim and Dave were glad to show what they could do in singing and playing. Also Jim's and Dave's oldest sons, Frank and Virgil, had guitars and were playing modern country and bluegrass songs. Lewis, Alex, and Sally showed an interest in the collecting but were not public performers, each for individual reasons. For instance, Mandy, Lewis, and Harrison had raised their children within the strong revivalist churches in the region. Alex was the type of mountain boy who, as Jim put it, "wouldn't open his mouth." Sally had so many children she didn't have time to perform. In a word, their father, Tom, had taught them all to sing and play and then had let them have their way with their talents.

With the family chart, my task of understanding and discussing the members of the family was easier. In general, traditions are carried down by the male line and performed at home and abroad by sons and grandsons. The women often sit back in the home circle, or even in a back room when men visitors are performing. Often they remain silent, until they suddenly prompt a teller or name a tale or song the performers have left out. In the Couch family tree, the excellent performances of Mary are an exception.

The genealogical chart may also be used to trace shifts in transmission of traditions. In the Couch family the lore of Tom did not necessarily die out with Sally. She had been a banjo performer and singer. Before she herself stopped singing, she may have taught her own sons and her husband a number of songs. I did not get to find out, because Jim had told me that she had quit picking years ago.

Two books resulted from my two years of collecting from the Couch and Harris families—*Sang Branch Settlers: Folksongs and Tales of a Kentucky Mountain Family* and *Up Cutshin and Down Greasy.*[3] Some months after I sent Jim and Dave a copy of *Up Cutshin*, I received some xeroxed materials from my publisher. I quickly recognized the handwriting on the enclosed letters. Jim Couch was suing the publisher and me for unlawfully distributing "that book." I rushed to the mountains and found Jim in his cabin looking sheepish, if not downright pleased, to see me. He said collectors had been pestering him—writing and coming to record stories for research papers: "I had to take my wife to the hospital and here come a dyked out feller with a quare name from New York, Philly, somewhere, wanting me to tell him tales." I was able to talk him out of a court case by promising early royalties, since the book was selling well.

My field study of oral tradition broadened my knowledge of the world and of human nature. I often say to others that I learned more by studying folklore than by studying letters.

NOTES

1. *Mountain Life and Work* 26:2 (Spring 1950): 16–17.
2. *Sang Branch Settlers: Folktales and Songs from a Kentucky Mountain Family* (Austin: University of Texas Press, 1974; rpt. Pikeville, Ky.: Pikeville College Press, 1980), p. 386.
3. Leonard Roberts, *Up Cutshin and Down Greasy* (Lexington: University of Kentucky Press, 1959).

Ronald L. Baker

The Folklore of Students

That folklore survives only among old folk is a popular mis-conception. In the United States, where the urban and suburban population is mobile and blocks and subdivisions often are not as homogeneous as neighborhoods and villages of the past, elementary and secondary students play an important role in developing and preserving local traditions.[1] They also maintain a stock of folklore restricted largely to their own age groups. As families relocate and students are promoted or graduated, the membership of student folk groups turns over every few years, but much of the lore remains, and new traditions arise.

On the school bus; before, between, and after classes; on the playground; in the cafeteria or soda shop; at parties, dances, and school functions; or even in the classroom, folklore is performed. Adults often feel that the riddles, rhymes, songs, jokes, legends, and games of their childhood are only dim memories, until their children reach school age and bring home some nearly forgotten lore like: "Knock, knock." "Who's there?" "Ilene." "Ilene who?" "Ilene over and you kiss my ass."*
Other traditions learned on the schoolbus or playground are not so familiar to parents, as they are recently created and sometimes inspired by popular culture, such as this parody of the theme from "The Beverly Hillbillies":

> Let me tell you a story about a man named Jed.
> One day he threw Granny into bed.
> He unzipped his pants and pulled out his worm.
> And out from the worm came a bubbling sperm.

As soon as teenagers are licensed to drive, the automobile becomes the setting of folklore content and performance. Cruising and parking, students swap jokes, sing songs, and play games. In fact, the automobile has contributed to modern parking legends like "Hook Man" and "The Boyfriend's Death," tales that tell of near-tragedy and tragedy while couples were parked on lovers' lanes and warn students to be careful when parking.[2] Local legends of ghostly lights, monsters, and haunted roads, cemeteries, and bridges have been kept alive by teenagers who hop in their

*See also James Leary's article on "Hangouts," p. 181, for a variant.

cars and visit the sites of the legends to neck, drink beer, or have a thrilling experience.

As students move on to college, they continue to perform folklore in the dormitory, fraternity or sorority house, coffee shop, tavern, or wherever else there is communal activity. Some college folklore is imported from lower levels of academe. For instance, at the University of Illinois, where one semester I collected nearly one thousand items of student folklore,[3] college students shared parodies of Mother Goose rhymes, bawdy book titles, depraved definitions, Confucianisms, and other traditions with elementary and secondary students, although sometimes the traditions were adapted to college life. Mother Goose vice-verse, nearly all scatalogical, was especially popular. A favorite was "Little Boy Blue, / And his mother knew."[4] Bawdy book titles, such as *The Cream of the Russian Army* by Ivan Yackinoff, can be collected from students in grammar school as well as in college, but the U. of I. students had one book title, *The Koch Book of Party Games*, that was unique to the Champaign-Urbana campus. Professor Leo Koch (pronounced "Cook") was dismissed from the faculty for his statements in the *Daily Illini* condoning premarital sex. College students recalled generally known depraved definitions, too, such as "What is virgin wool? A sheep that is faster than the shepherd"; however, some of their depraved definitions dealt exclusively with college life, for instance, "What's a fraternity pin? A crotch key."[5]

Various puns from Illinois also have versions in high school folklore, such as "Tonto, not knowing the Lone Ranger disguised as a canoe, stroked his paddle, and he shot across the lake"; and "She wasn't much of a wrestler, but you should see her box." Wanton daughter puns (e.g., "She was only the judge's daughter, but she was tried by every guy in the neighborhood") and punning rhetorical questions (e.g., "Did you hear about the plastic surgeon who made an asshole out of himself?") also are shared by high school and college students. Most Confucianisms from the U. of I. can be found among students generally, too, and most were sexual, as "Confucius say, 'Man who loses key to girlfriend's apartment get no new key,' " but again some of them were adapted to college life: "Confucius say, 'Bald-headed professor who stay out in sun too long have baked bean,' " for example. Other proverbs and sayings also were adapted to the university.[6] One informant said, "On this campus, a boob in the hand is worth two in the blouse," while another student offered, "Candy's dandy, but a frat pin's quicker."

Most of the folklore at Illinois, though, was not imported from lower levels of academe but dealt with campus life. Some of these traditions seem sexist today, but they are representative of college folklore collected from both male and female informants in the middle sixties. A migratory tradition incorporating an age-old motif (H411, "Magic object points out unchaste woman")[7] most frequently involved the Alma Mater statue. As one coed said, "The Alma Mater is a gigantic statue between the Union and Altgeld Hall. It is composed of three figures, one on each side of a large chair and the so-called Alma Mater right in front of the seat. When a virgin walks by, the Alma Mater is supposed to sit down." Another student suggested how folklore is made: "When I was a pledge, several of the other guys and myself carried a broken toilet bowl over to the Alma Mater and put it on the chair behind her. The word going around for the next several days was that if a virgin passed, the Alma Mater would shit." Sure enough, in one of several variant accounts, another informant maintained, "When a virgin passes in front of the Alma Mater, the statue is supposed to move her bowels."[8]

There were anecdotes about U. of I. coeds, too. A couple of male informants claimed that 99 percent of American coeds are beautiful, and the other 1 percent go to Illinois. Several traditions explained how girls become coeds. A female informant said a girl becomes a coed when she walks by the Alma Mater statue and it doesn't sit down, while a male informant maintained, "a girl becomes a coed if she is laid on the stadium steps." Legends also were told about "the girl with the golden arm," who supposedly was seen in a convertible in a residence hall parking lot "easing a Pi Phi's [sic] sexual tensions with her arm." Although another tale deals with a naive male freshman, it indirectly comments on U. of I. coeds. Walking by a girl's dorm, the freshman overheard one coed telling another that "There must be a mile of dick walking around here, and I'm not getting an inch of it," and the green freshman ran home.

Other familiar college tales, sometimes reported as legends and sometimes told as jokes, were told at the U. of I. as true stories. One informant swore that a coed walked into a class late one day, and the instructor told her, "You're just in time for a little quizzie." After looking over the exam, the coed said, "If this is one of your quizzies, I'd sure hate to see one of your testies!" Another student told of three coeds in an otherwise all-male class with a prof who began each lecture with a dirty joke. Fed up with the instructor's bawdy sense of humor, the coeds reported him to the department head and decided to walk out of class at the start of the next dirty joke. At the next class meeting, true to form, the instructor, who heard about the girls' plan, began, "Did you hear about the boat load of prostitutes going to England?" The three girls got up and were half way out of the classroom when the instructor gibed, "Wait a minute, ladies. The boat doesn't leave until next week."

Half-blind professors, boring professors, incompetent professors, and absent-minded professors also were the subject of tales at the U. of I. One professor was so blind that a different student attended class each day and answered roll for all the other students. Another professor had a glass eye, and all his students sat on the side of the room of the glass eye so they could cheat on exams. A boring law school professor noticed a student sleeping, so he stopped lecturing and asked another student to wake him. "Hell, no!" the student said. "You put him to sleep; you can wake him." Another professor finally gave up trying to lecture over the noise of a construction crew outside the classroom and told his class, "We'll have to dismiss. I can't even hear my own lecture." "Don't worry about it," some student quipped. "You haven't missed a thing." One absent-minded professor "unbuttoned his vest, pulled out his tie, and wet his pants."

According to college folklore, grading is not very objective. A migratory campus legend at Illinois dealt with a pledge who found a term paper in the house files and turned it in to his English instructor, who gave the paper an A and told the student, "When I wrote that paper twenty-five years ago I knew it deserved an A, and I think it still does." One student told about a U. of I. professor who spreads exams on the floor, dips his cat's paw in ink, and lets the cat walk freely among the papers. The papers marked by the cat get A's, and all the others get E's (i.e., F's). Another professor throws exams in the air, giving those that stick to the ceiling an A, those remaining in the air a B, those flat on the floor a C, and those standing on edge an E. When grades are due, another professor takes nature walks at night and gives students' names to the stars. The brightest stars get A's, and the dimmest get E's. Other professors assign grades by weight, length, or thickness of term papers. One tale has a student turning in a term paper with all pages blank except the first and last pages and receiving a *B*, while another tells of a student putting the World Series box scores in the middle of his paper and getting an *A*.

The tests themselves are considered illogical, insipid, and insignificant. According to U. of I. folklore, the questions on the psychology finals are not changed from semester to semester; only the answers are changed. Another tale dealt with the simplicity of the exams in physical education and the proverbial lateness of the Illinois Central. A student had a 9:00 P.E. exam and a ticket for an 8:50 train. He figured the exam would take only fifteen minutes and the train would be half an hour late, giving him just enough time to make the train, and he was right. Some tales warn that instructors do not take exams seriously, so hard work does not pay. A senior in electrical engineering worked diligently on a final exam, taking the entire three hours; however, when he left the classroom he found his semester grade posted on the door.

Since students consider grading subjective and tests unfair, they don't prepare but bullshit, guess, or cheat on examinations, according to college folklore. The most popular tale about an exam at the U. of I. concerned a single question on a philosophy final: "Why?" A student simply answered, "Why not?" or "Because," in variant accounts, and received the only *A* in the class. A question on an astronomy exam was, "Which is more important to the earth, the sun or the moon?" One student answered, "The moon because it shines when it is dark, while the sun shines when it's light anyway." A student who had a thousand-word paper due was not prepared, so he turned in a picture with a note that "a picture is worth a thousand words." Another informant said a student was seen flipping a coin during a true-false exam. Tales about cheating on exams were fairly common. For example, a student who worked for Clean-Towel had a key to the towel holders in the restrooms and before a final exam put his textbook in a towel holder. After looking over the exam, he asked to be excused, went to the john, took out the textbook, and looked up the answers.

Since students feel that exams are chancy, folk beliefs about exams have arisen. According to one tradition at Illinois, if a dog follows a student to an exam, the student will get a "dog" (i.e., a *D*) on the test. One informant related a legend with a variant of this belief: "One fellow last year went in to take a final with a *B* going for him. During the final a dog entered the room and sat down right beside him. He attempted to shoo the dog away, but to no avail. The student failed the final and got a *D* for the course."

On campuses where sports are emphasized, stories about star athletes are very common. The most popular tale about a jock at the U. of I. concerned Ed O'Bradovich's foul mouth. A blend of two subtypes of the tale runs:

O'Bradovich was a Sig Ep. Went to a dinner exchange to a prominent sorority. Sitting at the table, he said, "Pass the fucking salt." Complete silence. His date said, "You hear him. Pass the fucking salt." The Sig Eps were mad at Ed. Told him no more exchanges. He begged to go, so they made him promise not to say a word. Next exchange, Ed just sat there. His date was trying to draw him out of his shell with, "You played a good game Saturday." And, "Isn't this dessert good, Ed?" No answer throughout all this. Finally, she said, "Ed, you aren't saying a thing. How come?" Ed said, "Da, the guys are afraid I'll fuck up."

The proverbial dumb athlete was the subject of several U. of I. tales. One informant said star running back J. C. Caroline was put on defense when he turned pro with the Chicago Bears because he was too dumb to remember the plays. According to another student, at the half of the Michigan game at Ann Arbor the Fighting Illini were getting beaten badly, and the coach gave a rousing pep talk, ending with "Go out there and kill 'em!" Leading the fired-up team from the locker room, the co-captain took the wrong door, and the entire football team followed him into the swimming pool. A football recruit supposedly took his entrance exam and flunked the math part by saying that $7 + 6 = 11$. The coach pleaded with the examiners, arguing, "Oh, come on. He only missed it by one."

Stories about coaches also were popular at the U. of I. Occasionally, motifs from stories about professors enter tales about coaches, as the Illinois fencing coach allegedly was as absent-minded as professors. In Kansas City he pushed his team on a west-bound train but remembered he had left his hat in the station and ran back to get it. Returning, he boarded the right train heading east. Sometimes the incompetent coach surfaces, too. An Illini basketball coach was a poor recruiter, according to campus folklore, because he was a drunk. But more often, as Dorson has observed, the coach is "lofty and admired," while the professor is "lowly and comical."[9] Since Illinois had its last Rose Bowl team the year I collected, the football coach, Pete Elliott, especially was a campus hero. One of several tales told about Coach Elliott earlier was attributed to Bernie Bierman of the University of Minnesota[10] and involves an international motif, F624.4, "Strong man lifts plow": "When Pete Elliott looks for his linemen in the Southern Illinois farm regions, he drives along until he comes upon a college-aged boy plowing in the fields. He then asks him for directions to a nearby town. If the boy merely points in the direction with his hand, Pete drives on. But if when pointing, the boy picks up the plow and points with it, Pete starts talking about a football scholarship." As coaching is a risky business, coaches are sometimes superstitious. Former basketball coach Ray Combs supposedly put on a pair of red socks when his team won its first game and didn't take them off again until the team lost.

College folklore also includes fraternity or sorority rituals and customs. A common motif in campus tales is N384.4., "Fraternity initiate dies of fright." At Illinois, versions of these tales were common, although they did not always involve fatal incidents. In one tale, for example, actives put an ice cube on a pledge's chest after telling him they plan to brand the fraternity letters on his chest, and the pledge goes insane. In a related tale, though, the initiate is blindfolded after seeing a red-hot poker, which is then applied to a piece of meat placed before the pledge. At the same time a piece of dry ice is applied to the initiate's chest, and he dies of fright. The ubiquitous legend of "The Cadaver Arm" (Motif N384.0.1.1) was found in several versions at the U. of I. In one version, a pledge is put in a dark storeroom and warned that he should not turn on an overhead light. The pledge was not told that hanging from the pull chain of the light was a cadaver arm procured by a pre-med student, and when the actives returned for the pledge after six hours, they found the light on and the pledge huddled in a corner of the storeroom snarling and gnawing on the arm. A few initiation stories were humorous. In one U. of I. joke, a pledge is required to chug a bottle of whiskey, kill a polar bear, and have intercourse with an Eskimo woman. After a few days he returns all bloody and asks, "Where is that Eskimo woman I'm supposed to kill?"

A version of a mock funeral custom reported by Dorson also was performed at Illinois.[11] Every year Sigma Alpha Epsilon runs an ad in the *Daily Illini* for three days before and on Halloween. The first ad tells that an old alumnus, Paddy Murphy, is returning to visit the fraternity house, the second that Paddy has taken ill, and the third that Paddy passed away during the night and all friends are requested to attend funeral services at the fraternity house. At the funeral service a Halloween pledge party is held. A black hearse is parked in front of the house, and the living room is decorated like a funeral home, complete with flowers, a guest list, and a casket with a dummy in it. As couples pass the casket, they are led to a draped off area and are told to lie down on a platform that looks like a bed. After being warned that they will never return, a button is pushed, the platform retracts into the drapes, and the couple is led to the basement, where they find themselves in the midst of a party with a live band. Later in the evening, a eulogy is given for the deceased Paddy Murphy.

The games played by U. of I. students were mainly drinking games, although some were variants of adolescent kissing games. For instance, a game that the informant called "Checks" is a version of "Spin the Bottle." The players at a coed party form a circle, and a bottle is spun in the center. When the bottle points twice to one of the players, he or she has to move around the circle and kiss everyone's bare ass. The same informant offered another game called "Bounce." Male and female students sit on the floor in a circle, and, in a horizontal position, the girls are passed from male student to male student. "The idea of the game," according to this male informant, "is not to let the girls touch the ground while feeling the living hell out of them."

Songs, mainly bawdy drinking songs, were plentiful at Illinois. These songs were performed in the dorms and fraternity or sorority houses, at dances, parties, and hayrides, and especially in campus bars.[12] One evening during the breaks between the formal live entertainment shows in the overcrowded basement of Kam's, the most popular student bar at that time, I collected over a dozen songs from a group of fraternity men and their dates, who, after a few tall glasses of Bud, joined right in. On another occasion, during the intermission of a fraternity dance chaperoned by my wife and me, the couples spontaneously broke into song, including a long version of the most popular campus folksong, "Hey Loddy." The songs celebrated drink and sex, put down other fraternities and sororities, and extolled the students' own organizations. In short, alongside the official university loyalty and fight songs and the formal Greek songs were numerous informal songs, including the unofficial "Illinois Loyalty":

> We're the boys from Illinois.
> We live in caves and ditches.
> We scratch our cocks on jagged rocks.
> We're rugged sons-a-bitches.
> Illinois once, Illinois twice,
> Goddamned, cocksuck, rah, rah, fuck!

Generally, folklore at Illinois in the sixties revealed the same attitudes and concerns and served the same functions that Toelken observed in college folklore. As Toelken points out, college folklore is "full of stories, customs, remedies and rituals which run high with concern over pinning, engagement, finding a mate, virility and contraception . . . as well as with problems connected with the impossible daily load of reading, lectures, and homework."[13] Students see themselves at the mercy of an unfair system that imposes upon them too many unwanted professors and too much unnecessary homework; consequently, they feel a certain amount of rebellion and stealth to be justifiable. Students find an outlet for repressions through the symbolic action of anonymous folk traditions.[14]

According to Bruce Jackson, some of the forms of college folklore I have just described will soon be "as moribund as lumberjack folklore." Writing in the early seventies about tales of professors in particular, Jackson says that "the coherent campus now exists only at small colleges or out of the way places, places far from the urban scene and the world as most of us have come to know it. The modern multiversity simply does not offer the student or the faculty member the kind of social cynosure necessary for that sort of narrative to circulate and survive." Jackson feels that contemporary campus lore "has more to do with youth culture than campus culture—things like material folklore customs and techniques connected with grass, stories of busts and how you get across the border with your stash, the elan of bikes (which replaced convertibles), the argot, the different experiences with CN and CS, the rock music. . . ."[15] Since college students are youths too, naturally they will share popular culture and some folklore with noncollegiate youths. College students, like everyone else, belong to several folk groups at the same time—age, occupational, regional, ethnic, or religious, for example. At some urban universities or commuter colleges, a student's closest ties might remain with his ethnic, regional, or age folk groups; however, on virtually every campus, large or small, collegians have some occupational traditions that are not shared by other youths.

Acculturation is a fact of life, though, and in some times and places college culture, while retaining its discrete identity, might borrow an especially large number of traits and traditions from another culture. One need only contrast Dorson's seminal article on "The Folklore of Colleges" with the last section of his *America in Legend*, published nearly a quarter of a century later, to see how the youth culture of the late sixties and early seventies influenced campus life.[16] Beerlore indeed gave way to druglore, and student attitudes and values shifted as Greek life waned. Although the youth culture that Jackson speaks of certainly had an impact on college folklore during this period, the fraternities did not die, as Jackson predicted. Instead, Greek life and beer drinking gained new respectability, and the hippies of the sixties and seventies lost their charm, as did the Beats of the fifties, a counterculture of an earlier generation that also rebelled against the established society. College folklore, including tales of professors, has been more persistent than the folkways of these countercultures.

Still, college folklore, like all folklore, is dynamic. While the U. of I. lore from the middle sixties clearly reflects a concern with sex and the daily grind of lectures, homework, and exams, a collection of graffiti from male and female restrooms on the Champaign-Urbana campus in the early seventies suggests other concerns as well.[17] True, some of the graffiti were concerned with sex ("If it moves fuck it," from a male restroom; and "A hard man is good to find," from a female restroom), but the graffiti revealed a deep concern with political, social, and philosophical issues, too. Students were anti-Nixon, antiwar, anti–U. of I., and even antigraffiti

("Fuck all the people / who write on walls," from a female restroom). In fact, students, male and female, were nihilistic:

> Fuck All Authority
> Free Everything
> Socialize
> Religion is Superstition
> Leaders suck!
> Humanity is the measure of all things!
> Anarchy will win!
> All power to the imagination.

The graffiti revealed that male students generally were antigay: "The only good fag / Is a dead fag," while female students more often were progay: "Women, learn to think. Love your sisters! (You don't need men)." Male and female students alike, though, were prodrugs: "Don't vote! Smoke." Philosophically, male and female students agreed in their celebration of life: "Its [sic] always nice when you get something free . . . like LIFE!" (male); and "Life is the living we do and death is the living we don't do" (female).[18]

Most folklorists teach in colleges and universities, and in recent years they, as well as sociologists and anthropologists, have begun to examine the campus as a culture. Sociologists have offered a typology of student subcultures, examined the social forces and conditions that shape these groups, and explored the relations of college peer groups and their effects on the larger formal system.[19] Anthropologists have applied their intensive analytical methods of studying different cultures to familiar events on the college campus. For instance, Shirley Fiske studied college football at the University of Southern California and demonstrated that football functions as a rite of passage, an initiation into adulthood.[20] Other levels of education have been examined by anthropologists, too. Jacquetta Hill Burnett spent nine months in the "field" at a small midwestern high school in 1960-61 examining the rites and ceremonies of secondary students.[21] The folklorist, on the other hand, has been item-oriented, collecting especially songs, speech, and legends, or has examined folklore in breadth rather than in depth. Now that we have some very good, though dated, surveys of college folklore,[22] future studies of the folklore of academe might follow the more specifically pointed models of anthropology and provide intensive analysis of the traditional life of students.

NOTES

1. See Linda Dégh, "The 'Belief Legend' in Modern Society: Form, Function, and Relationship to Other Genres," in *American Folk Legend*, ed. Wayland D. Hand (Berkeley: University of California Press, 1971), p. 63. Kenneth A. Thigpen, Jr., in "Adolescent Legends in Brown County: A Survey," *Indiana Folklore* 4, no. 2 (1972): 141-215, includes 75 legend texts from students at Brown County High School in Nashville, Indiana. In the same number of *Indiana Folklore*, p. 96, John M. Vlach mentions 144 narratives he collected from fifth graders.

2. For examples with analysis of these two legends, see Linda Dégh, "The Hook," *Indiana Folklore* 1, no. 1 (1968): 92–100, and "The Boyfriend's Death," *Indiana Folklore* 1, no. 1 (1968): 101–106.

3. During the fall semester of 1964–65, I collected 990 items of college folklore from 44 undergraduate students at the University of Illinois, Champaign-Urbana. Controlling data are on file in the Indiana State University Folklore Archives.

4. For additional examples, see Joseph C. Hickerson and Alan Dundes, "Mother Goose Vice Verse," *Journal of American Folklore* 75 (1962): 249–59.

5. Bawdy book titles and depraved definitions are included in Alan Dundes and Robert A. Georges, "Some Minor Genres of Obscene Folklore," *Journal of American Folklore* 75 (1962): 223–24.

6. See Dundes and Georges, pp. 221–23, for further discussion and examples of punning rhetorical questions, wanton daughter puns, and Confucianisms.

7. All motifs cited are from Stith Thompson, *Motif-Index of Folk-Literature*, 6 vols. (Bloomington: Indiana University Press, 1955–58).

8. For variant accounts of this and other traditions on other campuses, see Richard M. Dorson, *American Folklore* (Chicago: University of Chicago Press, 1959), pp. 254–67.

9. Ibid., p. 257.

10. See ibid. for the same tale attributed to Bernie Bierman.

11. Ibid., p. 262, discusses the same tradition at Northwestern University.

12. For a collection of campus folksongs, see Richard A. Reuss, "An Annotated Field Collection of Songs from the American College Student Oral Tradition" (M.A. thesis, Indiana University, 1965).

13. J. Barre Toelken, "The Folklore of Academe," in Jan Harold Brunvand, *The Study of American Folklore: An Introduction*, 2d rev. ed. (New York: Norton, 1978), p. 387.

14. Ibid., pp. 375–76.

15. Bruce Jackson, " 'The Greatest Mathematician in the World': Norbert Wiener Stories," *Western Folklore* 31 (1972): 21–22.

16. Richard M. Dorson, "The Folklore of Colleges," *American Mercury* 68 (1949): 671–77; *America in Legend* (New York: Pantheon, 1973), pp. 253–310.

17. During the fall semester of 1972–73, a male and a female student in my folklore class at the University of Illinois collected 210 items of graffiti from male and female restrooms in university buildings and campus bars in Champaign-Urbana. For an analysis of campus graffiti, see Terrance L. Stocker, Linda Dutcher, Stephen M. Hargrove, and Edwin A. Cook, "Social Analysis of Graffiti," *Journal of American Folklore* 85 (1972): 356–66.

18. For contemporary campus lore reflecting similar sentiments, especially about drugs, see Dorson, *America in Legend*, pp. 253–310.

19. Theodore M. Newcomb and Everett K. Wilson, eds., *College Peer Groups* (Chicago: Aldine, 1966) exemplifies the sociological approach to student culture.

20. Shirley Fiske, "Pigskin Review: An American Initiation," in *Sport in the Socio-Cultural Process*, ed. M. Marie Hart (Dubuque, Iowa: Wm. C. Brown, 1972), pp. 241–59.

21. Jacquetta Hill Burnett, "Ceremony, Rites, and Economy in the Student System of an American High School," *Human Organization* 28, no. 1 (1969): 1–10.

22. The best surveys of college folklore are Richard M. Dorson, "The Folklore of Colleges," *American Mercury* 68 (1949): 671–77 (the material on college folklore in Dorson's *American Folklore* was drawn from this seminal survey article), and J. Barre Toelken, "The Folklore of Academe."

Alan Dundes

Office Folklore

In the nineteenth century and to some extent in the twentieth, the folk were thought to be rural and illiterate as opposed to urban and literate.[1] In addition, folklore was defined in part on the basis of the means of its transmission. Specifically, folklore was said to be *orally* transmitted from person to person and from generation to generation. The oral criterion was intended to distinguish folklore from written or literary materials. These definitions of folk and folklore essentially precluded the idea that a literate, urban folk might transmit written folklore. And yet literate urban officeworkers and others do in fact transmit written folklore. In earlier times, these traditional materials were handwritten; later they were typewritten or printed; most recently they circulate with the help of modern photocopier and Xerox machines. Such paperwork folklore (like all folklore) enjoys multiple existence; that is, individual items exist in at least two or more versions, and such paperwork folklore shows variation. In this regard, it is similar to other forms of written folklore: epitaphs, autograph book verse, the rebus form of the riddle, desk inscriptions, book-keepers (verses written in the front of school books often warning others not to steal the book), latrinalia (bathroom wall writings), and so on. Published collections of paperwork folklore have amply documented the nature of this thriving, emerging form of modern folklore.[2]

Individual items of paperwork folklore appear most often in offices—on public bulletin boards or taped to walls behind a desk. The larger the office (and the more bureaucratic), the more likely the display of paperwork folklore. It turns out that there are avid amateur collectors of paperwork folklore, just as there are enthusiasts of ballads, tall tales, limericks, and other genres of folklore. Sometimes, these devotees of xerographic folklore may be reluctant to share their accumulated collection of wallet cards, office memoranda parodies, folk cartoons, and the like with the inquiring folklore collector. The antiestablishment tone of some of the materials makes workers nervous about revealing the contents of their bottom drawers full of xeroxed items. It is one thing to have an anonymous cartoon on the office bulletin board making fun of bosses; it is another to be identified as the local source for such items. Other workers may feel that the contents of the folders hidden in their desk may not reflect a properly decorous image for them or for their office or company. Once convinced that the collector shares their interest in and enjoyment of paperwork folklore, however, they may allow the collector to copy their precious and well-guarded private storehouse. Some of the best collections have literally hundreds of examples and may represent materials gathered over a period of ten to twenty years.

One great advantage of xerographic folklore is that it allows virtually anyone to be a "performer." The performing skills required for a ballad singer or a joke-teller are not necessary for the communication of paperwork folklore. A person needs only enough manual dexterity to operate a Xerox machine! Typically, a visitor to an office will notice an exemplar of xerographic folklore attached to a wall or clipped to a desk blotter. If he likes it, he may ask to make a copy. He may then return to his own office where he in turn puts the item on display, or he may mail a copy to a friend he thinks would appreciate it. In the case of bawdy or obscene items, one would normally have to make a special request to see such materials, as they are typically kept out of sight.

Having collected examples of paperwork folklore, the folklorist should ask informants what they think the meaning and significance of the items might be. The next step is to try to annotate an individual item by comparing it with other (cognate) versions, an often difficult undertaking, since relatively few collections of paperwork folklore are in print, and many traditional items have not yet been reported by folklorists. Occasionally, a printed version of a piece of paperwork folklore will appear in daily newspapers, not infrequently in syndicated columns such as Ann Landers or Dear Abby. Sometimes, an array of commercially produced plaques or placards that reproduce folk mottoes or memoranda show up in novelty or gift shops. Without a convenient index of the content of syndicated columns or wall plaques, it is not always easy to find parallel texts in such sources. But as more and more collections of paperwork folklore are published, it will become easier to compare field collections with previously reported versions.

One of the problems in working with paperwork folklore is dating an item. Benjamin Franklin's "Advice to a Young Man in Love" (known under such titles as "Advice to a Young Man on the Choice of a Mistress") has been in existence for more than two hundred years and continues to circulate in xerographic form. Most xerographic folklore, however, has no known author and cannot often be traced back in time. Collectors should as a matter of course record the place and date of the items they find. Sometimes, informants can provide details as to their discovery of the item, but more often than not, informants cannot remember where or when they first obtained a particular wallet card or traditional letter.[3]

More than five hundred paperwork items circulate in the United States, and folklorists should realize that every single one represents a separate research problem. Moreover, indications are that new paperwork items are being created in response to current political, economic, social, and other crises in modern society. In other words, the study of paperwork folklore is just beginning, and it must become part of the ongoing study of American folklore.

The types of paperwork folklore include definitions (e.g., pseudo glossaries), business cards, greeting cards and letters, notices, mottoes, awards, instructions, tests, cartoons and drawings, extended double entendres, and parodies.[4] As an aid to would-be collectors of paperwork folklore, the following illustrative examples are offered.

The first example is a business card parody. It could be presented to someone who was speaking. It could be used to interrupt a speaker, or it might be passed to him after he had finished recounting some story. In either case, it is intended to jokingly impugn the credibility of the speaker (fig. 1).

My Card Sir

I AM SOMEWHAT OF A BULLSHITTER
MYSELF BUT OCCASIONALLY I LIKE
TO LISTEN TO A PROFESSIONAL.

PLEASE CARRY ON

FIG. 1

The second example is a notice or placard. In business and in life generally, a game metaphor is commonly employed, and in order to play the game, one has to learn the rules. The first rule involves knowing the power structure, as the following folk syllogism indicates:

Rule No. 1
THE BOSS IS ALWAYS RIGHT!
Rule No. 2
IF THE BOSS IS WRONG, SEE RULE NO. 1

The third example is a test or set of instructions. Although cast in business terms, it delineates one of the dilemmas facing career-oriented women in American society. If women conform to the male chauvinist stereotypes of passivity in speech and demeanor, they will not be competitive in terms of hiring; if, on the other hand, they reject the stereotypes, become active, and demonstrate leadership qualities, they run the risk of being labeled according to the following piece of paperwork folklore. The issue is whether the long-standing traditional double standard can be overcome.

HOW TO TELL A BUSINESSMAN FROM A BUSINESSWOMAN

A businessman	*A businesswoman*
is aggressive	is pushy
is good on details	is picky
follows through	doesn't know when to quit
stands firm	is hard
is a man of the world	has been around
is not afraid to say what he thinks	is mouthy
exercises authority diligently	is power-mad
is close-mouthed	is secretive
is a stern taskmaster	is hard to work for
drinks because of the excessive job pressure	is a lush

loses his temper because he
  is so involved in his job . . . . is bitchy
when he's depressed
  (hungover), everyone
  tiptoes past his office . . . . when she is moody,
                                         it must be "her
                                       time of the month."

    The fourth example is one of dozens of drawings and folk cartoons, one of the most popular forms of paperwork folklore. Such cartoons are rarely if ever signed, and they are not simply reproductions of cartoons appearing originally in the *New Yorker* or *Playboy*. The item in figure 2 sometimes is found in the form of an "award," that is, a cut-out circle. In any event, the accompanying inscription explains its function.

THIS IS AN INDISPENSABLE ITEM FOR EVERYBODY. FOR YEARS,
PEOPLE HAVE BEEN SAYING, "I'LL DO IT AS SOON AS I GET
A ROUND TUIT."

THE ABOVE IS A ROUND TUIT. CUT IT OUT, KEEP IT HANDY,
AND YOU WILL HAVE NO MORE TROUBLE GETTING ALL THOSE EXTRAS
DONE. YOU FINALLY GOT A ROUND TUIT!

FIG. 2

    The last example is intended to demonstrate that academic folk also have their own varieties of paperwork folklore. The existence of academic paperwork folklore makes it all the more surprising that this form of folklore wasn't recognized and collected years ago. The following parody of the essay type of final examination questions has been collected all over the United States.

FINAL EXAM

INSTRUCTIONS: Read each question carefully. Answer all questions. Time limit 4 hours. Begin immediately.

HISTORY: Describe the history of the papacy from its origins to the present day. Concentrate especially but not exclusively, on its social, political, economic, religious, and philosophical impact on Europe, Asia, America, and Africa. Be brief, concise, and specific.

MEDICINE: You have been provided with a razor blade, a piece of gauze, and a bottle of alcohol. Remove your appendix. Do not suture until your work has been inspected. You have fifteen minutes.

PSYCHOLOGY: Based on your knowledge of their works, evaluate the emotional stability, degree of adjustment, and repressed frustrations of each of the following: Alexander of Aphrodisias, Rameses II, Gregory of Nicia, Hammurabi. Support your evaluation with quotations from each man's work, making appropriate references. It is not necessary to translate.

ASTRONOMY: Describe the universe and give 2 examples.

SOCIOLOGY: Estimate the sociological problems which might accompany the end of the world. Construct an experiment to test your theory.

ENGINEERING: The disassembled parts of a high powered rifle have been placed on your desk. You will also find an instruction manual, printed in Swahili. In 10 minutes, a hungry Bengal tiger will be admitted to the room. Take whatever action you feel appropriate. Be prepared to justify your decision.

PUBLIC SPEAKING: 2500 riot-crazed students are storming the classrooms. Calm them. You may use any ancient language except Latin or Greek.

BIOLOGY: Create life. Estimate the differences in subsequent human culture if this form of life had developed 500 million years earlier, with special attention to its probable effect on the English parliamentary system. Prove thesis.

MUSIC: Write a piano concerto. Orchestrate and perform it with flute and drum. You will find a piano under your seat.

ECONOMICS: Develop a realistic plan for refinancing the national debt. Trace the possible effects of your plan in the following areas: Cubism, the Donatist controversy, the wave theory of light. Outline a method for preventing those effects. Criticize this method from all possible points of view. Point out the deficiencies in your point of view, as demonstrated in your answer to your last question.

POLITICAL SCIENCE: There is a red telephone book on the desk beside you. Start World War III. Report at length on its socio-political effects, if any.

EPISTEMOLOGY: Take a position for or against truth. Prove the validity of your stand.

PHILOSOPHY: Sketch the development of human thought, estimate its significance. Compare with the development of any other kind of thought.

GENERAL KNOWLEDGE: Describe in detail. Be objective and specific.

PHYSICS: Explain the nature of matter. Include in your answer an evaluation of the impact of the development of mathematics on science.

The above five examples are but a tiny fraction of the hundreds of distinct items of paperwork folklore currently circulating in the United States. The collecting possibilities for paperwork folklore are exciting, for it is certain that the rapid spread of office copier technology around the world will encourage the diffusion of paperwork traditions.

No doubt paperwork folklore traditions in different countries will reflect local, oicotypical worldview and value systems. If folklorists succeed in documenting the development of paperwork traditions both in the United States and elsewhere, they will have a rare opportunity to study folklore as it forms and as it adapts to the demands of different cultures. The collection and study of paperwork folklore will also allow folkloristics to keep pace with the modern world, since folklorists study not only folklore of the past but folklore of the present and the future.

NOTES

1. For further discussion of the definition of folk, see "Who are the Folk?" in Alan Dundes, *Interpreting Folklore* (Bloomington: Indiana University Press, 1980), pp. 1–19.

2. For more than one hundred examples, see Alan Dundes and Carl R. Pagter, *Work Hard and You Shall Be Rewarded: Urban Folklore from the Paperwork Empire* (Bloomington: Indiana University Press, 1978). For other collections, see Louis Michael Bell, Cathy Makin Orr, and Michael James Preston, *Urban Folklore from Colorado: Photocopy Cartoons* (Ann Arbor: Xerox University Microfilms, 1976), and Cathy Makin Orr and Michael James Preston, *Urban Folklore from Colorado: Typescript Broadsides* (Ann Arbor: Xerox University Microfilms, 1976).

3. For a fruitless attempt to discover the origin of an item of paperwork folklore going back at least to the 1940s, see Max Hall, "The Great Cabbage Hoax: A Case Study," *Journal of Personality and Social Psychology* 2 (1965): 563–69, and "26,911 Little Words," *The New Republic* 176: 17 (April 23, 1977): 9–10.

4. All the examples presented here were taken from Alan Dundes and Carl R. Pagter's unpublished manuscript "More Urban Folklore from the Paperwork Empire."

Bruce E. Nickerson

Factory Folklore

All occupations share a common body of occupational lore. For example, most occupations have stories about "fucked up" paychecks and "lousy bosses" (department chairmen, deans, vice-presidents, and so on.) Similarly, each subcategory of occupational lore has its own specific body of material, as well as sharing in the common body of occupational lore.

While scholars have studied occupations for some time, they have usually been concerned with "traditional" occupations, such as oil-field workers, cowboys, and loggers. Their interest in factory lore is recent.[1] Having agreed that there is a folk in the factory,[2] folklorists now ask: what is factory lore, how is it different from other materials, where can it be found and collected, and who are the twenty-one million blue collar workers[3] who generate such stuff?

Factory lore, the folklore generated by workers in factory settings,[4] includes verbal lore, material culture, and interpersonal relations. In one of the factories at which I worked, an inspector whose work station was inside a dark, light-tight booth could not find his work shoes. After an exhaustive search he found the shoes nailed to the underside of his work bench. This trick, of course, is a variant of the prank in which a lunch bucket is nailed to the bench. Shop towels, knotted to form a rough ball-shape about the size of a softball, made handy missiles to throw at other workers. This prank sometimes escalated into a full-scale war similar to snowball fights.[5] Factory lore, however, is more than pranks.

Factory lore lives in varied contexts, each of which introduces specific considerations. The interaction patterns that emerge in large plants differ from those in small shops, and this difference may affect the transmission of verbal lore. Concerns of workers in urban centers contrast with those in rural areas. For example, the individuals I worked with in a rural manufacturing plant often took jobs in industry specifically to provide enough income to keep their small family farms in operation. The urban workers just as often viewed their jobs as life-long careers. This difference had an impact on skills acquisition and perceived job mobility: the rural workers invested only enough of themselves to get a paycheck, while the urban workers were more willing to develop their industrial skills.

Assembly-line work, which restricts personal mobility and interpersonal interaction, and hourly paid jobs have important impacts on the transmission of verbal materials. A piece-work or incentive system that allows workers to keep a "kitty" or to "work ahead" frequently allows for "bull sessions," especially on the "off-shifts" (3:00 P.M.–11:00 P.M. and 11:00 P.M.–7:00 A.M.), which promote transmission of verbal materials.

The lack of written materials about factory lore makes the use of effective field methods extremely important. While not insisting that everyone interested in factory lore become a machinist, inspector, or rigger, I recommend that the fieldworker have an intimate, preferably firsthand, acquaintance with the factory. Unless the fieldworker understands factories well, simply interviewing informants will result in little more than a collection of trivia.

By the time I decided to study factory lore, I had graduated from a four-year apprentice program with an A.S. in Mechanical Engineering and had accumulated more than a decade of experience in a factory setting. I had worked as draftsman, mechanical inspector, machinist, and engineer. The participant-observer technique was an excellent and obvious way for me to collect materials. By working as a piece-work machinist in a large urban plant where I had worked before, I also had the collateral but important benefit of receiving a decent paycheck. During my eighteen months at the plant, my fellow workers accepted me as another "working stiff" and had no idea of my eventual goals. During my last week on the job, I told my friends that I had been working with them to gather material for my dissertation. They were pleased to learn that "one of us" would be telling their story.

The participant-observer technique is very effective in collecting factory lore, especially if the fieldworker is skilled in some blue collar occupation.[6] If it is useful for a collector of folk music to be able to play an instrument, it is almost essential that the fieldworker in the factory exhibit some degree of proficiency, or at least knowledge, in the use of tools. Such familiarity is respected by factory workers and can enhance rapport.

Contrary to the popular stereotype, blue collar workers are not exemplified by an ignorant Archie Bunker sitting with a can of beer in front of a television set after work. A tool and die maker typically has had four years of college level schooling in an apprentice program, plus several years of experience. Some workers may lack formal schooling, but their practical knowledge of the shop and the necessary shop math, combined with their shrewd knowledge of how to beat the system within the plant, indicates no mean level of intellectual ability.

The ethnic backgrounds of factory workers are varied, and their awareness of this background may change as a function of geography. In the New England area, industrialization and immigration of specific ethnic groups have been history long enough so that the workers, while aware of their ethnic backgrounds, by and large identify more strongly with their role as blue collar workers. Other areas, such as Gary, Indiana, may present a different situation, since the immigration of Eastern Europeans may be recent enough so that ethnic identity has not yet given way to blue collar identity and ethnic awareness.[7] This distinction between ethnic identity and ethnic awareness must be made so that ethnic materials collected in the factory are not confused with factory lore.

Factory lore can be divided into categories familiar to folklorists. Verbal lore includes both written and spoken material. Shop speech is both colorful and profane and gathers much of its idiom from the socioeconomic classes represented by the workers. The word "fuck" is an omnibus word, which, in Mencken's terms, soon becomes "dephlogisticated" by its frequent use.[8] Work is not ruined; it is "fucked up." Unsavory characters are "fuckin' assholes." Small measurements are frequently referred to as "just a cunt hair," or, if more accuracy is preferred, as a "red cunt hair" (no other color is ever used). Side by side with the profanity exists a large technical vocabulary (such as "mics"—pronounced "mikes"—for micrometers, "Bullard" for any vertical turret lathe, and so forth) and company- and shop-specific terms, such as "Q.R." (quality review form) and "M.R.B." (material review board form), to cite only two examples.[9]

The classic shop narrative concerns the industrial accident: the worker has just returned from the hospital after cutting off his finger on a machine. The shop safety manager comes over to the worker's area to ask how it happened; the worker begins to demonstrate, then yells, "Whoops, there goes another one!" I have collected this story in every plant context with which I am familiar.[10] *The Factory System Illustrated*, a fascinating account of the early factories in England,[11] indicates that the industrial accident story, which I consider to be the typical shop narrative, has preindustrial roots.

One of the functions of the industrial accident story is to warn workers about the dangers inherent in their work. It also functions to express workers' hostility toward and distrust of the company.

> In a variant of the lost finger story, when the worker reports to the plant dispensary, he is first asked if he was wearing his safety glasses and shoes when the accident occurred. In this instance, the worker is convinced that the company does not care for him as an individual, but is only concerned with their insurance premiums.[12]

Workers are also convinced that the company is more concerned with production than with people. In a story collected from a large urban newspaper, workers told me that a pressman was crushed by a roll of paper weighing over a ton. A crowd quickly gathered about the pressman, and the foreman, forcing his way through the crowd, knelt and felt the pressman's pulse. Looking up angrily at the crowd, the foreman said "All right, back to work, he can't help us now. We've got an edition to get out."[13]

Material culture in the factory is best represented by the ubiquitous "government job." Work done for oneself with company materials on company time exists in every factory.[14] At one time I was the proud owner of a Morris Minor that needed extensive engine work. I dismantled the engine and brought a number of the parts into work with me on the third shift. I enlarged and polished intake and exhaust parts, machined seats for dual valve springs, and lightened the flywheel on a lathe. Early one morning my foreman said, "Understand you're rebuilding an engine?"

"Yeah."

"Where is it?"

"In my drawer."

"A whole goddam engine?"

"Nope. Just parts."

"In your drawer?"

"It's a small engine."

"Well just make sure no one—"

"Don't worry, it's out of sight."

"Don't let any one see it. How you gonna get it out?"

"In my briefcase."

"And suppose the guards stop you?"

"I open my briefcase and show them books." (The guards recognized me and knew I was going to school, so this was a logical dodge.)

"O.K." my foreman said, "but I don't know anything about it. Let me know how it runs when it's together, O.K.?"

As in many instances, my foreman allowed me to do this work as long as my regular work was of the quantity and quality required and he could claim ignorance of my extracurricular activities. While the products of these government jobs are fairly traditional and unimaginative (knives made from old files are typical), workers' imaginations sometimes soar to great heights. One worker welded a menagerie of sixteen animals out of solid titanium, an interesting example of a folk sculptor emerging from a purely blue collar context.[15]

Costume, or on-the-job clothing, is an important aspect of factory material culture. Choice of clothing is limited to some extent by safety and utility, but apart from these considerations it exhibits a wide range of personal style. Even so, a worker's specific job category may be identified by the work clothes worn. Machinists will wear second-best sports clothes with short-sleeve shirts, frequently topped by an apron, while inspectors, who work in a cleaner environment, may wear long-sleeve shirts and a generally cleaner outfit sans apron.[16] One of the machinists I worked with preferred to wear less expensive sport shirts, bought especially for the purpose, rather than work shirts, because he didn't want to look "like a working slob."

In some occupations, clothing is determined as much by tradition as by other considerations. I once asked a letter press operator where he got his silly hat. He was wearing a square boxlike affair folded together from newsprint.

> "That's not a silly hat . . . if you knew anything about printing. That's an identification symbol."
>
> "It keeps your head clean?"
>
> "You can wear any kind of hat or cap for that. This here's different. It's a symbol."[17]

Factory workers express their individuality through decorating their work stations as well as in their choice of clothing.[18] Personalized work stations serve to offset the drabness of the factory and give the worker a sense of identity with the workplace. Family pictures, calendars, cartoons, and other similar items are taped to a flat surface of the machine or nearby wall, and many work stations have carefully crafted signs bearing legends such as "Hank's Haven."[19]

In one plant where I worked, the company told the workers they could paint their machines any color they liked. If they would paint the machines during "down time," the company would supply the paint. At first the workers' reaction was "Fuck 'em. If they want their machines painted, hire a painter." One by one they capitulated, however, worn down by the boredom of nothing better to do while waiting for machines to be repaired. The process accelerated until the plant became a veritable rainbow of color.[20]

Skills acquisition in the factory is usually by imitation or oral instruction and is much influenced by interpersonal relations. Even those who attend formal classes through apprentice programs or company-sponsored training programs must hone and develop their skills through imitation or verbal instruction from other workers. In many instances, established workers refuse to share their skills with newer workers, in order to protect their jobs from these newcomers. This job protection may involve hiding tools, refusing to communicate needed information, or withholding "tricks of the trade" that can make assigned tasks easier and more productive.[21]

Interpersonal relations in the shop generate many customs, the most widespread of which is the informal in-plant Christmas party. Generally not approved of by management because of the large quantity of alcohol consumed, the parties persist, and the foremen, while officially not approving, turn their backs and allow the festivities to continue.[22]

I worked third shift in one plant where we also managed a Thanksgiving party in addition to the Christmas bash. Our group contributed money, and we bought and brought into the plant the typical selection of beverages and food. For Thanksgiving we added a turkey, commandeered a heat treat oven, and later in the shift feasted on fresh roasted turkey.

Marriage celebrations may involve chaining a large piece of metal stock to the leg of the bridegroom-to-be as a symbolic ball and chain. Variations include coating the genitals of the bridegroom with layout bluing, an almost ineradicable substance.[23]

Initiation rites are common in the shop. The wild goose chase, where the new worker is sent to look for a left-handed monkey wrench, ten yards of pipe thread, or a bucket of steam has historical precedent dating back at least to the middle ages.[24]

Practical jokes, gambling, methods for beating the company's systems, horseplay, and informal systems of cooperative labor round out the area of interpersonal relations in the plant. While most of these activities are well known to people outside the plant context, "beating the system" requires further comment. Factory workers have developed ways to generate more pay without doing more work ("extra labor vouchers," time-clock punching groups), avoiding work (sleeping in the "shithouse"), and generally getting their own way and so exercising a degree of control over the work environment not permitted in the formal systems prescribed by the company.[25]

Research in factory folklore serves a number of important purposes. Most obviously, it helps define the whole area of occupational folklore. Because the shop is essentially a closed system with built-in controls, factory folklore has implications for a number of areas of folklore scholarship, such as rumor transmission, ethnicity, and the interdependence of folklore and interpersonal interaction

At a more practical level, an employer's knowledge of blue collar culture would help develop better working relationships between management and the workers. Recognition by management of the need for workers to exercise informal control over their work environment, for example, might prevent the institution of unnecessarily harsh, restrictive, and counterproductive systems. Plant location decisions could be made more effectively and with less damaging impact on local culture if management understood not only the local culture but how this culture affects the workers in the shop environment. General Motors, for example, employs a number of ethnologists on its national corporate staff for just such purposes.

Factory lore, then, has many exciting potential applications in business and industry. Its materials closely parallel traditional folklore genres and offer challenging opportunities for those concerned with refining, redefining, and broadening the study of American folklore.

N O T E S

1. See Robert H. Byington, ed., *Working Americans: Contemporary Approaches to Occupational Folklore* (Washington, D.C.: Smithsonian Folklife Studies, Number 3, 1978); and Camilla A. Collins, "Twenty-Four to a Dozen: Occupational Folklore in a Hosiery Mill" (Ph.D. diss., Indiana University, 1978).

2. Bruce E. Nickerson, "Is There a Folk in the Factory?" *Journal of American Folklore* 87 (1974): 134–39.

3. Arthur B. Shostak, *Blue Collar Life* (New York: 1969), p. 51. Note that this estimate is over ten years old, and that, despite the recent recession, the total number of mill and factory workers has risen markedly.

4. Factory and union lore overlap but are not synonymous. While union lore deals with the history of the labor movement, factory lore concentrates on the worker in the shop context.

Factory lore should not be confused with blue collar culture. These areas influence each other, as can be seen in common patterns of speech, humor, and sexual mores. The obscene joke is a good illustration of the distinction to be made. While these jokes abound in the factory context, my experience indicates that they are seldom occupationally related and seem to be more a reflection of the male socioeconomic culture represented by the workers than part of factory culture per se.

5. Bruce E. Nickerson, "Industrial Lore: A Study of an Urban Factory" (Ph.D. diss., Indiana University, 1975), p. 222.

6. Kenneth E. Goldstein, *A Guide for Fieldworkers in Folklore* (Hatboro, Pa.: Folklore Associates, 1964). Goldstein's material on the participant-observer field method is especially useful for the occupational folklore fieldworker who collects materials while "on the job."

7. Nickerson, "Is There a Folk in the Factory?" p. 136.

8. H. L. Mencken, *The American Language* (New York: Alfred A. Knopf, 1963), p. 399.

9. A more complete discussion of factory speech is found in Nickerson, "Industrial Lore," pp. 122–31.

10. Ibid., p. 133. In addition to the more expected verbal lore, Peter J. Oulette makes a case for the growth of a myth about a folk hero that has developed in a small shop in Springfield, Massachusetts, in " 'That Jerk is My Friend': An Analysis of a Folk Hero in an Industrial Setting" (Honors Thesis, Hobart and William Smith Colleges, 1978).

11. William Dodd, *The Factory System Illustrated, together with a Narrative of the Experience and Sufferings of William Dodd* (New York: Augustus M. Kelley, 1968).

12. Nickerson, "Industrial Lore," p. 145.

13. Ibid., p. 146.

14. Ibid., pp. 200–205.

15. Bruce E. Nickerson, "Ronnie Thiesse, Industrial Folk Sculptor," *Western Folklore* 37 (1978): 128–33.

16. Nickerson, "Industrial Lore," pp. 161–69.

17. Ibid., p. 162.

18. The need for industrial workers to express their individuality in a context that does not encourage such expression is illustrated humorously in David E. Whisnant, "The Craftsman: Some Reflections on Work in America," *The Centennial Review* 17 (1973): 215; and in Nickerson, "Industrial Lore," p. 171.

19. Nickerson, "Industrial Lore," pp. 170–77.

20. Ibid., p. 171.

21. Ibid., pp. 217, 218, and Nickerson, "Ronnie Thiesse," p. 130.

22. Nickerson, "Industrial Lore," pp. 207–11; and Oulette, " 'That Jerk is My Friend,' " p. 21.

23. Nickerson, "Industrial Lore," pp. 212–13; and Alan Smith, "Industrial Folklore in the Midlands," *English Dance and Song* 34 (1972): 8.

24. Allen Walker Read, "Non-Existent Objects: The Folklore of the Beguiler" (paper delivered at the annual meeting of the American Folklore Society, Boston, Massachusetts, November 20, 1966), is an excellent history of this type of behavior.

25. See Nickerson, "Industrial Lore," pp. 207–53, for greater detail on these and other factory activities.

Roger Mitchell

Occupational Folklore: The Outdoor Industries

Folklore research in the outdoor industries would appear to have followed the random interests of the individual collector. Folksong research is abundant, narrative scarce, deep-water sailing highlighted, the inland waterways largely ignored, the Northern lumberjack feted, the Southern logger little heard of, the glory days of horses and men much touted, their modern counterparts mentioned with muted voice. This combined favoritism of genre, occupation, time, and region makes the survey of occupational lore an uneven task at best.

Take the Reader's Digest Association's recent foray into our field, *American Folklore and Legend*. In addition to some folklore ("digested" of course), there is more popular history. The Courtship of Miles Standish, Jamestown and Poca-hontas, the Spanish conquistadors and their search for gold, the War of 1812 and Andrew Jackson: this mélange of subjects confuses tradition with the historical, while such topics as "Trailblazers and Trappers" illustrate some of the inequities of folklore scholarship.[1] Here is an outdoor industry with both a hoary past and a vital present. In company with guides and coon dogs, these outdoor types have for years provided the main diet for such magazines as *Field and Stream*, and the popularly written articles reveal their debt to oral tradition. The trapper-hunter-guide triad is but one of many outdoor industries that have been little explored by folklorists.

Farming qualifies as the original outdoors occupation, the mudsill of the American dream. But the lore of this enduring task has been sparingly harvested. While in the abstract, the tiller of the soil is part of our national mythology, the American farmer as farmer has not attracted folklorists. That stolid pilot of the tractor, dunging his fields, repairing his machinery, hoping to sell at profit so that he can stay in business—this is not the glittering stuff heroes are made of. Glamor fades in the near vicinity of the pigpen.

Shoulder to shoulder with the landed proprietor stands the migrant worker, who usually conjures up the image of the Chicano fruit-picker, but the migrant laborer is ubiquitous. Working with the farmer-woodsmen of Northern Maine, I often heard accounts of the "Harvest Excursion" to the grain fields of Western Canada and the United States. There is also the potato industry, which attracts part-time laborers from as far away as the American South. Within these personal narratives are motifs that repeat themselves in much work lore: food, the exacting boss, the romantic interlude with the boss's daughter, hell-raising of a Saturday night, the outstanding worker, accidents, and the return home, perchance with empty pockets. Details of this kind are often missing from studies in rural areas of folksong, dance, art, and architecture, and such omissions make it difficult for the outsider to appreciate the complex whole that binds owner and laborer alike to the land.

As yet, all too few folklore publications give us what can be found in Patsy Ginn's *Rough Weather Makes Good Timber*.[2] Here the reader can follow verbatim accounts from clearing the land to the first tractors, from folk medicine to bedbugs, childbirth, and the early automobile—the list is long and genuine. The result, a satisfying taste of farming lore, goes far in providing a deeper understanding of the period in Southern history that is the folksong collector's Golden Age.

How different appears that offshoot of farming and primitive transportation, the cowboy. Seated solidly astride the American imagination, the mythic figure of the man on horseback owes no small debt to romanticism and the collector. John Lomax, one of the first cowboy folklorists, was looking for ballads of the working man, and once he discovered them, he invested his subject with the mantle of the natural man: "The changing and romantic West of the early days lives mainly in story and in song. The last figure to disappear is the cowboy, the animating spirit of the vanishing era. . . . Dauntless, reckless, without the unearthly purity of Sir Galahad though as gentle to a pure woman as King Arthur, he is truly a knight of the twentieth century."[3]

This early interest in song has continued unabated. A recent compilation by the Fifes includes the cultural data often lacking in Lomax's work. Rich in variants and annotations, it gives an excellent overview of the cowboy, his songs, and his collectors.[4] D. K. Wilgus's classic work on Anglo-American folksong views cowboy song scholarship within the broader context of folksong collection and research.[5]

Wealth of song is not followed by a richness of narrative traditions in folklore collections. For this one must turn to nonfolklorists. Andy Adams's *Log of a Cowboy* (1903) and Jack Thorp's *Tales of the Chuck Wagon* (1926) give the insider's view of cowboy life and lore. Though a fictionalized account of a trail drive, Adams's work is nevertheless based on firsthand knowledge. Thorp's *Tales* is especially valuable since it represents the first and only venture into the cowboy narrative during this period.[6] In its newly edited form, Thorp's *Songs of the Cowboys* (1908) is also a must, for it includes Thorp's account of his first song-collecting days as he rode from camp to camp, plus a superb commentary by the Fifes.[7]

These many collected songs and few tales represent but a brief period in the saga of the rancher-cowboy. As early as 1888, we can find Theodore Roosevelt stating that the heroic days were nearly past.[8] What then of the last eighty-odd years? Today's cowboy rides a truck, and instead of soothing cows with song is himself caressed by his radio. Shorn of the romantic soubriquet of "cowboy," he has become a pragmatic stockman; the mule skinner drives a truck; and that eternal target of cowboy desperadoes, the stagecoach driver, is reining a Greyhound bus. Frederick Danker's recent article suggests that the long-distance trucker is America's contemporary man in the saddle. Danker presents truck-driver songs and narratives as sharing many elements in common with those of cowboys, rail-roaders, and teamsters, including rugged individualism, loneliness, hard work, greenhorns, and numskulls.[9] Certainly this continuity of tradition is worth further investigation. For ranching lore, help seems to be coming over the next rise. A team from the Library of Congress's American Folklife Center has begun a survey of ranch life in north central Nevada that will include local architecture, foodways, storytelling, and seasonal changes in ranch work. This many-faceted approach should go far in bringing the study of the cowboy into the twentieth century.

The waters recede when one turns to fishermen and sailors. Perhaps it is a case of heroes who peaked too soon. Before the ballad collectors began their search, the windjammers had struck their sails, and the deep-water men were largely to be found in Snug Havens. As for trotline tenders of the Great Lakes and sponge fishermen in Florida, they seem to have lacked the drawing power of Captain Ahab and his monomania. It comes as no surprise to find that songs of the sea have received the lion's share of academic interest.

A good place to start in this extensive folksong scholarship is William Doerflinger's *Songs of the Sailor and Lumberman*. He gives a broad sample of deep-water songs, ballads of the eastern fishing banks, and those relating to the West Indies trade, and includes copious annotations. Moreover, there are fine introductions to each section that allow the reader to see the songs within their original settings. The initial chapter sets the tone of the book with a cogent discussion of short-haul shanties, the where and when of their performance, the intricacies of ships' rigging, and a two-page labeled illustration of a ship under full canvas.[10]

Yet one supposes there were more storytellers than singers. Also what of the liner, freighter, trawler, tugboat, barge? Patrick Mullen's study of Texas fishermen amply demonstrates that diesel fumes have not smothered the narrative impulse, nor has modern technology quelled those doubts experienced by men who wrest their livelihood from an unpredictable sea.[11] It is especially significant that as fishermen have followed their prey from the East Coast to Texas waters, they did not leave their folklore behind. Weather is still second-guessed by observation of sun and moon, the flight of the birds, and the drift of smoke. In this weather lore Texas fishermen are akin to all those whose work must take into account the vagaries of rain and shine. Bad luck is averted, one hopes, by the avoidance of unpropitious days and acts, such as Friday beginnings and the placing of hatch covers upside down. Many of these same beliefs and cautionary tales are to be found on the Maine coast and in Michigan's Upper Peninsula.[12] Nor can one ignore Botkin's Mississippi treasury. Although gleaned largely from printed sources, it lays out well the folkloric riches of this great river's past.[13] Overall, one must say that the narrative lore of our rivers, lakes, and coasts has been sketchily reported.

Studies of occupational lore would have been poorer by far had not the newspaperman George Korson made an avocation of collecting mining traditions. Korson's discovery of this rich vein of lore came at a crucial time, for in the 1920s most collectors were still combing the countryside, bent on salvaging material believed to be fast disappearing before the onslaught of industrialization. Korson's forte was that he allowed no one genre to dominate his approach. His *Minstrels of the Mine Patch* gives an overview of mining not only in story and song but also in detailed vignettes of mining life itself. One views the panorama of farmers becoming miners; the ethnic mix of Germans, Irish, and Slavs; child labor and Molly Maguires; fun and tragedy. In *Black Rock*, Korson expanded his approach to include closely related materials on steel making, canals, and railroads.[14] A series of articles by Wayland Hand complements Korson's seminal efforts. Hand also puts mining lore in its proper perspective with his observation that while older mining traditions are disappearing, new traditions are taking their place.[15]

That the vein of mining lore is deep, broad, and awaiting further exploration can also be seen in Dorson's collection from the Upper Peninsula. There he encountered the lore of Cornishmen ("Cousin Jacks") and their fabled ability in the mines. We are given a tantalizing sample of mining talk, beliefs, strike lore, lucky finds, and the ever-present dangers of the underground.[16] All this fine work in mining folklore needs augmenting. Contemporary miners should be studied and the focus widened to include all types of mining: open pit, deep mine, fuels, metals, stone, even the lowly gravel pit.

A natural complement to mining lore is that of the oil industry. Many of the same general motifs are there: tragic accidents, chances for wealth lost, the oil-field character. But research in this field has barely tapped the hidden reserves, although opportunities would appear almost endless. The industry has become international and American oil workers are to be found around the world. Judging from my own relatives, there would seem to be a whole body of lore based on personal experiences on foreign shores, tales that have a certain sameness to them, as if the raconteurs were drawing on a common corpus of tales and motifs to spice up their workaday life histories. Most are job-related, and I have listened patiently to accounts of the dangers of the Alaskan highway, near-catastrophe on the high seas, foreign airports, and offshore drilling platforms. Some seem more akin to the lore of the American soldier and tell in great detail of astute dealing with foreigners, fabulous native women, and the monumental venality of alien police. Although each tale is plausible enough, it confounds the mind that these very pedestrian males undergo such transformation when abroad.

Thus far our knowledge of the traditions of the oil field is due largely to one folklorist, Mody Boatright, and his *Folklore of the Oil Industry*.[17] Combining taped interviews of oilmen with printed sources, Boatright makes it abundantly clear that the collective imagination of the oil industry is not fettered by its technology. His several publications bristle with the life and lore of a gutsy industry. Tall tales, folk figures, gushers, boomtowns, prostitutes—he sketched them all with a firm and steady hand. That the several oil-producing areas have their own tales to tell can be seen from Fields's article on the traditions of offshore oil fields.[18] But articles cannot do this complex topic justice. Needed now are several contemporary Boatrights to bring our scholarship up to date and to pursue the far-flung empire of oil.

The railroad is another occupation still living in its past. Railroad songs have been carefully collected, analyzed, and published, but narrative is another matter. Back in 1953, in their *Treasury of Railroad Folklore*, Botkin and Harlow pointed the way. Composed of selections and snippets from numerous printed sources, it paints a panorama of the glory days of steam, dealing with bosses, hoboes, engineers, and thieves in historical narrative, humorous tale, and ballad. The editors include this statement in their introduction: "Around this young giant there grew a mythology that made a romance of railroading, a romance not yet dead but now grown retrospective."[19]

There seems little reason for railroad lore to remain retrospective. The diesels roll on from coast to coast and thousands of men still make their livelihood following the rails. Residing in my hometown in northern Maine are families whose men have been employed for three generations by the Bangor and Aroostook Railroad. Theirs remains an arcane vocabulary filled with split switches and hot boxes. They tell with wry grins of Old Charley, the section foreman so demanding that he timed the boys when they went to the bush to relieve themselves. Still discussed are those skilled engineers who could ease a full load from a dead stop at Smyrna Mills crossing over the sharp grade going north on the Ashland Branch. Remembered too are the pranksters who would oil the rails and cause the train to lose its hard-earned momentum. Or Old Wobble Tooth of the tremendous appetite and low sex drive, who was aided (unknowingly) on the home front by his more virile section hands. Recent fieldwork by Jack Santino adds weight to my observations. Investigating railroads, airlines, and telephone companies, Santino has found storytelling very much alive. Pranks, accidents, noteworthy pilots and engineers, work performed in the face of adversity—this complex of motifs uncovered by Santino advertises the presence of a healthy worklore in the transportation industries.[20]

As for song, modern railroaders would seem to have joined the rest of us as spectators and listeners. Those of my acquaintance (along with farmers, truckers, and woodsmen) are addicted to the Nashville sound. But why do they listen? Will "canned country" be able to hold its own against the growing strength of pop music? How much narrative lore remains from the past; how much has been newly created for their posterity? The answers would add needed chapters to existing ballad scholarship and studies of the American legend.

And finally, lumbering. Here too favoritism in region, genre, and time remain strong. For example, we know little of the lore of whites and blacks toiling in their sweaty overalls in the chigger-infested pine woods of the South. Ruth Allen speaks to this omission in her study of East Texas lumbering and hazards a guess as to this lack of scholarly interest: "Timbering in the Sabine pines lacked the drama of the Pacific Northwest and the Lake states. . . . The colorful denizen of the Northern woods—the lumberjack with his deeds of derring-do, his outrageous flaunting of accepted codes of conduct . . . is not a hero of Texas legends."[21]

After the fading of lumbering's heroic age, when the lumberjack became a union man and his boss a timberland manager, the derring-do remained only in story and song of those fabulous days. Of these, the songs have come in for the most attention, with many fine compilations available, from Eckstorm and Smyth's *Minstrelsy of Maine* to Fowke's *Lumbering Songs of the North Woods.*[22]

Again, one must search hard for lumbering narratives, poring over Holbrook's *Holy Old Mackinaw*, thumbing through such collations as Gard and Sorden's *Wisconsin Lore*, and analyzing carefully the personal accounts left by such men as Ira Farrell and John Springer.[23] But still we are talking about logging as it was in limited portions of a spacious national timberland.

Quite obviously folkloristics cannot mature as a discipline when entire regions, eras, genres, and occupations have been thus haphazardly collected. As folklorists we pride ourselves on our comparative approach, yet generalizations based on this approach can only be as valid as the data that support them. There is a crying need for more fieldwork in occupational folklore, and I believe it would be best accomplished through regional studies. One such regional project is well under way at the University of Maine, where in 1958 two folklorists, Bacil Kirtley and Edward Ives, began editing the quarterly *Northeast Folklore*. Since 1962, Ives has carried on the work alone and changed the journal's format to a yearly monograph. The shift from article to in-depth study has resulted in a modest flow of publications unique in the shadowy world of occupational lore. The earlier volumes were genre-oriented, presenting tales and songs from Maine and nearby Canada. More recently the trend has been to autobiography and oral history.[24] In addition to his editorial duties, Ives has continued his own research on folksongs and their makers.[25] From these several volumes a satisfying portrayal of the Maine woodsman is emerging: his lore, life in the camps and on river drives, and the economic challenges of logging operations.

My own contributions to this regional lore are a direct result of Ives's encouragement. *George Knox: From Man to Legend*[26] grew from a student collection that my wife and I made for one of Ives's folklore classes. Volume 19 (1978) of *Northeast Folklore*, titled *I'm a Man That Works: The Biography of Don Mitchell of Merrill, Maine*, follows via the personal narrative my father's progress through a life of labor, from his first woods job at age thirteen to teamster to farmer to town official and retirement at age eighty. From this personal saga emerges a body of motifs common to worklore in general. There are the outstanding bosses, the strong men, the pranksters, the cautionary tales of accidents that could have been avoided, the ability to withstand adversity. The unifying element is the working man's code: honest labor demands fair pay; work well done is time well spent; and honesty pays off in the long run.

The monograph series is the most visible part of Ives's endeavors, but there exist also the Northeast Archives of Folklore and Oral History.[27] These extensive holdings go far beyond the published materials on lumbering. Fishermen, sailors, farmers, poachers, longshoremen—a varied lore from Maine's many occupations awaits the researcher. Moreover, there are several on-going indexes, including place and personal names, lumbering, and motifs.

The Maine program represents regionalism at its best, cutting across genre, time, and occupational specialties. Repeat this approach many times over within our national borders and folklorists would have available the kind of documentation that allows wide-ranging theory construction. And this fieldwork must be done. Folklore theory must of necessity remain tentative when huge areas such as occupational lore have been so incompletely researched. Otherwise folklorists could well be courting the same kind of theoretical disaster suffered by anthropologists, who at the turn of the century grandly raised their tower of cultural evolution on the sands of questionable data.

NOTES

1. *American Folklore and Legend* (Pleasantville, N. Y.: Reader's Digest Association, 1978), pp. 174–87.

2. Patsy M. Ginn, *Rough Weather Makes Good Timber* (Chapel Hill: University of North Carolina Press, 1977).

3. John A. Lomax, *Cowboy Songs and Other Frontier Ballads*, 2d rev. ed. (New York: Macmillan, 1933), xxiii.

4. Austin and Alta Fife, eds., *Cowboys and Western Songs: A Comprehensive Anthology* (New York: Clarkson N. Potter, 1969).

5. D. K. Wilgus, *Anglo-American Folksong Scholarship Since 1898* (New Brunswick, N. J.: Rutgers University Press, 1959).

6. Andy Adams, *The Log of a Cowboy: A Narrative of the Old Trail Days* (New York: Houghton Mifflin, 1931); Nathan H. (Jack) Thorp, *Tales of the Chuckwagon* (Santa Fe: Thorp, 1926).

7. Nathan H. (Jack) Thorp, *Songs of the Cowboys*, ed. Austin and Alta Fife (New York: Clarkson N. Potter, 1966).

8. Theodore Roosevelt, *Ranch Life and the Hunting Trail* (New York, 1888; reprint New York: Bonanza, 1978), p. 24.

9. Frederick E. Danker, "Trucking Songs: A Comparison With Traditional Occupational Song," *Journal of Country Music* 6 (1978): 78–89.

10. William M. Doerflinger, *Songs of the Sailor and Lumberman*, 2d rev. ed. (New York: Macmillan, 1972), pp. 1–4.

11. Patrick B. Mullen, *I Heard the Old Fishermen Say: Folklore of the Texas Gulf Coast* (Austin: University of Texas Press, 1978).

12. Richard M. Dorson, *Buying the Wind: Regional Folklore in the United States* (Chicago: University of Chicago Press, 1964), pp. 21–105; *Bloodstoppers and Bearwalkers: Folk Traditions of the Upper Peninsula* (Cambridge, Mass.: Harvard University Press, 1952), pp. 231–48.

13. Benjamin A. Botkin, *A Treasury of Mississippi River Folklore: Stories, Ballads, Traditions, and Folkways of the Mid-American River Country* (New York: Crown Publishers, 1955).

14. George Korson, *Minstrels of the Mine Patch* (Philadelphia: University of Pennsylvania Press, 1938); *Black Rock: Mining Folklore of the Pennsylvania Dutch* (Baltimore: Johns Hopkins University Press, 1960).

15. Wayland Hand, "Folklore from Utah's Silver Mining Camps," *Journal of American Folklore* 54 (1941): 132–61; "California Miners' Folklore: Above Ground," *California Folklore Quarterly* 1 (1942): 24–46; "California Miners' Folklore: Below Ground," *California Folklore Quarterly* 1 (1942): 127–53.

16. Dorson, "Miners," *Bloodstoppers and Bearwalkers*, pp. 211–30.

17. Mody C. Boatright, *Folklore of the Oil Industry* (Dallas: Southern Methodist University Press, 1963).

18. Mary C. Fields, "The View from the Water Table: Folklore of the Offshore Oilfield Workers," *Mid-South Folklore* 2 (1975): 63–76.

19. Benjamin A. Botkin and Alvin R. Harlow, *A Treasury of Railroad Folklore: The Stories, Tall Tales, Traditions, Ballads and Songs of the American Railroad Man* (New York: Crown Publishers, 1953), p. xii.

20. Jack Santino, "Characteristics of Occupational Narratives," *Western Folklore* 37 (1978): 199–212; " 'Flew the Ocean in a Plane': An Investigation of Airline Occupational Narrative," *Journal of the Folklore Institute* 15 (1978): 183–202.

21. Ruth A. Allen, *East Texas Lumber Workers* (Austin: University of Texas Press, 1961), p. 51.

22. Fanny H. Eckstorm and Mary W. Smyth, *Minstrelsy of Maine* (New York: Houghton Mifflin, 1927); Edith Fowke, *Lumbering Songs from the Northern Woods*, Publications of the American Folklore Society, Memoir Series, Vol. 55 (Austin: University of Texas Press, 1970).

23. Stewart Holbrook, *Holy Old Mackinaw: A Natural History of the American Lumberjack* (New York: Macmillan, 1939); Robert E. Gard and L. G. Sorden, "Lumberjack Lore," *Wisconsin Lore* (Madison: Wisconsin House, 1962), pp. 59–111; Ira Farrell, *Haywire: Growing Up in the Upper Peninsula 1905-1925* (New York: William-Frederick Press, 1961); John S. Springer, *Forest Life and Forest Trees: Comprising Winter Camplife Among the Loggers, and Wildwood Adventures* (New York: Harper, 1851).

24. Edward D. Ives, "Folksongs from Maine," *Northeast Folklore* 7 (1965); C. Richard K. Lunt, "Jones Tracy: Tall Tale Hero From Mount Desert Island," *Northeast Folklore* 10 (1968); Edward D. Ives, ed., "Fleetwood Pride, 1864–1960: The Autobiography of a Maine Woodsman," *Northeast Folklore* 9 (1967); Wayne R. Bean, "Me and Fannie: The Oral Autobiography of Ralph Thorton of Topsfield, Maine," *Northeast Folklore* 14 (1973). Some representative titles.

25. Edward D. Ives, *Larry Gorman, The Man Who Made the Songs,* Indiana University Folklore Series No. 19 (Bloomington: Indiana University Press, 1964); *Joe Scott: The Woodsman Songmaker* (Urbana: University of Illinois Press, 1978).

26. Roger E. Mitchell, "George Knox: From Man to Legend," *Northeast Folklore* 11 (1969). Study of a devil-possessed lumberjack.

27. Florence Ireland, "The Northeast Archives of Folklore and Oral History: A Brief Description and a Catalog of Its Holdings, 1958–1972," *Northeast Folklore* 13 (1972).

William M. Clements

The Folk Church: Institution, Event, Performance

On a summer evening, as you drive northwest out of Memphis along U.S. Highway 61 into the Delta flatlands of Arkansas, you are likely to notice two things. One is the landscape, flat and treeless except around farmhouses and along sloughs, but obviously fertile, as the rich fields of cotton and soybeans attest. Second, you notice the lively centers of activity along the road. Despite the lingering heat from the day and the diversions offered by television sets in air-conditioned homes, every small church that you pass is surrounded by cars and pickup trucks. A white clapboard building called "New Antioch Landmark Baptist Church," a cinder-block structure designated "Church of the Firstborn," even an abandoned filling station named "Interfaith Tabernacle" afford places for people to assemble for religious exercises. During the summer months in northeast Arkansas—in fact, throughout America—activity at the folk church is at its most intense. It is revival time, and evangelistic worship services occur almost every night of the week, as well as Sunday morning.

As a folklorist interested in traditional culture, you are intrigued enough to stop at one of the churches. It is 7:00 P.M., and the service is almost ready to begin. You park your car in a space alongside a rectangular building with fake-brick siding, whose gable end faces the highway. This is the Independent Full Gospel Assembly. When you enter the front door to sit in an uncushioned pew at the rear, you have entered the folk church. What you see and hear resembles workship experiences in folk churches throughout the country.

Though an outsider from the academic world, an observer rather than a true participant, and maybe even an unsaved sinner, you are immediately welcomed by many of the congregants with a handshake and a murmured "God bless you." The pastor may take some time to chat and extend the church's hospitality. He readily gives permission to record the service on tape (if not already arranged in advance).

The noise in the church strikes you immediately. Babies are crying; older children are scurrying down the aisles, banging doors shut; musicians are tuning their amplified instruments and practicing a few riffs. Most noticeable, though, is the sound of prayer. People kneel at their seats or along the altar rail at the front of the church. They pray aloud, often shouting, often sobbing, and—since the Full Gospel people believe in the Pentecostal gifts of the Holy Ghost—often breaking into unfamiliar, perhaps heavenly languages. The sound rises and ebbs as the prayerful folk are gripped by their emotions or their god.

The service seems to begin spontaneously. The cacophony of the instrumentalists becomes harmony as an electric guitar takes up the melody of a spiritual such as "Over in the Glory Land" or "Victory in Jesus." Then the drum set joins in, its rhythm reinforced when the song leader begins to rattle a tambourine. The piano comes in on the chorus. By this time everyone in the building is singing. Although a few hymnals may be scattered among the pews, no one needs them, for they have sung these songs hundreds of times.

Over and over, the verses of the song are repeated, each one followed by a rousing chorus. Before long many of the worshipers are clapping and waving their hands; a few may even be dancing in the Spirit at their spots in the church. After ten minutes or so of repetition, the music abruptly ceases. The clapping subsides more gradually, and during the lull you hear a few sobs and cries of "Thank you, Jesus," "Glory, glory, glory," "Praise the Lord," and "Hallelujah." Then the guitar begins again, and another song is under way. This song service may last half an hour, forty-five minutes, as long as the Holy Ghost directs. When it finally ends, with the crowd taut and fervent, the church's pastor replaces the song leader behind the podium.

The time for healing has come. A woman suffering from arthritis hobbles to the front of the church and is surrounded by many of the congregants. The pastor places a few drops of cooking oil on her forehead and lays a hand on her shoulder. Everyone prays aloud simultaneously. Although the woman limps just as painfully back to her seat, no one doubts that the Holy Ghost has initiated some sort of process to relieve her sufferings.

Although there are no printed programs for tonight's service, the congregation knows from experience that public prayer is next on the schedule. Individuals rise to request prayer for their families, their friends, or themselves. The pastor mentions several persons afflicted in body or soul who require special attention in prayer and calls for "unspoken requests." Hands shoot up around the room as people acknowledge their need for intercession regarding matters too personal for public declaration. Kneeling at their places or at the altar rail, the worshipers lift their voices in praise, thanksgiving, and supplication.

Once again music fills the church. The most musically gifted members of the congregation come forward to perform traditional spirituals and modern gospel songs, either alone or in groups. A thirty-year-old man, whose face, hands, and neck are deeply sunburned, tells how he had been a sinner, a slave to "dope and wine," until six months ago. He sings "Only a Tramp," as he chords the accompaniment on an acoustic guitar. A trio—two women and a man—performs "I'll Fly Away" and "Only a Dream." A little girl—maybe six years old—sings "a song she learned in Bible school" as the guitar, drums, and piano thunder around her. The worshipers respond to each piece with hearty applause and shouts of "Amen."

At the folk church everyone shares the limelight, for a period of testimony follows the special music. Virtually everyone in the building stands and expresses individual religious convictions. A few narrate specific events that have convinced them of the power of Jesus Christ, but most deliver formularized, set testimonies. Although it is unlikely that you will be expected to speak, you should be prepared. It is proper for you to thank the worshipers for their hospitality and to voice hopes that the evening's service will be successful; you need not publicly state your own religious views.

Once everyone has spoken, an offering is collected, and five- and ten-dollar bills turn up in the offering plate. The worshipers involve themselves in the activities of the folk church financially as well as spiritually.

After the collection money has been counted, the central part of the worship service—the preaching—begins. The pastor introduces the visiting evangelistic speaker, who has come all the way from West Memphis, where his own Full Gospel church flourishes. A fashionably dressed man in his mid-forties steps forward, shucks off his polyester sportcoat, and accepts the microphone from the pastor. Grinning at the congregation, he asks everyone who "truly loves the Lord" to say "Amen." Unsatisfied with the response, he requests to hear it again, this time louder. After the fourth try, the congregation replies with a deafening "Amen" that can probably be heard by the truckers as they roll by on Highway 61. The evangelist opens his King James Bible to the third chapter of John's Gospel and reads the account of the interview between Jesus and Nicodemus, laying particular stress on the concept of being "born again," which Jesus speaks of and Nicodemus cannot fathom.

He closes the Bible and repeats the words "born again" three times. With care and reason, he explains the idea to the congregation, trying to ensure that everyone present understands. Then he begins to cite some New Testament examples of second birth, to draw analogies between this spiritual experience and the homely affairs of the farm and factory folk whom he addresses, and to warn of Satan's nefarious attempts to prevent people from being born again. At some point during his message his style of delivery changes. No longer is the evangelist cool and deliberate; now he is flushed with emotion. His words flow in a rhythmic chant, ornamented with poetic devices such as alliteration and rhyme, punctuated at regular intervals with a grunted "Huh," and rising and falling in both pitch and volume. He thumps his Bible, pounds the podium, paces back and forth in front of the church, stretches his arms to the ceiling, crouches on the floor. Perspiration trickles down his cheeks.

And suddenly he stops. There is a moment of dead silence, broken when a woman rises and begins to speak in what seems to be gibberish. It is a message from the Holy Ghost transmitted in an unknown tongue through the voice of the woman. While the woman speaks, the evangelist clenches a fist at his temple, tightly shuts his eyes, and grimaces. The message in tongues lasts for several seconds, then ceases. After another moment of silence the evangelist speaks again. But now he is more subdued. His language resembles that of the King James Bible, and what he says is a conglomerate of miscellaneous quotations from the Old and New Testaments. Through the power of the Holy Ghost, he is interpreting the message just delivered. When he completes the interpretation, he bows his head. A hush has fallen over the church. He prays briefly. The preaching is over.

Now that the evangelist has put the crowd into a state of emotional and spiritual receptivity, the pastor reassumes control of the proceedings. He extends an invitation for anyone to come forward to "accept the Lord Jesus Christ as his personal savior" or to reaffirm a previously made Christian commitment. As everyone sings "Just As I Am," the pastor urges the unsaved to approach the altar. A few congregants stand beside friends and relatives who have not yet accepted Christ and add their arguments to those of the pastor. The pastor raises his hand to stop the singing and then tells of a young man who failed to heed a call to the altar. With tears streaming, he recalls how the young man died in an automobile accident that same night, missing his opportunity for eternal bliss. The singing resumes, and the period of invitation continues until the pastor is convinced that further pleas are useless. Then he calls on a man in the congregation to dismiss the group with a benedictory prayer.

You walk out of the church into the Arkansas night, having witnessed a series of folk performances integrated into a folk event at one of America's most common folk institutions.

Despite the Arkansas setting of this hypothetical worship service, it represents activities at folk churches throughout America. While my personal familiarity with the folk church stems from several years of field research (participant observation and interviewing) in northeast Arkansas as well as more casual contact with folk churches in west Texas and southern Indiana, I have found that my observations parallel those of investigators working elsewhere. Therefore, I conclude that the folk church constitutes the basic unit in American folk religion. If one assumes that folk religion is unofficial religion, it supplements what some commentators have called "mainline religion"[1]—the religious groups that constitute the sacred element in the American society's power structure. Folk religion exists "apart from and alongside the strictly theological and liturgical forms of the official religion."[2]

Any complex society has folk churches flourishing along its social, economic, political, and even physical margins. In America, folk churches have developed among peripheral social groups such as the Amish, among low-income economic groups such as factory workers in Southern cities, among politically disfranchised groups such as Native Americans, and among people on the wilderness frontier.[3] The worshipers at folk churches, existing outside the main currents of American culture, have not received religious fulfillment from mainline churches. Hence, their religious needs require other, more suitable institutions, engendered often in direct antithesis to the establishment churches. Folk churches emerge particularly at times of spiritual upheaval, such as the Great Awakening of the 1740s or the Kentucky Revival of the early 1800s, and respond to the needs of the new populations created by these upheavals.[4]

As an institution, the folk church manifests several characteristics.[5] From my own experience as a field researcher as well as from an examination of the findings of other students, I have isolated ten such characteristics of the folk church: general orientation toward the past, scriptural literalism, consciousness of Providence, emphasis on evangelism, informality, emotionalism, moral rigorism, sectarianism, egalitarianism, and relative isolation of physical facilities. Singly, none of these traits necessarily defines a church as folk, but together they provide an overview of this institution. Further research needs to be directed toward the historical roots of each trait, its distribution among folk churches, the functions it performs, and its parallels among mainline religious groups.

That research can be conducted in both the library and the field. Fieldwork must involve participant observation, for folklorists need to attend as many religious activities as they can. If they are interested in comparing degrees of informality at various folk churches, they will want to visit as many different churches as possible. If they wish to examine the function of sectarianism, they may choose to concentrate on a single church. Interviews with participants in activities at folk churches must supplement the folklorist's presence at the activities. Members of the folk church can provide commentary on happenings at the church and insights into their personal involvement with the institution, its doctrines, and its rituals. In all fieldwork dealing with religion, researchers must be aware that they are treating an especially sensitive topic. Many informants consider their religion the most important feature of their lives. Therefore, folklorists must treat the beliefs and practices observed with total respect, not blanching when a statement from an informant contradicts one's own cherished creed. For the purposes of religious research, folklorists must willingly suspend their own beliefs.

While the study of the folk church as institution should precede other areas of investigation, most folklorists probably feel more at ease dealing with what occurs at the folk church. As a folk event, the worship service can be studied through participant observation but should also be recorded on tape and film. The first task of the folklorist, no matter what kind of behavior studied, is to make a complete and accurate record. A folk event such as the hypothetical worship service described above produces a number of difficulties in making such a record. The actions of any one of the participants in the event are varied; he or she communicates through words, inflections in tone and volume of voice, gestures, body placement, and facial expressions. Therefore, making a tape recording of a preacher's words and actions does not adequately record the whole event. The use of film and videotape seems to be the most useful approach to recording the event, although several cameras focused on different parts of the congregation would be necessary for the most satisfactory coverage. In fact, several useful films depicting the worship exercises of the snake-handling groups in West Virginia have presented the total event in an admirable fashion.[6]

While the worship service is the most important event occurring at the folk church, researchers should not restrict their investigation to this one type of activity. Every folk church conducts other events for its members, and folklorists must record Sunday school classes, Bible study meetings, covered-dish suppers, all-day services with "dinner on the grounds," and special song services, which often occur on a designated Saturday evening each month.

Folklorists who record an event at the folk church may take several approaches toward understanding that event. They may wish to examine how the various institutional traits of the folk church affect the nature of the event, the relationship between one particular event and others that occur at the church, how historical and cultural factors shape the event, and the ways in which various aspects of the event interrelate to constitute an integrated whole.

When folklorists begin to work from the last perspective, they have begun to think in terms of folk religion as performance, for each aspect of the event constitutes a performance. No performance can be understood without thorough knowledge of its contexts, and after one kind of performance has been extensively analyzed in some isolation from other aspects of the event, it should be carefully related to the totality of the event. In a folk worship service, four kinds of performance seem especially fruitful for folkloristic research.

Singing. The spirituals performed at folk religious events are folksongs, usually learned and transmitted orally and performed in traditional singing styles. These songs have been studied by folklorists more than any other aspect of American folk religion. For example, George Pullen Jackson, in his *White Spirituals from the Southern Uplands,*[7] chronicles the history of shape-note singing schools, which attempted to provide musical competence for the musically illiterate. Jackson, who argued forcefully for the Euro-American origin of what are commonly called "Negro spirituals," published several collections of hymn tunes and texts taken from shape-note songsters.[8] Other singing styles, such as "lining out"—the practice of a song leader's reciting a line before the congregation sings it—deserve similar historical treatment. Additional areas of song research include the study of hymn composers, living and dead, whose works respond to the needs of congregations at folk churches; the examination of the repertoires of hymn performers; the determination of the relationship between song texts and the beliefs of the churches where they are sung; an inquiry into the influence of the media on folk hymnody; and the cultural context of songs and singing style.

Preaching. The central performer in the folk worship service is the preacher, whose prestige is bound up in his success as performer. Bruce A. Rosenberg has competently treated black folk-preaching style in *The Art of the American Folk Preacher*,[9] and many of his conclusions apply to white folk preachers as well. He points out that the rhythmic chant of folk preachers actually consists of repeated formulas, which are metrically consistent and easily remembered. These formulas can be varied in duration and intensity to mold and reflect the spiritual state of the congregation. Rosenberg's work is a model for stylistic investigation, but folklorists now need to undertake a deeper analysis of sermon content, a discussion of the relationship between sermon topic and the immediate context, and the effects of the individual preacher's temperament on his performance.

Ritual. The folk worship service is replete with ritual, for informality is not necessarily antithetical to ritualized behavior. If ritual is "action and beliefs in the symbolic order without reference to the commitment or non-commitment of the actors,"[10] then processes such as divine healing and speaking in tongues, which emerge in standardized patterns and persist almost independently of the individual psychologies of participants, are ritualistic. Perspectives developed by Arnold van Gennep in *The Rites of Passage*[11] and extended by Victor Turner in *The Ritual Process*[12] suggest that ritual often accompanies changes in identity and status. For example, the arthritic woman mentioned in the description of the hypothetical worship service was transformed, at least socially, from a state of affliction to one of incipient health by the Pentecostal healing ritual. In a non-Pentecostal folk church, such activities as the final invitation period have ritual elements. Folklorists can record these rituals, suggest their parallels with rituals in other cultures, interpret responses to ritual successes and failures, and relate the rituals to the folk churches' belief systems.

Testimony. A neglected aspect of folk worship, but one assuredly fruitful for folkloristic research, is the public testimony in which virtually every member of a folk church engages sometime. These brief public performances allow everyone a chance to be the center of attention during the worship event and can be excellent guides to the aesthetics of public performance at such events. Some testimony performers may choose to deliver highly stylized recitations such as the following:

> Truly I love the Lord tonight. And I praise him for all that he does unto me. And I praise him because he saw fit one time to reach down and save my soul and fill me with the Holy Ghost and show me this way. You all just pray for me that I'll always do what God tells me to do.

I thank the Lord tonight for what he means to me. I thank him and praise him for each and ever [*sic*] thing. God's been awful good to me, and I do praise him for it.[13]

Others may recount specific personal experiences that have religious significance, and a few may even use their testimony opportunities to preach brief sermons. Folklorists can treat testimonies from the same stances as they do sermons, focusing on such matters as content and style.

The folklorist's concern with the folk church does not end at the literal vestibule of the church building, for the religious folk take their religion with them as they go about their daily affairs after worship. They practice their religion, speak of it, and feel it deeply. The folklorist can look at several "extra-event" aspects of folk religion. For example, those who attend folk churches tell oral narratives to validate and illustrate their doctrines. These may be memorates, stories of personal experiences, or they may be third-person accounts of how others have encountered the wonderful workings of Providence.[14] Narratives may be collected that constitute a folk history of the religious group, or stories may focus on legendary individuals—saintly patriarchs and faithful matriarchs. The folklorist can also work toward codifying the belief systems of folk churches, recovering folk theology from narratives, generalizations about doctrine, and biblical proof-texts related by informants during conversations or in interviews. Although codification of beliefs may involve the imposition of the researcher's own attitudes on the material, the sensitive folklorist can strive to avoid this danger and ensure that the system described actually is that of the folk.[15]

No matter what aspects of American folk religion folklorists choose to address, they should be aware that their specific interest involves only a part of a complex of behavior. For example, those who follow the lead of many previous researchers and concentrate on singing must understand that the performance of any spiritual is part of the general event at the folk church and that this event responds to and reflects the institutional characteristics of the church. Religious folklore study must, of course, involve the basics of sound folklore research, but it must also fully account for the religious nature of the phenomena investigated at all levels: institution, event, performance.

NOTES

1. For example, see Martin E. Marty, *A Nation of Behavers* (Chicago: University of Chicago Press, 1976), pp. 52–54.

2. Don Yoder, "Toward a Definition of Folk Religion," *Western Folklore* 33 (1974): 14.

3. Works dealing with these folk churches on the margins of American society include John A. Hostetler, *Amish Society* (Baltimore: Johns Hopkins Press, 1963); Liston Pope, *Millhands & Preachers, A Study of Gastonia* (New Haven: Yale University Press, 1942); J. S. Slotkin, *The Peyote Religion, A Study in Indian-White Relations* (Glencoe, Ill.: The Free Press, 1956); and Charles A. Johnson, *The*

Frontier Camp Meeting, Religion's Harvest Time (Dallas: Southern Methodist University Press, 1955).

4. Of the many histories of American religion available, one of the best is Sydney A. Ahlstrom, *A Religious History of the American People* (New Haven: Yale University Press, 1972). The Kentucky Revival was particularly germinal in propagating Christianity among people for whom mainline religion was unsuitable. For discussions of this religious movement, see John B. Boles, *The Great Revival, 1787–1805: The Origins of the Southern Evangelical Mind* (Lexington: University Press of Kentucky, 1972); and Catharine C. Cleveland, *The Great Revival in the West, 1797–1805* (1916; reprint Gloucester, Mass.: Peter Smith, 1959).

5. I have discussed the traits of the folk church in "The American Folk Church in Northeast Arkansas," *Journal of the Folklore Institute* 15 (1978): 161–80; and in "The American Folk Church, A Characterization of American Folk Religion Based on Field Research Among White Protestants in a Community in the South Central United States" (Ph.D. diss., Indiana University, 1974).

6. The best films on the snake-handling groups are *Holy Ghost People*, produced by Blaire Boyd (McGraw-Hill Films, 1221 Avenue of the Americas, New York, New York 10020), and *The Jolo Serpent-Handlers*, produced by Karen Kramer (Karen Kramer, 22 Leroy Street, New York, New York 10014). For a discussion, see my "Review Essay: Snake-Handlers on Film," *Journal of American Folklore* 90 (1977); 502–506. The Indiana University Folklore Institute recently produced *Joy Unspeakable*, a 58-minute color cassette videotape on Oneness Pentecostals in southern Indiana (Indiana University Audio-Visual Center, Bloomington, IN 47405). For successful attempts to capture religious events in print and photographs, see William R. Ferris, Jr., "The Rose Hill Service," *Mississippi Folklore Register* 6 (1972): 37–56; *Foxfire* 7, No. 1 (1973): 5–75; and especially Jeff Todd Titon, "Some Recent Pentecostal Revivals; A Report in Words and Photographs," *The Georgia Review* 32 (1978): 579–605.

7. George Pullen Jackson, *White Spirituals from the Southern Uplands* (1933; reprint Hatboro, Pa.: Folklore Associates, 1964).

8. For example, see *Spiritual Folk-Songs of Early America, Two Hundred and Fifty Tunes and Texts With an Introduction and Notes* (1937; reprint New York: Dover, 1964). For a reprint edition of an original (1855) shape-note songster, see John G. McCurry, *The Social Harp*, ed. Daniel W. Patterson and John F. Garst (Athens: University of Georgia Press, 1973).

9. Bruce A. Rosenberg, *The Art of the American Folk Preacher* (New York: Oxford University Press, 1970).

10. Mary Douglas, *Natural Symbols, Explorations in Cosmology* (New York: Random House, 1970), p.20.

11. Arnold van Gennep, *The Rites of Passage*, trans. Monika B. Vizedom and Gabrielle L. Caffee (Chicago: University of Chicago Press, 1961).

12. Victor Turner, *The Ritual Process* (Chicago: Aldine, 1969). Turner's ideas have been applied to the rituals of American frontier folk in Dickson D. Bruce, Jr., *And They All Sang Hallelujah, Plain-Folk Camp-Meeting Religion, 1800–1845* (Knoxville: University of Tennessee Press, 1974), and I have used Turner's ideas to interpret rites of passage in contemporary American folk religion in "Conversion and Communitas," *Western Folklore* 35 (1976): 35–45.

13. The testimonies were recorded at the Apt Full Gospel Assembly in Apt, Arkansas (Craighead County), on 14 July 1973. Recent studies of testimony in folk churches include my "Public Testimony as Oral Performance: A Study in the Ethnography of Religious Speaking," *Linguistica Biblica* 47 (1980): 21–32.

14. Recent collections of religious folk narratives include Gopalan V. Gopalan and Bruce Nickerson, "Faith Healing in Indiana and Illinois," *Indiana Folklore* 6

(1973): 33-97; and my "Faith Healing Narratives from Northeast Arkansas," *Indiana Folklore* 9 (1976): 15-39.

15. I have examined one element in the belief system of folk churches in northeast Arkansas in "The Jonesboro Tornado: A Case Study in Folklore, Popular Religion, and Grass Roots History," *Red River Valley Historical Review* 2 (1975): 273-86.

William H. Wiggins, Jr.

The Black Folk Church

The black folk church is the central institution in the lives of many Afro-Americans. Its multiple rituals, belief systems, musical forms, plastic arts, and narrative types collectively constitute the largest and clearest reflection of the Afro-American folk ethos. To paraphrase a popular spiritual, the cultural impact of the black folk church is:

> . . . so high, you can't get over it.
> It's so low, you can't get under it.
> It's so wide, you can't get around it.
> You must come through at the door.

Black folk religion has its cultural roots in native West African and American Protestant beliefs and rituals. Slave narratives and travel accounts attest to the vibrance of American religious practices among the slaves. Frederick Douglass consulted Sandy, a root doctor, in an effort to escape his master's whippings.[1] Denmark Vesey used the slave shaman Gullah Jack to recruit men for his revolt.[2] From New Orleans have come accounts of Marie Laveau's voodoo ministry[3] and the dancing rituals of Congo Square.[4] In 1701 the Society for the Propagation of the Gospel in Foreign Parts, the American missionary agency of the Anglican church, began the first systematic attempt to Christianize the slaves. This agency's limited success was followed by the tremendously effective proselytizing efforts of the Methodists, Baptists, and Presbyterians during the Great Awakening.[5]

The resulting Methodist-Baptist model of the early Afro-American church is evident in these spiritual lyrics:

Call: My mother says it is the best
         There's a meetin' here tonight.
         To live and die a Methodist.
         There's a meetin' here tonight.

Response: I'm Baptist bred and Baptist born.
                 There's a meetin' here tonight.
                 And when I'm dead it'll be a Baptist gone.
                 There's a meetin' here tonight.

There are three black Methodist denominations. The African Methodist Episcopal Church was founded in Philadelphia in 1816; the African Methodist Episcopal Zion Church, in New York in 1822; and the colored [now Christian] Methodist Episcopal Church, in Jackson, Tennessee, in 1870. The National Baptist Convention, which is larger than the combined membership of the three black Methodist denominations, was chartered in Atlanta in 1886.

The urban migration in the twentieth century caused the splintering of this Methodist-Baptist folk church model. Pentecostal and Holiness sects emerged within the Afro-American religious tradition along with radical non-Christian sects like the Moorish Science Temple (1919), the Black Muslims (1930), and the Black Jews (1935). The despair of cramped urban neighborhoods also spawned the individual cult leaders Father Divine, Daddy Grace, Prophet Jones, and Reverend Ike.[6]

At first glance, the black folk church seems to be an extension of the following description by William M. Clements of the white American folk church: "This model consists of general orientation toward the past, scriptural literalism, consciousness of providence, emphasis on evangelism, informality, emotionalism, moral rigorism, sectarianism, egalitarianism, and relative physical isolation of church plants."[7] A closer look, however, reveals differences. Slavery and persistent racial injustice have caused the black folk church to interpret these traits very differently. For example, both black and white folk churches believe in the literal interpretation of such scriptures as Acts 17:26, "And [God] hath made of one blood all nations of men for to dwell on all the face of the earth. . . ." But, while the latter group tends to cite this text to promote racial separation, the former quotes the same scripture to affirm human brotherhood. The black folk church has personalized Clements's "consciousness of providence" tenet and believes itself to be the only institution through which God will be able to redeem America. "Egalitarianism" within the black folk church includes class and race, as the Civil Rights anthem so aptly proclaims: "Black and white together, we shall overcome someday." By the same token, the black folk church's "moral rigorism" goes beyond sexual codes of behavior to include a genuine love for all races of men. As the spiritual "Give Me That Old Time Religion" says, "It makes you love everybody." Black folk church buildings tend to be in the very center of the community, not isolated in outlying areas. In fact, many black communities are named after their churches.[8]

The folk genres of the black church are much easier to identify than those of the white folk church. Spirituals and gospel songs are its two distinctive musical forms. Fashioned by the slave community, spirituals were originally sung with no musical accompaniment and utilized the traditional AAAB form. For example,

A: Sometimes I feel like a motherless child.
A: Sometimes I feel like a motherless child.
A: Sometimes I feel like a motherless child.
B: A long way from home.

Many of their themes, such as Daniel in the lion's den, Moses before Pharaoh, and Samson and Delilah, are taken from the Old Testament. Toward slavery's end, white abolitionists began collecting Negro spirituals, and after the Civil War, the Fisk Jubilee Singers toured Europe performing these religious folksongs. Scholars have debated their origins, functions, and social implications. George Pullen Jackson's *White and Negro Spirituals, Their Span and Kinship*, Miles Mark Fisher's *Negro Slave Songs in the United States*, and John Lovell, Jr.'s *Black Song: The Forge and the Flame* and *The Story of How the Afro-American Spiritual Was Hammered Out* figure prominently in these discussions. Jackson theorizes that the slaves' spirituals evolved out of the camp meeting hymns and spirituals of their masters. John W. Work, a black music professor at Fisk University, who collected, arranged, and conducted the world-famous Fisk Jubilee Choir, refuted Jackson's origins thesis by citing structural, scale, and figure of speech differences between the Negro and white spirituals. Fisher postulates that the spirituals functioned as an expression of the slaves' desire to return to Africa. Lovell counters this proposal by offering the theory that the spirituals were directed more toward the free North, and that they are best explained as songs of social protest against the servitude of slavery.[9]

Gospel music emerged soon after the black urban migration began in 1910. Unlike those of the spirituals, the authors of gospel songs, such as Thomas Dorsey, who wrote "Precious Lord," and W. Herbert Brewster, who composed "How I Got Over," are known. The music is much more rhythmical, has instrumental accompaniments, primarily drums, tambourines, pianos, electric organs, and guitars, and the spiritual's AAAB form is often reduced to an AB rhymed couplet:

A: Precious Lord, take my hand.
B: Lead me on, let me stand.

Gospel themes tend to come from the New Testament, and many of the songs, for example, "In the Upper Room" and "Peace Be Still," center on the exploits of Jesus. Only one book has been published on this modern religious folk music form.[10]

The black folk church also has distinctive beliefs and rituals. Just as John Messenger has noted older Celtic beliefs and rituals among Irish Catholics on the island of Aran,[11] John Vlach has documented ancient African burial rites and beliefs still practiced by black Protestants in the American South.[12] The drum dancing at Pinkster (the slaves' Easter celebration),[13] John Canoe parades at Christmas,[14] and "broomstick" marriages disappeared from popular use at the end of slavery. The observance of Emancipation Day, the preparation and eating of black-eyed peas, greens, and pork on New Year's day to insure good luck, and the practice of baptism are still widely observed today by Afro-Americans. Baptism remains the primary adult rite of passage for black youth. In his autobiography, Bishop Richard R. Wright, Jr., an AME minister and the first black to earn the Ph.D. in sociology, gives us a clear insight into the cultural significance of baptism for most Afro-Americans:

There had been a current theological tenet that a child was not responsible for his sins until he was 12 years of age. Up to that time his parents, particularly his mother, were responsible for him. If he died before he was twelve, he was sure to go to heaven, whether converted or not; but if he died unconverted after twelve, hell would be his portion. For that reason, there was always a frantic effort for the boys of twelve and over to be converted. I was not sure of this belief but I did not want to take any chances.[15]

Newbell Niles Puckett's *Folk Beliefs of the Southern Negro* was the first serious study of the black folk church's rituals and beliefs. Puckett traveled throughout the South collecting religious beliefs and interviewing black root doctors.[16] Zora Neale Hurston published a more accurate monograph on hoodoo in 1931.[17] And in 1944 Arthur Huff Fauset published *Black Gods of the Metropolis: A Study of Five Negro Religious Cults in Philadelphia*, a seminal work on the rites and belief systems of the urban black folk church.[18] Gilbert Cooley has recently documented hoodoo practices and beliefs being observed by some urban blacks.[19]

The black folk church also has a unique preaching tradition. James Weldon Johnson recalls the traditional sermons:

I remember hearing in my boyhood sermons that were current, sermons that passed with only slight modifications from preacher to preacher and from locality to locality. Such sermons were, "The Valley of Dry Bones," which was based on the vision of the prophet in the 37th chapter of Ezekiel; the "Train Sermon," in which both God and the devil were pictured as running trains, one loaded with saints, that pulled up in heaven, and the other with sinners, that dumped its load in hell; the "Heavenly March," which gave in detail the journey of the faithful from earth, on up through the pearly gates to the great white throne.[20]

Perhaps nowhere else is style more important in the black folk church than in the delivery of these sermons. Black congregations expect their preachers to "whoop" or give them some "gravy" during the climax of their sermons. Bishop Wright mentioned the latter term in the following quotation, which demonstrates an aesthetic tension between a nonfolk and folk delivery of a sermon.

I have lived to see my style adoped by hundreds of succesful preachers. In my early ministry I was told, "You must give them gravy; gravy is what they want." My experience is that they are wanting, as well as needing, more meat in their preaching. I was accused of not putting on the "rousements," that is, appealing to emotions.[21]

Bishop Wright's "rousements" include traditional poetic descriptions of God as "water in dry places," "bread in a starving land," "a burden bearer," "a heart fixer," "a mind regulator," "a doctor who's never lost a patient," and "a lawyer who's never lost a case." The black folk preaching style demands that the preacher fully command this oral literature and use it with ease and creativity in his sermon's climax. The social function of the black folk sermon has been examined by William H. Pipes,[22] while Bruce A. Rosenberg[23] and Gerald Davis[24] have conducted extensive analyses into its metric structure. James Weldon Johnson has published a collection of poems based on folk sermons.[25] And Jeff Titon is currently analyzing the preaching style of the Reverend C. L. Franklin of Detroit.

My own research efforts have been directed toward black religious folk drama, which incorporates all the folk genres of the black church. "Ship of Zion," "The Child of the King," and "Heaven Bound" are some of the plays still staged in black churches. Many more of these religious pageants provided entertainment for black Americans before the urban migration of the early 1920s introduced the black masses to motion pictures and other forms of secular entertainment. These dramas transform the church sanctuary into a theater, utilizing handmade props and costumes, drawing their cast from the church rolls, and elevating worship to the aesthetic level of theater drama. "Heaven Bound" is the most researched of these dramas.[26] Much fruitful research remains to be undertaken.

Because of the multiplicity of genres and contextual dynamics, I decided to film one of these traditional dramas. My initial choice was "Heaven Bound," since it is produced each November by the choir of Atlanta's Big Bethel African Methodist Episcopal Church. My preliminary research revealed the play to be linear in progression. From the back of the church, down the aisle to the pulpit area, which has been transformed into heaven, comes a procession of the white-robed heavenly choir, the guardian angels, and St. Peter, who carries the keys to the kingdom and the book of life. The play's scenery includes white heavenly gates, blue heavenly clouds fashioned out of wrapping paper and blue and white paint, and hell, a red oilcloth enclosure in the back of the church, on which are painted images of a snake, a fire, and a red devil, replete with tail, horns, and pitchfork. Prominent props include a pair of oversized plastic dice, a ship's life preserver, wooden swords, a wooden shield, a wooden cross, an empty whiskey bottle, green palms, and a golden paper crown of life. The principal characters are the devil, two angels, who guard the heavenly gates, and a procession of twenty-four pilgrims. In the play, a narrator announces the journey of each pilgrim, while the choir and the heavenly traveler sing an appropriate song. For example, the hypocrite, dressed in a red dress, evokes much laughter from the congregation as she swishes down the aisle flirting with the devil and singing, "I Shall Not Be Moved." There is no dialogue. The play's drama comes from the miming antics of the devil and the pilgrims as they dance down the aisle toward the heavenly gates. The majority of the pilgrims enter the kingdom. But there are a few—the wayward girl, the young gambler, the hypocrite, and the rich man—who are denied entrance into heaven and are banished to hell. The play ends with the Christian soldier slaying the devil on the steps of the Heavenly Gates.

I was unsuccessful in my attempts to film "Heaven Bound," but later, a chance lecture gave me the opportunity to film another black religious folk drama. While showing slides of my ill-fated "Heaven Bound" field trip to my Afro-American folklore class, two students commented how much the play resembled "In the Rapture," an Indianapolis-based folk drama they had acted in before coming to Bloomington to study. They gave me the name, address, and phone number of the pageant's creator, Mrs. Margerine Hatcher, and, after a series of telephone calls, the first fruitful interview was arranged. It was followed by a videotaped home interview of Mrs. Hatcher and her family.

In the following weeks, we videotaped a rehearsal and performance of "In the Rapture" at the Church of the Living God, Temple #18 in Indianapolis. Props for this drama include a large plywood mountain, an eight-foot-high wooden cross, a six-foot-long boat mounted on shopping cart wheels, and cloth stumbling blocks made out of pillows from old living-room furniture. Jesus' big white throne dominates the center of the set. In addition to Jesus, the cast includes two angels, the devil, who is dressed in modern clothing and wears sunglasses, a female imp, the sinner, a beautiful woman, a female mountain climber, a narrator, and the choir.

Like "Heaven Bound," "In the Rapture" begins with a procession. White-robed choir members form two lines by clasping hands and then rock down the aisle to the heavenly choir stand, while singing the spiritual "Oh, Peter." At the end of the procession comes the sinner, who is stopped by the devil just before he enters heaven. This confrontation sets in motion a circular instead of linear plot. The sinner succumbs to the devil's "easy" temptations, which include a diamond ring, money, a beautiful woman, and a race car. When the sinner tries to end this relationship, Satan takes his heart, breaks it before the throne of Jesus, and brags to the congregation as he points at the weeping sinner: "Look at him! My right-hand man. Remember how clean he was? [The once nattily dressed sinner is now wearing a faded green work suit with frayed cuffs.] Look at him now. Raggedy. Shoeless. I don't need him. I've got all of you out there." During the harangue the angels give the broken heart to Jesus, who has now left his throne. The devil ends his speech by turning away from the congregation to look at Jesus, who has just completed putting the two pieces back together amid the crash of cymbals and shouts of "amen" from the audience. The play ends with a recessional; the choir sings "Oh, Happy Day!" as they leave heaven in a double line, shaking the hands of members in the audience as they pass by.

From our raw footage, we edited a fifteen-minute cassette tape to send along with a proposal to the National Endowment for the Arts, Folk Arts Division, which subsequently awarded us a sizeable grant. I also secured a matching grant from the Indiana Committee for the Humanities. It took almost two years to execute the plans outlined in my proposal. My first objective was to produce a technically sound film, free of unfocused frames and garbled sound. This criterion was met by Phil Stockton of the Indiana University Audio-Visual Department. He assembled a film crew of four cameramen, three stationary cameras and one mobile unit; several relay film carriers to supply the cameramen with fresh film and deposit the rolls of shot footage in a darkroom (where a file clerk labeled and stored it for processing); a sound engineer, who mixed the live audio portion of the performance; a photographer, who shot pictures of the set and scenes from the dress rehearsal; and two studio technicians, who prepared the fifteen-minute demonstration tape.

My second objective was to get the film crew to understand that I wanted this film to document the contextual dynamics of a live religious drama. Our film would be the first of its kind. William Ferris had filmed Sunday morning worship programs in two black churches,[27] but ours would be the first folklore film of a black religious folk drama. Like Ferris, I wanted to produce a film in which the actors' actions and the audience's reactions were central and the camera had a secondary role. Hence, instead of using the fine-art filming techniques in which the actors play to the camera, carefully noting stage markings and so forth, we reversed the roles and had the camera playing to the improvised actions of the actors and the instantaneous reactions of the congregation. This type of filming does not allow for retakes; either you capture the drama as it unfolds, or it is lost forever. I sensitized the crew to nuances of the plot by showing them my videotapes of the earlier rehearsal and performance. Later, we attended several live performances of the drama in Indianapolis, where I introduced the crew to the Hatchers and the play's cast. This familiarity with the production enabled Phil Stockton to orchestrate a plan for his crew, which not only filmed the entire drama but also effectively captured the play's highly dramatic scenes. For example, after viewing the drama several times we knew that one of the emotional climaxes occurs when the mountain climber struggles with the devil to scale the mountain and clasp the hand of Jesus. Because we were forewarned, the mobile camera focused on the struggling hands of the mountain climber and the devil as the climber reached up to the outstretched hand of Jesus, which is extended over the mountain. Meanwhile, the three stationary cameras recorded the reactions of three different segments of the congregation. This filming strategy allowed us to capture both the drama and the traditional congregational responses of weeping, hand clapping, and "amening."

My third objective was to produce a companion film that allowed the Hatchers and cast members to talk about the play's origin, evolution, and meaning. In this half-hour film, entitled *The Rapture Family*, I hoped to wed film to the folklore interview. The musicians talked about selecting only those songs "that have good acting parts to them"; Mr. Hatcher discussed his role as producer and stage decorator; Mrs. Gwen Parrish explained how her improvised narration stems from her own personal experiences; the devil, Mr. Joe Folson, and the sinner, Mr. Andy Crim, discussed the evolution of their characters; and Mrs. Hatcher spoke of how the play provides a sense of family for its cast members.

When we had edited the play down to ninety minutes, we invited the Hatchers to come to Bloomington to participate in the final editing of the film and indicate which scenes they felt could be eliminated without destroying their play's integrity. With their help we reduced the film footage to sixty minutes.

The final print of *In the Rapture* reveals much of the dynamics of Afro-American folk culture. First, the pageant presents a spiritual world view. The play dramatizes the folk belief that God and not man is the ultimate measure and controller of all things. God will terminate human history by calling his faithful followers up into an eternal heavenly rapture. Second, the drama presents man as being primarily spiritual and feeling in nature.[28] And, third, the play dramatizes the existential folk belief that life is to be lived; each member of the black folk community had vowed "to go and see what the end" of life will be. I feel this is why the mountain climbing scene is so popular with black audiences. The climber asks God for no special favor: "Lord, don't move that mountain!"; instead she requests: "Just give me the strength to climb it."

The film also dramatizes certain black folk aesthetics.[29] First, the drama is episodic in structure. Mrs. Hatcher shifts her play's ten songs around just as black bluesmen do their lyrics, jazzmen their riffs, narrators their folktale motifs, and preachers their sermon illustrations. In all these cases, the black folk artist manipulates the independent elements of the art form to fit the performance's creative mood. For example, Mrs. Hatcher never makes out the order of her songs until she arrives at the church; in some instances she has altered that order during a performance. Second, rhythm dominates the drama. Clarence Hatcher directs the choir as if he were playing a massive drum. By increasing the hand-clapping tempo he signals the coming of the spirit; slowing the rhythm in such songs as "His Eye Is on the Sparrow" creates a reflective mood among his hearers; and the sudden stopping of the rhythm in songs like "Climbing Up the Mountain" effectively builds dramatic tension and maintains the necessary audience-performer inter-action. And third, the Afro-American's marginal status is symbolized in the play's mountain, its stumbling blocks, and the angels' wings, all of which underscore the fact that the Afro-American experience has been an unending struggle to enter the mainstream of American society.

My initial research has uncovered three types of Afro-American folk dramas. "In the Rapture" and "Heaven Bound," prime examples of the first type, string together a series of songs with an oral thread of narration. While "Heaven Bound" is restricted by a prepared script, "In the Rapture" allows much more room for improvisation, through its flexible list of songs. This narrative freedom has kept its narration a vibrant part of the drama, while the printed text of "Heaven Bound" has become wooden over the years, yielding its dramatic importance to the singing and acting of the play. "Slabtown Convention" illustrates the second type of folk drama, which does not integrate music, mime, and narration as well as the first group. In this drama the songs, introduced by the convention moderator, seem to play much less of a thematic role. Music is used to reduce dramatic tension, as opposed to heightening it as it does in the first group. Set during a church convention, the principal characters are the various women delegates (the host pastor and visiting conference speaker are the only two male characters), the conference moderator, and the choir. The circular movement of this play evolves from the conversations between the moderator and the various reporting delegates. Whenever these conversations break into heated debates, the moderator diverts attention from the squabble by requesting a song from the choir. "The Womanless Wedding," an example of the third type of folk drama, makes little or no use of traditional black religious music. The setting is the church altar, where a pregnant bride and an anxious groom (these and all other roles are played by men) stand waiting to be married. The plot is one long series of distractions, which include such comical imbroglios as the groom's former wife and their children inter-rupting the marriage ritual by tearfully confronting the groom and begging him not to leave them. In this drama only the notes of sarcastic humor are sounded.

Afro-American folk dramas afford the folklorist a fresh look at traditional black American humor. Humor's didactic functions are evident in "In the Rapture" and "The Slabtown Convention." The former's comic portrayal of the devil affirms the cultural belief in the ultimate power of Jesus/God, while the latter's stereotypical conventioneers exemplify negative models of black womanhood. The use of sarcasm to control social behavior is evident in "The Womanless Wedding." The annual production of this play is a yearly reminder of the social ridicule that would be visited on any couple who breaks society's established sexual codes of behavior. William D. Piersen argues that this use of satire has West African roots.[30] And Dame Lorraine, a female-impersonated character found in the carnival parades of Trinidad,[31] reflects the all-male cast tradition of "The Womanless Wedding."

In conclusion, there is still "plenty good room" for future black folk church scholarship. All American folklorists have to do is walk through its door, "choose a seat and sit down."

NOTES

1. Frederick Douglass, *My Bondange and My Freedom*, introduction by Philip S. Foner (New York, 1855; reprint, New York: Dover Publications, 1969), p. 239.

2. Lerone Bennett, Jr., *Before the Mayflower: A History of the Negro in America 1619–1964*, 1st rev. ed. (New York: Penguin Books, 1975).

3. Robert Tallant, *Voodoo in New Orleans* (New York: Collier Books, 1962).

4. John Q. Anderson, "The New Orleans Voodoo Ritual Dance and Its Twentieth-Century Survivals," *Southern Folklore Quarterly* 28 (1960): 135–43.

5. E. Franklin Frazier, *The Negro Church in America* (Schocken Books, 1964), pp. 6–9.

6. Joseph R. Washington, Jr., *Black Sects and Cults* (Garden City: Anchor Press/Doubleday, 1973).

7. William M. Clements, "The American Folk Church: A Characterization of American Folk Religion Based on Field Research Among White Protestants in a Community in the South Central United States" (Ph.D. diss., Indiana University, 1974), p. 85.

8. Frazier, *The Negro Church in America*, p. 49.

9. For a complete discussion of the Negro-white spiritual origins debate, see: D. K. Wilgus, "The Negro-White Spiritual," in *Mother Wit From the Laughing Barrel: Readings in the Interpretation of Afro-American Folklore*, ed. Alan Dundes (Englewood Cliffs, N.J.: Prentice-Hall, 1973), pp. 67–80.

10. Tony Heilbut, *The Gospel Sound: Good News and Bad Times* (New York: Simon and Schuster, 1971).

11. John C. Messenger, "Folk Religion," in *Folklore and Folklife, An Introduction*, ed. Richard M. Dorson (Chicago: University of Chicago Press, 1972), pp. 217–32.

12. John Michael Vlach, *The Afro-American Tradition in Decorative Arts* (Cleveland: The Cleveland Museum of Art, 1978), pp. 139–51.

13. Melvin Wade, "Through the Rabbit's Eye: Critical Perspectives on African-American Folk Culture of the Nineteenth Century," Working Paper of the African and Afro-American Studies and Research Center of the University of Texas at Austin, 1977.

14. Dougald MacMillan, "John Kuners," *Journal of American Folklore* 39 (1926): 53–57.

15. Richard R. Wright, Jr., *87 Years Behind the Black Curtain: An Autobiography* (Philadelphia: Rare Book Company, 1965), p. 80.

16. Newbell N. Puckett, *Folk Beliefs of the Southern Negro* (Chapel Hill: University of North Carolina Press, 1926).

17. Zora Neale Hurston, "Hoodoo in America," *Journal of American Folklore* 44 (1931): 320–417.

18. Arthur Huff Fauset, *Black Gods of the Metropolis: A Study of Five Negro Religious Cults in Philadelphia Today* (Philadelphia: Publications of the Philadelphia Anthropological Society, 1944).

19. Gilbert E. Cooley, "Root Doctors and Psychics in the Region," *Indiana Folklore* 10 (1977): 191–200. Cooley has published a companion article in the same issue entitled "Conversations About Hoodoo": 201–16.

20. Floyd C. Watkins, "De Dry Bones in De Valley," *Southern Folklore Quarterly* 20 (1956): 136–49.

21. Wright, *87 Years*, p. 125.

22. William Harrison Pipes, *Say Amen, Brother! Old-Time Negro Preaching: A Study in American Frustration* (Westport, Conn.: Negro University Press, 1970).

23. Bruce A. Rosenberg, "The Formulaic Quality of Spontaneous Sermons," *Journal of American Folklore* 83 (1970): 3–20.

24. Gerald Lewis Davis, "The Performed African-American Sermon" (Ph.D. diss., University of Pennsylvania, 1978).

25. James Weldon Johnson, *God's Trombones: Seven Negro Sermons in Verse* (New York: The Viking Press, 1927).

26. Redding S. Sugg, Jr., "Heaven Bound," *Southern Folklore Quarterly* 27 (1963): 249–66.

27. William Ferris, *Two Black Churches* (New Haven: Yale University Design Studio, 1975).

28. LeRoi Jones, *Blues People: The Negro Experience in White America and the Music that Developed from It* (New York: William Morrow and Company, 1963), pp. 1–16.

29. William H. Wiggins, Jr., " 'In the Rapture': The Black Aesthetic and Folk Drama," *Callaloo: A Black South Journal of Arts and Letters* 2 (1978): 103–11.

30. See William D. Piersen, "Puttin' Down Ole Massa: African Satire in the New World," in *African Folklore in the New World*, ed. Daniel J. Crowley (Austin: The University of Texas Press, 1977), pp. 20–34.

31. Errol Hill, *The Trinidad Carnival: Mandate for a National Theatre* (Austin: The University of Texas Press, 1972), pp. 40–41.

William A. Wilson

Mormon Folklore

The study of religious folklore is one of the most rewarding tasks a folklorist will face, because the lore arising from a people's deeply felt religious needs will bring the folklorist close to other human hearts. The study of Mormon folklore is no exception.

On a spring morning in 1820, young Joseph Smith walked out of a grove of trees near Palmyra, New York, declaring he had just talked with God. In the following decade, he received further visitations from divine beings, brought forth a new body of scripture, and in 1830 founded the Church of Jesus Christ of Latter-day Saints—the Mormons.

From the outset Mormons found themselves in conflict with mainstream America. They steadfastly insisted that only they offered the road to salvation. They attempted to exercise political and economic control in areas they settled. And, to the shock of a Victorian America, they practiced polygamy. The result was antagonism and at times open warfare with their angry neighbors, who drove them from state to state, murdered their prophet, Joseph Smith, and in 1847 forced them to seek refuge in the mountains and deserts of Utah. There they subdued a hostile environment, colonized the Great Basin, sent out missionaries to gather in the elect, and single-mindedly devoted themselves to building a new Zion in preparation for the second coming of Chirst.

Out of these circumstances—out of a theology founded on the doctrine of continuing revelation and a belief in divine intervention in the affairs of man, out of a history of conflict and struggle—has developed one of the most vibrant bodies of folklore in America.

The first folklore having to do with Mormons was probably that created about them by their enemies. Scarcely had Joseph Smith announced his revelation to his unhappy neighbors when they began circulating yarns aimed at discrediting him, dark tales about his ignorant, superstitious parents and about the magic peepstones he used to divine both future events and the source of precious metals and great treasures hidden in the earth. In tale after tale, "Holy Joe" Smith is depicted as an unscrupulous mystic who defrauds the gullible and tricks them into believing in his supernatural powers. When Smith was murdered in 1844 and Brigham Young took his place, the emphasis in the anti-Mormon lore shifted from trickery to lechery. Young and his fellow church leaders, under whom the practice of polygamy grew to full bloom, are portrayed in a spate of yarns as sensual, fire-breathing patriarchs intent on seducing young virgins into their harems.[1] Though these tales have waned somewhat, they still persist. My students periodically turn in stories they have heard outside Utah about Mormon missionaries kidnapping young girls and sending them to a dungeon below the Salt Lake temple, where they are supposedly held prisoner and sexually abused. In one account, one of these girls escapes her captors, climbs to the spires of the temple, leaps into the Great Salt Lake (a jump of some fifteen miles), and swims to safety.[2]

In spite of the vicious anti-Mormon sentiment expressed in these tales, the church grew and prospered. As it did, and as members of this new Zion began to develop a sense of cultural identity, they began also to create a lore of their own. This religious lore, among the first to be brought to the attention of American folklorists, has been studied primarily by Mormon folklorists intent on using folklore skills to better understand their own culture. Since the 1940s, these scholars have produced a series of articles and four book-length studies. The most important of these, Austin and Alta Fife's *Saints of Sage and Saddle* (1956), recounts through legend and song major events in Mormon history: the revelations of Joseph Smith, the flight west, the struggles over polygamy, the taming of the desert, and, above all, the providential hand of God in all things. The other studies focus more narrowly on specific topics. Hector Lee's *The Three Nephites: The Substance and Significance of the Legend in Folklore* (1949) examines stories about three ancient American disciples of Christ known to the Mormon faithful through the *Book of Mormon* and believed by them still to be walking the earth, awaiting the return of the Savior, and giving comfort and aid to the physically and spiritually distressed. Thomas Cheney's *Mormon Songs from the Rocky Mountains* (1968) provides historical and theological contexts for Mormon folksongs, and his *The Golden Legacy* (1973) brings together anecdotes of the crusty, irreverent, but much-loved church authority J. Golden Kimball. Although Cheney's works are valuable social documents, they unfortunately lack the comparative notes needed to establish the material included as folklore.

Until recently, Mormon folklorists have tended to view the materials they have studied as cultural artifacts surviving from an earlier period, to be used primarily for the reconstruction of early Mormon social history. Thus Hector Lee wrote of the Three Nephites: "They afford an uncensored approach, through the substrata of Mormon thought, to pioneer concepts, attitudes, and impulses."[3] Implicit in this approach is the notion that in the more sophisticated world in which Mormons now live, the old tales, particularly the supernatural legends, are dying out. This is simply not the case. Mormons still hold fast to the visions of Joseph Smith and actively seek evidences of God's participation in their affairs. This fact is borne out by the stacks of supernatural stories contributed each year by Mormon students in university folklore classes. In the past decade, for instance, my own students, with no special prompting from me, have collected over 700 of the Nephite stories Hector Lee believed to be in a state of decline. (Lee's own study was based on some 150 texts.)

As this material has continued to flood in, Mormon folklorists have begun shifting their attention from the past to the present, realizing that just as pioneer Mormons created folklore as they responded to the circumstances of their environment, so contemporary Mormons generate lore as they come to terms with the joys and pains of their own lives. My "The Paradox of Mormon Folklore" (1976) is a first step toward an interpretation of this new material.[4]

To understand contemporary Mormon folklore, one must understand that Mormons consider themselves "a peculiar people," a kingdom apart, living in the world but not of it. They believe they belong to the "one true church," a church lost through apostasy following the death of Christ but later restored by revelation from God to Joseph Smith, and they believe they have an obligation, through vigorous missionary work, to share their restored gospel with the world.

The bulk of Mormon folklore functions to persuade church members that these beliefs are valid and that individuals must devote themselves valiantly to the cause—indeed, may suffer dire consequences if they fail to do so. In brief, this folklore falls into two broad categories: lore that shows how God protects the church in its battle with the world, and lore, remarkably like that of the early Puritans, that shows how God brings about conformity to church teachings by intervening directly in the lives of church members.

One of the best ways to prove the validity of a cause is to prove that God is on one's side. Thus Mormon tradition is replete with accounts of God fighting Zion's battles. From the mission field, for example, come numerous stories of beleaguered young missionaries saved from disaster by mysterious strangers, usually thought to be the Three Nephites, who appear suddenly to help the missionaries placate heckling crowds or to rescue them from angry mobs and then disappear. At times the Lord not only protects these missionaries from harm but also pours out his wrath on those who oppose them. For example, a Norwegian town that had treated missionaries badly was "completely leveled" by the Germans during the war. After the war, the repentant townspeople invited the missionaries back. In Taiwan a street where missionaries had been mistreated burned to the ground. In Costa Rica a town that had persecuted the missionaries "horribly" was hit by a flash flood that destroyed half the town and killed many people. And in Hawaii a town guilty of abusing missionaries was destroyed by a tidal wave.

Missionaries are by no means the only recipients of providential protection. According to one popular story, a Japanese pilot on the way to bomb Pearl Harbor on the morning of December 7, 1941, had flown over the radiantly white Mormon temple at Laie, Hawaii. Having failed to use all his bombs in the Pearl Harbor attack, he determined to destroy that white building on the return flight but was hindered from doing so because he could no longer find it, or because his bomb release, which had worked perfectly over Pearl Harbor, would no longer operate properly. After the war, the pilot traveled to Hawaii to find the building he could not destroy; he found both the temple and the church and eventually became a Mormon himself.

At the Hill Cumorah near Palmyra, New York, where Joseph Smith once received visitations from heavenly beings, the church holds an annual historical pageant attended by thousands. In one dramatic scene, a spotlight flashes on the darkened hill, revealing a white-robed figure, arms outstretched, representing the Christ. One year, according to recent legend, enemies of the church kidnapped the person playing Christ just before he was to appear on the hill. Yet when the spotlight cut through the darkness, a figure did appear in the light, a figure believed by many to have been the Savior himself.

To most Mormons the message of stories like these is clear: the Mormon church must be the true church of God, because he protects it from harm. In the narratives dealing with the conduct of church members, the same message is brought home again, the implication being that God would not concern himself with church members' obedience to gospel precepts if these precepts were not true.

If the wrath of God is kindled by outsiders who attack the church, it is more easily aroused by church members who fail to do their duty or who engage in blasphemous acts. A young man from southern Utah refused a mission call; a month later he died in an automobile accident. In 1860 Brigham Young dedicated a new irrigation project, Salem Pond, and promised that no drownings would occur there if no one swam on the Sabbath. The eight people who have since drowned in the pond were all swimming on Sunday. One widely circulated legend tells of two missionaries who decided to test their priesthood power by ordaining a coke bottle or, depending on the version, a fence post, a broomstick, a fire hydrant, or a dog or cat. In almost every instance the missionaries were struck dead immediately, usually by a bolt of lightning.

These accounts, in the words of one informant, show that "God will not be mocked." They persuade church members to do right by showing what happens if they do wrong. An even larger number of legends recount blessings that come from obeying God's commandments. Though these accounts are legion, one of them, which stresses the importance of temple activity, seems in recent times to have become more popular than any other. It will serve well as an example for the entire genre.

Mormons believe they have an obligation to save not only themselves and, through missionary work, their neighbors but also all their kinsmen who have died without benefit of gospel law. Thus they seek the names of their ancestors through genealogical research and then in their sacred temples vicariously perform for these ancestors all the saving ordinances of the gospel. In a recent narrative, a young mother attending a temple suddenly felt that something was wrong at home but was promised by a temple official that if she would complete the session everything would be fine.

> After the session was over she hurried home, and sure enough, there were fire engines and police cars all around her house. As she was running to her house, a neighbor lady stopped her and explained that her daughter had fallen into a ditch and couldn't be found. As the lady came to the house, there was her daughter soaking wet and crying. Her mother grabbed her and hugged her. After, the little girl gave her mother a note and explained that the lady who'd pulled her out of the ditch had given it to her. There on the note was the name of the [deceased] lady for whom that woman had gone through the temple that day.

Thus the dead woman, whose spiritual life had been saved through temple work performed on her behalf by the mother, had, in turn, saved the physical life of the mother's little girl.

This particular version of the legend was told as "an inspirational experience" by a young missionary instructor to a group of newly called nineteen-year-old missionaries about to enter the temple for the first time. Other people have heard the legend in different situations: in automobiles on the way to a temple, in the temple itself while waiting for the ritual ceremony to begin, in a genealogy class, in a Sunday School discussion, in family gatherings, from a clerk in a store, from a close friend while discussing spiritual experiences. And the legend has been told for a variety of reasons: to give spiritual uplift, to show that temple work is appreciated, to give testimony to the importance and sacred nature of temple ritual, and, above all, to demonstrate, as one informant puts it, "all the neat experiences that occur when one does work for the Lord. . . . This story is an example of His protection for His people who obey Him." The legend thus provides an excellent example of the way Mormon belief and conformity to that belief are strengthened by Mormon folklore.

In many ways, Mormon folklore has not changed from the days of Joseph Smith; God still leads the church, rewarding the faithful and punishing sinners. The world in which church members must meet the test of faith, however, has altered significantly. The pre-World War II agrarian society depicted by earlier scholars has given way to an industrial urban world. In this world, one of the Three Nephites, who might earlier have saved a rancher from a blizzard or watched over a farmer's fields so he could attend his church duties, now pulls missionaries from a flaming crash on a Los Angeles freeway or appears to a parking lot attendant about to be seduced by one of his lady customers and warns him "not to ruin his entire life for a few minutes of pleasure."

Mormon folklore, then, has not diminished or lost its vitality. It has simply changed to reflect the circumstances of a different world. As that world continues to change, we must continue to collect and reinterpret. The church has experienced radical transformation in recent years. It has dropped its ban against allowing blacks to hold the priesthood but has now taken a hotly contested stand against the Equal Rights Amendment. The church has also altered its organizational structure and has experienced dramatic growth (from two million in 1962 to five million in April 1982). Just as the trek west, the practice of polygamy (abandoned in 1890), and the struggle with the arid land shaped Mormon folklore in the past, so these recent events will give it form in the future. For example, the revelation in 1978 granting the lay priesthood to blacks has inspired a spate of humorous quips probably reflecting anxiety over the change: "Did you hear about the new Sidney Poitier movie—'Guess Who's Coming to Priesthood Meeting?' " "Did you know that tithing's been raised to twelve percent—to pay for busing?" "Did you hear that we've given the priesthood to the blacks—but we've taken it away from the Indians?" It has also inspired stories about the miraculous nature of the revelation, stories that assure church members that the change really came from God, not man.

As we look at new forms of Mormon lore, we must also look at forms neglected in the past. In the spicy anecdotes about the cussing church leader, J. Golden Kimball,[5] and in an earthy cycle of tales about erring Mormon bishops, lies a rich vein of folk humor that has been collected but not yet carefully analyzed. Also the large block of faith-promoting, but nonsupernatural, stories has been mostly overlooked. Mormons believe that if God is personally interested in their welfare, then they, as children of God, must be concerned with the welfare of others. Hence, while the missionary returning from the field will relate supernatural stories, he will talk also about the change of character he has observed in the lives of those who have accepted the gospel. He will tell stories about people who have abandoned their own interests to devote themselves to the service of others. These narratives must be included in any study that tries seriously to get at the Mormon mind.

Folklorists must also devise new ways of looking at Mormon lore. Most studies to date have assumed a cultural homogeneity that in reality has never existed. The fact is that rural and urban Mormons, educated and uneducated Mormons, male and female Mormons, born-in-the-church and converted Mormons quite often view the world through different eyes and respond to it differently in their lore. For example, converts to Mormonism living in the mission fields, away from church centers in the Mountainwest, may be little moved by tales of pioneer suffering and may know next to nothing of the exploits of the famous Three Nephites. Instead, they will know and tell stories of their own miraculous conversions and of the ridicule and suffering they endure, with the help of God, as they struggle to survive as the only Mormons in unfriendly and often hostile communities. In the Mountainwest, where many families can trace their roots to early pioneer times, the Nephite legend will be generally well known, though not universally accepted. Belief in it and in other supernatural legends will range from complete acceptance to guarded skepticism to outright disbelief. Some Mormons will even tell tales like the following, to poke fun at the entire Nephite tradition and at the gullibility of those who accept it so readily:

> A Mormon driving in his truck through a desolate area in southern California came upon an old man by the side of the road. He stopped and gave the man a lift. The old man asked to be let off at a point just as desolate as the one where he was when he was picked up. When the Mormon dropped him off the old man handed him a large round silver thing, rounded on one side—kind of convex. He told the Mormon to keep the object on a shelf for three years and after three years to look at it and he would find the old man's name written on it. So the Mormon put it on a shelf and just left it there for three years, not thinking much more about it. Then three years later he remembered what the old man had said and went to the shelf to get the round silver thing. As he rubbed the dust off it, sure enough, he found a name: "Chevrolet."

It is possible, I believe, to arrive at a consensus value center, an emotional core, that ties most Mormons together, but we must not lose sight of the fact that each Mormon is unique, different in some ways from all other Mormons, and that it may be as important to study how an individual uses folklore to manipulate the environment as it is to study that lore as an expression of the larger group.

Speaking of missionary work, Mormons often say that "the field is white and ready for the harvest." We can say the same thing about the study of Mormon folklore. The work has just begun. From it we can continue to learn not just about Mormons but about the behavior of religious people in general.

NOTES

1. For good examples of early anti-Mormon lore, see Austin and Alta Fife, *Saints of Sage and Saddle: Folklore of the Mormons* (Bloomington: Indiana University Press, 1956), pp. 109–25.

2. This and all others items of Mormon folklore discussed in this paper are located in the Utah State University Folklore Archives, Merrill Library, Utah State University, Logan, Utah 84322.

3. Hector Lee, *The Three Nephites: The Substance and Significance of the Legend in Folklore*, University of New Mexico Publications in Language and Literature, no. 2 (Albuquerque: The University of New Mexico Press, 1949), p. 126.

4. William A. Wilson, "The Paradox of Mormon Folklore," *Brigham Young University Studies* 17 (1976): 40-58.

5. See Thomas E. Cheney, *The Golden Legacy: A Folk History of J. Golden Kimball* (Salt Lake City: Peregrine Smith, 1973).

Gerald Warshaver

Urban Folklore

In a landmark paper, the sociologist Robert Park maintained that the city is more than a geographical location or a vast artifact containing congeries of individuals and constellations of institutions. As Park argued, "The city is, rather, a state of mind, a body of customs and traditions."[1] As folklorists move from the country to confront the urban state of mind and to research the customs and traditions of the city, they are apt to find their own undertakings getting away from them unless they develop a theoretical framework appropriate to the urban field. Conversely, without a perspective that sees the city and its peculiar culture as the object of investigation, the development of a coherent body of truly urbanistic folklore research is impossible. The principles that follow are intended to define a perspective and sketch out a framework for the study of the folklore of the city.

FIRST PRINCIPLE

The study of urban folklore should be seen as an historical activity whose logical starting point is the nineteenth century, the era of the beginning of modern industrial urbanism. Economic, demographic, technological, environmental, political, and other types of developments should be examined as they intersect with and influence the evolution of a given custom or tradition. As an historical undertaking, urban folklore should lead us into the present as we concern ourselves with contemporary continuities, discontinuities, or equivalent manifestations of tradition. How this principle might be applied can be seen in the custom of the urban promenade.

Before the full transition to industrial urbanism, America's urban elite ritually promenaded in the streets on Sundays after church and in the early evenings in spring and autumn. They exhibited themselves to each other and demonstrated their allegiance to their group by observing certain folk rules of "correct" promenade behavior. For example, along New York's Fifth Avenue, known to the elite as "The Street," women, children, and families kept to the eastern side, no matter how crowded it might be. Genteel gentlemen who smoked strolled on the "wrong side" (left) of the street.[2]

In the Gilded Age and after, the ambulatory promenade evolved into the equipage parade, the ritualized drive in the park. A partial list of the elements that influenced the evolution of this custom includes the commercialization of once exclusively residential areas, such as Fifth Avenue; the rise in the elite standard of living, which made private carriages and elaborate retinues affordable; the growth of urban population; the presence of new types of immigrants; the development of urban park systems; and the rise of country clubs and elite resorts.

Future research may reveal that the city is still a setting for patterned activities that are the functional equivalents of the promenade, insofar as they give members of the elite an opportunity to demonstrate their social commonality through the mutual display of "correct" behavior and appropriate deportment. Fieldwork may demonstrate that visitors to museums, art exhibits, or block and street fairs, members of self-awareness encounter groups, or perhaps even joggers could profitably be studied in this context.

SECOND PRINCIPLE

Urban folklore must be socially inclusive. It must embrace the lore of all types of urban groups. In my preceding example, I focused on an upper-class custom in order to emphasize that urban folklore ought not to restrict itself to the lower classes and ethnic minorities. In recent years, lower-class street rituals, such as "hanging out" (poorer people's version of the elite promenade), have been studied, but the contemporary field of middle- and upper-class urban rituals and customs remains an almost untouched subject.

THIRD PRINCIPLE

Because urban folklore views the city as a social organism, it seeks to discover and analyze the types of customary behavior and traditional beliefs that are shared as a result of city dwellers' participation in their everyday urban world. Sets of common urban behaviors that city dwellers take for granted as "the only right way to act" or "the normal way things are done" deserve special consideration as possible types of uniquely urban folklore.

The application of this principle may require a team approach to fieldwork or the use of videotape equipment. For example, the sociologist Michael Wolff and his team used videotape to analyze "pedestrian behavior" in a busy midtown business district. Wolff was able to identify several patterns of walking behavior that urbanites use to accommodate each other as they move at different rates and pass one another on the street. Janey Levine and her associates identified the customary ways subway riders communicate that they do not wish to communicate with their fellow passengers. Working alone, Lyn Lofland used interviews and personal observation to analyze how urbanites categorize strangers by means of traditional spatial rules.[3]

Urban folklorists must become familiar with the full range of everyday behavioral traditions and their underlying normative beliefs. Equipped with a knowledge of the forms and functions of all genres of oral communication, folklorists can make a special contribution by examining the informal (but formularized) communicative network that contributes to the maintenance and stability of these behavioral traditions. Urban talk that defines situations as either appropriate or inappropriate for customary behavior ought to attract the folk-lorist's attention immediately. For example, although we have Latané and Darley's fine sociological study of the situations in which urbanites will not intervene when others are in trouble,[4] we do not have a complementary study of the talk that justifies this "bystander apathy." We need studies of all the kinds of discourse about civic violence, antisocial types, and situations where it is dangerous to behave in a "normal" way. This kind of talk is especially significant because it can give rise to new patterns of behavior that in time become "normal," customary, traditional ways of acting in the city. For instance, beliefs about ways to identify, avoid, and contend with feral individuals are often transmitted in the form of superstitions: if you walk in the street and not on the sidewalk, you will escape attack; if you wear an expensive fur coat and reverse the fur and the lining so that the fur is covered by a plain fabric, you will be safe from muggers. Beliefs about street crime, beliefs about the misfortunes that befall innocent bystanders or those who do not observe the everyday behavioral traditions of the city are expressed as motifs in personal-experience stories, memorates, legends, and jokes.

What constitutes the full corpus of the folklore of everyday urban life? What are the social contexts in which urban folklore becomes the subject of urban talk? How is it incorporated in different genres? Which motifs occur most frequently and why? Finally, how and why does urban folklore differ from group to group, from city to city, and from one historical period to the next? The answers to these questions would greatly contribute to our understanding of the tenor of urban life in America today.

FOURTH PRINCIPLE

Urban folklore relates the repertoires of street folk to the ecology of the city. Hucksters, buskers, beggars, street musicians, pitchmen, pickpockets, children playing in the street and "bagpeople"—individuals who regularly camp in doorways or stand for days in the same spot, muttering and gesturing, with their three or four mysteriously filled shopping bags at their feet—all types of street folk invite the attention of the folklorist. This fourth principle ensures that the study of the textual and behavioral repertoires of these urban types will include an analysis of their environmental competence: their ability to effectively modify their performances to meet the needs of particular environmental conditions.

For example, an investigation of "three card monte," the urban version of the old shell game that has reappeared on the streets of New York after a seventy-year absence, should include the following five topics: a sketch of the pitchman's career; a study of the tricks of the trade that determine how the monte dealer manipulates his cards; a record and analysis of the formulaic pitch that he spiels to his audience; an inquiry into the code signals and dialogue shared by the dealer and his shills; and a study of the monte man's environmental competence. This study should analyze the unwritten lore that determines where the monte man sites himself and go on to deal with the manner and degree to which he will adapt his customary performance to the specific conditions of the layout of the street and the qualities and activities of the passing crowd.

The study of environmental competence calls for two kinds of fieldwork: observation and interviews. Still photographs and videotapes can help document the relationship between patterns of customary street performances and different categories of spatial and social environments. Interviews should be conducted with the end in view of learning how a group's folk speech or technical argot reflects the environmental conditions the group considers most relevant. David Maurer's *Whiz Mob*, a study of the folk speech and behavior of old-time pickpockets, provides a fine model. Maurer's interviews inform us why and how competent *canons* (pickpockets) *work* a *murderer's push grift* (a large, dense crowd) differently from the way they *hustle* the *spots* (the sites where people come together briefly, such as the bus stop), or *work* the *chutes* (the subways).[5]

FIFTH PRINCIPLE

By viewing the city as a multiple reality, a state of mind, urban folklore explores the image of the city that forms part of each group's stock of urban lore. In order to find their way in a strange city, tourists buy commercially produced maps. In

FIG. 1. Street ballad seller, 1870

FIG. 2. Licensed venders, 1870

FIG. 3. The tooth-powder man, 1870

FIG. 4. Flower vender, 1976

FIG. 5. Vender and cop, 1975

FIG. 6. Street musician, 1976

contrast, residents build up a mental image of the city that is a product of their particular place in the urban social mosaic. The work of Kevin Lynch and others who have studied the "maps" of the city environment that persons carry around in their heads and use as a means of orientation suggests that there are as many ideas of what constitutes the reality of a certain city (or a neighborhood) as there are different urban groups.[6]

Folklorists can get a graphic representation of their informants' picture of the city by requesting a freehand sketch. In my own fieldwork, I emphasize that individuals should "map out" the streets, districts, landmarks, meeting places, and boundaries significant to them. Since membership in particular social worlds generates particular images of the city, sketch maps can serve as a guide to the version of the city that is "real" to a given group.[7]

Interviews can be used to elicit the symbolic meaning of the mapped items. Personal experience stories, anecdotes, memorates, legends, jokes, and folk names reveal the emotional significance informants attach to the items on their maps. Knowledge of a group's mental map of the city provides the folklorist with a useful tool for delineating the communicative network that reflects the everyday urban behavioral customs and beliefs discussed in the preceding section.

Old neighborhoods, commercial sites, recreational areas, and landmarks that no longer exist as part of the actual cityscape may persist as part of the mental map of the elderly or those who are the bearers of urban folk history and legend. This lore, which researchers have termed "after-images,"[8] merits careful investigation, for it demonstrates how traditional dimensions of past folk experience interpenetrate present "readings" of the reality of the city. "After-images" signify how knowledge of a past social milieu projects itself as a behavioral reality into the present.

Freehand sketch maps of informants' neighborhoods can teach us how the folk idea of a neighborhood differs from the image held by outside "experts." Folk who share a spatial image of a neighborhood perceive their "true" or "real" neighborhood as a small territory nesting within a larger residential district. Although this larger district usually bears the official name of the neighborhood (though informants may give it their own folk name), informants perceive the smaller territory to be their primary field of urban acquaintanceship. That is, residents feel the "true" or folk neighborhood to be the behavioral environment where "everyone knows who belongs and who doesn't." Folk neighborhoods can be as small as a few apartments (in a high-rise environment), a dozen houses, or a street. They seldom comprise more than several city blocks.[9]

Folklorists interested in studying the cultural processes involved in urban "neighboring" must avoid thinking in terms of units alien to their subjects' definition of the situation. Patterns of traditional sociability found in rural communities may be discovered in the city if folklorists make an adjustment in their scale of inquiry.

Information about how a group pictures the city gives us insight into the group's urban beat, its customary range of activity. For example, inner-city street gangs tend to possess a finely articulated mental map of their "turf," their folk neighborhood. Like the inner-city poor in general, they tend to have a very limited mental map of the city. Their restricted images signify truncated beats. Similarly, although various groups of middle- and upper-class city dwellers may indicate areas inhabited by the poor on their sketch maps, their knowledge of these areas is rarely a function of their own urban beat.[10] Although a considerable amount of research is needed before we can come to any definite conclusions, I would offer, as a theory to be tested, the notion that images of neighborhoods that are not a product of a group's beat are the product of a mixture of gleanings from the media and a group's traditional beliefs about the neighborhood's inhabitants. William H. Jansen has termed the traditional ideas one group has of itself and supposes others to have of it "esoteric folklore." He has called the traditional beliefs one group holds of another and that it thinks the other group has of itself "exoteric folklore."[11] The role esoteric-exoteric folklore plays in the meaning urbanites give to their image of the city and its role in shaping an urban beat are topics of interest to be pursued by urban folklorists in the future.

The principle of studying the city as a state of mind has ramifications that go beyond the field of the urbanist. Since mental maps are subjective knowledge structures—generalized and abstract models of the world—they may prove to be a useful concept for folklorists and literary critics interested in the structural study of narrative. I suggest that mental maps of the city might be useful as a concept to explain how certain folkloric narratives are structured. For example, labor reminiscences and immigrant autobiographical stories frequently strike the researcher as "formless" or merely episodically additive. Using the concept of the mental map, future researchers might disclose that these narratives are structured in accordance with the mental image of the city that tellers share with their natural audiences. Armed with sketch maps and interviews, researchers might find that as the tellers name the streets lived on, the neighborhoods lived in, the paths and direction taken to work, they externalize the process by which mental maps of the city were formed. At the same time they might be understood to be giving form to their narratives, demonstrating in yet another way how the city is rooted in the minds of its inhabitants.

In conclusion, I would like to stress the autonomy of urban folklore. The principles proposed in this essay assume that urban folklore is an integral part of the city, not an intrusive survival from the rural past. The perspective informing these principles sees urban folklore as a product of the urban environment and a force that affects the way the city is perceived. From this point of view, the task of the urban folklorist is no less than the elucidation of the native traditions of America's urban civilization.

NOTES

1. Robert E. Park, "The City: Suggestions for the Investigation of Human Behavior in the Urban Environment," in Robert E. Park, Ernest W. Burgess, and Roderick D. McKenzie, The City (Chicago: University of Chicago Press, 1925), p. 1.

2. Mariana Van Rensselaer, "Fifth Avenue," Century Magazine 47 (November 1893): 12–13; Elizabeth Duer, "New York Society a Generation Ago," Harper's Monthly 105 (June 1902): 109–14.

3. Michael Wolff, "Notes on the Behavior of Pedestrians," and Janey Levine, Ann Vinson, and Deborah Wood, "Subway Behavior," in People in Places: The Sociology of the Familiar, ed. Arnold Birenbaum and Edward Sagarin (New York: Praeger, 1973), pp. 35–48, 208–16; Lyn Lofland, A World of Strangers (New York: Basic Books, 1973).

4. Bibb Latané and John Darley, The Unresponsive Bystander: Why Doesn't He Help? (New York: Appleton, 1970).

5. David Maurer, Whiz Mob: A Correlation of the Technical Argot of Pickpockets with Their Behavior Pattern (New Haven: College and University Press, 1964), pp. 173–80.

6. Kevin Lynch, The Image of the City (Cambridge: M.I.T. Press, 1960); Roger M. Downs and David Stea, eds., Image and Environment: Cognitive Mapping and Spatial Behavior (Chicago: Aldine, 1973); Florence C. Ladd, "Black Youths View Their Environment: Neighborhood Maps," Environment and Behavior 2 (1970): 74–99; Barry Goodchild, "Class Differences in Environmental Perception," Urban Studies 11 (1974): 154–69.

7. Anselm Strauss, "Life Styles and Urban Space," in Environmental Psychology: Man and His Physical Setting, ed. Harold M. Proshansky, William H. Ittelson, and Leanne G. Rivlin (New York: Holt, 1970), pp. 303–12.

8. J. Douglas Porteous, "Design with People: The Quality of the Urban Environment," Environment and Behavior 3 (1971): 159.

9. Terence Lee's research strategies and his typology of neighborhood schemata should be of interest to urban folklore; see Lee's "Urban Neighborhood as a Socio-Spatial Schema," in *Environmental Psychology*, ed. Proshansky et al., pp. 349–70.

10. Grady Clay, *Close-Up: How to Read the American City* (New York: Praeger, 1973), pp. 110–26; David Karp, Gregory P. Stone, William C. Yoels, *Being Urban: A Social Psychological View of City Life* (Lexington, Mass.: D.C. Heath, 1977), pp. 145–49.

11. William H. Jansen, "The Esoteric-Exoteric Factor in Folklore," in *The Study of Folklore*, ed. Alan Dundes (Englewood Cliffs, N.J.: Prentice-Hall, 1965), p. 46.

Richard A. Reuss

Suburban Folklore

Historically, folklorists have most often studied those peoples furthest away from themselves. The natives of distant exotic lands, the peasants of Europe, the frontier families of yesteryear and rural dwellers of today, the poor everywhere have not lacked for folkloristic scrutiny. Recently, new considerations of the folk process have led scholars to study urban folklore. But even though the majority of academics in the United States live the greater portion of their lives in suburban communities, hardly any folklorists have ventured with notebook or tape recorder into their own neighborhood to study the traditions of middle- and upper-class America at home.

Much folklore found in the suburbs is common to or a carry-over from urban (defined here as inner city) or other American subcultures: commonplace ritual greetings ("Beautiful day, isn't it"), ethnic foods and holiday customs, jokelore, children's rhymes and games, occupational traditions, sports superstitions, and much more. The emphasis in this essay, however, will be on describing some of the many traditions that in terms of content, function, or context are primarily, if not exclusively, attached to suburban living and lifestyles.

In sociological terms, a "suburb" is a politically independent residential community that is substantially dependent economically, and to some extent socially, on an urban center, and that supplies the city or greater metropolitan area with a labor force in return for needed goods and services. In general, the socioeconomic status of suburbanites is higher than that of the average central city dweller; the geographic and social mobility is greater; and participation in community affairs is proportionately increased. Homes generally are single-family dwellings, and households are organized along the lines of nuclear family (parents and children) rather than extended family (parents and children plus grandparents and other relatives). Factories and heavy industry are absent; stores and shopping centers are confined to adjacent areas by both custom and zoning ordinance. Debate continues, however, among social scientists as to whether suburban residents are more or less neighborly, politically conservative, or morally conventional than inner city populations.

Many suburbs are the subject of folklore stereotyping in surrounding populations. The residents of Marin County, outside San Francisco, are nationally depicted as proponents of hot tubs, divorce, and a liberated lifestyle. Mention Beverly Hills, California, and one inevitably is greeted with images of mansions and movie stars. Other suburban areas may be identified with particular ethnic groups, Levittown or "little boxes" architecture and social values, racist attitudes and notions of lily-white purity, college living, and so on. Suburban communities have their own folklore about themselves, too. Grosse Pointe, Michigan, on the eastern outskirts of Detroit, is known to most people in that greater metropolitan area as the home of the snobbish and the rich; Grosse Pointers harbor this stereotype of themselves as well, but most believe that the wealthiest elite live in some other neighborhood in the Grosse Pointe area than their own. Traditions about each suburb are based in part on its physical characteristics and on observable behavior that transpires within, but otherwise tend to be both reductionist and speculative in character. During the Detroit riot of 1967, one survey found that suburban dwellers who neither lived nor worked in the inner city had a much more inflated notion of the chaos, damage, and behavior of the rioters than those actually present downtown during the several days of disturbance. Typically, all residents of a given community are apt to be labeled with the preconceived characteristics in spite of the fact that there is usually considerable digression from the stereotypic traits within even the more homogeneous suburbs.

Any person living in a suburb will soon internalize a largely unspoken folk concept of his or her neighborhood. Almost always smaller than the suburb as a whole, the "folk" neighborhood may comprise just a few streets and adjacent areas such as school yards, ball fields, the nearby Dairy Queen, and so on. The folk boundaries may be busy street crossings, undeveloped lots, brooks, fences, railroad tracks, or whatever; they may overlap school district lines, less often town political boundaries, and will tend to shift somewhat in the minds of residents living in different parts of the same neighborhood. All the same, the general outlines of the "folk map" will be clear to anyone who bothers to check. Inherent in the folk concept of neighborhood are all the associated notions of home, security, territoriality, and license. One who ventures outside this inner sanctum will find different ground rules. Outside their own neighborhood, children on their own do not make so much noise or move about so freely, or at least their casual behavior will not be tolerated for as long without sanction. Adults in a strange neighborhood can be presumed upon less freely for information or assistance in time of need, and cooperative efforts will be fewer and less intense than similar efforts made with strangers who live within a commonly identified folk neighborhood.

Within each suburb, the houses, lawns, gardens, garages, sidewalks, and other landscape features are arranged in patterns dictated by custom as much as by zoning laws or town regulations. One does not usually plant a vegetable garden on his or her front lawn, build the garage directly in front of the house, or construct tall "spite fences" around one's property without evoking the criticism and contempt of one's neighbors. Much of what is done ostensibly for convenience can be explained by more profound social and psychological truths. Placing the mailbox by the front rather than the side or rear door, for example, may be rationalized in terms of saving the postman time and steps; yet the milkman, meter readers, garbage men, and assorted repair persons frequently are encouraged or expected to utilize the more distant entrance route to the house when such is available. The difference is that though the individual mail carrier may have been a familiar face on the block for twenty years, his role represents the formal callings of society upon the family of the home dweller. Other servicemen of the type described above have a stronger degree of association with portions of the family's more personal and private existence (eating, regulating fuel, controlling waste). Similarly, friends of the family's children are often exhorted to use side rather than front door paths once they are accepted by parents as close intimates of their offspring. Intimacy as well as curtailment of grimy footprints and distribution of empty water glasses is inherent in these entreaties: "Come to the side door—we *know* you now," the youngster is told.

The folk dichotomy between public and private life-space is replicated in the ways in which suburban homes and lawns and gardens typically are utilized. Families used to have formal sitting rooms or parlors (from the French *parler*, to speak), which were reserved for use when important company was received. A "living room" for more casual and intimate family gatherings was frequently found in the interiors of such homes. Sometimes the kitchen doubled as a social center as well, a pattern particularly characteristic of ethnic American families. Today most suburban homes do not have parlors; the latter's function has been subsumed by the living room, whose original purpose in turn has been replaced by a "family room," den, or finished basement. Bedrooms and bathrooms associated with the family's most private activities are ordinarily located at the very back of the house or on another floor. All of this house organization, clearly demarcated in, though not totally unique to, suburban housing, is folkloric custom rather than public health code prescription or legal necessity. Similarly, in a seminal article published in *Western Folklore* in 1972, E. N. Anderson studied traditional suburban arrangements of lawns and gardens in southern California.[1] In addition to identifying the front-public, back-private folk polarization associated with these and related landscape features about the home, Anderson and his students noted that the reasons offered by homeowners for the existence of their lawns and gardens, such as to provide a place for children to play, to grow one's own fruit and vegetables, to offer shade, and so forth, usually bear little reality to the facts. Children generally are kept off well-manicured front lawns and only given the run of less tended and more private back or side yards; the shade offered by most trees and shrubs is minimal or eschewed in favor of sun; and the effort expended in raising a limited amount of produce does not economically or emotionally justify the labor or time involved to grow them. Anderson postulates that the more profound reasons why suburbanites devote portions of their weekend and spare-time energies to cultivating well-ordered lawns, shrubs, and gardens instead of playing golf or watching television are tied to issues of social and peer group status, and to innate human needs to distance the individual and society from the outwardly chaotic and unmitigated wildness of nature.

Within each suburban neighborhood, there can be found a variety of indigenous place and local-character lore, vivid and significant to area residents but meaningless to outsiders. The local deli is advertised as Gumpert's on its store marquee, but children will shout and adults whisper its better-known and mildly pejorative folklore name of "Ickle-Bickle." Certain houses or other buildings outwardly indistinguishable from nearby structures are traditionally associated with mysterious events or strange owners: a murder, an alleged drug pusher, a mad octogenarian with a bankroll stashed in her mattress, or an "Amityville Horror" poltergeist. Many of these reported doings are local variations of floating stories; others originate at and are anchored to specific settings, but in any case the accounts stubbornly persist in neighborhood memory even after the original participants are long gone from the scene. Individuals who are the subject of local lore frequently are singled out for attention because of their departure in some fashion from local standards of normative behavior. Henry Ford is remembered today in one upper-class Detroit suburb not so much for his mass production of the automobile and other public activities as for the fact that he and his wife failed to join the right clubs and social organizations after they became affluent. I myself know of a retarded man in a Long Island middle-class community who became a figure of legend because he peddled old clothes, did not shave, dressed unkemptly, and habitually scavenged for old newspapers in other people's trash baskets. Neighborhood children regarded him as a bogeyman, and grownups viewed him with a mixture of uneasy tolerance, sympathy, and disdain. Stories abounded attesting to his sudden and silent appearances on the streets and private property of local residents, or his "irrational" anger when children ventured near his apartment in a relative's garage or taunted him with catcalls or hurled crabapples and other missiles at him. Local lore about "Edgar" served both as a reminder of community values of neatness and order and as a folk definition of "craziness" for years after he died.

Another major component of the verbal lore of contemporary suburbia is the so-called urban legend, which perhaps deserves equal billing in the folklorist's lexicon as the "suburban legend," since so large a percentage of these narratives are set, either explicitly or implicitly, in a suburban locale. These narratives typically are brief accounts of anonymous people caught up in bizarre and traumatic, occasionally supernatural or humorous, circumstances because of the violation of some unspoken community or social norm. They are most intensively communicated among teenagers but are widely disseminated throughout the rest of the suburban population as well. One cycle of these stories revolves around babysitters left alone with their young charges. In one narrative the parents call to notify the sitter of a later returning time only to be informed by the teenager spaced out on LSD that all is well and "the turkey is in the oven." Knowing no such food is in the house, the parents speed home to find their baby roasting in the oven. Another familiar tale, recently recast into a Hollywood horror movie, concerns the sitter harassed by a series of obscene phone calls, which eventually are traced by the police to an unknown caller phoning from an upstairs bedroom.

Numerous other narratives tell of similar startling incidents. A lady who allows a postman to use her bathroom is surprised by his sudden reemergence in the living room totally nude. A sidewalk construction worker who arrives home at midday unexpectedly finds his wife in bed with another man and takes his revenge by filling the lover's car with wet concrete. Sometimes the scene shifts to the neighborhood shopping center, where centuries-old mutilation tales with racial overtones are localized as having occurred in department store restrooms. Or customers die from bites caused by poisonous snakes hatched from eggs in clothes shipped in from the Orient for resale to cheap chain-store outlets. Or patrons of fast-food eating establishments purchase some variety of fried rodent instead of chicken, fish, or ribs, or find insects in soft drinks. All these stories and many others circulate nationally, yet they are invariably placed in a neighborhood setting; if they did not originate in the suburbs, they have followed the suburbanites to their current domiciles from either the city or the country. Moreover, they help shape behavior, since each contains both a submerged taboo violation and a prescription for "safe" as well as acceptable behavior. Parents should take cognizance of their teenagers' lifestyle; young women should not stay in strange houses alone for hours on end; cheap foreign goods and mass-produced fast foods are apt to be suspect at times, and so on. All the class values and prejudices of today's suburbanites are inherent in such narratives. Presented for the most part as essentially factual, their retelling serves to perpetuate and reinforce community norms better than any moral didacticism on the part of parents or teachers.

The suburban environment also offers a wealth of customary expressive behavior for the folklorist to examine. In a provocative unpublished study, Diane McCallum describes the traditional shopping activity of suburban teenage girls in an affluent Detroit suburb, noting the similarity in the patterns she observed to those reported by older women from comparable backgrounds of her acquaintance.[2] Typically, such shopping, carried out on both weekday afternoons and Saturdays, is leisurely, highly ritualistic, and social in character, sharply in contrast to the purposeful "errand-running" of others. Adolescent girls habitually walk to and move about the center in groups, frequenting principally those stores where they may congregate comfortably together and which sell goods that relate to personal appearance and social identity. Clothing stores, jewelry shops, and cosmetics counters are mandatory stops each trip. If time permits, a coke and french fries break or an occasional foray into a book or record store will be added, but hardly ever will these girls venture into a hardware store, no matter how conveniently located. Typically, the girls test, feel, try on, and discuss at length with clerks and each other the objects they are appraising, but only now and then do they make an actual purchase, and that is usually an incidental one. For these girls it is a time to see and be seen, to communicate, to learn about colors, textures, and fabrics, as well as material qualities and traditional values, and to find support and new self-awareness within the peer group. Their behavior passes almost unnoticed by their fellow shoppers, but its unique and ritualistic qualities are immediately apparent to store salespersons and the discerning observer.

Other folkloristic suburban teenage activity involves use of the automobile, the mobile social hall of today's youth. In a 1974 article in *New York Folklore Quarterly*, Michael Licht documents a variety of play activities traditionally engaged in by suburban adolescents and young adults in New York.[3] "Chicken," where two cars race toward each other at high speed with the nominal winner being the driver who turns the wheels of the car aside last, is more talked about than actually played. "Mooning" involves the sudden exposure of buttocks or genitals to pedestrians or other passing cars with the intent of generating a startled or shocked response. Catcalling is yelling crude and sexually suggestive insults at persons, particularly women, on the streets ("Hey, Crisco, too much fat in your can"). In a "Chinese Fire Drill" (also called "redlight-greenlight" and other names), the occupants of a car stopped at an intersection leap out and race around the vehicle pell-mell while yelling and screaming, creating as much of a disturbance as possible before piling back into the car and driving off when the light changes. Drag-racing presumably is well known to most readers. Likewise, the favorite suburban automotive pastime of "cruising," that is, driving certain streets slowly for show, in search of action, and for the purpose of finding friends and members of the opposite sex, has been noted widely by scholars, news media, and film-makers (*American Graffiti*). In all these play activities there is an aura of self-testing and violation of responsible adult norms of behavior, which is age-appropriate and normative, though aggravating to parents, police, pedestrians, and polite society.

Teenagers are not the only ones who engage in folkloric behavior with regard to the automobile. Adults invest their cars with names and personalities, animating their existence as primitive man enlivens stones, trees, and other objects with projections of his soul. The suburban folk likewise endow their cars with protective magic talismans: St. Christopher statues, lucky rabbits' feet, oversize dice, or other symbolic magical accoutrements, usually prominently displayed on the dashboard or suspended from the rearview mirror. The objects themselves are mass produced, and reference to the magical implications of these charms is minimal. Yet the folk behavior of attempting to protect oneself and one's family in a prized and familiar, but high-risk, environment through the use of charms is age-old.

Festival behavior in the suburban context has hardly been considered as yet, be it the neighborhood block party or the annual commemoration of some unique event or characteristic earmarking the community as distinct and apart from others. In some localities, the residents of particular streets traditionally engage in the display of creative and extensive outdoor Christmas lights and decorations, occasionally in competition with other neighborhoods. Though there are no formal announcements, rules, or public commentary, the reputations of such streets are perpetuated by word of mouth, and considerable peer group pressure is exerted on the newcomer to one of these blocks to participate and maintain the prestige of his or her neighborhood. The impact of the suburban milieu on festival behavior associated with rites of passage, such as weddings and funerals, likewise has received little attention.

In substantial part this inattention proceeds from a view of suburban traditions as mundane, uninspiring, and hardly worthy of notice, particularly in contrast to colorful ethnic customs, antique costumes, and rural folk habits of a vanished America. Yet suburban folklore is equally functional in its importance. Like folk traditions everywhere, it identifies community norms and values, entertains while it educates or reinforces individuals in expected behavior patterns, and provides creative outlets for individual expression and collective release of tensions within socially approved channels. To find the folk expression of today, the scholar and curious layperson need scarcely leave home; they need venture no further than their own doorsteps.

NOTES

1. E. N. Anderson, Jr., "On the Folk Art of Landscaping," *Western Folklore* 31 (1972): 179–88.

2. Diane McCallum, "Shopping Behavior of Teenage Girls in Grosse Pointe, Michigan," unpublished ms. in Wayne State University Folklore Archive, Detroit, Michigan, 1975, 8 pp.

3. M. Licht, "Some Automotive Play Activities of Suburban Teenagers," *New York Folklore Quarterly* 30 (1974): 44–65.

James P. Leary

"Hanging Out": Recreational Folklore in Everyday Life

Slouched in chairs on a country store's front steps, swaggering on city street corners, sharing coffee in farm kitchens, or leaning against backyard fences, Americans (rural, urban, young, old, male, female, of varying ethnic and class backgrounds) periodically gather to relax and socialize, to "hang out." Considerable folklore is learned and performed on these occasions. And, although few researchers have investigated "hanging out" in any systematic fashion, its practice by diverse sociocultural groups may be reduced to some basic concepts.

Occurring away from work and domestic responsibility, hanging out necessarily demands a gathering *place*. The "hangout" may be fixed along the local tavern's wooden bar, beneath some corner street lamp, in a basement "recreation" room; it may move seasonally from a fish-laden lake to a duck blind; it may also roughly encompass a geographical area or mental map like the "neighborhood turf" marked by urban streets and suburban backyards, or the rural roads and secluded spots around a small town. Likewise, the *time* for hanging out is not random, but determined by tradition. It may fall regularly on rainy days and wintry mornings, during weekends or vacations, on a week night, in the late afternoon when school or work have ceased, or during intervals amidst these activities.

Participants are a variable lot. Late adolescents roaming the streets and unattached young adults prowling singles bars temporarily inhabit a developmental phase: they are "running wild" before "settling down" to inevitable employment and marital responsibility. Likewise, "senior citizens"—retired from jobs, their children gone—spend waking hours in the company of peers. For some adults, hanging out extends from adolescence to old age as a dominant interactive mode or lifestyle. So radical an occurrence may result from personal choice or occupational necessity, as in the case of socially marginal people ("bums," "drifters," entertainers, gamblers); it may also be affected by the chronic unemployment plaguing certain rural areas and urban ghettoes, or as the result of inheritance ("jet setters," the "idle rich"). For middle-aged adults, hanging out is far more frequently an occasional style of interaction, having diminished into an often secondary component of everyday life (breaks from work, stops at the tavern, card parties, bowling nights) or become one aspect of multifaceted annual events: fishing trips, conventions, reunions, athletic contests.

Finally, hanging out is a cultural activity or *process* involving a concerted, creative departure from workaday reality through artful behavior. Speech is not used seriously to convey information, but playfully to foment sociability. Drink and the consumption of "treats" (sweets, junk food, pizzas) often accompany this transformation. Meanwhile, folklore genres—nicknames, good-natured gibes, boasts, proverbs, jokes, and personal experience stories—are uttered in jocular tones or through the assumption of comic personae. Laughter, spontaneous actions (elaborate handshakes, shoulder punchings, arched eyebrows, embraces), dancing, and formalized games (played with cars, cards, darts, dice, horseshoes) may nonverbally convey camaraderie.

The identification of place, time, participants, and process is, however, only a preliminary step toward understanding. Hangers out in two given spaces and moments may be moved by differing aesthetic impulses; consequently, their cultural processes may well satisfy contrasting social and personal ends. The A & P parking lot in Bloomington, Indiana, and central Wisconsin's Ritz Tavern offer concrete examples.

Located in downtown Bloomington, the A & P lot, until its recent purchase by a liquor store, was frequented after hours by working-class male adolescents who arrived, uninvited, in growling "hot rod" cars to drink beer, smoke marijuana, broadcast "heavy metal" rock music, strut, prank, and indulge in tire-squealing, engine-taxing, "show-off" driving. Emerging from autos, they engaged in verbal sessions frequently dominated by irrepressible raconteurs like Paul Wilson. A stock boy at a local grocery, pilot of a 1957 Chevy Nomad, Paul reeled off raunchy parodies of AM radio songs and commercials. Even more popular were his grotesque yet imaginative characterizations of the parking lot scene.

Posing as a news reporter (that media figure equated with "truth"), Paul borrows from the baseball poem "Casey at the Bat" to disparage Bloomington as "Mudville," a nowhere place where "bad" things happen. Three characters are scornfully introduced: the chicken, a beast associated with cowardice and stupidity; "Little Missy Prissy," a hoity-toity nursery rhyme take-off; and cartoon boob Elmer Fudd, frequent prey of trickster Bugs Bunny. Each experiences difficulty with some routine physical process: digestion, menstruation, defecation. Accordingly, all suffer severe punishment: decapitation, mutilation, sterilization. Escaping danger are Missy's well-hung boyfriend and numerous "hot rodders" wearing protective mud valves.

Oh, let me tell you somethin'. Y'know what happened down in Mudville today? Say, today was bad news in Mudville. Two chickens got their heads chopped off. One of 'em swallowed a peach and was chokin' to death. Little Missy Prissy woke up with a goddam tampax crossways. They had to cut her pussy hole bigger. But that's good because her boyfriend had too big a dick. Then Elmer Fudd woke up, got a turd crossways. They just had to give him a whole histarextomy [*sic*] and a half. So, it was bad news in Mudville [a car roars by]. News today in Mudville—more mud. Say-hey, we got any hot rodders comin' down in Mudville, they better get their mud valves on.

Belittling women, the weak, the awkward, the unfortunate, celebrating machismo, Paul's routine is stylistically congruent with crude and "tough" verbal exchanges elsewhere on the lot.

Hailing each other by nicknames ("Mad John") or derogatory epithets ("shit for brains," "queer face"), youths traded put-downs ("A" drives up in a car, "B" queries "anybody hurt in that wreck?") and boastful threats ("I'll hit you so hard your ancestors'll feel it"). Inflated narratives generally ensued concerning boldness (releasing a greased pig in school), driving ability (laying a "patch" on main street), and sexual activities ("Hey, it only took me five minutes to get into Marlene's pants"). "Dirty jokes" were also performed amidst nudges and leers.

The preceding evidence argues that these hangers out in Bloomington shared an aesthetic of violence and outrage. As A & P regular Mike Cazee put it:

> What's neat's bein' up here of a Friday night. See these assholes in the back row [of the parking lot] throwin' beer cans at guys in the front row. That smartass A & P manager gettin' smacked. Cars slidin' sideways out in the street. Cops hidin' behind the Marathon station. [Pause.] Some chick gettin' banged over behind the garbage cans.

On a sociological level, Mike and Paul's beered-up, foul-mouthed, "horny" tradition functioned to create an adolescent niche independent of childish innocence; rebelliously defying "managers" and "cops," they simultaneously rejected adult respectability. More personally, by challenging one another and the surrounding world, participants strove to acquire a sense of their own "manhood."

Like the A & P lot, Dominic Slusarski's Ritz Tavern lies just off a downtown square, but there similarity stops. One of Stevens Point's "old timer" bars, the place's decor has altered little in Dominic's thirty-seven years of operation. A long bar fronts well-stocked liquor shelves, beer-company clocks tell the time, a venerable Wurlitzer alternates C & W tunes and polkas. There are few all-day customers; habitués arrive to cluster in constantly shifting groups, departing after a shot of brandy or a 16-oz. "shupe" of local Point Beer. Patronage predictably swells on rainy days, during winter cold spells, or on weekends. Like Dominic, the clientele is largely Polish, but Germans, Norwegians, and multiethnic "half breeds" intermix; most are farmers, tradesmen, retirees. Except during weekend dances, when live concertina music sets couples spinning, the tavern is primarily a male preserve.

Men at the Ritz and related establishments shake dice, make bets over six packs, buy each other drinks, share "snoose," and, most importantly, talk. Discussions and good-natured arguments over politics, economics, morality, meteorology, and athletics are invariably localized, fattened with expressive language ("That'll show 'em where the bear shits in the buckwheat"), and punctuated by witty aphorisms ("My home is in heaven, I'm just here on vacation"). Observations on the present stray into the past as talkers reminisce, frequently exaggerating, about the time "a tornado tore off the barn roof and twirled it around three times," or that "tough old moonshining Polack who'd worked in the pinery." As conversation warms, jokes are interjected to illustrate points, or for their own sake. Popular narratives celebrate hunting and fishing, farming, and married couples. Perhaps because few patrons are WASPs, opening all to ribbing over national heritage, jokes about ethnic buffoons are most prevalent.

"Where's Ben?", a story about a wily bartender's bamboozling of some ethnic character (interchangeably a "Polack," a German, or a Norwegian), is typical:

This fellow went into a bar. The bartender was playin' jokes on him every day, y'know. He'd come in there, bartender'd say, "Where's your buddy, Ben?" "Ben who?" He says, "Bend down and kiss my ass." Next day, same thing'd happen. . . . So, he went and told his buddy about this. He says, "Gee, that guy is gettin' me every time with them jokes." He says, "Well, I'll tell you what to do." He says, "When you go in there, before he has a chance to say anything, you ask him where Ilene is. And he'll say 'Ilene who?' And you say, 'I lean over and *you* kiss *my* ass.' " "Oh, good." So, he goes in there, y'know. Comes up to the bartender, "You seen Ilene around?" "Yeah," he says, "she just went out with Ben." He says, "Ben who?"

Spoken in a bar, before ethnics, amidst constant gaming, this text eschews the violent language of Paul Wilson's commentary. No less bungling than the chicken, Missy Prissy, or Elmer Fudd, the simple dupe nevertheless has a chance to retaliate; even with ultimate failure, he suffers no lasting harm, but is only, once more, victim of "them jokes." So it is with tavern-goers at the Ritz.

"Where's Ben?" reflects a cultural aesthetic of friendly competition, of "give and take," dominating hanging out at the Ritz. Participants utilize folklore resources to tease gently, draw out, and involve one another in a common activity. Ted and Alvin Konkol refer to the integrative function of barroom loitering:

Ted: There's all kinds here. The people get along good here
            because there's . . .
Alvin: There's all kinds.
Ted: There isn't one nationality here. . . . Used to be, years ago,
            when I was a kid, yes, if you weren't Polish, you wasn't
            nobody, y'know. But that's changed. I know a lot of
            people I don't know what the hell they are. It don't make a
            lot of difference to me what the hell they are either.

In a more emotional vein, Dominic put it this way: "People like to come to my bar because they have a good time."

For the dedicated folklorist, places like the Ritz and the A & P lot will ultimately make the most sense on a similarly personal, experiential level. Aspiring fieldworkers *must* hang out with their chosen group. If one lacks an "in," strategy is required.

Before approaching the A & P group, I racked my brain to recall the jokes, stories, and brags I'd once relied on, for as a teenager I'd had experiences with analogous youths. With repertoire dredged up and a six-pack of beer stuffed into a knapsack, I walked to the lot as the grocery closed, accosting the first friendly looking arrival—Paul Wilson. Wary of being viewed as either "narc" or "nut," I introduced myself as what I was: a student wishing to conquer term-paper boredom by writing about the street scene. Enlisting his antiacademic sympathies, I recounted a few teenage activities. Paul offered a "toke" of marijuana, I handed him a Fehr's beer, and the evening unfolded pleasantly.

Breaking the ice at Dominic's was a similar matter. I entered the tavern early on a summer afternoon; only a few were present. Through tourist questions about the local beer, small talk was easily initiated; conversation soon led to my occupation. Replying, to quizzical looks, that I was a folklorist, I illustrated my interests by telling a Hoosier-Kentuckian joke. They laughed and Richie W. slid a can of Copenhagen snuff in my direction. Suppressing fears of swallowing the stuff, I stuck a pinch in my cheek, met Richie's eyes, and bought him a beer. In recompense, he matched my story with a long Norwegian dialect joke. Two hours later I emerged into daylight, filled with stories and drink. Here again, trust was gained by meeting a few individuals at a time when socializing wasn't full blown, defining a role for myself, demonstrating interest, a little esoteric knowledge, and exchanging commodities.

Repeated visits solidified fledgling friendships. At first, I made no attempt, beyond post-gathering notation, to document occurrences. Practicing patience, I let events unfold, thereby gaining an important "natural" understanding of hanging out, while simultaneously devising appropriate recording techniques. At the lot, where speakers roamed the blacktop, spontaneously commenting on emergent situations, I asked permission to record participants (provided the tapes were played back to them) by putting the machine in my backpack, with the microphone strung down my sleeve and taped to my wrist. While Dominic's patrons were less mobile, a constantly shifting clientele, noise from adjacent conversations, and polka music conspired against extensive taping. Sessions over brandies and beer were scheduled with gifted raconteurs either in their homes or around tables in quiet taverns.

With problems of rapport and recording overcome, fieldwork became especially rewarding. Not only were hangers out regularly accessible at a specific place and time, but they also gathered for the distinct purpose of performing folklore forms. Finally, within this heightened context, they were often willing to comment on the aesthetics, function, and meaning of their expressive behavior.

William E. Lightfoot

Regional Folkloristics

Norma Turner is an active and accomplished performer of folk traditions who lives up the Left Fork of Beaver Creek in Drift, Kentucky, which is situated in Floyd County near the center of the Appalachian highlands. During a conversation I had with Norma Turner in 1974, she sang several folksongs, including the following version of "Sam Adams" (Laws dF 62), which she learned from her mother:

> In the state of old Kentucky
> One dark and stormy night,
> A horrible crime [was] committed
> And later brought to light.
>
> A man was cruelly murdered,
> Sam Adams was his name,
> His body cut to pieces;
> They accused Joe Huster's gang.
>
> He left his home one morning
> Employment to seek;
> He told his loving family
> He'd just be gone a week.
>
> He went down to Auxier,
> One week he went to stay,
> But little did he think that
> It was his fatal day.
>
> That night did Samuel Adams
> Lay down upon his bed;
> They crept into his room
> And knocked him in the head.
>
> They cut and maimed his body
> So powerful to behold;

They buried him in the river bank
Down in the sand so cold.

His friends soon grew uneasy;
They searched for him in vain
From Jack's Creek down to Auxier,
But nothing did they gain.

But God with all his power,
To see what He could do,
He sent a whirling flood
That washed him into view.

His body was discovered
And placed beneath the clay,
For there it may remain
Until the Judgment Day.

Joe Huster was arrested,
And all his foreign band,
For murdering Samuel Adams
And burying him in the sand.

Their faces they grew pale
As the jury it filed in;
The foreman read the verdict:
It was life in the Frankfort Pen.

Norma Turner performed the ballad exceptionally well, but it failed to make a strong impression on me. I realized that the song was a "murder" ballad, but I understood very little else about it: Who was Sam Adams? Why was he killed? Who was Huster? Foreign band? Jack's Creek? Auxier? After discussing the ballad with Ms. Turner, I was able to see it through a more appropriate frame of reference, and the song immediately began to acquire more meaning. From the stories Norma Turner told, I learned that the ballad is a "true story" that describes in part the horrible death of a local man at the hands of "foreigners," and that the event occurred only a few miles from Drift some fifty years ago. The oral history that Norma Turner provided enhanced my understanding of "Sam Adams" considerably.

After leaving Drift, I drove on up Beaver and over to Big Mud Creek, still in Floyd County, to the home of George Tucker, who is also a folk musician. Mr. Tucker sang "Black Jack Davy," a version of "Barbara Allan" that lasted a good ten minutes, and some other folksongs. After a while, I mentioned my visit with Norma Turner and asked Mr. Tucker if he knew the ballad about Sam Adams. He knew not only the song but, like Ms. Turner, quite a bit about the history of the events it partially describes. After talking with Mr. Tucker and, subsequently, many others, I began to appreciate even more the ballad Norma Turner performed, and I began to see what it might mean to folks in the area. Moreover, I was forced to disagree with the American ballad scholar G. Malcolm Laws, Jr., who believes that "The Death of Samuel Adams" is in doubtful currency in oral tradition.[1]

Laws's failure to recognize "Sam Adams" as a traditional native American ballad and my initial inability to appreciate the song—my weak level of "receptive competence," in other words—point to two important facts: that there is a highly local body of folklore up Left Beaver that requires some scholarly attention, and that this folklore needs to be studied from a regional point of view if it is to be understood fully and appreciated properly. Indeed, the meaning of many specific folkloric performances, such as Norma Turner's, may be obscured or lost completely without an understanding of the sociocultural matrix, or context, in which the performances occur.

It is sometimes difficult to determine the pertinent sociocultural context of a folkloric event, because it may very well exist within a system of contextual concentric circles. For example, Norma Turner's version of "Sam Adams" was performed in the eastern United States, in the South, in the Upland South, in Kentucky, in eastern Kentucky, in the Appalachian highlands of eastern Kentucky, in the Cumberland Plateau, in the Big Sandy Valley, in Floyd County, up the Left Fork of Beaver, in Drift, in a certain neighborhood, and in a particular family's home. All these "regions" (sections, districts, areas, territories) may constitute bases for corresponding ICENs, or folk groups, of which Norma Turner is a part.[2] It appears that the event described in the ballad, though known beyond Floyd County, is not familiar to people throughout the Cumberland Plateau; the Big Sandy Valley region is, then, the crucial sociocultural context of Norma Turner's performance of "Sam Adams."[3] The context is so crucial, in fact, that the ballad does not "exist" outside the region; "Sam Adams" is a truly regional folksong.

Folklorists have long been aware that culture—especially folk culture—exhibits regional variations.[4] Distinctive clusters, groupings, or patterns of such variations constitute folk regions. Regional folklore exists in a reflexive relationship with a particular geographical area: a region shapes folklore, and folklore helps shape a region.[5] The process of studying folklore that displays regional integrity, or "regionalization," by identifying and assembling it and then analyzing it in terms of the sociocultural context that produces and encloses it may be designated "regional folkloristics." Folksongs such as "Black Jack Davy" and "Barbara Allan" appear widely and can be appreciated generally, but a ballad like "Sam Adams" not only invites but demands a region-oriented folkloristic strategy if full understanding is to be achieved.

The concept of regionalism is new neither to social scientists nor to humanists, and although a great deal of confusion surrounds the notion of what, exactly, constitutes a "region," most theorists would agree that "whatever else regionalism may or may not be, its first essence is to be found in the geographic factor. The mudsill of the idea of regionalism is that social phenomena may best be understood when considered in relation to the area in which they occur as a cultural frame of reference."[6] The regional concept has been utilized effectively by sociologists, historians, literary scholars, linguists, anthropologists, ecologists, economists, political scientists, geographers, and others, but, until recently, has lain largely fallow in the theoretical fields of American folklorists.[7] There has of course been quite a bit of folklore *collecting* within regions in the United States, but not very much attention has been paid to regional theory, methodology, or analysis.[8]

Folklorists in America have, however, long recognized the value of the concept of regionalism and have called for its use as a method of folkloric research. For example, Herbert Halpert, after surveying the state of American regional folklore scholarship in 1947, reported that the regional collections, which consisted mostly of songs and beliefs, were little more than lists of texts with inbred notes, and that the collectors failed to provide adequate contextual information for the cultures with which they were concerned. Halpert called for more sophisticated regional studies, remarking that much of past regional folklore work had been done in very broad areas, and that the "need now is to gain a more complete understanding of the folk culture of smaller regions. . . ."[9]

Richard M. Dorson voiced similar criticism twelve years later in the "Regional Collectors" section of "A Theory for American Folklore." Dorson complained that regional folklore scholarship in the United States was "motivated chiefly by convenience and emotional identification with a locality," and that although some of the regional collections were technically excellent, they remained nevertheless "on the level of text-hunting." Dorson urged that American regional collecting "be tied to theoretical questions," and suggested certain works of the sociologist Rupert Vance, the linguist Hans Kurath, and the anthropologist Melville Herskovits as possible theoretical guidelines.[10]

Although the need for a responsible regional approach to folk culture seems to have been established long ago, pleas for a regional folkloristic methodology continue.[11] Clearly, the concept of regionalism can be valuable to American folklorists, but, shelved away, it has gathered considerable dust. Perhaps some of the dust can be whisked away if the problems connected with the relationship between folklore and regionalism are clarified through a consideration of a suitable method for studying regional folklore. Five steps seem basic to such a method: (1) selection of the region, (2) delimitation of and familiarization with the region, (3) careful collection and classification of the folklore, (4) interpretation and analysis of the folklore in relation to its context, and (5) comparison of the folklore with the folklore of other regions.

SELECTION OF THE REGION

As numerous regional studies attest, "there are almost as many regional theories as regional theorists."[12] A maze of varying conceptualizations of "region" confronts anyone studying the literature: "provincial locality," "physical character-istics," "group-of-states," "homogeneous traits," "distinguishing traits," "state of mind," and on and on.[13] This maze may be negotiated through the realization that there are only two basic kinds of regions: ontic (natural, real), and ad hoc (hypothetical, contrived, artificial). Ad hoc regions exist foremost in the minds of "alien" observers and are drawn according to whatever criteria the investigator chooses for their delimitation, whether they be patterns of rainfall, covered bridges, or methods of barbecuing meat. These kinds of regions usually preclude considerations of "group," group consciousness, or folkloric expressions of group consciousness.

Ontic regions, on the other hand, owe their existence to geographical, social, or cultural "facts," such as mountains, rivers, settlement history, or whatever else, and may or may not have within them corresponding cultural groupings. It is, of course, ontic *cultural* patterns or areas that are of interest to folklorists. Cultural geographer Wilbur Zelinsky describes such a region:

Let us define a culture area as a naively perceived segment of the time-space continuum distinguished from others on the basis of genuine differences in cultural systems. The two characteristics that set it aside from other varieties of geographic region are: (1) the extraordinary number of ways in which it is manifested physically and behaviorally; and (2) the condition of self-awareness on the part of participants. . . . One must insist that if self-consciousness is lacking . . . , then we are examining something other than a genuine cultural area.[14]

Regional folklorists, then, are interested in groupings of people who have acquired self-perceived notions of location, identity, differentiation, and homogeneity, and who share common sets of experiences, attitudes, and values that give them a distinct regional character.

Among such regions that have been studied by folklorists are "Little Egypt" in southern Illinois, Michigan's "Upper Peninsula," "Wiregrass" Georgia, "Little Dixie" in Missouri, northern Indiana's Calumet region, the Ozarks, middle Virginia, the Texas Gulf Coast, the Schoharie Hills of New York, and Maryland's eastern shore.

Numerous other regions remain to be studied. In Kentucky alone, for example, there are five physiographic regions, according to the P. P. Karan and Cotton Mather *Atlas of Kentucky*: Jackson Purchase, Western Coal Field, Pennyroyal, Bluegrass, and Mountains. Although these regions are "natural," they do not in every case correspond to cultural groupings. An attempt by a state agency to divide Kentucky into subregions based upon "common problems and goals because of similar geographical conditions and cultural backgrounds" has produced a fifteen-region division much closer to areal cultural patterns. Some of these subregions, such as the Purchase and the inner Bluegrass, are in line with the physiography of the state, but others, like the Pennyrile, are not.

Moreover, it is doubtful that all these areas are true regions. Of the five subregions in eastern Kentucky, for example—Fivco, Gateway, Big Sandy, Kentucky River, and Cumberland Valley—Big Sandy seems to be the only ontic region. I suspect that the others are regions "between places," that is, regions of residual convenience that do not possess true regional character and self-consciousness. Regional folk-cultural research in these and other sections of the state would help determine if they are, in fact, culture areas.

Fieldwork I conducted in the Big Sandy Valley indicates tht Big Sandy is indeed a self-conscious region. Folks "up Sandy" think of themselves as "Big Sandians," have a fairly uniform idea as to the boundaries of the region, and even possess a regional motto: "Big Sandy Against the World (By God)!" And there are, of course, distinctive folk traditions up Sandy that express this regionality.

A regional folklorist, then, should select a self-recognized region, rather than "drawing" one according to single-factor variables. *Is* there a Fivco culture area? A Texas Panhandle cultural region? A San Francisco Bay Area region? A Mississippi Delta region? (According to southerners, the Delta begins in the lobby of the Peabody Hotel in Memphis.) Clearly, folklore materials can teach us much about areal cultural variation in America.

DELIMITATION OF AND
FAMILIARIZATION WITH THE REGION

After choosing a region for investigation, the folklorist should learn as much as possible about the area and its inhabitants. In order to understand the folklore, an investigator must be acquainted with both the physical environment and the sociocultural milieu.

The observer should clearly delimit the region under consideration by determining its boundaries. The best way to do this, as well as to ascertain the nature and strength of identification with the region, is by combining etic (alien, exoteric, objective) observations with emic (native, esoteric, subjective) notions.[15] The perimeter of the region—and the corresponding cluster of folk-cultural variations—may be established most effectively by beginning at the core, the common point of reference or the primary source of shared identity, and proceeding outward until distinctions and factors of identification either cease or become vague and blurry. For example, although the forks of the Big Sandy River head in Virginia and West Virginia, Big Sandians do not consider these sections part of "their" region. Upon crossing Tug Fork to the east or Pine Mountain to the south, one is unequivocally outside Big Sandy. Distinctions are less pronounced to the west, but there is a consensus that Salyersville, which is not "on the waters of Sandy," lies beyond the region. Big Sandians agree that Ashland-Catlettsburg marks the northern boundary of their region.

In an effort to determine what has been variously called the "spirit," "tone," "personality," "character," "nature," and "genre de vie" of the regional group, the folklorist should give careful attention to the collective history, experiences, thoughts, feelings, attitudes, and values of the region. This will enable the investigator to begin to understand the dominant concerns, the ethos, the consciousness, and the world view of the region. World view is expressed through folklore, and folklore, in turn, tends to reinforce and validate world view.[16] This reciprocal process, or reflexive relationship, is central to regional folkloristics, whether the investigator is primarily interested in folklore forms or in the regional group itself. Indeed, there is no better way of understanding a culture area than by studying its folk culture. Traditional speech, art, customs, beliefs, crafts, and literature tell us infinitely more about a group of people than does popular culture, which is largely the same everywhere, or idiosyncratic cultural behavior, which is not shared and is therefore not representative of group behavior. In other words, in order to understand regional folklore one must understand the region, and in order to understand the region one must understand its regional folklore. To understand Delta blues, one must understand the Delta; to know the Delta, one must know Delta blues.

COLLECTION AND CLASSIFICATION
OF THE REGIONAL FOLKLORE

Ideally, all the folklore within a region should be collected in order to determine which items best exhibit areal variation. Since this would be impossible even with a team of collectors, the regional folklorist is forced to concentrate on those items which seem best to represent the regional corpus and reflect the world view of the inhabitants.

Variation in regional folk culture occurs in at least three ways: structurally, stylistically, and thematically. A collector interested in the formal variability of folklore may choose to investigate generic regionalisms, concentrating upon those forms typical of the region (e.g., corridos, I-houses, crab shanties, ice sculptures, or sand paintings).[17] Or the investigator may be primarily concerned with stylistic regionalisms, or with the *manner* in which the folklore is performed ("constructed" in the case of material culture).[18] A third alternative is to study the thematic content of a region's verbal folklore.[19] Through verbal forms—and especially stories and songs—a folklorist is able to discern the major interests and dominant concerns of a folk group.This approach lends itself particularly well to regional analysis, because the subjects of songs and stories—whether the Three Nephites, whaling experiences, dust storms, the mining of coal, or local feuds—can be highly indicative of regional consciousness.

Still another problem to be resolved is the *degree* of the folklore's regionality. While some folklore within a region is not in any sense distinctive, some items, like "Sam Adams," are so region-specific that they simply do not appear, nor are they understood, outside the region. Other items are migratory and exist throughout many regions (or in none at all). Complicating the matter further are local versions of migratory materials (oikotypes) that are in tradition within regions. It is necessary, then, to classify the folklore according to its varying degrees of regionality.[20] A continuum may be employed, at one end of which can be assembled the most regional (enchorial), and at the other, the least regional (nonenchorial) folklore. Clearly, folklore that owes its existence and perpetuation to a particular geographic area is much more indicative of regional consciousness and is more subject to regional interpretation and analysis than is nonenchorial folklore such as "Barbara Allan," "knock-knock" jokes, or the proverb "Haste maskes waste." A distinction should be made, in other words, between regional folklore and the folklore of regions.

INTERPRETATION AND ANALYSIS

Regional folklore must be studied in relation to its regional context; this is the "mudsill" of the idea of regionalism and of regional folkloristics. As pointed out above, both the nature and function of regional folklore are inseparably linked to its physical and cultural environment. The folklore is both product of and stimulant to regional consciousness, and it is this reflexive process which constitutes the primary target of regional folkloristics.

A major interpretive benefit of collecting folklore within a regional frame of reference is that it allows for a more thorough coverage of subjects and genres than does collecting oriented toward individuals or small groups. What we know of Sam Adams, for example, comes from composite narrative portraits provided by several Big Sandians. Moreover, a regional approach brings out cross-generic relationships; the death of Adams is recounted in *both* story (local legends) and song up Sandy. These benefits, as well as the general ones of regional folkloristics, can be illustrated when we look at "Sam Adams" from a Big Sandy point of view.

Persons alien to the region would hear, at most, a "horror" ballad: an unfortunate fellow is cruelly murdered and dismembered, and his killers are found and sent to prison. Obviously, most outsiders would be unfamiliar with Adams, Huster, Auxier, Jack's Creek, and the river that God flooded. The meaning of "foreign band" would be obscure, and the reason for Adams's death would be completely unknown.

Big Sandians, through their common fund of esoteric knowledge and associations—their regional consciousness—would respond to the song much more fully. They would automatically associate Jack's Creek with upper Floyd County and the mining town of Wheelwright, and would know about the extreme isolation and violence that characterized upper Beaver Creek during the twenties. They would know that the coal companies had imported hundreds of European laborers to work in the mines, and that these workers, "who couldn't even talk good English," were thought of as "hunkies" and "damned furrin sons-of-bitches" by many mountaineers. They would know also that Auxier is some thirty miles down Levisa Fork of the Big Sandy River, where the river is wider and more subject to flash flooding.

The ballad is surely more meaningful to Big Sandians than to outsiders; the regional consciousness adds dimension to the collective Big Sandy receptive competence. Familiarity with the geography, characters, and place-names contributes substantially to the coherency of the ballad. The horror of the event is intensified for Big Sandians because it happened close to home and involved local people. Sympathy for the Adams family (Norma Turner was acquainted with Adams's wife), and especially for Adams, who was killed by the "hunkies," is increased considerably. Strong sympathy for Adams in opposition to strengthened racist attitudes toward the foreigners of course heightens tension in the song. For Big Sandians, then, the ballad is both local history and solid, coherent verbal art.

Furthermore, some Big Sandians would perhaps know, as did several persons with whom I talked, that Adams was a "mean," "bad-principled," coal-company-hired "policeman" at Wheelwright, who was relentlessly intolerant of and biased toward the foreign workers. They would know that Huster (sometimes "Schuster") and his "band" of friends were "from around Iran, Turkey, or Russia, or somewhere in there," and that after objecting to being cheated by Adams at poker, Huster was severely "pistol-whipped" by Adams. And they would know that Huster and his friends then moved down-river to Auxier and enticed Adams to join them by writing him that they had found him a job. Norma Turner's ballad, after two introductory stanzas, takes up the story at this point (omitting the fact that pieces of Adams's corpse were found by a young boy while fishing in the river).

Viewed from this perspective, the ballad acquires still new meaning. Sympathy for the *workers* is evoked, and Adams's death is seen as suitable punishment for a racist, bullying thug. Assuming that this crisscrossing of responses exists both individually and collectively throughout the region, the folklore concerning Adams—the song *and* the stories—expresses ambivalent attitudes toward Adams's death. From one perspective, Adams is seen as a hero, victimized while trying to protect the integrity of the region from invading outsiders. From another view, Adams is a villain and an "outlaw" who violates both fundamentalist religious principles and the social order and is duly punished.

The Big Sandy region was going through a period of intense social flux during this decade, and much of its folklore expresses, and perhaps helps mediate, the strong conflict in the minds and hearts of Big Sandians between the freedom and insularity of the frontier and the restraints and cosmopolitanism of "civilization." Clearly, while "Sam Adams" is perhaps meaningless to outsiders, it is distinctly charged with meaning for Big Sandians. And it should also be clear that knowledge of the regional context is absolutely essential to a full understanding of the ballad.

COMPARISON WITH OTHER REGIONS

After the folklore of a region has been collected and interpreted, it should be mapped and collated with other regional collections. As cultural geographer Robert Wildhaber remarks,

> The modern geographical method in folklife may be called a representation of items by cartographical means and therefore a way of looking at these items in their regional surroundings and location, and of drawing those conclusions that can safely be drawn. . . . What you should see in well-drawn maps are culture areas . . . and cultural frontiers . . . , that is, you may see indicated the specialities of a folk-group or of a region, or the influences from and connections with other groups and regions.[21]

The laborious task of mapping American culture—both folk and nonfolk—has been undertaken by the Society for the North American Cultural Survey (SNACS), a consortium of geographers, folklorists, anthropologists, and historians, which has begun work on an atlas of North American cultures. The goals of SNACS and of regional folkloristics are identical: to indicate what is known about the geographic aspects of the traditional cultures of America in their many varied forms and, perhaps equally important, what is yet to be learned.[22] When these goals are achieved, we may come to understand more about how folklore functions in culture, how culture is linked to environment, and how the cultural parts of America are related to the whole.

NOTES

1. G. Malcolm Laws, Jr., *Native American Balladry*, American Folklore Society Bibliographical and Special Series, vol. 1, 2d rev. ed. (Philadelphia: The American Folklore Society, 1964), p. 271. Laws classifies "Sam Adams" as dF 62, the "dF" indicating that the two variants known to him were texts "sung only by people who have since died."

2. ICEN is an acronym for "interactional, communicative and experiential networks." See Beth Blumenreich and Bari Lynn Polonsky, "Re-evaluating the Concept of Group: ICEN as an Alternative," in *Conceptual Problems in Contemporary Folklore Study*, Folklore Forum Bibliographic and Special Series, no. 12, ed. Gerald Cashion (Bloomington: Folklore Forum, 1974), pp.12–17.

3. The Big Sandy Valley region is defined by the Big Sandy River and its tributaries. For both emic and etic descriptions of the region; a fuller discussion of the folklore concerning Sam Adams; a survey of the use of the concept of regionalism by geographers, anthropologists, and folklorists; and an application of the methodology discussed below to the folklore of Big Sandy, see William E.

Lightfoot, "Folklore of the Big Sandy Valley of Eastern Kentucky" (Ph.D. diss., Indiana University, 1976).

4. For a recent discussion of folklore and regionalism, see Suzi Jones, "Regionalization: A Rhetorical Strategy," *Journal of the Folklore Institute* 13 (1976): 105.

5. See Archie Green, "Reflexive Regionalism," *Adena* 3 (1978): 5; and Barre Toelken, "Folklore, Worldview, and Communication," in *Folklore: Performance and Communication*, ed. Dan Ben-Amos and Kenneth S. Goldstein (The Hague: Mouton and Co., 1975), pp. 265-86.

6. Howard W. Odum and Harry E. Moore, *American Regionalism* (New York: Henry Holt and Company, 1938), p. 227.

7. European folklorists have not neglected the regional concept; see, for example, Sigurd Erixon, "Regional European Ethnology," *Folk-Liv* 1 (1937): 89-108. For discussions of the use of the concept of regionalism by various scholarly disciplines, see Odum and Moore, pp. 277-419, and Part III (pp. 215-310) of *Regionalism in America*, ed. Merrill Jensen (Madison and Milwaukee, 1951; reprint, Madison and Milwaukee: The University of Wisconsin Press, 1965).

8. Collections of American regional folklore are far too numerous to list here. For a good bibliography of regional collections in America as well as examples of the folklore of seven regional American groups, see Richard M. Dorson, *Buying the Wind: Regional Folklore in the United States* (Chicago and London: The University of Chicago Press, 1964).

9. Herbert Halpert, "American Regional Folklore," *Journal of American Folklore* 60 (1947): 363.

10. Richard M. Dorson, "A Theory for American Folklore," *Journal of American Folklore* 72 (1959): 200-201.

11. For example, see Maja Bošković-Stulli, "Regional Variations in Folktales," *Journal of the Folklore Institute* 3 (1966): 306; and Jones, 107.

12. Odum and Moore, p. 301.

13. For several more examples, see Odum and Moore, p. 29; Louis Wirth, "The Limitations of Regionalism," in *Regionalism in America*, pp. 382-391; and Rupert Vance, "Region," in *International Encyclopedia of the Social Sciences* (New York: Macmillan, 1968), pp. 377-82.

14. Wilbur Zelinsky, *The Cultural Geography of the United States* (Englewood Cliffs, N.J.: Prentice-Hall, 1973), pp. 112-13.

15. For a recent discussion of emic and etic units of conceptualization, see Pertti J. Pelto and Gretel H. Pelto, *Anthropological Research: The Structure of Inquiry*, 2d rev. ed. (Cambridge: Cambridge University Press, 1978), pp. 54-66.

16. See Toelken, pp. 265-86. World view, perception, and culture can be influenced significantly by environment; see Yi-Fu Tuan, *Topophilia: A Study of Environmental Perception, Attitudes, and Values* (Englewood Cliffs, N.J.: Prentice-Hall, 1974).

17. See, for example, Henry Glassie, *Folk Housing in Middle Virginia: A Structural Analysis of Historic Artifacts* (Knoxville: The University of Tennessee Press, 1975); and *Pattern in the Material Folk Culture of the Eastern United States* (Philadelphia: University of Pennsylvania Monographs in Folklore and Folklife, no. 1, 1969).

18. Alan Lomax is one folklorist who is concerned with stylistic regionalisms; see his *Folk Song Style and Culture*, American Association for the Advancement of Science Publications, no. 88 (Washington, D.C.: American Association for the Advancement of Science, 1968).

19. Among the best collections of American regional verbal folklore are Emelyn E. Gardner, *Folklore from the Schoharie Hills, New York* (Ann Arbor: The University of Michigan Press, 1937); Richard M. Dorson, *Bloodstoppers and*

Bearwalkers: Folk Traditions of the Upper Peninsula (Cambridge, 1952; reprint, Cambridge: Harvard University Press, 1972); Leonard Roberts, *South from Hellfer-Sartin: Kentucky Mountain Folktales* (Lexington, 1955; reprint, Berea, Kentucky: Council of the Southern Mountains, 1964); George B. Carey, *A Faraway Time and Place: Lore of the Eastern Shore* (Washington and New York: Robert B. Luce, 1971); the works of Vance Randolph, which range from *The Devil's Pretty Daughter* (New York: Columbia University Press, 1955) to *Pissing in the Snow and Other Ozark Folktales* (Urbana: University of Illinois Press, 1976); and Patrick B. Mullen, *I Heard the Old Fisherman Say: Folklore of the Texas Gulf Coast* (Austin: University of Texas Press, 1978).

20. Although she overlooks folk speech, which is perhaps most subject to regionalization, Suzi Jones suggests some folklore genres that are particularly susceptible to regional influences; see "Regionalization: A Rhetorical Strategy," pp. 111–18. It is of course *local* speech, legends, ballads, character anecdotes, and techniques that carry the most regional weight.

21. Robert Wildhaber, "Folk Atlas Mapping," in *Folklore and Folklife, An Introduction*, ed. Richard M. Dorson (Chicago: University of Chicago Press), pp. 481–482.

22. This statement, slightly paraphrased here, appears in the prospectus for *The Cultural Patterns of North America: A Cartographic Anthology*, which was prepared by SNACS in September 1977.

Marta Weigle

The Southwest:
A Regional Case Study

The American Southwest may be operationally defined as comprising Arizona, New Mexico, the El Paso, Texas, area, and parts of southern Colorado. Ideally, portions of northern Mexico should also be included, but the rationale is too complex and problematic for adequate discussion below, so the political border between the two countries will be considered an actual barrier. This working perspective follows cultural geographer D. W. Meinig's incisive historical study, *Southwest: Three Peoples in Geographical Change, 1600-1970*. Meinig indicates the main physical boundaries of this territory, which "has tended to be set apart on the west, north, and east by broad zones of difficult country—the Mohave-Sonoran desert, the Colorado River canyonlands, the Southern Rockies, and the Llano Estacado—lands which long were and mostly still are thinly populated."[1] Basically semiarid, the region encompasses climate and life zones ranging from desert to alpine, with few areas readily or consistently hospitable to human habitation. The Gila River, the Rio Grande, and their tributaries have long provided the main foci and support for permanent settlement. Before the late 1800s, Santa Fe, El Paso del Norte, and Tucson were the most important Spanish communities; today, Albuquerque, El Paso, and Phoenix are the key urban centers.

The designation "American Southwest" is clearly ethnocentric, since the area lies north of Mexico and Latin America and is central to the sacred worlds of the various Native Americans who have lived there for centuries. Spanish exploration began in the sixteenth century and colonization in the seventeenth. Mexican rule was established in 1821, and these lands were ceded to the United States by the 1848 Treaty of Guadalupe Hidalgo and the 1853 Gadsden Purchase. Hispanic southern Colorado was detached from northern New Mexico in 1861, and the Arizona Territory established in 1863. Texas achieved statehood in 1845, Colorado in 1876, and New Mexico and Arizona not until 1912.

Until recently, the population of this vast area was relatively sparse. Popularly thought to be tricultural—Indian, Spanish or Mexican, and Anglo—in fact, the Southwest was and is remarkably pluricultural. Early Spanish records document a number of different Indian and Spanish-Mexican-Indian settlers. In 1970, anthropologist Edward H. Spicer tentatively identified forty-two different ethnic groups in the states of Arizona, New Mexico, Sonora, and Chihuahua during the 1960s.[2]

His work was part of an important conference on "Plural Societies in the Southwest," during which various scholars addressed basic interpretive and planning issues raised by such long-standing and persistent cultural diversity. Although folklore received scant notice in these papers, it plays an important role in maintaining and creating this pluralism, and folklorists working in the Southwest can both contribute to and profit from the theoretical and practical questions raised.

When faced with such ethnic complexity, the folklorist finds basic questions of concern, e.g.: How do members of one group perceive and express the differences between themselves and members of other groups? How do they accommodate and manipulate these differences when they are with their own "kind" and when they are interacting with members of other groups? What do people themselves consider the most distinctive features of their own heritage and way of life? When and how do they express these significant features in daily and ceremonial life? Both anthropologists and sociologists have argued for answering such questions in individual rather than collective terms, and some folklorists are developing theory and field studies in these directions.[3] Instead of compiling checklists of traits and genres from ideal, "bounded" groups, they look at the ways individuals negotiate ethnic boundaries "situationally" in their interaction with one another. One's Indian or Chicano or Anglo identity may be less important at the laundromat than at a political rally, for example. This orientation is fairly recent in Southwest studies, however, and the folklorist must cull the available sources to derive an historical sense of the dynamics of multiple ethnic identities and lores and to design new field studies.

Most of the folklore collected to date in the Southwest will not be directly relevant to elucidating dynamic ethnic identities and patterns of interaction. The lore is presumed to be preserved by idealized, isolated, and homogeneous groups of Indians, Hispanos, and Anglos. It is fruitful to reexamine these archival and published materials for evidence of how one group viewed other groups and how the difficulties and delights of interethnic relationships were expressed in song, story, custom, or whatever. Focusing on humor and horror will often uncover "boundary-establishing-and-crossing" expressions in previously collected folklore and local history.

Humor plays with many kinds of natural, social, and intellectual boundaries.[4] Thus, when an Hispano wryly refers to Anglos as *bollos* (sometimes *bolillos*), or rolling pins, when cowboys on the Llano Estacado stage mock Indian fights to amuse each other and frighten tenderfeet, and when Pueblo clowns wear alarm clocks and cameras to burlesque Anglo neighbors and tourists during certain dances, perceived differences are made apparent and differential ethnic identities clarified. Anxieties about interethnic communication and conflict are revealed in serious accounts of "horrors." Navajo stories of the Long Walk period in the 1860s tell of a people beleaguered by Anglos, Mexicans, and other Indian tribes. Except for the Long Walk itself, much of this narrative is comparable to Hispanic and Anglo tales of pillage, ambush, raid, enslavement, captivity, and massacre. An especially promising area of investigation in this regard would be to explore documented cases of witchcraft trials involving interethnic accusations. For example, in 1733, a Spanish couple brought charges against an Indian from Isleta Pueblo who had apparently given them a peyote-based mixture to drink. After investigation, lashes were administered to the chief sorcerer of the Pueblo, who allegedly commanded both Indian and Spanish souls.[5] Humor and "horrors" are both playful and serious expressions of interethnic differences and important factors in determining ethnic boundaries as understood and manipulated by the people involved.

Government agencies and universities have sometimes sponsored research important to folklorists investigating inter- and intra-ethnic identification and communication in the Southwest. From 1949 to 1955, Harvard University's Laboratory of Social Relations sponsored a "Comparative Study of Values in Five Cultures" project in western New Mexico. Anthropologist Clyde Kluckhohn's heuristic summary analysis of "expressive activities" covers dimensions of concern to folklorists, namely: the arts, recreation, sports, games, humor, aesthetic standards, and emotional expression among Navajos, Zunis, Spanish-Americans, Mormons, and Texan homesteaders who inhabit the same general area.[6] In the early 1960s, the New Mexico Rural Health Survey sponsored fieldwork on contrasting Hispano and Anglo health-disease systems, and handbooks were prepared to help public health officials trying to implement modern medical programs in rural areas. The extensive literature on bilingual-bicultural education is also well worth consideration.

The WPA federal arts projects in the late 1930s and early 1940s are very important sources for regional folklorists. In general, the publications of both state and national art, music, theater, and writers' projects (and to a lesser extent the Historical Records Survey) represent only a small portion of the local history, folklore, and folklife collected by fieldworkers and edited by office personnel in-state and in Washington. For example, research in two Santa Fe repositories for Federal Writers' Project documents uncovered several hundred manuscripts describing nearly every aspect of Hispano folklife and lore in northern New Mexico. Some two hundred of these had been collected, transcribed, translated, and composed by one bilingual, bicultural fieldworker, Lorin W. Brown. Interviews with Brown and further investigations showed that little of this valuable documentation was published, and much of it had been ignored or unfairly criticized by FWP officials in Santa Fe and Washington.[7] Work comparing what was published or prepared for publication and what was submitted and filed could thus provide evidence for both "official" and "folk" conceptions of folklore, ethnic identities, and possibly the Southwest as a whole.

Besides rereading and reviewing archival and published sources to develop a processual view of the multiple ethnic lores in the Southwest, folklorists must also investigate the region as a whole. Is there a continuing or recently emerging southwestern identity? Officially, politically, administratively, and analytically, there have been various "Southwests" recognized for many years, but these are generally outsiders' conceptions or convenient labels.[8] The folklorist's challenge is to discover whether there have been or are now coming to be "native" or "folk" or "unofficial" conceptions of the region, which are expressed symbolically and manipulated by residents as well as outsiders. In other words, is there a southwestern folklore or only folklore from the Southwest? Is there an identifiable, traceable, and analyzable southwestern expressive culture that transcends ethnic, political, occupational, and other groupings? This is much more difficult to document, and little if any fieldwork has been oriented in this direction.

Historically, one must look first at the Spanish borderlands, particularly the mission system and policies, with respect to Indians and land grants. These attempts at colonization and administration still mark the region in everything from place-names and language forms to land and water adjudication, which figure prominently in many residents' sense of "The Southwest." However, a possible "northern provincial" folklore in the seventeenth, eighteenth, and early nineteenth centuries has yet to be investigated, although imaginative research requiring linguistic and paleographic skills might delineate some features. Church visitation reports, travel accounts, and some civil records would provide likely sources, as would extant material culture. The reconstructed expressive culture of these northern provinces might then be compared to expressive cultures in other parts of early Mexico that are better documented from a folklorist's standpoint.

Guidebooks and travelogues from both the nineteenth and twentieth centuries are also important for identifying and tracing a southwestern expressive culture. Journalists like Charles Fletcher Lummis describing *Some Strange Corners of Our Country: The Wonderland of the Southwest* in 1892, writers like Agnes C. Laut reporting a trip *Through Our Unknown Southwest* in 1913, the editors of *Look Magazine* presenting the 1947 *Look at America: The Southwest*, and the anonymous compilers of railroad, Chamber of Commerce, automobile and travel guides all contribute to an imposed (and often accepted) definition and sense of region. Such materials and the people who read, use, and act in terms of them affect and sometimes effect southwesterners' expressions of themselves and their region's distinctiveness. In fact, tourism is an important economic factor in the Southwest and a powerful influence on all expressive cultures there.[9] To date, however, little has been done to describe the extent and nature of such influences upon either regional or ethnic customs and lore.

The Southwest also boasts a rich literary and artistic tradition. Both artists and writers have produced creative and interpretive pieces about the region. In many ways, such interpreters are intuitive folklorists interweaving library research, direct observation, local history, folklore, and revealing personal "field" experiences to present a coherent, compelling picture of a distinctive expressive culture in the region. Thus, when Erna Fergusson contends that "the arid Southwest has always been too strong, too indomitable for most people"—a land "infinitely productive of the imponderables" and a "wilderness where a man may get back to the essentials of being a man,"[10] she is not only a literary artisan but also a "folklorist" who has long heard such values expressed in various ways by her fellow native New Mexicans. Similar interpretive essays by noted writers such as Mary Austin, Edwin Corle, Harvey Fergusson, Paul Horgan, Oliver La Farge, Haniel Long, and Frank Waters have helped shape at least Anglo notions of a southwestern expressive culture and way of life.

Interpretive southwestern studies have a further significance in the search for regional folklore. These impressionistic accounts sometimes resemble an informant's ruminations and reminiscences and may thus suggest ways to conduct, record, and analyze both formal interviews and informal field observations. For example, Haniel Long's "Stories by Way of Epilogue" to his 1941 *Piñon Country* can be viewed as typifying the memorates, anecdotes, and observations a field-worker might expect to hear and elicit in conversations with Anglo southwesterners and maybe Hispanos as well. Long devotes most of this final chapter to recounting his own and his friends' experiences with various Indians, ranging from a Pueblo boy's first encounter with a toilet seat to mention of several myths and tales that demonstrate Indians' close involvement with nature. Long's

Hispano narratives center on language differences, politics, folk medicine, and folk religion, while the Anglo stories deal with an English "land grab," Mormon honesty, and a Czech murder case on Barela Mesa. While each narrative individually may not be emblematic of "The Southwest," all together they suggest underlying conversational patterns of both appreciation and concern (with land, with water, with cultural differences) that characterize the talk and behavior of those who consider themselves southwesterners. Of course, not all interpreters of the Southwest are as clearly "colloquial" as Long attempts to be, but careful analysis of interpretive essays can contribute significantly to field and analytical studies of a common regional expressive culture.[11]

Celebrations should also be studied as possible manifestations of a southwestern expressive culture. State fairs, rodeos, and fiestas are all occasions likely to elaborate important common values and symbols of the region. For example, civic and religious celebrations in Santa Fe, New Mexico, known as La Fiesta de Santa Fe and formerly held on Labor Day weekend, vividly dramatize both ethnic and community identities. Among the events are the burning of Zozobra ("Old Man Gloom")—a 1920s creation of local artist Will Shuster—a melodrama satirizing current city and state affairs, parades, the crowning of a fiesta queen (a Spanish woman with an ethnically mixed court), masses and public religious processions, and a public pageant reenacting the *entrada* of Don Diego de Vargas into Santa Fe after his supposedly "bloodless" reconquest of the city in 1692. Religion scholar Ronald L. Grimes has traced the history of these carefully orchestrated and consciously elaborated events and analyzed their significance as the expressions of "a uniquely symbol-conscious city." (Note that in many respects the Southwest may be "a uniquely symbol-conscious" region.) He finds that "artists, politicians, Indians, and non-Hispano groups also have considerable interest in the natural, religious, civic, and ethnic symbols of these celebrations, even though Indian and Anglo participation in them is not as central as Hispano involvement."[12] Such occasions can thus be viewed as expressive microcosms of the Southwest.

By most definitions, the American Southwest is a borderland region marked by environmental adversity and persistent cultural diversity. Both the land and the people have attracted scholars, artists, and interpreters of every description. Folklorists studying the area face a dual task: first, to describe, trace, and analyze inter- and intra-ethnic processes of artistic communication and group identity, and second, to identify, trace, and analyze folk expressions of regional identity and to compare them with official and analytic conceptions. Today more than ever, perhaps, in this rapidly changing, so-called energy-producing, Sun Belt area, there is a need to understand plural societies and meaningful regional identities and dynamics that can inform public policy and individual living strategies. This is a challenging enterprise to which folklorists should make substantial contributions while at the same time furthering knowledge in their own and related fields.

NOTES

1. D. W. Meinig, *Southwest: Three Peoples in Geographical Change, 1600–1970* (New York: Oxford University Press, 1971), p. 6. See also his "American Wests:

Preface to a Geographical Interpretation," *Annals of the Association of American Geographers* 62 (1972): 159–84.

2. Edward H. Spicer, "Plural Society in the Southwest," in *Plural Society in the Southwest*, ed. Edward H. Spicer and Raymond H. Thompson (Albuquerque: University of New Mexico Press, 1972), p. 31.

3. Cf., e.g., Stephen Stern, "Ethnic Folklore and the Folklore of Ethnicity," *Western Folklore* 36 (1977): 7–32. See also the case study of a Mexican-American woman by Rosan A. Jordan, "Ethnic Identity and the Lore of the Supernatural," *Journal of American Folklore* 88 (1975): 370–82. Studies heuristic to folklorists are also in E. Lamar Ross, ed., *Interethnic Communication*, Southern Anthropological Society Proceedings, no. 12 (Athens: University of Georgia Press, 1978).

4. Cf., e.g., Mary Douglas, "The Social Control of Cognition: Some Factors in Joke Perception," *Man*, n.s. 3 (1968): 361–76; Walter P. Zenner, "Joking and Ethnic Stereotyping," *Anthropological Quarterly* 43 (1970): 93–113. For South Texas Mexican-American examples, see Américo Paredes, "Folk Medicine and the Intercultural Jest," in *Spanish-Speaking People in the United States*, ed. June Helm (Seattle: University of Washington Press for the American Ethnological Society, 1968), pp. 104–19.

5. Marc Simmons, *Witchcraft in the Southwest: Spanish and Indian Supernaturalism on the Rio Grande* (Flagstaff, Ariz.: Northland Press, 1974), pp. 30–32. Navajo "horrors" are recounted in *Navajo Stories of the Long Walk Period* (Tsaile, Ariz.: Navajo Community College Press, 1973), a collection of oral narratives in which, according to project supervisor Ruth Roessel, "for the first time, Navajo history is looked at, interpreted and presented by Navajos for Navajos."

6. Clyde Kluckhohn, "Expressive Activities," in *People of Rimrock: A Study of Values in Five Cultures*, ed. Evon Z. Vogt and Ethel M. Albert (Cambridge, Mass.: Harvard University Press, 1966), pp. 265–98.

7. Lorin W. Brown, with Charles L. Briggs and Marta Weigle, *Hispano Folklife of New Mexico: The Lorin W. Brown Federal Writers' Project Manuscripts* (Albuquerque: University of New Mexico Press, 1978), pp. 19–29 and *passim*.

8. For a cogent review of such constructs, see Vernon Carstensen, "The Development and Application of Regional-Sectional Concepts, 1900–1950," in *Regionalism in America*, ed. Merrill Jensen (Madison and Milwaukee: University of Wisconsin Press, 1951), pp. 99–115. This symposium also included a paper by John W. Caughey, "The Spanish Southwest: An Example of Subconscious Regionalism," pp. 173–86.

9. Cf., e.g., Valene L. Smith, ed., *Hosts and Guests: The Anthropology of Tourism* (Philadelphia: University of Pennsylvania Press, 1977); William Wroth, ed., *Hispanic Crafts of the Southwest* (Colorado Springs: The Taylor Museum of the Colorado Springs Fine Arts Center, 1977); and Charles L. Briggs, *The Wood Carvers of Córdova, New Mexico: Social Dimensions of an Artistic "Revival"* (Knoxville: University of Tennessee Press, 1980).

10. Erna Fergusson, *Our Southwest* (New York: Alfred A. Knopf, 1940), pp. 18–19. Also see her *New Mexico: A Pageant of Three Peoples* (1951; rev. ed., Albuquerque: University of New Mexico Press, 1973).

11. Besides Haniel Long, *Piñon Country*, American Folkways Series (New York: Duell, Sloan and Pearce, 1941), and Erna Fergusson (op. cit.), see, e.g.: Ross Calvin, *Sky Determines: An Interpretation of the Southwest* (1934; rev. ed., Albuquerque: University of New Mexico Press, 1965); Edwin Corle, *Desert Country*, American Folkways Series (New York: Duell, Sloan and Pearce, 1941); idem, *The Gila: River of the Southwest*, Rivers of America Books (New York: Rinehart and Company, 1951); idem, *Listen, Bright Angel: A Panorama of the Southwest* (New York: Duell, Sloan and Pearce, 1946); Harvey Fergusson, *Rio Grande* (New York: Alfred A. Knopf, 1933); Paul Horgan, *The Heroic Triad: Essays in the Social Energies of*

Three Southwestern Cultures (New York: Meridian Books, World Publishing Company, 1971); Frank Waters, *The Colorado*, Rivers of America Books (New York: Rinehart and Company, 1946). Useful background on most such interpreters can be found in Van Deren Coke, *Taos and Santa Fe: The Artist's Environment, 1882–1942* (Albuquerque: University of New Mexico Press, 1963), and Marta Weigle and Kyle Fiore, *Santa Fe and Taos: The Writer's Era, 1916–1941* (Santa Fe: Ancient City Press, 1982).

12. Ronald L. Grimes, *Symbol and Conquest: Public Ritual and Drama in Santa Fe, New Mexico* (Ithaca, N. Y.: Cornell University Press, 1976), p. 22. See also James S. Griffith, " 'Tucson, Meet Yourself': A Festival as Community Building," *Southwest Folklife* 1 (Winter 1977): 1–7. For other approaches, see, e.g.: Robert Jerome Smith, "Festivals and Celebrations," in *Folklore and Folklife, An Introduction*, ed. Richard M. Dorson (Chicago: University of Chicago Press, 1972), pp. 159–72; idem, *The Art of the Festival*, University of Kansas Publications in Anthropology, no. 6 (Lawrence, Kansas, 1975); Roger D. Abrahams and Richard Bauman, "Ranges of Festival Behavior," in *The Reversible World: Symbolic Inversion in Art and Society*, ed. Barbara A. Babcock (Ithaca, New York: Cornell University Press, 1978), pp. 193–208.

Jan Harold Brunvand

Regional Folk Speech and Sayings

Newcomers living among the Mormons in my home state of Utah are often confused and bemused by things they hear the Latter-day Saints saying. Why do they speak of going to an "LDS steak house" or to the "ward" on the "Lard's day" for worship? What are "ZCMI" and "Deseret Industries," where Utahans may go shopping? Why are Jews called "gentiles" here? And in a car, where is the "jockey box," in which the map is kept on a drive down to "Dixie" or to "the Four Corners"?

Gradually—if they stay long enough in Utah—repeated local usage and explanations will clarify these expressions and others for the outsider. "Stake" (not "steak") and "ward" are units of LDS (Latter-day Saint) congregational organization. The Lord becomes "Lard" following a typical pattern of regional pronunciation. "ZCMI" (or just "ZC") stands for "Zion's Cooperative Mercantile Institution," a large department store with several branches, which is the outgrowth of a church effort, started in 1869, to counteract the influence of "gentile" (i.e., non-Mormon) businessmen in the Saints' promised land, or "Zion." "Deseret" is a *Book of Mormon* word meaning honeybee, and the beehive is still the Utah state symbol, signifying cooperation and hard work; the motto surmounting the hive on the state seal is "Industry." Like the word "Zion," "Deseret" is frequently used in Utah for business names. "Deseret Industries" operates a thrift shop based on donations of used goods as part of the LDS church welfare program. "Jockey box," only occasionally heard nowadays for the "glove compartment" in cars, is a survival of a term for the supply box on pioneer wagons. Southeastern Utah is called "Dixie" because of its warm climate and early attempts to grow cotton there, and in the far southeastern corner of the state there is a unique coming together of the boundaries of four states: Utah, Colorado, New Mexico, and Arizona.

Thus do local geography, culture, and history contribute to the formation and retention of folk speech (more accurately, "dialect"), the traditional variation in spoken language from standard usage taught in school and used in formal discourse. It is speech characteristic of members of folk groups when communicating among themselves, whether the groups are defined by age, social status, occupation, region, religion, or other factors. Folk speech includes variations in pronunciation ("greasy" vs. "greazy" or "wash" vs. "worsh"), in vocabulary ("cherry pit" vs. "seed" or "stone"), and in grammar ("dived" vs. "dove" or "div"). The study of folk speech to some extent also includes place-names, salutations, replies, intensifiers, swearing, euphemisms, slang, the jargon of professions and trades, and some proverbial expressions.

Since everyone grows up as a native speaker of one or more regional or social dialects, most travelers have had similar experiences to those of the typical newcomer to Utah. Even within one's own folk group or groups, a person may note folk speech simply by paying close attention to special terms and usages in the context of group interaction. These nonstandard speech patterns reflect the larger context of folk groups' oral, customary, or material traditions. Therefore, as a Utah folklorist, I am less interested in local speech itself than in folk expressions appearing in such forms as tales, songs, games, or the folk names for handmade artifacts.

For example, as a newcomer myself to Utah some years ago, and as a "gentile," I felt some puzzlement in collecting stories about young Mormons' missionary experiences, which are often told by "return missionaries." I soon learned (with the help of my folklore students) some of the special vocabulary of the group: new missionaries in the field are called "greenies"; much of their time is spent "tracting" (distributing religious tracts door-to-door); and they seek "golden contacts," people who are ripe for conversion to the LDS faith. Missionaries often ask the "Golden Questions": What do you know about Mormonism? Would you like to learn more? When missionaries are close to their time for returning home, they are said to be "riding the trunks." Since missionaries abide strictly by the *Word of Wisdom*, some of them make use of sham swearing, also called "missionary swearing," like "cheese and rice got damp in the cellar!" (Say it fast and you will understand how it allows for letting off steam in a vocalization close to "real" swearing, but without breaking the commandment.) All of this prepared me to understand and appreciate an inside joke about a pope who died and went to heaven; he was asked by St. Peter about what progress the Mormons were making on earth, but he confessed to not knowing much about this group. St. Peter, evidently a *true* "Saint," responded, "Would you like to learn more?"[1]

In the general context of Utah's predominant religion, I detected many traditional usages, which I defined and alphabetized on cards as a flexible working glossary of the folk speech likely to be encountered in other Utah folklore. Appointed church leaders, for instance, are termed "bishops," "counselors," and "patriarchs." "Primary" and "Mutual" (the "Mutual Improvement Association," abbreviated "MIA") are the children's and youth's religious-education and social groups.

Phrases that have moved from formal religious contexts to everyday use are "to bear my testimony" (declaring one's personal witness to the faith) and "the laying on of hands" (healing by the prayerful blessing of one who holds the priesthood). Missionaries are warned in cautionary tales against "shaking the dust from their feet" (following a biblical example), a forbidden means of cursing places that show strong anti-Mormon tendencies.[2] The "Three Nephites," people whose history is in the *Book of Mormon*, are the subject of a widespread oral legend cycle. Besides the town of "Nephi," other Utah place-names that echo the *Book of Mormon* include "Moroni" and "Lehi," while early LDS leaders are commemorated by the names "Brigham City" and "Heber City."

Anti-Mormonism as well as the impartial observations of outsiders in Utah and surrounding states have added to folk speech such terms as "Mormon buckskin" for baling wire, "Mormon iron" for rawhide, "Mormon dip" for a bland milk gravy, and "Mormon tangle" for a packer's knot. All these phrases reflect the notion of Mormons as sometimes inept frontiersmen trying to make do with available resources. More complimentary terms are "Mormon shovel" (used in irrigating crops) and "Mormon derrick" (a hay stacker), both referring to the positive LDS contributions to ranching and farming in the arid Great Basin. Some gentile westerners refer to "land fit only for sagebrush and Mormons," or they say about anyone's quick departure, "He took off like a Mormon on a mission." Along similar lines, the Mormons themselves refer to less-than-devout Latter-day Saints as "Jack Mormons," and a drink of hot water with cream and sugar (to satisfy the *Word of Wisdom* prohibition against stimulating beverages) is called "Mormon coffee" or "Mormon tea." A restorative herbal tea made from a local plant is known as "Brigham tea," and any sweet nonalcoholic drink served at LDS receptions is "Mormon punch."

Many Utah speech patterns are not tied to religious practice or belief. The community names "Provo," "Ogden," and "Escalante," for example, are drawn from non-Mormon pioneers. Local people, whether Mormon or not, pronounce the place-names "Heber" and "Weber" (a county and a river) as "Hee'-ber" and "Wee'-ber"; the town of "Toole" is pronounced "Two-ill'-uh"; "Hurricane," a town in southern Utah, has the last syllable slurred to "-kin." (One folk etymology attributes the name Hurricane to an actual big wind storm during the period of pioneer settlement, while another tale humorously relates the region to the Garden of Eden and the name to a cry from the departing occupants, "Hurry, Cain!") Sections of Salt Lake City are called "Swedetown" (because of early residents there), "the Avenues" (because of local street-naming patterns), and "the East Bench" (for topographic reasons). The whole Salt Lake Valley is sometimes called "Happy Valley," in ironic reference to prevailing LDS positive thinking.

While folklorists may elicit items of folk speech in interview situations by asking about odd expressions in oral texts or by questioning local people concerning cultural institutions, they may hear many other terms in the course of everyday life. In either case, when one records, the context of use should always be noted. For example, in Utah the terms "elastic" for rubber bands and "bottling" for canning or preserving foods are current in daily office or home use and occasionally appear in journalism or advertising. The expression "to sluff school" is used orally as well as in official directives against "playing hookey" or "skipping," as the practice may be termed elsewhere. Youngsters talk of working as "baby tenders" (rather than "sitters"), and so do their employers. Not only the young or slightly educated in Utah pronounce "picture" as "pitcher": a local FM radio station announces the playing of the musical work "Pitchers from an Exhibition." Policemen and broadcast journalists here, like the rest of the folk, usually speak of "vee'-hickles" in their accident reports. Such contextual notes help establish the general currency of folk expressions in a community.

Probably the most obvious Utahism is the frequent reversal of the vowel sounds "a" and "o" before the consonant "r." Just how this came about is not clear, but evidently it has become something of a prestige dialect trait among Utah Mormons. In their speech "horse" becomes "harse," "fork" becomes "fark," and the words "barn" and "born" reverse their usual pronunciations so that a proverbial expression is rendered in Utah as "Were you barn in a born?" The term "ward" so often used by Mormons rhymes with "hard," as illustrated in a couplet from the Utah folksong "Echo Canyon": "Our camp is united, we all labor hard, / And if we are faithful, we'll gain our reward." This "horse/harse" syndrome has led to sample statements that circulate in oral tradition to show "how they talk in Utah." People are supposed to have said, "Let's go to the ward and warship the Lard" and, less believably (since there are variants), "Good Lard, Darthy, what a gargeous arange argandy farmal!" The towns of "American Fork" and "Spanish Fork" both become "Farks"; musicians play the "horpsicard"; and phrases like "hard core pornography" come out strangely mangled in much Utah speech. Thus the study of this folk speech phenomenon should become a unified inquiry into actual usage plus the other folklore spinoffs and echoes of it.

Besides using localized folk speech as one marker of distinctive traditional culture patterns, researchers also study dialect as an important trait distinguishing or defining a larger region. This kind of research attracts both folklorists and language specialists, and students of regional folk speech should familiarize themselves with some of their methods and findings.

The American Dialect Society was founded in 1889, the year after the organization of the American Folklore Society, for the specific purpose of fostering regional speech studies. Prominent charter members included George Lyman Kittredge and William Wells Newell (first president of AFS). The ballad scholar Francis James Child was first president of the ADS, and folklorist Louise Pound first editor of the society's journal, *American Speech*, in 1925 and later president of the society. She characterized the fields of folklore and dialect this way: "Surely dialect is a species of folklore, though the two subjects are usually treated independently."[3]

Research in American dialects investigates deviations from British usage, borrowings from other languages, specialized vocabularies, social stratification of speech, and especially "linguistic geography"—the distribution of regional speech patterns. An early and highly influential endeavor was H. L. Mencken's book *The American Language*.[4] Collecting terms from published sources produced such useful references as Mathews's *Dictionary of Americanisms*,[5] but most effort has focused on the living language, sampled by questionnaires or interviews and analyzed with statistical methods. The results are often publications that tally and map the findings in great detail.[6] A useful summarizing work is Hans Kurath's *A Word Geography of the Eastern United States*.[7] Eastern American folk speech, Kurath shows, includes variant terms for older rural and household items like andirons (sometimes called "fire dogs"), frying pans (called "spiders" in some areas), and burlap bags (variously termed "grass sacks," "crocker sacks," or "tow sacks"). After such variations are recorded on maps, "isoglosses" (usage areas) are drawn, and where several isoglosses coincide, a "dialect boundary" is marked.

Linguistic geographers' findings may be used by folklorists for identifying areas where a highly localized folk tradition might exist. Richard M. Dorson, for example, was attracted to a Maine community for fieldwork by the "relic" speech areas described in the *Linguistic Atlas of New England*.[8] An excellent job of collaboration by a folklorist with a linguistic geographer is Vance Randolph and George P. Wilson's work on Ozark folk speech.[9] This dialect is found throughout Randolph's many collections of tales, songs, superstitions, and other forms, so in this folk speech survey the authors frequently elucidate usages by quoting folk texts. For example, two methods of swinging a girl in a square dance are known in the Ozarks as "biscuits" (waist-swinging) and "cornbread" (hand-swinging). This explains a line in an old dance call that goes, "Meet your pardner, pat her on the head, / If she don't like biscuits, feed her cornbread."

A formal linguistic-geography approach to western American speech is Atwood's *The Regional Vocabulary of Texas*,[10] in which the author reports responses to typical questionnaire items like "Name for male bovine (with original equipment)," which yielded the variants "bull," "surly," euphemistically "male," and, in the Southwest portion, "toro." A larger word list, but without precise identification of sources and distribution, is Adams's *Western Words*.[11] Adams defines both "surly" and "toro," but he also includes many combinations with the word "bull," such as the logging terms "bull chain," "bull cook," "bull donkey" (an engine), and "bull prick" (a metal tool); the cowboy terms "bulldog," "bull hides" (heavy leather chaps), and "bull nurse" ("a cowboy who accompanies cattle on the train to their ultimate destination"); and the more general terms "bull cheese" (sliced dried buffalo meat), "bullwhacker" (freight-wagon driver), and "bull whip." In *The Cowboy Says It Salty*[12] Adams gathered sayings mentioning bulls: "as far as I could throw a bull by the tail," "as full of pride as a bull is of wind in corn time," and "snorin' like a choked bull." Such glossaries and studies should be checked against specific local usages within a region. For example, neither Atwood's systematic study nor Adams's wide-ranging surveys include the name "bull fence," sometimes heard in Utah as an alternative for "rip gut," a fence made of branches or tree roots woven together. A folklorist's essay on American pioneer fences, although containing valuable dated quotations and descriptions of such types as "brush fence," "cactus fence," "sod fence," and "worn fence," also lacks "bull fence."[13] Even from this very limited example, it is clear that some regional folk speech patterns have not yet been collected by the specialists; that is, there is still work for local folklore collectors to do.

When larger-scale systematic fieldwork in linguistic geography for the Rocky Mountain area is attempted, certain special conditions must be allowed for. The settlement period is much shorter than in the East or South, and many older people who might be prime informants in other regions moved west as adults and are not native speakers of local dialect. The student who wishes to work in the area will find that some standard questionnaire items about flora, fauna, and geography are inappropriate for the West, while terms like "aspen," "potgut" (a name for ground squirrel), "gulch," and "arroyo" must be added. And finally, as dialect specialists have written, "One of the most important problems in any large-scale study of the Rocky Mountain area is the way in which the various streams of culture from further east have met and intermingled against a new geographical background."[14]

For folklorists working on dialect and folk speech in any region, problems of linguistic questionnaire design, informant selection, and data analysis are not crucial, since what they want from folk speech material is additional indicators of traditional attitudes and the folkloric genres typical of communities. Western folk comparisons collected in Colorado that reflect range and ranch life, for example, are "lost as a dogie," "loco as a steer," "knee-high to a jack rabbit," and "chuckleheaded as a prairie dog." A proverbial saying about riding broncs comments on excessive pride: "There ain't no horse that can't be rode; there ain't no cowboy [or 'buckaroo'] that can't be throwed." Common phrases in the western vernacular include "to hit the trail," "to dry gulch," and "to head for the high country." Some typical sayings heard recently in Nevada are "to put a burr under your saddle," "as busy as a horse's tail in fly time," and "a long rope and a hot iron." The last expression refers to cattle rustling and is employed in the opening verse of a folksong from Arizona: "I used to make money a-runnin' wild cattle, / In them good old days 'fore the business went wrong, / When a hot runnin' iron and a good long riata / Was all that was needed to start you along."[15]

All regions have distinctive folk-group speech and dialects, which might be collected as demonstrated here for Utah and the Mountain West. A good beginning is to compile special glossaries. Menu terms, children's talk, the jargon of sports or hobbies, and teenage slang are all promising subjects. A euphemism, such as "Rocky Mountain two step" for diarrhea, might be "green apple quick step," "Montezuma's revenge," "Delhi belly," or simply "travelers' disease" elsewhere. The speech of immigrants and the related dialect stories should be collected. Several states have "panhandles," while other local folk place-names are "the Eastern Shore" (Maryland), "The City" (New York), "The Big Bend" (Texas), and "The U.P." (Michigan's upper peninsula). State residents' nicknames include "Webfoot" (Oregon), "Hoosier" (Indiana), and "Sooner" (Oklahoma).

Folk speech, like all folklore, is not just old words found in isolated regions. Many college students have discovered, in the process of trying to collect others' folklore, that they themselves employ folk speech in such forms as abbreviations for campus buildings ("SUB" for Student Union Building), terms for passing tests ("to CLEP out" for taking tests in the College-Level Examination Program), expressions for flattering a teacher ("to brown nose"), and nicknames for courses ("Rocks for Jocks" is beginning geology).

Folk speech may be defined simply as the language used by anyone communicating within a folk group, and the study of folk speech begins with the systematic collection of the language and its contexts, a job that local folklore enthusiasts may helpfully perform.

NOTES

1. See Jan Harold Brunvand, "As the Saints Go Marching By: Modern Jokelore Concerning Mormons," *Journal of American Folklore* 83 (1970): 53-60; and *A Guide for Collectors of Folklore in Utah* (Salt Lake City: University of Utah Press, 1971).

2. See Roger M. Thompson, "The Decline of Cedar Key: Mormon Lore in North Florida and Its Social Function," *Southern Folklore Quarterly* 39 (1975): 39-62.

3. Louise Pound, "Folklore and Dialect," *California Folklore Quarterly* 4 (1945): 146-53; quoted from the reprint in *Nebraska Folklore* (Lincoln: University of Nebraska Press, 1959), p. 211.

4. Published in 1919 and revised or supplemented several times. See the abridgment by Raven I. McDavid, Jr. (New York: Alfred A. Knopf, 1963).

5. Mitford M. Mathews, *A Dictionary of Americanisms on Historical Principles* (Chicago: University of Chicago Press, 1951).

6. See Hans Kurath, *Linguistic Atlas of New England*, 3 vols. (Providence, R. I.: Brown University Press, 1939-43); Harold B. Allen, *The Linguistic Atlas of the*

Upper Midwest, 3 vols. (Minneapolis: University of Minnesota Press, 1973); and Gordon R. Wood, *Vocabulary Change: A Study of Variations in Regional Words in Eight of the Southern States* (Carbondale and Edwardsville: Southern Illinois University Press, 1971).

7. Hans Kurath, *A Word Geography of the Eastern United States* (Ann Arbor: University of Michigan Press, 1949).

8. See Richard M. Dorson, *American Folklore* (Chicago: University of Chicago Press, 1959), p. 122.

9. Vance Randolph and George P. Wilson, *Down in the Holler: A Gallery of Ozark Folk Speech* (Norman: University of Oklahoma Press, 1953).

10. E. Bagby Atwood, *The Regional Vocabulary of Texas* (Austin: University of Texas Press, 1962).

11. Ramon F. Adams, *Western Words: A Dictionary of the American West*, rev. ed. (Norman: University of Oklahoma Press, 1968).

12. Ramon F. Adams, *The Cowboy Says It Salty* (Tucson: University of Arizona Press, 1971).

13. Mamie Meredith, "The Nomenclature of American Pioneer Fences," *Southern Folklore Quarterly* 15 (1951): 109–51.

14. Marjorie M. Kimmerle, Raven I. McDavid, Jr., and Virginia Glenn McDavid, "Problems of Linguistic Geography in the Rocky Mountain Area," *Western Humanities Review* 5 (1951): 264.

15. From "The Cowman's Troubles" composed by Gail Gardner and sung by him on *Cowboy Songs*, Arizona Friends of Folklore Limited Editions, no. 33-1 (Flagstaff, Arizona, [1972]).

Edward D. Ives

The Study of Regional Songs and Ballads

Anyone who collects English-language folksongs within a particular area will find that most of that area's repertoire is not indigenous but imported.[1] Most songs, in fact, will have come to this country with the settlers from Great Britain. These will include the so-called Child ballads like "Lord Randal" and "Barbara Allan" and the later and more popular broadsides like "The Wexford Lass" and "The Battle of Waterloo." Other songs, most of them modeled on the broadsides, will be of American origin, such as Civil War pieces like "The *Cumberland*'s Crew," occupational pieces like "The Jam on Gerry's Rock," or murder ballads like "Henry Green." In addition, there will be late nineteenth- and early twentieth-century parlor and sentimental songs like "The Baggage Coach Ahead" and "The Black Sheep," and even more recently composed country-and-western pieces. All such songs, as I say, will have come to the area from elsewhere, but always there will be some pieces that (the collector will be told) were made up "right around here," often by some readily identified songmaker. Frequently these will be humorous or satirical in tone and full of references and allusions that make sense only to local people "in the know," but often enough, they will be ballads or sentimental pieces on the imported models. It is these various kinds of locally composed songs that will be discussed here.

To begin with, we should not think of local songs so much as belonging to a special genre as sharing a special provenience. Every song was a local song once, but most of the older ballads have shed their origins to time and the effects of oral tradition. "Barbara Allan," for example, was surely composed by some local songmaker working at a particular time and place, responding to specific circumstances, and composing within a chosen artistic tradition—the ballad form. But at the present time there is no chance of our ever being able to flesh that bare-bones assumption out with any facts. Ignorance of specific origins tempted early scholars like Gummere to suggest that ballads were in fact authorless.[2] Later scholars, although conceding the possibility of individual authorship, denigrated it, claiming that a song became a folksong only after it had been submitted to the process of oral tradition.[3] Collectors emphasized salvage archeology, in an attempt to rescue the remains of an old tradition before it was too late. A few local songs were included at the back of most regional collections,[4] but no one paid much attention to them or thought of them as relevant to the study of creation and distribution in traditional cultures.[5] Attitudes are changing now.

What I have to say in the following pages is based on over twenty years of collecting and studying local songs in Maine and the Maritime Provinces of Canada, particularly the lives and works of three songmakers: Larry Gorman, Lawrence Doyle, and Joe Scott. Gorman, originally from Prince Edward Island, spent most of his life in the lumberwoods of Maine and New Brunswick and was famous for making up scathingly satirical songs on people he worked for and lived among. Doyle, a farmer from the east end of Prince Edward Island, also made up satirical songs, but they were of a more gentle nature. Scott, on the other hand, was not a satirist at all but a maker of ballads in the broadside tradition, and his ballads have become part of the standard repertoire of singers throughout the Northeast.[6] In spite of my parochial emphasis, there is evidence that local songs and songmakers are part of the cultural landscape wherever traditional songs are sung, and the methods suggested here for their study should be useful anywhere.[7]

Although collecting local songs presents no special problems, once singers know that someone is interested in them, I have found that it helps to ask about a specific songmaker or even a specific song.[8] Failing that, direct questions such as "Did anyone around here ever make up songs?" or "Do you know any songs about things that happened right around here?" are perfectly good openers. Oftentimes a letter published in the local newspaper will help not only in locating knowledgeable singers but also in making the collector's name and mission familiar to people in the area.

Folklorists should gather as many versions of each local song as possible, keeping careful notes on all controlling data (where and when collected, from whom, where and when the singer learned it, whether it was elicited or volunteered). But the questioning should continue: who made the song up, did the event really happen the way the song says it did, were there other songs about that event, does the singer know other songs like it or by the same author, were there other people around who made up songs? Undoubtedly, the collector will need to clarify puzzling references ("What's it mean in there by 'political gallus?' "), although such explanations usually come more easily in a follow-up interview. In due time, the collector should also thoroughly check all relevant regional collections and archives, and perhaps even drop a line to others who have collected in the area to see if they have come across the song or have versions of it. Since, as we have seen, the emphasis of published collections has not been on local songs, it may well be that collectors have such material but simply never got around to publishing it.

The time limits must also be delineated in much the same way as the spatial limits. Is the song still being sung, or is it something that *used* to be sung? To this end, one should ask not only the usual questions, such as "When did you learn that song?" but also "When did you last sing it?" I have frequently asked that question when I re-collected a song from an informant, only to find the answer was, "The last time you were here," a pretty good indication that the song is no longer part of a vital tradition.

Manuscript versions are especially useful in studies of local songs, but again, careful distinctions are necessary. Frequently, people have written down versions of a song for me as they remember it, which means the manuscript represents the tradition as it is at present. But sometimes I have received copies that were written down many years ago, representing the tradition as it was at an earlier point in time. Manuscript copies should be as carefully controlled as oral versions—and datable early manuscript copies are obviously very valuable.

Three other sources should be mentioned. First, local songs occasionally have been published in whatever newspaper was read in the area. Second, songmakers sometimes have had their pieces printed by a local press and then sold them around for so much a copy.[9] Third, in recent years local songmakers have made considerable use of radio and, more especially, recordings to distribute their work.[10] All such versions are very much part of a song's tradition.

Even the question of acceptance into tradition must be seen in its local context, and the collector should pay close attention to the song that occurs in only one version in order to attempt to determine why it did *not* enter tradition. There are several possibilities. Perhaps the song was locally thought of as its maker's property, something that others would have felt awkward appropriating. A song known *to* other people though not sung *by* them would still have been very much part of local tradition.[11] On the other hand—and this is especially true of topical or satirical songs—a song might have been extremely well known at one time but forgotten in the course of years, save for its chance remembrance by one elderly singer. Either way, the chances are that the collector will find people recalling odd fragments or remembering that there was such a song and that "it was a corker." We should never forget that traditional songmakers do not create for posterity but for the moment, and that continuity in time is (from the creator's point of view) largely an accident and might even be (if he saw the song as *his*) an annoyance. Yet continuity is about the best available index of how well a song *was* accepted into local tradition, and therefore the chance survivor that did not make it assumes great negative importance.

One special case deserves mention: the satirical song made up to be sung for a very select audience or even for no audience at all. I know a man who, feeling he had been cheated out of wages by his employer, made up a song that he never sang for anyone for fear it might "get back" to its subject. He was, though, willing to sing it for me, an outsider, years after the event.[12] Such songs never enter tradition, yet since they are part of an individual's repertoire and seem to function as personal safety valves, they should be collected whenever possible. Frequently, these songs come up in response to a question such as "Did you ever make up a song yourself?"—followed by discreet probing when the answer is a diffident disclaimer.

A final caveat on collecting. It is a rather sterile exercise to study the distribution of locally composed songs (or any songs, for that matter) without knowing the performance traditions of the area. Songs are not abstractions; they exist only in performance (or, between performances, in the dark at the back of the mind). Where and under what circumstances were songs performed? (And it should be remembered that publication in a newspaper or distribution by radio or record constitutes a special type of performance.) If, for example, it was the custom to have singing during the "breaks" at dances, it would help to know from how large an area people attended and how such areas might interlock. If a songmaker had access to a local radio show, how large a hinterland did the station reach? Information on singing can be gathered as a folklorist collects the songs, but frequently a good deal of probing is required. That is, asking where songs were sung will often be answered by, "Oh, just around at parties and things," at which point the interviewer gets to work: parties where and when, how would songs come up at parties, who would sing them?

Such distributional studies yield two types of information. First, taken in conjunction with a knowledge of performance traditions, there is no better way to delineate regions than by observing the geographical spread of local songs. Sometimes a whole group will be known only within a particular area and completely unknown outside it. Regions often overlie and interlock with each other, at times in a most bewildering fashion, but once their boundaries have been discovered, it is almost always possible to explain both their existence and their interrelationships through demography, economics, or a combination of both. Lawrence Doyle's songs, for example, were almost entirely confined to a few townships on the eastern end of Prince Edward Island, an area that was the hinterland of a couple of small ports and hence economically self-contained—people moved freely within it, but there was no need for them to move beyond. Within this area I also found men who knew Joe Scott's songs well, and Joe's songs—having been created within lumber-camp tradition—were familiar to people throughout northern Maine and the Maritimes, and once again their distribution can be adequately explained by historical developments within the lumber industry.[13]

Two cautions: first, having established the limits of a song's distribution, the scholar should test them rigorously to assure that they are truly limits and not simply the product of either regional loyalty or myopia. Second, the songs of people who move to a new area should in no way be thought of as part of the tradition of the new area unless they are accepted and performed by persons outside the immigrant group. I collected several of Lawrence Doyle's songs in Melrose, Massachusetts, from a man who moved there from near Doyle's home on Prince Edward Island. Another man learned one of Doyle's songs when he went down to Watertown, Massachusetts, to work, but he learned it from another recent P.E.I. emigrant, and I later collected the song from him back on P.E.I. some years later. In neither case can the songs be said to have migrated to Massachusetts and become part of local tradition there.[14]

The second and perhaps most important thing we can learn from distribution studies of local songs is what actually happens to a song in tradition. My own work has shown me, for instance, that the concept of communal re-creation (that a song becomes a folksong through the process of being passed on) is simply not true or, at best, explains very little. While most of Joe Scott's ballads, for example, showed all the changes one might expect from oral transmission, these changes in no way can be said to have affected the essence, the whatness, the identity of any one of them. A folksong is no different from any other work of art; it becomes what it is in the mind of its creator, not through the effects of its means of preservation and distribution. One problem arises here: in order to study change, we must know what the song was at its beginning. Ideally, we should have a copy of it as the author wrote it. Frequently, such an original (at least of relatively recent compositions) is available, in the form of either a printed slip or a recording. If not, it is sometimes possible to construct one, but any conclusions drawn on the basis of such a construction should be carefully qualified.

At this point, let us turn our attention from what happens to a song once it has been created to how it came into being in the first place. To this end, it will help to think of a song as the resultant of three vectors: an "event" or set of facts, a song tradition, and an individual talent.

To begin with, many local ballads are about events recorded in printed sources, thus available to scholars who may wish to reconstruct them. Murder ballads, for example, are relatively easy to document through local court records, vital statistics, and the like. Once the date of the event is known, other sources will open up, notably newspaper files. Frequently, however—and this is especially true with satire—the researcher will find nothing directly to the point in documentary sources, the event being too trivial for official records or inappropriate for newspapers. Yet documentary sources may contain extremely important *indirect* material. Census records, deeds, wills—all can help establish not only the existence of people mentioned in a song but also where they lived, when, and what relationship they bore to each other. Simply reading through the local newspaper around the time an event is supposed to have happened can uncover useful details. Lawrence Doyle, for example, wrote a song about a "picnic" or "tea party," and while I was unable to find specific mention of it in the local papers, I found that tea parties were regular summer events, and I developed a very good idea of what they were like from browsing through newspaper accounts of other such occasions. Finally, I have found that a walk through the local cemetery will turn up all kinds of unexpected data, a cemetery being, after all, an easily and pleasantly available cluster of vital statistics.[15]

Very seldom will all information on a song come from documents, nor are they necessarily the best or richest sources. Usually the most they can offer is a series of clear blazes and reliable benchmarks around which to order other data. I emphasize documents here largely because folklorists are apt to neglect them. But most of our knowledge of events behind a local song will come from oral sources, the sort of talk that comes after the song has been sung, in response to questions such as, "Did that really happen?" or "Did this man live around here?" All this information should be carefully recorded, and the various accounts should be compared, with due consideration being given to the reliability and authority of the informant. A warning here: a folklorist must be careful, while temporarily playing the historian's game, not to fall into the historicist trap of only trying to establish what "really" happened.[16] What people *say* happened is important as well, even though known to be "wrong." In addition, a song will often live in symbiosis with a parallel narrative tradition, which sometimes carries additional information about the song's content, sometimes something quite extraneous. Joe Scott's ballad "Howard Carey," for example, is about a man who hanged himself in his rooming house in Rumford, Maine, and the room in which he died became a tradition in its own right. The point is that *all* information—intrinsic, extrinsic, clearly true, and patently false—has value. In fact, in terms of what a song means to the people who sing or listen to it, subjective truth is far more important than history.

Still, in order to compare what happened with what the ballad says happened, we need to come as near as we can to objective historical truth, but if we are going to avoid a second historicist trap, we need something more: we need to know the *songmaker's* perception of the truth. It may well be that the researcher, having court records and vital statistics to hand, will know much more about what happened than the songmaker ever could have known, and while it is altogether elegant to be able to say that the songmaker was mistaken about something, such an assertion says little about creativity. On the other hand, it would be very much to the point to be able to show either that the creator was working with common gossip—what was passing for truth at the time—or that he obviously knew the truth but chose to ignore or distort it. As a final note, it would be especially interesting to discover that the "event" was entirely fictional, which would raise the question of whether the songmaker thought he was telling the truth or was intentionally presenting a fiction. And if he knew it was fiction, where did he get his idea?

That brings us to the second of our three vectors, the tradition itself. Many times in ballad-making the truth is distorted or adjusted to make the known facts square with the conventions of a particular song tradition. Therefore, the scholar must have a thorough knowledge of the local repertoire (*including tunes*), especially as it would have been known to the songmaker. It is not enough, for instance, to know there was a tradition of murder ballads: specifically what murder ballads would the songmaker have known or been likely to have known? It may be that in composing a particular ballad the creator followed the tradition carefully. On the other hand, perhaps the usual models were bypassed in favor of a new direction. Joe Scott, for example, certainly knew the murder ballads that circulated in Maine lumber-camp tradition, but he ignored them all in writing "Benjamin Deane," turning instead to pirate ballads like "The *Flying Cloud*" or "Charles Augustus Anderson" for his model.[17] Either way, be the songmaker carefully conservative or wildly innovative, out of the fusion of facts and tradition in the alembic of the creator's mind comes newness—a work of art that is both unique and similar to others.

Finally, we come to the third vector, the individual artist. Although it is not always possible to discover him, he is always there, and his identity is known often enough to make the search for him worthwhile.[18] If he is still alive, he should be interviewed in detail, not only to get the facts of his life but, even more important, to find out why he chose to write about certain subjects in just the way he did, what he used for models, what his expectations were, and what other songs he has written. If he is not still alive, every attempt should be made to answer those same sorts of questions both by consulting public records and by conducting extensive interviews. If it is possible to bring together a number of songs, they should be examined carefully to see if they exhibit anything that could be called a style, something that makes them distinctive. That is apt to be a very subtle matter, and it should never be forced; in traditional songmaking, idiosyncrasy and originality were far less apt to lead to an individual's work being accepted than a skillful following of convention. Even so, in the three extended studies of songmakers I have done, I have always been able to find some evidence of personal style.

To sum up, the study of local songs can show us the entire art process from creation to distribution within a traditional culture. One of the results of such work will be a better understanding of the place of art in human affairs, partly through its demystification, partly through its democratization. Yet in the end, the wonder of it all will be increased.

NOTES

1. The best surveys of ballads widespread in American tradition are Tristram P. Coffin, *The British Traditional Ballad in North America*, supplement by Roger

deV. Renwick, Publications of the American Folklore Society, Bibliographical and Special Series, 2d rev. ed. (Austin and London: University of Texas Press, 1977); G. Malcolm Laws, Jr., *American Balladry from British Broadsides*, American Folklore Society, Bibliographical and Special Series (Philadelphia: American Folklore Society, 1957); idem, *Native American Balladry*, rev. ed., American Folklore Society, Bibliographical and Special Series (Philadelphia: American Folklore Society, 1964).

2. For the communal theory of origins, see any of the works of Francis Barton Gummere or, better yet, D. K. Wilgus's admirable survey and critique of Gummere and his successors, in *Anglo-American Folksong Scholarship Since 1898* (New Brunswick, N. J.: Rutgers University Press, 1959), pp. 3-52.

3. See Phillips Barry, "Communal Re-creation," *Bulletin of the Folk-Song Society of the Northeast*, No. 5 (1933): 4-6, although Barry was very alert to the concept of individual creation; Gordon Hall Gerould, *The Ballad of Tradition* (New York: Oxford University Press, 1932), pp. 163-68.

4. When Helen Creighton met Ben Henneberry of Devil's Island, Nova Scotia, for the first time and asked him to sing, the first song he chose was "Meagher's Children," a local song. However, when her first book was published, this song appears as number 135 out of 150. See *Songs and Ballads from Nova Scotia, Toronto and Vancouver* (J. M. Dent, 1932; reprint, New York: Dover, 1966), pp. xiii-xiv, 292-96.

5. A notable exception is Herbert Halpert, "Vitality of Tradition and Local Songs," *Journal of the International Folk Music Council* 3 (1951): 35-40.

6. Edward D. Ives, *Larry Gorman: The Man Who Made the Songs* (Bloomington: Indiana University Press, 1964; reprint, New York: Arno Press, 1977). Idem, *Lawrence Doyle: The Farmer Poet of Prince Edward Island* (Orono: Maine Studies No. 92, University Press, 1971). Idem, *Joe Scott: The Woodsman Songmaker* (Urbana: University of Illinois Press, 1978).

7. For a survey of at least one aspect of this local songmaking tradition, see Edward D. Ives, "The Satirical Song Tradition in Maine and the Maritime Provinces of Canada" (Ph.D. diss., Indiana University, 1962; University Microfilms 63-242), pp. 265-383.

8. For some general suggestions on finding informants, see Edward D. Ives, "Common-Man Biography: Some Notes by the Way," in *Folklore Today: A Festschrift for Richard M. Dorson*, ed. Linda Dégh, Henry Glassie, Felix J. Oinas (Bloomington: Indiana University, RCLSS, 1976), pp. 260-63.

9. See Ives, *Joe Scott*, pp. 54-57, 76, 426-27; idem, *Larry Gorman*, pp. 112-21; Roger D. Abrahams, "Charles Walters—West Indian Autolycus," *Western Folklore* 27 (1968): 77-95.

10. See Neil V. Rosenberg, "Goodtime Charlie and the Bricklin: A Satirical Song in Context," *Canadian Oral History Association Journal* 3 (1978): 27-46.

11. The best study of such a song is Henry Glassie, " 'Take That Night Train to Selma': An Excursion to the Outskirts of Scholarship," in *Folksongs and Their Makers*, ed. Henry Glassie, Edward D. Ives, and John F. Szwed (Bowling Green, Ohio: Bowling Green University Popular Press, 1970), pp. 1-68. See also Steven A. Schulman, "Howess Dewey Winfrey: The Rejected Songmaker," *Journal of American Folklore* 87 (1974): 72-81.

12. See Ives, *Larry Gorman*, pp. 177-79.

13. Ives, *Lawrence Doyle*, pp. 249-50; idem, *Joe Scott*, pp. 414-19.

14. Ives, *Lawrence Doyle*, p. 145.

15. For more on documents as sources for folksong study, see Ives, "Common-Man Biography," pp. 251-60.

16. John Foster West's *The Ballad of Tom Dula* (Durham, N.C.: Moore Publishing Co., n.d.) is not concerned with the ballad at all. In fact, it ignores the

ballad and simply tries to establish the facts of the case. On the other hand, Peter Aceves, "The Hillsville Tragedy in Court Record, Mass Media and Folk Balladry: A Problem in Historical Documentation," *Keystone Folklore Quarterly* 16 (1971): 1-38, is a model study, showing how each of these media illuminates the others.

17. See Ives, *Joe Scott*, pp. 249, 412.

18. In addition to the works by Ives, Glassie, Szwed, and Schulman cited above, see Loman D. Cansler, "Walter Dibben, An Ozark Bard," *Kentucky Folklore Record* 13 (1967): 81-89, and idem, "He Hewed His Own Path: William Henry Scott, Ozark Songmaker" in John A. Burrison, ed., *Studies in the Literary Imagination* 3 (1970): 37-63 (published by Georgia State University, Atlanta, Georgia).

José E. Limón

Folklore, Social Conflict, and the United States– Mexico Border

The post-1821 arrival of increasingly larger numbers of Anglo-Americans in the borderlands set in motion a series of political and economic changes leading to the social subordination of the area's Mexican population. The Texas War for Independence (1835–36) was the prelude to the more significant United States–Mexican War, which ended in 1848. The United States victory resulted in the annexation of the borderlands and the incorporation of the very small native Mexican population of some eighty thousand into the United States. What is much more important is that the United States military invasion and victory added to the disruption of Mexican politics and society, thereby contributing to the events leading to the Mexican Revolution of 1910. In turn, that revolution created social chaos, which produced a massive and still continuing immigration of largely impoverished Mexicans into this country. These immigrants, together with the small native Mexican group, took an economic position as largely labor-dependent workers in the United States political economy. As such, they became the objects of economic exploitation and racial-cultural prejudice and discrimination.[1] Such practices are still characteristic of social relations in the area, although in an attenuated form.

While this process of social subordination certainly affected areas like California and New Mexico,[2] the Texas-Mexican population suffered a more virulent experience under the new socioeconomic order. In turn, this special regional experience generated a much more extensive folklore of social conflict, which folklorists have analyzed. For these reasons I will emphasize the Texas experience.

Social contact and conflict in Texas occurred in two broad phases. Between 1848 and 1890, an Anglo ranching society established itself among the native (also ranching) Mexican population, living with them in a rough social equality. However, beginning in the 1890s, a clear racial-cultural stratification and subordination began to emerge, as a new wave of Anglo-American entrepreneurs and farming interests established a political and economic hegemony over the native population as well as the thousands of Mexican immigrants entering the area after 1910. While initially constituting primarily a rural work force, between 1920 and the present, the Mexicans began to urbanize in the cities of San Antonio, Corpus Christi, Houston, and other, smaller towns. With few exceptions, this total population—rural and urban, native and immigrant—became the victim of class-racial exploitation and mistreatment. In 1910, a young Mexican was arrested near Rock Springs, Texas, and charged with the murder of an Anglo-American woman. Antonio Rodriguez never came to trial. A mob of townspeople took him from the jail, tied him to a tree, and burned him to death.[3] Not so long ago, in 1973, a Dallas policeman questioned a twelve-year-old Mexican boy about a minor burglary by holding a pistol to his head "just to scare him." The gun went off, in what was later called "an unfortunate incident." The courts gave the officer a five-year sentence.[4] That same year a Sheriff Hayes in southwest Texas questioned a Richard Morales by holding a shotgun to his stomach. That gun also went off.

These are simply the more public and dramatic manifestations of a racial discrimination and oppression that still affects the lives of Mexicans in Texas and other parts of the United States in terms of housing, education, labor, and culture. In 1977, for example, the County Tax Assessor/Collector of San Antonio, Texas, issued to employees a ban on speaking Spanish in the office—this in a city with a 50 percent Mexican population. To be sure, the Mexican community has countered this assault with political and economic resistance.

Social oppression and resistance to that oppression are obviously articulated primarily in political and economic modes, but they are also articulated through folkloric expression from both groups in the conflict. It is a bit ironic that both the Mexican and the Anglo folkloric responses to social conflict have best been studied and summarized by the Texas-Mexican scholar Américo Paredes. This review essay owes a substantial debt to his work. I will particularly draw on his most recent summary of this question[5] and begin with American folklore.

Anglo-Americans generated an exoteric folklore out of this conflictual relationship, albeit one of limited generic range and symbolic significance. We may begin and end almost exclusively with the minor genres. The most simple folklore to be noted is a corpus of folk ideas—Anglo stereotypes about Mexicans. Like all stereotypes, these may be transmitted as conversational folk expressions: "Oh you know how Mexicans are . . . they're so—"; or they may inform major genres such as folk narrative; or they may be codified in mass cultural expression such as popular written literature or advertising. In this particular cultural case, these Anglo-American stereotypes would render the Mexican as lazy, dirty, thieving, devious, conspiratorial, sexually hyperactive, and overly fond of alcohol. On the other hand, to this same folk, the Mexican can also be carefree, romantic, poetic by nature, debonair, and charming. Mexican women constitute a special case; here, the dominant image is the sultry, tempestuous, and sexually tempting female, often a prostitute, but one who falls in love with an American male.[6]

Like stereotypes, structurally simple ethnic slurs also emerge in conditions of sociocultural conflict and subordination. While Mexicans out-produce Anglos in this particular folkloric matchup, we can nevertheless note Anglo-American slurs based on language play (Meskin, Mex, Spic, Paydro) or on food behavior (greaser, pepper belly, frijole guzzler).[7] A third, closely related minor genre recently collected by Ed Cray is the derisive adjective. Cray notes that "the names of races, nationalities, and locales are often pressed into service as adjectives," usually in a disparagement of the group or locale's technologically or economically adaptive practices. A makeshift "tin can stuffed with steel wool mounted on an exhaust pipe" may be referred to as "a Mexican muffler," or an "increase in rank or title without an accompanying pay raise" is a "Mexican promotion."[8]

Again, Américo Paredes has noted the recent emergence of more complex forms, such as the mock riddle, although one may question its pervasiveness or endurance in American oral tradition.[9] Nevertheless, according to Paredes, today one can hear Anglo-American youth asking,

What's brown and fries chicken?
Answer: Colonel Sanchez.

Or, to cite another example from my own field experience:

What's brown and rides a golden palomino?
Answer: Roy Rodriguez.

Finally, an older and more enduring item of American lore is the ethnic joke directed against Mexicans. In this joke cycle, the butt of the joke is the whole Mexican group and its seeming inability to cope with modern American culture, especially technology. An example is the now standard story about the international submarine contest to be judged on the basis of which nation's sub can stay down the longest. The Mexicans win because their submarine never comes up.[10]

The preceding items summarize our scholarly knowledge of the Anglo-American folklore of social conflict. It is a meager scholarly output, probably reflecting the general weakness of such a folkloric tradition. To be sure, a great deal has been said about Mexicans in American popular literature and in mass, institutionalized cultural expressions such as film, but these are not my primary concern here.

Yet the minimal Anglo folklore that has been collected does play a crucial role in the social relationship between the two peoples. Generally speaking, we might say that it furnishes a psychological rationale—an expressive justification—for the social subordination of Mexicans in the Southwest. In his now classic and standard formulation, Allport notes that a "stereotype is an exaggerated belief associated with a category. Its function is to justify (rationalize) our conduct in relation to that category.[11] Justification and rationalization are certainly some of the functions of Anglo folklore about Mexicans. The continued social mistreatment of Mexicans is surely made psychologically easier if one can think of them either as less than morally complete humans or as happy, romantic people satisfied with their lot. The psychological effects of slurs, I suspect, are much the same. They reduce, dehumanize, and shape our social conduct toward the object of the slur.

The rest of the pertinent Anglo-American folk tradition—the derisive adjectives, mock riddles, and ethnic jokes—also justifies and rationalizes social domination, but perhaps in a more focused manner. In all three expressive cases, the Mexican is depicted as technologically or economically inept—not capable or worthy of socioeconomic mobility or technological and thereby contemporary social power. This perception is, perhaps, most clearly expressed in the mock riddles, which are also, of course, joking riddles designed to produce humor and laughter. The humor of being a brown Sanchez and owning a chain of fried chicken outlets lies not merely in the wordplay between "Sanders" and "Sanchez" but in the incongruity between being Mexican and having such a socioeconomic position as a Colonel Sanders. The riddles offer a momentary symbolic existence for what is, in effect, generally impossible or at least rare in society, and it is this incongruous interplay between the symbolic structure and the social reality that produces the humor. Pervasive socioeconomic mobility for Mexicans in the United States is, in effect, still a joke, and, as Mary Douglas has commented, "If there is no joke in the social structure, no other joking can appear."[12] Birnbaum has offered a summarizing statement on the final social intent of slurs, ethnic proverbial sayings, and, by implication, other forms of folklore.

> . . . one has to admit that the reason for them may not only be intolerance toward the manifestations of alien cultural phenomenon . . . but also a response to a recognized economic threat: competition. . . . Slurs and proverbial sayings against immigrants can, therefore, be largely viewed as attempts at defaming their "national character" in order to assure the continued control of the "natives."[13]

Yet such social effects are partially muted by the apparently negligible quantity of such American folklore in this context.

Nevertheless, despite the apparent current and historical paucity of such folklore, much still remains to be done in future research and analysis in at least three broad areas. The first approach would revisit the known genres in the context of new social issues and with contemporary conceptualizations. For example, Birnbaum has noted the possible intensification of slurs and other forms of ethnically aggressive folklore in direct relationship to the growing political power of Mexicans in the Southwest.[14] And what will be the folkloric effect of the latter taken together with an even more significant social phenomenon—the massive immigration of undocumented Mexican workers? These areas remain almost wholly unexamined.

Contemporary performance-oriented folkloristics offers us another way of reapproaching known Anglo-American folkloric material. How exactly—by whom and under what sociolinguistic conditions—are slurs and other forms of folklore performed in actual conversational situations? What, for example, are the performance contexts of mock riddles? Or, to take a more specific example: we know that Anglo-Americans and Mexicans often do interact socially, especially in the workplace and related social settings such as diners and bars. How is ethnicity negotiated folklorically in social interaction structured by differential identity?[15] Sometimes, otherwise socially abrasive folklore-like slurs can acquire an inverted significance in such interactions, leading to the humorous release of anxiety and the development of social bonds beyond ethnicity.[16]

A second research area is the process of folkloric borrowing, adaptation, and conversion. For example, how do we handle those cases where Anglo-Americans perform traditional Mexican materials in an unselfconscious folkloric way? In the literature, we have the case of an Anglo-American providing a Mexican legendary narrative,[17] and the historical example cited by Romano in which an Anglo-American becomes a patient for a Mexican folk healer.[18] The material is Mexican, but the bearers and performers are American. How widespread is this sort of adaptive borrowing, and what is its sociocultural significance? One might conduct a similar inquiry into the relationship between traditional Mexican folklife and mass, institutional American popular culture. We have already noted one such articulation between folk stereotypes and mass advertising. What about others? For example, an intriguing topic is the current "cook-off" festival behavior so popular among Anglo-Texans and often based on cooking traditional Mexican folk foods such as *chili, tamales, menudo,* and the less "traditional," yet very Texas-Mexican, *fajitas* (broiled skirt steak). Klymasz points out how such ethnic festivals can serve as antidotes to the homogenizing effects of mass culture for ethnic groups.[19] Might not they do the same for the dominant society—a temporary fantasy escape from its own homogenization? Still another related intriguing area for further exploration is the folklore that results from contact between Mexicans and blacks as the latter come into the Southwest either as slaves, freed slaves, or settlers. Peter Narvaez has given us a fine start on this scholarly path with his work on the relationship between Mexican musicians and the bluesman.[20]

Finally, as another point of departure for future research, we may question one of the basic contentions of this review, namely the very notion of a small amount of clearly American folklore emerging from the social contact along the border. I suspect that we may add at least a bit more to the tiny corpus noted earlier. Is American folksong production as bleak as Paredes believes when he tells us that ". . . the English speaking Texan . . . disappoints us in a folkloristic sense. He produces no border balladry"?[21] While I believe Paredes is fundamentally right on the ballad form, can one nevertheless argue a folklore case for songs originally based on printed popular materials and poems of known authorship but later sung as "traditional" songs in folk scenes such as cowboy camps? Admittedly there are substantive problems of authenticity and methodology.[22] Yet some of these quasi-folksongs quite clearly reveal ambivalent attitudes toward Mexicans, especially women—songs such as "A Border Affair" by Charles Clark.[23] Indeed, according to the Fifes, the image of "a wild and adventurous Anglo-American who provokes the undying love of a Mexican maiden" would emerge as a moving theme in American folksong.[24] The ambivalence in attitudes toward Mexicans would occasionally extend to males as well, as in "The Texas Cowboy and the Mexican," reported by John A. Lomax as an anonymous folksong. While the song notes the intense racial prejudice "ag'in' the whole Mexican race," the hero of the song is an Anglo cowboy, a stranger with "a cold blue eye" who saves a Mexican from certain death at the hands of a mob of Anglo ranchmen.[25]

Other genres and categories might also be profitably reexamined. Legend creation is of particular interest here. Recently, McWilliams has demonstrated the formation of the pervasive and powerful legend of the battle of the Alamo.[26] Do Mexicans figure in other legends as well? Did the real or alleged military threat from Mexico after 1848 and into the years of the revolution generate legends among the Anglo-Americans living along the border? Children's folklore remains largely unexamined on this issue. What sort of attitudes toward Mexicans, if any, do Anglo children express in their folklore? Either historically or at present, do these children manifest an anti-Mexican sentiment equivalent to that expressed against blacks?[27]

These, then, are some of the generic areas and conceptual approaches that might be examined in the future study of the American folklore produced by social contact in the borderlands. While we may not find an overwhelming amount of new raw data, I believe the area merits continuing analytical interest.

If most of Anglo-American folklore in this context is an expressive justification for social domination, then Mexican folklore in the United States may in large measure be understood as a defensive reaction to and criticism of that social domination. Again, we are deeply indebted to Américo Paredes for our knowledge of this folklore. Consider, for example, the minor genres, such as the folk stereotypes of Anglos held by many Mexicans. Anglos are thought to be arrogant, intrusive, and impolite in their social dealings.[28] Morally and culturally they may be regarded as cold, insipid, and sexless—in short, something like cold ham. And, indeed, this food symbol furnishes an image for an early ethnic slur—*jamones* (the ham eaters)—used to name Americans. A few others are *bolillo, gavacho, paton, mister,* and the well-known *gringo.*[29] In keeping with their special relationship to the Mexican community,[30] the Texas Rangers merit a slur all of their own— *rinche*—which exploits the highly negative emotional associations of the suffix *-inche* in the Spanish language. The latter sound carries a great deal of the insult in the common children's taunt:

> Rinche pinche
> Cara de chinche!
> (Mean Ranger
> Face of a bug!)

The major genres, especially narratives, lend greater support to the notion of folklore as defense and resistance. Again, Paredes has shown us how Mexicans have developed joke forms that take a critical account of the diminant society, symbolizing the latter in the figure of the Stupid American constantly victimized by a clever Mexican trickster figure.[31] In a recent study I have extended his findings to jokes that Mexicans tell about group members—*agringados*—who collaborate with the dominant group.[32]

Legendry also plays a part in this matter of resistance and criticism. The reader will recall the burning of Antonio Rodriguez in 1910 cited earlier. Consider this legend collected in south Texas in 1972:

> Well, this boy was named Antonio Rodriguez and he came to the little town of Rock Springs and there he was taken prisoner because the Americans said that he killed an American woman . . . and they took him to a tree and they burned him alive. . . . And, you know, after awhile, God sent a tornado and it hit the town of Rock Springs, but it only hit the American side of town; it did nothing to our people, and in that way, God punished those people.[33]

In this narrative we have a clear rendition of the opposing forces in the social order as seen expressively in 1972. "Our people" are opposed to "those people," and the latter suffer God and nature's retribution for their evil deed.

Finally, we may turn to the extensive corpus of song narratives—the *corridos*— many of which speak directly or indirectly to the question of social conflict. Two major books by Paredes have collected and interpreted the ballads of border conflict that criticize American social injustice and celebrate Mexican opposition.[34] This critical ballad tradition continues in a modified fashion into the 1980s. Today one may hear "El Corrido de Morales," concerning the Morales killing mentioned earlier. I quote a verse from this ballad:

> Las prisiones estan llenas
> de inocentes mexicanos
> No dudo Hayes quede libre
> Por ser un americano.

(The prisons are full
of innocent Mexicans
I do not doubt Hayes will go free
Since he is an American.)

And, in a recent publication, Dan Dickey studies the *corridos* about a famous American who defended the rights of Mexicans.[35]

Dramatistic and static genres may also be interpreted in a conceptual framework of resistance, although perhaps in a more indirect mode. They do not contest the social order through the direct symbolic statement of opposing values. Rather, such a generic performance offers contestation by limiting the hegemony of the dominant culture in the lives of the native population. As folk behaviors, they stand as critical alternatives to those imposed from without and from above in the social structure.[36] For example, the historical and still effective charisma of the Mexican folk healer yields to an analysis of his inverting and subverting symbolic power in a context of American-induced social change.[37] In the area of food behavior, Alicia Gonzalez provides ample evidence for an understanding of the integrating role of the Mexican *panadero* (baker) in a community threatened by economic fragmentation.[38] Finally, the contemporary dancing of the Texas-Mexican polka in dance halls throughout the Southwest creates ludic arenas of *communitas* inverting and mitigating the effects of social subordination.[39]

Social contact and conflict along the border have also created another corpus of folklore that speaks to *intra*-Mexican tension and self-questioning induced by the social change created by Americans. For example, Mexicans may often borrow Anglo-American slurs and jokes about Mexicans and use such folklore among themselves in an ambivalent fashion (see note 13). We know of jokes that Mexicans tell about their own folk traditions,[40] jokes told about undocumented workers and other recent Mexican immigrants,[41] *corridos* that are critical of Mexican drug smugglers operating within the community,[42] and, finally, legend narration as an affirmation of ethnic identity in a world of acculturative pressure.[43]

As is evident, the Mexican side of the folklore of social conflict continues to receive considerable scholarly attention. Nevertheless, much new research and analysis remains to be done. Four major broad areas require attention. First, we need more detailed contextual analysis of all genres in terms of social conflict. How are proverbs used interactionally? What actually happens to audience and participants during a *corrido* singing session? In folk medicine, how do illness complaints, diagnosis, and treatment reflect the socioeconomic tensions of life? Second, the relative omission of non-Texas folklore in this review points to a geographically keyed scholarly need. The study of the Mexican folklore of New Mexico and California, for example, has been limited by the dominance of the historic-geographic or folk-culturalist approaches.[44] The analysis of these regional folklores from contextual and conflictual perspectives has simply not been done. A third intriguing area for more research is the effect of Chicano ethnic nationalism on the performance and the study of folklore.[45] Finally, the entire corpus of such Mexican folklore along the border needs to be summarized and interpreted holistically within a critical theory of culture and society. This review represents an initial step in that direction.

I have delineated the scholarly status of folklore produced by social contact along the United States–Mexico border. It would appear that one group has produced a great deal of folklore (and a number of folklorists) while the other has not. I have tried to summarize and interpret both groups and their folkloric productions in a conceptual framework of conflict and subordination. Paredes offers a final comparative statement on this entire question.

> . . . the Mexican stereotype of the Anglo appears in songs and narratives belonging to a truly folk tradition (artistic but unreflecting expressions of a whole people), while the Anglo anecdotes about the Mexican most often betray the reflective eye of the conscious artist or would-be artist. . . . On the other hand, except for names and ethnic jokes of a fairly general kind, Anglo folklore almost ignores the Mexican. One might say that he has been observed by the Anglo, while the Anglo has been experienced by the Mexican.[46]

We can perhaps add a bit more and thereby speak to the cross-cultural significance of folklore in situations of social conflict and oppression. Perhaps another significance of folklore in social domination lies in its very absence. Should we account for folkloric silence as well as for its expression? Richard Bauman has noted "the clear bias in the ethnography of speaking" toward groups in which speaking is markedly important.[47] That is, we do not often account for groups or social situations in which speech, including expressive speech forms such as folklore, has a minimal presence and meaning. Why does social conflict along the United States–Mexico border produce such a large amount of relevant folklore in one cultural group and not in the other? If, as Abrahams tells us, folklore is a set of "traditional expressions and implementations" used by social groups to attack recurrent anxieties and social problems,[48] then, perhaps, a converse implication is also true. To the extent that a social group does not view others in its environment as a threat or a problem, it will offer a minimal folkloric response. For Anglos, the Mexicans in the Southwest have not posed a threat or a problem, because they have been so fully and completely dominated by institutional means. In this case, folklore may not be a necessary expressive mechanism for the social and psychological control of the environment; its relative absence tacitly speaks to the totality of Anglo institutional control. Its much greater presence among Mexicans overtly speaks to the need for a symbolic criticism and limitation of that control in the absence of other, institutional resources.

NOTES

1. Juan Gomez-Q., "The Origins and Development of the Mexican Working Class in the United States: Laborers and Artisans North of the Rio Bravo, 1600–1900," in *El Trabajo y los Trabajadores en la Historia de Mexico/Labor and Laborers Through Mexican History*, ed. Elsa Cecilia Frost, Michael C. Meyer, Josefina Zoraida Vasquez, and Lilia Diaz, Proceedings of the Fifth Meeting of Mexican and Northamerican Historians, Patzcuaro, 1977 (Mexico City and Tucson: El Colegio de México and University of Arizona Press, 1979), pp. 463–505.

2. See Leonard Pitt, *The Decline of the Californios: A Social History of Spanish-Speaking Californians, 1846–1890* (Berkeley: University of California

Press, 1966); George I. Sanchez, *Forgotten People: A Study of New Mexicans* (Albuquerque: Calvin Horn Publishers, 1968).

3. José E. Limón, "El Primer Congreso Mexicanista de 1911: A Precursor to Contemporary Chicanismo," *Aztlan: An International Journal of Chicano Studies* 5 (1974): 84–117.

4. Shirley Achor, *Mexican Americans in a Dallas Barrio* (Tucson: University of Arizona Press, 1978), pp. 148–53.

5. Américo Paredes, "The Problem of Identity in a Changing Culture: Popular Expressions of Culture Conflict Along the Lower Rio Grande Border," in *Views Across the Border*, ed. Stanley Ross (Albuquerque: University of New Mexico Press, 1978), pp. 68–94.

6. Ozzie Simmons, "The Mutual Images and Expectations of Anglo Americans and Mexican Americans," *Daedalus* 90 (1960): 286–99.

7. Paredes, "The Problem of Identity in a Changing Culture," p. 79.

8. Ed Cray, "Ethnic and Place Names as Derisive Adjectives," *Western Folklore* 21 (1962): 27–34.

9. Paredes, "The Problem of Identity in a Changing Culture," pp. 88–89.

10. Américo Paredes, "The Anglo American in Mexican Folklore," in *New Voices in American Studies*, ed. Ray Browne (Lafayette: Purdue University Press, 1966), pp.113–27. While Paredes notes the performance of this joke among Mexicans, he acknowledges its probable origins in Anglo oral tradition.

11. Gordon W. Allport, *The Nature of Prejudice* (Garden City, N.Y.: Doubleday, 1958), p. 187.

12. Mary Douglas, "The Social Control of Cognition: Some Factors in Joke Perception," *Man* 3 (1968): 366.

13. Mariana D. Birnbaum, "On the Language of Prejudice," *Western Folklore* 30 (1971): 247–68.

14. Ibid., p. 258.

15. Richard Bauman, "Differential Identity and the Social Base of Folklore," in *Toward New Perspectives in Folklore*, ed. Américo Paredes and Richard Bauman (Austin: University of Texas Press, 1972), pp. 31–41.

16. Edward K. Miller, "The Use of Stereotypes in Inter-Ethnic Joking as a Means of Communication," *Folklore Annual* 7 & 8 (1977): 28–42.

17. George D. Hendricks, "Four Southwestern Legends," *Western Folklore* 27 (1968): 255–62.

18. Octavio Romano V., "Charismatic Medicine, Folk Healing and Folk Sainthood," *American Anthropologist* 67 (1965): 1151–1173.

19. Robert D. Klymasz, "From Immigrant to Ethnic Folklore: A Canadian View of Process and Transition," *Journal of the Folklore Institute* 10 (1973): 131–40.

20. Peter Narvaez, "Afro-American and Mexican Street Singers: An Ethnohistorical Hypothesis," *Southern Folklore Quarterly* 42 (1978): 73–84.

21. Américo Paredes, *With His Pistol in His Hand: A Border Ballad and Its Hero* (Austin: University of Texas Press, 1971), p. 15.

22. John O. West, "Jack Thorp and John Lomax, Oral or Written Transmission?" *Western Folklore* 26 (1967): 113–18.

23. John White, *Git Along Little Dogie: Songs and Songmakers of the American West* (Urbana: University of Illinois Press, 1975), p. 135.

24. N. Howard [Jack] Thorp, *Songs of the Cowboys*, ed. Austin and Alta Fife (New York: Clarkson N. Potter, 1966), p. 104.

25. John A. Lomax, *Songs of the Cattle Trail and Cowcamp* (New York: Macmillan, 1919), p. 11.

26. Percy McWilliams, "The Alamo Story: From Fact to Fable," *Journal of the Folklore Institute* 15 (1978): 221–34.

27. Kenneth Porter, "Racism in Children's Rhymes and Sayings, Central Kansas, 1910–1918," *Western Folklore* 24 (1965): 191–96.

28. Simmons, "The Mutual Images and Expectations of Anglo Americans and Mexican Americans," pp. 286–99.

29. Américo Paredes, "On Gringo, Greaser and Other Neighborly Names," in *Singers and Storytellers*, ed. Mody C. Boatright, Wilson M. Hudson and Allen Maxwell (Dallas: Southern Methodist University Press, 1961), pp. 285–90.

30. Paredes, *With His Pistol in His Hand*, pp. 22–23.

31. Paredes, "The Anglo American in Mexican Folklore," pp. 113–27.

32. José E. Limón, "Agringado Joking in Texas-Mexican Society: Folklore and Differential Identity," *The New Scholar* 6 (1977): 33–50.

33. A brief but intriguing discussion of this legend may be found in Américo Paredes, "Mexican Legendry and the Rise of the Mestizo," in *American Folk Legend: A Symposium*, ed. Wayland Hand (Berkeley and Los Angeles: University of California Press, 1971), pp. 97–107.

34. Américo Paredes, *With His Pistol in His Hand*, and *A Texas Mexican Cancionero: Folksongs of the Lower Border* (Urbana: University of Illinois Press, 1977).

35. Dan William Dickey, *The Kennedy Corridos: A Study of the Ballads of a Mexican-American Hero* (Austin: Center for Mexican American Studies, The University of Texas, 1978).

36. For a theoretically limited but still provocative discussion of folklore as contestation, see Luigi Lombardi-Satriani, "Folklore as Culture of Contestation," *Journal of the Folklore Institute* 11 (1974): 99–121.

37. José E. Limón, "Folk Tradition and Social Change in Mexican South Texas," unpublished paper read at the annual meeting of the American Folklore Society, Pittsburgh, Pennsylvania, 1980.

38. Alicia Maria González, " 'Guess How Doughnuts Are Made?': Verbal and Nonverbal Aspects of the Panadero and His Stereotype," in *"And Other Neighborly Names": Social Process and Cultural Image in Texas Folklore*, ed. Richard Bauman and Roger Abrahams (Austin: University of Texas Press, 1981), pp. 104–22.

39. José E. Limón, "Texas-Mexican Popular Music and Dancing: A Symbological Analysis," unpublished paper read at the Conference on Chicano Culture, University of California at Berkeley, 1975. A publication that pursues a similar line of analysis with respect to Mexican dancers in California is Manuel Pena, "Ritual Structure in a Chicano Dance," *Latin American Music Review* 1 (1980): 47–73.

40. Américo Paredes, "Folk Medicine and the Intercultural Jest," in *Spanish Speaking People in the United States: Proceedings of the 1968 Annual Spring Meeting of the American Ethnological Society*, ed. June Helm (Seattle: University of Washington Press, 1968), pp. 104–19; José E. Limón, "Metafolklore and the Vanishing Hitchhiker: A Performance Analysis," unpublished paper read at the annual meeting of the California Folklore Society, 1979.

41. José R. Reyna, *Raza Humor: Chicano Joke Tradition in Texas* (San Antonio: Penca Books, 1980). See especially pp. 27–32.

42. Maria Herrera-Sobek, "The Theme of Drug Smuggling in the Mexican Corrido," *Revista Chicano-Riqueña* 7 (1979): 49–61.

43. Rosan A. Jordan, "Ethnic Identity and the Lore of the Supernatural," *Journal of American Folklore* 88 (1975): 370–82.

44. Américo Paredes, "El folklore de los grupos de origen mexicano en los Estados Unidos," *Folklore Americano* 14 (1966): 146–63.

45. For example, see Nicolás Kanellos, "Folklore in Chicano Theater and Chicano Theater as Folklore," *Journal of the Folklore Institute* 15 (1978): 57–82. A

related area also deserving of greater, more sophisticated attention is the use of folklore in Chicano written literature. For an example, see Jane Rogers, "The Function of La Llorona Motif in Rodolfo Anaya's *Bless Me Ultima*," *Latin American Literary Review* 5 (1977): 64–69.

46. Paredes, "The Problem of Identity in a Changing Culture," p. 89.

47. Richard Bauman, "The La Have Island General Store: Sociability and Verbal Art in a Nova Scotia Community," *Journal of American Folklore* 85 (1972): 330–43.

48. Roger D. Abrahams, "Personal Power and Social Restraint in the Definition of Folklore," in *Toward New Perspectives in Folklore*, pp. 17–18.

Robert B. Klymasz

Folklore of the Canadian-American Border

The boundary that separates the United States from its northern neighbor has been widely hailed as one of the world's longest undefended borders. This situation has seemingly failed to generate the kind of striking folklore discussed by Limón in the previous chapter[1] or, looking further abroad, that produced by the celebrated Scottish border, where "there is scarce a rock or stone, scarce a patch of benty grass or tuft of heather that has not had its stain of blood that flowed, century after century, from the veins of warriors."[2] In the history of the Canadian-American border, armed conflict is a minor characteristic, and the pronounced predilection for peace and friendship shared by both countries has hardly yielded the kind of tension-filled folklore corpus that typifies these other border traditions.

Nonetheless, the simple, bare notion of a boundary line conjures up a need to distinguish between "them" and "us," and even friendly borders can set the scene for folkloric activity. Every summer, for instance, large numbers of visitors travel to participate in a series of special events held at the International Peace Garden, a 2,200-acre park that straddles the Manitoba (Canada) and North Dakota (United States) boundary. Research into these festivities would very likely reveal folkloric processes and details similar to those recorded in ancient Rome, where Terminus was ritually honored every year as the god of boundaries:

> O Terminus, whether thou art a stone or a stump buried in the field, thou too has been deified from days of yore. Thou art crowned by two owners on opposite sides; they bring thee two garlands and two cakes. An altar is built. . . . The simple neighbours meet and hold a feast, and sing thy praises, holy Terminus; thou does set bounds to peoples and cities and vast kingdoms; without thee every field would be a root of wrangling. Thou courtest no favour, thou art bribed by no gold: the lands entrusted to thee thou dost guard in loyal good faith.[3]

For most Americans and Canadians today, the boundary that separates them is taken as a fact of nature, almost an act of God, which no one thinks of changing. The indigenous segment of the continent's population, however, approaches the

White Man's line with a completely different set of sentiments. Each year the Iroquois stage a border-crossing parade that by force violates the values of both the laws and the nationalism of Americans and Canadians. As parade, festival, and mass-media drama, the event helps to set the native people apart from all others, in a symbolic act that validates their identity. It also serves as a social event and an annual holiday ritual for Indians in the border area. On July 17, 1976,

> the Ladies Auxiliary of the Native Canadian Centre of Toronto chartered a bus to Niagara Falls, Ontario for the 49th Annual Border Crossing Parade. There they neatly lined up with other Indians from Tuscarora, Six Nations, the Indian Defense League of America, and the surrounding towns. The Oneida Drum and Brass Band, wearing large Plains-style feather war bonnets, led the parade. They were followed by The Indian Majorettes, the Tuscarora Indian Princess of 1976, and then the regular marchers—mostly women and children.[4]

After crossing over to the U.S. side, everyone went to a park to continue with the celebrations: booths were set up to sell Indian crafts and foods; a "Miss Indian Defense Association of America" was chosen; guest speakers were made honorary members of the border-crossing organization; and prizes were given for "traditionally" dressed babies, such as those wearing feather war bonnets.

The border that generates this kind of folkloric behavior is over 5,500 miles in length.[5] Cutting through a string of terrains—cultural and historical as well as geographical—it links a series of criss-crossing phenomena that have paved the way for a concomitant assortment of folkloric responses. Together these constitute a variegated border tradition that forms a kind of regional folklore complex by both countries.[6] As a result, then, the folklore of the Canadian-American border is not monolithic in terms of either form, context, or content. Instead, we have a complex of folkloric materials composed of individual clusters that surface in response to specific events or conditions. These pockets of folklore, so to speak, vary from one stretch of the border to another and from one kind of experience to another. A wide range of moments in the history of Canadian-American border relations provides the backdrop for this folkloric process and for a special genre of folk narrative: the border-crossing story.

Millions of Americans cross over into Canada every year, and for many of them this is an everyday, back-and-forth type of occurrence. Living within the vicinity of the border, these residents tend to regard the line "merely as a nuisance which slightly delays their arrival at Saturday night dances" on the other side. Others find that, except for the difference in the price of, say, cigarettes, the border is not really noticeable at all.[7] In 1937, Canada's popular humorist Stephen Leacock (1869–1944) expressed his view of the border situation in the following delightful manner:

> If you want to see the real Canadian-American frontier you must go, not to the forty-ninth parallel, but to the Niagara-Buffalo boundary,—Go in summertime, round the first of July or the fourth,—they hardly know which is which. Go on a holiday and see the Stars and Stripes and the Union Jack all mixed up together and the tourists pouring back and forward over the International Bridge: immigration men trying in vain to sort them out:

Niagara mingling its American and Canadian waters and its honeymoon couples, Canadians buying curios in the States and Americans buying querrios in Canada,—and such a chattering and fraternisation that it is no wonder that foreigners can't tell which is which of us. Or go to the Detroit-Windsor frontier and move back and forward with the flood of commuters, of Americans sampling beer in Windsor and Canadians sampling lager in Detroit: there you don't really cross the frontier at all, you drive under it in a tunnel. Or come down here to Montreal and meet the Dartmouth boys playing hockey; or take the Eastern Townships of Quebec where Lake Memphremagog refuses to recognize any separation, and people out bass fishing hook up the international boundary; or go to a "Ball-game" of the International League and sit in your shirt-sleeves and root and try to remember which is your nationality.[8]

Not all border-crossing experiences reflect the easygoing camaraderie depicted above. Many are unusual and personally crucial. Narratives in this particular category usually view the border as a gateway that leads to a kind of otherworld, which promises wealth, adventure, exotica, safety, and refuge. Missing today are the classic folkloric motifs describing this otherworld as protected and impenetrable because of barriers such as fearsome fires, glass mountains, witches, or walls of silver.[9] A hint of such a formidable barrier appears in the following excerpt from a text allegedly sung by fugitive slaves as they crossed over into Canada in the second half of the nineteenth century:

> Oh, righteous Father, wilt thou not pity me,
> And help me on to Canada, where all de slaves are free.
> Oh I heard Queen Victoria say,
> That if we would forsake,
> Our native land of slavery,
> And come across de lake,
> Dat she was standing on de shore,
> Wid arms extended wide,
> To give us all a peaceful home,
> Beyond de rolling tide.[10]

A true border-crossing story points to the obstacles that test and, of course, underline one's mettle and purity of intentions. One must be prepared to meet and submit to the scrutiny of garrulous customs officials, vicious police dogs, immigration authorities, patrols—a modern-day version of the dreaded Scylla and Charybdis that serves as a grueling ritual of control at international borders the world over. As such, then, the crossing into Canada can develop into a harrowing undertaking that is emotionally draining and full of anxiety for the average American. The various aspects of this particular motif are strikingly reflected in the following excerpts from narratives recorded among American draft dodgers who in the sixties and early seventies crossed into Canada to avoid military service in Vietnam:

(1) There were four people and a car full of luggage in a VW, and we couldn't lay down and things like that. We just sat up. It took us 38 hours straight

through. We slept sitting up. Another source of fear was that we were stopped in Nebraska by the state patrol for driving five miles over the speed limit, and we were afraid that since my father had turned me in, and because I had a secret security clearance, they would have already given my name to the FBI. . . .

(2) Those who had traveled . . . had little concern about crossing the border. . . . However, tensions were sometimes exacerbated by wives who expected real difficulty. . . . "My wife was really neurotic about it. . . . She was really scared. She thought there were going to be U.S. troopers there at the border and we would have to drive through their blockade. . . ."

(3) Yeh, man, I really felt good when I came across that border. WOW! I felt like somebody had taken a heavy stone off my back. When I was in the States everybody was talking about the draft. Everything you did was in reference to the goddamn draft. Everybody was worried about it. The second you come over the border, man this just disappears like smoke. You don't worry about it anymore. You can tell them to fuck it. That's the end of it. I felt pretty damn good, and there isn't all that paranoia—that's over.[11]

Besides the narratives of fugitive slaves and draft dodgers, the folklore of the Canadian-American border also includes a considerable quantity of material that emerged in response to what was perhaps the most spectacular border-crossing episode in the history of Canadian-American relations: the Klondike Gold Rush, 1896 to 1899. The epic dimensions of this story include a rich array of legendary characters and a cast of thousands—the largest ever single rush of United States citizens across the border to Canada. In the space of fewer than eighteen months, some fifty thousand American men and women participated in this epidemic of gold fever. In Dawson, and indeed almost everywhere, the Americans outnumbered the Canadians by at least five to one.[12] In a manner that is reminiscent of the barrier motif mentioned earlier, eyewitness accounts focus on the treacherous trails that led into the Canadian gold fields. One of the largest of these led through the Chilkoot Pass, which straddled the international border between Alaska (United States) and British Columbia (Canada):

Who would have thought that this wall of glittering white, with a slope so precipitous that no animal could cross it, would turn out to be the most effective way to reach the gold-fields? Who would have thought that, in spite of its steps of solid ice, its banshee winds, its crushing fall of snow, and its thundering avalanches, the Chilkoot was to be the funnel through which the majority of men would attain their goal?[13]

Brought up with the social, legal, and political traditions of the United States, the Americans found themselves living temporarily under a foreign flag, obeying, however reluctantly, foreign regulations and encountering a foreign bureaucracy and officialdom. A popular anecdote triggered by the situation describes the confrontation of a bewhiskered British judge and an American charged with assault:

"Prisoner . . . I understand you come from the other side of the line. We will not put up with your bullying here. The fine is one hundred dollars."

"That's all right, Judge," came the reply. "I've got that right here in my breeches pocket."

"And six months' hard labour. Perhaps you have that in your other pocket!"[14]

Other amusing moments in the Canadian-American folklore complex include quips about American tourists arriving at the Canadian border on a hot summer's day loaded down with furs and skis. At least one commentator has traced the source of this stereotypic image of Canada to Hollywood, with its almost six hundred movies about Canada.[15] Several movie titles refer directly to the border, for example, *Over the Border* (1922), *Border Blackbirds* (1927), *Border Saddlemates* (1952); and the opening subtitle of *The Northern Code* (1925) claimed that "beyond the Canadian border lies a land of lengthy shadows and strange forget-fulness. . . . A land where the natives, ruled by primitive passions, practised the one code they learned from nature—'the survival of the fittest.' "[16] Hollywood's "Great Canadian Theme" between 1918 and 1925 was that of an American accused of a crime (almost always wrongly) who escapes into foreign, Canadian territory to reach the anonymity and peace of the Great Woods. Besides asylum, Canada also offered a chance to forget—the past, an unfaithful wife, or a dead sweetheart. The Royal Canadian Mounted Police were seen as a kind of local and conveniently accessible Foreign Legion, where a man could bury the past. Women, small children, household pets, and even zoo animals made it over the border: in *Soul of the Beast* (1923) Ruth Lorrimor, abused by her wicked stepfather, a circus owner, escaped to the Canadian woods along with the circus's prize performer, Oscar the Elephant.[17] For all and sundry, then, the Canadian border developed into a folkloric motif that held the promise of a second chance—a portal that inevitably led to the safety and comfort of still another New World version of the mythic Elysium.

On hot and humid summer evenings, the so-called Canadian snow pictures that depicted Canada as a wintry land were especially useful as coolants to sweating audiences, who sat, without the later benefits of air-conditioning, in airless, stifling theaters. One enterprising theater owner, capitalizing on his showing of *Over the Border*, made it clear to his patrons exactly how frigid conditions were over the American-Canadian border. To contrast the climate on both sides of the boundary line, he divided his lobby into two sections: the left side, representing the United States, garlanded in green foliage and bathed in hot lights; the right side, representing Canada, framed by cotton-topped fir boughs and lit by frigid blue. The resultant "snow lobby" was crowned by a sign that tooted: "You Can Go 'Over the Border' Inside!"[18] In this manner, then, Hollywood brought the lore of the Canadian-American border to millions who would never have the opportunity to experience it in any other way.

Still other aspects of Canadian-American border folklore await exploration. Of special interest are the nature, role, and specific features of the barrier-gateway dichotomy, which, as suggested earlier, pervades the entire complex as its basic theme. Also, tourism and nonborder points of entry, such as airports, warrant attention as contributing new elements to the storehouse of Canadian-American border folklore.

NOTES

1. See also Américo Paredes, *A Texas-Mexican Cancionero: Folksongs of the Lower Border* (Urbana: University of Illinois Press, 1976).

2. Jean Lang, *A Land of Romance: The Border, Its History and Legend*, 2d ed. (London: T. C. and E. C. Jack, Ltd., 1930), p. 3.

3. Publius Ovidius Naso, *Fastorum libri sex: The Fasti of Ovid*, ed. and trans. James George Frazer (London: Macmillan and Co., Ltd., 1929), vol. 1, pp. 96–97.

4. John A. Price, *Native Studies: American and Canadian Indians* (Toronto: McGraw-Hill Ryerson Ltd., 1978), p. 228.

5. In this regard, it is interesting to note that the United States–Mexico border is a little over 1,900 miles in length, and the celebrated Scottish border is only 73 miles long.

6. In this connection, see, for instance, many of the entries listed in Edward D. Ives and Bacil Kirtley, "Bibliography of New England–Maritimes Folklore," *Northeast Folklore* 1 (1958): 19–28; 2 (1959): 19–23; 3 (1960): 20–23; and Luc Lacourcière, *Oral Tradition: New England and French Canada* (Québec: Archives de Folklore, Université Laval, 1972).

7. National Film Board of Canada, Still Photography Division, Ottawa, *Between Friends / Entre Amis* (Toronto: McClelland and Stewart Ltd., 1976), pp. 217, 249.

8. Stephen Leacock, *My Discovery of the West* (Toronto: Thomas Allen, 1937), pp. 165–66.

9. See motif numbers F140 to F149.1, as listed in Stith Thompson, *Motif-Index of Folk Literature*, 6 vols. (Bloomington: Indiana University Press, 1966).

10. Robin W. Winks, *The Blacks in Canada: A History* (Montreal: McGill-Queen's University Press, 1971), p. 243.

11. Roger Neville Williams, *The New Exiles: American War Resisters in Canada* (New York: Liveright Publishers, 1971), p. 45; Kenneth Fred Emerick, *War Resisters Canada: The World of the American Military-Political Refugees* (Knox, Pennsylvania: Knox, Pennsylvania Free Press, 1972), pp. 92–94. Additional materials can be found in Jim Christy, ed., *The New Refugees: American Voices in Canada* (Toronto: Peter Martin Associates Ltd., 1972), pp. 81–85, 113–14, 121, 146; and Lawrence M. Baskir and William A. Strauss, *Chance and Circumstance: The Draft, the War, and the Vietnam Generation* (New York: Alfred A. Knopf, 1978), pp. 175–76.

12. Pierre Berton, *Klondike: The Last Great Gold Rush, 1896–1899*, rev. ed. (Toronto: McClelland and Stewart Ltd., 1972), p. xii.

13. Ibid., p. 236.

14. Ibid., p. xv; see also additional variant on p. 308.

15. Pierre Berton, *Hollywood's Canada: The Americanization of Our National Image* (Toronto: McClelland and Stewart Ltd., 1975), p. 12.

16. Ibid., p. 78.

17. Ibid., p. 54.

18. Ibid., pp. 50–52.

Roger Mitchell

Americanization of Folklore in U.S. Possessions and Territories

American influence is ebbing fast in the Caribbean, and the Virgin Islands alone remain U.S. possessions in an area once seen as an American lake. The situation is quite different in the Pacific, where recent political developments suggest that American possessions will increase rather than diminish. While the American presence in Polynesia holds steady with the state of Hawaii and the Territory of Samoa, the same does not follow in that island world called Micronesia. Following World War II, the United States not only regained the territory of Guam but also assumed responsibility for much of Micronesia, called the Trust Territory of the Pacific Islands. This trust is now entering its last years, and already the Mariana Islands District has voted overwhelmingly to cast its lot with the United States. Two other island groups, Palau and the Marshalls, have also indicated that they too may seek some sort of permanent alignment. The relative poverty of the central districts suggests that they have few options other than continuing as some kind of American dependency if they wish to maintain their technological gains.

It would seem long overdue that folklorists interrupt their love affair with the Oceanic past and consider Polynesian and Micronesian folklore in relation to the American experience. Charles Skinner pioneered this approach nearly a century ago.[1] It was an ambitious effort and included lore from both the Caribbean and the Pacific. Although popular in its appeal and deficient in the control data that are de rigueur among folklorists today, Skinner's book reveals the deep inroads made by westernization in the aboriginal lore of Hawaii, Guam, and the Philippines. My own collecting in this general area would indicate that this melding of the Oceanic and the western has continued unabated.

The comparative basis for such an approach is substantial. In her *Hawaiian Mythology*, Martha Beckwith performed an epic task in bringing order to the voluminous research on Polynesian oral traditions. Katharine Luomala later rounded out this landmark work with a summary of well over a century of folklore research in the area.[2] But missing from this mountain of scholarly exertion are major efforts that would document the changes wrought in their folklore as Hawaiians and Samoans have been pulled into the American cultural mainstream. As Luomala showed in her study of the Vanishing Hitchhiker legend and Kikuchi reinforced in his recent article on ghostly fireballs, Hawaiian lore is changing with the times. Ghostly hitchhikers have merged with old Hawaiian goddesses, and contemporary Caucasians, native Hawaiians, and Japanese-Americans now share the Hawaiian-Japanese belief in supernatural fireballs.[3]

Even better opportunities for research on the Americanization of Oceanic folklore are to be found in the Trust Territory of the Pacific Islands and the Territory of Guam, since the region includes island cultures that range from grass skirts on the Yap Islands to McDonald's Hamburgers on Guam. The inhabitants of the Trust Territory still boast a strong native folklore, although this varies in accordance with the receptivity of each group to culture change.[4] As with Samoa and Hawaii, there exist excellent collections of aboriginal lore that allow in-depth comparisons between the past and present. Outstanding is the multivolume work of a group of German scholars.[5] These early publications show that Micronesians were quick to expand their native lore by incorporating both sacred and secular stories introduced by the early missionaries. Many of their narratives are thinly disguised accounts of the crucifixion of Christ, the Tower of Babel, Jack the Giant Killer, and the tar baby, to mention a few. In my own fieldwork of the last two decades, I have collected similarly modified accounts of dragon slayers, maligned wives, and evil trolls.[6] These western intrusions have been accompanied by reductions in native lore. Micronesian mythology has been decimated by Christianity. As some islanders have departed their isolated atolls for district centers, they have not passed on to their descendants the lore of their natal islands. Years spent in American schools have placed additional barriers between other young Micronesians and their heritage.

On the other hand, American popular culture has taken the islands by storm. Dances, basketball, gangs, television, bars, movies—everywhere one turns, the burgeoning growth of the American way of life is evident. Whatever form Micronesian folklore takes in the future, it will assuredly have a strong American component.

Nowhere in Micronesia has this process of westernization gone farther than on Guam. The over four hundred years stretching from Magellan's landfall (1521) to the hectic post–World War II years have transformed the land, its people, and its folklore. Very few myths and *Märchen*-type tales remain from Guam's past, and fewer still survive in oral tradition. Instead, they appear from time to time in newspapers or in some other ephemeral publication. A few legends remain, telling that this rock was dropped by a supernatural being, or over that cliff leaped two thwarted lovers. The most vigorous forms of native lore are the many tales of fearful encounters with the spirits of the pagan dead, the *taotaomonas*. Narratives left from the long Spanish period are more plentiful and have kept alive the memories of martyred priests, miraculous statues, and Hispanic tricksters.

American lore is more diffuse. Along with the X-rated film, the erotic yarn has great popularity on the island. Graffiti, especially in men's rooms at the University of Guam, are well acclimated and reflect the sexual, racial, and political tensions of the island's mixed population. Traditional American folklore has been introduced in the schools and through the newspapers, in articles timed to coincide with American holidays. The personal narrative is especially rich, for this includes the trying experiences of the Japanese invasion and occupation during World War II and the subsequent reinvasion in 1944, with July 14 serving as the functional equivalent of the Fourth of July.

As this American lore infiltrates Guamanian tradition, the islanders are making some fascinating cultural accommodations. For example, the Vanishing Hitchhiker legend on Guam has absorbed the early Spanish tradition of the White Lady who haunts a bridge, along with the still more ancient Guamanian tradition of the *taotaomona*.[7]

Other changes in and additions to Guamanian folklore show the influence of American popular culture and a growing tendency toward fakelore. Guam has a mermaid legend, a composite of a Micronesian base and a strong Spanish component, with a few fillips added during American times. There is now a Miss Mermaid day, complete with fish tail, beauty contest, and Chamber of Commerce hoopla.

There would seem then to be strong reason for bringing the study of Oceanic folklore out of the realm of cultural anthropology and into the purview of American folkloristics. As indicated, cultural transformation is afoot in U.S. territories and dependencies, and the American experience is and will continue to be a major catalyst. Many of these islanders are already American citizens; more will become so in the near future. Their expanding contacts with America and their fellow Americans are fast changing their lives and lore, and these changes are deserving of more attention from folklorists than they have been given thus far. Research opportunities are both numerous and of deep significance to the study of folklore. At what rate are these divergent people absorbing our national mythology? What functional shifts are being made as American lore is reduced to island size? In turn, will this island world continue to grip the American imagination as have Samoa and Hawaii? The answers to such questions await investigation.

NOTES

1. Charles M. Skinner, *Myths and Legends of Our New Possessions and Protectorate* (Philadelphia, 1900; reprint, Ann Arbor: Gryphon Books, 1971).

2. Martha Beckwith, *Hawaiian Mythology* (New Haven, 1940; reprint, Honolulu: University of Hawaii Press, 1970); Katharine Luomala, "Survey of Research on Polynesian Prose and Poetry," in *Folklore Research Around the World*, Indiana University Folklore Monograph Series, No. 16, ed. Richard M. Dorson (Bloomington: Indiana University Press, 1961), pp. 135-53.

3. Katharine Luomala, "Disintegration and Regeneration, the Phanto.n Hitchhiker Legend," *Fabula* 13 (1972): 79-97; William K. Kikuchi, "The Fireball in Hawaiian Folklore," in *Directions in Pacific Traditional Literature: Essays in Honor of Katharine Luomala*, Bishop Museum Special Publication 62, ed. Adrienne L. Kaeppler and H. Arlo Nimmo (Honolulu: Bishop Museum Press, 1976), pp. 157-72.

4. See Roger Mitchell, "Micronesian Folklore and Culture Change," *Journal of the Folklore Institute* 9 (1972): 28-44.

5. Georg Thilenius, ed., *Ergebnisse der Sudsee-Expedition 1908-1910*, Hamburgische Wissenschaftich Stiftung und Notgemeinschaft der Deutschen Wissenschaft, 16 vols. (Hamburg: Friederichsen, De Gruyter, 1914-38).

6. Roger Mitchell, "A Study of the Cultural, Historical, and Acculturative Factors Influencing the Repertoires of Two Trukese Informants" (Ph.D. diss., Indiana University, 1967), pp. 589–604.

7. Roger Mitchell, "Ancestral Spirits and Hitchhiking Ghosts: Syncretism on Guam," *Midwestern Journal of Language and Folklore* 2 (1976): 45–55.

American Entertainments

Folklore research has concentrated largely on Americans at work, first in the outdoor occupations, and recently on the assembly line and in the office. Americans in their leisure pursuits also become involved with folklore, as these three exploratory articles on theatrical performances, festivals, and sports events make evident.

At various moments and in particular forms in the history of the American stage, actors and playwrights have drawn upon folk character types, folk humor, and folk speech to delight audiences with a sense of the familiar. Where theater is improvisational, flexible, informal, and intimately enmeshed with theatergoers, declares Robert Toll, the folklorist will find a happy hunting ground. Yankee farce, comic monologues, minstrelsy, vaudeville, ethnic theater, and regional theater have at various periods incorporated trickster pranks, tall talk, patter and repartee, traditional songs, tunes, and dances, and popular legends into their acts. One of the sensational moments in American theatrical history occurred in 1848 when the actor Francis Chanfrau impersonated on stage a Bowery folktype known as the "b'hoy." The jerry-built musical drama, "A Glance at New York," that featured Mose the Bowery b'hoy, appealed at first to the b'hoys in the Bowery theater and subsequently to audiences in every city of size in the land. Such long-run Broadway hits captured Jewish-immigrant and poor-white folktypes in enduring portraits.

Festivals seem more at home in almost every other country than the United States, a point strongly made by Harvey Cox in *The Feast of Fools* (1969). Cox contends that the work ethic has driven the sense of festivity and fantasy out of American life, and in comparison with the great feast-days and ceremonial events in other cultures, the United States has indeed seemed barren and bereft of joyous occasions. A new vein of festival research, about which Beverly Stoeltje writes in her essay on "Festival in America," has uncovered a number of community celebrations of an indigenous kind, from rodeos to tulip festivals, which extol the product or personality identified with the region. The festival is itself a folk form, a blend of many separate genres, and requires sophisticated attention on the part of one or more folklorists in order to unravel its structure and symbolic behavior. Boosterism, hoaxing, beauty pageants, fairs, and contests all get mixed up in

American festivals. At Churubusco, Indiana, a farmer sighted and gave chase to a monster turtle, which he never captured, but Churubusco now celebrates an annual Turtle Day Festival in honor of the Beast of Busco, and vendors sell turtleburgers and turtleneck sweaters and celebrants stage turtle races and choose a Turtle Queen.

In place of the religious holidays of other climes, Americans indulge in sports extravaganzas. The Superbowl, the World Series, the NCAA and NBA basketball championships catapult them into annual frenzies. As Elizabeth Peterson suggests in her essay on "American Sports and Folklore," these occasions partake of the nature of festive events that Stoeltje examines. But they belong with a separate spectrum of interests and activities that extends to participation in and observance of collegiate, high school, country club, and sandlot sports. For all the impact of sports and athlete celebrities on American life, folklorists have as yet made but a few gingerly approaches to the subject, and these mainly addressed to verbal items and genres. Peterson makes a plea for consideration of the cultural meaning of sports traditions and ethnographic analysis of sporting events. The folklorist might assess for instance the concept of "fair play" and "being a good sport" versus the advocacy of gamesmanship and winning at any cost, an ethical conflict that extends into business and war. I still remember my shock at the injunction of a camp counselor to do anything we could, by fair means or foul, to win our tennis match with the rival camp, and to see him put the action to the word by miscalling a crucial shot in the match he was refereeing, in favor of his players. What are the traditional codes that coaches instill in their players? The question is of more than passing interest. A feature article in *Time* magazine about a successful football coach (September 29, 1980) explicitly states the ambivalence of the codes.

> To the rabid, almost reverential followers of his University of Alabama football teams, Paul William ("Bear") Bryant is a nearly mythic figure, a man who embodies the traditional American values: dedication, hard work, honesty and, above all, success. To the frustrated fans of the legions of teams he has defeated, he is a relentlessly slippery recruiter, a ruthless win-at-all-costs tyrant.

In these several areas of American pastimes and recreation our contributors have presented analytic models for folkloric probings that can yield rich results.

Beverly J. Stoeltje

Festival in America

The discipline of folklore has seen a resurgence of interest in festival in recent years, with a strong emphasis on the current social significance of traditional celebrations.[1] Scholars as well as the general public and public institutions have rediscovered festivity, and the term *festival* has been adopted by many of the burgeoning popular events that share few generic features. Events which *do* share such features, however, rarely use the term to name the event. This discussion centers on festivals of the latter kind, held within a community setting, expressing traditions meaningful to that community and produced by and for its members, not for outside consumption.[2]

In the United States community festivals reflect the diversity of American traditions, including ethnic celebrations, religious fiestas, and festivals connected with region or occupation. Traditions from both the ancient and the more recent past are celebrated, as well as those that fuse the two. Czech-American harvest festivals illustrate this fusion, as Svatava Pirkova-Jakobson demonstrates in her study illuminating the meaning of the event in both Czechoslovakia and America.[3] The vital festival, then, encapsulates elements of relevant shared experience in public presentation.

The complexity and immediacy of festival demand that the study of festival be grounded in a conceptual framework. Toward that end the following framework is suggested for use in planning research and interpreting data.

CONCEPTUAL FRAMEWORK FOR FESTIVAL RESEARCH

The framework approaches festival through three categories: (1) generic features; (2) festival structures; (3) symbolic action.

(1) *Generic features.* Two features dominant in vital festivals will be considered here: the repertoire of festival communication and the expressed dimensions of temporal reality.

Festival can incorporate every art and play form in the culture, combining them in infinite variations, manipulating both form and content, and transcending routine perceptions through intense participation in artistic and ludic expression.

Perhaps it was this transcendent quality that stimulated Nietzsche to speak of "the art of the festival" as "that higher art."[4]

The repertoire of socioaesthetic forms used to communicate in festival includes not only all local genres, but a multiplicity of codes and scenes for the performance of them.[5] Noise, smells, food, costume, rhythm, and action bombard the senses, using every semiotic code. These are expressed in local genres of music and dance, drama, feasts, verbal art, and display forms, and presented in multiple scenes, both scheduled and spontaneous, many of which occur simultaneously.

Such complexity often gives rise to an impression of chaos and disorder, especially to members of modern society trained to isolate the senses and limit communication to visual, literate forms based on principles of sequence.[6] Festival involves us in a shift from the communicative forms of routine, modern life to the multiple communications of celebration, based on principles of repetition and simultaneity.[7] These principles of communication so determine festival experience that to ignore them results in piecemeal interpretations rather than the comprehension of the special folk genre of festival, characterized particularly by humor, complexity, intensification, and participation.

Like communication, the temporal reality of festival has multiple dimensions. Festivals with ancient roots have been associated with changing seasons and annual cycles. Linked with religious holidays, some festivals mark a sacred time period, celebrate a saint's day, or honor the ancestors. Secular cultures associate festivals with historical events. Some American communities, for example, celebrate the Fourth of July with a festival, and Juneteenth celebrates emancipation from slavery.[8]

Periodicity and recurrence function consistently throughout these various contexts. The impersonal, predictable movement of time provides the stimulus for festival independent of any human agent. This impersonal force is not a rite of passage or a curing ceremony but is equally relevant to all members of the social group, relating them to the cosmos or to social history through principles of periodicity and recurrence.

A second dimension of temporal reality focuses on the dialectical process of tradition and change. Substance in festival derives from traditions based on common identity; thus festival emphasizes the past. Yet festival occurs in and for the present; thus social change emerges. Specifically, if contemporary themes and styles are not incorporated in festival, it fails quickly, but if the traditional substance becomes lost, the festival dies with the passing of the contemporary. This process then constitutes a dimension of human action where two temporal realities, the past and the present, function in tandem.[9]

Sometimes operating subtly and at other times explosively, the process requires sensitive and diligent research to be identified in some festivals, for it is affected by the heterogeneity of American community life, clearly manifested in the interpretations of a festival given by participants. Collecting these from officials, performers, peripheral individuals, special interest groups, and both older and younger generations allows the researcher to construct a synchronic image of this diachronic process.

These dimensions of temporal reality expressed during festival—cosmic, historical, and present—serve to relate the individual to the social group of festival, to larger cultural units, and to the defined cosmos through participation and performance in festival.

(2) *Festival structures.* To an outsider any given festival may seem mysterious, for structure and organization are rarely visible, but apparently unstructured and spontaneous activity appears everywhere. In reality, structures serve to organize the artistic and social expressions in festival through the manipulation of time, space, genre, and role, and to determine time and space for unstructured expression. Essentials of this structural complex are discussed below.[10]

a. *Time and Place.* A special date is determined to accord with the festival purpose and announced publicly in advance; a particular space is designated and transformed into the festival grounds.

b. *Opening Ceremony.* The festival begins with an official opening ceremony, usually a parade or a procession, depending on the sacred or secular nature of the event. Such a ceremony usually displays the existing social structure and confirms the values dominant within the community. For example, at the Texas Cowboy Reunion, a celebration of cowboy heritage held on July 4, an afternoon parade officially opens the event. Leading the parade are two cowboys on horses carrying the state and national flags. This unit joins the symbols of the state and nation—the flags—together with the local symbol—the cowboy—to create a unified image. Further, the cowboy flag carriers are foremen on the large ranch which provides leadership for the event itself so the riders represent a specific element in the cowboy community.

Cowgirl contestants in the rodeo barrel race ride in a group near the front of the parade, and they are required to dress in colorful Western attire. Each girl represents a town, a ranch, or a business located in the larger region and wears its name on a satin ribbon pinned to her shirt. Grouping the cowgirls together constitutes them as a special category and placing them near the front of the parade acknowledges the importance of the category: the dress requirements point to an association between females and beauty, and their representative capacity emphasizes their relationship to a community or institution.

Social structure is apparent in each of the other categories of the parade, such as the individuals who are displayed in convertible automobiles. These include politicians from the area and a woman who has been chosen as the Hostess of the Reunion. Business and civic organizations construct floats, and neighboring towns send riding groups known as Sheriff's Posses. The parade concludes with a large group of mounted cowboys and cowgirls of all ages, including fathers and grandfathers who place their children and grandchildren on the saddle with them. This unit displays the cowboy element of the social structure: the individual rider or family group, who is not affiliated with an institution and exhibits no identification other than the self on the horse.

Thus a careful examination of each unit within the parade and of the parade as a sequential whole will reveal a body of information about the social group that has been chosen as appropriate for public communication.

c. *Ritual.* A ritual event attracts a devoted group of participants who have a personal involvement in the ritual purpose. Rituals of religious festivals are central to the celebration and involve many participants, but more modern secular festivals tend to situate the ritual privately where a limited group attends. An example is the ritual that crowns and presents the queen of the festival to a select audience; less common are religious services in which lay leaders figure prominently.

d. *Drama and Contest.* Eliciting broad participation and a large audience, the folk drama or competitive event enacts social conflicts, reverses orders, or articulates tension. In traditional societies throughout the world folk drama occupies this position, and the folk clown often has a prominent role. Contemporary American Indian clowns often parody the behavior of Anglos in folk drama, and Hasidic Jews in New York adapt Bible stories to contemporary themes in the folk drama known as Purimspiel.[11] In modern American society, competitions and contests have assumed this position. They situate relationships of opposition within the boundaries of a playing field or arena in place of a stage, and reflect the preoccupation with competition characteristic of modern life. Competitive events are generally interpreted to the audience by an announcer who articulates specific themes; but values are further communicated through the performers in the action, the heroes and heroines of the event, and even through the subject itself which has been selected as worthy of competition: the fiddle music in a fiddle contest, the watermelon in a watermelon auction, oxen in an ox pull. Thus car races at the Indy 500, horse races at the Kentucky Derby, a community rodeo or circus, or a football game at Homecoming, all serve as dramatic performances expressing relationships of opposition in culturally defined forms of competition.[12]

e. *Concluding Event.* In contrast to the opening ceremony of a festival, the closing event exhibits much less structure. Festival exhibits a pattern of action beginning with the formal and moving to the informal. Often it concludes with dancing in the streets, large feasts, or displays of fireworks. At this time excess and licentiousness reach their peak.

f. *Music and Food.* Festivity rarely, if ever, occurs without music and food. At times they are the subject of scheduled events such as feasts or performances, but they also have a continuous and spontaneous character. Both are powerful means of expressing the identity of the group or groups represented in the festival. The processes of selection and preparation, means of presentation, and identity of the performers and presenters all serve to define the nature of any participation in the festival.

g. *Outside Performers.* Common to festival everywhere are the traveling vendors, performers, and "amusement makers." At times they are clustered together in carnival. In more recent years craftspeople and traders have become popular additions to festival. Individual specialists such as fortune tellers, magicians, or portrait painters may be set apart in a space of their own. These marginal, traveling people offer the exotic, strange, and unusual to the community for consumption. The choice of "outsiders" and the relationship between them and the community inform any study of the social parameters that define the event. "Outsiders" and their products also display the current preoccupations of the local participants (arts and crafts, antiques, fortune telling, tattoos, tee shirts). In contrast to local performers, the itinerant specialists offer the strange in the impersonal interaction of commerce, and often the result is an object or memory which remains long after the occasion (say, a souvenir or a fortune).

h. *Participation.* Actual festival behavior can be fruitfully examined with the concept labeled "structure of participation." Although participation may appear chaotic, there are nevertheless structures that guide the choices the participants make. Categories resulting from these structures include age and sex divisions, ethnic groups, performers and audience, drinkers and nondrinkers, and numerous others. For example, when participants are members of more than one ethnic group, the first relevant data to obtain about these groups will be the nature and location of participation by the groups. If the groups are divided by ethnicity, one will want to obtain data on why they are separated, who makes decisions, and what actually happens in the separate spaces. Further, one will want to know how the boundaries are determined and maintained, who may cross them, and for what purposes. Answers may suggest economic or political factors, racism, personal taste and so on, but the important objective is to gain an accurate picture of the participation itself. By eliciting these organizational data, the social structure of the community and the relationship of festival to routine, "normative" life become apparent.[13]

(3) *Symbolic action*. Festival removes or transforms the behavioral environment into a space and time markedly different from that of routine life, i.e, into what Victor Turner labels the *liminal* for preindustrial society and the *liminoid* for modern society.[14] This transformation has often been described as a licensed relaxation of the norms and rules governing social life, a negation of the social order. Other interpretations stress the themes of regeneration and revitalization, suggesting that symbolic action in festival brings about a triumph of life over death, affirming the identity of the folk group. This ambivalence saturates festival in themes of negation and creation, expressed particularly through humor and directed at both the folk group and outsiders.[15]

Activities at festival manipulate structures so that themes are perceived through enactment.[16] Sacred/historical subjects (cosmological, commemorative, or religious) are reflected in ritual and ceremony, and secular/present subjects (interaction between tradition and change) are enacted through drama, contests, feasts, music, and dance. (In reality, of course, no event deals with one domain exclusively.)

Symbolic inversion, the reversal of established orders such as social hierarchies and male/female roles, characterizes festivals around the world. In hierarchical societies symbolic inversion creates egalitarianism during festival or carnival. Recent studies point out that reversal can replace equality with hierarchy in societies where egalitarianism is the stated norm.[17] Throughout America festivals and celebrations present queens and princesses and their escorts as representatives of the communities during festival. Not only does this process create an aristocratic hierarchy from a society committed to egalitarian principles, but the selection of a regal female to represent a social group in a country primarily governed by male leaders reverses the norm for sex roles as well.

A second means of creating hierarchy in American festival exists in the competitive event. Participants begin with equality and without differential status. Through agonistic action the event establishes winners, a hierarchy of superior competitors, dividing the participants into the victorious and the defeated and creating differentiation out of sameness.

The winner becomes a hero or heroine, and the queen reigns throughout the festival. When the festival is over, though the memory will remain, these individuals return to their social position in routine life. (In some cases the individual's social position may be enhanced, but queens do not reign nor is a nonprofessional's career altered by the festival competition.)

These inversions may be observed easily because of their public nature, but symbolic actions may also be communicated more subtly, as in drama or music.

THE RESEARCH PROJECT

Festival research requires careful planning if the investigator is to avoid being seduced into oblivion by participation or stunned into paralysis by observation. A conceptual framework should be mapped onto the information obtained in advance from the schedule, contacts within the community, old newspaper articles. A team effort is advisable with a division of labor agreed upon in advance. *Several* members of the team should take the responsibility for laying out, individually, a spatial arrangement of the festival grounds and personnel. Research methods should include recorded interviews, recorded events, detailed notes on paper or spoken into a tape recorder, photographs, slides, videotapes, and the collection of any relevant printed matter. Politeness should govern all interactions, recognizing that politeness systems vary, not only across ethnic lines, but from rural to urban, east to west, and north to south. General data on the following festival elements should be gathered before concentrating on specific activities, determining what position, if any, each occupies in the overall event: food and drink, music and dance, dress and costume, symbols, ethnic and social groups, occupations, institutions and organizations, special performers.

American festivals reflect infinite variety, quite beyond the ethnic and regional diversity we associate with American culture. The subject chosen by the community as its festival theme generally but not always functions also as its identificational symbol, and as such is enacted, displayed, verbalized, and transformed in festival action.

Agricultural products often provide the symbol in rural areas. The Watermelon Thump of Luling, Texas, where watermelons are raised as a major crop, serves as such an example. In contrast to the product symbol, in Peru, Indiana, performance itself becomes a symbol when the annual community circus, featuring all local children as the performers, serves as the focus of celebration. Rodeo, featuring the cowboy, transforms an occupational role into a festival symbol in some communities. Italian, French, Hispanic, and Slavic communities in Brooklyn, New Orleans, Los Angeles, Detroit, and Santa Fe as well as the small towns of America create festival by combining sacred and secular themes in symbolic representations drawn from the Catholic religion. The oldest American festivals are still celebrated among Pueblo Indians with ritual dramas to mark the solstices or equinoxes. And finally, perhaps the most modern festival transforms the automobile into a festival symbol at the Indy 500.

To determine, then, what a particular community celebrates in festival, each festival event must be attended and the themes and symbols identified, noting what the structured and unstructured activities actually express in symbolic action as well as what is officially stated.

Lest one think that because festival research is pleasurable it is, therefore, easy, caution should be exercised in setting project goals in order to ensure that the capacities of the research team match the goals. Even one long day of gathering data in the blazing sun with large groups under noisy conditions can be frustrating for an inexperienced researcher. Thus the wise student of festival will evaluate and prepare the human resources as well as the recording equipment when undertaking the journey into that multidimensional reality we label festivity.

NOTES

1. Festival studies by folklorists that demonstrate contemporary approaches include a special festival issue of *Western Folklore* 31 (1972) with articles by Abrahams, Bauman, Newall, Smith; Alan Dundes and Alessandro Falassi, *La Terra in Piazza* (Berkeley: University of California Press, 1975); Robert J. Smith, *The Art of the Festival* (Lawrence: University of Kansas Publications in Anthropology #6, 1975).

2. For a discussion of the contrast between festival and festivals that have become spectacles or objects of consumption, see Marianne Mesnil, "The Masked Festival: Disguise or Affirmation?" *Cultures* 3:2 (1976): 11-29.

3. Svatava Pirkova-Jakobson, "Harvest Festivals in America," in *Slavic Folklore: A Symposium*, ed. Albert Bates Lord, American Folklore Society Bibliographical and Special Series, 6 (Philadelphia: 1956), pp. 68-82.

4. Friedrich Nietzsche, *Joyful Wisdom* (New York: Frederick Ungar Publishing Company, 1960), p. 124.

5. I am using the term *code* here in a general semiotic sense to mean a sign system such as costume, food, language. The term *scene* refers to locally defined, meaningful contexts of action.

6. For a brief report relating to this topic see Edmund Carpenter, "If Wittgenstein Had Been an Eskimo," *Natural History* (February 1980): 72-77.

7. A detailed discussion of this semiotic system, labeled the "carnival semiotic," can be found in Barbara Babcock, "The Novel and the Carnival World," *Modern Language Notes* 89 (1974): 911-37.

8. For a discussion of calendrical rites and rites of reversals see Edward Norbeck, "Rites of Reversal of North American Indians as Forms of Play," in *Forms of Play of Native North Americans*, ed. Edward Norbeck and Claire R. Farrer (New York: West Publishing Company, 1979); for an example of a fiesta in the Southwest see Evon Z. Vogt, "A Study of the Southwestern Fiesta System as Exemplified by the Laguna Fiesta," *American Anthropologist* 57 (1950): 820-39; for discussions of American historical festivals see William H. Cohn, "A National Celebration: The Fourth of July in American History," *Cultures* 3:2 (1976): 141-56; Beverly J. Stoeltje, "Rodeo as Symbolic Performance" (Ph.D. diss., University of Texas, 1979); William H. Wiggins, Jr., " 'Lift Every Voice': A Study of Afro-American Emancipation Celebrations," in *Discovering Afro-America*, ed. Roger D. Abrahams and John S. Szwed, pp. 46-57 (Leiden: E.J. Brill, 1975); idem, "January 1: The Afro-Americans' 'Day of Days,' " *Prospects* 5 (1979): 331-45.

9. Harvey Cox, *The Feast of Fools* (New York: Harper & Row, 1969), p. 56.

10. Generic distinctions of ritual ceremony, drama, and contests are productively compared in Max and Mary Gluckman, "On Drama, and Games and Athletic Contests," in *Secular Ritual*, ed. Sally Falk Moore and Barbara G. Myerhoff (Amsterdam: Van Gorcum, 1977).

11. Claire R. Farrer, "Singing for Life: The Mescalero Apache Girls' Puberty Ceremony," in *Southwestern Indian Ritual Drama*, ed. Charlotte Frisbie (Albuquerque: School of American Research/University of New Mexico Press, 1980); and Shifra Epstein, "The Celebration of a Contemporary Purim in the Bobover Hasidic Community" (Ph.D. diss., University of Texas, 1979).

12. The Indy 500 has been thoroughly documented with a special emphasis on the features of competition in Ron Dorson, *The Indy 500: An American Institution Under Fire* (Newport Beach, Calif.: Bond/Parkhurst Books, 1974).

13. Roger D. Abrahams and Richard Bauman, "Ranges of Festival Behavior," in *The Reversible World*, ed. Barbara A. Babcock (Ithaca: Cornell University Press, 1978).

14. These terms are explicated in a particularly useful study for the purposes of comparing preindustrial and modern festival in Victor Turner, "Liminal to Liminoid, in Play, Flow and Ritual," *Rice University Studies* 60 (1974): 53–92.

15. The theme of death-and-regeneration has long been an essential of festival action. This inseparable association as found in popular festivals of early Europe is explored in depth in Mikhail Bakhtin, *Rabelais and His World* (Cambridge: MIT Press, 1968).

16. Roger D. Abrahams, "Toward an Enactment-Centered Theory of Folklore," in *Frontiers of Folklore,* ed. William R. Bascom (Boulder: Westview Press, 1977).

17. Louis A. Hieb, "Meaning and Mismeaning: Toward an Understanding of the Ritual Clown," in *New Perspectives on the Pueblos,* ed. Alfonso Ortiz (Albuquerque: University of New Mexico Press, 1972); Roberto Da Matta, "Carnival in Multiple Planes," paper presented at the Burg Wartenstein Symposium No. 76, Cultural Frames and Reflections: Ritual, Drama and Spectacle, Wenner-Gren Foundation for Anthropological Research, 1977.

Robert C. Toll

Folklore on the American Stage

Folklore played a central role in the development of American stage entertainment. In the age of live performances and vocal, mass audiences, when show business was perhaps the nation's most democratic institution, entertainers shaped their shows to suit the tastes and desires of the masses of common people who paid for them, which meant that the songs, dances, stories, and humor of the American folk became part of show business. Over the years, folklore periodically revitalized stage shows. Yet, folklorists and theater historians have virtually ignored the potentially rich areas of collecting, researching, and analyzing the uses of folklore on the American stage.

Between the War of 1812 and the Civil War, Americans concentrated on national development and on putting their democratic ideology into practice. It was the age of the common man, of Andrew Jackson and the birth of modern political parties, of westward expansion and urban growth, of attacks on monopolies and special privileges, and of an outburst of unpretentious, entertaining literature and stage shows that glorified everyday Americans and mocked aristocrats and Europeans. The demand for entertainment everyone could afford, understand, and enjoy seemed unlimited, especially in the burgeoning cities of the East. Performers who had been traveling around the nation found they could make a lot of money by bringing the culture of country folk to entertainment-hungry city dwellers.

These performers were among the first collectors to seek out America's unique folklore. But they were entertainers, not folklorists; their purpose was to make money, not to reproduce material authentically or to distinguish between what they borrowed and what they created. The interaction of folk and popular cultures quickly became very complex and blurred. Folk material from one group would become part of the popular culture only to be adapted by another folk group and then picked up by still other popular entertainers. Many of the folk elements can be identified by specialists, but in some cases the boundaries between folklore, adaptations of folklore, and folklike fictional material are difficult to separate, especially because serious folklore collecting did not begin until after these processes had taken place. This problem requires care, sophistication, and the use of methodologies from related fields such as history, music, dance, and theater.

Folklore played a more important role in popular stage shows before the Civil War than at any other time. The reasons were simple. The public liked the culture of common people far better than highbrow drama. But show business and popular song and play writing were in their infancies, so performers turned to folk cultures for ready-made sources of appealing material. Finally, the performers could use bits of folklore basically as they found them because the broadly based, eclectic stage shows of the period combined drama, variety acts, and farce, the elements that would later develop into separate entertainment forms. Even when tragedies such as *Hamlet* were performed, variety entertainers of all sorts appeared between the acts, and the evening ended with a comedy farce. Within these flexible slots, folklore made its first great impact on the American stage.

In the 1820s and 1830s, performers traveled widely and were always on the lookout for unusual American characters and lore. In 1828, Thomas D. Rice, a song and dance man who wore burnt cork makeup and did Negro dialect routines, saw a crippled black stablehand, Jim Crow, singing a catchy song and doing an odd dance. Rice learned the song and dance and became a star with his "Jump Jim Crow" act (fig. 1). Other white performers took whiskey and banjos to Southern plantations to collect material from slaves. Some entertainers "studied" the lore of the Western frontier. Others looked to the East. George H. Hill, a native New Englander, became a star using the dialect and lore he grew up with to portray Yankee characters.

These native folktypes were so popular that they gave birth to cycles of plays and to a new entertainment form. Brother Jonathan, the generic Yankee country boy, who was proud, independent, and nationalistic, used his common sense and sharp tongue to outsmart city slickers and to ridicule the high-falutin. He was what the public wanted to believe American farmboys were like. One Yankee boasted of his ability to do everything:

I'm the boy for a race, for an apple-paring or quilting frolic—fight a cock, hunt an opossum, or snare a partridge with any one. Then I'm a squire, and a county judge, and a brevet ossifer in the militia besides, and a devil of a fellow at an election to boot.[1]

The Yankee was joined by backwoodsmen who bragged of being invincible frontier supermen, by rowdy riverboatmen who loved to sing and fight, by daredevils who would try anything, including jumping off waterfalls, and by goodhearted city toughs who fought for their neighbors against con men and exploiters. America's first popular culture heroes were drawn from American folklore. They allowed common people to believe in themselves in a period when the central issue was establishing American democratic identities and institutions.

While the American stage used folklore to create positive images of white common people, it also addressed itself to the issues of slavery and race, which dominated America by the 1840s. In 1843, the first uniquely American entertainment form, the minstrel show, was born when a full evening of blackface song, dance, and comedy about plantation life proved a great hit. Soon, minstrel shows performed by whites in burnt cork makeup sprang up around the country, shows so flexible that minstrels could adjust their material to audiences during the performance. The first generation of traveling minstrels picked up the lore of both white and black folk groups. In their black dialects, they used the songs of Western

MR T. RICE
as
THE ORIGINAL JIM CROW
New York Pub. by E. RILEY N.º 29 Chatham St.

FIG. 1. Thomas D. Rice, the first blackface star, in his ragged "Jim Crow" outfit (Harvard Theatre Collection)

boatmen, the tall tales of the frontier, and the boasts of backwoodsmen. One blackfaced character bragged:

> My mammy was a wolf, my daddy was a tiger
> I'm what you call de ole Virginia nigger;
> Half fire, half smoke, a little touch of thunder
> I'm what dey call de eighth wonder.[2]

But in the 1840s, what distinguished minstrels was the material they drew from Afro-American culture, which made its first great impact on American show business in early minstrel shows. American tap dancing emerged when minstrels combined Afro-American rhythms with European dances such as the jig; the forerunners of jazz appeared in syncopated banjo tunes; and a distinctively American popular music developed when minstrel songwriters such as Stephen Foster blended Afro- and Euro-American music. Minstrels also adapted black street vendors' cries, trickster tales, superstitions, and symbolic animal stories in which the small and weak outwitted and defeated the strong and powerful. In one minstrel version of "Jim Crack Corn," the blue tail fly devoured a slave master while his slaves watched with glee:

> Poor mass did scream, de fly didn't care
> He eat till de shoe alone war dere
> An all ob de old Massa dat we could spy
> Stuck out ob de troat ob de Blue Tail Fly.[3]

But by the mid-1850s, the folklore content of minstrels declined, as stereotypes replaced folktypes and a second generation of urban-based minstrels, who had little time to collect folklore, emerged. After the Civil War, white minstrel shows grew slicker and more lavish, leaving their folk roots behind.

The second phase of American stage history began in the 1850s when eclectic stage shows fragmented into separate entertainment forms. In drama, a new generation of actors relied heavily on fixed scripts crafted by professional writers. As a result, folklore seems to have played a greatly diminished role in most plays of the period, even the popular plays that toured the American heartland, such as *Rip Van Winkle*, a great late nineteenth-century hit with Joseph Jefferson III playing the lead for nearly forty years (fig. 2). The play, first written in 1828, was based on Washington Irving's short story which retold German and Dutch folktales about a rustic tippler, Rip, who signed away his property in a tavern and later drank an elves' brew with Henry Hudson's ghost and then slept for twenty years. The play did not become a hit until professional playwright Dion Boucicault in 1865 rewrote and romanticized it (making Rip a charming, naive, young man) and removed it even further from its folk roots. Perhaps the clearest change was in the Yankee, whose most popular late nineteenth-century reincarnation was Uncle Joshua, who had to leave *The Old Homestead*, an idyllic New Hampshire farm, to rescue his son, Reuben, who had gone to the big city, been corrupted, and become a hapless drunk lying in a New York City gutter. All Joshua could do was take Reuben home and nurse him back to health. In the age of industrialism, the brash, self-confident rural folk characters who earlier had challenged the city and won were reduced to quaint, helpless victims of progress. In Joshua, Rip, and their many spin-offs, nostalgic, sentimentalized folksiness had replaced the optimistic vitality of earthy folk characters (fig. 3).

Two cycles of post–Civil War popular plays seem to offer greater potential for the folklorist. *Uncle Tom's Cabin* (fig. 4) was so popular that many traveling actors performed nothing else. Drawing on stock scenes and speeches and adding attractions such as animal acts, comedians, dancers, and singing groups, the "Tommers" varied their shows to suit local audiences and actually performed a wide range of shows under one title. With their great flexibility, diversity, and responsiveness, Tom shows bore striking resemblance to pre–Civil War plays and probably included considerable folklore from mid-America, where they enjoyed their greatest popularity. In the 1870s and 1880s in New York City, Edward Harrigan and Tony Hart starred in a series of musical comedies focused on Dan Mulligan and his Irish, German, and black working-class neighbors. These shows put the urban folk on the stage. A song in *McSorley's Inflation* (1882) described a typical cast and setting:

> It's Ireland and Italy, Jerusalem and Germany,
> Oh, Chinamen and nagars, and a paradise for rats,

FIG. 2. Joseph Jefferson III as young Rip Van Winkle (Harvard Theatre Collection)

FIG. 3. The folksy warmth of *The Old Homestead* (Harvard Theatre Collection)

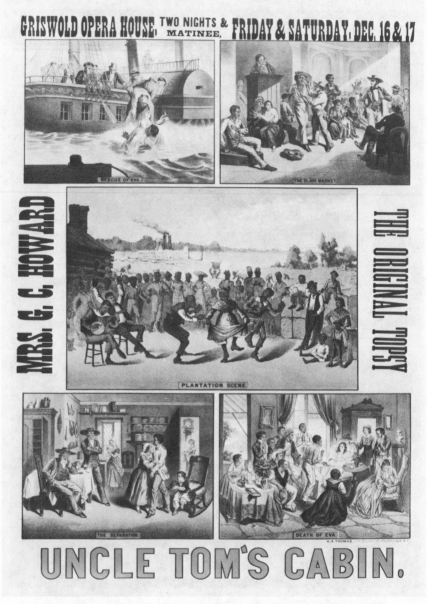

FIG. 4. Poster for a lavish late nineteenth century production of *Uncle Tom's Cabin* (Harvard Theatre Collection)

All jumbled up togayther in the snow or rainy weather,
They represent the tenants in McNally's row of flats.[4]

For their partially improvised shows, Harrigan and Hart drew material from the streets, from the same workingmen who shouted out cheers of recognition to the stage characters, undoubtedly indicating that Harrigan and Hart used a lot of urban folklore in their hit shows. But until folklorists study the uses of folklore in Tom shows, the Mulligan plays, and the other popular plays of the period, it will be impossible to determine whether the loosely structured, partially ad-libbed shows made greater use of folklore than the set, scripted shows, as impressionistic data suggest.

When the first generation of American black entertainers broke into minstrel shows after the Civil War in segregated troupes, they brought large amounts of Afro-American folklore with them. Singing groups from Southern black colleges introduced northern whites to spirituals, but it was black minstrels who took these religious songs to every part of America. In their religious songs, black minstrels could openly express the sentiments they otherwise had to mask. They sang of a heaven where "de white folks must let de darkeys be," where no one would be bought or sold, and where everyone would have enough to eat even if they "ain't got any money."[5] Blacks had made gains, and they were determined to keep them.

> An' I'll never turn back no mo'
> An' I'll never turn back no mo'
> An' I'll never turn back no mo'
> I'm a ridin' up in de chariot
> It's so early in de morning
> An' I'll never turn back no mo.'"[6]

Black minstrels also relished the antics of wily tricksters, the pleasures of soul food, and the joys of freedom. "I nebber will forget, no nebber, de day I was sot free," sang black minstrel Sam Lucas.[7] With the sounds of black dialects, the humor of black lore, the rhythms of black music, and the sight of black dances, black performers made places for themselves in show business and added humanity and diversity to stage portrayals of blacks, using folklore as their vehicle and their weapon.

In the late nineteenth century, the most promising area of inquiry for the folklorist is vaudeville, the successor to minstrelsy, in which a new wave of first generation performers brought new life to the American variety stage (fig. 5). By the 1880s, public concern was shifting from blacks to the massive immigration of southern and eastern Europeans. Minstrels in blackface tried to portray immigrants, but they could not compete with the flexibility of vaudeville which featured ethnic types and dialects of all sorts—blacks, Irish, Germans, Italians, and Jews. As vaudevillians, these immigrants and their children probably drew on their folk traditions, though no studies as yet confirm this speculation. Not only could such research investigate what folklore was used, but also how it was adapted, how its use varied from group to group, and how its use by ethnic group members and nonmembers differed.

A related and promising topic is the foreign language entertainment that thrived in the nation's ethnic neighborhoods, from New York's Lower East Side to San Francisco's Chinatown. Beginning in the 1880s, cities with large populations of

FIG. 5. Lew Fields and Joe Weber in one of their classic vaudeville
comedy bits (Harvard Theatre Collection)

Jewish immigrants, for example, developed a full range of Yiddish plays, variety
shows, musicals, comedies, and stars. Popular Yiddish dramatists like Moyshe
Hurwitz and Joseph Lateiner cranked out scripts as fast as they could by translating
and "Yiddishizing" popular plays and biblical stories, using settings, names, and
character types familiar to the Yiddish audience. The plays were often literally
finished on stage, as actors ad-libbed to fill in the writers' outlines and to please
audiences. These and other such foreign language shows, which cushioned the
shock of emigration and eased the adjustment to the new world, must have drawn
on traditional folklore. Analyses of the nature and function of ethnic folklore in
these in-group shows and in general American shows could suggest answers to
critical questions about the acculturation, impact, and image of immigrants in the
age of immigration, questions that the folklorist has unique tools to answer.

Professional performers also developed occupational folklore of their own. They
told stories and wrote dressing room graffiti about audiences, agents, boarding
houses, hotel clerks, theater managers, restaurants, traveling, and each other. In a
profession rife with insecurity, they developed a rich lore of superstition, believing
bad luck would result from whistling in the dressing room, seeing a bird on a
windowsill, throwing away old dancing shoes, or a host of other such transgressions. Good luck, which was much harder to find, might come from wearing
undershirts inside out, from touching a hunchback, or from the well-known wish,

"break a leg." This rich, virtually ignored area of stage folklore can be approached either through field collection or through printed sources.

By the end of the 1920s, sound movies and radio were replacing live stage shows as the major sources of popular entertainment. Since mass media carried the same performance to audiences throughout the nation, studio and network executives, who had little, if any, contact with audiences, became the arbiters of entertainment, standardizing and homogenizing the shows in their quest for the broadest popular appeal. The ethnic dialects of vaudeville gave way to the middle-American sound of radio and movies, and folklore seems to have played a diminished role in popular entertainment. But the mass media were also a source of folklore, as people around the country took material from the shows they shared and circulated it in oral tradition, a process folklorists should document and analyze to help assess the impact of mass media on American culture.

Stage shows using folklore certainly did not disappear in the twentieth century. Serious dramatists like Frederick H. Koch, Robert E. Gard, and Paul Green consciously tried to craft folklore into a distinctively American dramatic art, an attempt which contrasted sharply with the offhand way popular entertainers incorporated folklore into their shows. This process apparently continued in the Toby plays of Fred Wilson, Neil Shaffner, and others. Toby, a latter-day version of the farmboy as hero, stood for the virtues of rural America. He attracted small-town audiences for over fifty years, from 1911 to 1962. Toby loved to ridicule city slickers who knew nothing about farm life, such as the woman who believed pigs had to be oiled to keep them from squeaking. He was also often the butt of jokes, but when pushed too far, he blurted: "Next time he does that, I'll whale him with a whiffletree."[8] Toby shows, like Tom shows, had a basic format but were often partially ad-libbed to suit local audiences, who felt Toby was one of them. Studying the uses of folklore and mass media material in the Toby shows could provide important insights into the nature and functions of rural folklore in the age of mass media.

This survey, which offers more questions than answers, does suggest several hypotheses for future studies. Folklore seems to play an important role in the early stages of popular entertainment forms that are flexible and diverse. It is frequently found where an intimate interchange between vocal audiences and creator-performers exists. The first generation of entertainers in a new field seems to draw heavily on folklore, while its importance appears to decrease as popular entertainment forms grow more established and rigid. Folklore seems to play important roles in formal dramatic art when writers consciously seek out native material and themes. The mass media's greatest significance for folklore studies may be as sources of a new, national folklore, rather than as bearers of tradition. In any case, it is time that folklorists examine the complex relationships between America's folk cultures and its entertainment forms, the institutions that more than any others were created of, by, and for the American people.

NOTES

1. M. M. Noah, *She Would Be a Soldier* (New York: 1819), p. 19, quoted in Richard M. Dorson, "The Yankee on the Stage—A Folk Hero of American

Drama," *New England Quarterly* 13 (1940): 471.

2. E. P. Christy, *Christy's Plantation Melodies #1* (New York: 1851), p. 47, quoted in Robert C. Toll, *Blacking Up: The Minstrel Show in Nineteenth Century America* (New York: Oxford University Press, 1974), p. 41.

3. Ethiopian Serenaders, "Jim Crack Corn," (n.p., n.d.), quoted in Toll, p. 49.

4. E. J. Kahn, Jr., *The Merry Partners* (New York: Random House, 1955), p. 64.

5. Toll, pp. 239–40.

6. *Sam Lucas' Plantation Songster* (Boston: n.d. [1857]), p. 15, quoted in Toll, p. 241.

7. Sam Lucas, "De Day I Was Sot Free" (Boston: 1878), quoted in Toll, p. 247.

8. Neil E. Shaffner with Vance Johnson, *The Fabulous Toby & Me* (Englewood Cliffs, N.J.: Prentice-Hall, 1968), p. 5.

Elizabeth Peterson

American Sports
and Folklore

Jacques Barzun once remarked, "Whoever wants to know the hearts and minds of America had better learn baseball."[1] While Barzun's claim about baseball's importance is perhaps exaggerated, scholars have given little serious consideration to the magnitude and significance of sport in American life. Yet, from the improvised pick-up softball or football game to complex sporting events such as the Indy 500 or the Kentucky Derby, sports now permeate most of our social institutions and touch our daily lives. Sport metaphors commonly appear in casual conversation—in political and business rhetoric as well as religious language. Today even the most disinterested observer of sports, for instance, knows the meaning of such sport-derived aphorisms as "out in left field," "below the belt," or "bush league." Society at large, then, may recognize an element of truth in Barzun's comment about American culture but scholars until recently have tended to take sports, play, and games for granted, and have often considered their presence in American life as trivial.

Folklorists, in particular, have tended to view the highly bureaucratic and rule-bound aspects of sports as antithetical to the informal variations of traditional play and games. Because they have emphasized fluidity and variation in transmission as the defining characteristics of folklore, they overlook genres which stress fixed structural elements and exhibit a high degree of verbal or behavioral formalization. A recognition of a continuum of structural variation and formalization in traditional expressive behavior will allow folklorists to investigate phenomena such as sports in its many cultural manifestations: from street games, in which rules are adapted to fit the number of participants and the physical environment, to professional ball games, whose rules are enforced by organizations and institutionalized judgment.

Treatment of sport as a contest requires explication of the formal elements of a particular event. From this perspective, any sport may be defined as a competitive physical activity between at least two opposing sides which requires some display of physical skill or prowess.[2] Although most people think of sports as competitive events between two individuals or two teams, such activities may also involve competition between an individual or team and animal (i.e., bullfighting), a person and the natural environment (i.e., mountain climbing), and an individual and an ideal standard (i.e., setting a record for the mile run). Using this approach, a folklorist might document instances of varieties of stickball to determine changes in traditional sports or regional variations and dissemination. These kinds of informal changes are in contrast to the binding decisions of governing bodies in organized sports.

In *Sports and Social Systems,* sports sociologists John Loy, Barry McPherson, and Gerald Kenyon delineate three other levels of analysis which folklorists may employ.[3] They suggest that sport as an institutionalized game might be considered an abstract but distinct pattern of cultural behavior and social structure having its own values, norms, sanctions, and roles. These are expressed in team organization, sponsorship, technological skill and training, and symbolic features of ritual and ceremony.[4] While many of these elements in modern American sport are codified in written regulations, oral tradition and ritual conduct also perpetuate attitudes regarding appropriate role behavior and values. Such attitudes are the proper study of the folklorist.

Secondly, sport may be considered as a social institution with highly developed means to "organize, facilitate, and regulate human action in sport situations."[5] At this level, sport not only includes the informally organized neighborhood football game, but also club sports, municipally sponsored sports such as Little League, college sports, and professional sports clubs. Each type displays an increasing concern with specialization and leadership, and each affords the folklorist an opportunity to study the formation and social dynamics of folk groups. Voluntary, informal, and part-time sporting events which need little organization provide a time and place set apart from routine living. Membership in this type of sports group is rarely dependent on outside social, religious, or economic factors, but emerges from the activity itself. Traditional shared knowledge of the sport, its beliefs and heroes, the jargon, the use of uniforms or caps are all folkloric means which enhance the boundaries and perpetuation of the group. At the other extreme, a professional sport organization such as a football or basketball team exemplifies an occupational group for whom play is a livelihood. Whereas the informal sports group may generate limited and fragmented traditions, professional athletes constitute an occupational group with a highly developed code of behavior, distinctive values, and beliefs, legends, tales, jokes, and aphorisms.

Finally, the folklorist may look at sport as a form of social involvement.[6] In this sense, we may consider the consumer of sport as well as the participant. Sport involvement for many Americans is vicarious; fans may attend their alma mater's homecoming game, watch the World Series with friends at a local bar, or watch Monday night football with family and friends at home. Sport, then, provides a focal point for people to express group loyalties and identify with heroes in traditional ways. In a broader perspective, patterns of social involvement in sports may also be interpreted as a means of socialization. As William Beezley has suggested, college homecoming weekends may best be studied as "festivals involving college rituals, occasions for the socialization of students and the sharing of a common experience."[7] American small towns sometimes treat their high school football or basketball games as community festive events, and their players as local heroes.[8] A humorous anecdote, commonly collected among various ethnic groups, which relates the misinterpretation of a baseball game by an immigrant, further underscores the importance of sports as a means of socialization and assimilation. One version, presented in Richard M. Dorson's *Folklore and*

Fakelore, tells of an old Frenchman—or Finn—who is persuaded by his sons to attend a World Series game.[9] While the sons hope that the father's attendance will soften his and other parents' resistance to such modern American foolery, the father reaches the opposite conclusion. To him, the playing field and diamond are nothing more than a "cow pasture" with a "rabbit path," and the catcher looks ridiculous wearing a "birdcage" on his head and a "mattress" over his torso. Unaware of baseball rules and terminology, the father is equally puzzled when he overhears the fans seated in front of him state that the batter has "one ball" because the Frenchman considers this comment to be an insult to the batter's masculinity. In this instance, the comical narrative serves as an index of assimilation into American culture: the Frenchman, unacquainted with the codes of baseball conduct and the sensibility that motivates the national game, is not fully assimilated in American culture, while his sons have made the transition from Frenchmen to French-Americans.

These suggestive analytic approaches to sport proposed by Loy, McPherson, and Kenyon point to the need for conceptual frameworks and scholarly rigor in sports folklore. As a complex phenomenon stressing competition between opposing sides, a sporting event incorporates many traditional genres which occur simultaneously as well as sequentially. On the playing field or in the stands, sports include elements of traditional nonverbal behavior, speech, music, food, or costume. In a larger cultural context, however, sport is also a model of and for behavior; it endorses certain cultural ideologies and values regarding social status and class. In the United States, folk ideas of masculinity and femininity, for instance, shape and are shaped by the notion of sport as a masculine domain of knowledge and activity. During the 1976 summer Olympics, the U.S. press specifically emphasized the fact that the East German women's swim team, who won the lion's share of the medals, trained by lifting weights. The implications were readily apparent: the East German women were manly while the U.S. women swimmers who gave a disappointing performance nonetheless retained their femininity. Similarly, women now entering the higher echelons of corporate business sometimes find themselves treated as outsiders by the "old boy" network. In these situations, a woman's lack of knowledge about sports and locker room talk and camaraderie is occasionally exploited by male associates to mark her exclusion from what is still essentially a male domain. As a contest form, sport also dramatizes and encapsulates this idea and other dominant cultural values, themes, and conflicts. Sports folklore, thus, may be studied in its immediate game context, as a social institution, or in a larger cultural and historical milieu.[10]

Until recently, folklorists have ignored these conceptual possibilities. Nineteenth-century folklorists in the United States, like their colleagues in Europe, evinced little interest in the traditional elements of sports. Folkloristic studies and collections of children's play and games reached a peak near the close of the century with the publication of William Wells Newell's *Games and Songs of American Children.*[11] Using anthropological theories prominent at the time, Newell documented the diffusion and adaptation of English and European games to American soil. He provided thorough cross-cultural comparisons and in many cases suggested that children's games were survivals of ancient rituals or festivals. Displaying many of the same interests as his contemporaries, Newell emphasized games and pastimes with strong verbal components—counting-out rhymes, songs, rounds—and often overlooked sports. Discussing ball games, Newell provided only cursory descriptions of handball, football, hockey, cricket, and baseball. Especially telling are Newell's remarks on baseball. While he recognized baseball as "the national game," he excluded the institutionalized version from consideration, instead treating secondary ritualized elements such as tossing a bat "to choose up sides."[12] Similarly, American anthropologist Stewart Culin catalogued several variations of baseball among boys in New York City, but offered little comment on its historical significance or relationship to other games.[13]

Sport competitions and school sport programs became institutionalized throughout the United States at the turn of the century, but folklorists regarded them as nontraditional. Also, folklorists showed little interest in traditional games and recreations. Major collections of games appeared only occasionally in the first half of the present century, and these rarely differed from the approach advocated by Newell, Culin, and others. Paul G. Brewster's *American Non-Singing Games* and Leah Rachel Clara Yoffie's article "Three Generations of Children's Singing Games in St. Louis,"[14] for instance, added quantity to the corpus of American children's games but provided little theoretical innovation. Adapting the theoretical orientations of folk narrative scholarship, folklorists continued to stress the verbal aspects of play and games and emphasize the folkloric text or item.

Sporadic treatments of sport traditions have appeared in folklore journals since World War II. These modern investigations also focus primarily on the verbal elements of sports folklore. Many approaches can be applied to sports folklore: two major organizing principles are by genre and by folk group. Folklorists examine legends, anecdotes, speech, beliefs, and rituals of athletes as an occupational group or study the legends, anecdotes, and stereotypes about athletes held by outsiders. Thus, while the lore generated by and about sports is finally receiving attention from folklorists, the sport event itself continues to be overlooked.

At present, Tristram Coffin's *The Old Ball Game: Baseball in Folklore and Fiction* (subsequently reissued as *The Illustrated Book of Baseball Lore*) is the only book-length study by a professional folklorist devoted to sports.[15] Writing primarily for a popular audience, Coffin confines himself to the occupational folklore of professional baseball, and to treatments of baseball in journalism and literature. Employing the idea that professional baseball players develop a body of folk traditions that enforce and perpetuate a professional code of behavior and maintain boundaries between insiders and outsiders, Coffin examines slogans, aphorisms, anecdotes, proverbial phrases, beliefs, and legends surrounding heroic figures such as Babe Ruth, Ty Cobb, and Ted Williams. Coffin further identifies traditional motifs told in similar anecdotes about different players at different times, such as the pitcher who calls in the outfield and then proceeds to strike out a side.[16] In related studies, Gerard Reese compiled a motif index of baseball stories culled from books written by players and managers; Bonnie McGuire's "Babe Ruth" expands Coffin's contentions regarding Ruth as an American hero—and everyman as well as superman.[17] Similarly, in "Superstitions of Baseball Players," Lee Allen provides a lengthy catalogue of beliefs used by players to aid their batting and hitting.[18] While Reese, McGuire, and Allen provide ample confirmation of Coffin's survey by indicating the range of traditional motifs and beliefs in baseball lore, the interests of the authors are primarily literary and the mode of presentation sometimes does not go beyond a catalogue. None of the authors systematically considers the usage or the cultural meaning of these traditions to the players or fans.

Recently, folklorists have written articles emphasizing psychological and sociological aspects of professional football and baseball traditions. Although each author delineates a specific topic for consideration, the theoretical orientation is still primarly item-oriented. On the one hand, William Beezley's "Locker Rumors: Folklore and Football" enumerates the occupational folktypes of coach and team jokers revealed in anecdotes and the implicit maxims expressed in exemplary stories that constitute the player's code of behavior and standards.[19] In contrast, Alan Dundes' renowned "Into the Endzone for a Touchdown: A Psychoanalytic Consideration of American Football," examines units of football folk speech and aphorisms and asserts that football functions symbolically as a ritual masculinity contest and male homosexual combat.[20] Yet another approach is taken by anthropologist George Gmelch's "Magic in Professional Baseball." Testing Malinowski's hypothesis that "magic appears in situations of change and uncertainty,"[21] Gmelch clearly demonstrates that ritual, taboos, and fetishes are most often employed in batting and hitting, two activities of chance, but rarely used in fielding, where a player has more control of his actions.[22]

Even though professional American sports have triggered the most interest among folklorists, college sports also offer many research opportunities. Elements of campus folklore such as dormitory legends and fraternity and sorority initiations are addressed in folklore scholarship, but campus sports are an equally integral part of college life. In 1959, for instance, Richard M. Dorson noted the existence of folk stereotypes, jokes, and anecdotes surrounding athletic coaches and "dumb jocks."[23] Few scholars have followed Dorson's lead by examining the range of such traditions and their functions in university life, but a recent study by James Wise explores legend variants about a college football player who singlehandedly vanquishes a group of attackers in terms of three different sets of social oppositions and tensions: college vs. town, white vs. black, and athlete vs. nonathlete.[24] Although Wise situates his study within the trends of past scholarship, his work is a noteworthy attempt to investigate the many cultural meanings and values invested in a seemingly straightforward college sports legend. Folklorists pay scant attention to the calendrical nature and ritualistic elements of college events such as homecoming or athletic training. Shirley Fiske, however, has interpreted the yearly cycle of American collegiate football as an initiation ceremony for players that dramatizes the status change from adolescence to male adulthood.[25]

Although folklorists have limited their research largely to baseball and football, two recent studies on professional wrestling by John Gutowski and Mark Workman depart from the traditional concerns of folklorists by examining the structural and formulaic qualities of wrestling as a folk drama which articulates moral tensions between good and evil.[26] Football and baseball may be "the national games" in symbolic terms, but stock car and auto racing and horse racing are the most popular spectator sports in the United States today.[27] Other sports such as basketball, golf, and tennis have also been overlooked.

The directions of research suggested by Fiske, Gutowski, and Workman raise fundamental problems in American folkloric treatments of sports. By emphasizing the occupational nature of this lore, folklorists have produced a body of data and research applicable to sport as a social institution but they have left unanswered many questions regarding sport as a type of social involvement or a distinct cultural form. They have made little use of new research undertaken by sociologists, anthropologists, and psychologists in the areas of play, games, sport, festival, and ritual. Most folkloric studies of sport are now conducted separately from research on children's play and games, and fail to note the continuity between children's and adults' play, or the relationships between informal and organized leisure activities. If folklorists in the past have sometimes emphasized the components of sports, recent anthropological and sociological research in festival, ritual, and play stresses the event as a genre of behavior in itself. Much like festival and ritual, the sport event subsumes many traditional genres and provides a unified context in which to observe generic interrelationships. This shift in focus helps us to understand sports as a unique cultural and historical form and makes sensible the many traditions which occur within it and emerge from it. Here again, Gary Alan Fine's research on Little League Baseball culture, and Brian Sutton-Smith's work in play, games, and sport in general are exceptions to the rule.[28]

Vince Lombardi has been credited with the saying "Winning isn't everything, it's the only thing," while the phrase "nice guys finish last" is attributed to Leo Durocher. The origins of these proverbial aphorisms are not in question. Instead, both sayings embody what folklorist Alan Dundes and anthropologist George Foster have termed "folk ideas as units of worldview."[29] Contained in each saying are certain American notions about competition and hierarchy. As many scholars have suggested, the conflicting ideas of democracy and individualism, of equality and hierarchy display fundamental tensions in American culture. While this ideological tension is present in most aspects of American life, it may be that American sports symbolically express these oppositions in a highly condensed and visible fashion.[30] As a public contest form, a primary objective is to ensure the equality of chance and opportunity to opposing sides in order to make the victory one which is based on individual or team skill and merit. During the event, hierarchy is created. We see this particular articulation of opposition and resolution every time we participate in or watch sports—in the informal street games of stickball as well as Little League games, homecoming games, and major sporting events. As Beverly Stoeltje has suggested, major American competitive happenings such as the Indy 500 or the Kentucky Derby are best considered as modern American festive events which highlight contest through specific mediums (e.g., automobile and horse).[31]

Outlined briefly, these new perspectives may free folklorists from an over-emphasis on traditional sport items and genres. Beginning with the sport event, folklorists need to relate the content, style, and form of sports hero legends, anecdotes, jokes, and customs more directly to the social, cultural, and historical contexts in which they occur. What, in fact, do these "items" tell us about sports, their values, and American culture in general? The newly created discipline of sports sociology as well as organizations like the Association for the Anthropological Study of Play provide theoretical directions upon which folklorists may draw.[32] But, to paraphrase Richard M. Dorson's statement about American folklore, the best books in American sports folklore remain to be written.

NOTES

1. Jacques Barzun, *Science: The Glorious Entertainment* (New York: Harper & Row, 1964), p. 5.

2. John Loy, Barry D. McPherson, and Gerald Kenyon, *Sport and Social Systems* (Reading, Mass.: Addison Wesley Publishing Co., 1978), p. 21.

3. Ibid., pp. 3-21.

4. Ibid., pp. 10-14.

5. Ibid., p. 15.

6. Ibid., pp. 16-21.

7. William H. Beezley, "Locker Rumors: Folklore and Football," *Journal of the Folklore Institute* 17 (1980): 196.

8. Robert S. Lynd and Helen Merrell Lynd, *Middletown: A Study in Modern American Culture* (New York: Harcourt, Brace, & World, 1929), pp. 212-13.

9. Richard M. Dorson, *Folklore and Fakelore* (Cambridge, Mass.: Harvard University Press, 1976), pp. 235-37, 242, 244.

10. See Richard Bauman's article "The Field Study of Folklore in Context" in this *Handbook* for further explication of types of context.

11. William Wells Newell, *Games and Songs of American Children* (New York: Dover Publications, 1963).

12. Ibid., pp. 184-85.

13. Stewart Culin, "Street Games of Boys in Brooklyn, New York," *Journal of American Folklore* 4 (1891): 221-37.

14. Paul G. Brewster, *American Non-Singing Games* (Norman: University of Oklahoma, 1953), and Leah Rachel Clara Yoffie, "Three Generations of Childrens' Singing Games in St. Louis," *Journal of American Folklore* 60 (1947): 1-51.

15. Tristram Coffin, *The Old Ball Game: Baseball in Folklore and Fiction* (New York: Herder & Herder, 1971); idem, *The Illustrated Book of Baseball Folklore* (New York: Seabury Press, 1975).

16. Coffin, *Illustrated Book of Baseball Folklore*, pp. 33-34.

17. Gerard Reese, "The Baseball Story: A Motif Index Derived from Stories Found in Books Written by Baseball Players and Managers between 1946-1973" (M.A. thesis, SUNY Cooperstown, 1975), and Bonnie McGuire, "Babe Ruth," *New York Folklore* 1 (1975): 97-108. For a brief treatment of folk legends about Babe Ruth from an American historian's perspective, see Marshall Smelser, *The Life That Ruth Built* (New York: Quadrangle/New York Times Book Co., 1975), pp. 562-65.

18. Lee Allen, "The Superstitions of Baseball Players," *New York Folklore Quarterly* 20 (1964): 98-109.

19. Beezley, pp. 196-221.

20. Alan Dundes, "Into the Endzone for a Touchdown: A Psychoanalytic Consideration of American Football," *Western Folklore* 37 (1978): 75-88.

21. George Gmelch, "Magic in Professional Baseball," in *Games, Sports, and Power,* ed. Gregory P. Stone (New Brunswick, N. J.: *transaction,* 1972), p. 139.

22. Ibid., pp. 128-37.

23. Richard M. Dorson, *American Folklore* (Chicago: University of Chicago Press, 1959), pp. 257-58.

24. James Wise, "Tugging on Superman's Cape: The Making of a College Legend," *Western Folklore* 36 (1977): 227-38.

25. Shirley Fiske, "Pigskin Review: An American Initiation," in *Sport in the Sociocultural Process,* ed. Marie Hart (Dubuque, Iowa: Wm. C. Brown, 1976), pp. 413-30. See also Gerald Weales, "Ritual in Georgia," *Southern Folklore Quarterly* 21 (1957): 104-109.

26. John Gutowski, "The Art of Professional Wrestling: Folk Expression in Mass Culture," *Keystone Folklore Quarterly* 17 (1972): 41-50, and Mark E. Workman, "Dramaturgical Aspects of Professional Wrestling," *Folklore Forum* 10 (1977): 14-20.

27. Loy, McPherson, and Kenyon, p. 310.

28. Gary Alan Fine, "Small Groups and Culture Creation: The Idioculture of Little League Baseball Teams," *American Sociological Review* 44 (1979): 733–45. For an anthology of Sutton-Smith's work, see Brian Sutton-Smith, *The Folkgames of Children* (Austin: University of Texas Press, 1972).

29. Alan Dundes, "Folk Ideas as Units of Worldview," in *Towards New Perspectives in Folklore*, ed. Américo Paredes and Richard Bauman, pp. 93–103 (Austin: University of Texas Press, 1972), and George M. Foster, "Peasant Society and the Image of Limited Good," *American Anthropologist* 67 (1965): 293–315.

30. Loy, McPherson, and Kenyon, pp. 413–15.

31. Stoeltje, personal communication.

32. For more information on T.A.A.S.P., contact Alyce Cheska, Department of Physical Education, University of Illinois, Champaign-Urbana, Illinois 61801.

American Forms
and Performers

Until very recently, folklorists sorted out the items they had collected in the field into convenient categories called genres. They referred to the items by the umbrella names for these genres, such as folktales and folksongs, and more precise labels for subdivisions of the genres, such as tall tales and ballads. This sifting could be carried still further, for instance, to hunting tall tales and native American ballads, and yet further, to bear-hunting tall tales and native American murder ballads. Through the genre approach we can learn about thematic emphases in American folklore, such as the popularity of bear-hunt yarns, which reached their artistic climax in Thomas Bang Thorpe's *The Big Bear of Arkansas* (1845), the classic sketch in the humor of the old Southwest, and of tearful ballads of girls murdered by jealous lovers, as in the Indiana ballad of Pearl Bryan.

The genre approach has limitations, however, and sufficient resources exist for those who wish to pursue this avenue. For American folktales Ernest W. Baughman has provided an indispensable *Type and Motif-Index of the Folktales of England and North America* (1966), and in *Native American Balladry* (1950, revised edition 1964), G. Malcolm Laws has introduced a basic classification and surveyed the themes of this song corpus in an authoritative essay. In *The Study of American Folklore* (1968, revised edition 1978), Jan H. Brunvand divides his chapters according to genres, and the contributors to *Folklore and Folklife, An Introduction*, a volume I edited (1972), similarly address the genres of their specialties. But genres in the broad sense are international rather than national. Folk narrative, folksong, proverb, riddle, belief, folk dance, folk craft, folk games will be found in every culture. Then a good deal of folklore cannot be neatly squeezed into these genres—for example, folk religion, folk medicine, and folk festivals, which involve several genres as well as patterns of social interaction that lie outside the genres. A category such as folk speech seems too loose and fluid for systematic treatment; how does one distinguish folk from dialect from regional from uneducated speech?

Two essays in the following section deal with the borderlines of narrative genres that are now attracting the attention of folklorists. Sandra Stahl advances the thesis that all Americans—perhaps all people—are storytellers, to the extent that we repeatedly relate experiences that have befallen us and left an indelible mark on our memories. Some of us are more addicted than others to this kind of narrative performance, and Stahl has even identified the editor of this *Handbook* as such a personal narrator and analyzed one story in his repertoire. In the companion piece, Sally Yerkovich explores the appearances of folkloric expression in ordinary conversation, to make the point that folklore continually weaves in and out of our talk, and need not be set apart by staged performances from the rhythms of daily life.

In looking beyond the genres, folklorists today are concentrating more closely upon the bearers, reciters, and transporters of tradition. As a consequence fieldworkers now seek out and report the biographies, styles, repertoires, and shaping influences upon folksingers, storytellers, folk musicians, craftworkers, folk healers, and comparable performers in the folk arts. While folk performers operate within traditional forms, they stamp their individual imprints upon the texts and objects they transmit and fashion. From the ranks of the obscure mass of the population some folk artists have now risen to a status of visibility and even a limited fame. John and Alan Lomax took the Negro ex-convict blues and ballad singer Leadbelly on tour. Edward D. Ives devoted his researches to reconstructing the lives and compositions of Maine-Maritimes woodsmen-songsters: Larry Gorman, Lawrence Doyle, Joe Scott. The life story and marvelous cures of Don Pedro Jaramillo, the healer of Los Olmos, New Mexico, are on record in a book-length study. Michael O. Jones devotes the major part of *The Hand-Made Object and Its Maker* to an Appalachian chairmaker, Chester Cornett. In this mode of field investigation the folk performer, if living, becomes a collaborator, partner, and coworker with the folklorist, perhaps a coauthor. Almeda Riddle invited folklorist Roger Abrahams to edit for publication her folksong collection. The once faceless names attached to texts have now taken on the dimensions of full-bodied human beings.

Four articles in this section deal with singers, storytellers, craftworkers, and healers under the rubric "Performers." The performing folksinger seems a natural enough designation, since we are accustomed to think of song as directed to an audience. Storytelling requires a little more stretch, since it does not constitute a major part of our public entertainment today, but it, too, involves a listening audience and dramatic devices on the part of the narrator, and so a case for performance can be persuasively argued. With healers, hoodoo doctors, water witches, fortune tellers, psychics, and that whole genus of practitioners in the magic arts, the concept of performance may appear out of bounds. But the cures, charms, and visions can be analyzed as a series of ritual acts—the presenting of the problem to the wonderworker, in a specified setting; the consideration of the problem, with appropriate props, utterances, motions, countenances; and the resolution, in the form of a prescription or revelation from the sage. So the magicmaker too is enacting a performance for his private audience, and the larger circle that will surely hear of his exploits from that audience. In his painstaking analysis of the Afro-American hoodoo system, written as an Indiana University folklore dissertation, Michael Bell employs the term performer in speaking of the hoodoo magicians.

When we come to artisans and craftworkers, we speak of their performances more in a metaphorical sense. They select their materials, design, shape, mold, color, and ornament them, exhibit and sell them. Yet by analogy with folk musicians, tale-bearers, and shamans we can refer to basketmakers, quilters, potters, carvers,

blacksmiths, and sundry other craftspeople as engaging in creative performance—
an analogy that John Vlach draws in his essay on "Folk Craftsmen." In his piece on
the study of artifacts in the section "Methods of Research" Henry Glassie does refer
to the craftsman as "performing" while engaged in his process, even if he lacks an
audience. In all these cases, from workers in wood, metal, and stone to spinners of
fictions and prescribers of remedies, folklorists now seek to document the
personalities that influence the course of traditional forms.

Sandra K. D. Stahl

Personal Experience Stories

The remnants of European tale-types or variants of the Child ballads still found in America may offer the folklorist valuable insights into our past and prove an aesthetic delight to the researcher, but for someone who wants to investigate a folk narrative form that is a vital part of the social life of nearly every American today, perhaps no genre is so appropriate as the category loosely termed "personal experience stories." It would be a rare adult who has not at one time told such a story or who did not have at least one or two such favorite stories in a ready repertoire. And this of course is part of the appeal of the genre for the student of American folklore. Though there certainly are some people who "specialize" in telling personal experience stories and have an active repertoire of twenty to thirty well-polished tales, tellers of such stories are not an elite or even a separable group. The typical American adult will have an active repertoire of at least three or four such stories. Often these casual tellers of personal experience stories are not even aware that they have a blossoming repertoire of tales or that they ever participate in folk narrative telling events. More likely a friend, spouse, or other family member will surprise the teller with recognition of "the story" and the request to tell "about the time you did such and such."

The experience recreated in the narrative may be an amusing incident from the teller's childhood, a school or work experience, a once-embarrassing social mishap that time has turned into a humorous *faux pas*, perhaps an encounter with the supernatural or unexplainable, or maybe a painful lesson in the proverbial school of hard knocks. Whatever the experience, the story itself is a narrative creation of the teller, and it uses not only the experience itself as a base but also many traditional aspects of storytelling—predictable form, evidence of cultural and personal stylization, conventional functions. This combination of nontraditional content—the teller's unique experience—and the traditional aspects of form, style, and function is what makes the personal experience story a challenging research topic in contemporary American folklore.

Personal experience stories are first-person narratives usually composed orally by the tellers and based on real incidents in their lives; the stories "belong" to the tellers because they are the ones responsible for recognizing in their own experiences something that is "story worthy" and for bringing their perception of those experiences together with the conventions of "story" in appropriate contexts and thus creating identifiable, self-contained narratives. Any single personal experience story tends to become increasingly polished in terms of form and style as the teller repeats it in varying contexts. Without pushing the metaphor too far, we might say that the first telling of a personal experience story serves as an *ur-form* for the teller; retellings always consciously or subconsciously take into account the form, style, and content of that first telling. But, through context-sensitive "re-creation," the teller polishes the story until it becomes a fairly stable performance piece incorporating those consistent aspects of style and content that the teller deems essential to a good rendition. If the story is successful, if it effectively entertains, teaches, or awes the audience, then the teller is likely to repeat it whenever the context—like the context for a proverb or pun—is appropriate.

RELATIONSHIPS TO OTHER GENRES OF FOLKLORE

Not all folklorists consider the personal experience story either an identifiable genre or even "folklore" in its broadest sense. The content is, after all, non-traditional; it cannot be corroborated in the indexes nor in other published or archived texts.[1] Some stories (*memorates*) do involve traditional beliefs, but even then the stories themselves are idiosyncratic in content and confined to the repertoires of the individuals whose experiences they reflect.

A temptation might be to view the personal experience story as a modern replacement for the entertaining *Märchen* or for the informative and instructive oral legend. But the personal experience story as a genre has been a part of oral tradition for a long time. Its current popularity more than likely results from increased scholarly interest: I would hesitate to speculate on a rise in modern man's introversion or personal creativity simply on the basis of the number of personal experience stories now being collected. Rather I would argue that the genre has always been popular. Probably the strongest evidence for this assertion is the well-established tradition of first-person tall tales, jokes, anecdotes, and even *Märchen* that make use of the audience's assumed familiarity with the form and style of a personal experience story.

In addition to forms that rely upon a familiarity with the personal experience story as a genre, a number of folklore genres share many of the features that identify personal experience stories. For instance, the smaller legend categories—family stories, anecdotes, gossip—exhibit the same limited circulation, idiosyncratic content, or relatively short life as do personal experience stories. In fact, as Juha Pentikäinen has pointed out, distinguishing the personal account from other legend categories is often quite difficult. Two other researchers, Dégh and Vázsonyi, have even suggested that the hypothetical "proto-memorate" is so necessary to a discussion of legend that it becomes a moot point for the scholar whether a particular narrative is a personal experience story that may become a legend or a legend that has been cast in a first-person format.[2] Furthermore, it seems arguable that personal experience stories themselves might be further subdivided on the basis of content rather than simply their first-person form.

The term "memorate" (coined in 1934 by the Swedish scholar C. W. von Sydow) has long been accepted to identify personal accounts of experiences with the supernatural or first-person stories that illustrate beliefs. In 1952 Richard M.

Dorson published a collection of Michigan lore in which he included a group of personal narratives collected from informants he dubbed "sagamen."[3] Though Dorson cited von Sydow's comments on the memorate as a precedent for his inclusion of such stories, most of what he collected involved neither the traditional beliefs nor supernatural figures associated with the genre but extraordinary experiences of realistic or "secular" nature, such as Swan Olson's story of beating the farmer he worked for and getting paid for it or Charlie Goodman's account of an incident in the winter of 1895 when he effectively intimidated the deputy game warden.

My own reasons for stressing the secular nature of what I have called "personal narratives" arise from the differing functions such stories serve among people who tell or listen to them. Because they involve traditional beliefs, memorates represent personal testimonials either supporting or denying the validity of established elements of culture. A story of an encounter with a revenant is surely a very personal account, incorporating perhaps a strong emotional response on the part of the teller. But, like many of the death omen and ghost narratives in Montell's *Ghosts along the Cumberland*, memorates usually reflect either the teller's acceptance or questioning of the traditional belief at the base of the story.[4] A secular personal narrative, on the other hand, may reinforce or deny a traditional value or attitude, but such a core of content material is not easily extractable (as an indexed belief or motif) or perhaps even widely shared by the storytelling community. The secular personal narrative, in other words, represents a segment of the teller's personal system of ethics. The storyteller's own values influence the perception of experience, encourage the casting of the incident in a story form, and prompt the repetition of the story in various contexts.

IDENTIFYING TELLERS, TEXTS, AND REPERTOIRES

We are surrounded by personal narrative raconteurs ranging from kindergarteners who tell us what they "did at school today" to senior citizens recounting lengthy life sagas. Of the "real storytellers," perhaps two kinds are distinguishable— those who are "other-oriented" and those who are "self-oriented." The first group tells stories that resemble representatives of the various legend categories. They underplay their personal role in the story to emphasize the extraordinary nature of things that happen in the tale. These stories might easily be categorized as memorates rather than as the more secular personal narratives, or perhaps as anecdotes in which the narrator serves mainly as witness and recorder of incidents in which other people are the primary participants. Like Lüthi's "legend character," such a storyteller hopes to impress the audience with the testimony that life does indeed confront us with some of the strange and awesome happenings hidden behind the beliefs and rumors of earlier generations.[5]

The "self-oriented" tellers delight in weaving fairly elaborate tales that build upon their own self-images and emphasize their own actions as either humorous or exemplary. These tellers tend to offer the audience stories that resemble the tall tale, joke, parable, or realistic *novella*. The difference between a "self-oriented" teller and an "other-oriented" teller might be seen more clearly through a comparison of two sample texts. The teller of the first text, Shirley Fisher, is basically other-oriented: she has a small repertoire of personal experience stories, mostly involving traditional beliefs or events in which other people are equally important participants. The second storyteller is Richard Dorson, editor of this *Handbook*, whose particular oral text I have selected because the story content is already documented as a self-conscious performance piece by the teller himself. His is, of course, a "self-oriented" narrative.

The "Other-Oriented" Narrative

The story below was recorded at the teller's home in Andrews, Indiana, October 3, 1974, in the evening. At the time of the recording the storyteller, Shirley Fisher, was thirty-three years old. A native of Huntington, Indiana, Shirley lived with her husband, Bill, and four children in the small town of Andrews, about six miles from Huntington. Present at this particular storytelling were the teller (SF); several of her children; the collector's sister, a friend of Shirley's, Carol Wallace (CW); and the collector (SKDS). The incident is one Shirley has often discussed; Carol specifically asked for the story. Involved is the folk belief in a magic "charm" to heal burns. Dorson reports a similar story in his *Bloodstoppers and Bearwalkers*, where he records Bert Damour's story about Louie Toine, who charmed the burn away when boiling maple-bark water spilled on Bert. In volume six of the *Frank C. Brown Collection of North Carolina Folklore* are several examples of "blowing" or "talking" the fire out of burns, along with conventional home remedies for burns. Harry M. Hyatt in *Folklore from Adams County Illinois* records three "magical" cures for burns. One informant, like Shirley, insists that "a man has got to tell this to a woman, or a woman to a man." In only one text does the healer actually blow on the burn itself; as Shirley suggests, the term "blowing" is usually used metaphorically. Shirley commented briefly that her grandmother could also stop the bleeding of a wound; bloodstopping is a similar folk remedy involving a curative charm learned from another bloodstopper.

In this instance the burn incident takes place at a factory—Utah Electronics in Huntington, a plant that has employed the collector, her sister, and Shirley at one time or another. "Grandma" and "Bill" are Shirley's grandmother and husband, respectively.

SF: When I got burned at the factory—hot wax. A wax pot busted and fell on me. And hot wax went down on me, you know. Course I called Grandma right away and told her. And she said, "Well, I'll start working on you." And they took me out to the hospital, and they said, "Oh, you'll be all scarred," you know. And I don't have a scar from it!

CW: What did she do to you?

SF: "Blew out the fire"—there was things you read out of the Bible, you know.

CW: She didn't come and actually blow on you did she?

SF: No, huh-uh. You don't have to be right there. Just as long as you're working on it and you know who it is and all that. Same as with stopping bleeding—she could always do that with it.

SKDS: Did she ever tell anybody her . . . ?

SF: A man has to tell a woman and a woman has to tell a man. It can't—she couldn't teach me. She coulda told Bill, and Bill coulda taught me. But she's gone now—and nobody ever learned it. And the last few years of her life, she wasn't—it takes a lot out of you to do that, and she couldn't do it anymore, we never did learn how to do it.

This memorate or other-oriented text resembles the belief legend in form, following a dialogue pattern rather than an individual "performance-piece" format. The text bears the appearance of being rough and spontaneous rather than polished—even though the teller has told the story many times before. With such a story it is to the teller's advantage to appear unselfconscious in the telling; the technique of simulating spontaneous form lends an air of sincerity and immediacy to the storytelling, qualities that might be undermined by an extremely polished performance.

The "Self-Oriented" Narrative

Richard Dorson's self-oriented text, on the other hand, is polished, well-organized, and entertaining. A version of the story was recorded at the teller's home in Bloomington, Indiana, December 7, 1974. At the time of the recording, the storyteller was fifty-eight years old. A native of New York City, Dorson came to Indiana in 1957 as director of Indiana University's folklore program. Present at this particular storytelling were the teller; his wife, Gloria; the collector (SKDS); and the collector's husband, Mark Stahl. The storyteller was well aware of the kind of story I wanted; he had told the story many times previously and considered it an established part of his repertoire. Typically he began the story with a recital of his failing efforts in "Pop" Whitman's American History course at Exeter. He had slowly brought his grade up from an F to a B+ through some methodic self-instruction on "how to study."

Then one day Pop announced a prize competition annually given by the Daughters of the Society of Cincinnatus to the best student essay on the cause of the American Revolution. So—I was thinking, I had been at Exeter four years and a summer session and I'd never won any academic honor—and this is my one chance. So I stayed in my room that weekend. I got all of the books on the American Revolution out of the library. I put them all around me—took something out of this, something out of that—[laughter]—combined it into an essay. I cut the Saturday night movie. This was the top occasion at Exeter. You waited all week long for the Saturday night movie to begin—a Laurel and Hardy film. And I didn't go to that. I cut Sunday morning church; I had somebody sign in for me—that was compulsory. And I wrote this thirty-five-page paper on the causes of the American Revolution, and I handed it in to Pop.

And now the scene shifts to the very last ritual occasion of my Exeter career—Prize Night, in the assembly hall where we had our chapel services. And seven hundred Exeter boys are seated there. They now have girls, but at that time—it was a completely, uh, monastic institution. [Laughter.] So I'm sitting at the back of the hall, as a senior. And Doc Perry, our principal—a very benign, benevolent figure—is up front announcing the prizes and all the faculty are seated behind him. And he's reading off the list of winners. And one prize after another goes to John Aloysius O'Keefe. He won the Bandler Latin Prize, the Heald Debating Prize, the Stilton Mathematics Prize—it is incredible how many prizes are going to this one individual. And he's mounting up this big pile of books and medals and certificates. But I wasn't paying much attention because I wasn't involved in any of these competitions—but just the one that I was waiting to hear about. And finally we reached that point. And Doc Perry says, "And now it is my pleasure to announce the winner of the prize annually given by the Daughters of the Society of Cincinnatus for the best essay on the cause of the American Revolution. The winner is—John Aloysius O'Keefe. [Laughter.] Honorable mention: Richard M. Dorson." So I sat there—crushed, despondent. I later learned that John Aloysius O'Keefe had written a sixty-three-page paper on the causes of the American Revolution.

So, I'm feeling very, very blue, grim. Four years and a summer session at Exeter and nothing to show in the way of any academic achievement. In fact, I was very lucky just to graduate because I had to get a tutor to get a D in physics. [Laughter.] So, I'm sitting there with my head in my hands not paying any attention to what's going on because that's the only prize I had a chance for—that I entered the competition for. And then—suddenly I heard my name called. And, and, I looked up, and there's Doc Perry waiting for me to come up, and I had to walk the whole length of the assembly up to the front. Seven hundred boys all applauding, and Doctor Perry smiling, and he has a big handful of books there—six books from the Biographies of the Great Americans, with my name inscribed in Latin: Ricardo Mercienis Dorsonibus. And so I'm loaded down with these books, and Doc Perry announces, "I am pleased to award to you the prize annually given to the Exeter student who has made the greatest improvement in American History." [Laughter.] So I didn't quite know how to respond to that, but anyway—I had won a prize, the kind of prize you can't really enter into the competition for. [Laughter.] And so, I am now able to say that I came away with one academic distinction [laughter]—a rather curious kind of distinction.[6]

Clearly the teller's self-image is the unifying element of the fairly long narrative. He skillfully creates a sense of the naiveté and academic ineptitude of his boyhood and by implication allows the audience to compare these with his present level of academic achievement. The young boy in the story is charming rather than pathetic because the teller's attitude toward his experience is positive and secure, one that allows for humor and amuses both the teller himself and his audience.

Humor seems a technique and a perspective particularly valued by the teller. In this story, for example, he could have left out the entire segment in which he competes for the prize given for the best essay on the causes of the American Revolution. The basic story (and a true account) would still be there: he improved his study skills in American History and thus won the unexpected prize awarded to the student most improved in American History. But the story would be very dry, lacking the important image of rivalry, and it would not serve to demonstrate the teller's obvious high regard for humor, both as an aesthetic technique and as a way of creating meaning. Furthermore, I am sure the teller would argue that the story would not accurately represent the teller's experience without this segment he perceives as important. To another teller, one who valued humor and artistry less and serious moralizing more, the competition for the American Revolution Prize and the list of prizes won by the rival, John Aloysius O'Keefe, might seem tangential, amusing perhaps but not integral to the real message of the story. For Richard Dorson the humor is necessary—not for the sake of entertainment, not for the sake of truth, but clearly for the sake of the story, *his* story. Along with his audience he can laugh at his own "Sad Sack" persona as he desperately holds out against the inevitable victor, Mr. O'Keefe, and he can play up his dramatic disappointment when the battle is lost because he knows that in the end he will win the war. In this case, he does succeed in the more serious business of learning how to learn, how to be a scholar. And this lesson or value is perhaps the most important one created through the story. As George Carey writes, in essense the story relates "how one man got on the long road to becoming a scholar."[7]

The character presented in Dorson's story is protected by the humor and the entertaining style of the storyteller. But the storyteller himself is quite vulnerable. I think the personal experience story as a genre is appealing in great measure because of this vulnerability of the storyteller. Nothing creates intimacy quite so well as some confession or exposure of the self; the storyteller offers a welcome gift to a cold world, a moment by the fire of self. The conventions of the story make self-revelation acceptable and entertaining, but the courage of the storyteller in articulating usually covert values makes the storytelling an engaging experience, for the teller and the audience. In effect the narrator tests personal values—practical, moral, social, aesthetic—with every story repetition. The willingness to bring forward values for the scrutiny of the audience makes the narrator vulnerable: but like Achilles or Siegfried, the teller proves heroic not by hiding that vulnerability but by courageously accepting responsiblity for the story, more so than the teller of fanciful *Märchen* (for it is tradition that asserts the worth of the story) or the master of parable and fable (for the experience story is real, not hypothetical). Existentially, the personal experience narrator not only acts or experiences but "thinks about" his action, evaluates it, learns from it, and tells the story—not to express his values, but to build them, to create them, to remake them each time he tells his stories.

Opportunities for collecting personal narratives are nearly limitless. A number of formal situations have traditionally served as contexts for the telling of personal experience stories. Sermons, classroom lectures, television or radio interviews or "talk shows," after-dinner speeches, or revivalistic testimonials frequently incorporate memorates or personal narratives. Usually such stories are fairly well-rehearsed and serve a clear didactic or illustrative function. In addition to such formal situations, innumerable informal contexts encourage or even provoke the exchange of personal experience stories. Parties, coffee or lunch breaks, family dinners, happy hour at the local tavern—all are natural contexts.

The would-be collector might logically seek out such contexts for the exchange of personal experience narratives and simply record each storytelling event in its entirety. Such collecting situations would be ideal in many respects; they would certainly allow for more effective functional or stylistic analysis than would the formal elicitation of narrative texts. Nevertheless, valuable material can be collected by asking the teller to recall stories told in the past or by asking friends or family to suggest stories they remember hearing before. One advantage to the out-of-context collecting would be the collector's certainty about the traditionality of the story in the teller's repertoire. And, when the story is thus regarded as a "text" rather than part of an interactional event only, it can be studied comparatively, either as it varies over time or as it may contrast with a story based on the "same" incident as told by another person.

The researcher's method of collecting personal experience stories and the subsequent analysis of them are intimately related. In order to incorporate an elaborate discussion of function, verbal cues, and meaningful stylization in the analysis, the collector will necessarily capture the item in context, as, for example, Barbara Kirshenblatt-Gimblett has in her study of "A Parable in Context."[8] A patient collector may even witness the kind of polemic exchange that sometimes occurs when two people involved in the same incident simultaneously create individual stories. Or the storytellers may engage in a heated contrast of their already well-established versions.[9] On the other hand, the researcher may wish to focus on the content of the stories and perhaps even ignore the form and style of individual items for the sake of broad thematic generalizations.[10] Other analytic approaches might involve refining the definition of the genre through the use of textual examples; relating the repertoire, personality, and social roles of individual storytellers; investigating in depth the style of various storytellers, noting their responses to varying contexts, their use of exaggeration, perhaps even their techniques for moving from one medium to another, as one might do with the written and oral versions of the Exeter story.[11]

Studies of personal narratives could help in the exploration of American beliefs and values. Lauri Honko's fine study has already explored the relationship between the memorate and traditional folk beliefs.[12] I am convinced that the personal narrative can be useful in discovering the more secular values of contemporary Americans as well. Students can learn to assess the aesthetic values and techniques used in the telling of oral stories.[13] Ethical values, personal goals and hopes, dominant themes and guiding principles—all of these covert but dynamic forces are hidden in these unassuming, everyday tales.[14] Curiosity charms us into asking why these personal experience stories are so pervasive in American culture. Why do our parents and grandparents guide and entertain us with their own personal tales? Why does Richard Dorson tell his Exeter story when—like his informant Douglas Suggs—he must surely know a hundred traditional stories? Why does the Austrian immigrant working in a Houston department store tell her tale of trading the Russians perfume for food after Vienna was three-quarters destroyed? Obviously there are many reasons why we tell such stories. One outstanding reason is that through personal experience stories we articulate and then test the values that identify our selves.

NOTES

1. See Sandra K. D. Stahl, "The Personal Narrative As Folklore," *Journal of the Folklore Institute* 14 (1977): 9–30, and idem, "The Oral Personal Narrative in Its Generic Context," *Fabula* 18 (1977): 18–39, respectively, for a lengthy consideration of the personal experience story *as folklore.*

2. Juha Pentikäinen, "Belief, Memorate, and Legend," *Folklore Forum* 6 (1973): 217–41; Linda Dégh and Andrew Vázsonyi, "The Memorate and the Proto-Memorate," *Journal of American Folklore* 87 (1974): 225–39.

3. Richard M. Dorson, *Bloodstoppers and Bearwalkers* (Cambridge, Mass.: Harvard University Press, 1952), pp. 249–72, and esp. note, p. 298.

4. William Lynwood Montell, *Ghosts along the Cumberland: Deathlore in the Kentucky Foothills* (Knoxville: University of Tennessee Press, 1975).

5. The differing characters of the legend and tale heroes are discussed in an excellent article by Max Lüthi, "Aspects of the *Märchen* and the Legend," *Genre* 2 (1969): 162–78.

6. Dorson includes a written version of the story in "The Legend of the Missing Pajamas and Other Sad Sagas," *Journal of the Folklore Institute* 14 (1977): 115–24; George Carey discusses the story briefly in "The Storyteller's Art and the Collector's Intrusion," in *Folklore Today: A Festschrift for Richard M. Dorson*, ed. Linda Dégh, Henry Glassie, and Felix J. Oinas (Bloomington: Indiana University RCLSS, 1976), pp. 81–91.

7. Carey, p. 81.

8. Barbara Kirshenblatt-Gimblett, "A Parable in Context: A Social Interactional Analysis of Storytelling Performance," in *Folklore: Performance and Communication*, ed. Dan Ben-Amos and Kenneth S. Goldstein (The Hague: Mouton, 1975), pp. 105–30.

9. Linda Dégh contrasts two such tellers, Steve Boda and his wife, Ida, in "Symbiosis of Joke and Legend: A Case of Conversational Folklore," in *Folklore Today*, pp. 101–22.

10. See, in particular, Richard M. Dorson, "Hunting Folklore in the Armpit of America," *Indiana Folklore* 10 (1977): 102–104.

11. For a study of one personal narrative teller's performance in both oral and written media see Sandra K. D. Stahl, "Style in Oral and Written Narratives," *Southern Folklore Quarterly* 43 (1979): 39–62.

12. Lauri Honko, "Memorate and the Study of Folk Belief," *Journal of the Folklore Institute* 1 (1964): 5–19.

13. See Mark B. Stahl, "Using Traditional Oral Stories in the English Classroom," *The English Journal* 68:7 (1979): 33–36.

14. Kenneth S. Goldstein recognizes even overt politicizing in the telling of personal narratives to children in "The Telling of Non-Traditional Tales to Children: An Ethnographic Report from a Northwest Philadelphia Neighborhood," *Keystone Folklore* 20:3 (1975): 5–17.

Sally Yerkovich

Conversational Genres

"Tuck up your sleeves and loosen your talktapes," shouts the washerwoman in *Finnegans Wake* as she settles down by the river Liffey to wash clothes and to gossip with her companion. We may not always have as much gossip to thrash over as the washerwoman, but like her, we all know the pleasures of a good conversation.

Many scholars, including linguists, sociologists, and anthropologists, work to unravel the mysteries of conversation. Folklorists have as their focus the artfully patterned aspects of everyday discourse. Here we will examine both the directions and results of previous work as well as the possibilities presented by relatively untried approaches. Our subjects will range from jargon to proverbs, from curses to jokes, from narratives to artistic styles of speaking.

When someone asks a folklorist about the kinds of verbal art found in conversation, the folklorist is most likely to begin by talking about the shorter forms of traditional expression used in everyday discourse: proverbs, superstitions, taunts, curses, charms, spells, and the like.

These genres were first dubbed *conversational* by Roger D. Abrahams in "A Rhetoric of Everyday Life: Conversational Genres." Abrahams' approach indicated a recognition of the importance of context to the meaning of the traditional expressive forms. New questions had then to be asked about these forms: who can use them? speaking to whom? when? where? Abrahams' study leads us to realize that without some knowledge of context we cannot understand the meaning and intent of these genres.

Abrahams also noted that the conversational genres exhibit similar dramatic structure and "they set up a protagonist-antagonist relationship between the speaker and spoken-to, and proceed to only suggest a possible resolution to the conflict."[1] For example, I could use the proverb, "Don't wash your dirty linen in public," to advise a friend to keep his private concerns to himself. In so doing, I would be putting myself in a dual role as a person able to make a judgment about the situation and as someone capable of influencing another's behavior. In a similar manner, conversational genres can be used to apply strategies of argument in situations where conflict needs to be resolved, where a position needs reinforcing, where a summary needs to be made.

A few years later Abrahams added other genres to the conversational list—local names, jargon, slang, intensifiers, and all forms of special languages. These both embellish speech and identify users as members of certain social or cultural groups.[2] Just as secret handshakes are nonverbal signs of membership for some social groups, bureaucratese and academic jargon identify their users' professional affiliations. In a similar manner, conversational genres can be used to apply strategies of argument in situations where conflict needs to be resolved, where a position needs reinforcing, where a summary needs to be made.

Studies of folkloric genres such as those proposed by Abrahams yield important information and insight into the meaning of conversational forms. Through them we can identify the speaker, listener, place, and time of genre use. A listing of these features, however, is not necessarily sufficient for our understanding of the subtleties of the forms. We can go further and begin to look at the interrelationship of these features. We then shift our focus slightly and examine the dynamics of the conversational situation, observing how folklore fits into the processes of our everyday lives.

If we look at social interaction as a process—a flow of human behaviors—rather than as a series of discrete events, we recognize other less obvious genres of conversational folklore. We can begin to pick out forms of folklore that are longer than any individual utterance. For example, some kinds of stories occur in conversations. They are seldom presented by one speaker as monologues but are constructed over conversational turns by several individuals. The term *conversational genre*, then, can be expanded to its fullest sense, one which encompasses the many kinds of artfully structured behaviors we use as we act and interact with one another.

When we recognize the processual nature of human interaction, we focus on the social situation, how it is constituted, and how folkloric performances arise from it. We acknowledge that we are looking at a complex interrelationship among a number of factors that may allow for the appropriate use of an expressive form. For example, in order for a proverb to have for its user the desired social effect, it must be used correctly. The user must size up the conversational situation, understand its flow and the roles of the various participants in it, understand the particular generic device to be used, and then strategically place it within the flow of interaction. As you plant so shall you reap. A misused conversational genre can embarrass where we intend to praise, can divide where we intend to unify, and can turn a social situation upside down.

A focus upon the social situation also allows us to move from the short conversational genres embedded within sentences that have long been considered folkloric to explore the possibility of other folklore genres being conversational. We can now turn to genres like jokes, legends, and stories which are constructed over conversational turns during the course of social interactions. When we begin with a social situation, the interaction within the situation becomes of primary importance. We look not only at where we are (e.g., a living room) but also at how we happen to be there and who is there with us. The people who make up the "cast of characters" in a particular social scene are of utmost importance, because through their presence and interrelationships, they create the situation and shape what may or may not be said there.

We all know that we tell jokes to our grandparents differently from the way we tell them to our close friends and peers, and furthermore, that the jokes we tell will vary from group to group and individual to individual. Just as we choose what we talk about according to our listeners, our listeners shape what we say. When a joke is introduced, "Say, did I ever tell you the one about . . . ," we know too well that the listeners aren't immediately silenced. Their verbal and nonverbal responses to the joke telling shape the joke significantly. In fact, whether a joke is funny or not may depend totally upon just how all of the components of the joke-telling situation mesh. The joke itself unfolds as the telling progresses. It is emergent, that is, a unique product of a particular interaction.

We should note here as well that the realization of the joke as an expressive form, its performance, is emergent from the situation in which it is told. A joke becomes folklore in this respect only as it is successfully told, as the teller assumes both the aesthetic and the cultural responsibility for its telling. When the performance of a joke fails, that is, when the listeners do not acknowledge that a joke is funny or corny or whatever it is intended to be, the content of the joke is still folklore. The teller, however, may opt for distancing himself from the performance of the joke *as* folklore. "I can never remember punch lines," "I'm not very good at telling jokes," or "When Mary told it, it was funny" are all kinds of statements to qualify the performative nature of the joke telling. Statements such as these change the situation from that of joke telling, where a competent performance is expected, to that of reporting a joke. In the latter case, the joke teller is distanced from the responsibilities involved in successfully telling a joke. Although the information exchanged is folkloric, the nature of the situation is no longer one in which artistic performance is required.

I have used jokes here as an example of a folklore form not usually considered a conversational genre. In fact, jokes are only one of the many narratives which emerge from conversational situations. We can consider legends as well as certain kinds of rumors and stories in a similar manner. Careful observation as well as extensive audio recording of conversational interactions is necessary for us to discover and analyze the narrative forms of folklore which are products of our everyday discourse.

Still we have only begun to explore the possibilities for analysis which the social situation provides. We have yet to deal at any length with the conversational process itself and with the parts of that process which are artistic in their own right. As we do this we must at all times remember that we are dealing with not just an individual speaker but with two or more speakers involved in an interactive exchange. Thus we do not focus solely upon ways of *speaking* but instead upon ways of *conversing*, and we begin to explore those kinds of conversations which may be considered genres in and of themselves.

Here we observe the varying kinds of conversations which occur in particular places with specific individuals present. We can see the relationships that obtain among the speakers and how, if at all, these relationships affect the kinds of conversing they participate in. We can note the names which the individuals use in referring to their own conversations ("Oh, we were just *chatting*"; "We've been *talking shop*") as well as any evaluations which they might make of their conversations ("Talking to him puts me to sleep"). With this data we can then begin to sort out those kinds of conversation which have a potential artistic or expressive element to them and, further, exactly which factors must be present in order for an interaction to be artistic.

The shift to artistic conversation may be seen as a shift into performance in folkloric terms. Here, we view performance as the actualization of the expressive or artistic potential of behavior. There are certain ways of speaking which lend themselves to a performance mode, for example, reminiscing or "holding forth." Performance in this case might occur as a professor recounts stories of his encounters with well-known individuals in his field. In dealing with conversational interaction, however, performance must be viewed in a slightly different manner. As we noted earlier, conversation implies an exchange among two or more individuals. Performance in conversation, then, must be applied to that interactional exchange among individuals rather than to the speaking of only one participant. Performance in conversing occurs not because of a single individual's contribution to the situation (although particularly artful talkers may be able to control the expressive level of a conversation more than most) but because of the collective actions and interactions of all of the participants in the situation. The individuals in the group, then, collectively take the responsibility for maintaining the performance mode in their conversing.

The performance mode of conversing relates closely to Georg Simmel's concept of sociable conversation. Simmel calls this the art form of conversation, in which people talk simply for the sake of talking. This comment does not imply, however, that sociable conversation is trivial. As Simmel points out, although

the topic is merely the indispensable medium through which the lively exchange of speech unfolds its attractions, . . . the content of sociable conversation . . . must be interesting, fascinating, even important. But it may not become the purpose of the conversation.[3]

When it does, sociability is no longer present. Emphasis upon the subjective, upon the self, upon the serious, all cause the conversation to shift from its sociable state.

Sociability is the pure form of conversation: one in which the flow of the exchange—the conversing—is an end in itself. The speaker changes frequently and in spite of the momentary dominance of each participant, no one person controls the overall interchange. Everyone participates as if they were equals in order to maintain the sociability of the situation. At this level, our way of conversing becomes a kind of performance, one in which each individual accepts the responsibility not for his own aesthetic presentation but for maintaining the ambiance of artful conversational interplay.

When we join in sociable interaction, we engage in a celebration of the act of conversation itself. As we might hunt for the pleasure of the chase, we participate in artistic conversation for the pleasure of associating with others. We conjoin to acknowledge the importance of groupness to our lives.

But we still have a great deal to discover about that groupness and about our ways of associating which express it. We have only begun to investigate the ways of speaking and the kinds of conversing that are central to our daily lives. With the recognition of conversation as a fertile ground for the study of expressive behavior comes a responsibility for further investigation. We need to understand how we distinguish between different ways of talking and what these distinctions mean in terms of our social interactions. We need to explore the various styles of speech that we use in different kinds of talking and conversing and to discover which elements of style are important when we define certain speaking as artistic. We need to know the structure of our expressive actions and interactions and the structure of the situations which allow them. There is no such thing as useless prattle. When we tuck up our sleeves and loosen our talktapes, we participate in a process of association, the need for which is at the core of our humanness.

NOTES

1. Roger D. Abrahams, "A Rhetoric of Everyday Life: Traditional Conversational Genres," *Southern Folklore Quarterly* 32 (1968): 51.

2. Roger D. Abrahams, "The Complex Relations of Simple Forms," *Genre* 2 (1969): 113.

3. Georg Simmel, *The Sociology of Georg Simmel,* ed. and trans. Kurt H. Wolff (New York: Free Press, 1950), p. 52.

David Evans

Folk Singers
and Musicians

For most of the history of American folksong scholarship, folk-lorists were content to collect and publish texts and sometimes the tunes to which they were set. The performer's identity, if it was noted at all, was usually accorded about as much significance as the place and date of collection and could be summarized in a few words that provided name, age, sex, occupation, and little else. But today an emphasis on the singer or musician has become one of the dominant scholarly approaches. The impetus for this turnabout actually developed out of the interests of the early textual scholars such as Phillips Barry. A preoccupation with folksong origins led Barry in 1912 to attempt to identify and learn something about the life of a ballad composer. His concern with textual variation later prompted him to explore the relationship between a ballad variant and the singer's personality.

A growing sociological awareness among folklorists in the first three decades of the twentieth century resulted in a search for performers whose songs seemed to typify the themes and genres of particular folk groups. Howard W. Odum, who began collecting black folksongs after the turn of the century, published in 1928 the first of three novels about "Black Ulysses," a composite character based on the many itinerant singers of blues and worksongs Odum had encountered in his fieldwork. Only five years later John and Alan Lomax discovered Leadbelly (Huddie Ledbetter) in the Louisiana State Penitentiary. Leadbelly must have seemed like the living reality of "Black Ulysses." Accompanying himself usually with a twelve-string guitar, he sang blues, reels, prison worksongs, field hollers, spirituals, children's songs, ballads, and assorted other pieces. With the help of the Lomaxes, Leadbelly was released from prison and presented to the American public as an authentic representative of the black folksong tradition. The venture proved moderately successful, and since the 1940s a string of performers who seemed to typify the best that a regional or ethnic musical tradition has to offer have been written about in books and articles and presented on the concert and festival circuit. Outstanding examples are Woody Guthrie, a composer with a social consciousness who drew upon the traditions of the Oklahoma Dust Bowl; Almeda "Granny" Riddle, an Ozark Mountain ballad singer *par excellence*; and Bessie

Jones, a performer of play songs and other pieces form the black tradition of the isolated Georgia Sea Islands.

Folklorists have combined their interest in authorship, variation, and individual embodiment of whole traditions with a new attention to performance, artistry, and creativity. Interest in these latter subjects began to develop in the 1940s as phonograph records and live performances brought authentic folk music directly to large numbers of Americans who had never heard it before. Record collectors of early jazz, blues, and "hillbilly" music researched the lives of the great performers who had made commercial recordings since the 1920s, and in some cases these performers were brought out of musical retirement to a round of concerts and festival appearances. Among the outstanding "rediscoveries" of this sort are Ferdinand "Jelly Roll" Morton, Mississippi John Hurt, Big Bill Broonzy, Son House, and Skip James in black tradition, and Buell Kazee, Dock Boggs, Clarence Ashley, and Sam and Kirk McGee in southern white tradition. These and many other fine performers serve as models for scores of folk revivalists who try to learn their songs and vocal and instrumental styles. Although this interest in artistry and performance generated many excellent books, articles, and phonograph records during the last twenty years, most of this scholarship existed outside of or on the fringes of academic folklore study. Folklorists have too often considered these artists to be tainted by commercialism through their recording activities (and hence not to be true "folk" performers) or have looked askance at the hordes of "folkniks," "blues freaks," and "pickers" who frequently mix radical ideology or clumsy musicianship with a sincere desire to know more about the lives and music of these performers. Then too, very few folklorists have been trained to understand performance techniques or the history of commercial recording of folk music. Since the ability to recreate folk music performance is an important key to understanding and analysis of the music, and since folk performers have been exposed to phonograph records and other mass media for more than half a century, folklorists interested in studying performers would do well to learn more about these subjects. Universities offering training in folklore need to build collections of commercial recordings and encourage students to learn performance styles from traditional artists.

Anyone can now read about the lives and music of hundreds of folk performers, hear generous samplings of their repertoires and styles on phonograph records, and observe their music directly in live performances and visual media presentations. It is no longer an innovation in folklore scholarship to publish more than the barest biographical details of one's informants or to point out that folksongs can be viewed as performances rather than texts allied to tunes. We must go further to determine the significant factors in the music and careers of performers and identify those performers most in need of our attention.

Most folklorists would probably prefer to find and study performers with the large repertoires of a Leadbelly or an Almeda Riddle, as these people tend to be easy to collect from and appear to be representative of the best and broadest features of their respective musical traditions. Such performers are indeed worthy of study, but they are not necessarily typical, and a preoccupation with these star informants can distort the nature of a tradition which depends for its continuity largely on individuals with more modest repertoires. Performers such as Leadbelly and Almeda Riddle may be said to more closely resemble song collectors than typical folk performers. Leadbelly, in fact, would often preface or intersperse his songs with spoken explanations of their meaning, much as a folklorist might annotate a published text, and Almeda Riddle has developed a highly self-conscious awareness of her sources and her songs' artistic value and has not been averse to improving fragmentary or corrupt texts through reference to the collection of Francis James Child. Folklorists should recognize that singers who make the effort to learn several hundred folksongs are generally highly cognizant of the tastes of their audiences—including folklorists and folk revivalists—and will try to provide the kinds of performances that they think are desired.

If we are to study star performers, we must devote equal attention to those who have attained this status in the eyes of their community. Leadbelly, for all his greatness as an artist and his influence on folk revivalists, had virtually no impact on the southern black folksong tradition. His synthesis of the many strands of this tradition would have represented a dead end if his career had not made a fortuitous detour into the realm of folksong scholarship and the folk music revival. On the other hand, the songs of Mississippi blues singers Tommy Johnson and Charley Patton are still performed today by many other folk blues singers, even though their recording legacies are smaller than Leadbelly's and their songs often appear to be textually incoherent and partly improvised. Many performers who are stars in their own communities make recordings or are professionals, and undoubtedly such recordings enhance their reputations as well as supplement oral transmission in disseminating their songs. Johnson and Patton were primarily improvisors and rearrangers of traditional material, and their musical careers were semi-professional and carried out on a local level. Others, like Bob Wills, Muddy Waters, Bill Monroe, Blind Willie McTell, Jelly Roll Morton, Uncle Dave Macon, and Jimmie Rodgers, represent thorough professionals and in some cases stylistic trend setters, who perform traditional material and popular songs, compose new pieces which sometimes achieve traditional status within their folk groups, and leave rich recorded legacies of their performances. While such individuals can be studied from the standpoint of popular music and culture, the folklorist should be especially equipped to evaluate the extent to which they utilize and transform traditional musical material as well as shape and contribute to tradition.

One of the chief reasons for concentrating on individual performers is to determine their relationship to folk tradition and thereby reveal aspects of folk process. The interplay of imitation, memorization, revision, composition, and improvisation can be fascinating. Different performers will sometimes specialize in one or another of these processes or use several of them in their handling of a particular piece. In order to study these processes properly the folklorist will generally have to work with an informant over an extended period of time and record the same pieces on multiple occasions. It would also be desirable to record the people from whom the informant learned songs and those who have learned from the informant. In this regard family musical traditions are especially interesting and notable studies have been made of two southern white mountain families, the Ritchies and the Hammonses.

In examining the processes of tradition, the folklorist should realize that performers may have both active and passive song repertoires as well as different repertoires for different audiences. For example, Leonard "Baby Doo" Caston began his musical career as a folk blues singer and guitarist in Mississippi, moved to Chicago and entered the world of popular blues, vocal groups, and jazz, and has finally wound up in Minneapolis playing guitar and keyboard background music at a cocktail lounge. He has obviously left folk music far behind, though he is still able to perform it. Big Bill Broonzy also started as a folk singer in Mississippi, but when he first recorded in Chicago in 1927, he was performing and composing blues in a currently popular style. He continued to set and keep up with popular blues trends until the early 1950s. At that time he was discovered by folk revivalists and induced to recall some of the earliest songs he had learned as well as to compose new blues with political themes. When Broonzy dictated his autobiography in 1955, he emphasized these oldest and newest aspects of his music, vastly downplaying the quarter of a century during which he was one of the top stars in commercial blues recording. Blind Willie McTell, on the other hand, maintained specialized repertoires throughout his entire career for different audiences. He could perform blues and rags for black house parties, spirituals and gospel songs for churches, and hillbilly and popular songs for serenading in the parking lots of white-only drive-in barbecue stands. When John A. Lomax visited him in 1940, McTell was even able to record five ballads as prizes for the folklorist.

In addition to studying the repertoires and performance processes of folk singers and musicians, the folklorist can investigate their lives to reveal whether the performer plays any special roles in the community. The careers of professional performers can be seen as a series of significant musical events, such as travels, performance engagements, recording sessions, associations with other performers, and personal activities which affect the performer's musical career. Others, especially nonprofessionals, may provide more significant information on their lifestyles than their lives. For example, Blind Log (Lord Randolph Byrd) of Savannah, Georgia, was unable to date many events in his career, but he gave me a rich account of what it was like to be a blind itinerant musician: his encounters with police, robbers, and mean dogs, his different reactions to white and black audiences, the routes he would travel in pursuing his living, the kind of money he made from his music, the places where he played, such as house parties, barbershops, churches, railroad stations, livery stables, tobacco warehouses, storefronts, hotels, bars, and on the streets, and the characters of his musical associates, such as Blind Willie McTell, Blind Ivory Moore, and Blind Benny Paris.

Ideally the performer should be given as much opportunity as possible to present his life and music in his own terms. A good number of autobiographical accounts now exist, many with song examples, by such diverse individuals as Dust Bowl composer Woody Guthrie, blues singer Big Bill Broonzy, professional country music singer Alton Delmore, and professional jazz and blues pianist Jelly Roll Morton. There are also song collections compiled by cowboy singer Glenn Ohrlin, ballad singer Almeda Riddle, bluesman Brownie McGhee, and children's game song performer Bessie Jones. All of these works have been compiled with the help of a folklorist or folk revival enthusiast. The folklorist, however, has an obligation to correct exaggerated claims and other misstatements, fill in significant omissions, and delve into topics of interest to the discipline but perhaps insignificant to the performers, or aspects of the folk process, difficult for performers to articulate, that lie at the very heart of their performance styles and their handling of musical material.

Folklorists should not neglect the historical study of important and influential performers. Details of the lives and repertoires of deceased folk singers and musicians may often be reconstructed through the use of public records, newspaper accounts, phonograph records, and interviews and recordings of relatives, friends, and musical associates. Lengthy accounts based on such sources have been made by folklorists of the lives and music of northeastern woods composers Larry Gorman and Joe Scott, Mississippi blues singer Tommy Johnson, and Georgia songster Blind Willie McTell. Of course, there is a danger that not all of the folklorist's sources will provide a consistent account of the subject. For example, one of Tommy Johnson's brothers, Reverend LeDell Johnson, was convinced that Tommy was a drunkard and a sinner who had sold his soul to the devil in order to learn to play the guitar, while his other brother, Mager Johnson, thought that Tommy was simply a good fellow who liked to have fun and who never harmed anyone.

Finally, it should be pointed out that many performers are specialists in one particular genre or style of folk music. J. B. Smith, a black Texas convict, for example, specializes in composing prison worksongs and field hollers. Jack Owens of Bentonia, Mississippi, whom I have recorded extensively since 1966, has never performed anything except blues. We need further studies of such specialists, particularly in the traditions of occupational groups such as sailors, railroad men, and hoboes, and in such genres as religious folksongs, "dirty" songs, and various instrumental traditions. And in general there is a need for folklorists to investigate the lives and music of performers in traditions other than southern black and white folk music. The many fine and varied studies that have been made of southern performers plus a few from other regional and ethnic traditions should serve as models and sources of stimulation for folklorists as they expand their interests in the future.

Richard M. Dorson

Folktale Performers

Readers of folktale collections would never know until recent years that tales issued from human throats. Following the model set by the Grimms, nineteenth- and twentieth-century collectors emphasized the narratives, gave them polish and literary style, and ignored the tellers. Today a new perspective gives proper due to the oral text and the narrators who impart their personality and creative touches to the traditional plots. One modern school of American folklorists stresses the performance aspects of folklore expression and refers to the narrator as a performer in a storytelling event. A collector in the field should not only record stories but obtain the tellers' life histories, observe audience reaction and interaction, take notes and photographs of the milieu, and, back home in the study, consider the aesthetics, the histrionics, and the repertoire of each narrator. For folktales do not exist in a vacuum, but come to life only when delivered by individuals skilled in the art of oral entertainment, and no two tellings are identical.

We now are in a position, thanks to various ethnographic reports and careful studies, to consider and compare a small number of American folktale artists. Although lengthy narratives are seldom told in the United States, the available information shows a considerable range of style and content among the nation's storytellers.

MÄRCHEN TELLERS

English-speaking readers customarily think of fairy tales as the main form of folk narratives, but they seldom are heard in the United States, and even in western Europe the decline of peasant culture has led to their demise in what was once their stronghold. Yet on occasion a weaver of fairy tales—usually called *Märchen* by American folklorists, borrowing the German term, but also known as wonder tales and magical tales—will be discovered. These fictions stress aristocratic and supernatural characters, underdog heroes undergoing perilous adventures, and large doses of magic and enchantment. Clearly these *Märchen* are imported from abroad.

From England has come the one cycle of magical and trickster tales to be found in the English-speaking tradition in the United States. A sampling of the cycle first appeared in the *Journal of American Folklore* in 1925,[1] and a book of *The Jack Tales* followed in 1943, collected by Richard Chase, who took editorial liberties but obtained excellent notes from Herbert Halpert. Subsequent collectors have printed and issued recordings of Jack Tales, so that some fifty tales associated with the hero Jack are now available, all emanating from the southern Appalachians and in particular the Beech Mountain area of northwestern North Carolina. A cluster of families, the Harmons, Wards, and Gentrys, have specialized in telling them. The September 1978 issue of the *North Carolina Folklore Journal* was devoted to examples and analyses of the Jack Tales.

Marshall Ward

An article in that issue by C. Paige Gutierrez, a doctoral candidate in anthropology with a master's degree in folklore from the University of North Carolina, examines the narrative style of Marshall Ward, an accomplished teller of Jack Tales.[2] Gutierrez interviewed Ward twice in 1974, consulted his oral autobiography recorded in 1969, and viewed a videotape of Ward telling a Jack Tale; with the article she supplied two photographs of him in storytelling action. We have thus at hand a close-up of a master narrator in the most elaborate tale tradition in the United States. In another article in the same issue Gutierrez considered the properties of the Jack Tale as a narrative subgenre.[3] She thus was equipped to analyze both the teller and his cycle.[4]

The facts of Ward's life are straightforward. He was born in Beech Mountain, North Carolina in 1906, never left the area, farmed all his life, and taught fifth grade at Banner Elk for thirty years until his retirement at sixty-five. None of his seven brothers and sisters tell Jack Tales. He claims he knew his repertoire by the time he was five, and would relate tales to his siblings until they fell to snoring. As a teacher he told the stories weekly for three decades to his mountain school fifth-graders.

In his repertoire Marshall Ward both remains faithful to and departs from the Jack Tale narrative tradition. His Jack conforms to the stock Americanized and Appalachianized version of the hero in standard European tale-types, a farm boy who speaks and behaves like any Beech Mountain youth, but undergoes remarkable adventures and encounters. But Gutierrez points out that Ward modifies and softens violent and cruel episodes which offend his middle-class values. In the tale of "Jack and the Heifer Hide," Jack deceives his brothers into letting him drown them in sacks, and Marshall Ward comments in the text: "He felt a little sad about his brothers—he killed them—but they's a-gonna kill him. It's him or them; that's all there was to it. He tried to play fair with them in every way he could, but he couldn't."[5] In "Jack and the Doctor's Girl" Marshall Ward introduces social questions not raised in the variants told by Ray Hicks and R. M. Ward. Marshall portrays the doctor as a greedy hypocrite, and hence subject to criticism, since doctors should be humanitarian. Jack's fight against the doctor becomes a fight for justice. But the doctor also shows remorse, and emerges as a guilt-ridden individual rather than a stereotyped villain. Besides moralizing, Marshall Ward injects into the tales practical information about measurements, meat packing, medical treatment, and details of daily living, which expands his texts to greater length than those of other tellers. Also he lets his imagination roam over the properties of magic objects, such as a magic playaway club that cleared land, built a house, dug a lake, and carried Jack's dad and brothers home. Marshall Ward's inventive powers extended to the composition of wholly new fictions, which conform to the lack/lack liquidated structure of the typical Jack Tale.

In terms of delivery, Marshall Ward displays considerable histrionics. Narrating from a seated position, he indulges in sweeping gestures, animated expressions of happiness, sadness, and surprise, mimicry of animal calls and the voices of giants, witches, and drunks. He changes his pitch, intonation, and speed according to the action and characters. Marshall recognizes that another Jack Tale teller, Ray Hicks, employs a quite different oral style: "droll long voice—he doesn't tell nothin' like I tell 'em—almost a different story."[6] Both traditional and individual elements interact in the telling of Jack Tales.

Joe Woods

A teller of European *Märchen* relating fictions in English is rarely reported in American folklore publications, but at Crystal Falls in Upper Michigan I met such a one, who was cited to me as "full of crazy stories." I hunted up Joe Woods (née Wojtowicz), born in Csanok in Austrian Poland in 1887. He had migrated to America at twenty-one and traveled throughout the northern states working in the woods, on the harvest, and down in the mines, where he contracted rheumatism. Stocky and cross-eyed, Joe proved a spell-binder as he reeled off wonder tales and satirical jests, right out of the Aarne-Thompson type index it seemed. But his texts differed from those in the books, for he delivered them in pungent, colloquial English, flavored with mispronunciations and idiomatic dialogue, so that the fairy tales, which seem unreal and remote in print, crackled with life on his lips. One stylistic device he employed effectively was the insertion of direct questions during the action: "Well, what's shoemaker going to do? Is he going to steal that horse?" Untroubled by his immigrant speech, Woods simulated plaintive, subdued, and angry tones, followed his complex story line clearly and confidently, steered clear of ambiguous pronouns, and painted detailed settings and graphic accounts of Old Country peasant life. He never floundered or groped for a word, although this was the first time he had related tales in English, and he spaced his incidents in natural paragraphs. In the mines and lumber camps Joe entertained his fellows in "Polock" and "Slavish" (he also knew Russian, Croatian, Bohemian, and Serbian); they would place tobacco and cigarettes in his mouth so he would continue a second night. Joe remembered hearing tales told by a wooden-legged beggar in his boyhood, and by men at village fairs, and never forgot them. He was always in complete control of his often complicated texts. While apologizing for certain indelicacies, he did vouchsafe an original text of riotous scatological humor, "The Two Brothers." What impressed me most about Joe Woods was his power to rivet attention with these fairy tales supposedly meant for children.[7]

Cecilia Meléndez

In the course of a field project in East Chicago, in the Calumet Region of northwest Indiana, Philip B. George encountered Cecilia Meléndez, 56, who alone of her Puerto Rican family poured forth *Märchen*, animal tales, jokes, and riddles. She had left Puerto Rico in 1948 to join her husband, who had moved to East Chicago a year before to work for Inland Steel. In Puerto Rico even in her teens Cecilia had shone as a *Märchen* reciter (in Spanish) but in the urban environment, with the demands of the mill's work hours and the competition of the media, there were no congenial social gatherings at which she could entertain responsive audiences. Hence she resorted to two alternatives: she told *Märchen* to herself as she did her housework, and she adjusted her repertoire in her family and church circles (she and her husband and son converted to the Baptist faith in East Chicago) toward jokes, personal experience narratives, and riddles, as more appreciated story fare. Her personal annals dealt chiefly with incidents of growing up with her brother Miguel in Puerto Rico, and of supernatural occurrences there (her father dated a witch). She spoke less, and with less relish, about her life in Indiana. Cecilia did continue, on limited occasions, to relate *Märchen* and animal tales about Compay Conejo (the Puerto Rican Brer Rabbit), Juan Bobo (the Latin American trickster), and such household favorites as "Hansel and Gretel" and "The Tar Baby" to her immediate family. George recorded over twenty of these structured tale types from Mrs. Meléndez. He describes her as "an excellent and constant performer with a good memory, a large variety of hand and facial expressions, a variable voice, and a vivid imagination at her command."

Besides her storytelling, Cecilia maintains her Puerto Rican identity in other ways through traditional foods, participation in ethnic organizations, and involvement in the Puerto Rican congregation of her church. George concludes that the transition from her homeland to East Chicago has not erased her ethnic personality but compelled her to reassert it through new channels.

In transcribing and translating five of Cecilia's narratives, George commented on the problem of capturing the vitality and exuberance of the performance in a printed text, especially her episodes with Miguel, which "must be read out loud, shouting the exclamations, pausing and changing voice tone. One should try to imagine a lively little lady bouncing around, waving her arms, and laughing as she tells the tale." Since the printed vignette simply sketches Cecilia's childhood memory of hunting birds with her brother, who would call "Pullijo" (a meaningless term), to make the birds freeze, much of the story's appeal must lie with the delivery. On that score George assures us of its dramatic and didactic power. Kids in Puerto Rico grew up, maintains Cecilia, with healthier, more innocent attitudes than those in crime-ridden East Chicago.[8]

TALL TALE HEROES

If *Märchen* tellers derive their sustenance from Old World sources, narrators of tall tales speak in a distinctly American vein. As the *Märchen* characterizes European storytelling, so the tall tale exemplifies American storytelling, but generalizations must be used cautiously, for the fictive exaggerations of the German soldier-adventurer Baron Münchausen, published in 1785, set the model for his American counterparts. But late nineteenth- and early twentieth-century conditions in the United States seemed particularly propitious for the propagating of Münchausen figures. Spread-eagle oratory, Manifest Destiny, and the idea of progress all reinforced the tall tale, and tellers around the country attached these fictive exploits to themselves. After their deaths other lesser narrators continued to reproduce their narratives, now told about them rather than by them, and perpetuated their self-created legends. Jim Bridger in the Rocky Mountain trapper country, John Darling in the Catskills of New York, Jones Tracy on Mt. Desert Island off the Maine coast, Hathaway Jones in the Rogue River region of southwest Oregon, Len Henry in northern Idaho, Daniel Stamps in western Illinois,

Abraham Smith from southern Indiana and eastern Illinois, and Gib Morgan from the oil fields all fit this mold. The latter two are especially renowned.

"Oregon" Smith

The most complete study to date of an American tall-tale teller is William Hugh Jansen's 1949 dissertation, *Abraham "Oregon" Smith, Pioneer, Folk Hero and Tale-Teller*, reproduced in book form in 1977 by Arno Press. Jansen, a folklorist trained under Stith Thompson at Indiana University in Bloomington, heard Bloomington residents talking about "Lying Abe" Oregon Smith and followed the trail of the notorious storyteller. Abe spent his last years in Chrisman, Edgar County, Illinois, where he died in 1893 aged 97. A sojourn in Oregon from 1852 to 1859 had enlarged his repertoire with whoppers about the far west and earned him his sobriquet. The surviving photograph printed by Jansen shows an erect, imposing figure with sparkling eyes and white hair, sporting a bow tie and vest, and holding a cane in his left hand. Jansen unearthed a surprising amount of documentation and oral tradition about this obscure farmer and homesteader. In addition to six chapters of biography he furnished one chapter of folk-memory about Smith, one analyzing Smith's narrative technique, and seventy-two texts, with variants, recovered from tellers who attributed the tales to Smith. Lying Abe was both a disseminator of tales that others retold, and a subject of legends about his personal traits and habits, such as his youthful strength, his selling of sassafras medicine, for which he was also known as "Sassafras Smith," and his penchant for exaggerated stories. In one popular legend he "attained such a reputation for falsehoods that he became a town scandal and finally he was 'churched' by the officials of the Church of Christ. He was called to account in a regular church trial for his tales about Oregon."[9] At the trial Smith admitted his sins and said he had "shed barrels and barrels of tears over them."

From folk-memories Jansen was able to reconstruct the performance techniques of Lying Abe. Smith assumed the role of an entertainer and showman, and held the stage for himself, unlike other exaggerators who enjoyed swapping or matching lies. He held court in loafing places, such as grocery stores and street corners, and often workers on the job or crowds at a political rally spotting him would gather round and call for stories. Smith narrated them with a straight face and serious mien, to convey the impression of sincerity, and some auditors thought he had told his lies so often he believed them himself. He confined himself to a fairly limited repertoire, in which he played the hero, and attached stock tall tales of remarkable deeds to himself. He did not tell dirty stories or seek to moralize. Animated gestures and a "shrill penetrating kind of voice" enlivened his presentations. Observers commented on his artistry and imagination as a raconteur, and Jansen considered his ability to convince listeners that his folktales were his own invention a mark of his storytelling genius.

Gib Morgan

Oregon Smith may be compared with another tall-tale performer, Gib Morgan, likewise studied after his death by a folklorist. Mody Boatright, a University of Texas professor, published *Gib Morgan, Minstrel of the Oil Fields* in 1945, with five biographical chapters, one chapter analyzing Gib's style, and fifty-one tales imputed to Gib, unfortunately in paraphrase and without informant data or comparative notes. Morgan lived from 1842 to 1909 and followed the oil fields from

Pennsylvania to the Midwest as an oil driller. His photograph in the uniform of a Civil War veteran reveals a mild-looking, almost mousy, chap with a full mustache and large ears. Gib became celebrated as a yarnspinner and his tall tales about his exploits, like Smith's, passed into the retellings of others.

In several ways, however, Morgan's performances differed substantially from Smith's. The oil driller's repertoire consisted largely of occupational tall tales requiring some knowledge of oilfield technology and of gushers and sudden fortunes and freakish happenings, alongside which Gib's tales seemed not so incredible. Where Abe sought to impress hearers with the truth of his lies, Gib through his farfetched yarns aimed at arousing skepticism of much oilfield promotional blarney. Also, he used his tales for satiric purposes to deflate blowhards and bullies. Gib produced an apt lie with a spontaneous air as if he had contrived it on the spur of the moment. According to Boatright, "he could so link a tale up with the circumstances of the moment that the hundredth telling sounded like the first."[10] This quality of adapting his lies to the audience and the situation did not apply to Oregon Smith, who delivered his tales in consistent form as set pieces. Commentators have praised Morgan's wit and inventiveness, and opined that only too strong a taste for John Barleycorn kept him from greater fame as a humorist. His favorite haunts were saloons, and he is pictured at a bar with a bottle and glass in hand reeling off wisecracks and whoppers to a laughing circle. Where Oregon Smith's lies earned disapproval from some of his churchgoing fellow-townsmen, Gib Morgan's oilfield buddies recognized that he did not lie to deceive. One friend remarked that a better description for Gib than "the biggest liar in the oil country" was "the best entertainer in the oil country."[11] Like Smith, he avoided the obscene, the violent, and the vulgar.

AFRO-AMERICAN NARRATORS

By general consensus Afro-American folklore is recognized as the most fertile vein of oral expressive culture in the United States, and its carriers are praised as talented performers, especially bluesmen, jazzmen, and gospel singers. While the oral narratives of black storytellers are fairly well collected, individual narrators have received nothing like the recognition given Leadbelly or Blind Lemon Jefferson or Bessie Smith or B. B. King in the musical traditions. Yet the performers of prose pieces deserve their due fully as much as the singers and musicians. The two outstanding tale-tellers I encountered when collecting Afro-American folklore in southwestern Michigan, James Douglas Suggs of Calvin Township and John Blackamore of Benton Harbor, differed as day and night. Suggs, sixty-five when I met him, a laborer on public works, brimmed over with excitement in delivering his tales, which covered the spectrum of Afro-American prose traditions. He projected himself into the action, sometimes switching from third to first person as he identified with the chief actor. Comic tales he spun of preachers, Irishmen, and fools evoked bursts of laughter from him, but he had his somber side too, and turned solemn when discoursing of hants and hoodoos. His thick Mississippi Delta dialect receded when he opened the stops of his inflectional range to simulate the shrieking sister at the revival meeting, the rumbling tones of the preacher, or the bumpy motion of a ghost train. Like other black tale-tellers I met, Suggs had performed before audiences; he had played with a touring minstrel company, and he also sang folksongs to banjo accompaniment. A Suggs narration embodied two special features: a swift recap of the story, or its final episodes, and a moralizing post-commentary, sometimes pointed up with an apposite incident from his own personal knowledge.

John Blackamore, thirty, a foundry worker and landlord, might have come from a different world, although some of his tales overlapped with those of Suggs'. Blackamore recited his richly detailed, realistic narratives without inflection, in a dead flat monotone. But his texts were letter perfect, unerringly delivered, and swelled with minutiae of daily life to two and three times the length of standard variants. Thus Blackamore will take a standard Afro-American tale, such as "The Coon in the Box," the most popular in the Southern Negro repertoire, which most tellers, even Suggs, relate in a dozen sentences or so, and flesh it out into a full-bodied sketch. Where the average teller simply states that Old Marster's favorite slave John had the reputation for being a diviner, Blackamore fills in the characterization by having John eavesdrop on his master and so anticipate the jobs for the next day. Blackamore then details these jobs, such as rounding up the livestock, cleaning up the stable, plowing the west forty acres, and creates a running dialogue between the astonished landowner and his all-knowing serving-man. Updating the milieu to post-slavery times, Blackamore changes Old Marster to Old Boss, the slave to a handyman, and the patterollers to crackers. The resulting vignette brings to life the drama in which John luckily guesses that a raccoon is hidden under the box. "You got the old coon at last," the handyman acknowledges, referring to himself, when he has failed to discover in advance what is under the box, but he has won the bet wagered by his boss that John knows everything. Blackamore's verbal portraiture compensates for his flat delivery, and equalizes Suggs's animation of voice and gesture.

When I first met John Blackamore he was tying his tie in an inner room and my contact, his roomer, yelled from the hallway, "Hey, John, tell this fellow a story." Without inquiring further Blackamore launched into an animal tale, all the while continuing to get dressed, and completed the tale as he went out the door. In later sessions I found him just as responsive and prolific. But up north he had lost his audience, and several of his buddies walked out of the room while he was reciting to me. Back in Charleston, Missouri, he had narrated tales to the fellows there in all-night sessions.

DOWN-EAST LOBSTERMEN

Regional occupations provide another spawning ground for American folktale lore, but collectors have concentrated their energies mainly on the folksong vein of cowboys, lumberjacks, miners, sailors, and railroaders. We are beginning now, with such field reports as Mody Boatright's *Folklore of the Oil Industry* (1963) and Patrick Mullen's *I Heard the Old Fishermen Say* (1978) to redress the balance.

In my own fieldwork on the high Maine coast in 1956 I encountered two excellent folk narrators of sharply contrasting styles from the same regional-occupational subculture of Maine's coastal fisheries. Curt Morse of Kennebec was known throughout Washington County as a wag and humorist, and related sixty-one tales to me. Jim Alley of Jonesport enjoyed no such reputation, and appeared dour and moody, but he willingly let me record 151 texts. Both were retired lobstermen, in their seventies, who shared the down-East folkways of the coastal and offshore-island traditional society that lived off the lobster and herring fisheries and clam digging. Both related comic anecdotes about the local characters that abounded in Washington County, supernatural legends about local witches, blasphemous wind-buyers, and birth-marked babies, and tall tales and jokes. Their narratives ran from fifty to seven hundred words, and never transcended the single episode. Yet their repertoires also notably differed. Curt specialized in the personal tall tale, wrapped around his family and relatives and himself. Often he simply adapted standard lying tales usually told, as Jim Alley told them, in the third person. Curt also relished humorous personal-experience incidents which he developed into wry little vignettes, such as his first and last trip inland to the potato country, or the time he was knocked out by a croquet ball, or how he fooled some city fellows from New York. These adventures perfectly suited Curt's persona of the clown and wit, and indeed he was constantly on camera, every afternoon walking up and down the main street of Machias, the county seat, greeting friends and cracking wise, or regaling groups with his drolleries; the first time I met him a couple was tailing him, bursting into peals of laughter every time he uttered a word.

Jim Alley told no tales on himself. He narrated a swatch of jokes, twenty-five about Irishmen, as well as half a dozen fabliaux dealing with infidelity, none of which appeared in Curt's store. Terse, spare, economical, impersonal were Jim's pieces, and I never did learn on what occasions he released them, for when I met him he seemed to care little for companionship and dispensed his endless series of brief tales mechanically and with never a laugh. Yet on eight meetings with him he always produced new stories, and I can only guess at the extent of his full repertoire.[12]

SAGAMEN

Ordinarily we think of folktale tellers as narrating *Märchen*, tall tales, legends, or jokes, but American folklorists now recognize that master narrators may specialize in personal experiences, which contain their own elements of wonder, terror, and humor. These raconteurs are just as much performing storytellers as the others we have been discussing, and their tales, if not derived from tradition, become traditional within a limited circle. I met several such tellers in the Upper Peninsula on my field trip there in 1946 and dubbed them "Sagamen" in the resulting book, *Bloodstoppers and Bearwalkers*.[13] The most astonishing was Swan Olson, seventy-three, born in Sweden, who at seventeen immigrated from Stockholm to Minnesota, and had passd his life working on farms, in the mines, in lumber camps, and, in his old age, as mason, plasterer, bricklayer, and carpenter. In a barbershop in Negaunee I heard Swan telling the barber an episode from his youth about eating a fly-pie. We arranged to meet later in a tavern, and he spent the evening recounting events in which he had bested drunken bosses, wild lumberjacks, and highway robbers, graphic scenes all, cut from the same cloth; in each one the hero-teller defeats one or more ogres by his wits and agility. A gentle old man, his head swinging from side to side, Swan seemed the antithesis of the dashing resourceful figure he portrayed. I surmised that he had perfected his stories through repeated tellings for half a century. He relied on no verbal tricks but let the tale carry the burden.

A match for Swan Olson's personal sagas set in farms and lumberwoods are those of Wilbert Harlan set in the city. A black steelworker, forty-nine when I met him in Gary, Indiana, in 1976, Harlan like Olson recounted chapters in his life history in a continuous flow in one protracted session. Olson I could follow very clearly, with each adventure separately framed, but Harlan poured forth his narrative in a relentless torrent so packed with detail that I could not absorb it at the time and had to digest the transcript to follow the story line. But in the transcript the narrative units emerged clearly: proving himself, in his first job at thirteen, cleaning a soda fountain; contending to be the first black laborer on the floor in the "Big Mill," U.S. Steel; coaching a high school girls' track team to victory in Olympic trials. A friend who knew Harlan from the mill stated that he talked just as volubly at work, in his position as washroom janitor (to which he had been relegated after straining his back shoveling manganese into the furnace). The virtuosity of his performance depended not on histrionics of delivery but on the dramatic power and mnemonic control of his theme, the penniless black youth making his way in a white world. Harlan used no gestures, no inflections, no pauses but charged ahead in a harsh monotone with machine gun velocity.

MOUNTAIN WOMAN

Ever since the pioneering field expeditions of Cecil Sharp to the southern Appalachians in 1916 and 1917 the public and the folklorists have regarded that region as a mecca for folklore collectors. What seemed to be the ideal conditions for the perpetuation of traditional culture—isolation, illiteracy, superstition, poverty, ignorance, simplicity—became associated with Appalachia. We now question the stereotype and the premise as we learn about folklore in the city, but Appalachia does continue to yield traditional riches.

One sample of these riches, published in 1977, presents the written and oral narrative repertoire of a mountain widow, Sara Cowan, 75, from the settlement of Pebble Creek near Greensboro at the foot of Black Mountain, Kentucky, a progressive town on the Appalachian plateau. Folklorist Willard B. Moore, the author-collector, made all these names pseudonymous, pleading the sensitivity of the materials, which are conventionally folkloric. Moore, then living in California, had read Cowan's column in the Greensboro Weekly *Courier* reporting on traditional mountain folklife, with occasional folktales inserted, and began a correspondence which culminated in a visit in 1974 and a tape recording of Sara's tales. In 1977 a whole issue of *Indiana Folklore* was devoted to Moore's report on "The Written and Oral Narratives of Sara Cowan." His account contained ten excerpts from Sara Cowan's column, extracts from his field diary, pertinent observations and comments on the recording sessions, and a total of forty-three oral narrative texts recorded over four days with an appendix listing four tale types and twenty-six motifs identified in the tales. Since Moore provides a running chronicle of the week he, his wife and children spent as guests in Sara Cowan's home on Pebble Creek, with the recorded texts in their chronological place in the week's activities, he has given us the fullest statement yet of an American female storyteller.

Sara had lived all her life in that mountain area, and only once or twice had visited the outside world. While her columns depicted her as poor, feeble, helpless, and religious, he discovered her to be comfortably housed, vigorous, and critical of Pentecostal and Holiness excesses. Moore did not describe her appearance or furnish a photograph, although he delineated her house in some detail. He found Cowan a willing and fertile storyteller, and the reader of her texts is struck by her vivid colloquial speech, adroit use of dialogue, and realistic etching of details in the mountain settings. They carry conviction and convey the sincerity of the narrator, and that is the chief fact about her repertoire: she is telling true stories. In contrast to Jack Tale tellers like Marshall Ward, whose wonder tales immediately mark him as an out-of-the-ordinary fabulist, Sara Cowan relates the incidents and experiences commonly known to mountain and pioneer and backcountry folk. Her repertoire is stocked with remarkable accounts of snakes—"Snake tales is all I'm good to tell"—faith healers, witches, ghosts of murdered peddlers, buried treasure, the great flood of 1927—these are her fullest and richest narratives, in contrast to the rare tall tale and jest she intersperses in her flow of local happenings. Her own formulaic beginnings and endings for these anecdotes and legends emphasize their accuracy: "Now another true story"; "This is a true story"; "And ever' word of it is true if I ever told a truthful word in my life"; "That's a true story if thar ever was one told." Even during the visit of Bill Moore and his wife, Sara added to her series of true faith-healing tales an episode that had just transpired, in which Sara asked the healer, Hassie Cornett, to help the Moores, who had just come down with headaches; Hassie prayed and they recovered by next morning. Thus overnight Sara minted a fresh personal experience narrative to add to the wondrous cures she told about Hassie, and pointed the moral: "Now, I believe that was to show them what faith they should have in her, give 'em faith that she *could* do these things."

Analyzing Cowan's narrative style and personality, Moore credits her with several devices that heighten the dramatic immediacy of her presentation. She introduces prophetic omens and warnings that foreshadow catastrophes, and embellishes her diversified snake stories to make herself the heroine, one who cuts off the head of a blacksnake with a butcher knife. But she felt uncomfortable with tall tales and did not make herself the fabulous hunter when she told about the "breathing tree" stuffed with raccoons. Moore characterizes her as an "aggressive" teller, who will outdo a rival teller of true narratives with ones yet more remarkable, much as one liar tops another in a liars' contest, and who interrupts younger tellers to give the "right" version.[14]

FACULTY WIFE

Performing storytellers may be found in the midst of mainstream middle-class and upper-crust society as well as in off-center traditional cultures, and we all know the "life-of-the-party" type gifted with a flow of jokes and anecdotes. Perhaps the most successful such performer in my circle of friends and acquaintances was Jennie Clifton [pseudonym], wife of a former linguistics colleague of mine, who possessed a seemingly endless repertoire of off-color jokes with which she regularly broke us up at cocktail and dinner parties. I once noted titles of at least forty jokes she had delivered. Jennie when I knew her was in her late thirties, mother of four, trim, blonde, attractive, informal, fast-talking but with clear enunciation. She seemed the last person who would listen to, let alone relate, dirty jokes, but she could take material that in print was quite coarse and transform it into something refreshingly frank. Only once did I publish a text of hers, in a Foreword to *Folktales of Japan*, as it offered an unusual analogue to a Japanese humorous story.[15] A man traveling in a bus down south felt the need to pass water. The bus stopped for repairs in the middle of a country road, without a tree or bush in sight. The man walked over to a Negro digging, stood behind him, and engaged him in conversation, until the deferential black man said, "Say, boss, is you peein' on me?" In another of her tales that stayed with me, a voluptuous woman sits in an airplane next to a young man, who becomes so excited that he ejaculates all over the seat. Wiping off the sperm, he turns to his companion and asks, "Do you mind if I smoke?" In yet another of her favorites, delivered in mock Negro dialect, a black man afflicted with diarrhea seeks a diagnosis from a pompous physician, who informs the patient that he is suffering from "lockage of de bowels." When the sufferer protests that his ailment is just the reverse, the doctor amends his diagnosis to say it is "lockage of de bowels in de open position." The contrast between the vulgarity, racism, and sexism in the jests and Jennie's genteel and ladylike presence provoked storms of laughter. At the same time she possessed a sure control of her texts and spoke without false starts or stops.

The faculty wife must be considered a stellar raconteur as much as the mountain woman, though their repertoires are as far apart as the poles. Sara deliberately eschewed off-color jokes, although she shared one privately with Bill's wife, but primarily she related narratives to impress and instruct her listeners. Conscious of her audiences, she withheld overly personal accounts of crimes and scandals that might affect any of those present. Jennie too knew her audience, and indulged in her jocose pieces only under appropriate circumstances, with intimate friends in a party mood, several drinks under their belts, egging her on and already grinning and ready to guffaw. Sara specialized in the serious and didactic; Jennie, in the ribald and uproarious. Sara's stories reaffirmed faith in mysterious forces. Jennie's stories poked fun at the social mores. What a private audience will relish may shock a public audience, and we have seen the political disgrace that befell Secretary of Agriculture Earl Butz when the media broadcast a couple of his private jokes, of the kind Jennie customarily relayed to her friends as sure-fire hits.

DIALECTICIAN

A special folk narrative genre that flourishes in the United States as a consequence of immigration is the dialect story, a product of the propínquity of the foreign-born with the American-born. Native speakers of American English mimic the language mispronunciations and malapropisms of immigrants wrestling with their new speech. These dialect stories, some short jests, some elaborate pieces, vary according to the characteristics of the mother tongue when applied to English. In the Upper Peninsula where the Finns, French Canadians, and Cornishmen ("Cousin Jacks," bringing over an English county dialect of their own) live in close proximity, dialecticians for all three groups abound, with a scattering of Swedish and Italian mimics. In the southwest one can hear Mexican dialect stories, in Pennsylvania dialect jests with German accents, throughout the nation Jewish dialect jokes. Not only language mistakes but also cultural mishaps befalling the immigrant, on his first visit to a baseball game, or a carnival, or the big city, create the humor. Both stock jests and original scenes furnish source materials for dialect treatment. The same tale may turn up in several dialects, and the description of the baseball game is known in French, Finnish, and Italian versions.

Every native Peninsularite seemed to know some dialect squibs, but in each town at least one individual had gained a reputation as a dialectician and would perform on the programs of lodge meetings, church socials, and even high school commencements. The first dialectician I met, Burt Mayotte, an auto mechanic at Sault Ste. Marie, held the position of *raconteur* for the Allouette singers, the local

French-Canadian club, and regularly narrated at their entertainments. Wiry, energetic, dark-haired, under forty, Burt himself came from French-Canadian stock and identified admirably with the protagonist of his recitations. In the act of narrating he simulated the *Canadien* with darting eyes, nervous twists of head and shoulders, and gesticulation of hands, all adding up to a spasm of physical activity that marked the excitable, befuddled Gallic character of his tales. Mayotte's phrases fell into a rhythmic beat as he poured forth the *conte*, the French nasal intonations providing neat upswings on which to pause, so that the prose of the tale veered toward the cadences of verse, or at least singsong. The effect of the comical French-Canadian dialect and dialogue—"Woke up, Joe, woke up, we're not here at all, we're twelve miles from here" (said by one *Canadien* to another when their boat breaks loose from its moorings during the night)—is heightened by the correct English Burt employs in introducing the tale or linking up its incidents. There is no question about Burt Mayotte's being a performer, for on or off stage he was putting on an act.[16]

POLITICIAN

Public speakers, whether preachers, college presidents, toastmasters, or politicians, rely heavily on the apt anecdote and applicable joke, careful always not to offend sensibilities but eager to relax their audiences and win their sympathy. No more successful raconteur adorns our political history than Abraham Lincoln. He possessed a limitless fund of comic stories, upwards of one hundred and fifty that were recorded by contemporaries. "I can't resist telling a good story," he remarked, and once he roused a friend in the middle of the night to do just that. In a time-honored folkway he matched yarns with other tellers, appreciated their good ones, and introduced an acquaintance as the author of "The Slow Horse Story." He claimed that he remembered every story he ever heard. In the White House he became celebrated for his storytelling, seated at the left of the open fireplace, tilted back in his chair, with his long legs reaching over to the chimney jamb. In the telling he mimicked characters, acted out parts, reproduced a stutterer's peculiar whistle, twanged in dialect, and gyrated his arms and legs. Under the spell of the tale his melancholy face glowed with animation, his eyes gleamed, he chuckled, he rubbed his hand down the side of his leg. The tale tradition he drew upon came from small midwestern market towns and dealt with farming and back country scenes: horse trades, cock fights, ploughing, courting the farmer's daughter. A number of his yarns we can recognize as well-known folktales, for example the "kush-maker" story, told by Davy Crockett and popular in World War II, about a self-styled producer of kushes (or some other strange-sounding object) who, called on to explain his occupation, drops a piece of iron into the water, which goes "kush."

But one aspect of Lincoln's performance distinguishes his style and technique from those of other master narrators: he utilized comic anecdotes to point a political moral when confronted with a thorny problem of office. A typical situation for a Lincoln tale falls into three segments: the posing to the president of the problem by some troubled person; Lincoln's relating an appropriate humorous story; and his application of the story to the matter in question. General William T. Sherman inquired of Lincoln in March 1865 what was to be done with the Confederate leaders, particularly their president, Jefferson Davis. Lincoln replied that he hoped Davis would depart the country but could not say so openly. "As usual," recalled Sherman, "he illustrated his meaning by a story." The president told about a heavy drinker who had taken an abstinence pledge, and asked for a lemonade when offered a drink at a friend's house. But if the friend poured some brandy into the lemonade, added the teetotaller, unbeknownst to him, he would not object. So Lincoln would not object, if, unbeknownst to him, Davis were tipped off. On another occasion Lincoln responded to the same question with the anecdote of the small boy who caught a coon and hoped it would escape so he wouldn't have to kill it.[17]

Lincoln performed his funny stories before citizens, Cabinet officers, patronage seekers, and generals. After his death they reached still wider audiences in jestbooks, and in our day Carl Sandburg has rescued a great many in his six-volume biography. But without Lincoln's presence the stories become barebones.

We have seen a spectrum of American folktale performers: men and women (children remain to be studied in the United States, as Jean MacLaughlin has done in Peru[18]), blacks and whites and ethnics, the unknown and the famous, people from marginal cultures and from the main culture. Some tellers specialize in magic tales, some in personal sagas, some in bawdy jokes, some in unusual true happenings, some in dialect humor.[19] Tellers may seek to amuse, to inform, to instruct, to surprise, to extol. What they have in common is the ability to make oral narratives come to life and enrapture listeners. Ordinarily we think of singers and dancers as performers, but the evidence now makes clear that tellers too should be classed as performers, even though in the United States they do not recite long epics and romances.

NOTES

1. Isobel Gordon Carter, "Mountain White Folk-lore: Tales from the Southern Blue Ridge," *Journal of American Folklore* 38 (1925): 340–74.

2. C. Paige Gutierrez, "The Narrative Style of Marshall Ward, Jack Tale-Teller," *North Carolina Folklore Journal* 26:2 (1978): 111–26.

3. C. Paige Gutierrez, "The Jack Tale: A Definition of Folk Tale Sub-Genre," ibid., pp. 85–110.

4. The Jack Tale issue also contains a transcript of an introduction by Marshall Ward to a Jack Tale in which he informs his youthful audience how he learned the tales from his daddy, who had learned them from his great-great uncle Counce Harmon, and how he himself had been telling them for sixty-five years, and had given Richard Chase fourteen of the sixteen stories he put into his book. This preamble has itself become traditional and formulaic with Marshall Ward.

5. "Four Beech Mountain Jack Tales," ed. Thomas McGowan, ibid., p. 66.

6. Gutierrez, p. 116.

7. See Richard M. Dorson, "Polish Wonder Tales of Joe Woods" and "Polish Tales from Joe Woods," *Western Folklore* 8 (1949): 25–53, 131–45; "The Two Brothers" in *Folktales Told Around the World*, ed. R. M. Dorson (Chicago: University of Chicago Press, 1975), pp. 493–98; "Oral Styles of American Folk Narrators," in Dorson, *Folklore, Selected Essays* (Bloomington: Indiana University Press, 1972), pp. 108, 112–13.

8. Philip B. George, "Reaffirmation of Identity: A Latino Case in East Chicago" and "Tales of a Puerto Rican Storyteller" in *Indiana Folklore* 10 (1977): 139-48, 149-58. Quotations from pp. 143, 149.

9. William Hugh Jansen, *Abraham "Oregon" Smith, Pioneer, Folk Hero and Tale-Teller* (New York: Arno Press, 1977), pp. 230-31.

10. Mody C. Boatright, *Gib Morgan, Minstrel of the Oil Fields* (n.p.: Texas Folk-lore Society, 1945), p. 48.

11. Ibid., p. 36.

12. See Richard M. Dorson, "Tales of Two Lobstermen," in Dorson, *Folklore and Fakelore* (Cambridge, Mass.: Harvard University Press, 1975), pp. 212-22.

13. See Richard M. Dorson, *Bloodstoppers and Bearwalkers* (Cambridge, Mass.: Harvard University Press, 1952), pp. 250-57.

14. Willard B. Moore, "The Written and Oral Narratives of Sara Cowan," *Indiana Folklore* 10 (1977), p. 91. Quotations from pages 78, 28, 40, 42, 73. Kentucky mountain family true stories are in Leonard Roberts, *Sang Branch Settlers* (Austin: University of Texas Press, 1974).

15. Keigo Seki, ed., *Folktales of Japan* (Chicago: University of Chicago Press, 1963), p. xii.

16. For Burt Mayotte see "Oral Styles of American Folk Narrators," pp. 110, 114-15; *Folktales Told Around the World*, pp. 487-90.

17. For the Jefferson Davis stories, see B. A. Botkin, *A Civil War Treasury of Tales, Legends and Folklore* (New York: Random House, 1960), pp. 510-11; Richard M. Dorson, *American Folklore* (Chicago: University of Chicago Press, 1959), p. 72. For Lincoln as storyteller see *American Folklore*, pp. 70-73, and Dorson, *Folklore: Selected Essays*, pp. 118-25. Also for Lincoln's Sykes yellow dog story see, in Part II of the *Handbook*, my article, "A Historical Theory for American Folklore," in the section entitled "The Civil War."

18. See Jean MacLaughlin in *Folktales Told Around the World*, pp. 530-45, for informant data and tales of thirteen- and fourteen-year-old Peruvian boys.

19. Extended discussions of Suggs, Blackamore, Woods, Alley, Morse, Mayotte, and Lincoln are in Dorson, "Oral Styles of American Folk Narrators," pp. 99-146. For a folklorist's report of the performance style and technique of a woodsman storyteller, Ham Ferry, in an evening in a barroom, see Robert D. Bethke, "Storytelling at an Adirondack Inn," *Western Folklore* 35 (1976): 123-39. Ferry tells the American blend of tall tale, anecdote, and personal narrative.

John Michael Vlach

Folk Craftsmen

Surprisingly little is known about American folk craftsmen. Craft occupations have been studied, but usually as general roles excluding particular individuals. It is ironic that craft works of former times have recently become valued as antiques and thus cherished as quaint treasure while the craftsmen who made them remain anonymous. Existing research consists mainly of catalogues of traditionally manufactured things grouped into categories and assigned to historical periods. In some books objects are almost given a life of their own existing independently of craftsmen. This is, of course, a faulty assumption but one that will be tacitly supported as long as craftsmen remain nameless and faceless folk. Folklorists were once only interested in tales not taletellers and songs not singers, but in recent years, they have deliberately refocused their attentions on performers. Now that the domain of folklore is widely understood to include material as well as verbal and gestural expressions of tradition, more consideration may be given to craftsmen rather than craft objects.

The processes of craft occupations are very complex even though the final products might seem modest and simple. Clients must be engaged, objects designed, materials obtained, tools and technical means employed, and products marketed. A craftsman's work is related directly to his social context, immediate ecology, historical period, and economic circumstances as well as his personal training, development of skill, and expression of talent. In order to approach this intricate web of relationships folklorists need to construct detailed and involved life histories that match the complexities of their careers. Armed with such studies we might soon dismiss the omnipresent and facile assumption that people who work with their hands are simple and quaint. The four examples given below summarize studies that focus on particular craftsmen, and together they illustrate: (1) the relationship of tradition to individual creativity, (2) the symbolic meaning inherent in crafted items, (3) the ingenuity manifested in craft technology, (4) the interplay between craft and personal philosophy, and (5) craft as an expression of distinct ethnic heritage.

A leader among the few folklorists who have researched individual craftsmen is Michael Owen Jones. Since 1967 he has produced a series of articles on aspects of chairmaking in Kentucky, culminating in his book *The Hand-Made Object and Its*

Maker (1975), which not only presents a definitive portrait of Chester Cornett, a chairmaker, but also lays the theoretical groundwork for the study of the individual craftsman.

Jones relentlessly pursues the minute details of Cornett's life in order to trace his development as a chairmaker. By tracking down the many pieces of furniture Cornett has made during his long career (and which had been scattered throughout the community), Jones was able to document important changes in Cornett's repertoire and convincingly show how his chairs were the product of a private and idiosyncratic vision. To be sure, traditional precedents had an impact on his works, but what Jones makes clear is that tradition is only a starting point for the craftsman; it is the conceptual raw material which the individual may reshape and reorder. Cornett at first made slat-back chairs very similar to those of his maternal grandfather, but as his artistry matured, he gained greater competence as a woodworker, and changed his chairs until they resembled no others in the community. Through a close look at the work and life of Chester Cornett, Jones warns us against viewing tradition solely as a social restraint that enforces repetition of historical habit, and he demonstrates that folk craftsmen can be as highly creative and imaginative as any fine artist.

Another folklore study which honors the scholar's responsibility to his informant is by Henry Glassie on William Houck, a maker of Adirondack pack-baskets. Glassie first presents the complex technology Houck employs and then sets his baskets in their historical and regional context. One of the most noteworthy aspects of Houck's work is his use of white ash, a troublesome medium for basketry. As Houck says, "The Devil and Hell can't cut it."[1] Once a tree is located and felled, it is quartered and further split into "bars." These bars are then pounded in much the same fashion that a blacksmith strikes iron bars on his anvil. In this way, the wood is softened enough to be made into "splints" which become parts of the basket; the wider, thicker pieces are used as "set-ups" or "stays," while the thin pliable "braiders" are woven between the stays. After soaking this material in water, it is shaped around a collapsible five-piece wooden form which is removed once the basket is finished. After the basket dries out the material becomes almost as hard as it was in its original state. Thus, the pounded ash Adirondack pack-basket is extremely durable and probably will not need to be replaced during the life of its owner.

In a later study of American craft, Glassie attempted to plumb the deeper significance of Houck's baskets.[2] Employing a sophisticated method of analysis derived from the works of Claude Lévi-Strauss, Glassie postulated that an artifact like a basket embodied a statement of the craftsman's relationship to the natural environment. In his early years as a logger, Houck made his living attacking trees, clearing them from the land. Now in semi-retirement as a dairy farmer and basketmaker, he returns to select the most difficult tree possible for his work. He literally beats the wood into submission and reassembles it according to his plan, his will. The tree submits to man, taking on his shapes and purposes; the media of nature become the artifacts of culture. Through the craft process Houck achieves a goal that he could only approach as a logger. Once the opponent, he has become a victor over nature. If this particular analysis seems high-flown or wide of the mark, it nevertheless suggests how attention to the nature of the materials used, the specific processes, and certain significant shifts in biography indicate that craft objects can legitimately be treated as symbolic of the way an individual relates to his physical environment. This theme, while not immediately apparent in Houck's basketry, is no less real. Glassie's scholarship reminds us that once we have recorded the ethnographic details of craft we should turn to more fundamental interpretation utilizing all the theoretical hypotheses available. In this way we may come to understand the craftsmen more completely than they can consciously permit.

Earl Westfall, of Higbee, Missouri, is another basketmaker who uses his work, albeit in an indirect manner, to demonstrate his prowess in the natural realm. In a conversation with folklorist Howard Wight Marshall he demonstrates his knowledge of white oaks, the source of his materials.

> HWM: Well, I guess it's pretty hard to pick just exactly the right tree?
>
> EW: Well, yeah, sometimes you go into the woods that looks like it's nice timber and you can run over forty acres and not find a stick of timber that'll make a basket. Yessir. It's got to be so tough and straight-grained and no knots in it. It's got to be just right or it won't work. If you don't get timber that'll work, I can't split it out and nobody else can.
>
> HWM: Can you tell just from looking at a tree?
>
> EW: No, you've got to take your ax and take a chip out of it . . . down toward the bottom of the tree. Just take a good chip out of it with your ax and you can tell whether it's straight-grained, whether it'll split for you. The bark's got a lot to do with it. You can look at a tree and tell whether it's twisted or not, you know. Lotta times you can look at it and tell that it's too brash. Why if you split it open, it'd just break . . . and of course that wouldn't be no good. It'd split good into a post or somethin' . . . but it won't make no basket.[3]

Westfall's craft has provided him with more than an intimate knowledge of the central Missouri landscape. A man with deep-rooted religious convictions, he sees basketry as descending from the "old Bible days." Thus, his work and his belief reinforce each other, because every basket perpetuates a "Biblical tradition" while simultaneously his religion validates his basketmaking. Only by questioning a craftsman closely and taking note of his personal perspective can we get at important issues concerning the meaning and intention of traditional crafts. We can then go beyond a simplistic assumption that craftsmen are engaged solely in an economic venture and probe deeper levels of significance.

Philip Simmons of Charleston, South Carolina, whom I myself have studied, is a blacksmith with an alternative tradition. As an Afro-American he is heir to a legacy of style and creativity different from most Anglo-American smiths.[4] His distinct ethnic heritage is hidden in his work and can only be sensed after a consideration of his life history within the context of his community.

Since the mid-eighteenth century Charleston has been a noted center of wrought-iron decoration. There is a well-developed local style for the design of balconies, gates, fences, window grills, lamp stands, and hand rails. As a child, Simmons grew up surrounded by wrought-iron tracery. He would walk a certain route to school each day just to pass by the elaborate gate at No. 16 Charlotte Street. At the age of thirteen he apprenticed himself to Peter Simmons (no relation), an ex-slave blacksmith, and before he reached his nineteenth birthday in 1931 he was a full-fledged ironworker, what he terms with pride "a general blacksmith." This title subsumes the trades of the angle smith who bends iron, the wheelwright who makes and repairs wagons and wheels, the farrier who tends horses' hooves, and the toolmaker. Decorative ironwork was included too, but because of the high demand for his practical skills he didn't do any ornamental pieces until 1938. When horses "went out" he realized that only by redirecting his efforts to decorate iron could he survive as a blacksmith. The transition was not difficult: "I could mash out a leaf just as easy as a horseshoe. They both got the same principle." Thus, the premises of pragmatic craft became the basis of decorative art. As a decorative ironworker Simmons had a vast number of examples in Charleston to use as patterns and he deliberately developed a competence with the major motifs: the S- and C-scrolls, the spear point, circle-scroll combinations, and floral clusters. With each commission he attempts to match the work (gate, grill, or whatever) to its neighborhood context. As he says, "You have to follow what they have." Thus, Simmons has become the custodian of the entire Charleston tradition.

Simmons's work closely resembles Charleston's traditional decorative iron, and his career as a black ironworker seems little different from that of a Euro-American smith. But there is an important difference in the way he formulates his designs; they are in the Charleston mode but achieved via a distinct improvisational mind set. Simmons does not just design and then make a gate. Rather, he postulates a limit for variations and then arranges various elements in experimental arrays until his "vision" is fulfilled. Simmons describes the process:

> It isn't always a thing gonna be set in your mind and when you just about half way you can see you ain't gonna like it. Sometime I draw the whole thing and don't like it myself—not the customer. But one thing . . . you can visualize, it give you a background. Like this thing [drawing] here, I may not like all these scrolls when I start but still I see it that way after puttin' it in and I see where I can improve it.

A gate thus "grows" by fits and starts as Simmons's creative abilities are deployed. The finished product gives no hint of his mental agonies during the creative process. In it are no clues that his performance with wrought iron is analogous to blues composition or improvised jazz dance. But there is, in fact, a shared Afro-American aesthetic in force which fosters a high degree of individuating improvisation: "That is what I like about the blacksmith trade—doin' it from scratch and arriving at the idea from my own mind, my own thoughts. That's the part I enjoy." Again, only by close attention to the working processes of the craftsman do the most significant aspects of meaning in craft products emerge. Attention to the stylistic process of Simmons's blacksmithing opens a vista on his work that is not obvious when his gates and balconies are merely seen in their final contexts.

Folklorists have created a record of other craftsmen: cane makers, quilters, rope makers, broom makers, weavers, dry stone wallers, carpenters, stone cutters. Much insight into American folklore can be gained by studying craftsmen, but we have far to go. In the torrent of recent books on quilting, for example, almost no attention is paid to the creators of a great art form; the concentration is on "how-to" descriptions. Perhaps it would be profitable to take note of the methods of description and evaluation used in the discipline of art history, which carefully retraces the training and development of artists and associates them with other creative personalities of the place and period. The elaborate biographies that result from rigorous and meticulous research provide a rich and detailed record of the achievements of Cezanne, Picasso, Klee, and hundreds of other well-known artists. Such studies allow further judgments to be made with some measure of precision and certainty. These qualities, sorely needed in folkloristics, may be attained if the craftsman becomes the focus of craft study.

NOTES

1. Henry Glassie, "William Houck: Maker of Pounded Ash Adirondack Pack-Baskets," *Keystone Folklore Quarterly* 12 (1967): 26.

2. Lecture given by Henry Glassie at a symposium on "American Folklife" held at Towson State College, Towson, Maryland, in February 1976.

3. Howard Wight Marshall, "Mr. Westfall's Baskets: Traditional Craftsmanship in North Central Missouri," *Mid-South Folklore* 2 (1974): 46.

4. John Michael Vlach, *The Afro-American Tradition in Decorative Arts* (Cleveland: The Cleveland Museum of Art, 1978), pp. 108–21.

David J. Hufford

Folk Healers

Folk medicine and its practitioners have never really found a comfortable or consistent place in the generic organizational scheme that has characterized folklore scholarship since its inception. Most often in American folklore studies folk medicine has been considered a subdivision of the "minor genre" called superstition (a term now generally avoided because of its pejorative connotations) or folk belief. Since the general concept is derived from the study of literature it naturally leads one to think in terms of discrete products of language such as poems or novels. Consequently, the study of folk healing began with the collection and listing of cures and "beliefs" such as "The seventh son of a seventh son can carry goiter away by rubbing it."[1] Contemporary folklorists have increasingly noted the limitations of this generic approach, stressing that both the personal and cultural context and the depth of belief must also be studied to achieve a broad understanding of the belief *per se*. Nonetheless, some very useful scholarship dealing with questions of origin and geographical distribution has resulted from this enumerative method. Also, annotated belief collectanea provide invaluable tools for the location of specific beliefs and cures scattered throughout the folklore literature. The premiere example of scholarly annotation of beliefs in American folklore is volumes VI and VII of the *Frank C. Brown Collection of North Carolina Folklore*, edited by Wayland D. Hand.

A major limitation of the generic approach is that it treats "belief" as a static thing when in fact it is a dynamic *characteristic* that varies from person to person and time to time. For example, although "touching a toad can cause warts" is a widespread traditional statement, many from whom this proposition can be collected do not believe it. Such statements are even found within what may be called "traditions of *dis*belief." This is the case when an informant says something like "Some people believe that touching a toad can cause warts, but that is just because a toad's skin is all bumpy and looks like it has warts on it." The

---

Folk medicine as a subject of study has developed in both anthropology and folklore. While there has been mutual influence in these developments, the picture is quite different in each field. Therefore, the present article is limited as much as possible to the topic *within folklore studies*.

proposition persists in its most frequently collected form, but the nature of the belief characteristic attached to it is very different from that which we might infer from the bare text. Many well-known propositions of this sort are as easily collected in their disbelief settings as in contexts of genuine belief.

In viewing folk medicine as a series of discrete beliefs and recipes, scholars have been hindered in recognizing these materials as parts of systems. Seen as free-floating items which might either persist or perish on their own, the beliefs have been thought of as survivals from a less enlightened period. Their endurance has been more often attributed to flaws in the American educational effort than to continuing functions. This understanding paralleled the anthropological view of simple cultural evolution and the inevitability of progress (with progress defined as increasing similarity to the culture of the scholar).

HEALTH SYSTEMS APPROACH

In contrast, a "health systems" approach includes the healer and patient within the basic study of folk medicine so that people and materials may be examined together as integral parts of a functioning unit. "System" is used here in its most general sense to suggest a combination of elements arranged in more or less orderly relationships to form a whole. Health systems may be viewed in either of two ways: as the consensus among a number of people; or as an individual's collection of health related information and attitudes. "Curanderismo" in the American Southwest or "powwowing" centered primarily in Pennsylvania are examples of consensual health systems. Such consensual systems comprise all aspects of what are most often called "folk medicine traditions." The individual's system, on the other hand, always differs to some extent from the traditions on which it draws, even in the case of full-time healers. This divergence is caused by the unique combination of life experiences of each individual and the rich variety of approaches to health which run throughout North American culture. Both of these complementary perspectives—the consensual and the individual—are necessary for a thorough examination of folk medicine.

INTEGRATION

An essential characteristic of a health system is the interrelatedness of its components, a quality which may be termed integration. The greater the number of orderly relationships that exist among the components, the more integrated and, therefore, stable, the system. In the case of folk health systems it is their integration which has prevented their reduction to a few survivals by the advance of modern medicine. The orderly connections among the cures and other propositions have allowed each to resist change with some of the weight of the whole system. For example, Vance Randolph quotes a folk herbalist as saying "God Almighty never put us here without a remedy for every ailment."[2] Such a statement illustrates a link between a belief in the efficacy of herbal remedies and a belief in Divine Mercy. This common kind of connection not only lends general stability to the herbal healing tradition, but does so in a way that is rather inaccessible to the arguments of skeptical modern medicine. One consequence of these relationships is that a healer with a great memorized knowledge of a healing tradition may be a weak custodian of that tradition while another with fewer "facts" may be a very effective tradition bearer because of superior integration. This difference is especially important to note in fieldwork since it indicates that a "star informant" may not be as important in a given healing tradition as others who cannot supply as many "beliefs." Of course many other factors such as communication style and skills are also crucial in determining the effectiveness with which a healer functions to maintain a given tradition.

The connections of a folk healing tradition with its cultural context are also important for understanding healers and their patients. A tendency to focus on individual traditions as being discrete and self-contained has resulted in part from too great a dependence on modern academic medicine as a model for analysis. In recent centuries Western academic medicine has undergone a more or less intentional process of separation from other facets of culture. This separateness, though still more apparent than real, appears very unusual when compared with the situation in other cultures, where health systems are strongly related to such other aspects of culture as religion and artistic expression.

The integration of folk health systems with their surrounding culture has important consequences for the study of folk healers in America. First of all, it is difficult at times to separate the processes of folk health systems from those of popular culture, since folk healers working in very old and conservative traditions often utilize printed sources. An excellent example of such influence is the Pennsylvania German "powwow" tradition. Called *Brauche* or *Braucherei* in the Pennsylvania German dialect, this tradition was imported to the American colonies from the German-speaking areas of Central Europe. Heavily occult in nature, it operates primarily on the basis of either spoken or written charms. Since 1820 healers in this tradition have extensively used a book originally entitled *Der lang verborgene Freund* first published in that year in Reading, Pennsylvania. Compiled by a German immigrant named Hohman, this book has been through a great many editions in both German and English, alternatively as *The Long Lost Friend* and *The Long Hidden Friend*, and is still in print and in use.[3] Also in print and in use are such books as the apocryphal *Sixth and Seventh Books of Moses* and *The Egyptian Secrets of Albertus Magnus*. Though reliance on print has traditionally been considered a definitive difference between popular and folk tradition, it is clear that powwowing is a folk healing tradition. Even when dealing with the influence of current printing on a healing tradition we must be very cautious about labeling one healer "folk" and another "popular" on this basis. Given the conditions of modern American culture, the role of print must always be part of the study of folk healers.

In addition to such modern processes, folk healing is also extensively inter-connected with the contents of both academic and popular health systems. It is well known that folk medicine contains treatments once in use among academically trained physicians but now surviving only in folk tradition. The substantial contributions of folk medicine to modern medicine are less known. For example, the extremely important cardiotonic medication digitalis (the dried leaf of the herb purple foxglove) was in use among both American Indian and European folk herbalists long before its official discovery in England in the eighteenth century. And that discovery was made by one William Withering, who learned of it from an old woman who was a healer in the vicinity of Birmingham. Hundreds of such substances have made the transition from folk tradition to official status in *The Pharmacopeia of the United States,* and no doubt many more await "discovery."

The greatest amount of cross-influencing probably takes place between folk and popular health systems. By "popular health systems" we refer to those which are too print-oriented to be clearly folk but which do not sufficiently dominate the cultural mainstream to be considered "official." This rubric would include such systems as chiropractic, "health foods,"[4] psychic healing, and Christian Science. In view of the positive sanctions surrounding standard academic medicine today, it is useful for some purposes to consider popular traditions together with folk healing under the heading "unorthodox." This is true, for instance, of the application of the study of healers to medical education and consultation, an area with excellent prospects for further development by folklorists.[5] I have worked with a number of healers who illustrate this popular-folk connection very well. One, for example, was an organic farmer who was very knowledgeable on the subject of health foods, who opposed vaccination on the basis of chiropractic theory, practiced healing within a basically folk religious framework, and referred some of his clients to a local folk herbalist. Such eclecticism is very much the rule among modern folk healers. It is therefore necessary that scholars of folk healing be familiar with popular traditions. Without a knowledge of such principles as "the creative innate intelligence" (chiropractic) or "auras" (psychic research) many statements of typical folk healers appear disjointed, when in fact they relate logically to a complex conceptual framework.

Another kind of interconnection exhibited by folk healing traditions is the manner in which they bridge ethnic lines. The powwow tradition is again a good example. The term has now been accepted throughout the region to refer in general to folk healers (powwows) as well as their practice (powwowing). As a result this word, which was originally borrowed from the Algonquin languages by English and then became attached to a specifically Pennsylvania German tradition, is now often applied to healers of many different ethnic backgrounds whose practice may range from herbalism to spirit mediumship. Such bridging may be found throughout the United States, although many cultural affinities are still clear in such traditions as conjuration (black) and curanderismo (Mexican-American) and will no doubt persist for a very long time.

NATURAL VS. SUPERNATURAL

Historically, folklorists have classified healers and their approaches as either natural or supernatural. In the Pennsylvania tradition, for example, herbalists have been considered "natural healers" and powwows supernatural. Although in some ways this classification is workable and advantageous, it tends to break down under close scrutiny. Herbalists often harvest their materials according to astrological principles and frequently administer them together with a verbal formula or prayer. Similarly, many powwows use natural materials such as tobacco, turpentine, or herbs as well as charms. A more serious problem with this classification scheme is that it tends to be ethnocentric and to overlook the systematic nature of healing traditions. As a result the "natural" category is often called "empirical" or "rational," and the supernatural "irrational." In fact the implications of these terms are simply incorrect.

The use of verbal charms to remove warts (supernaturally) is based as much on accurate observation as is the use of flour or cobwebs to stanch the flow of blood (naturally), and therefore it is just as "empirical." Both practices work quite consistently. Whether the effect of the wart charm is considered to be magical or psychosomatic has no bearing on its empirical foundation. The same is true for practically all of the beliefs and practices of folk healers. If there were no observations suggesting that they work, they would not continue to be used. The analysis and interpretation of observations is a very complicated activity and certainly folk healers and medical doctors would be able to argue at great length with one another about the validity of their conclusions. But such disagreements do not make the folk healer and his patient any less empirical.

The rational-irrational distinction is just as problematic. For example, there are those who argue that illness may be caused by an imbalance or inadequacy of certain kinds of energy, that some healers have the ability to collect or focus that energy and then heal by laying their hands on the patient and allowing that energy to pass through. Such a position is rational in the sense that it can be logically derived from a few basic assumptions. The fact that these assumptions differ dramatically from those employed by modern medical science does not make the conclusions less rational. Of course, being rational is not the same as being correct, as is demonstrated by countless outdated medical theories—such as that miasmas were the cause of disease—theories which were empirical, rationally derived, and incorrect.

In the final analysis these uses of empiricism and rationality, common though they are in the academic study of belief, really refer to the willingness of the academic world to agree with a practice or believed proposition. It would be more forthright to use such words as "correct" or "efficacious," although such decisions would be in constant need of revision. The current situation, however, is most unfortunate because it makes a superficial label of two of the processes of folk tradition which are most in need of investigation: the accumulation and ordering of observations; and the logical interpretation of those observations using the assumptions present within a given tradition.

FOLK PSYCHIATRY

More than any other method, functionalism (the modern successor of survivalism) has acknowledged the empirical and logical nature of folk healing. Frequently this approach has been employed in the study of folk psychiatry (also called ethnopsychiatry or transcultural psychiatry), which assumes that therapies relying extensively on verbal techniques are psychotherapies.[6] Hence all supernatural medicine is considered to be folk psychotherapy. While other functionalists have attributed to healing traditions such positive functions as social control and maintenance of group identity, they have generally avoided the question of whether or not supernatural folk medicine might actually heal anything. Transcultural psychiatry has the virtue of suggesting that the answer is "yes," and of providing a theoretical framework for the examination and explanation of that function. However, if the scholar forgets that the various theories of psychotherapy are themselves cultural constructs there is a danger of merely translating folk terms into psychiatric terms without gaining any insight.

One of the most challenging subjects for careful objective study in this area is the individual healer himself. While perhaps the largest amount of folk healing of all kinds is carried out by nonspecialists on a first-aid basis, the full- or part-time specialist is especially fascinating. Generally these healers are the bearers of the most complex and well-integrated systems, and their personal histories frequently illustrate the most powerful patterns of healing. The organic farmer–folk-healer mentioned above will again provide a good illustration. Until his late thirties this man had been an ordinary farmer without any special interest or activity in the area of healing. He was, though, beset with major problems. His farm was not prosperous, he was experiencing family difficulties, and he was apparently quite ill. He considered the illnesses from which he suffered to be physical, although it is possible that they included psychosomatic and psychological problems (this would be the inference of transcultural psychiatry). He told me that eventually the illnesses brought him to the verge of death. "I know what it is like to reach the end of your rope, tie a knot, and hang on." At that point he lapsed into a period of unconsciousness in which he believed that he was transported to heaven and received a thorough explanation of his problems and the actions he could take to correct them. From this point on he gradually convalesced, helped back to health by a friend who brought him a special diet of organically grown produce. All of this produced very dramatic changes in this man's entire world view. He acquired a complex, but coherent, system for understanding a variety of threats to himself and his family: social, economic, and political pressures (a conspiracy including international banking concerns, the United Nations, FBI, CIA, and Food and Drug Administration); health issues (e.g., food additives, modern medicine); and moral concerns (much of modern technology and education). He also acquired a system of resources for addressing those threats: organic farming; a low technology living style; a reliance on herbalism and healing by prayer for sickness; and an interesting version of conservative, millenarian Christianity. These changes dramatically revitalized not only the man himself, but also his family and his farm. During the period that I worked with him he was quite prosperous and very well known throughout the area among those who shared similar beliefs. Such a process is very complex and cannot be fully explicated here. This seems to be a rather common pattern among those who become healers in their adult life: disorder and illness, often in a period of great stress; a crisis; inspiration, sometimes accompanied by mystical experiences; some help and input from an "expert"; revitalization which is generally stable over time provided that some social support is available. Anthropologists have found this pattern typical of the development of shamans in other cultures,[7] but not enough attention has been paid to the life histories of North American folk healers to be certain of its frequency and distribution in our culture. My own fieldwork would suggest that it is surprisingly common, especially among healers whose methods are heavily supernatural. Of course there are many other ways of becoming a healer, including inheritance, accidents of birth such as being a seventh son of a seventh son, and apprenticeship to an established healer.

FOLK ILLNESSES

Folk healers treat practically the whole range of ills known to modern man— warts, arthritis, colic, sexual dysfunction, skin disorders, cancer, etc.—and in addition some that are unrecognized by medical science, such as *mal ochio* or evil eye, soul loss, and the effects of witchcraft. Some of the symptoms involved in such diagnoses can be adequately described in conventional diagnostic terms, while others cannot. In the latter case, it can be very tempting to reduce the folk category to an apparently similar medical term such as depression, hysteria, depersonalization, epilepsy, and so forth. And while such a reduction may sometimes be appropriate, its veracity cannot be taken for granted unless it is carried out with all of the care and precision associated with good diagnostic work.

In my work with memorates and the experiential components of supernatural belief I have encountered a set of traditions which well illustrates the problems involved in attempting to view folk categories as corresponding directly to the categories of modern medicine. The experience of awakening during the night to find oneself unable to move is apparently fairly common. Less well known is the fact that in a surprisingly large number of such cases, people also either strongly sense a "presence" nearby during the attack of paralysis or hear, see, and sometimes even smell something which either threatens or physically attacks them at this time. They frequently feel the attacker pressing on them or holding them tightly, and experience a variety of sensations which are difficult to describe.[8] Amid the welter of recurring details there is a very clear pattern in the phenomenology of the event, one which appears to exist all over the world with little if any variation (except in interpretation) in different cultures and subcultures. Examples of folk names for the attacks include the old hag (Newfoundland), nightmare (British), witch-riding (British and black traditions), Cauchemar (French), and attack by evil spirits (Mormon traditions). Various branches of medicine have from time to time shown an awareness of some aspects of the experience and have made efforts to connect it directly with a standard medical category. One psychiatric interpretation considers this an "angst attack" on the basis of the fear, paralysis, and the fact that victims are in a supine position about 90 percent of the time. Other physicians have called it a fanciful elaboration of an angina pectoris attack because it sometimes involves a feeling of pressure on the chest. I have found at least four other distinct medical explanations in the literature. Each one conflicts to some extent with the others and relies on a description of the phenomenon that is less complete and accurate than that found in the various folk traditions. Indeed, information from the folk tradition has made it possible to assemble a more systematic description of this experience than has previously been available, and to demonstrate the inadequacy of most of the medical comments about it. Some of the findings proceeding from folk tradition have implications for both diagnostic and therapeutic issues. This is another example, then, not only of the complexity of the relationships between folk and medical categories, but also of the possibility of usefully applying information from the study of folklore to medical goals.

Scholars of folk healing have long sought to find out *about* their subject. By way of the functionalist approach, especially ethnobotany and folk psychiatry, scholars have now begun the effort to learn *from* it. Such work can be of great practical importance to the daily problems of modern health care, especially if the full context of folk healing traditions is kept in view, including not only herbalism, folk psychiatry, and folk categories of disease, but also foodways and nutrition, the role of traditional narratives in determining the compliance of patients with medical regimens, the role of folk religion in coping with pain and bereavement, and a host of other topics which are at once of folkloristic interest and medical importance.

CONCLUSION

The study of folk healers and healing has long been relegated to "minor genre" status within folklore. This has been because of problems in fitting it into the basically literary organization of materials which has long characterized folklore, and because of the difficulties of trying to deal objectively with believed traditions. It is, however, possible to overcome these difficulties and bring the study of folk healing to the position of major importance that it merits. The UCLA Conference on American Folk Medicine convened by Wayland Hand in December of 1973 seems to have marked a turning point in that process, and the Smithsonian Institution's symposium "Folk Medicine: Alternative Approaches to Health and Healing" held in September of 1979 is one of many signs of growing interest. The success of the venture depends upon careful scholarship; a balanced consideration of materials, context, and process; and a synthesis of the work accomplished so far with new insights. The results will be well worth the effort.

NOTES

1. Wayland D. Hand. ed., *Popular Beliefs and Superstitions from North Carolina*, The Frank C. Brown Collection of North Carolina Folklore, Vol. 6 (Durham, North Carolina, 1961), p. 201.

2. Vance Randolph, *Ozark Superstitions* (New York, 1947), p. 93.

3. For an excellent discussion of the powwow tradition and its connections with both print and general religious tradition, see Don Yoder, "Hohman and Romanus," in *American Folk Medicine*, ed. Wayland D. Hand (Berkeley: University of California Press, 1976), pp. 235-48.

4. For a consideration of health food practices from a folklore perspective, see David Hufford, "Natural/Organic Food People as a 'Folk Group': Nutrition, Health System and World View," *Keystone Folklore Quarterly* 16 (1971): 179-84.

5. For an example of such an application, see David Hufford, "Christian Religious Healing," *Journal of Operational Psychiatry* 8 (1977): 22-27.

6. For example, see Ari Kiev, "The Study of Folk Psychiatry," in *Magic, Faith and Healing*, ed. Ari Kiev (New York: Free Press, 1964), pp. 3-35; and Kiev, *Transcultural Psychiatry* (New York: Free Press, 1972).

7. See Anthony Wallace, *Religion: An Anthropological View* (New York: Random House, 1966), pp. 145-52.

8. See David J. Hufford, *The Terror That Comes in the Night: An Experience-Centered Study of Supernatural Assault Traditions* (Philadelphia: University of Pennsylvania Press, Publications of the American Folklore Society, 1982).

John H. McDowell

Children's Folklore

Children's folklore encompasses a great variety of verbal and nonverbal activities, whose common denominators are first, that they circulate primarily among children, and second, that they incorporate playful or artistic motives with some standing in community tradition. Children of four years of age already produce and enjoy routines clearly belonging to this realm of activity, and this initial competency derives from intense preparation during infancy and early childhood. With the onset of adolescence, a new period of folkloric expressivity begins, and again, the new developments are founded on previously acquired capabilities, especially those elaborated during the critical span of five to eight years of age.

Children's folklore is a species of children's play, but the two categories are not coterminous. The play motive common to all forms of children's folklore produces a sense of make-believe or secondary reality, premised on ordinary reality but in some manner distanced from it, perhaps by the allocation of a special play space, or by a reversal of real-life contingencies, or by some other factor.[1] The boundary between children's play and folklore is not always a clear one, but a broad guideline would recognize as children's folklore precisely those forms of children's play exhibiting the collective dimension to which we have alluded.

The distinction between playful and artistic motives is an important one. Play involves a more or less free and inventive manipulation of resources, somehow set apart from the productive activities of what we think of as ordinary life. Similarly, art entails a manipulation of resources within a special context, but the play of art is carefully attuned to collective preoccupations, and is in fact dressed for public consumption. The emergence of art from play in children's folklore is a central theme, and the transition from one to the other is largely secured during the critical period of five to eight years of age. The play motive is evident in the earliest productions of a folkloric character, while artistic performance comes later, and indicates a grasp of community values and aesthetics.

The primary habitat of children's folklore is the juvenile peer group, which may convene in any number of neighborhood settings. This social unit retains considerable autonomy from adult supervision, and therefore must be treated as an institution indigenous to childhood. Within the juvenile peer group the performance of folklore occupies a position of major importance. In a community relatively uninfluenced by writing, oral performance transacts a good deal of community business.[2] Basic legal maneuvers such as establishing ownership, defending a territory, or scolding a miscreant are accomplished through recourse to verbal and kinesic formulas drawn from local tradition. Negotiation of status within the group or between groups often involves the display of virtuosity in one or another form of folklore. Oral tradition and more specifically the verbal forms of folklore are the very fabric of peer-group interaction.

Since the child participates in vertical as well as horizontal social relationships, two additional channels for the performance of children's folklore are indicated. The adult-to-child channel contributes formal models and novel content which are selectively adapted and introduced into the child's folkloric repertoire. Some forms of folklore readily lend themselves to propagation through this channel, and others like the dandling rhyme and nursery tale are premised upon it. Age discrepancy among participants may be a positive factor in many performance settings, allowing for an agreeable exchange between differential repertoires. The adult-to-child channel generally seeks to interpret adult orientations in terms intelligible to children, and thus contains interesting clues concerning adult notions of childhood.

In the child-to-adult channel, the child adapts his expressive repertoire to what he considers to be adult standards. Folklore entering into this conduit draws selectively on peer-group repertoire, often utilizing those portions which are most orderly and sober, and thus attuned to the apparent expectations of adults.

Principal among these channels of children's folklore is the format of peer-group interaction. Here the children are released from the positional hierarchies of adult society into a vibrant world of play among peers.

COLLECTION

In collecting children's folklore, a number of methodological options are available. The two major variables defining these options are the particular communicative channel tapped, and the strategy adopted for presenting oneself to the children. We limit the discussion to the collection of materials autochthonous to childhood, and thus are concerned with only two channels of folkloric performance, the child-to-child and the child-to-adult.

The collector may reproduce the child-to-adult format by inviting the child to perform folklore for the collector's benefit. If adequate levels of rapport are forthcoming, a great deal of children's folklore emerges in these sessions. But there are two inherent limitations to this method. First, only certain children respond favorably when isolated with an unfamiliar adult and requested to perform. This method thus selects for certain personality types among children, and there is no guarantee that the repertoires of these bolder children are entirely representative. Second, even those children who are willing to perform will tend to adapt their repertoire to what they perceive to be adult standards, thus emphasizing some portions of their repertoire and neglecting others.

Moreover, to speak of performance in this setting is a bit odd. Deprived of the familiar peer-group ambience, the child is often constrained merely to report on folkloric routines rather than to perform them. The resulting productions may be fragmentary and colorless in comparison to their peer-group counterparts.

The frailty of this research method can be illustrated with reference to the work of child psychologists utilizing folkloric materials.[3] The standard practice is to isolate the child in a room with an adult investigator who is a stranger or virtual stranger to the child. In one research design the child was exposed to riddles in this setting, and his responses were measured by two indicators—funniness ratings, or explicit evaluations of humor in a given riddle, and mirth response, or visible indications of amusement.[4] The researchers were puzzled by the failure of their two indicators to correlate, a troublesome discrepancy which to some extent vitiated their findings. The folklorist immediately detects the problem: the artificiality of the interactional setting, depriving the experiment of ecological validity, or conformance to real-life situations.

Any effort to obtain a comprehensive and reliable portrait of children's folklore requires the monitoring of peer-group interaction. But here we confront a basic methodological dilemma: the juvenile peer group is premised on the exclusion of adults. It is a fragile social construct either dissolved or radically altered by the presence of adults. If the collector approaches a peer group in action, the most likely impact is the fragmentation of the scene into a sequence of child-to-adult interactions, with a heightened affect due to the presence of peers as an audience. The collector becomes the center of attention and the children produce routines characteristic of the child-to-adult channel. Valuable material may emerge, but the authentic peer-group material remains elusive.

To surmount these obstacles two tactics are available. First, the collector may lurk about quietly until the intensity of peer-group interactions supersedes the disruptive impact of the collector's presence. The second tactic is to incorporate oneself into peer-group dynamics by presenting oneself as someone other than an adult authority figure. This feat of self-definition is brought about by adopting a playful attitude toward the children, and signalling one's disregard for certain elements of adult mentality. For example, assuring the children that they can use "bad words," if they want to can produce speedy results. In one memorable collecting session I so thoroughly convinced the children that I was not to be taken as an authority figure that I began to receive the harassment normally accorded a new kid in the neighborhood. In the process, I recorded a valuable store of insults.

Neither of the strategies developed here is absolutely reliable, but each affords some possibility for penetration into the world of peer-group interaction. A triangulation of all available strategies is perhaps the researcher's best hope. The child-to-adult format will produce large inventories of folkloric items; observation of child-to-child interaction allows the folklorist to locate these items in their natural contexts, and to round out the inventory by including items not readily incorporated into child-to-adult intercourse.

REPERTOIRES

The forms of children's folklore are usefully classified according to the comparative importance of kinesic and verbal components. Kinesic forms involve the flexing of muscles according to a set of socially sanctioned regulations. These forms are often games, or playful activities of a competitive nature, in which the rules guarantee an equal chance of victory to all participants. Games such as "Hide and Go Seek" and "Tag" are widely distributed in cultures throughout the world, and familiar to most of us from our childhoods.[5] In kinesic forms there is no intrinsic verbal component; the point is, rather, to leap and bound, feint and spin, in an expression of sheer physical dexterity.

The second category of children's folklore involves a balanced focus on verbal and kinesic faculties alike. In some of these the two components are segregated and sequenced in the play, as in the games known as "Mother May I?" and "Red Rover," where a verbal formula alternates with segments of kinesic activity. Other forms such as jumping rope and handclapping forge an intricate synchrony of verbal and kinesic elements. In handclapping, for example, a traditional rhyme must be recited to the timed meeting of the hands. The availability of several styles of handclapping allows for the development of real virtuosity.

The third category includes forms centering on the verbal faculty, involving the manipulation of sounds and concepts rather than body limbs. We will pause over some of these forms in slightly greater detail.

Children's riddling is a comtemplative affair, at base an inquiry into the epistemological foundations of culture. Riddles point to linguistic and conceptual anomaly lodged within familiar cultural codes. Consider the old standard:

What's black and white and red all over? *A newspaper.*[6]

This riddle derives from semantic duplicity present in the linguistic code, which allows two meanings to attach to the single phonetic sequences /red/ and *all over,* the former being either the color or the verb, the latter either an adverbial or adjectival modifier. A riddle incorporating conceptual duplicity, and thus focused on the cognitive code, is the following:

A thousand lights in a dish. *Stars.*

Here the riddlee is forced to make a novel association between familiar tokens of experience in order to solve the riddle. These exercises in metaphor challenge or reassemble cognitive orders founded on everyday experience, and thus retain a capacity to vitalize the ordinary.

Riddling is an inherently social activity, providing for a rapid exchange of turns and roles. In order for riddling to proceed at all, participants must agree on the ground rules. But within this consensus there remains much to negotiate. Legalistic disputes arise over the taking of turns, the proper fulfillment of roles, the aptness of proffered solutions. The negotiation of riddling in a peer-group setting is an art in itself, an art only revealed to the researcher who has managed to observe child-to-child interaction.

Children's rhymes and songs verse the child in native poetic discourse, and alternately mock and celebrate the received orders of society. They provide the child with performance space, or allow for communal recitation of a familiar ditty. The bifurcate content of these poetic designs is striking. Consider these examples:

(a)   John and Mary sitting in a tree
      K-i-s-s-i-n-g
      First comes love, then comes marriage
      Then comes Mary with a baby carriage.

(b)   Down by the river, down by the sea
      Johnny broke a bottle and he blamed it on me.

I tell ma, mama tell papa
Johnny got a whippin' and a haw haw haw.

(c)   I had a little brother
His name was Tiny Tim,
I put him in the bathtub
To teach him how to swim.

He drank up all the water
He ate up all the soap,
He died last night
With a bubble in his throat.

(d)   Way down south where bananas grow
Grasshopper stepped on the elephant's toe.
The elephant said with tears in his eyes:
—Pick on somebody your own size.

The first two of these examples presents societal orders as we normally encounter them. Thus the continuation of society appears in the orderly sequence of love, marriage, and childbirth; and maintenance of social order appears in the proper dispensation of justice within the family. But the last two examples reverse the common orders: a sister calmly drowns her little brother, and a tiny animal bullies a larger cousin. These parody rhymes could be thought of as miniature rites of reversal.

The power of patterned speech is manifest in these rhymes. Each of the examples cited above evidences isochronic meter, the folk meter of English hymns, ballads, and nursery rhymes, as well as some manner of end rhyme. The corpus of children's rhymes and songs provides an invaluable introduction to the forms of poetic discourse.

Children's narrative produces a verbal icon of a child's experience, and like all narrative seeks to capture the joy, pathos, or mystery of existence. Unlike riddles, which focus on the intimate realms of experience, narratives may roam the world at large in search of a topic, and even transcend the limits of actual experience. If the riddle may be said to restrict itself to the inner circles of the child's cosmology, and to vitalize this domain through the cultivation of anomaly, then to narrative must be attributed not only this same capacity but also the inverse capacity to harness the unfamiliar and through verbal representation deprive it of some of its vitality. Evidence for this assertion is found in the prominence of witches, ghosts, devils, bears, crocodiles, and panthers in children's narrative, and their complete absence from children's riddles.

THEMES

The study of children's folklore articulates a number of themes of transcendent interest, and has in fact become a stimulus of considerable theoretical activity in recent years. In concluding this brief survey of children's folklore, I will mention a few of the themes historically or currently deriving from the study of children's folklore.

Children's folklore as residue. The first volume of the *Journal of American Folklore*, published in 1889, contains a contribution from H. Carrington Bolton that is illustrative of nineteenth-century approaches to children's folklore.[7] He cites the leading British anthropologist of the day, Edward Tylor, to the effect that "things which occupy an important place in the life history of grown men in a savage state become the playthings of children in a period of civilization." Directing his attention to the counting-out rhymes of children, Bolton concluded: "I hold that 'counting-out' is a survival of the practice of the sorcerer . . . and that the spoken and written charms originally used to enforce priestly power have become adjuncts to these puerile games."[8]

Children's folklore was thus construed as the residue to customs belonging to former stages of civilization. As conserved among children they were fragmentary, meaningless survivals, lacking the force and vitality they enjoyed in their proper social contexts. This interpretive schema exemplifies what Alan Dundes has termed "degenerative theory" in folkloristics, referring to those theories that conceive of folklore as an inferior version of something grander.[9] With the demise of the global theory of cultural evolution, this mode of interpretation lost its force, and a long hiatus in interpretive activity ensued.

The process of acquisition. The student of children's folklore observes artistic competence at its inception. Early folkloric productions exhibit the constitutive principles of the performance genres in skeletal form. Early narratives may stumble over the creation of temporal disjunction, a necessary sequencing of two events, without which there can be no narrative.[10] Consider these examples, collected from children at the verge of narrative competence:

Once upon a time there was a little boy, his name was Ricky, he hit my sister.

Once upon a time there was a bear and a ginger bread man and the bear eat the ginger bread man, and he is fat, and she had a baby bear, and he, she is a girl, and her name is baby bear and that's all.

In each instance, there is some use of framing formulas, and some attempt to create temporal disjunction, but these are surely marginal narratives, lacking the coherency and poignancy of narrative production in later years. Children learn to weave together multiple instances of temporal disjunction; they begin to tamper with the iconicity of narrative by cueing one episode as prior to another already related. And eventually they develop the ability to select poignant themes, and communicate them to an audience in such a way as to amuse or startle, as the following story from an eight-year-old girl illustrates:

My uncle when he was about your age he used to, every night he go to the railroad tracks, and then there he saw a man, and that man he was turning on, he was turning on matches in the night, and then he, he said: "What are you looking at?" Then that man got up like that, and he didn't have no nose.

In riddling children initially produce routines exhibiting the proper riddling form, but departing from standard practice in one of two ways: either by eliminating the deceptive move, thus producing simple descriptive routines; or by creating puzzling routines which lack proper solutions. These two options are illustrated below:

What's red? *A rose.*
What's big big big like the fig in the dog? *You.*

In the sixth year, riddles incorporating correct forms of deception begin to appear, especially the simpler forms such as those based on homophonic pairs. The seventh year is pivotal, as the more complex forms of reversal appear in the child's riddling. By taking a longitudinal slice, the researcher sees artistic competence in these genres unfold in an orderly fashion.

There appear to be interesting connections between the process of acquisition in children's folklore and what Jean Piaget calls psychological development.[11] The seventh year figures as a watershed in both areas. In psychological development the child moves from the preoperational stage into the stage of concrete operations, to adopt Piaget's terminology. He becomes aware of classes and the reversibility of operation. The forum of children's folklore apparently interacts with the spontaneous intellectual development of the child, providing an arena for the rehearsal of new-found conceptual skills.

SOCIAL PROCESS

Society demands of the individual the ability to cooperate with others in the elaboration of social tasks. The simplest conversation is a social edifice founded on an elaborate but mostly unarticulated set of mutual understandings. From the individual's point of view, social conventions must be negotiated and manipulated in the pursuit of personal goals.

Children's folklore, in all three of the channels we have identified, constitutes one important locus of socialization. The forms of children's folklore are for the most part inherently social activities. The child is constrained to master the social conventions, for example, the rules of the game, and then turn this knowledge to advantage in the crucible of social interaction.

The verbal genres of folklore develop in the child skill in the negotiation of personal interests subject to the restraints of social convention. In riddling, the riddler enjoys the position of absolute authority, a privilege rarely available to the child. But the riddler must yield a turn promptly, to facilitate a brisk exchange of riddles. Children prolong their turns as riddler through several moves, such as denying a correct solution, providing clues instead of the riddle solution, and even chastising a lethargic group of riddlees. Yet one must not overly try the patience of the group, or risk future access to the role of riddler. In narrative sessions, children jostle for the floor in concerted fashion, and a comparable negotiation of etiquette takes place. In these forums the child becomes adept at turning the social contract to personal advantage.

CONCEPTUAL PROCESS

Recent definitions of culture have emphasized its conceptual nature, as a set of recipes for getting things done, or a set of cognitive systems.[12] In much of children's folklore, two basic conceptual skills are practiced: the ability to articulate conceptual orders and the ability to reverse, transcend, or parody these same orders.

In riddling the child produces both descriptive routines, with their orthodox renditions of primary sensory experience, and riddles proper, founded on a block element or germ of ludic reversal. Rhymes evince a similar duality of intent, in some cases recapitulating societal orders, in others turning them on their heads. Narratives likewise alternately display and subvert the received orders. Thus a good many stories celebrate the role of motherhood, in its benign aspect; but others present this hallowed figure in quite another light: "Hey you know the little girl, she had a mother but the mother was a witch. . . . "

One primary function of these rather disparate conceptual lessons is described by Ian Hamnet in the following terms:

> Classification is a pre-requisite of the intelligible ordering of experience, but if conceptual categories are reified, they become obstacles rather than means to a proper understanding and control of both physical and social reality. The ability to construct categories and also to transcend them is central to adaptive learning.[13]

ENCULTURATION

Children's folklore thus constitutes a major enculturative forum paralleling the institutional educational process. The forms of children's folklore rehearse a broad range of physical, social, and conceptual skills. In the stimulating arena of peer-group intercourse, the child is exposed to the very foundations of culture, and gradually encouraged to display mastery of them. Notably, school operates in quite a different manner, imposing a discipline and orientation extrinsic to the world of childhood. Children's folklore is an uneasy adjunct to the formal educational process, though some interesting attempts to corral this spontaneous learning forum have been reported.[14] Further progress can be anticipated, especially as educators become more sensitive to the distinguishing features of children's folklore.

But with or without the nod of institutional authority, as long as children assemble in peer groups maintaining some autonomy from adult supervision, they will continue to assimilate basic cultural skills through indulgence in the forms of children's folklore.

NOTES

1. Johan Huizinga, *Homo Ludens: A Study of the Play Element in Culture* (New York: Pantheon Books, 1939); Roger Caillois, *Man, Play and Games* (New York: Free Press, 1961).

2. Iona and Peter Opie, *The Lore and Language of School Children* (Oxford: Oxford University Press, 1959).

3. P. E. McGhee, "Children's Appreciation of Humor: A Test of the Cognitive Congruity Principle," *Child Development* 47 (1976): 420–26; Kenneth Whitt and Norman Prentice, "Cognitive Processes in the Development of Children's Enjoyment and Comprehension of Joking Riddles," *Developmental Psychology* 13 (1977): 129–36.

4. Whitt and Prentice, op. cit.

5. Brian Sutton-Smith, *The Folkgames of Children* (Austin: University of Texas Press, 1972).

6. The examples of children's folklore quoted in this article are drawn from my own fieldwork in Austin, Texas, during the years 1974–75, partly written up in my own volume, *Children's Riddling* (Bloomington: Indiana University Press, 1979).

7. H. Carrington Bolton, "The Counting-Out Rhymes of Children," *Journal of American Folklore* 1 (1880): 31–37.

8. Ibid., p. 36.

9. Alan Dundes, "The Devolutionary Premise in Folklore Theory," *Journal of the Folklore Institute* 6 (1969): 5–19.

10. William Labov and Joshua Waletzsky, "Narrative Analysis: Oral Versions of Personal Experience," in *Essays on the Verbal and Visual Arts*, ed. June Helm (Seattle: American Ethnological Society, 1967).

11. Jean Piaget, *The Child and Reality: Problems of Genetic Psychology* (New York: Viking Press, 1973).

12. Ward Goodenough, "Cultural Anthropology and Linguistics," *Monograph Series on Languages and Linguistics* 9 (1964): 167–73.

13. Ian Hamnet, "Ambiguity, Classification and Change: The Function of Riddles," *Man* 2 (1967): 385.

14. Richard Bauman, "The Ethnography of Children's Folklore," draft prepared for Colloquium on Ethnography and Education: Children In and Out of School, University of Pennsylvania, 1978.

PART II INTERPRETATION OF RESEARCH

In the earlier period of American folkloristics collectors would hunt for tales, songs, beliefs, and proverbs with no thought beyond the excitement of the chase and the trapping of the game. Today no trained folklorist would publish a collection without some exegesis of the materials. Such interpretation need not involve an all-embracing master theory, but may rest with cultural and historical analysis of the items discovered. To take two recent publications: in *I Heard the Old Fishermen Say*, Patrick Mullen presents dozens of texts of local treasure legends, fishing tall tales, and local character anecdotes related by the coastal and deep-water fishermen of the Texas Gulf Coast. But he surrounds these texts with commentary on their functions in the culture, narrative style, and genre distinctions, as well as ethnographic details. In *Joe Scott: The Woodsman Songmaker*, Edward Ives resurrects the biography and song repertoire of a dead and forgotten Maine ballad composer. With each recovered ballad text Ives provides evidence for the authorship and the oral circulation, and builds a case for his interpretation of the song's layers of meaning to Scott and his audience.

Because this new era of American folklore scholarship is just commencing, we cannot single out many volumes of this sort, but we can confidently predict that future reports from the field will include interpretive discussion. Interpretation does not, however, necessarily connect theory to *American folklore*, but may regard *folklore in America* as part of a universal model. One kind of interpreting is not in itself superior to the other, but we need to distinguish between universal and national models. For instance, Alan Dundes continually calls for, and exemplifies in his own work, efforts by folklorists to fathom the import of folklore in the lives of the people among whom it percolates. In some of his essays he does address American character traits, such as the expression of male chauvinism, or the attachment to the number three, or the homosexual implications in football, in American folk speech and other folklore. But his basic model, the psychoanalytic, can be applied to folk materials in any culture. One may seek national characteristics through psychoanalytic readings of folklore, and indeed Gershon Legman in his exhaustive two volumes on *Rationale of the Dirty Joke* does arrive at a conception of American society as male-dominated and homoerotic. The great spate of dirty jokes that form the staple story fare in American life demonstrates, according to Legman, that men regard women as sexual toys and reserve their primary esteem and admiration for each other. Leslie Fiedler reaches similar conclusions in his Freudian approach to literature in *Love and Death in the American Novel*, by citing such examples as Huck and Jim interacting on the raft. Such an interpretation, if it is to receive much acceptance, needs to be supported by other kinds of evidence, for instance the findings of sexual researchers.

In my own thinking I have attempted to design a folklore model from the elements of the American historical experience, rather than from any *a priori* assumptions—save that the stuff of history generates the stuff of folklore. This model therefore requires a close partnership between folklorists and historians, but few have as yet entered this partnership, and the first three centuries of American history remain largely terra incognita to students of folklore. My thesis is set forth in the opening essay in Part II.

One of the few historians who have utilized American folkore sources—indeed the only one at this writing to construct a major work—is Lawrence Levine, who contributes a statement on interpreting American folklore historically. His piece dovetails with mine, for while I proposed that folklorists look at major themes of American life in chronological sequence, from colonization to industrialization, to see how folklore spins off from them, Levine is asking historians to look at available folklore as usable sources for the reconstruction and understanding of past eras. He meets head on the misgivings felt by the historical profession about relying on such apparently flimsy sources, and even adds to the suspicion by presenting examples of how folklorists arbitrarily select and unconsciously misinterpret the materials they collect through preconceived biases, e.g., "the folk are simple." Proper examination of Afro-American slave songs and tales reveals, in Levine's eyes, continuities with African culture patterns that rebut the upholders of the thesis, advanced by Stanley Elkins, of slavery's corrosive effect on the African heritage. Since interpretations differ, I must refer to the position held by the black scholar Arthur Huff Fauset and myself, that the African origins school have overstated their claims, and that much Afro-American folk culture has developed from its own energies and historical circumstances. But with Levine's main thrust I certainly agree, that slave folklore used as a historical source provides a means of illumining the slave mind in all its vigor and fertility.

From another perspective Roger Abrahams considers two of the most frequent ways in which folklorists in the United States analyze their data: what he calls the sociological, which emphasizes the social context and the folk; and what he calls the ethnographic, which emphasizes the manners and morals and the lore. He does not divide the two concepts sharply, but as a matter of emphasis: on the membership of the group or on the performance by the individual. In his comments on "the new ethnographers" he indicates a shift from concerns with the major institutions of the culture to the everyday modes of behavior, and how these modes relate to the spectacle occasions in the culture. Speaking of the sociological folklorists, he suggests that their preoccupation with marginal groups in society, like gypsies and cowboys, whose folklore is immediately visible, may be redirected toward the solid center of the population. Both strategies look behind the folklore into the living processes from which it emerges. They depend for their data on thorough field observation, and consequently these studies are restricted to the contemporary scene. That detailed ethnographies of past periods may be constructed from printed and manuscript sources is seen in the brilliant social history of

Rockdale (1980), a Pennsylvania mill town in the nineteenth century, written by the anthropologist Anthony F. C. Wallace. The method of ethnohistory combines documentary research to establish the historical baseline with up-to-date field investigation, and the one example of such a work in American folklore is Lynwood Montell's *The Saga of Coe Ridge* (1970). Montell interviewed former residents of the abandoned Coe Ridge settlement of black families in southern Kentucky, and examined court records, newspaper files, local histories, and similar sources to reconstruct Coe Ridge's history. The methods of interpretation outlined by Abrahams provide rich detail for the contemporary settings of folklore but bypass the historical dimension.

No matter what theoretical position or school of thought American folklorists identify with, or even if they choose to maintain a posture of objective detachment, all possess ideology, contends Archie Green in the final essay of this section. He states that no attempt has been made to place folklore scholars in the stream of American intellectual thought, and he himself offers suggestive judgments along this line. Green quotes me as opposing the ideal of disinterested truth pursued by the scholar to the *idées fixes* of Old Left liberals and New Left radicals, but I must qualify the ideal and agree that none of us escapes ideology. The ideals of truth itself, fair play, equality, democracy, freedom, and the work ethic constitute an American ideology, to which almost all American folklorists will subscribe, and which will color their interpretations and govern their collecting. Vance Randolph believed in the values of an older, rural America and found them in his Ozark folklore. George Korson sympathized with the Pennsylvania coal miners in their hard lot and reported ballads and legends portraying their exploitation and dangers. John Greenway in his leftist youth published *American Folksongs of Protest* and in his rightist later years published a selection of eulogistic Americana in *Folklore of the American West*. Folklore lends itself to liberal, populist interpretation, because of the easy identification of the folk with the people, yet the traditional folk in the old agrarian sense are themselves conservative, God-fearing, capitalistic. Green comments on the paradox of liberal and conservative ideologues sharing the same folk festival platform. He further traces the increased role of the federal government in recent years—a role which his own energetic lobbying effort was instrumental in fixing—in public support of folk culture activities. The exhibits and publications that result from such support confirm the national ideology of consensus, progress, contentment. But wherever folklorists find themselves, in the public or private sector, in the academy or the marketplace, in the museum or at the festival, they will take an ideological stance.

Richard M. Dorson

A Historical Theory for American Folklore

Theories of folklore abound, but they tend to take a universal rather than a national approach. The present generation of folklorists in the United States applies structural, or oral-formulaic, or sociolinguistic, or psychoanalytic models to the exegesis of folklore materials. Never do they begin with the American scene and then develop a model. Universal models are certainly legitimate, given the cross-cultural nature of folklore, but so are national models, and all the more so in the case of colonized countries. A theory for United States folklore begins with the distinction between Old World and New World nations, between the continents of Asia, Africa, and Europe and the continents of North and South America and Australia. In our theory we week to divide folklore in America from American folklore. Forms of folk tradition and folk behavior that could be recorded and studied anywhere in the world comprise the first category, and those derived from American historical and cultural experience the second. Folklorists in America tend to use the genre and concept approach and American folklorists must use the historical approach.

Several symposia published in the 1970s illustrate the trends and directions among an emerging generation of theoretical folklorists in the United States and their concern with genre and concept. In *Folklore Genres* (1976), edited by Dan Ben-Amos, the essayists depart from the conventional view of genres as static categories to interpret them as "modes of communication . . . in the lore of peoples." This view is expressed and developed in three other symposia: *Toward New Perspectives in Folklore* (1972), edited by Américo Paredes and Richard Bauman, *Folklore: Performance and Communication*, edited by Ben-Amos and Kenneth Goldstein (1975), and *Frontiers of Folklore*, edited by William Bascom (1977). The titles of these works themselves tell volumes, for performance and communication are the two prestige terms in the new dialectic, and these theorists see themselves as trail-blazers. Synthesizing these new perspectives, Barre Toelken titled his textbook *The Dynamics of Folklore* (1978). One of the folklore frontiersmen, Richard Bauman, paid special tribute to Dell Hymes's "seminal essay" of 1962 on the ethnography of speaking as the most influential in conceptualizing the study of folklore as communication.[1] Under the banner of the rapidly expanding field of semiotics, the concept of communication now embraces nonverbal behavior: signs, signals, gestures, kinesics. In 1980 Bauman was elected president of the American Semiotics Society and editor of the *Journal of American Folklore*.

These are the ideas currently in vogue in American folkloristics, and intriguing as some find them, they have nothing to do with a theory for American folklore. One of the purposes of this *Handbook* is to redress the balance so that the national model attracts attention and discourse along with the universal models. These are by no means mutually exclusive paradigms, and the historical folklorist can look for performance and communication data in documentary sources. But they do represent quite different intellectual formulations and research methods. Folklorists in America seek their primary data in the field, while American folklorists in addition to fieldwork rely heavily on the library as they strive to cover the whole range of American history, from the seventeenth century through the twentieth. The fieldwork emphasis also will notably differ.

COLONIZATION

In the historical theory the story of American folklore coincides with the beginnings of American history, that is, with the period of discovery, exploration, and colonization. The national model for United States folklore thus forms part of a larger model applicable to all nations colonized in modern times, as a result of the expansion of Europe from the fifteenth century on. These nations came into existence as a result of European settlements in alien lands where the indigenous population was too scattered and weak to resist subjugation, assimilation, or dispersal. Where then does one find the folklore? The various European traditions may accompany their human hosts overseas, but they are bound to change character three thousand miles and more from their *Heimat*. Local legends attached to landmarks, for example, do not readily transplant. Meanwhile the unfolding drama of colonization, with its sea voyages, Indian encounters, survival struggles in the wilderness, mingling of European peoples, and importation of African slaves, was establishing new institutions and reference points. American folklore is born in this atmosphere heavily charged with heroics, catastrophes, and supernatural agencies. Any colonial era will generate a corpus of larger-than-life legendary annals, for these are among the most stirring times in history.

The folklore model for colonized nations thus takes into account the clash and merging of invading and aboriginal cultures, an exotic flora and fauna, and the birth of a new people. But each country under this model requires its own submodel, adjusted to its special historical circumstances. Canada, Mexico, Brazil, Australia will display different combinations of ingredients in the colonial brew: French or Spanish or English or Portuguese settlers intermarrying with or eliminating indigenous peoples who exist in varying degrees of nomadic or agricultural advancement, with the African element another inconstant factor. In the submodel for the future United States, the chief elements forming folk traditions include the English supernatural legacy of witch, ghost, devil, and providence; English interaction with the coastal Indians and their mythology and shamanism; the planting of German, French, and Spanish settlements alongside the English; the introduction of African slavery ; and the flurry of rumors, reports, horrors, and wonders about America circulating in English pubs and counting houses and American cabins, stockades, and plantations in the wilderness.

We do not need to ask the question, what is English or Spanish or French—or Japanese or Turkish—folklore, in the same way that we ask what is American folklore, since the heritages of these peoples are well established, and stretch back to the dawn of history. If Americans simply borrow, can they be said to possess their own folklore? Alexander Haggerty Krappe, whose *The Science of Folklore*, published in 1930, still provides a useful introduction to the European genres, flatly said no. Folklorists no longer raise this particular question, satisfied with the mounting evidence that Americans have produced folklore, but they spend little time examining the seedbed of home-grown American traditions. The reason is simple; they are at home in the field, not among historical sources. What few efforts have been directed toward the colonial scene stem from an older generation or from nonfolklorists. George Lyman Kittredge, the famous Shakespearean scholar, made two notable contributions in *The Old Farmer and His Almanack* (1904), identifying English folk beliefs, sayings, and facetiae tucked into the eighteenth-century file of Robert B. Thomas's almanac series, and *Witchcraft in Old and New England* (1929), demonstrating the transport of witch fears to the New World. Another literary scholar, Percy G. Adams, mined a rich vein in his *Travelers and Travel Liars, 1600–1800* (1962), which defined the genre of the fabulous but allegedly accurate tales of New World natives, beasts, plants, and landscape that travel writers liberally sprinkled through their overseas adventures. These "true" tales would grow into tall tales by the nineteenth century and become a fixture in American yarnspinning. Otherwise studies of colonial folklore are sadly lacking.

THE REVOLUTION

If colonization sets in motion the American story, the Revolution ushers in the United States story, and similarly gives rise to a set of legend-incrusted events, from Paul Revere's midnight ride to Cornwallis's surrender at Yorktown.

But popular tradition is not folk tradition, and folklorists have done very little with the available wealth of those hallowed years 1775–1783. The one book-length attempt, *Uncertain Glory, Folklore and the American Revolution* (1971) by Tristram P. Coffin, probes erratically at spy narratives, ballads, hymns, and warrior-heroes, and never develops a firm methodology.[2] By contrast, Karl G. Heider's microstudy in the *Journal of American Folklore* on "The Gamecock, the Swamp Fox and the Wizard Owl" skillfully winds through printed sources— personal narratives of the Revolution, state histories, oral histories, biographies— to reconstruct the legendary nomenclature attached to three South Carolina generals.[3] In the War for Independence, Frances Marion, Thomas Sumter, and Andrew Pickens fought adroitly against the British and earned their appellations, which, Heider's evidence shows, were first applied by the foe as epithets and subsequently converted by admirers to sobriquets. Heider further points out and suggests in his subtitle, "The Development of Good Form in an American Totemic Set," that the triadic names possess symbolic meanings: three is a revered number in American culture; the generals lived in three regions of South Carolina—Low Country, Midlands, and Upcountry—and the creatures with whom they were associated reflect the linkage: a ground animal for the low country (Marion), a bird for the upcountry (Pickens), and a ground bird for the midlands (Sumter). The evolutionary process of folk legend dictated the final "good form" of three totemic heroes. How many comparable nuggets of heroic legend can be uncovered by the folklorist from those halcyon days? In *America Rebels* (1953) I assembled a selection of personal narratives written down by Revolutionary patriots, usually half a century or so after the events, when a golden haze had settled over the War for Independence, and veterans transferred their oral recitals of war into print for a new generation. Only in 1980 has the great cache of Revolutionary adventures encased in pensioners' applications to Congress been brought to public notice.[4]

THE FRONTIER

Following colonization and revolution, the next, and most significant, event in American history, as pointed out by Frederick Jackson Turner, lies in the drive west that conquered the continent. The westward movement created a sequence of successive frontiers that molded the American character, in Turner's analysis of 1893, and shaped an American mythology, in the interpretation Henry Nash Smith presented in 1960 in *Virgin Land, the West as Symbol and Myth*. This mythology limned a fertile western preserve that produced fabulous crops and a stalwart breed of frontier heroes, but was itself, according to Smith, based on a myth to which Turner succumbed, the myth of the West as an earthly paradise. In fact much of the West included the grim Middle Border of Hamlin Garland and the great southwestern desert. Meritorious folklore studies of the frontier myth following Smith's lead are not yet written, but some penetrating examinations of frontier humor, the special brand of exaggeration and comic delineation of character that flowered in the states of the old southwest before the Civil War, have been achieved, by literary scholars rather than folklorists. Noteworthy are Constance Rourke's *American Humor* (1931), tracing the continuities of the ring-tailed roarer frontier boaster, along with the down-East Yankee and the blackface minstrel, in the nation's comedy and literature; Bernard De Voto's *Mark Twain's America*, linking Mark Twain with the oral humorous yarn and comic newspaper sketch of the southwestern frontier; and Walter Blair and Franklin J. Meine's restoration of *Mike Fink, King of the Mississippi Keelboatmen* (1933) from fugitive antebellum sources.

Because the frontier itself acquired a legendary aura, episodes and personalities in frontier history lend themselves to folkloric treatment. An excellent example is afforded in the folk history of the Mormons, recounted in *Saints of Sage and Saddle* (1956) by Austin and Alta Fife, who follow the march of the Latter-day Saints from western New York to Illinois to Utah through the marvels, providences, and ballads attached to Joseph Smith, Brigham Young, and the saints. The mountain men engaged in the Rocky Mountain fur trade became the subjects of admiring yarns, but no folklorist has yet done justice to Jim Bridger—scout, trail-blazer, Indian fighter, and recounter of wonders about Yellowstone Park. One stream of oral legendry concerning another mountain man, John Johnson, the notorious eater of Crow Indian livers—hence his sobriquet, Liver-Eating Johnson—has found its way into print, and thence into film.[5] Border warfare between Indians and whites has also lent itself to myth-making about Indian oratory, cruelty, heroism, and fatalism. Bruce Rosenberg has written on *Custer and the Epic of Defeat* (1974), viewing the annihilation of Custer at the battle of the Little Big Horn in 1876 in terms of epic narrative structure. A classic primary source filled with folklore matter and concepts is James Mooney's *The Ghost-Dance Religion and the Sioux Outbreak of 1890* (1896), an ethnographic-historical narrative of the last revivalistic and militaristic effort of the Plains tribes. Prophecies, visions, hallucinations, spirits, music, dance, white stereotypes of Indian behavior, the mystique of Sitting Bull, all commingle in this report. In sum, the bright promise held out to students of frontier, humor, and mythmaking remains, in Smith's title, virgin land for the folklorist.

SLAVERY

Slavery, the "peculiar institution," also imparts a special character to American history and to American folklore. The legal importation of African slaves by the American colonies and states until 1808, primarily for work on cotton plantations, and the continued domestic breeding of slaves until the Civil War established a large subordinate black culture possessing the richest of folklores. Forced into illiteracy, the slaves developed a vibrant verbal, musical, and dance culture of animal and bird tales, Old Marster tales, hant stories, hymns, spirituals, gospel songs, hollers, work songs, cries, shouts, jigs, reels, breakdowns, rhymes, and taunts that continued and expanded under freedom into new forms such as jazz, blues, ragtime, toasts, and the dozens. Collectors have captured these genres, but only with Lawrence W. Levine's *Black Culture and Black Consciousness: Afro-American Folk Thought from Slavery to Freedom* (1977) did a trained historian utilize these folk documents for purposes of historical interpretation. Levine contends that the history of black Americans can be written from the black point of view, rather than from the standard white sources, by using folklore materials. Such history cannot reproduce precise chronological events but it can recreate attitudes and climates of opinion in broad historical periods—in this case the antebellum decades of the nineteenth century and the postbellum years to the 1940s. Where slaves expressed a covert defiance of their masters through their folklore, blacks in freedom times moved to more overt folkloric statements of their independence and disdain of whites. Levine asserts that "the crucial change marking black folklore after emancipation was the development of . . . heroes who confronted power and authority directly, without guile or tricks, and who functioned on a secular level."[6] He tends to overpress his thesis of black militancy against whites, and largely bypasses hoodoo, the core of Afro-American folk belief, which is used by blacks against blacks and rarely crosses racial cultures. On his most solid ground Levine deals with cult figures in twentieth-century Afro-American music and shows concretely how composers and singers such as Thomas A. Dorsey, Mahalia Jackson, and Mamie Smith merged the sacred and secular folk-musical styles. Levine succeeds in demonstrating the creative energies and resilience of black Americans under slavery and under freedom conditions, with collective and individual examples. A complementary work is needed to illustrate the folklore elements connected with events of black history, such as Nat Turner's Rebellion of 1831, or the operation of the underground railroad, or the great northern migration of the 1920s.

The possibilities for historical research in Afro-American folklore both in the field and in the library can be seen in several dissertations undertaken at Indiana University. Working through a great range of colonial writings, William D. Piersen pieced together a picture of black "governors" and their assemblies as they evolved in seventeenth- and eighteenth-century New England, in sub rosa imitation of the white governments, with their own pageantry and ritualism.[7]

Interviewing the descendants of slaves in the District of Columbia and Maryland, Gladys-Marie Fry chanced on a vigorous oral tradition of body-snatching night doctors or night riders, who, the white masters claimed, would capture runaway slaves and sell their bodies to medical schools. In her dissertation and subsequent book Fry linked the night doctors to a chain of bogey figures, from ghosts to patterollers to white-sheeted Ku Klux Klanners, that maintained social controls over the black population.[8] From black communities all over the country William A. Wiggins amassed documentation and testimonies to freedom celebrations held by freed slaves and their offspring in counterpart to the white man's Fourth of July, but at variable dates depending on local traditions.[9] Analyzing the vast body of data on hoodoo recorded by Harry M. Hyatt in southeastern states, Michael E. Bell has contended that hoodoo practitioners perform within a coherent and orderly system of magical beliefs and practices and do not, as observers have thought, act idiosyncratically.[10] These original investigations suggest the rich rewards available to historically minded scholars of Afro-American folklore.

THE CIVIL WAR

As the most traumatic chapter in American history, the Civil War—known in the south as the War Between the States—left in its wake traditions concerning military and naval officers, Billy Yank and Johnny Reb in the ranks, civilian officials, women behind the lines and at the front, spies, traitors, prisoners, raiders, Negroes. No event, or series of events, so fully involved so many of the American people and generated so many hero and ogre figures and symbolic points of reference: Lincoln, Lee, Grant, Sherman, Stonewall Jackson, Jefferson Davis; Fort Sumter, Bull Run, Pickett's charge, Gettysburg, Vicksburg, the Monitor and the Merrimac, Appomattox Court House. Where some two to three million Americans lived at the time of the American Revolution, the population had reached thirty-one million by 1860, and none could escape the impact of a fratricidal war fought within the heart of the country. Yet again folklorists have largely ignored these historical traditions. Leonard Roberts snared a handful of Civil War escapades in the context of the Couch family saga along with bear and deer hunts, witch doings, healings, and other such Kentucky mountain story topics.[11] D. K. Wilgus and Lynwood Montell have composed a model study of "Beanie Short: A Civil War Chronicle in Legend and Song," placing on record the oral accounts about the southern guerrilla leader remembered by hillfolk in Monroe and Cumberland counties in southern Kentucky.[12] Some informants seemed proud that he had killed their ancestors. These accounts deal with his often brutal raiding activities, his gruesome death at the hands of avengers, and the stolen treasure he buried. A little fiddle song memorializes, "Old Beanie Short, / He'll never be forgotten."

These promising indicators point the way to what folklorists may accomplish in Civil War fieldwork. The one panoramic treatment is B. A. Botkin's *A Civil War Treasury of Tales, Legends, and Folklore* (1960), the most successful of his grab-bag treasuries since it alone is organized around a historical-chronological frame. From the enormous literature spawned by the war he turned to the publications of veterans' organizations, encyclopedias of wartime anecdotes, participants' memoirs, and regimental histories for human-interest narratives that portrayed the intimate side of the conflict. As Botkin himself recognized, the popular style of the time ran to the falsely genteel, with damn and hell dashed as too powerful to spell in full, so a good deal of the guts of oral tradition gets dissipated in the sources. Still the themes and clues for a thousand folkloric investigations lie in these writings. One motif that particularizes the Civil War is its fraternal and fratricidal nature. In one tale after another the enemies behave like allies, friends, and brothers; generals cannot distinguish one side from the other; West Point classmates greet each other across the field of battle; sentries converse with the foe; prisoners escape easily back to their camps; captors and captives consort in high spirits. Speaking the same language, reared under the same flag, the combatants exchanged many gallantries and pleasantries, as if war were unifying rather than dividing them. As counterweight, in this bloodiest of all wars, the motif of carnage, butchery, and destruction also recurs in personal narrations.

The Civil War is intertwined with the Lincoln legend, and the savior-president rapidly became the subject of countless anecdotes, including those he told himself. Lincoln stories stress his humanity, his humbleness, his fearlessness, his physical grotesqueness, and his shrewd humor. Some have become national property, like his reported response to the charge that General Grant drank heavily: "If those accusing General Grant of getting drunk will tell me *where he gets his whiskey*, I will get a lot of it and send it around to some of the other generals."[13] This witticism thus linked two heroes. A master raconteur of humorous folk yarns, Lincoln typically applied his tales to vexing political situations. Again subjected to criticisms of Grant, this time for paroling the southern army he had defeated at Vicksburg, Lincoln thought of the story about Sykes' yellow dog, who was blown to bits by small boys putting a cartridge at the end of a long fuse into a piece of meat. Sykes picked up one scrap of the dog and said, "Well, I guess he'll never be much account again—as a dog." Lincoln opined that the Vicksburg army would never be much account again—"as an army." Grant's critics looked for their hats.[14] Such stories about Lincoln's stories shaped the legend of a sage who spoke in the idiom of the people. A full folkloric study would juxtapose anti-legends with admirational legends of the Civil War heroes. Of Stonewall Jackson it was said he gained his sobriquet because he stood against the Federals at Bull Run like a stone wall, and he refused to come to the relief of his fellow generals but remained rooted like a stone wall.[15] We await folklore monographs on the Civil War investigating myriad such matters.

IMMIGRATION

After the Civil War waves of immigrants poured into the United States from southern and eastern Europe, attracted by advertisements and promotional literature from railroad and steamship companies and industrial corporations. The rise of heavy manufacturing, stimulated in large part by government contracts during the war, created the demand for a cheap labor pool, while the casualties of the war had diminished the nation's manpower. Historians have commented on the shift in immigrant stocks following the war from British, German, and Scandinavian to the less assimilable strains from Italy, Poland, the Balkans, and the Baltic countries. These latter peoples entered into a double kind of folk migration: in one sense as a great folk movement from one continent to another, and in another sense as a movement of folk, i.e., of peasant populations rooted in traditional cultures, and now becoming, in Oscar Handlin's title, *The Uprooted*. The folklorist should therefore be concerned with the migrants' common shared experiences of *The Atlantic Crossing*, in Marcus Lee Hansen's title, and their acculturation to American life. The resulting series of culture shocks, in disease-ridden ships' holds and urban ghettoes, bred its own saga and traditions. Also the folklorist wishes to inspect the transplanted customs and folkways that take root or grow new shoots on American soil. The first objective concerns the immigrants as participants in a historic folk movement; the second, the immigrants as carriers of inherited folklore.

American historians agree on the signal importance of immigration as a force contributing to the economic, political, and cultural strength and growth of the American people. The land of the free was indeed open to virtually all comers until the quota impositions of the 1920s began closing the door. These large population groups of distinct nationalities pose inviting targets to folklorists, but their first researches, chiefly in the form of doctoral dissertations in which the writers investigated their own stocks, concentrated narrowly on Old World survivals in the new setting. Even when such survivals were collected, they fell into the category of "memory culture," recollected by immigrants from their Old Country youth but no longer functional in the American context. With the relabeling of the immigrant as ethnic, in the 1970s, a shift in perspective occurred on the part both of scholars and the nationalities. Instead of immigrants being homogenized in a melting pot, they and their children and grandchildren now proudly asserted their ethnic diversity. Further, the ethnic concept included stocks that never undertook the Atlantic or the Pacific crossings, like the Mexican, or even the Puerto Rican, born under the American flag but a minority folk in terms of language and culture.

Only one book-length field study by a professional folklorist has yet been achieved, but it brilliantly exemplifies the rewards awaiting the informed folklore approach to American immigrant communities. In *The Two Rosetos* (1974) Carla Bianco examined in depth the town of Roseto in northeastern Pennsylvania, eighty miles from Philadelphia, at the foothills of the Poconos, whose 1,630 souls (census of 1960) were colonized from Roseto, Valfortore, a mountain village in southern Italy nestled in the Appenines. Bianco conducted fieldwork in both Rosetos, accumulated clippings, letters, artifacts, memorabilia from both places, published a bibliography of Italian-American folklore, undertook comparative fieldwork in metropolitan Italian neighborhoods in New York, Chicago, Long Island, and New Jersey, and subjected her rich data to historical and cultural analysis. She concentrated on two questions: how did the traditional culture of the American village compare with the way of life in its Italian parent village; and what changes had occurred in the lifestyle of the Pennsylvania Rosetans from their town's founding by slate-quarry workers in 1882 up to Bianco's field trips in 1965–66. Bianco was able to document answers to these questions in rich human detail. The voices of the folk sound through her pages, in refreshing contrast to the ethnic histories listing arid dates of the founding of organizations, churches, and newspapers. She reported new traditions that set off the American from the Italian Rosetans, especially in personal historical accounts, which she recognized as "a form of authentic traditional narrative [that] concerns the critical points of the migratory process: emigration, arrival, search for work, primitive standards of living, the fight for survival against established settlers, and first accomplishments."[16] Every immigrating stock in America could furnish orally recited sagas following these motifs. From such personal experience chronicles, and other folklore of ballads and tales, Bianco extrapolates a dual myth of America: the land of opportunity and fabled riches, and a land of injustice and exploitation.

> What can we find in America?
> Mountains of gold and mountains of work,
> A golden cross, but still a cross
> A diamond cross is still a cross.[17]

Here we see perpetuated the twin images of America dating from colonial times, the Earthly Paradise and the Howling Wilderness, linked in William Jennings Bryan's cross of gold metaphor. Bianco also looked closely at the continuities of Old World folk forms and saw in the first generation a loss of folktales and work songs due to changed conditions but a high degree of retention in such matters as folk religion and folk medicine. Credence in the mischievous little demons known as *munaceddi*, in the evil eye *malocchio*, and in the power of iconic saints and madonnas remained as powerful in Roseto and pan-Italian America as in Italy. In one instance an Italian woman in Brooklyn kept a little Statue of Liberty on her bureau and invoked it as Santa Liberata, thus syncretizing icons of the two cultures.

But Bianco noted as well major changes taking place in the life rhythms of Pennsylvania's Roseto that were causing conflicts between the generations. From 1915 to 1940 a great sense of community prevailed, reinforced by the homogeneity and physical apartness of the American Rosetans, who felt all the more need to band together because of the derisive attitude of nearby English and Welsh and Germans—the "Northerns"—toward the "Wops." But in the next quarter of a century the gulf separating the intimate culture from mainstream American culture closed for the younger generation who, influenced by the mass media, the schools, and the mobility of American life, abandoned communal for private activities. Coincidentally, the rate of heart attacks in the town now rose from near zero to the national average. Roseto had attracted the attention of medical researchers because of the low incidence of heart disease among her obese, pasta-eating citizens.[18] One theory suggests that shared rituals and ceremonies insulated the Rosetans against stress and heart failure, but with the withering of their communal folklife, they became as susceptible to cardiac arrest as other gut-driven Americans.

The shafts of light on ethnic behavior thrown by *The Two Rosetos* could and should be beamed by folklore researchers on every nationality stock in the United States.

INDUSTRIALIZATION

The great age of American industrial expansion commences after the Civil War, with the completion of the transcontinental railroads and the erection of manufacturing empires in steel, oil, rubber, chemicals, and other basic products for a mass market. Modern America, the nation of big business, advanced technology, and sprawling cities, begins to take shape in the 1870s. This urban, industrial, mechanized America we know today would seem at the furthest pole from the kind of rural, agrarian, backward-looking society in which presumably folklore flourishes. Recent revisions of folklore theory and field strategy have altered this premise and led folklorists to regard the city, the factory, the mill, the office, and indeed all industrial work sites as promising arenas for their researches. Hence modern America, instead of damping out folklore, becomes a breeding ground for all kinds of unsuspected folkstuff.

This new departure in American folklore studies will seem less radical if we review the series of transitional steps moving the "field" from the outdoors to indoors. The concept of collecting from economic occupations characterizes conscious fieldwork in the United States from its first ventures in 1908 and 1910 with the recording of cowboy songs by N. Howard "Jack" Thorp and John Lomax. By the 1920s and 1930s collectors in Maine and Michigan were issuing volumes of lumberjack songs, and although the days of sail had lapsed, collections of sea shanties too made their appearance. These ballad-singing workmen of the range, the woods, and the deep seemed natural conveyors of folklore, for, if not rooted in the soil like the peasantry, they lived and worked in the open on the fringes of society far from urban centers. One day a journalist covering the mining towns in Pennsylvania asked himself, "Do miners sing songs?" and finding no books on the subject Goerge Korson set out in the '30s and '40s to record the balladry of anthracite and bituminous coal miners. The next step was taken by Mody Boatright, the Texas folklorist, who did extensive interviewing of oilfield workers in the '40s and '50s. In 1945 he placed on record a tall-tale telling hero, *Gib Morgan, Minstrel of the Oil Fields*, and in 1963 he assembled his data from printed and oral sources in *Folklore of the Oil Industry*. Where earlier collectors of occupational lore had concentrated narrowly on songs (although Korson did branch out into amateur ethnography), Boatright had perforce to deal with other forms of tradition since singing played no part in the occupational life of oil drillers. Rather they indulged in tall tales, often, in Gib Morgan's versions, of a highly technological nature, and in legends of fabulous strikes, tragic near-misses, marvelous oil-finding equipment, and eccentric spending of oil riches. Oil drillers, like miners and lumberjacks, worked outdoors or underground, but the oil industry involved greater use of machinery, and still it generated a folklore.

What about workers living in cities and laboring on assembly lines inside buildings? In 1970 I raised the question, "Is There a Folk in the City?" in the *Journal of American Folklore* and in 1974 Bruce Nickerson in the same journal queried, "Is There a Folk in the Factory?" Both articles presented affirmative responses. Nickerson himself had worked in plants in Indiana and Massachusetts and recorded information on the job, and written a doctoral dissertation on factory folklore outlining the tricks, pranks, unwritten codes, and work routines that united assembly-line employees into a folk. The manifesto for the new perspective on industrial folklore came in 1978 in a special issue of *Western Folklore*, "Working Americans: Contemporary Approaches to Occupational Folklore" (reprinted that year as Smithsonian Folklife Studies Number 3). The five contributors shared the conviction that the workaday world of all occupations, white-collar as well as blue-collar, firemen and waitresses and telephone company workers, merits attention from folklorists. They mapped out this unfamiliar terrain with statements of definition, field strategy, characteristics of the newly revealed genres, and wide-ranging bibliographical resources on a sophisticated level of discussion. "The complex of techniques, customs, and modes of expressive behavior which characterize a particular work group comprises its *occupational folklife*," wrote Robert S. McCarl.[19] McCarl and Jack Santino singled out the occupational personal experience narrative as a major genre of industrial lore, in which the hero-worker exhibits traits of wiliness and deception as he outwits the management hierarchy with whom he continually does battle. Preindustrial heroes prided themselves on their strength and loyalty to the company.

My own field trips among the steelworkers of Gary and East Chicago in 1975 and 1976 confirmed the hypotheses set forth in *Working Americans*. Posing to myself the question, was there a folklore of steel, I talked with numbers of "millrats" but until I had toured the mills and learned something of the work processes, I could not comprehend or recognize the traditions of steel. Eventually streams of personal narratives poured into my tape recorder, grouped around such themes as grim industrial accidents, goofing off on the job, mill thefts, vandalism, the size and ferocity of rats, odd characters, and union versus management. The message that came through spelled out disgust with the work conditions and resentment against the company, yet in an earlier day, before the unions, the first generation of east European laborers had found deep satisfaction in their jobs. Their children, owning cars, attending college, looked down on mill labor as degrading, and put in hours only for the easy spending money.

As matters now stand, the field of occupational-industrial-urban folklore and folklife lies wide open, with enough results tabulated to ensure rewards to future investigators. The vein of xeroxed folklore that circulates primarily through offices has been exposed by Alan Dundes and Carl Pagter in *Urban Folklore from the Paperwork Empire* (1975). Several folklorists have dealt with rumors of foreign objects in processed foods and drink, such as the fly in the coke bottle, worms in hamburgers, and rats in Kentucky fried chicken, rumors that have cost the parent corporations tens of thousands of dollars in rebuttal advertising. At every stage of the industrial complex, from manufacturing to distributing to consuming, folklore enters the picture. Who would comprehend modern America needs must be informed about industrial folklore.

In these great themes—colonization, the Revolution, the westward movement, slavery, the Civil War, immigration, and industrialization—can be found the pulse of the American historical experience. On no one of them has more than a start been registered in uncovering their folkloric riches.

NOTES

1. In *Frontiers of Folklore*, ed. William R. Bascom (Boulder, Colorado: Westview Press, 1977), p. 122.

2. See my review in *Journal of American Folklore* 87 (1974): 380–81.

3. *Journal of American Folklore* 93 (1980): 1–22.

4. *The Revolution Remembered: Eyewitness Accounts of the War for Independence*, ed. John C. Dann (Chicago: University of Chicago Press, 1980).

5. Raymond W. Thorp and Robert Bunker, *Crow Killer: The Saga of Liver-Eating Johnson* (Bloomington: Indiana University Press, 1958).

6. Lawrence W. Levine, *Black Culture and Black Consciousness* (New York: Oxford, 1977), pp. 385–86.

7. William D. Piersen, "Afro-American Culture in Eighteenth Century New England: A Comparative Examination" (1975). This was done in history, but Piersen took his M.A. in folklore.

8. Gladys-Marie Fry, "The Night Riders: A Study in Techniques of the Social Control of the Negro" (1967). This was published by University of Tennessee Press in 1975 as *Night Riders in Black Folk History.*

9. William Wiggins, " 'Free at Last!': A Study of Afro-American Emancipation Day Celebrations" (1974).

10. Michael E. Bell, "Pattern, Structure, and Logic in Afro-American Hoodoo Performance" (1980).

11. Leonard Roberts, *Up Cutshin and Down Greasy* (Lexington: University of Kentucky Press, 1959), pp. 84–88.

12. In *American Folk Legend, A Symposium*, ed. Wayland D. Hand (Berkeley: University of California Press, 1971), pp. 133–56.

13. B. A. Botkin, *A Civil War Treasury of Tales, Legends and Folklore* (New York: Random House, 1960), p. 244.

14. Ibid., pp. 365–66.

15. Ibid., pp. 30, 579.

16. Carla Bianco, *The Two Rosetos* (Bloomington: Indiana University Press, 1974), p. 35.

17. Ibid., p. 45.

18. Ibid., pp. xi, 56, 133, 154.

19. *Working Americans*, ed. Robert H. Byington (Washington, D.C.: Smithsonian Folklife Studies Number 3, 1978), p. 3. The sophistication of *Working Americans* contrasts with the naiveté of T. P. Coffin and H. Cohen, *Folklore from the Working Folk of America* (New York: Doubleday, 1973), deficient in ideas and contents.

Lawrence W. Levine

How to Interpret American Folklore Historically

In 1909 Howard Odum complained that "Posterity has often judged peoples without having so much as a passing knowledge of their inner life, while treasures of folk-lore and song . . . have been permitted to remain in complete obscurity."[1] Although there has been progress, the problem Odum identified over seventy years ago remains with us. In 1974 the eminent historian C. Vann Woodward urged his fellow historians to end their neglect of the oral interviews with ex-slaves collected by the Federal Writers' Project (FWP) in the 1930s. Yet, one of his passing remarks deserves comment. Woodward noted that in 1945 "B. A. Botkin published a small book of excerpts from the FWP interviews consisting mainly of anecdotes and folklore, *but* containing quite enough material of historical value. . . . "[2] Woodward's "but"—segregating folklore from "materials of historical value"—typifies an attitude still plaguing historians. Trained to use books, newspapers, diaries, letters, official reports—the written remains of the highly literate portions of society—historians too often neither know what to do with orally transmitted folk materials nor see the need to preserve them. Yet without such preservation and use many of the varied voices that make up any society as large as ours are stilled and we are lulled into the belief that those voices that are recoverable from traditional printed sources are the only ones there were.

To be sure, there are grave problems involved in utilizing the materials of folklore for the purposes of history. Their time and place of origin, the identity of their creators, and their geographical distribution are usually difficult, often impossible, to determine. But though the scholarly challenge presented by folklore is real, it is neither unique nor insurmountable. Historians have learned to use other imperfect sources with wisdom and insight. They can do the same with folkloristic sources.

In the world of folklore, the historian quickly learns that things are not always what they seem. Lydia Parrish's important *Slave Songs of the Georgia Sea Islands*, which she collected from the twentieth-century descendants of the slaves, affords a good example. A fieldworker who observed Parrish closely noted that she knew just what she wanted. "She would not give in one millimeter. The performers must sing the songs of their forefathers or sing nothing. . . . She would make the singers dig deep into the recesses of their minds until they had unearthed the desired treasure."

One day Parrish asked a group of black women for slave songs. They began with "Swing Low Sweet Chariot" and "Gimme Dat Ole Time Religion." Parrish tolerated these "quasi spirituals" but when the singers began "Standing in de Need of Prayer," she said sharply: "Oh no! I don't want that. Sing something your grandmother used to sing." The women had a conference, shook their heads, and said that the years had robbed them of the songs. But Parrish persisted and finally, under great pressure, the women dredged from their memories songs that satisfied the collector. The danger for the historian is that without clear knowledge of her methods (which her book does not supply) one could get the impression that all of the songs she collected were still in the living tradition in the twentieth century.[3]

Historians must also understand that folklorists often gathered and presented materials under their own moral guidelines. Newman White was typical in excluding from his collection many songs "that deal brutally and nauseously with pure sexual lust."[4] John Lomax received songs from a collector who feared that many of them "are too smutty to send through the mail. I left off several verses from the songs I enclosed on that account."[5] Censorship was practiced not only by folklorists but also by their subjects. When Elsie Clews Parsons asked one of her informants for a specific tale, he responded: "Oh, you want dem kin' o' tales too! I could tell you a heap o' dem tales, but I blush fo' you."[6] This urge of people to censor their own lore came not only from a sense of morality but also from the group's perceived need to protect themselves from outsiders. As generations of blacks put it:

> Got one mind for white folks to see,
> 'Nother for what I know is me;
> He don't know, he don't know my mind.[7]

Thus it is crucial for the historian utilizing folklore to know as much as possible about the conditions under which the material was collected and the attitudes of the collector.

Folklorist Tristram Coffin has complained of those of his colleagues whose reformist sentiments make them too prone to see social protest in folksong, but then illustrates the very danger he warns against by insisting that in true folksong, social protest is almost never present since "the folk just don't look at the world the way the reformer does. The folk are simple. They accept their lot."[8] But why approach folklore with either set of assumptions? Isn't the fundamental reason for the historical study of folklore the attempt to understand the consciousness of its creators? With folklore, as with other sources, scholars who are certain of what they will find before they look will inevitably find only that which they already "know."

This pitfall is particularly well illustrated in the area of Afro-American folklore. In 1912 W. H. Thomas collected and published *The Railroad Blues*, containing such lyrics as:

> My mother's dead, my sister's gone astray,
> And that is why this poor boy is here to-day

and commented that it was the only song in his collection "in which I think I detect insincerity. Now the negro may have periods of despondency, but I have never been able to detect them."[9] Five years later, John Lomax printed these lyrics:

> White folks go to college, niggers to de fiel';
> White folks learn to read an' write, niggers learn to steal.
> Ain't it hard, ain't it hard,
> Ain't it hard to be a nigger, nigger, nigger?

and confessed that he found it "difficult to say" why blacks should sing songs of discontent since "There surely exists no merrier-hearted race than the negro," possessed of "a nature upon which trouble and want sit but lightly."[10] When Elsie Clews Parsons failed to find the traditional tales for which she was searching from twentieth-century blacks, she concluded that the folktale was "in the last stage of disintegration." In fact, the new tales and alterations of old tales that she collected were signs not of disintegration but of transformation, affording the historian a superb view of the changes taking place in Afro-American consciousness.[11]

These examples, which could be multiplied many times, make it clear that historians must allow folklore to speak for itself and must understand that it will only speak to those who are willing to take the lore and its creators seriously. Those who confine the history of the intellect to the educated elite and who share *Webster's New International Dictionary*'s conception of the folk as "the masses of people of lower culture" will inevitably miss the rich and complex expression, perception, imagination, and imagery that so often characterize folk thought. Intellectual history, as Joseph R. Levenson defined it, is "the history not of thought, but of men thinking," and few sources reveal the process of people thinking more clearly than the songs, tales, aphorisms, proverbs, jokes, and memorates that collectively constitute folklore.

Historians not only must approach folklore openly but also with knowledge of the cultural and social context in which the lore was created and transmitted. For instance, W. C. Handy has shown that the following song, which he heard in the 1890s—

> Got my dungeon loaded
> Bound to blow you down;
> I just got back
> From Wheeling today.

—would be incomprehensible without the knowledge that "dungeon" meant pistol, that Wheeling, West Virginia, was the site of a prison, and the prisoners often sang of the vengeance they would wreak on the men romancing their women while they were away.[12] Similarly, when Frances Kemble heard her slaves sing:

> Jenny shake her toe at me,
> Jenny gone away

she dismissed it as a nonsense verse. But, as Chadwick Hansen has shown, she probably heard not the English word "toe" but an African-derived word meaning "buttocks," which would explain the hilarity and delight with which slaves sang and heard the verse.[13]

The uses and importance of folklore to the historian can be demonstrated by examining how these sources have allowed recent scholars to move beyond assumptions which for too long structured historical understanding of black life and culture in slavery: the assumption that African culture disappeared almost completely in the English colonies and that slaves were left no choice but to meekly copy white culture; the assumption that the vast gulf between African and European culture made it impossible for a blend of the two cultures to take place; the assumption that black slaves and their descendants had little sense of group cohesion, pride, or history and had no sources of power or authority independent of the whites.

A careful understanding of slave song weakens the foundation of each of these influential beliefs. Though slaves in America engaged in widespread musical exchanges with the whites around them, their song style and performance remained much closer to Africa than to Western Europe. This was so not only because of the isolation in which many slaves lived but more importantly because for all the differences between Afro- and Euro-American music in rhythm, harmony, and performance, there were crucial areas of similarity such as the shared diatonic scale which allowed a syncretic blending of the two musics and which meant that musically the slaves were influencing their masters at least as much as they were being influenced by them.

In function, too, slave music remained close to its African roots. In Africa music served the dual purpose of preserving communal values and of allowing the individual to transcend societal restrictions by expressing feelings which ordinarily could not be verbalized. It was common for African peoples to utilize song, dance, and tales to express their feelings about each other and their leaders. Slaves in the United States preserved this traditional practice everywhere they lived. Priscilla McCullough recalled that when young women on the plantation where she was a slave strayed from the moral code, other slaves "sing bout dat girl and dey tell all bout uh. . . . Den ebrybody know an dat girl sho bettuh change uh ways."[14] Nor were whites safe from the slaves' candor. "We raise de wheat," slaves sang, "Dey gib us de corn";

> We peel de meat,
> Dey gib us de skin;
> And dat's de way
> Dey take us in.[15]

In their music, then, slaves preserved an independent voice in which they could communicate their attitudes to each other, to the whites, and to their God. Close scrutiny of slave spirituals reveals the full extent of this independence. While white spirituals were pervaded by other-worldliness, rejected the temporal present, and focused upon Jesus and Heaven, slave spirituals focused upon this world, identified with the Children of Israel, relived the stories of the Old Testament, and transformed Jesus into an Old Testament warrior. Although white preachers urged slaves to be humble in this world so they might be saved in the next, slaves delighted in singing of David, Daniel, Jonah, Noah, Joshua, and Moses, all of whom won their victories in *this* world.

Spirituals reveal not only how discriminating slaves were in choosing which parts of the white man's religion to emphasize, but also how close slaves remained to aspects of African cosmology. The gods and heroes the slaves sang of were not remote, abstract beings but as intimate, personal, and immediate as the gods of Africa had been. This sense of personal immediacy was based in part upon the sense of time and space the slaves brought with them from Africa where the lines between the past, future, and present were not rigid and the gods and ancestors were part of this world as well as the next.

In the area of religion and folk beliefs, as well as that of music, it is clear that the African and West European systems, long assumed to be totally different, had enough in common to facilitate interchanges between whites and blacks. Both Africans and many of the Europeans they met in America lived in a universe populated by spirits and witches, by supernatural omens and signs, by charms and magic, by conjuring and healing. Thus slaves could accept so many European beliefs not because their African culture had been wiped out but because these beliefs were so familiar and were a source of comfort in a world that often seemed so hostile and unpredictable. They were also a source of independent power. Nature spoke to those who knew how to listen. "Old people had signs for everything then," an ex-slave reported. There were signs forecasting the weather, prophesying bad or good luck, warning of impending whippings or the approach of white patrols, predicting imminent sickness or death. Signs did not have to be accepted passively; they were often calls to action. A screech owl's cry—a sign of death—was countered by turning shoes upside down at your door; a black cat crossing your path was bad luck unless you spit on the spot where your paths met; an itching left eye foretold a whipping which could be avoided by chewing roots which would soften the master's heart.

Being able to "read" and understand the natural universe also helped one deal with sickness. "There were no doctors back there," an ex-slave testified. "If you got sick, you would go dig a hole and dig up roots and fix your own medicine."[16] Thus bags of gum resin were worn by children to protect them from almost every conceivable ailment; herb teas and soups warded off whooping cough; a tarred rope worn around the waist cured rheumatism; a nutmeg hung from the neck was effective for neuralgia; there were innumerable cures for poisons and snakebite. In their folk beliefs and folk medicine, slaves were able to carry on the traditions of their African past, blend them with many of the Euro-American practices they encountered in the New World, and use them to provide their own source of power and protection and to derive some sense of control over their own lives.

Slave folktales are equally revealing to the historian willing to learn something of African as well as American lore. In their tales, nineteenth-century white Americans tended to deal with forces greater than themselves by featuring such gargantuan individuals as Davy Crockett who would boast: "I'm half-horse, half-alligator. . . ." In precisely the same period, slaves dealt with their fears and insecurities not in the characteristic American manner of magnifying the individual but in the African tradition of dealing with the powerful through the guile, wit, and cunning of such physically insignificant tricksters as Brer Rabbit. Once again we find proof that the patterns of African culture did not suddenly disappear in the face of mindless black acculturation to the ways of their white masters.

Finally, historians must learn to analyze not only the content of folklore but also its structure. For instance, slave music continued to feature the overriding African antiphonal (call and response) structure which placed the individual in continual dialogue with the community and allowed for both individual and communal expression. It is simply not reasonable to suppose that this musical structure could have remained so dominant had slavery been able to completely destroy the central sense of community Africans had brought with them. The same lesson can be derived from examining the structure of slave dance performance and looking carefully at the communal setting in which tales were told.

This brief overview indicates how valuable folklore can be to the historian in reconstructing a people's thought and culture. The historical use of folklore helps us to gain some sense of a people's angle of vision, to better understand the inner dynamics of a group and the attitudes of its members, and to comprehend the strategies and mechanisms a people employ to guard their values and maintain their sense of worth. Folklore helps us to overcome what William James called "a certain blindness in human beings" which prevents them from understanding the significance and consciousness of other peoples.

NOTES

1. Howard W. Odum, "Religious Folk-Songs of the Southern Negroes," *American Journal of Religious Psychology and Education* 3 (July, 1909): 265–66.

2. C. Vann Woodward, "History from Slave Sources," *American Historical Review* 79 (April, 1974): 470. Italics added.

3. This description of Parrish's collecting techniques is by C. S. Murray in the WPA manuscripts, South Carolina file, in the Archive of Folk Culture, Library of Congress. See also Lydia Parrish, *Slave Songs of the Georgia Sea Islands* (1942; reprint ed., Hatboro, Pa.: Folklore Associates, 1965).

4. Newman White manuscripts, Houghton Library, Harvard University. See also Newman I. White, *American Negro Folk-Songs* (1928; reprint ed., Hatboro, Pa.: Folklore Associates, 1965), p. 312.

5. John A. Lomax, *Adventures of a Ballad Hunter* (New York: Macmillan, 1947), p. 37.

6. Elsie Clews Parsons, *Folk-Lore of the Sea Islands, South Carolina*, Memoirs of the American Folk-Lore Society, Volume XVI (Cambridge, Mass.: American Folk-Lore Society, 1923), pp. xix–xx, 102–103.

7. See Lawrence W. Levine, *Black Culture and Black Consciousness: Afro-American Folk Thought from Slavery to Freedom* (New York: Oxford University Press, 1977), pp. xii–xiii.

8. Tristram P. Coffin, "Folksong of Social Protest: A Musical Mirage," *New York Folklore Quarterly* 14 (Spring, 1958): 2–9.

9. W. H. Thomas, *Some Current Folk-Songs of the Negro* (The Folk-Lore Society of Texas, 1912), p. 9.

10. John A. Lomax, "Self-Pity in Negro Folk-Songs," *The Nation* 105 (August 9, 1917): 141–45.

11. Elsie Clews Parsons, "Tales from Guilford County, North Carolina," *Journal of American Folklore* 30 (April–June, 1917): 168–200; Levine, *Black Culture and Black Consciousness*, ch. 6.

12. W. C. Handy, *Father of the Blues: An Autobiography* (1941; New York: Collier paperback ed., 1970), p. 147.

13. Frances Anne Kemble, *Journal of a Residence on a Georgian Plantation in 1838–1839* (1863; reprint ed., New York: Knopf, 1961), pp. 163–64; Chadwick Hansen, "Jenny's Toe: Negro Shaking Dances in America," *American Quarterly* 19 (Fall, 1967): 554–63.

14. Georgia Writers' Project, WPA, *Drums and Shadows: Survival Studies among the Georgia Coastal Negroes* (Athens, Georgia: University of Georgia Press, 1940), p. 154.

15. Frederick Douglass, *Life and Times of Frederick Douglass* (rev. ed., 1892; reprint ed., New York: Collier, 1962), pp. 146–47.

16. Fisk University, *Unwritten History of Slavery: Autobiographical Accounts of Negro Ex-Slaves*, ed. Ophelia Settle Egypt, J. Masuoka, and Charles S. Johnson (Nashville, 1945), p. 180; Levine, *Black Culture and Black Consciousness*, pp. 55–80.

Roger D. Abrahams

Interpreting Folklore Ethnographically and Sociologically

The term *folklore* has come to mean the accumulated traditions, the inherited products and practices of a specifiable group, a social unit which has some notion of its own groupness. Not only traditional texts of performance and material objects are studied but the process of making and the doing as well. In the main, we choose to do so as a means of getting at basic notions of the *authentic*. And establishing authenticity has remained a central concern of folklorists. Recent workers in the field have become somewhat less focused on the historic past and more on the processes, social and cultural, of the present. In such a case, folklore is employed as a term for the accumulated wisdom and practice of a social group, one in which there is a close relationship between the producers and the consumers: the makers and the users in the case of material culture; the performer and the audience with regard to expressive culture.

Those who are concerned with the present uses of the practices of the past like to distinguish between two ways of approaching the basic term of the discipline, one which emphasizes the *folk*, the other which underscores *lore*. The first draws on folklore as an essentially *social* (or more pointedly, *sociological*) term; the second is more centered on the cultural dimension. The distinction is important, simply because stressing one or the other may determine how the process and products of tradition are depicted. The study of folklore begins with the collection of these data of tradition. But should the investigator wish to place the lore in its context, a choice is generally made whether to fill in the record by describing the society in which the tradition is maintained, or by situating the traditional practices and performances within the expressive system of the group—that is, within the system of interaction (often what we call the *manners*), and the way such behavior is endowed with meaning and value (the *morals* of the group). Thus we have two larger, significant ways in which folklore in context may be studied: the sociological and the ethnographic. Both relate the materials of tradition to a larger world view or ideology, the former primarily to the entire range of symbolic and value-laden structures and the latter to notions of social order and social norms and deviations.

The term *lore* invites us to look at the expressive dimension of the cultural system in which folklore tradition endures. On the other hand, using *folk* intimates that such tradition exists within describable social units. Observing the enactment of traditions has made us aware that the context of the enactment (whether the situation is one of work or play, performance or celebration) often provides us with some of the basic information as to how we might go about describing the boundaries of the group. That is, working together and playing together (or both) means expending energy in common by observing shared rules and practices. To do this there must exist some dimension of previous experience of such activities, and thus, some preexisting patterns of expectation carried into the interaction by both the makers (players, performers, craftspeople) and the users (audience, spectators, consumers). In this sense, the enactment of traditions provides us with a good deal of our basic feeling for who makes up the group, the community.

Moreover, investigation of the content of the lore often gives us some of the quickest and most forceful evidence of how this group presents itself to itself and then breaks itself up into smaller segments. By this I simply mean that folklore often involves an open depiction of the way in which, say, an opposition between men and women is projected by the group, or between the older and younger members of the community, between different moieties (like clubs, fraternities, schools), and so on. And, perhaps most important, in a good deal of lore (especially in jokes) one begins to get a feeling for who the significant nonmembers of the group are: those who are depicted as the enemy, the strangers, or the despised ones. One also learns who the half-members are, the ones like deranged people, morons, bogie-men, criminals, alcoholics, or drugheads. Studying folklore by picking up on such factors means using lore to understand the social structure of the society. In this sense folklore is studied sociologically. The ethnographic approach, on the other hand, underscores how folklore operates within a behavior and performance system. The two overlap at many points and must be regarded as complementary ways of studying the content and context of the materials of tradition.

COMING AT FOLKLORE ETHNOGRAPHICALLY

"Ethnography is the task of describing a particular culture," note Spradley and McCurdy in their introduction-by-doing manual, *The Cultural Experience*.[1] This definition is so straightforward and uncomplicated it gives us the impression that ethnography might be done by anyone. In a sense, all of us *do* ethnography all of the time—whenever we observe behaviors or performances with sufficient self-consciousness to recount the happenings later and make judgments of the goings-on. But doing folklore and ethnography in a professional manner implies a high level of self-conscious monitoring and reporting, and a deeper sense that what is recorded is a part of the system of action and interaction between human and human, man and nature. We regard culture as a whole way of life in which all of the pieces of behavior somehow fit together.

Adequate ethnographic description takes into account the existence of organic relationships between the inception and outcome of action, relationships that underline the purposes of the activity. Therefore, we assume that a system and a set of regularities underlie the actions. The task of ethnography is to collect data and to describe them in sufficient detail that the materials may be reported in their relation to the system. In essence, the purpose becomes one of "writing the rules" of a culture.

The question "What is a culture?" is easy to comprehend in the abstract and extremely difficult to answer in the specific. A particular culture is a group that shares a language and has developed a sense of groupness or community. But defining our purpose in such a cut-and-dried fashion can mean that we choose to do fieldwork only in those places which exhibit such a shared language and such activities in common. These groups already have developed the self-conscious sense of community that provides the collector with quick insights into the way the system works, because native commentary on behavior and performance is as collectable as the activity itself.

By limiting ethnography to such enclaves, our data for culture and, by extension, for folklore come from already existing groups. What is meant by "a culture," "a community," and especially "a folk group" is now, in great part, determined by the information derived from ethnographies which demonstrate only that such groups do in fact exist—an obviously circular argument. A great number of these enclaves have been usefully described, but many other kinds of units and individuals, who live neither within boundaried communities nor as a segment of a complex society, have received little attention from ethnographers. To pursue the ideal of the ethnographer, one should describe the entire range of cultural situations, not just those in which people from stable communities get together to entertain and instruct each other.

To a certain extent, a shift in this imbalance has already begun to occur in folklore study, for the very notion of what constitutes a folk group has been modified. Though the homogeneous, self-sufficient agrarian community remains our ideal collecting situation, folklorists for some time have been observing and describing the emerging lore of part-time social units and segments within complex societies and cultures: groups which engage in intensive work, play, or recreation together. In the main, such study has been primarily concerned with the use of the emergent lore in giving evidence of (and in producing) a sense of social solidarity.

There are, of course, crucial differences of emphasis between folklorists who attack their field problems ethnographically and ethnographers who find it useful to include the collection of folklore as part of the field experience. We can best reveal this difference by noting where the energies of the fieldworker are directed. For example, if an ethnographer is engaged in a special study of the governance system of a Native American community, it would be useful not only to look at household relationships, kinship, and quasi-kinship networks, ways in which friendship groups are established, but also how traditional speechmaking enters into the decision-making processes of the group, and by extension at the expressive means of conveying powers and duties. On the other hand, the folklorist perceives the ethnographic task, before the fact, as one of observing and collecting the entire range of traditional expressive acts and events as they are put into practice by members of a culture. The ethnographic strategy would be to make as complete a catalogue of these acts, scenes, and events, and as full a lexicon of native terms for these as possible, to produce an inventory of expressive forms and situations.

Culture used to be commonly defined as the ways people devised to live with each other in groups. Under such a broad definition the ethnographic strategy usually employed is to gather as much information as possible about the makeup of the community and the way in which family, religion, government, and economy operate. Recently anthropology has witnessed a subtle but openly stated shift in the definition of culture. As put forth by those called *the new ethnographers*, culture has come to mean what one needs to know on a second-by-second, minute-by-minute basis to get along and be understood in a group. Among other things, this new definition underscores the importance of the "givens" of culture, including traditional products and practices. Whereas the systems of greatest interest in ethnography had been the institutions of a culture, now the systems of manners and decorum come more to the fore. Through structured and regulated interactions the larger systems are put into practice. "Family," the new ethnographer implicitly argues, is ultimately defined by how people in certain relations treat each other, and how they operate when group members break such rules of manners. Ethnographically inclined folklorists have been profoundly affected by these newly articulated concerns of the anthropologist-ethnographers. We have come to recognize how discovery procedures and analytic techniques might be employed so that the patterns of behavior of everyday expressive life may be related to the way in which the larger display events (from festivals and rituals to games and sports, as well as performance occasions) are related in basic structure and in thematic content. Thus a useful dialogue has been established between folklorists and the group of ethnographers calling their subdiscipline "the ethnography of communication."

SOME SOCIOLOGICAL APPROACHES

Folklorists have also been increasingly concerned with the ways in which lore enters into the process of making—and sometimes unmaking—the social structure of a group. Indeed, analyzing folklore with regard to the light it casts on social structure has made folklorists more sensitive to how narrowly *folk* has been defined. Definitions restricted to a peasantry have been gradually broadened to include any nonliterate group which celebrates its sense of community through activities-in-common. Even as the concept of folk has become more broadly based and less tied to a highly stratified society, however, the social units which have continued to interest folklorists have been those that share with the peasantry a geographical or social isolation: mountain people, Afro-Americans, children, ethnic minorities—especially those who have chosen to stay together in their own enclaves because of religious connections. Thus, we know a great deal about the life and lore of some of the most insular communities in America, like the Amish and the Shakers. These enclaves could hardly be called important in the formation of American ideas and a sense of national cultural identity. Yet it is their very smallness and cultural difference which has most attracted folklorists.

The same might be said of the occupational groups which folklorists have chosen to study, for they too are depicted as folklike in their isolation, in the homogeneity of their values and life-ways, and in the nonurban character of their folklife and lore: cowboys, for instance, or lumberjacks, sailors, hoboes, fishermen, and miners, those primarily male occupations which attracted the rootless (and some would say shiftless) element of American society. Folklorists, like sociologists, have been fascinated by the life of the outsiders and the outcasts, the deviants and the roisterers. But whereas sociologists came to the study of these groups from a theoretical fascination with those who most test the stability and the norms of the social structure, folklorists came to look at these communities because of the creative or productive dimension of their lives and have delighted in the implicit relationship between social isolation or "marginality" and creativity in performance, festivity, and other kinds of play. Here, too, folklorists have extended their definition of "the folk" to include less than full-time groups—in this case, communities of self-designated derelicts ("hoboes," "gypsies"), groups made up of citizens or rank-and-file workers who in one phase of their lives place themselves in the position of "outsider," if only temporarily. Folklorists are attracted to those people in marginal positions in society who tend to be segregated (or self-segregated) and produce more in-group expression in direct relation to the amount of time spent together under intense conditions. From time to time, calls are sent out from members of the profession to study elite and professional groups, but few have so far taken up the challenge.

Another sociological perspective has been employed by folklorists, often the same investigators who have pursued ethnographic methods. This approach focuses on the role of the tradition-bearer in society; especially the performer. Most of these monographic studies are of singers, especially bluesmen in the South and local songsters in New England and the Canadian Maritime provinces, and they attempt to relate the context of the songs to the way of life of the singer living between communities, and thus to the similarities and differences between social roles and relationships as they are lived and as they are depicted.

Finally, one other social area that has interested folklorists—perhaps more in our theorizing than our practice—relates to the ways in which folklore embodies stereotypes both of others and of self. Here the pioneering overview of the subject by William Hugh Jansen points out the important factors of sociological perception by which the manifest content of much story lore explores the relationship between out-group (or exoteric) notions of group traits and the in-group (or esoteric) complex of traits projected by the group both upon itself and significant others. This stereotyping dynamic Jansen calls the esoteric-exoteric (or S-X) factor of folklore.[2] He notes that by closely attending to the ways in which a social group depicts itself and reacts to others' depictions of it, and by combining this with the counter-stereotypes this group has of those who impose such a stereotype, folklorists can add a great deal to an understanding of intergroup dynamics. Folkloristic studies following the path pointed out by Jansen have noted that such stereotyping is a very "deep" dimension of the cultural dynamic, and that even in situations in which it becomes bad manners to continue to stereotype others in this way, the pattern of trait-attribution simply becomes deflected onto other marginal creatures: morons, drunkards, dopeheads, crazies, strange large animals like elephants and whales who suddenly become like members of the human family; or onto ethnic groups (like the Italians or the Poles) who have already been assimilated into the American polity and who will "take" the jokes, in the main, as goodhearted joshing.

Both the ethnographic and sociological ways of coming at folklore, then, cause the investigator to look closely at the sociocultural *setting*—or, more actively, the *situating*—of the lore. They direct the observer and analyst both to how enactment and content features are part of the process of living in groups, and how these characteristics reflect some of the most important ways in which the social trouble spots are named, projected, and played with. The dimension of this process thus far given short shrift by folklorists has been the place of *playing with, playing at,* and *playing around.* Most of the lore which has been collected in the history of folkloristics comes from play settings and situations; yet folklorists have only recently developed preliminary strategies for discovering and describing the way in which these play worlds operate. To do this will necessitate a fuller understanding of how the distinctions between work and play are constituted.

Moreover, a few folklorists have come to recognize that some of the most interesting traditional forms arise and persist not *within* groups but *between* them. Jazz, for instance, is a musical form that seems to arise at the intersection between black and white communities, and the same is true of sea chanties. Fairs and festivals are also events which call for a playing together of people who otherwise do not know each other. With the growing interest in studying celebrations and festivals, we are certain to see new sociological insights within folkloristics.

NOTES

1. James P. Spradley and David W. McCurdy, eds., *The Cultural Experience: Ethnography in a Complex Society* (Chicago: Science Research Associates, 1972), p. 3.

2. William Hugh Jansen, "The Esoteric-Exoteric Factor in Folklore," in *The Study of Folklore*, ed. Alan Dundes (Englewood Cliffs, N.J.: Prentice-Hall, 1965), pp. 43–51.

Archie Green

Interpreting Folklore Ideologically

Scholars throughout the world hold ideological positions, although it is the belief of many empiricists that they are immune from the virus of ideology. Within the United States, most folklorists (whether trained in language, literature, or anthropology) place a high premium on detachment from politics, which distancing they see as precondition to the search for truth. Aversion to "ideology" flows from the unmanageable breadth built into the word; often it connotes malicious propaganda, distorted analysis, and cruel subversion. Yet this same word also indicates the systematic theories which gird any polity—the underlying charter of a tribal people or a giant sovereign state.

Folklorists eschew "ideology" as commonly used for two reasons: they do not wish to see themselves as dealing with insubstantial forms; they do not wish to appear as committed to insidious guides. Nevertheless, "ideology" in its technical sense cannot be expunged from the vocabulary. We hold philosophic positions whether stated clearly, carelessly, or else unstated. Further, we live in societies—ours and theirs—denominated "open" or "closed," "libertarian" or "authoritarian," "democratic" or "totalitarian"—umbrellas for the complex structures of thought and deed which shelter everyday life.

Few American folklorists interpret their data by conscious metaphysical design. They do not sit in an archive straining songs or stories through an ideological sieve. Rather, they accept mainstream norms as natural or orderly. In this sense, scholars absorb values as they breathe ever-present air. Only a handful of folklorists during the past century in this country have identified with radical theses challenging majoritarian consensus. From William Wells Newell and Francis James Child to the semioticians and the symbolists of today, most American folklorists have accepted dominant ideology: empiricism, pragmatism, individualism, parliamentary democracy, progressive reform, free market economics. There are, of course, alternate names for these intertwined constructs; they combine and recombine differently from decade to decade. We use no unitary catchphrase, like "apple pie," to encompass America's major theories. Nevertheless, our central ideology, best labeled "secular liberalism," is as cemented together by deep assumptions as is Soviet life by Marxism.

Historians, while considering national continuities and discontinuities, have sought to identify synoptic beliefs. These are well described by David Potter: Americans before the Civil War "cherished a fierce devotion to the principles of personal independence and social equalitarianism. They shared a great pride in the Revolutionary heritage, the Constitution, and 'republican institutions,' and an ignorance about Europe, which they regarded as decadent and infinitely inferior to the United States. They also shared a somewhat intolerant, orthodox Protestantism, a faith in rural virtues, and a commitment to the gospel of hard work, acquisition, and success."[1] Other writers have reworked these elements endlessly, altering emphasis by period or region. Sociologist Daniel Bell, focusing on the interplay of grinding work and pleasurable acquisition, today sees the state's needs as contradictory in its requirement for puritanical producers and hedonistic consumers—all united by notions of individual fulfillment.[2]

Folklore in the United States has never been surveyed within the special frame of the history of intellectual thought. When this task is undertaken, we shall deal with figures such as John Locke, Thomas Jefferson, William James, John Dewey, Franz Boas, and Horace Kallen. Despite differences, these liberal thinkers unite under the encompassing terms "empiricism" and "pragmatism." Whether or not folklorists are conscious of basic philosophic debts, they are not scholars lacking ideology. In fact, the study of folklore is weakened when it neglects the widest frame within which expressive culture is generated, enacted, and comprehended. To link the words "folklore" and "ideology" then demands dual explication: (1) philosophic concerns of folklorists, and (2) the state's response to folk culture.

No simple graph exists upon which to pin the ideas of leading folklorists from right to left. Not only do we lack a published history of the discipline in the United States, but particular biographical articles generally ignore partisan questions. To illustrate: Joel Chandler Harris popularized Negro tales in the very years when English and German notions of folklore as science reached our shores. We know the full details of his life and have questioned the authenticity of Brer Rabbit texts, but we have not placed Harris in the stream of the debate which engulfed Booker T. Washington and W. E. B. DuBois. While black people struggled to firm notions of accommodation and nationalism or integration and separatism, Uncle Remus settled in mainstream mythology as an exemplar of gentility and adjustment. In paying close attention to Brer Rabbit as a trickster hero, we overlooked Uncle Remus as a model citizen.

In contemporary folklore study, we must pose ideological questions about pioneers, especially those with influence beyond the academy. Was George Lyman Kittredge a proud Tory like his Harvard peer Barrett Wendell? When Kittredge studied New England witchcraft, did he ponder Henry Cabot Lodge's antipathy to immigrants—latter-day witches in the New Jerusalem? Why did John Lomax, exposed to populism in his Texas youth, come to scorn Franklin Delano Roosevelt's reforms? Lomax, in championing American balladry, typed songs of down-and-out classes (outcast girl, dope fiend, jail bird, tramp). Was this not an implicit statement bridging populist and New Deal values? Did Professor Stith Thompson, conversant with Native American literature, comment on John Collier's critical plans in the mid-1930s to reorganize the Bureau of Indian Affairs? Did Thompson see Collier as one who literally fashioned the then-future setting for tribal tales?

In time, folklorists will delve into their discipline's guiding precepts, and unearth foundations of ideological concern held even by scholars of anti-ideological (value-free) persuasion. Only recently did historian John A. Williams attempt to divide the discipline into two camps—comparative (historical-geographical) and functionalist (radical)—likening left-wing political response of the 1930s to right-wing (Cold War) response of the 1950s. Professor Richard M. Dorson, in rebuttal, made the distinction that New Left historians "approached the folk with an a priori philosophy; the folklorist . . . approached them with an open mind." To elaborate, Dorson identified desired professionalism as "the search for truth and standards of excellence."[3] This poses well the classic confrontation between turgid polemics and dispassionate truth, or activism and the ivory tower.

The period during which America's shared ideology was most questioned was that of the Great Depression, when a number of alternatives surfaced: socialism, communism, fascism. Those associated with foreign powers posed the greatest threat to our well-being. In the 1930s, Marxist ideology made a deeper inroad into American intellectual life than did fascist thought. The "Red Decade" precipitated an extensive history; however, the major folkloric thesis about this period by Richard A. Reuss remains unpublished.[4]

Charles Seeger, like other intellectuals, was touched by Marxist thought and, ultimately, pulled away or synthesized a residue into new statements. Responding to the deep poverty about him in New York City, and to the failure of public servants to explain the Crash, Seeger turned to the left. He joined the Composers Collective in offering revolutionary music to the masses and Marxist analysis to the temple. With "On Proletarian Music," he posited a sterile view of culture as a decorative superstructure mounted tenuously on a concrete base of economic production. Communists in the years 1928–34 believed capitalism to be in its final stage, and employed a mechanistic and sectarian rhetoric to trumpet views. Late in 1935, Seeger accepted a position in Washington within the New Deal's Resettlement Administration, where he shifted to anti-fascist and united-front formulas. In New York he had asserted that melancholy folksongs helped "slaves endure their lot." In Washington he heard Appalachian song as a vibrant bonding voice in migrant camps and rural homesteads.

In examining one individual's transition from revolutionary to reformist postures, we contrast rival interpretive modes for the data of folklore. Also, by placing Marxist attention to folksong in a time frame, we learn something of the integration of tactical and theoretical concerns, often in seeming opposition. Eventually, agit-prop and popular-front material spilled over into the folksong revival, finding a way to 1960s protest song. Yet to be resolved is the paradox that, during Cold War years, some folksong enthusiasts merged radical and conservative values, often on the festival platform. Also, this platform on the National Mall gave Congress in the 1970s a palpable sense of folklife.

In the years of Vietnam and Watergate, when New Left activists extended classical Marxism, folklorists seemed largely immune to these European intellectual currents. This point is underscored by reference to two contributions by scholars outside our field. Tim Patterson examined country music from the perspectives of communists Georg Lukács and Antonio Gramsci, asserting that Nashville had robbed the folk of its consciousness by reifying its culture, by turning emotion into a commodity, and by using the product to establish class hegemony.[5] Carl Boggs, with more depth, examined Afro-American blues living "beneath the surface of bourgeois cultural mediations."[6] He pegged his cogent analysis of blues—simultaneously enervating and freeing—to a lengthy review of Paul Garon's *Blues and the Poetic Spirit*, a book synthesizing ideas from Karl Marx, Sigmund Freud, and André Breton. I find it significant that criticism of the material of American folklore from the ideological perspective of Patterson and Boggs has not yet appeared in our folklore journals. In a recent exchange on the term "folk," between ethnomusicologist Charles Keil and Richard M. Dorson, the former uses Marxist thought to make "leverage points for liberation." In time, radical folklorists will follow this lead.

To move from the apparatus of contemporary neo-Marxism to the mind-set of public sector folklore is a long step in time, place, and thought. Folklorists in state agencies, like their academic peers, accept mainstream ideology and work within the bounds of secular liberalism. In dealing historically with the American government's response to folk culture, we learn that its role differs substantially from that of European nations. King Louis XIV and his minister Colbert, during the 1660s, established an enduring system of French royal patronage of fine art. We did not employ a parallel model (democratic) until the mid-1960s and, to date, have not fully accepted the matter of indirect subsidies by the National Endowment for the Arts. Nor did we emulate Finland's nineteenth-century path, where a dedicated cadre of scholars used folk literature of the *Kalevala* to vitalize nationalism (a process carefully detailed by Professor W. A. Wilson). Generally, we have relegated our legend making away from the government—George Washington's cutting the cherry tree to Paul Bunyan's felling the towering fir—to popular-culture hucksters.

Conscious of America's egalitarian heritage, we have reacted most negatively to the state's manipulative use of culture in fascist and communist societies. The United States has not followed European states by establishing a ministerial post for culture, but, instead, has developed an alternate set of decentralized agencies and tax codes in this area. Normally, we divide culture into segments—high, pop, folk, tribal—and assign supportive roles to philanthropy and to private enterprise, respectively, for high and popular material. Largely, folk expression has been unsupported by the federal government, while tribal life has been simultaneously protected and eroded. In the main, federal bureaus have themselves served national assimilative strategies.

Only in the 1970s did the government pay direct legislative attention to folk culture, stimulated partly by the previous decade's "folksong revival," by the search for ethnic roots, by the rhetoric of diversity, and by the coming together of movements for natural, historical, and cultural conservation. These disparate concerns led to statutory action by Congress in the American Folklife Preservation Act (January 2, 1976). Essentially, Congress asserted that folklife (traditional expressive culture shared within groups—familial, ethnic, occupational, religious, regional) was worthy of preservation and presentation. Further, the act established at the Library of Congress an American Folklife Center to undertake this assignment.

Folklife legislation was first introduced by Senator Ralph Yarborough (Texas) on March 20, 1969. Previously, he had been impressed by the Festival of American Folklife staged by the Smithsonian Institution. In 1967, the festival's director Ralph Rinzler had borrowed the label "folklife" from Professor Don Yoder, who had learned it in European usage (material culture, regional ethnology). Smithsonian staff members extended "folklife" broadly to encompass dramatic and musical performance, craft demonstration, decorative art, and ritualistic behavior by a wide variety of people. Through four Congresses (91, 92, 93, 94), individual legislators equated the words "folklore" and "folklife," and defined each largely in commonsense terms of rurality, ethnicity, and artisanship.

In contrast to the Folklife Center's statutory base, the previous public unit dealing with folk material, the Archive of Folk Culture (orginally named the Archive of American Folk-Song), was established in 1928 administratively (and penuriously) within the Library of Congress's Music Division. Robert Winslow Gordon, a Harvard-trained ballad scholar with an affinity for the lore of ordinary citizens and an interest in technology's effect on oral tradition, was the Archive's organizer. Gordon did not serve beyond the Depression years; his successors in the 1930s were father and son John and Alan Lomax.

By placing the Center and the Archive at poles, we scale and evaluate federal effort. The former was created after legislative debate and launched by tax funds; the latter was created by internal decision and funded initially by private philanthropy. Without real growth until the New Deal's experimental years, the Archive lapsed back into quietude after World War II. The Archive, by asserting the worth of American folksong, rooted itself in the long campaign to free belletristic works from European authority. Although Gordon hunted songs, his "ancestors" were Irving, Hawthorne, Longfellow, Melville, and Twain—builders of American literature. The Center, at its start in 1976, benefited from timely attention to Horace Kallen's concept of cultural pluralism—a key formula used to modify previous national models of Anglo-conformism and melting pot synthesis. In the gradual shift from the Archive's position to that of the Center, we can see public sector folklore pragmatically tempering ideology's metal.

To appreciate tax-supported collecting of folklore is to know the colloquial phrase, "working on the project." Between 1933 and 1943, Congress set up the Works Progress Administration primarily for relief employment. Units in art, writing, music, and theater all gathered data and distributed findings through state guidebooks, slave narratives, historical building surveys, sound recordings, documentary photographs, and hortatory drama. Folklorist Ben Botkin, Harvard-trained and versed in southwestern regionalism, brought a lively sense of social ethics and concern for the "forgotten man" to his position as WPA folklore editor. One example of an invaluable collection compiled by the WPA is the Index of American Design, holding thousands of careful drawings of handicrafted objects. Holger Cahill, the son of Icelandic immigrants and a pioneer in museum folk art exhibition, assembled this New Deal treasure (now housed in the National Gallery of Art).

The prime governmental agency in folklore in the United States during the nineteenth century was Major John Wesley Powell's Bureau of American Ethnology (1879) within the Smithsonian Institution. Powell, an objective scientist dedicated to studying Indian tribal languages, was also a partisan of native life. His dualism is typical of early scholarly and liberal attitudes toward the folk. He considered Indian life doomed and, as an antiquarian, wished to save its last remnants; conversely, he recognized the intrinsic worth of Indian culture and, as an activist, he sought to keep it alive.

Pioneer attention to folk culture by federal agents appears in the work of William Francis Allen, Charles Picard Ware, and Lucy McKim Garrison. Their book, *Slave Songs of the United States* (1867), grew out of a healthy mix of abolitionist conviction and practical experience as teachers of contraband slaves at the Carolina Sea Islands during the Civil War. Although some wartime attention to Negro lore was funded by the government, no one in America was then ready to advocate a discrete public unit committed to cultural preservation. The War Department, and later the Freedmen's Bureau, dealt every day with members of folk society, but saw the government's mission as that of preparing former slaves for large society. Allen, Ware, and McKim accepted this goal but mediated its assimilative function by a concomitant belief in Negro worth. Lucy McKim could hear the differences in African and European song, and puzzled to understand New World interaction. Beyond study, she believed deeply in the intrinsic value of folk culture: a spiritual held meaning transcending chains.

This sketch from the Folklife Preservation Act back to Civil War collecting of slave songs is highly compressed. Central in importance to the chronology is this kernel: Sea Island collectors in the 1860s expended federal tax funds, while others in the 1970s used similar money to bring Sea Islanders to the National Mall. The United States drifted haltingly to any forms of artistic support—libraries, museums, endowments; within these major institutions attention to the folk has been mainly negative and, more recently, casual. Nevertheless, we generalize that public effort on behalf of folk culture has reflected in large measure the shared ideological assumptions which shore the state.

Attention to the connection between folklore and ideology within the public arena relegates to the sidelines consideration of activity in academic and commercial institutions. To comment on the private sector is, in part, to employ an assumption of "natural" use of folk material as against use labeled "artificial." For example, a sea chanty paces rhythmic work, but when the Yale Glee Club sings the same chanty its function changes to that of mild entertainment for those outside the maritime community. Shift in function for given material is constant in a multilayered society, and ideological design may be attributed to such change when lore becomes harnessed to large ends.

Two interpretive illustrations make this point. In 1910 John Lomax published his initial collection *Cowboy Songs*, with a preface by ex-President Theodore Roosevelt. Songs in these pages served neither to herd cattle nor to cheer cowboys, but to assert that homespun poetry held an honorable pedigree, and to help establish a national mythology. Specifically, this collection, like the dime novel or Wild West Show, highlighted the cowboy's Americanism. In the mid-1920s Henry Ford subsidized old-time fiddlers in performance. His Model T had already broken patterns of rural life and conservative morality. Troubled by such change, the industrialist found in string-band and square-dance music a tested substance—a balm evocative of the past, yet appropriate to the politics of his friend President Calvin Coolidge. Accordingly, we can follow one item of expressive culture from natural use to ideological symbol, if we employ sophisticated analytic tools which account for origin, form, utility, and meaning.

In drawing together the guiding assumptions used by academicians with those used in public agencies, I have sought binding threads from Lucy McKim's time to the present. Abolitionist collector, Indian ethnographer, popular journalist, archive editor, festival planner, and college teacher emerge as close cousins. Some students of folklore express surprise upon learning that they inhabit a powerful mansion, for, in day-to-day work, they call attention to people set apart or in minority sets. We seem especially drawn to the culture of the neglected; after we gravitate to lonesome ditties, to legends plowed under, we declare ourselves folklorists. Still, to be drawn to minority life does not automatically turn scholar into rebel. In the United States, for two centuries, assorted populists, agrarians, greenbackers, free-thinkers, progressives, and visionaries have competed with anarchists and socialists for the agora. Throughout, it has been easier to articulate change in Lockean than in Marxian terms.

During the 1960s, tension springing from rival perceptions of disciplinary role was channeled within the American Folklore Society into debate over the single word "applied." In this coded usage we have been less fortunate than peers in anthropology. Edward Spicer talks objectively about the triadic application of knowledge: academic channels, popular forums, organized interaction between scholars and civic policy-makers.[7] From 1935 to 1938, an Applied Anthropology Unit functioned in the Office of Indian Affairs. In the 1970s the Center for Applied Linguistics prepared handbooks on contract with public agencies. By contrast, folklorists have eschewed the formulaic term "applied," equating it with "ideology" as debasing scholarship.

By coming to grips with pejorative overtones in the word "ideology," we strengthen understanding of interpretive tools both in the classroom and in the federally funded office. When we comprehend the contradiction posed by differences in values between marginal folk and mainstream scholars, we untangle our own ideological roots. Francis James Child as well as John Wesley Powell (and their successors) produced song or tale anthologies, ballad studies, language handbooks, collections of vernacular objects, and art portfolios. These works, in addition to holding great documentary value, were animated by commitment to the souls of slaves and Indians, of balladeers and craftsmen. Not only did the folk hold special status in the eyes of scholars, but generally a tradition carrier was set apart physically from campus or laboratory. Symbolically, folk artists were as hidden in verdant hollows as Jack Tales or cornstalk dolls.

Issues of status and class continue to demand the most serious attention from folklorists, for these touch the bedrock of social organization. Many scholars confine themselves to the classroom, but even these folklorists by subject-matter preference work among people touched by marginality. This voluntary choice imposes the necessity to question whether full integration of folk artistry within national life is desirable, as well as to negate the limits of esthetic standards which base culture only in settings of wealth and power.

To close, American folklorists, from the beginning, have worked mainly within empirical and pragmatic frames. Further, they have been content to fill in taxonomic details of expressive life rather than to ponder the meaning of such life. Individual scholars, on campus and in public bureaus, have sought to complement their study with concern for minority culture. This tie of scholarship and action is not often facile, nor have its practitioners always been articulate in their course. It has been easier for us to paint with small than with large brushes.

The challenge to folklorists is constant; in collection and interpretation we face major American polarities: assimilative/pluralistic, sophisticated/naive, central/marginal. Daily questions of ideology are unending and relentless. The debate at the turn of the century between conservationists and timber trusts continues today between Sierra Club land-ethic enthusiasts and lunch-bucket job developers. Even folklorists who wish to avoid politics may be caught on both sides of the barrier—some folk wish to live undisturbed in mountain cabins, while others seek to bring blue-collar factories to the mountains. The dilemma for the folk is often excruciating; folklorists usually have the luxury to distance themselves from problems on the firing line.

Within their home of liberal thought, cloistered folklorists have occupied many parlors: self-conscious antiquarianism, sentimental romanticism, show-business hucksterism, Anglo-conformism, melting-pot fusionism, cultural pluralism. A few souls have also wandered to radical closets. On the whole, we have not explored attic or cellar links in the terms "folklore" and "ideology," nor have we identified the hidden value positions of progenitors. Whether we tag ourselves variously as teachers, journalists, curators, archivists, preservationists, presenters, or cultural documentarians, we feel, in the 1980s, that we cannot escape our chosen mission of explaining American tradition. To articulate appreciation of language and literature, of art and artifact, prepares us to shed "ideology" of its negative connotation and to understand this word in its technical sense. Precision in language is prelude to clarity in ideological position. Ultimately, American scholars spin the fibers of popular sovereignty and democratic equity, of enlightenment rights and communal needs. While interpreting the folk's cultural emblems, folklorists also embroider diverse ideological banners.

NOTES

1. David M. Potter, *The Impending Crisis 1848–1861* (New York: Harper & Row, 1976), p. 472.

2. See Daniel Bell, *The Cultural Contradictions of Capitalism* (New York: Basic Books, 1976).

3. See John A. Williams, "Radicalism and Professionalism in Folklore Studies: A Comparative Perspective," *Journal of the Folklore Institute* 11 (1975): 211–39. The quoted material is from Richard M. Dorson's "Comment on Williams" in the same issue, pp. 236, 238.

4. Richard A. Reuss, "American Folklore and Left-Wing Politics: 1927–1957" (Ph.D. diss., Indiana University, 1971).

5. Tim Patterson, "Notes on the Historical Application of Marxist Cultural Theory," *Science and Society* 39 (1975): 257–91.

6. Carl Boggs, "The Blues Tradition: From Poetic Revolt to Cultural Impasse," *Socialist Review* 8 (1978): 115–34.

7. Edward H. Spicer, "Early Applications of Anthropology in North America," in *Perspectives on Anthropology*, ed. Anthony F. C. Wallace (Washington, D.C.: American Anthropological Association, 1977), pp. 116–41.

PART III METHODS OF RESEARCH

In a semiliterate letter to her brother who had encouraged her to collect folklore as a therapeutic measure, Minnie Hyatt Small set forth in all her innocence and total ignorance of the subject her experiences "in the field." Her field was Adams County in northwestern Illinois, and she produced—under her brother's name, though the work was mainly hers—a masterpiece of local collecting of beliefs and belief tales, the amateur classic, *Folklore of Adams County Illinois* (1935, rev. ed. 1965). Such a work would never be accepted today by professional folklorists, and some measure of how the study of folklore has progressed may be gained by contrasting their field reports with that volume of some 12,000 texts laid out seriatim, giving only the sparest hint of a source ("Negro," "German") and no other comment. The platform for the new fieldwork model is firmly announced by Richard Bauman in his opening essay on "The Field Study of Folklore in Context," which avers that the text represents merely the tip of the iceberg. Under the tip lies a whole complex of behavioral patterns that folklorists must expose before they can begin to understand, and explain to their readers, how the beliefs, tales, songs, sayings, and other traditions manifest themselves in the culture and what they mean to the people. Disembodied collections in the old sense are dead. Modern collectors must relate their folklore to the life and thought of the community, and Bauman outlines interrogative procedures for achieving this end.

In his observations on collecting musical folklore and folksong, D. K. Wilgus also stresses the obligation to record folk music in context, rather than in a studio situation, and to supplement such recording with interviews to expand knowledge of the context. He further points out the difficulty of drawing an easy line between folk and other musics—popular, commercial, professional, ethnic—and counsels the collector to err on the inclusive rather than the exclusive side. But tales, songs, and music are simple matters compared to the still largely untouched area of field research on artifacts, ranging from gravestones to whole landscapes, that Henry Glassie urges folklorists to enter, as a means of giving solid underpinning to free-floating oral traditions. Glassie advocates not simply a reporting on the manner of making a banjo or log house but a perception of the social and moral values expressed by these objects. Hence the fieldworker must interrogate makers and users, and investigate documentary sources, to complete artifactual research.

No longer, as in Minnie Hyatt Small's day, can the folklore collector stroll into the field with pad and pencil. Now the fieldworker calls on an arsenal of technological aids: still camera, tape recorder, videorecorder, motion picture camera. These resources provide much fuller context, aurally and visually, for the folkloric event than a written ethnography can convey, but at the same time they add to the intrusive elements that distort the event. Articles by Carl Fleischhauer, Richard Blaustein, and Sharon Sherman consider the merits and liabilities of these audiovisual machines, and give technical pointers on the selection of equipment and its deployment in the field situation. They touch on such mundane matters as the advisability of unplugging a noisy refrigerator before recording, along with more philosophical concerns, as how best to capture the essence of the event without engaging in media overkill. Once in Okinawa, where a Japanese folklore group was conducting a folk-cultural tour, I beheld a *matsuri*—a village ritual—involving half a dozen farmers offering rice bowls to a shrine deity under an arch. A dozen Japanese scholars and technicians in business suits holding film and still cameras of sophisticated make zoomed in on the peasants, encircling them and drawing closer until the cameras practically touched their faces. Had I possessed a camera myself I would have shot the picture-takers as an example of media overkill in its most aggressive form. This particular *matsuri* had already been filmed and photographed extensively; I held in my hand a picture book showing the scene that was now being shot yet again.

In writing about American folklore films Sharon Sherman moves from the level of technical suggestion in filmmaking to the level of critical analysis of completed films. This inventory of folkloric films, now of fairly impressive extent, provides a new kind of research resource for folklorists, to supplement and complement the printed word. Thus students of the folktale can view the narrative performances depicted in *Ray Lum, Mule Trader*, and scholars concerned with ethnic behavior can behold the variety of Serbian traditions captured in *The Popovich Brothers of South Chicago*. Sherman indicates criteria by which folkloric film documents may be evaluated in terms of content and form.

In a related essay exploring another underused source, Archie Green surveys the poorly charted area of sound recordings of folk music, which run the gamut from field-recorded discs and tapes to commercial releases. All kinds of recordings within the continuum have contributed to the knowledge of American folksong and folk music, Green demonstrates, and he points to scholarly critics in record review columns who assess the value for research purposes in recordings made under very different conditions, and by quite different artists. Popular recordings of folksongs, such as Merle Travis's "Nine Pound Hammer" and Paul Robeson's "Water Boy," both preserved and changed tradition, and so present intriguing problems for the folklorist, comparable to those arising from the interaction of literary and folk versions of traditions.

Many field-collected materials find their way into special repositories known as folklore archives, and the scholarly folklorist must consult such archives at one point or another in his researches. While American archives have not attained the professional scope and stature of their European counterparts, some fifteen now exist as respectable resources strong in their regional area. Using archives requires special investigative techniques, as Langlois and LaRonge explain in their collaborative article. Only historians among the sister disciplines rely on archival sources to any degree, and these consist of state and federal documents bearing little resemblance to the texts and ethnographies consulted by folklorists. The recent emergence of oral history archives does invite a closer comparison with folklore archives, since both types contain transcripts of interviews, but generally speaking the oral historian makes appointments with prominent persons while the folklorist follows trails among the unknown and unheralded.

Completing the quadrant of field, library, and archives is the museum, as requisite research center for the folklore scholar. As the folklore archive extends the available texts of oral tradition beyond the hoard of the individual collector, so does the folk museum widen the cache of objects that the artifactual researcher may observe. The fieldworkers' problem of supplying contexts for the texts of tales and songs they collect is matched by the folklife curators' task of supplying contexts for the objects they exhibit. To do so, Willard Moore points out in his article on folklore museums, curators are reinforcing their display materials with oral family histories and documentary records of ethnic and farming life. Also they share with scholars of oral traditions the perennial issue of fakelore, for museums, whether devoted to elite or folk culture, tend to emphasize the nostalgic, idyllic aspects of the American past. Moore refers to a number of folklife museums whose holdings may assist the student of folk art and folk architecture, occupational and ethnic groups, folk religion, and folk medicine. In their search for the cultural data in which folklore lies embedded, folklorists must familiarize themselves with the treasures in specialized museums as they do in specialized archives and specialized libraries.

But they must also venture outside these repositories of artifacts, tape transcripts, and books on their subject, accumulated and systematized by others, and strike out on their own into the welter of printed sources that may yield buried folklore. Folklorists are more accustomed to recording informants than to poring through files of newspapers and periodicals and examining publications that may contain supernatural and humorous lore, but, as Francis de Caro makes plain in his survey of these printed sources, they should cultivate this garden for several compelling reasons. Older variants, national legends, occult wonders, contextual data, cultural myths, popular jokes, folklore in the news—all can be gleaned from print. American folklorists must continually ponder over the intricate interrelationships between spoken and printed words, and de Caro cites a number of studies that have made a beginning in this direction.

One particular form of printed sources rich in folklore is American literature, but works of fiction, drama, poetry, and other writings of artistic merit require separate consideration from nonliterary publications, since their authors adapt folkloric materials to their own creative purposes. Sandra Stahl gives such consideration, and presents a new comprehensive methodology for studying the intersecting points of folk and literary criticism. She enumerates a list of these points that goes beyond the customary procedure of identifying folk elements in literature and assessing their role in the work. Stahl suggests the folk-literary critic attend to a number of matters that unite and divide the two fields, from basic assumptions to audience reactions and responses. Fruitful lines of research that can illuminate the omnipresence of folklore in American literature and the influence of literature upon American folklore are indicated in this statement.

The eleven essays in this section discussing methods of research to be pursued by American folklorists deal with conceptual, technological, and data-location questions. Collectively they indicate the complex nature of this many-sided research as it has gathered momentum since mid-century.

Richard Bauman

The Field Study of Folklore in Context

Scholars have been objectifying folklore for centuries, concerning themselves with the life history of folklore items as they persist over great periods of time, travel vast distances across the world, settle down in widely separate locales, or fill up anthologies and archives. Approached from this perspective, folklore appears to have a life of its own, subject only to impersonal, superorganic processes and laws. In many ways, this view of folklore is an abstraction, founded on memories or recordings of songs as sung, tales as told, spells as chanted. The symbolic and expressive forms we call folklore have their primary existence in the action of people, and are rooted in the social and cultural life of those people. The texts we are accustomed to viewing as the raw materials of folklore are merely the thin and partial record of deeply situated human behavior. If we are to understand what folklore is, we must go beyond a conception of it as disembodied superorganic stuff and view it contextually, in terms of the individual, social, and cultural factors that give it shape, meaning, existence. This reorientation in turn requires us to broaden the scope of our fieldwork; a contextual perspective on folklore makes the enterprise of folklore fieldwork much more ramified and complex than the simple butterfly-collecting approach—the collecting of anachronistic antiquities—that often passes for fieldwork in folklore.

One need not necessarily document the whole of social and cultural life to do meaningful fieldwork; the purpose of this essay is not to legislate, intimidate, or overwhelm the potential fieldworker with ambitious and prescriptive guidelines.[1] Rather, what follows is an attempt at a reasonably comprehensive conception of folklore in context, of sufficient scope to allow for the formulation of a great many specific and closely focused projects. What remains essential is a basic conception of folklore as *situated in a web of interrelationships*, a frame of reference which may allow for the pursuit of specific connections and patterns, depending upon the investigator's interests and resources, while keeping in view the broader range of relevant factors as well.

My emphasis will be on aspects of context most immediately accessible through fieldwork, with a primary focus on verbal folklore.[2] We may divide the broad range of contextual relations into aspects of *cultural context*, having to do with systems of meanings and symbolic interrelationships, and *social context*, having to do with matters of social structure and social interaction.

CULTURAL CONTEXT

Context of Meaning

Perhaps the most fundamental aspect of cultural context with regard to folklore centers on the problem of understanding. In other words, what is the information one needs to know about the culture and the community in order to understand the content, the meaning, the "point" of an item of folklore, as the people themselves understand it? The dimensions of meaning implicated here extend across the entire scope of culture itself. What aspects of the people's way of life are expressively represented, projected, transformed in their folklore? What systems of belief and value underlie the relations of interdependence, cause and effect, motivation and choice, modes of action, symbolic and metaphoric relations, and other semantic dimensions, as these give shape to folkloric expression? What expectations with regard to production and interpretation are raised by the generic shape of the folklore?

The scholar studying the folklore of an exotic society more easily recognizes the need to attend to contextual matters of this kind.[3] In working with a familiar culture in one's own country, as folklorists often do, there is a natural tendency to assume that the meaning of folklore is readily accessible because the people are. But as both laymen and scholars become more aware of society as an organization of diversity,[4] we should come to recognize that meaning is problematic in all cultures, subcultures, and communities, especially in our own complex and heterogeneous society. Here, trained folklorists who are themselves members of the groups whose folklore they study, can perform a valuable service by elucidating the cultural meaning of materials gathered from those groups. Américo Paredes's masterful analysis of a series of jests recorded from Mexican-American narrators in Brownsville, Texas, is an effective case in point.[5] These jests, on their face apparently aiming ridicule at practitioners of traditional folk medicine, clearly require of the reader, as of the original audience, some degree of knowledge of relevant aspects of the folk medical system and the ways those are recounted in narrative form, all of which Paredes duly provides. Their full import, however, rests in the specific nature of cultural contact and conflict on the Texas-Mexican border, apparent as an element of meaning in the jests only to one as fully knowledgeable about the area as Paredes is. With the benefit of Paredes's informed presentation, the stories emerge as parodies of *casos* (belief tales), and reflections of the ambivalence of Mexican-Americans who are at the same time loyal to and frustrated by their traditional culture on the one hand, and by mainstream Anglo culture on the other.

As Paredes points out, much of meaning is conditioned by situational factors (see below, *Context of Situation*), but some variation in interpretation is rooted in the variability of human knowledge, understanding, and experience. The moral here is not to take meaning for granted. By taking advantage instead of the frequently licensed position of the fieldworker and asking people to explain the point and meaning of their folklore, the investigator may uncover unanticipated dimensions of significance in apparently familiar traditions.

Institutional Context

A broader but related aspect of cultural context may be approached in terms of the anthropological notion of institution, a functionally organized system of purposeful activity, made up of interrelated ideational, behavioral, and social elements. An institution may be as broadly encompassing as politics, religion, kinship, or economics, or as restricted as neighboring, initiating, celebrating, or barn-raising.[6]

The chief value of the notion of institution is as an analytical integrating concept, focusing attention on how aspects of culture fit together, and on what is related to what else. From the point of view of the folklorist, how does a particular item or genre relate to other aspects of cultural life to make up larger interrelated configurations? Where does it fit into the culture, and how does it function? For example, in a large section of East Texas, part of the institutional context of stories about shrewd traders, of a kind popular in American folk tradition since the early nineteenth century, is the institution of coon dog trading, conducted regularly in Canton, Texas, as part of the larger institution of a First Monday Trade Day. The stories function in a variety of ways, as a means of enhancing the teller's personal image as a man of wits and words, as sociable entertainment, as guides to action, and so on. Investigation of the institutional context of a folklore form reveals in a general sense the spheres of action within which it finds its place in the culture, and the generalized ends served by its use.

Context of Communicative System

A further set of cultural interrelationships of increasing interest to scholars in recent years has to do with the organization of the domain of folklore itself from the folk point of view, the systems of folk categories and labels for the genres and speech acts in terms of which people organize their folklore.[7] Here one would want to know the range of expressive forms that make up the folkloric repertoire of the culture, and the set of natively meaningful terms and distinctions people employ to differentiate between them or group them together. More broadly, how do the communicative forms that make up the folklore of the community relate to the entire communicative system of the culture? These larger systems of expressive interrelationship constitute a context for each distinct form, and give it meaning in terms of cultural expectations and norms for its content, form, use, and evaluation. For example, Roger Abrahams develops a taxonomy of ways of speaking on the street in Black American culture, in which such forms as playing the dozens, performing toasts, telling jokes and other kinds of stories are implicated. The taxonomy illuminates the interrelationships of these folkloric forms to each other and to other verbal forms along several culturally significant dimensions, including the relative status of the interactants, the tone of the interaction, and the spontaneously conversational vs. aesthetically stylized performance character of the speaking.[8] The question, then, is how a particular form of folklore relates to other folklore forms within the culture.

SOCIAL CONTEXT

Social Base

The concept of folklore as the collective expression or possession of a people has been basic to folkloristic thought for more than two hundred years, and continues to exercise a powerful influence on the discipline today. The social base of folklore—the group or collectivity within which it is current—represents an important aspect of its social context. Here we ask, with which feature(s) of social identity is the currency of a particular piece or body of folklore associated?

Much of the recent discussion by folklorists concerning "who are the folk?" is addressed essentially to this point.[9] For nineteenth-century folklorists, the answer was simply peasants, but contemporary folklorists have expanded their view of the social base of folklore to *"any group of people whatsoever* who share at least one common factor."[10] Most of American folkore study, though, has been and continues to be confined to a more limited range of social organizing principles, such as region, ethnicity, occupation, and age.[11] The family as a social base of folklore is just beginning to receive attention, while the community, representing the social matrix within which much of folklore is learned, used, and passed on, has been largely overlooked.

Individual Context

If folklore is the collective expression of social groups, it is also the personal expression of the individuals who use it. Just as social groups and social life constitute the context in which individuals acquire and use folklore, the life history of an individual and the structure and evolution of an individual's repertoire represent important contextual frameworks for understanding the place of folklore in human life.

For any given item in a person's repertoire, we may productively investigate such matters as how and when it was learned, and what factors, both social (e.g., role eligibility) and individual (e.g., personal taste), have influenced its status as an active or passive part of the repertoire at any given time.[12] How does it relate to the repertoire as a whole? What selective factors and organizing principles, again both social and individual, give structure to the individual repertoire? In the few life histories and repertoire studies that folklorists have published about—or better yet, in collaboration with—their informants, we are just beginning to sense the factors shaping a folk performer's career and the ways in which an individual's life represents an illuminating contextual framework for the study of folklore.[13]

Situational Context

The most recent dimension of context to capture the attention of folklorists, though adumbrated more than fifty years ago by Malinowski,[14] is situational context, the ethnographic study of folklore in use, in the actual conduct of social life. The basic frame of reference here, and the unit of description and analysis, is the communicative event. (The term event designates a culturally defined, bounded segment of the flow of behavior and experience, constituting a meaningful context for action.)[15] A sampling of folkloric events described in the recent folklore literature might include sociable encounters at the general store, women's rap sessions, family gatherings, blues performances, and even telephone conversations.[16]

The structure of folkloric events is a product of the interplay of numerous situational factors, including physical setting, participants' identities and roles, cultural ground rules for performance, norms of interaction and interpretation, and the sequence of actions, making up the conventional scenario of the event itself as a cultural scene.

As with every aspect of culture, there is a conventionalized, patterned organization to folklore events, amenable to generalized ethnographic description. At the same time, every event will have a unique and emergent aspect, depending upon the distinctive circumstances at play. These factors will condition the choice of items for performance, the strategies employed in their use, and often the shape of the emergent text and the structure of the specific situation itself. They will also give a dimension of meaning to the items of folklore employed, above and beyond their generalized cultural meaning (see above, *Context of Meaning*).

Attention to situational context requires us to ask of a given tale or song or proverb, what does it mean in this particular situation, as used for these immediate purposes, in the interaction of these particular people? One of the best demonstrations of this approach at work is William Labov's subtle analysis of the use of a specific ritual insult in a particular situation as a key both to the generalized cultural roles for such ritual insults (playing the dozens), and to the uniquely creative rhetorical effect of that specific performance.[17] Labov's analysis is an extensive elucidation of one "sound" (ritual insult), "your mother's a duck," demonstrating how it is artfully employed as a means of establishing a particular situation as play, and thus retroactively reframing a prior command to shut up, susceptible of being taken as a serious challenge, as not to be taken seriously. Ritual insults are clearly to be understood as play—we both know that your mother is not a duck. But if you take the command to shut up as a serious challenge, linked as it is to "your mother's a duck," you are tacitly admitting that your mother could be a duck, thus losing face. In this situation, the element of meaning that is foregrounded is "this is play."

"Natural" Context

Folklorists demonstrate a persistent impulse to strive for the so-called natural context of a folklore form, an impulse generally resting on a conception of the way things were in an ideal time before progress or the intrusive presence of a folklorist corrupted the folk. To the extent that we have a legitimate historical interest in the way things used to be, or an ethnographic interest in the way things work in a community when the folklorist isn't there watching, trying to account for natural contexts is useful. But the concept rapidly becomes unproductive if it fosters the notion that any departure from our traditionalist conception of natural context is therefore unnatural, and outside the purview of folklore, that a folksong is contaminated when accompanied on an electric guitar. Novelties occur, changes happen. The threads of continuity in human expression are also threads of change. American folklorists have been unashamedly interested in European tales among the North American Indians,[18] but a French *conte* told to an Ojibwa by a seventeenth-century *voyageur* was no less natural or unnatural than a Cree tale performed to an American folklorist today. Indeed, we can learn a great deal about the creative process by which a performer adapts his performance to situational circumstances from a close contextual description.[19]

CONCLUSION

The field study of folklore in context is a multiplex undertaking. To be done effectively, the contextual dimension must be attended to directly, built into the field investigation as a central focus from the beginning, not simply relegated to the status of a residual or secondary category of complementary information, to be correlated or conflated with the folklore materials at some later stage of the analysis. The fieldworker seeking to comprehend folklore in terms of the web of contextual interrelationships that define its essence will find it useful to organize the gathering of field data around the six broad foci outlined above: (a) *context of meaning* (what does it mean?); (b) *institutional context* (where does it fit within the culture?); (c) *context of communicative system* (how does it relate to other kinds of folklore?); (d) *social base* (what kind of people does it belong to?); (e) *individual context* (how does it fit into a person's life); (f) *context of situation* (how is it useful in social situations?).

To use this outline as a kind of checklist, though, would be to misunderstand the purpose for which it is presented. More important than any checklist is the basic contextual frame of reference, the conception of folklore as fundamentally rooted in the richness of human social and cultural life—not simply folklore and culture, or folklore in culture, but folklore *as* culture.

NOTES

1. Space does not permit the presentation here of detailed methodologies for fieldwork, which are best sought in the growing number of available guides to ethnographic practice. Especially useful for folklorists are Kenneth S. Goldstein, *A Guide for Field Workers in Folklore* (Hatboro, Pa.: Folklore Associates, for the American Folklore Society, 1964); Joel Sherzer and Regna Darnell, "Outline Guide for the Ethnographic Study of Speech Use," in *Directions in Sociolinguistics: The Ethnography of Communication*, ed. John Gumperz and Dell Hymes (New York: Holt, Rinehart & Winston, 1972).

2. There are other dimensions of context that I do not treat here, because they are not directly a part of fieldwork, e.g., the historical context out of which a particular tradition or item emerged. Nor is the contextual perspective limited only to the direct field study of living traditions; it can also be employed effectively in the study of documentary historical cases or of memory culture. See for example Richard Bauman, "Quaker Folk Linguistics and Folklore," in *Folklore: Performance and Communication*, ed. Dan Ben-Amos and Kenneth S. Goldstein (The Hague: Mouton, 1975), and Richard Bauman, "The La Have Island General Store: Sociability and Verbal Art in a Nova Scotia Community," *Journal of American Folklore* 85 (1972): 330-43.

3. The best examples of work of this kind tend to be found in the anthropological literature. See for example William A. Lessa, " 'Discoverer of the Sun': Mythology as a Reflection of Culture," *Journal of American Folklore* 79 (1966): 3-51; Melville Jacobs, *The Content and Style of an Oral Literature* (Chicago: University of Chicago Press, 1959); and Dell Hymes, "The 'Wife' who 'Goes Out' Like a Man: Reinterpretation of a Clackamas Chinook Myth," in *Structural Analysis of Oral Tradition*, ed. Pierre Maranda and Elli Köngäs Maranda (Philadelphia: University of Pennsylvania Press, 1971).

4. Anthony F. C. Wallace, *Culture and Personality*, 2nd ed. (New York: Random House, 1970), pp. 23-24.

5. Américo Paredes, "Folk Medicine and the Intercultural Jest," in *Spanish Speaking People in the United States*, ed. June Helm (Seattle: University of Washington Press, for the American Ethnological Society, 1968).

6. Bronislaw Malinowski, *A Scientific Theory of Culture* (New York: Oxford University Press, 1960).

7. Dan Ben-Amos, "Analytical Categories and Ethnic Genres," in *Folklore Genres*, ed. Dan Ben-Amos (Austin: University of Texas Press, 1976); Gary H. Gossen, *Chamulas in the World of the Sun* (Cambridge, Mass.: Harvard University Press, 1974).

8. Roger D. Abrahams, "Black Talking on the Streets," in *Explorations in the Ethnography of Speaking*, ed. Richard Bauman and Joel Sherzer (New York and London: Cambridge University Press, 1974).

9. Alan Dundes, "Who Are the Folk?" in *Frontiers of Folklore*, ed. William R. Bascom (Boulder: Westview Press, for the American Association for the Advancement of Science, 1977).

10. Alan Dundes, *The Study of Folklore* (Englewood Cliffs, N.J.: Prentice-Hall, 1965), p. 2, emphasis in the original.

11. Richard Bauman and Roger D. Abrahams with Susan Kalčik, "American Folklore and American Studies," *American Quarterly* 28 (1976): 360–77.

12. Kenneth S. Goldstein, "On the Application of the Concepts of Active and Inactive Traditions to the Study of Repertory," in *Toward New Perspectives in Folklore*, ed. Américo Paredes and Richard Bauman (Austin: University of Texas Press, 1972).

13. See, for example, Roger D. Abrahams, ed., *A Singer and Her Songs: Almeda Riddle's Book of Ballads* (Baton Rouge: Louisiana State University Press, 1970); and Bessie Jones and Bess Lomax Hawes, *Step It Down: Games, Plays, Songs, and Stories from the Afro-American Heritage* (New York: Harper & Row, 1972).

14. Bronislaw Malinowski, *Myth in Primitive Society* (London: Kegan Paul, French, Trubner, 1926), pp. 29–30. See also Alan Dundes, "Texture, Text and Context," *Southern Folklore Quarterly* 28 (1964): 251–65.

15. Richard Bauman and Joel Sherzer, "The Ethnography of Speaking," in *Annual Review of Anthropology*, vol. 4, ed. Bernard J. Siegel (Palo Alto, Calif.: Annual Reviews, 1975), pp. 27–30, 40–42.

16. Richard Tallman, "Where the Stories Are Told: A Nova Scotia Storyteller's Milieu," *American Review of Canadian Studies* 5 (1975): 17–41; Richard Bauman, "The La Have Island General Store"; Susan Kalčik, " '. . . like Ann's gynecologist or the time I was almost raped': Personal Narratives in Women's Rap Groups," in *Women and Folklore*, ed. Claire R. Farrer (Austin: University of Texas Press, 1975); Barbara Kirshenblatt-Gimblett, "A Parable in Context: A Social Interactional Analysis of Storytelling Performance," in *Folklore: Performance and Communication*; Charles Keil, *Urban Blues* (Chicago: University of Chicago Press, 1966), pp. 114–42; Linda Dégh, "Two Old World Narrators in [an] Urban Setting," in *Kontakte und Grenzen: Probleme der Volks-, Kultur-, und Sozialforschung. Festschrift für Gerhard Heilfurth zum 60. Geburtstag* (Göttingen: Otto Schwartz, 1970).

17. See William Labov's "Rules for Ritual Insults," in *Rappin' and Stylin' Out*, ed. Thomas Kochman (Urbana: University of Illinois Press, 1972).

18. Stith Thompson, "European Tales among the North American Indians," *Colorado College Publication*, Language Series, vol. 2, no. 34 (Colorado Springs: Colorado College, 1919); Richard M. Dorson, *Bloodstoppers and Bearwalkers* (Cambridge, Mass.: Harvard University Press, 1952), pp. 58–59.

19. Regna Darnell, "Correlates of Cree Narrative Performance," in *Explorations in the Ethnography of Speaking*.

D. K. Wilgus

Collecting Musical
Folklore and Folksong

In approaching the collecting of traditional music and song in North America one cannot escape considering what has been done, what should have been done, and what remains to be done. I shall be emphasizing fieldwork in the Anglo-American and Afro-American traditions because it has been the most prolific (which tells us something already) and because those areas are most familiar to me.

When one thinks of collecting folk music, one thinks of the deliberate expedition—of John Lomax riding into a cow camp with a cylinder recording machine balanced on the pommel of his saddle and the morning glory horn rolled up in an oilskin behind; of Cecil Sharp and Maud Karpeles setting out in a jolt wagon for remote Appalachian settlements; of Robert W. Gordon's historic four-year trek through many areas of North America; of John and Alan Lomax trucking recording apparatus through the "state farms" of the prison systems of the South.[1] But there have been long-term investigations by single collectors such as W. Roy MacKenzie and Vance Randolph.[2] There has been the directed work of many subcollectors, as in *The Frank C. Brown Collection*. Actually collectors and collecting have been of many types, and their very disparity has contributed to our knowledge of the material, of the tradition, and of methodology.

Certainly there may be wrong ways to collect, but there is no right one. The enthusiastic Northern white youth who ventured to Parchman Prison Farm in the company of a local black who was packing a pistol was not using good methodology—or good sense either. One readily knocks on the door of a Kentucky farmhouse and announces a quest for "old songs"; but one hesitates to do so in the suburban San Fernando Valley—though under some circumstances it might work. Different areas, different traditions require somewhat different methodologies. And every field situation is to some extent unique. But there are factors in the musical traditions themselves and in the aims of the collectors that provide guidelines.

Ideally one should strive for the most accurate audiovisual recording (one must presuppose electronic equipment) of the full repertoire of a tradition in its natural context, together with "native" reactions to and interpretations of the musical events. Note that this could not be achieved *in situ* with any number of television units. Investigation beyond the immediate event is required. The full repertoire might never be available in "natural context" within the collector's period of investigation. And a recording in "natural context" is almost certainly not even an ideal, but a chimera, unless one resorts to means which, even if possible, are dangerous and unacceptable.

Certainly, one of the first problems confronting the fieldworker in any area of folklore is what to "collect." No fieldworker can "collect" everything, and if anyone could, the results might well be the dust heaps of any "vacuum cleaner" method. Selectivity is necessary—just as this chapter is selective in discussing the collecting of folk music. One kind of selectivity is unavoidable, as it involves the performer's perception of the interests of the fieldworker and usually the performer's desire to satisfy (or perhaps on rare occasions to defy) those interests. On the other hand, the fieldworker's specific focus must never involve the rejection of any material presented by a performer. The problem indeed is not selectivity itself, but conclusions based on that selectivity. On the basis of forty-six weeks of fieldwork in the Southern Appalachians from 1916 to 1918, the experienced English collector Cecil Sharp concluded—or more accurately others concluded on the basis of his observations—that traditional singers in the area did not use instrumental accompaniments, and that the only instrumental music was provided by fiddle and dulcimer—at a time when there well might have been a banjo picker behind every bush. Sharp also learned to ask for "love songs" so that he would not be given hymns, in which he was not interested. Of course, if one keeps in mind the title of his collection, *English Folk Songs from the Southern Appalachians*, there is less difficulty accepting his narrow focus—though the "howler" of treating "John Henry" and "Wild Bill Jones" as "street ballads" is hard to swallow.

Selectivity involves both the choice of the general tradition being investigated—e.g., black music in south Chicago, Lithuanian singing in southern Pennsylvania, rural white performances in south-central Kentucky—and the concentration of interest within that tradition: a survey of available performances of all musics assumed to be traditional, or a selection based on one or more subgenres of material, source, or function. Selectivity also involves the questions—consciously or unconsciously formulated—the fieldworker seeks to answer. Collecting techniques are sometimes determined by the use envisaged for the recorded results. Are they destined for archival preservation and study or for circulation through commercial or educational media? Selection involves not only material and techniques, but locale. (There is a story that an unnamed English folksong collector ultimately failed because he was a teetotaler and did not collect in pubs.) Choices may also be made on grounds of age or sex. (Because such choices in the past have seldom been explicit, it is difficult to determine, for example, the extent to which older Anglo-American ballads have depended on female tradition.) And of course choices are sometimes forced on the collector by members of the community or by local "experts." That members of a community seek to influence the collector to document particular performers and performances or specific materials may be a significant ethnographic datum in itself, but the collector may consequently overlook "underground" traditions, important but nonrespectable performers. The "local expert," however, is more dangerous in attempting to isolate the collector on the basis of a nontraditional half-educated attitude.

A paradox faced by the fieldworker is that one needs to know beforehand much of what is being sought. That is, in order to be successful at collecting folk music in a given tradition one should know a good deal not only of folk music tradition in general, but of a specific folk music tradition in particular. To effectively collect a certain kind of material, the collector should know in advance who performs what, where, at what time—ironically, the exact information often sought. The results of previous investigation can often serve as introductory handbooks to the music traditions of specific American cultures: A few general observations may be helpful in preparing for the trip. The fieldworker can look first at a series of distinctions based on materials, performance, and function which may be useful even though they overlap to some extent. The traditions so distinguished are: Domestic, Social, Institutional, Occupational, and Professional.

MUSICAL TRADITIONS

Domestic Tradition

One must first distinguish between domestic *tradition* and domestic *performance*. In terms of actual collection of materials, items of all traditions distinguished have often been collected in domestic *situations*, that is, presented to the collector in the home of a performer, whatever their "normal" incidence. Domestic *tradition*, on the other hand, refers to the musical materials regularly performed within a family and among families in a traditional community. Quite obviously materials from other traditions can and do enter domestic tradition, so that, for example, a female singer in the Northeast may have in her repertoire a song of the logging camps. The fact that such songs are now in domestic tradition, the way in which they entered the tradition, and their status within the tradition are part of the problems faced in considering the content, function, performance, and history of songs normally performed within the family. The fieldworker must attempt to establish the "domesticity" of the materials not so much in terms of origin, but in terms of performance and function. Are there distinct men's songs and women's songs within the domestic tradition? Is there sex linkage within the domestic tradition?

Social Tradition

The extent to which one may distinguish social from domestic tradition varies greatly among traditional cultures, and even within what one would define as a traditional culture. Music designed or performed for group entertainment and enjoyment may be accepted or rejected within the same general culture. Dance and "frolic" music, including songs associated with social activities, may be excluded from the domestic tradition of parts of a traditional community, while readily accepted among others. In Anglo-American tradition the fieldworker will normally record items from social tradition in a domestic situation, collect information about social performances from nonparticipants, and rarely document a "frolic." (Unusual indeed was the situation I encountered in Dover, Tennessee, in which a lay fundamentalist preacher and her banjo-picking husband reached a compromise of a weekly event in a vacant house owned by the wife, which involved a shared meal, secular song and dance, and a midnight sermon and prayer service.) On the other hand, the social tradition may be so generally accepted that it is difficult to separate from the domestic tradition.

Institutional Tradition

Music traditions connected with institutions—chiefly religious and political— have also been too often documented as reflected in domestic situations. The ingrained belief among American collectors that folk music belongs to rural knitters and spinners in the sun has too often militated against documentation of performances directly associated with institutions. Anglo-American and Afro-American religious music might seem an exception, but in truth there has been less documentation than one might expect, at least in terms of structure and function. Material associated with contemporary institutions has been suspect to the folklorist for a number of reasons. One reason of course is the natural use of commercial media by institutions, for the folklorist has yet to find a way to fit contemporary media transmission into any paradigm. Another is the matter of "revivalism," which is seen as any "artificial" or conscious use of folk materials. Thus the music and dance associated with the local Polish-American hall would be viewed as not "really" a folk tradition, and the songs of the Civil Rights Movement considered suspect because folklorists of the "applied folklore" persuasion were associated with them. Even the songs of the Southwestern farm workers and the *La Raza* movement do not escape question. Since I share some of the misgivings, I can only emphasize that the material and information are worthy of collection and study, however one classifies them. Furthermore it should be stressed that this music—basically ceremonial, as is the music of the New Orleans Mardi Gras "Indians"—is usually a "public" music and requires techniques not normally used by American folk music collectors.

There is institutional music in another sense—perhaps more recognizable under the rubric *ritual* music—which has been easily avoided by the collector of Anglo-American folk music because of its paucity. Music connected with such rites of passage or seasonal celebrations as weddings, funerals, or Christmas has been generally considered nontraditional in the Anglo-American tradition. If not the musics themselves—"Oh Promise Me," "Nearer My God to Thee"—then their use can be considered traditional. But non-Anglo groups in North America do have a variety of traditions accompanying such celebrations.

Occupational Tradition

Occupational songs, with some exceptions, have been associated by American folklorists with male groups separated from the rest of society by reasons of their trade, e.g., sailors, loggers, cowboys, soldiers. Because the "isolation" in which the traditions developed has now disappeared—and had largely disappeared by the time folklorists began investigating the traditions—collection has been undertaken primarily in domestic situations. Sedentary occupations such as mining or textile work produced bodies of song which have tended to blend with domestic tradition and can and have been collected with other material. With a few exceptions, such as the work songs of blacks, continued to some extent on prison farms, the work place has been avoided as a milieu for recording, at least partly because the exclusiveness of the tradition makes the folklorist more an intruder in the work place than in a domestic situation. Of course if one cannot collect railroad songs in a caboose, there is more opportunity in a railroad bar.

Professional Tradition

The fact that there can be—and is—a professional folk music tradition has been a bitter pill for many students of American folk music to swallow, particularly since the medieval minstrel and latterly the Appalachian banjo minstrel had been made the scapegoats for the "degeneration" of traditional song. I am not referring here to material derived from commercial sources, nor am I treating directly the problem of the commercialization of performances, though the line between the two is thin. Thin also is the line between professional tradition and other traditions discussed. The place of professional folk performers has been usurped by the commercial media to the extent that performers who cannot "make it" in translating their art through commercial media are absorbed back into the domestic tradition, and the collector is, as usual, dealing with the reminiscences of folk professionals. The minstrel no longer sings on the courthouse steps, and the traveling medicine show seems to have vanished. Less frequently encountered are the community string band playing at local dances and the blues performer performing at crossroad jukes. But the professional tradition is not dead and the fieldworker must face the various problems involved. Must one compensate the black blues performer? Should one record the local bluegrass band at a tobacco auction? How should one deal with the sophisticated tamboritza band at the wedding? The answer begins with the recognition of the tradition and must end where the individual fieldworker "draws the line." If the blind singer on Chicago's Maxwell Street is of interest to the folk music collector, what of the electrified blues performer in the nearby lounge? We can beg the answer to such questions by turning to problems of technique involved in collecting material from whatever traditions the fieldworker chooses to investigate.

PROBLEMS OF COLLECTION

It has often been charged that the American folk music collector has chosen to record folk music—other than that in domestic tradition—"out of context." In truth, material is always collected "in context," but the context has often been that of the interview rather than the "natural context." The interview context is not one that I shall be heretical enough to say should be preferred, but one which I shall say is necessary. Of course the interview context has been enforced upon fieldworkers by their own beliefs that the traditions they are investigating are at the least dying and can be salvaged only in this way. But the interview context is necessary even in a tradition recognized as vibrant. Let us assume that by the most sophisticated means a traditional music performance is recorded in its natural context—be it a work song, a curing song, a frolic tune. The interview technique is still necessary for significant contextual information. The investigator has secured a "one-time" performance. Was it representative? Can the informant or informants provide variants? What is their opinion of the performance in terms of its aesthetics of effectiveness? And one may wish to re-elicit the performance for a technically superior recording or for comparison with the performance in natural context.

I emphasize collecting by interview not only because it has been the prevalent technique, but because it is the most significant and actually the most demanding for the fieldworker. The problems of collecting folk music *in situ* can be largely technical and difficulties encountered often merely seem insurmountable. For example, in documenting the music of a black church service (more properly the entire church service) there are choices to be made—where, what, and how to "mike," where to place cameras, etc. But that is the result of certain technical decisions, and must then be followed by interviews and interpretive techniques. Certainly the bare recording of such a "happening" is valuable, but it must be considered perhaps the midpoint of the process necessary for the fieldworker.

It should be pointed out that the folk music collector, like the proverb collector, cannot wait around until the event takes place. Quite often it is a solo performance for the individual's benefit or part of a structured/familial relationship. The investigator cannot follow the performer driving home the cows, waiting for a spontaneous burst of song, though he may sometimes let the performer sit on the buck rake because the activity helps recall the song. One may well record in the highly structured context of an Appalachian fiddle contest or a Bavarian wedding, but these situations must always be supplemented by in-depth interviews of the performers. And the collector of folk music is more fortunate than investigators of some other genres in that traditional music performances tend toward the "fixed text" side of the scale. The collector of anecdotes had better catch his bird on the wing, for the request to repeat the story may well result in an inferior production—the listener has already "got the point." A musical performance, on the other hand, might well improve in a later repetition—certainly it is less likely to deteriorate.

Although the problem varies among traditional cultures, the fieldworker can never assume that any given recording captures *the* performance. Performances may vary not only over time, but in accordance with the situation as well. One must be willing to accept and sometimes encourage repeated performances, particularly under differing circumstances. Nor should a collector avoid a previously recorded item. One is consequently torn between the possibility of garnering "new" items and the need to investigate the dynamics of a performer's tradition. So one must also determine whether to concentrate on the active or current tradition of a number of performers in a community or group, or attempt to penetrate into the passive or historical repertoire of one musician. For purposes of archiving and publishing, transcriptions of items performed are often organized by various principles unrelated to the sequence in which they were performed. The original tapes will preserve the sequence and possibly suggest associations that have affected the performances. Subsequent recording of the materials in differing sequences may then answer questions raised by the original sequence.

I have already emphasized the selectivity necessarily engaged in by the fieldworker. No longer does the collector of Anglo-American folksong go armed with the abridged edition of Child's *The English and Scottish Popular Ballads* and query informants to see if they recognize any of the items. And I presume that workers in other areas have not such "Childish" attitudes. But our current "enlightenment" does not mean that we must be passive recorders. It is all well and good to set out to record "what is"—but sometimes "what is" must be solicited by the fieldworker. One extreme, perhaps, is that of the "local song." Not only may the material be "sensitive," but the performer may not volunteer it because of a feeling that the collector would not be interested in such esoteric items. Unless the collector deliberately and successfully conveys his interest in songs of local reference, he can only stumble on the songs. The process becomes one of "rifle collecting"—specific requests of performers and following leads to informants who are acquainted with the items. Especially important here is information *about* the musical materials—more than the minimal information such as the stated source from whom the performer learned the material.

The collector directly and indirectly indicates to the traditional performer what is sought; the performer generally responds with what he thinks the collector wants. If the collector doesn't ask why this fiddle tune has such a "funny" name or what story is connected with it, the performer won't bother. When the performer does respond to a collector's question with an answer at variance with the collector's "knowledge," that answer must be weighed carefully. Sometimes the answer is factually correct—proving a validity in folk tradition. Sometimes the answer has a "folk truth" that the collector should recognize—e.g., that a new song is made by changing proper names. Sometimes, of course, an informant—usually an important one—devises a nonce answer; this should not be rejected, but carefully considered. Unfortunately the collector does not always know the right questions. Logger songs in the Northeast have invariably been collected out of context, that is, not in the shanties in which they were originally performed. The Irish influence on the latter songs is apparent. The Irish *declamando* technique—speaking the last line or word of the song—is well documented. But there is another Irish custom in song performance—the interaction of the audience with the performer in uttering words of encouragement between stanzas of the song: "Good man"; "Fine lad." This custom still exists in Irish pub singing both in Ireland and in eastern cities of the United States. Did it exist in the logging camps? I have found no evidence that anyone ever asked.

Accounts of collecting experiences and techniques often appear in the introductions and sometimes notes to published editions of folk music. (And in "editions" one should include LP recordings, whose importance is rightly increasing.) The editions, whether directed to regions, occupations, or genres, not only furnish "how to" and "how not to" advice (sometimes unwittingly), but are in other ways guides which must be consulted by the potential fieldworker. Both what is present and what is absent in such editions can be helpful in establishing needed directions. While feigning ignorance is sometimes a useful ploy for the fieldworker, stupidity is not. And a collector who seems less than knowledgeable about the tradition studied soon loses the respect of the performers. Without knowledge the collector will simply not ask the necessary questions. One Oklahoma cowboy singer who had previously been recorded commercially and been an informant for the Library of Congress was not so identified by later collectors, who consequently failed to ask significant questions about his previous experiences.

Such lapses would lead one to respond to the title "Collecting Musical Folklore and Folksong": *Don't*, if by collecting is meant simply the recording of sound materials with little concern for their function, their relation to the lives of the performers, and the culture of the community in which they appear. Certainly "the text is the thing,"[3] but how is one to understand the text?

NOTES

1. John A. Lomax, *Adventures of a Ballad Hunter* (New York: The Macmillan Company, 1947); Cecil J. Sharp, *English Folk Songs from the Southern Appalachians*, ed. Maud Karpeles (London: Oxford University Press, 1960); Robert Winslow Gordon, *Folk-Songs of America*, National Service Bureau Publication No. 73-S (New York: 1938).

2. W. Roy MacKenzie, *The Quest of the Ballad* (Princeton, N.J.: Princeton University Press, 1919); Vance Randolph, *Ozark Folksongs*, 4 vols. (Columbia, Mo.: State Historical Society of Missouri, 1946-50).

3. D. K. Wilgus, "The Text Is the Thing," *Journal of American Folklore* 86 (1973): 241-52.

Henry Glassie

Folkloristic Study of the American Artifact: Objects and Objectives

However one chooses to talk about folklore, as tradition or as communication, it is apparent that objects made of wood as much as objects made of words can be folk things. The key principles of folk process lie in banjoes as surely as in songs. Both are created out of personal experience within particular situations and are, therefore, simultaneously of the past and of the present, traditional and emergent. Both embody ideas of right form, correct behavior, and effective use of resources; thus both incarnate aesthetic, ethical, and economic values. These principles of personal creativity and cultural value are displayed in artifacts as well as in verbal arts. By comparing across media, we are carried past material and verbal detail to spiritual essences. Yet, as an instance of the art-critical heritage of the discipline of folklore, distinctions in media are basic, and generally one group of folklorists studies "material culture" and another studies "oral literature."

This seems inefficient. But division is necessary. Not as a goal, but as a way to pry reality open, to enter and order it for meaningful synthesis. Facing things as they are without presuppositions sounds good, but innocent description would be infinite. There would be no place to stop, no reason to describe one thing and not another, no means for distinguishing between them in the first place. So folklorists come into their world assuming it is not absurd: it is patterned and the patterns separable from the ground of chaos are the product of human planning.

There are particular and powerful reasons for scholars to concentrate on artifactual expressions of culture. These reasons suggest ultimate goals for research which guide in the valuation of some artifacts over others and determine methods of field recording and modes of interpretation. Two foci may be distinguished within the field of artifactual research. One has to do with history, the other with the enactment of values.

The central historical issue is simply stated. To write about the past, one needs information from the past. If the only variety of information taken into account is literary, the vast majority of the world's people are dismissed from historical scrutiny. Most societies have been nonliterate. In the past, most members of literate societies were illiterate, and even today in preponderantly literate societies, most people do not set their thoughts into writing for posterity. Since history is based on literature, it is a chronicle stressing anguish in which a few people, the writers and their patrons, are taken seriously and named leaders, and most are condemned to anonymity with the following masses.

Clever work with the literature left us by the mostly wealthy, mostly white, mostly male, mostly urban, mostly Protestant writers of the European-American past, and subtle analysis of the oral history preserved in little communities can help redress historical inequities. But writing by the few about the many is sometimes prejudiced, often inaccurate, and always indirect, and oral history tells more about its tellers than about its historical subjects. The answer is to encounter the direct cultural expressions of past people, even though this means, in general, facing nonverbal documents, things like broken pots and old houses, and making them the central documents of history. Literally, artifacts persist through time. You cannot hear a medieval song or a colonial sermon, but you can touch a medieval reliquary and walk within a colonial church.

When all the historian has is chipped flint points and some fragments of bone, then history must be written out of them. When more remains, choices can be made. The most useful artifacts are tenacious, situated, and complex.

American historical archeologists develop their basic schemes out of ceramics not because pottery is more important than other classes of object, but because potsherds endure abundantly in archeological sites. Inherent material tenacity brings us things in numbers great enough to be organized into meaningful structures, and from stretches of time long enough to allow for the erection of useful chronological sequences.

The archeologist's ceramic fragment does not exist in its original context as part of a plate under a chicken on a table in the midst of a domestic row. But its exact place in the earth helps locate the spatial and temporal coordinates of that original context. Time can often be inferred from place. By getting carried around, some artifacts, such as furniture, have associations shaken off and become more difficult to study than others, such as houses and gravestones, which usually stay put. Of all the artifactual desiderata, complexity is the most important. Furniture's complexity makes up for its portability. The more complex an object is, the more decisions its design required, the more a particular mind in operation can be discovered behind it. Cultural understanding requires the analyst to become imaginatively the maker of the object being studied, the poet of the poem, the potter of the pot. The trouble with many artifacts is the trouble with many written documents, such as tax lists, inventories, or census reports: they do not incorporate an alien mind richly enough to resist the scholar's advances. Shattered shards, scattered facts are too easily ordered to reflect back the scholar's image. The richer the artifact, the more resistant it is to manipulation and forcible entry, the more helpful it is to earnest inquiry.

It is no surprise that historically oriented folklorists have concentrated on architecture, which is tenacious, situated, and above all, complex. Architecture divides space for differential experience. You see it and feel it, both inside and out; you look out from within, move in from without. Architecture is to be seen: it is an arrangement of shapes, colors, textures; it is an end in itself, an artwork. Architecture is to be used: it is hollow, a shelter, a shell for life; it is a means to other ends, a tool. Architecture, symbol and object, bodies forth and conjoins aesthetic with utilitarian drives at different conceptual levels: the room, the building, the urban lot or farm, the community, the entire landscape.

The grandest of artifacts, whole landscapes are collective products. Made by many people who lived at different times, they present the student with interpretive difficulties. That is no excuse for the limited attention American landscapes have been given;[1] still, the real problems in landscape interpretation explain why research has centered on buildings. The building was originally the projection of a plan held in a lone mind. Since it is a materialization of one person's intentions, it represents a unified concept, and the conflicts and complexities it embodies are those of one person, one culture, one time, not those of different people, cultures, or times. A house is designed to contain more kinds of activity than any other building. A piece of sculpture, a machine for food processing, a school, workshop, and dormitory, a stage for entertainment, the house incorporates the greatest complexity within a unitary plan; it is the logical center for American history.

By establishing the goal of providing history for common people, the folklorist is guided to certain sources of information. It is not that houses are the only objects to study, but that houses most fully exemplify the desiderata of the historical folklorist. They are universal, lasting, and complicated. Other historical sources, written, oral, and artifactual, are useful insofar as they approximate the house's virtues.

Knowing why and what to study, the folklorist knows how to record information in the field. The house or gravestone is not to be used as mere illustration for previously established schemes. Schemes, perhaps challenging, startling schemes, must be built afresh from objects read as the tangible record of vanished consciousness. Simply, the goal for recording is completeness. The ideal account enables its readers to reproduce the object being described by making again all the decisions the original designer had to make in order to create this house or that gravestone.

Much time is lost while the fieldworker debates whether or not to record a fact. Record it. Modern folktale scholars do not fret over which words of a story to record; their analysis demands full, verbatim texts. Facing a gravestone, serious field-workers are similarly free from worry. They simply photograph the whole stone, its details, and they transcribe the epitaph exactly as it appears. From much experience, I know it is best to form habits of architectural recording that guard against fragmentary documentation. Rough measures are only roughly useful. The rule is: measure the shortest distances, so that the width and height and placement of rooms, walls, moldings, windows, doors are precise not vague. Nothing is uninformative. Nothing can be omitted. In making good measured plans, the whole object is encountered and its form is accurately miniaturized.[2]

The exact measured plan, the architectural fieldworker's *sine qua non*, represents but one major aspect of an artifact: its basic form. Two other aspects demand the fieldworker's attention. One is decoration, the other is technology. While each of these three holds wide explanatory potential, within each there is one especially powerful structure of meaning.[3]

Basic form is proposed out of one mind into confrontation with many minds. It exists, therefore, as a social connector and separator. A house's exterior covers its inhabitants with a meaningful mask: conventional or eccentric, it presents its viewer with an image of social cohesion or disjunction. A house's interior serves to draw people together or push them apart. Visitors step over the threshold into the house's living center or they are blocked and channeled by corridors. Sleepers snore and snuggle together or are isolated into private chambers. Cooks bustle amid entertaining conversation or conduct their business behind partitions in efficient work spaces. Basic form helps arrange social action, either through individualistic or collective, rationalistic or organic visions of order.

Decoration results from conceptual play and projects consciousness as clearly as basic shape. But, being less tied to environmental problems (a house can be pretty, but it should be warm) and social needs (a house can be warm, but it must shelter the mental health of its inhabitants), decoration is more variable. An architectural historian, spotting brackets under the eaves of a home, pronounces it "Italianate," and reduces it to an instance of national taste. A folklorist, recognizing the same house's basic form, proclaims it "I house" and reduces it to an instance of local tradition. Both are right. And wrong. Fashionable detail proves the builder was aware of the latest modes. Traditional basic form shows he was unwilling to surrender to them. The conflict of fashion and tradition, national and local culture, is resolved in the building of real houses. Most join old form and new detail, exhibiting a hierarchy of values that is basically local and conservative, super-ficially national and progressive. Thus compromising, builders reveal themselves to be neither witless followers of a national line nor the bondslaves of tradition. They are volitional beings whose houses display their potential for choice, becoming for us, thereby, valuable historical documents.

Technology is the means by which nature is made cultural. The mind directs the hand to intervene and the trees become ships, stones become statues. As natural materials are transformed, cultural attitudes toward nature are written into artifacts. Some people see themselves as participants in nature, others alienate themselves from nature to exploit it morally as a resource. Some enjoy reminders of nature around them—flashes of wilderness in their parks, the natural colors of wood and textures of stone in their homes. Others wish to celebrate human freedom and man's conquest of nature through the utter elimination of natural origin from their artifacts; they prefer the mountain pasture cleared of trees, the log trimly hewn, the planed and painted chest or boat.

With their basic forms, decoration, and technology described, artifacts are made potentially meaningful in terms of individual-collective, local-national, and natural-cultural dialectics. The problem of selectivity remains. Perhaps this accurately recorded house is weird, an improper representative, not so significant after all. Fortunately, quantitative research is not difficult among artifacts. An initial, quick and shallow but complete, survey will isolate an intuitively repre-sentative collection of objects. From complete descriptions of them, a list of key traits can be developed enabling great numbers of things to be recorded, minimally but rigorously, thus providing quantitative support for qualitative accounts.

Oral history loses power as time depth increases; it cannot account for the earliest eras. Written history loses power as social breadth increases; it cannot account for most people. There are problems with the artifactual record. We have more early works from men than women, more from the upper and middle classes than the lower class. But some early textiles and slave quarters do survive, and if silent artifacts are less than we would wish for, they are still the deepest, broadest, best historical source we have. As artifacts are made meaningful and set into spatial and temporal patterns, a new history begins.

The second major concern of the folkloristic student of artifacts is the enactment of values. The folklorist's historical goal is rescuing common people, people like ourselves, from historical oblivion. Now the goal is rescuing common people from subhuman status. Full humanity appears in principled decisions, choices made with philosophical consistency. But most people do not codify their philosophies into treatises any more than they fossilize their historical minds in writing. They act. The scholar's task is to construct the logic behind action, describing how values are arranged and embedded in daily life and artistic activity.

This task must be approached historically through the analysis of products. But the theoretical issues are best addressed in living situations where study will not concentrate on products—banjoes and songs—but on people in action, making banjoes, singing songs.

The center of study is the person taking control of culture, accepting active responsibility for the creation of tradition. Once paper dolls and model planes are abandoned, many modern people surrender their right to conceive and create artifacts, but they continue to talk. It is reasonable, then, for the ethnography of the enactment of values to develop its theories more out of speaking than making.

History requires the artifact. Things—books, letters, houses, gravestones—are all we have once oral historical memory has run out of accuracy. The second philosophical concern of the folklorist does not emphasize artifactual evidence. Still, good reasons remain for continuing to attend to material modes of cultural expression.

First, studying people in action with various media will help folklorists keep their attention on the issue of values. When concentrating on verbal arts alone they seem often tempted by premature satisfaction. They will offer a description as complete when it consists of no more than a list of the steps in a procedure, the rules of a process. A fine start is a disappointing conclusion. Process is but a fancy way to talk about form. The issue is not forms and how they are developed and presented; it is values, cultural priorities, and how they are ordered and enacted.

Second, the full range of cultural values involves complexities most apparent in the creation of artifacts. Students of verbal arts sometimes reduce folklore to a leisure time activity, to fun—important fun, to be sure, but fun nonetheless. Studying artifactual creativity, folklorists will be reminded of utilitarian values and economic realities, since most artifacts are overtly tools.

Third, studying the creation of artifacts, the manipulation of materials, helps us site people in their environments. It seems possible to study speech events as though people were floating in the air. Understanding their artifactual creativity will relocate them on the earth as real beings with physical as well as social constraints, economic as well as aesthetic problems.

And fourth, the fieldworker's task is simplified by certain aspects of artifactual creation. The process at which study begins can be literally observed. The most important dimensions of both verbal and material creativity are hidden in the performer's mind. But it is useful to be able to watch while things are formed in the air, visually following the progress of creation. Further, the craftsman making a banjo can be comfortably stopped in midprocess for explanations of decisions in a way that a singer cannot be. And, accustomed to performing without the immediate support of a familiar audience, the craftsman can perform efficiently and redundantly with only the fieldworker present.

Historical research is founded upon complete descriptions of objects. Complete descriptions of process are the base for research into the enactment of values. These descriptions begin with the accumulation of materials, when the basketmaker tramps through the snow to his woodlot to select a young oak as thick as the span of his hand, or the quilter collects old clothes in a basket. They follow exactly as the oak is riven and split, shaved and woven, as the cloth is cut into patches and strips, pieced, backed, and quilted. Descriptions do not end with baskets or quilts; they follow the objects through marketing into their new situations, where the basket is used by the basketmaker's neighbors to gather sweet corn in the fields of autumn, and the quilt becomes an ornamental hanging in a suburban home owned by a young couple who met at a folk festival. The maker's biography, centered upon learning and developing the craft, the maker's feelings toward manufacture and marketing, the user's attitudes toward the object and its creator—information on these topics provides some flesh for the technological skeleton.[4]

Any process, from making a mudpie to a nuclear submarine, might be described, but the folklorist's interest is drawn to processes over which people have control. When a process is controlled by a person or face-to-face group from accumulation through marketing, it will more fully express culture and satisfy personal needs than one that is fragmented. Delegating accumulation and marketing can leave individuals with a sense of the end product's being their own work. But when manufacture is broken into separate jobs done by separate people, the maker's control is abandoned to the design, and the product, the latest Ford automobile, is more the designer's than the maker's; it seems more the product of circumstance than of culture. Work in factories often entails more personal creativity than is realized by people whose notion of factory work comes off the assembly line in Chaplin's *Modern Times*, and workers do take pride in the soaring concrete viaducts they helped make, but since folklorists want to understand how culture is manifested in artifacts, they are drawn to objects that enact an intellectual and experiential unity, that were made by the people who designed them. It is logic, then, not nostalgia, that draws folklorists to men who make baskets, women who make quilts.

Control alone does not attract the folklorist. Intimacy, the object's capacity for meaningfully joining maker and user, is the other principle folklorists use to define their enterprise. This is the issue of communication and the rationale of tradition. It is logical for the folklorist to be drawn more to the artist struggling with social realities to enact collective values than to the artist struggling in the tangles of the psyche to express the ego. While the aficionados of "folk art" are fascinated by humble artists who thrash like the outlaws of recent art history, splattering idiosyncrasy over canvas, professional folklorists study chairmakers, santeros, quilters, cooks—artists whose products less celebrate the precious troubled soul than come forth as appropriate communication, as traditional expression. True folk artists lack neither individual talent nor personal spirit, but comfortably or painfully they subordinate these to group needs and received ideas.

Where artistic expression and social being, thought and action converge, there is the folklorist's focus. Folklore scholarship is not a matter of materials—banjoes and songs—but a tradition of inquiry and discourse. Within their tradition, folklorists decide what to study and how to talk about it. The key to deciding correctly is knowing what value relation is at stake. Other important relations could guide study—the relation of the sacred to the secular, for instance—but the essential one in folklore has been the aesthetic-ethical. The aesthetic is the senses' search for their own pleasure: the production of beauty for its own sake. The ethical is the just ordering of people: the production of a moral society. By studying their interpenetration, powerful matters like the relation of art to utility and the individual to the group are opened for serious discussion.

Why study folk artifacts? Within folklore scholarship, increased attention to material culture will help balance study. Recently folklorists have passed through a foolish phase of disregarding historical realities, leaving effects without causes, phenomena without explanations, and the status quo without challenge. Because they survive from times past, artifacts can transport us backward to deepen our understanding. Recently folklorists have drifted into an ethereal notion of human action. Artifacts, tools most of them, earthly all of them, will help snap us back to reality.

But folklorists should not study artifacts and verbal arts. They should, we should, attend to all modes of expression while studying things as they are. We should not collect banjoes and songs and singing events. We should be interested in all of what happens. Only through intense engagement with reality can we begin to answer our most serious questions. Must things be as they are?

NOTES

1. Important American studies of the landscape do exist. John Fraser Hart has given us a good survey in *The Look of the Land* (Englewood Cliffs, N.J.: Prentice-Hall, 1975). Among the fine, closer studies are: Donald W. Meinig, *Imperial Texas: An Interpretive Essay in Cultural Geography* (Austin: University of Texas Press, 1968); Peter O. Wacker, *The Musconetcong Valley of New Jersey: A Historical Geography* (New Brunswick, N.J.: Rutgers University Press, 1968). But the American land deserves work like Richard Weiss, *Häuser und Landshaften der Schweiz* (Erlenbach-Zurich and Stuttgart: Eugen Rentsch Verlag, 1959). W. G. Hoskins and E. Estyn Evans have both produced studies of sweeping scope and beautiful exactitude; see, for examples, Hoskins's *The Making of the English Landscape*, 1955 reprint (Harmondsworth: Penguin Books, 1971) and *The Midland Peasant: The Economic and Social History of a Leicestershire Village* (London: Macmillan, 1965); and Evans's *The Personality of Ireland: Habitat, Heritage and History* (Cambridge: Cambridge University Press, 1973) and *Mourne Country: Landscape and Life in South Down*, 1951 reprint (Dundalk: Dundalgan Press, 1967).

2. For the techniques of architectural recording, see: R. W. Brunskill, "A Systematic Procedure for Recording English Vernacular Architecture," *Transactions of the Ancient Monuments Society* 13 (1965–66): 43–126; Harley J. McKee, *Recording Historic Buildings: The Historic American Buildings Survey* (Washington, D.C.: U.S. Department of the Interior, National Park Service, 1970); Thomas B. Renk, "A Guide to Recording Structural Details of Historic Buildings," *Historical Archaeology* 3 (1969): 34–48; Warren E. Roberts, "Fieldwork: Recording Material Culture," in *Folklore and Folklife, An Introduction*, ed. Richard M. Dorson (Chicago: University of Chicago Press, 1972), pp. 435–39.

3. The use of technological and decorative detail as historic sources involves treating them, after the fashion of basic shape, as form. For examples of how this is done, see: Henry Glassie, "The Variation of Concepts within Tradition: Barn Building in Otsego County, New York," in *Man and Cultural Heritage: Papers in Honor of Fred F. Kniffen*, Geoscience and Man, 5, ed. H. J. Walker and W. G. Haag (Baton Rouge: School of Geoscience, Louisiana State University, 1974), pp.

177-233; Marcus Whiffen, *American Architecture Since 1780: A Guide to the Styles* (Cambridge, Mass.: The M.I.T. Press, 1969).

4. Studies of artists in action provide the best models for the student. The most notable works on American manual and mental process are: Michael Owen Jones, *The Hand-Made Object and Its Maker* (Berkeley and Los Angeles: University of California Press, 1975); Ruth L. Bunzel, *The Pueblo Potter: A Study of Creative Imagination in Primitive Art*, New York, 1926, reprint (New York: Dover Publications, 1972); Bernard L. Fontana, William J. Robinson, Charles W. Cormack, Ernest E. Leavitt, Jr., *Papago Indian Pottery* (Seattle: University of Washington Press, 1962). Minor works include: Henry Glassie, "William Houck, Maker of Pounded Ash Adirondack Pack-Baskets," *Keystone Folklore Quarterly* 12:1 (1967): 23-54; Howard Wight Marshall, "Mr. Westfall's Baskets: Traditional Craftsmanship in Northcentral Missouri," *Mid-South Folklore* 11:2 (1974): 43-50; John Michael Vlach, "Philip Simmons: Afro-American Blacksmith," in *Black People and Their Culture: Selected Writings from the African Diaspora*, ed. Linn Shapiro (Washington, D.C.: Smithsonian Institution, 1976), pp. 35-57. Useful comparison may be made with J. Geraint Jenkins's descriptive survey of British workers, *Traditional Country Craftsmen* (London: Routledge & Kegan Paul, 1965).

Carl Fleischhauer

Sound Recording and
Still Photography
in the Field

Successful use of media equipment in folklife fieldwork involves both selecting the right machine and using it effectively. Technically superior equipment is expensive and requires more sophistication of its user, but good work can be produced with even modest equipment if it is used well. Fieldworkers who are self-confident and who establish a comfortable working relationship with the people they visit are able to gracefully integrate equipment into any field situation.

SOUND RECORDING

Fieldwork most frequently involves audio recording, and the quality of this recording depends upon a variety of factors ranging from the situation itself to the type of tape recorder. For machines of similar quality, fidelity tends to be proportional to tape velocity and the width of the recording track. Broadcasters typically use machines that record the full width (full track) or half the width (half track) of the tape and operate their machines at 7½ inches per second. The open reel recorders sold for home use have two recording tracks one-quarter the width (quarter track) of the tape; tracks recorded in opposite directions are alternated on the tape (fig. 1). Among the drawbacks of audiocassette recording are the slower 1⅞-inches-per-second tape velocity and the relatively narrower track width. Cassettes are also mechanically more complex than reels and therefore more likely to jam, and harder to splice should the tape break.

But the preference of professional recordists for open reel recording over cassette recording goes beyond these problems. Because the most commonly used cassette recorders control the recording level automatically, they exaggerate background noise. In addition, they are usually equipped with built-in microphones that add the sound of the machine's own motor to recordings, although use of a separate microphone will overcome this drawback. Only the more expensive cassette recorders permit manual control of the recording level and contain special noise reduction circuits.

If the selection of a recorder were based solely on these technical considerations, the first choice would be a full track or half track reel-to-reel recorder. The next choice would be a reel-to-reel recorder with the quarter track format, followed by a

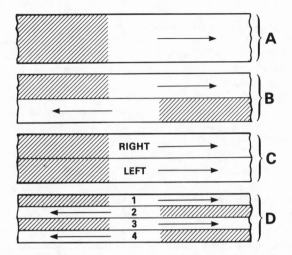

FIG. 1. Recording track formats. A: Full track mono. B: Half track mono, recorded in both directions (double track). C: Half track stereo. D: Quarter track stereo, recorded in both directions.

sophisticated cassette recorder, and, finally, a cassette recorder with automatic level control.

Anyone selecting a recorder, however, must also consider handling ease, which unfortunately often decreases as features to improve fidelity increase. Sophisticated cassette recorders weigh more and are a little harder to operate than the automatic ones, while most quarter track machines are heavy and awkward to move. Some half track and full track recorders share these drawbacks, although Nagra and a few of the other fully portable reel-to-reel machines are as small and light as the better cassette recorders and no more difficult to use.

Greater handling ease influences many fieldworkers to choose the simplest machines, but their decision is also reinforced by two widespread beliefs: first, that the standards of fidelity for recording the spoken word need not be as high as those applied to music, and, second, that more sophisticated or larger equipment intimidates informants. To argue that the spoken word does not deserve the same care as music is to argue that speech is not as precious as song or that the style and content of narrative is less than that of music. And although not all recordings will find their way onto a record album or a radio program, they may be deposited in an archive where future listeners deserve clarity of sound.

Certainly, in some situations equipment makes informants self-conscious or shy. Still, the most frequent recording task of folklorists is the interview-conversation, during which it is unlikely that a bigger machine intimidates any more than the mere fact of visiting and recording itself. Just as a tense interviewer will make informants uncomfortable, so the interviewer's uneasiness with machinery will quickly be communicated.

When I plan to record a person during a first visit, I often begin without my equipment and run back to the car for it after a comfortable interview has begun. I am usually able to set the recorder up as I carry on the conversation, but this process is greatly facilitated when I am joined by a second worker. During the American

Folklife Center's 1977 field project in Georgia, Alan Jabbour and I drove into the small town of Lenox one afternoon and started to chat with the storekeeper. As the talk became interesting, I slipped out to the car and brought in the recorder and cameras while Alan kept the conversation flowing. After the tape was safely rolling, I kept an eye on the recorder, interjected remarks and questions from time to time, and photographed the event.

The most critical factor in the recording situation is microphone placement, for a properly situated microphone will mitigate the shortcomings of a modest recorder. One common directional pattern is called "cardioid," often illustrated by a figure in the shape of a heart or semicircle (fig. 2). A classic radio announcer's setup consists of a cardioid microphone suspended eighteen or twenty inches from the mouth and slightly above the breathstream so air does not blow directly across the microphone (fig. 3). In the field, this setup can be duplicated with a microphone stand and boom arranged to allow the informant a clear line of sight to the interviewer. As the conversation progresses, the informant's attention is drawn to the interviewer and the microphone and stand at the periphery of vision become less distracting. Sound quality nearly equal to that of a cardioid microphone on a stand will be provided by a lavalier or clip-on microphone easily fastened to the informant's clothing. It may, however, limit movement slightly or be sensitive to the rustling of fabrics.

An unlimited number of techniques can enhance the quality of sound recording. Reverberation will be reduced by setting up in a room with carpets and draperies. In many homes, however, conversation normally occurs in the kitchen, where the

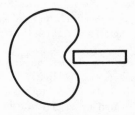

FIG. 2. (*Above*) The cardioid pattern. The microphone "hears" somewhat better in the direction it faces; most sounds coming from behind are also "heard," but with an off-mike quality.

FIG. 3. (*Right*) Interview microphone setup. A cardioid microphone is suspended about eighteen inches above and in front of the subject's head, leaving open a clear line of sight to the interviewer.

floors and walls are bare. Echoing here can be reduced if the subject sits in a relatively open space rather than against a reflecting surface. Similarly, the noise from kitchen appliances burdens a recording with a very bothersome hum, which is eliminated if the appliances are turned off or unplugged during the recording session. If the interviewer poses questions in a slightly louder than normal tone, the responses will also be spoken more loudly and the clarity of the recording improved.

Dwight Diller, Alan Jabbour, and I, for instance, had recorded the Hammons family in West Virginia intermittently for two years, but good takes of some of Burl Hammons's fiddle tunes continued to elude us. Finally, on a particularly noisy and hectic weekend at Burl's home, we rented a motel room for a few hours and—in an echo of the pioneer days of commercial recording—taped the music there. When I recorded West Virginia fiddler Melvin Wine a few years later, the interfering sounds were likely to come from a television set in the next room, but his family would always graciously sacrifice their viewing for an hour or two while we recorded.

Melvin, like most fiddlers I know, tended to think of taping a tune as a kind of demonstration and would customarily play the tune for three repetitions lasting about a minute and a half. Such brief takes make unsatisfying selections on a phonograph record, and so I would time Melvin as he played and signal to him after two and a half minutes that it was safe to stop.

Many aspects of fieldwork run counter to the accepted norms of polite behavior. Fieldworkers often find it a little hard to visit someone solely to elicit information rather than for friendly conversation. Similarly, fieldworkers are even more uncomfortable in suggesting that microphones on visible stands be set up or refrigerators unplugged. Still, I believe the act of interviewing itself is the source of discomfort and not the manner of its execution. Folklorists who work carefully with good equipment convey to the informant how much they value his words and thus produce a flattering and positive effect. To introduce equipment without adding tension to the field situation, fieldworkers must act calmly and confidently. The behavior required resembles a physician's bedside manner or a professional photographer's way of coping with nervous portrait sitters.

Fieldworkers record performances, activities, and events as well as interviews. The best possible recordings in these more difficult circumstances require a stereo recorder, multiple or special-purpose microphones, a mixer, or even a studio. A preacher who traverses the church during his sermon might be recorded with a wireless microphone, a conversation in a workplace might be captured with the aid of a highly directional "shotgun" microphone, and a semiprofessional musical ensemble might best be recorded in a studio. The basic equipment needed for a simple interview will be far less adequate in these situations. A modestly equipped fieldworker might concentrate on clearly recording one or two aspects of a situation and then accept moderate to poor recording quality for the rest of the situation. For instance, a single microphone in a church could be placed to favor congregational singing and provide only fair coverage of the preaching. Or, with two microphones and cables but no mixer, one microphone might be placed to cover the singing and the other the preaching and the cables plugged and unplugged as needed.

A useful setup for stereo recording consists of a pair of cardioid pattern microphones whose tips very nearly touch and whose bodies are on the same plane at an angle of ninety degrees (fig. 4). A clamp on the microphone stand holds the microphone in the correct position. The pair delivers a stereo "picture" covering

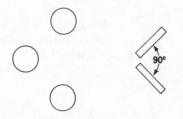

FIG. 4. Recording a trio in stereo with a coincident-tip microphone setup. A pair of cardioid microphones are placed on a stand about five or six feet from the trio. The musician in the middle will be centered on the recording; the other two musicians will be off-center, but the trio will blend smoothly from left to right without exaggerated stereo separation.

about 180 degrees, blending the left channel across to the right. If placed in relation to a single source of sound as a single microphone would be, the solo voice or instrument is recorded equally on both channels, providing the effect of monaural or center-channel sound. Sounds such as doors closing, chairs squeaking, pets or farm animals calling, or the interviewer's questions will be louder on one channel than the other with the overall effect suggesting ambiance and directionality without exaggerated stereo separation.

A balanced musical ensemble, usually one accustomed to performing without a public address system, can be recorded with a single microphone or stereo pair at a distance sufficient to cover the entire group. Many professional and semi-professional groups rely upon sound reinforcement to perform and therefore need a separate microphone for each sound source to make a balanced recording, as well as a microphone mixer and a setup in which the sound recorded on the tape can be monitored separately from the sound in the air. Headphones that shut out ambient sound may suffice, but it may be necessary to monitor the audio in an adjacent room. Some ensembles are best recorded in a studio.

STILL PHOTOGRAPHY

Many professional photographers use larger film format cameras, but cameras that take 35mm film are ideal for many tasks and serve as excellent general purpose tools, especially if they accommodate interchangeable lenses. The normal lens sold with most camera bodies is not necessarily the most useful lens for fieldwork and a potential buyer may wish to substitute one or more other lenses.

Lenses are differentiated by their focal lengths (usually expressed in millimeters), which define the angle of view. For cameras using 35mm film, normal lenses are ones with focal lengths of about 50mm; wide-angle lenses have shorter focal lengths, and telephoto lenses have longer ones. The maximum aperture (or opening size) of a lens is also an important distinguishing feature, especially when comparing lenses of the same or similar focal length. Lenses with larger apertures admit more light and can be used more easily in dimly lit situations. With a light-sensitive black-and-white film like Eastman Kodak Tri-X, a lens opening of f2 can be used in a typical home interior with a shutter speed of 1/60th of a second, while a lens with a smaller f2.8 aperture would require the use of a 1/30th of a second shutter speed for an equivalent exposure. This longer shutter speed makes it more difficult to hold the camera steady.

Lenses with a wide angle of view are essential for photographing human activities. Wide-angle lenses with focal lengths from 35mm to about 20mm will frame pictures of two or more persons and their activities. Depending upon distance to the subject and the viewing angle, any lens may render perspective differently from the way the eye perceives it, an effect especially noticeable with wide-angle lenses. Still, if human activity is in the foreground and is the principal picture element, it can often be well represented in spite of perspective distortion. If the subject matter, on the other hand, is something like architecture, careful placement of the camera can help make the perspective seem normal even when a wide-angle lens is used.

The narrow angle of view of telephoto lenses makes them suitable for photographing details. Portraits are customarily made with a lens whose focal length is slightly longer than normal. With 35mm cameras, face or bust portraits are customarily taken with lenses whose focal lengths vary from 85mm to 105mm. Such lenses are manufactured with relatively wide maximum apertures and are also useful when photographing details of work process, sections of a landscape, and the like. Lenses with focal lengths over 135mm rarely have wide maximum apertures nor are they capable of focusing closer than eight or ten feet and are therefore more useful outdoors where the details to be photographed are further away and more light is available. Zoom lenses provide a range of focal lengths in a single optic, but trade off this versatility for greater size and weight and smaller maximum apertures.

Most camera manufacturers offer "micro" or "macro" lenses whose focal lengths are close to those of normal lenses and capable of taking close-ups of small objects or copying old photographs as well as shooting normal scenes. These lenses usually do not offer wide apertures since they are designed to provide high resolution and flatness of field. They can be especially helpful if a fieldworker already has other lenses with wide apertures.

The presentation of photographs is most effective if close-ups are mixed with photos showing larger portions of a scene. The more lenses and camera positions used to collect a variety of images, the easier the editing. Most photojournalists expose twenty times the number of pictures they expect to need, thus providing more coverage for the editor, increasing the likelihood that significant or fleeting moments in action or gesture are recorded, and permitting sets of pictures to be made at slightly different exposures. This variation of exposure, called bracketing, compensates for uncertainty about the best exposure in any given situation.

Characteristics of the subject matter may dictate the choice of color or black-and-white film, but the decision is often more sensibly made in terms of the intended use for the pictures. Color transparencies are generally used for presentations in a class or meeting and for most color reproduction in printed publications. Publications, however, reproduce black-and-white photographs from positive prints and the best results are obtained if the original photography is done on black-and-white negative film. Such prints will also give the best results in an exhibit where the photographic print itself is displayed. Black-and-white prints may be derived from color slides, but the results are inferior, especially if the color film used is a grainier, high-speed film like Ektachrome. Since black-and-white photographic materials have a longer life span than color materials, archival considerations have led the

American Folklife Center to encourage fieldworkers to use two cameras and create separate sets of color and black-and-white images whenever possible.

The ability of any given type of film to produce a sharp image is proportional to the film emulsion's sensitivity to light; films that require more light ("slower") generally produce sharper pictures. This difference is more striking in the case of color films and many press photographers use a high-speed black-and-white film such as Tri-X in most situations but switch from less sensitive Kodachrome to a higher speed Ektachrome in situations where light levels are low.

While fieldworkers may compensate for underexposed film by increased development ("pushing"), this technique also increases granularity and contrast. At some point every photographer must add light in dark places and may do so by replacing existing light bulbs with ones of higher wattage where this will not cause a safety hazard. The amount of light can also be increased by using additional fixtures. Turning lights on during an event is disruptive and can be avoided by turning lights on before people enter a room, or by turning special lights on at the same time as the normal ones.

Flash units are very portable and are brighter than photographic lights whose illumination is constant. These advantages are offset, however, by the obtrusiveness of the flash itself. In addition, because flashguns are often aligned with the camera lens, they give very flat illumination, unlike the modeling effect of off-axis lighting. This unattractive direct light may be avoided by bouncing the flash from the ceiling or by using one or more units at a distance from the camera. Moderately priced flash units equipped with automatic exposure control in both direct and bounce modes are available.

Photographs made in the field include posed pictures of people, pictures of inanimate objects or scenes, and images made in more or less candid fashion. Pictures of the first two sorts permit the use of a tripod or other camera support, thus allowing the photographer to eliminate camera unsteadiness, use smaller lens openings for a deeper zone of focus, and shoot fine grain films. Exposures of several seconds or more will permit photography in very dim interiors.

People are distracted from the camera when they are engaged in activity, thereby permitting the fieldworker to make more naturalistic photographs. Through actions, movements, or gestures a photographer's reactions to a scene will be communicated to the subjects. By changing position when the movement will be least distracting, shooting from less prominent or obtrusive positions, or simply waiting for the right moment to shoot, the photographer can reduce camera-motivated behavior.

Equipment must be attentively operated to realize its full potential; rapport must be maintained with informants in order to make a visit productive. This dual demand requires intense concentration but, as with any professional skill, ability increases with experience. The more familiar a worker is with the equipment, the more energy can be devoted to the human relationship. Media documentation shares with other aspects of fieldwork a need for a sense of purpose that gives a worker a certainty of manner.

Just as a writer's prose is often improved by an editor, a media editor can help a maker of non-print documents assess and structure images or sounds. The memories of the time when photographs or recordings were made often blind a worker to their omissions or weaknesses. Like finished writing, edited presentations of pictures and sounds involve the manipulation of symbolic forms, and their success as items of communication can be judged by others.

Janet Langlois and Philip LaRonge

Using a Folklore Archive

Traditional figures of speech such as "between the devil and the deep blue sea" and "on the horns of a dilemma" accurately describe the position of a researcher who needs to make use of folklore archives. On the one hand, a researcher must rely on an archive for adequate coverage of the folk process. Barre Toelken, author of *The Dynamics of Folklore*, comments, "Folklore collections are more than merely the playground for scholars, for in folklore archives is the most telling evidence of the vitality of cultural tradition in our country as well as elsewhere."[1] And George List, former director of the Archives of Traditional Music, observes, "The folklore archive serves to record these traditions as an aid to the study of cultural change."[2] On the other hand, the user may find working in an archive a most difficult task, because of the incompleteness, inaccessibility, and sensitivity of folklore collections as recorded cultural traditions.

Knowing What You Want: The Nature of Archival Collections
American folklorists have many points of view about the methods of collection, the data to be collected, and the meaning of folklore for the participants and for the analysts. This theoretical diversity is reflected in the individualistic quality of American folklore archives, each one usually mirroring the particular concepts of the organization with which it is associated. The oldest folklore archive in the United States, the Archive of Folk Culture at the Library of Congress, founded in 1928, like an archaeological site, reveals successive layers of theory in its changing systems of cataloging and in the types of material accessioned over the years.

Some folklore archives specialize in certain genres, such as the Archives of Traditional Music at Indiana University and the National Storytelling Research Center in Jonesborough, Tennessee. Others, especially those connected with universities and local historical societies, tend to be rich in the traditions of the areas in which they are located. The Wayne State University Folklore Archive contains extensive holdings of urban and ethnic materials, thanks to its location in Detroit, the nation's fourth largest metropolitan area. Archives affiliated with academic institutions often contain specialized materials unrelated to their location because of student or faculty interests; the large collection of Micronesian materials at the Indiana University Folklore Archives, for example, is directly attributable to Roger Mitchell's fieldwork in the South Pacific.

Archival records range from index cards, manuscripts, audio recordings, photographs, slides, films, and audiovisual tapes to objects and artifacts. Earlier records tend to emphasize text while the later ones emphasize context and performance.

The adequacy of each record, regardless of the medium in which it is preserved, depends on the training and skill of the field collectors and the equipment available to them. Because folklore archives in the United States, with the exception of the Archive of Folk Culture in the Library of Congress, are not operating with sizeable budgets, they become depositories for collections rather than research facilities. Accordingly, they depend on nonprofessional collectors, often students in college or university folklore classes, for their materials although professional folklorists have made contributions as well. The strength of this system of recording folk traditions is that nonprofessionals often have entrée to situations unknown to professionals; the weakness is that cultural records are less complete and less accurate than they might be.

Researchers, then, must judge the appropriateness of the resources for the project at hand. Assuming they accept that "half a loaf is better than none," their next step is to locate archival materials and master the finding aids available in each institution.

Finding What You Want: Location of Archives and Classification Systems

Unfortunately, there are no guides to folklore archives currently available which list specialized holdings within the archives themselves. However, there are several options open to researchers. One is to check standard bibliographic references for listings such as Gale Research's *Special Libraries Directory*, the Library of Congress's *National Union Catalogue for Manuscript Collections*, and the Society of American Archivists' *National Archives Directory*. Another is to refer to the *Folklore Archives of the World: A Preliminary Guide*, published as *Folklore Forum*'s first number of its Bibliographic and Special Series,[3] and to *A List of Folklore and Folk Music Archives and Related Collections in the United States and Canada*, published in Washington, D.C., by the Archive of Folk Culture in the Library of Congress. A third is to request information from individual archives, since several publish guides indicating the types, sources, and format of their collections while some publish holdings lists arranged by genre or ethnic origin.[4] Initiatives of the Archiving Section of the American Folklore Society under the direction of Richard Thill and Dan Ben-Amos and the publication of *Archiving News*[5] promise centralized information on archival locations and holdings.

A researcher's visit to an archive is preferable to a mail inquiry. Although most archives do have some policy for handling research correspondence, this approach is generally more difficult, frustrating, and time-consuming than direct consultation. Preliminary contact with the archive, stating areas of interest as specifically as possible, will allow archival staff to make some preparations for the researcher and thus allow the researcher to use time allotted more efficiently. Too general a subject will only lead to confusion; most archivists have at least one favorite anecdote about the lady who wanted to see "everything you have" about German superstitions or cures for the common cold. On the other hand, if the researcher is looking for a particular German superstition among a certain group in a certain time—say, second-generation Germans living in Chicago—the project's scope will be manageable.

Specificity will give the focus needed to use the various finding aids, the nature of which are determined largely by the arrangement of materials in each archive. In genre-based archives, collections are broken up physically and each item filed in folders or boxes according to genre or the ethnic or occupational origin of the material. At the University of California at Berkeley, for example, a researcher interested in Portuguese jokes goes first to the Portuguese file, then to the folder within that file marked "jokes." There is no concordance or card catalogue for the collection, simply a master list of categories in the file and a list of informants' names.

Far more common is the system by which collections are kept together physically as much as possible and their contents indexed. This method has the advantage of keeping data obtained by the same collector together with accompanying contextual material. The cross references by genre, ethnicity, and subject are compiled into a card catalogue. For example, a collection of Mexican songs, tales, and foodways is indexed by four catalogue cards representing the culture and each of the three genres found in the collection. Some card catalogues go further and index specific titles, motif numbers, and names of persons and places mentioned in the text. Access to the needed material is thus assured, although the researcher must often read through a large and varied collection to find it.

The computerization of folk archival catalogues and indexes is one of the goals of the American Folklore Society's Archiving Section. Transforming multiple finding aids into a standardized input system open to national and international usage is a monumental task. Nevertheless, the Computerized Folklore Archive at the University of Detroit and the Folklore Archive at the University of Nebraska at Omaha have not only computerized catalogues but computerized collections as well.

Using What You Want: Ethical Questions and Research Suggestions

Although physical protection of the collections in terms of appropriate storage facilities and preservation techniques is the responsibility of the archive,[6] the researcher's obligation is the other side of the same coin. Archival materials are usually irreplaceable and proper handling while doing research is essential to prevent damage.

Ethical protection of the collections is a responsibility also shared by archives and researchers and one that has far-reaching implications for folklore research. Although most archives have some system of contracts with donors and informants, the ownership and use of archival materials is an area fraught with legal problems, many as yet unsettled in the courts, to say nothing of the ethical questions involved in the collection and use of folkloric materials in general.

Perhaps the researcher's greatest problem is to strike a delicate balance between conserving sensitive or esoteric cultural materials and publishing information vital to the understanding of culture for the scientific community. Some practical advice about ethical use of archival holdings may be helpful at this point. When examining materials, it is best not to quote directly without the archivist's permission, especially if the collection is under restrictions. Wayne State University Folklore Archive staff follow this rule with collections concerning drug-related, prison, and police folklore since members of these folk groups can be recognized by style of speech and other indicators.

The researcher who wishes to copy parts of a collection or make use of it in a publication should check the archive's policy on these matters. Some archives will obtain the donor or the collector's permission before sending the materials. Others, such as the Archive of Folk Culture, will charge the researcher with that responsibility; a permission slip is generally provided with the inquiry form, and by signing it the researcher frees the archive of any involvement in the misuse of the materials.

The researcher hoping to use folklore archive resources for publication purposes may feel somewhat like the ancient voyager caught between Charybdis and Scylla, given the alternatives discussed above. Several different types of research have been successfully completed, nevertheless.

(1) Research proper. A survey of the representative *Readings in American Folklore*, edited by Jan Harold Brunvand, shows that many articles in the first two sections, "Collections of American Folk Materials" and "Folklore in Context" respectively, focus on field-collected and archive-deposited records of the folk process. In "The Surpriser Surprised: A Modern Legend," William Hugh Jansen compares various archival texts of the urban narrative in which a man, expecting a sexual encounter with his secretary, finds himself nude at his own surprise birthday party.[7] Sylvia Ann Grider's " 'Con Safos': Mexican-Americans, Names and Graffiti" utilizes text and context, collected by students in Texas, to examine relations between writings on walls and belief systems.[8]

The articles in the last two sections of *Readings* move the focus from archival materials themselves to their analysis and to theoretical perspectives in folklore in general. Cultural records become the empirical base for theory, either as concrete examples in Alan Dundes's article on "Games Morphology" or as general reference in Roger D. Abrahams's "Folklore in Culture."[9]

(2) Preliminary research. For the researcher planning individual fieldwork, archival collections can furnish background information. They can be useful in initial selection of research topics, in modifying research designs, and in locating geographical and cultural areas for study. Depending on archival policy, the resources of folklore archives may supply the researcher with names of potential interviewees.

(3) Supplemental research. Once the researcher has completed field research, archival material can be used as backup data. Kay L. Cothran acknowledges her debt to the Georgia Folklore Archive in her study on narrative performance, "Talking Trash in the Okefenokee Swamp Rim, Georgia,"[10] and Roger Abrahams thanks the Western Kentucky University Folklore Archives in the opening pages of his *Deep Down in the Jungle: Negro Narrative Folklore from the Streets of Philadelphia*,[11] to cite but two instances. Archival cross-referencing contributes to the authenticity of the published study and sets up a network of footnotes and bibliographies for other researchers interested in related topics.

Perhaps the final relation of archive and researcher to be mentioned here is the one in which the researcher either donates material to an already established archive, develops an original archive, or encourages those interviewed to set up their own community archive. In the first case, contracts between donors and archives are designed to protect the personal and literary rights of researchers and those interviewed while opening up the data to a wider audience. In the latter cases, basic manuals about archive procedures are published by the Society for American Archivists. Most folklore archives will send guidelines upon request. Archival consultants are available through state and federal granting agencies, most notably in the program of the National Endowment for the Humanities on Local, State and Regional History. Using a folklore archive can be a rewarding experience for all researchers. Developing, maintaining, and augmenting archives are necessary means to this end.

SELECTED AMERICAN FOLKLORE ARCHIVES

INDIANA UNIVERSITY:

Archive of Traditional Music
Maxwell Hall
Bloomington, IN 47405

Folklore Archives
Folklore Institute
510 N. Fess
Bloomington, IN 47405

LIBRARY OF CONGRESS:

Archive of Folk Culture
Washington, D.C. 20540

MADISON COUNTY
HISTORICAL SOCIETY:

Traditional Craft Archive
435 Main St.
Oneida, NY 13421

UNIVERSITY OF CALIFORNIA
AT BERKELEY:

Folklore Archive
Department of Anthropology
Berkeley, CA 94720

UNIVERSITY OF CALIFORNIA
AT LOS ANGELES:

Archive of California and Western
Folklore
Center for the Study of Comparative
Folklore and Mythology
1037 GSM - Library Wing
405 Hilgard Ave.
Los Angeles, CA 90024

UNIVERSITY OF DETROIT:

Computerized Folklore Archive
4001 W. McNichols Road
Detroit, MI 48221

UNIVERSITY OF MAINE:

Northeast Archives of Folklore
and Oral History
South Stevens Hall
Orono, ME 04469

UNIVERSITY OF NEBRASKA
AT OMAHA:

Folklore Archive
Omaha, NE 68182

UNIVERSITY OF OREGON:

Randall V. Mills Memorial Archive
of Northwest Folklore
Department of English
University of Oregon
Eugene, OR 97403

UNIVERSITY OF PENNSYLVANIA:

Folklore Archive
Folklore and Folklife
Room 415, Logan Hall CN
Philadelphia, PA 19104

UNIVERSITY OF TEXAS:

Center for Intercultural Studies
in Folklore and Ethnomusicology
Austin, TX 78712

UTAH STATE UNIVERSITY:

Fife Folklore Archive
Department of English
UMC 32
Logan, UT 84322

WAYNE STATE UNIVERSITY:

Folklore Archive
Wayne State University
448 Purdy Library
Detroit, MI 48202

WESTERN KENTUCKY UNIVERSITY:

Western Kentucky Folklore, Folklife
 and Oral History Archive
University Libraries
Western Kentucky University
Bowling Green, KY 42101

NOTES

1. Barre Toelken, "Folklore Archives" in *Dynamics of Folklore* (Boston: Houghton Mifflin, 1979), p. 307.

2. George List, "Archiving" in *Folklore and Folklife, An Introduction*, ed. Richard M. Dorson (Chicago: University of Chicago Press, 1972), p. 455. See also the journal *The Folklore and Folk Music Archivist*, volumes 1–10, published at Indiana University, Bloomington, under the editorship of George List, 1958–68.

3. Peter Aceves and Magnus Einarsson-Mullarky, comp., *Folklore Archives of the World: A Preliminary Guide*, *Folklore Forum* Bibliographic and Special Series No. 1 (November 1968), 27 pp.

4. *Guide to the Indiana University Folklore Archives* (Bloomington, 1976) and *Folkstore One at the University of Detroit* (Detroit: University of Detroit Computerized Folklore Archive, n.d.) are good examples of the former, while Wayne State University Folklore Archive, *Afro-American Folklore Collections*, Annotated Holdings List No. 1 (Detroit, 1977), *Polish and Polish-American Folklore Collections*, Annotated Holdings List No. 2 (Detroit, 1978), and *German and German-American Folklore Collections*, Holdings List No. 3 (Detroit, 1980) are good examples of the latter.

5. *AFS Archiving Section Newsletter* 1:1 and 1:2 published at the University of Nebraska at Omaha by editor Richard S. Thill. The Society of American Archivists, 330 S. Wells, Chicago, IL 60606, publishes a quarterly journal, *The American Archivist*, and a monthly *Newsletter*.

6. See Toelken, pp. 308–11.

7. Jan Harold Brunvand, ed., *Readings in American Folklore* (New York: Norton, 1979), pp. 64–90.

8. Ibid., pp. 138–51.

9. Ibid., pp. 334–44 and pp. 390–403.

10. Ibid., pp. 215–35.

11. Roger D. Abrahams, *Deep Down in the Jungle: Negro Narrative Folklore from the Streets of Philadelphia* (Hatboro, Pa.: Folklore Associates, 1964).

Richard Blaustein

Using Video in the Field

A good craftsman always tries to use the right tool for the job, and the person setting out to collect folklore would do well to keep this bit of folk wisdom in mind when choosing equipment for fieldwork projects. Portable video, like any collecting medium, has its own particular advantages and limitations, and the fieldworker must carefully consider these in relation to the desired end product. First of all, portable video is still very new, and improvements and changes are taking place constantly. The black-and-white half-inch reel-to-reel Portapak, commercially introduced by the Sony Corporation in 1968, has been rendered virtually obsolete for most purposes by the various portable color-capable videocassette recorders now available for professional broadcasting and home use, and there are all sorts of options and accessories to suit a wide range of needs and budgets.[1] If the fieldworker's objective is to produce a documentary for educational distribution or television broadcast, 16mm sound film should be seriously considered as an alternative to video. Broadcast-quality three-quarter-inch portable equipment, now extensively used in television news coverage, is commercially available, but is at least as technically demanding as film and is quite expensive ($5,000 for the recorder itself, plus an additional $10,000 to $85,000 for a professional color camera).

If broadcastable audiovisual quality is not an overriding concern, however, there are many ways in which the folklorist can effectively use portable half-inch videocassette equipment (designed for home use) in the field. First of all, such equipment is relatively inexpensive ($800-1200 for the recorder, $300-500 for a black-and-white camera, $1000-1500 for a color camera), compact and reasonably durable, though constant maintenance is *absolutely essential* to keep it in working order. Secondly, the equipment is easy to operate; a beginner can be taught the basics of shooting video in half an hour. For the beginner, another attractive feature is the low cost of videotape as compared to film ($11-20 for a one hour Beta or half hour VHS cassette); practice tapes can instantly be reviewed and erased to be used again, if initial results are unsatisfactory. Depending on the format of the particular videocassette recorder, it is possible to shoot from a half-hour to six hours of uninterrupted action. These features not only make portable video an excellent learning tool for the beginning fieldworker but also open up for the seasoned researcher exciting possibilities unavailable with other collecting media.

In addition to allowing extensive, in-depth documentation of situations and activities, portable video's instant playback capacity enables the researcher to gain a better understanding of the participant's perceptions of sociocultural events, through the process of making video recordings, playing them back to informants, and taking note of their comments and responses.[2] As part of a video documentary that my students and I were doing on the quilting tradition of a small upper East Tennessee farming community, we shot landscape footage to provide background and supplement the interviews and activities we had already recorded. When we showed the landscape footage to the quilters, most of whom happened to be from old established prosperous families in the community, their responses were surprising and revealing. As long as they saw scenes of lush meadows, fat cattle and freshly painted houses, they were content, but as soon as scenes of run-down cabins, sagging fences, and ramshackle sawmills appeared on the screen, they protested, with comments such as, "Cut that out of the tape! That's ugly! That's Appalachian!" Since their comments and suggestions were to be the basis for our edit outline, we followed their wishes and did exclude the bits of local landscape they found offensive. Other investigators may wish to lay different ground rules for a similar situation, but the point is that the playback capacity can be used to elicit the socioeconomically determined ways in which individuals selectively perceive and evaluate their physical environments. This unique advantage can be taken a step further by teaching informants to make their own video recordings; their tapes then become objective indicators of cultural, perceptual, and cognitive style.[3] To those modern folklorists who define their interests in terms such as "the ethnography of play," "the ethnography of communication," and "expressive culture," the appeal of portable video lies in its ability to document lengthy sequences of communication and interaction and also to facilitate the investigation of the insider's interpretation of folkloric events through the playback process. But even if the fieldworker doesn't share such high-level theoretical concerns and is simply interested in recording folk performers and craftspeople, portable video still has a lot to offer.

The nature of the subject or event to be recorded largely determines the type of equipment and number of people involved in a particular video documentation project. Generally speaking, video works best when its subject matter involves physical action, such as music-making, dancing, or crafts; verbal folklore, such as stories, jokes, and proverbs, usually does not come across well on video, unless the informant happens to be a particularly lively raconteur or there is an audience other than the fieldworker with whom to interact.

As in any fieldwork situation, it is essential that the researcher be capable of establishing rapport with prospective informants; a relaxed atmosphere minimizes the potentially distracting and intimidating effects of the recording equipment. The video equipment itself also can be a great help in establishing rapport. The fieldworker whose goal is to record individuals or small groups of people engaged in relatively sedentary home activities, such as singing, playing musical instruments, or making handicrafts, needs to have a small portable TV set in addition to a video recorder and camera. Before getting down to serious taping, the fieldworker can show informants how the equipment works (a wonderful ice-breaker in itself), play previously recorded tapes of other people engaged in similar activities, and also let informants become comfortable with the taping situation by viewing themselves on TV. Aside from the additional information that reviewing tapes with informants can provide, it also gives the fieldworker and subjects an opportunity to unwind after a taping session. A family of old-time musicians I recorded came to look upon these tape-viewing sessions as their own TV show and would invite friends and neighbors to join them. These rapport-establishing techniques are even more effective when the tape is played back on the informant's own TV set.

If color is not absolutely essential to the end product, satisfactory black-and-white quality can be obtained indoors with a 300-watt light bulb screwed into an overhead light fixture. With color equipment, a floodlight, with its attendant discomfort from heat and glare, will be necessary (unless the researcher uses one of the new Panasonic or JVC color cameras capable of producing satisfactory images at light levels as low as 3 footcandles). Of course, the recording could be moved outdoors, though this course of action takes an event out of its natural context. The single fieldworker shooting indoors can employ a variety of techniques, such as hand-holding the camera at eye level, placing it on a tripod at chest height, or holding it on the lap and using a small TV set placed between the camera operator and subject as a monitor. There are tradeoffs involved in all these approaches. For instance, hand-holding provides more freedom but requires a very steady hand (unless you are using one of the newer lightweight cameras that can be comfortably balanced on the shoulder), and there is also the problem of confronting the subject with a glaring lens rather than a pair of human eyes. Conversely, while lap-holding makes it possible to operate the camera and yet maintain something like normal eye contact, it is hard to keep from fidgeting and wobbling the camera.

Although a single fieldworker can produce reasonably satisfactory results, actually the best solution is to adopt a team approach, letting one fieldworker take the role of interviewer while the other stays in the background to operate the equipment. This method usually results in superior content and technical quality and is much less distracting to all concerned. The team approach becomes absolutely necessary when working outdoors, especially if the activity to be recorded involves a lot of movement. Depending on the nature and location of the event, as well as the availability of house current, there are various ways in which the video recorder can be used outdoors. If the activity occurs close to a source of electricity, the video recorder can be placed on the ground and powered with an extension cord; a long camera extension cable will give the camera operator optimum freedom of movement, otherwise a tripod and a telephoto lens may be required. If, however, the activity involves a great deal of continual movement, such as following an herb-gatherer up a steep mountain path to get to a patch of wild ginseng, the video recorder will have to be battery-powered, which will permit only a half-hour of shooting time, and the interviewer will have to manage the recorder and microphone to leave a partner free to handle the camera. Modified backpack frames set up to hold the recorder and camera are available, but I have found that these are rather cumbersome and can easily throw a person off balance, especially when hiking over rugged terrain. When shooting outdoors, a windscreen for the microphone is a must; in a pinch, one can be improvised with foam plastic and adhesive tape.

Videotaping formal staged events such as fiddle contests, bluegrass festivals, or revival meetings is entirely another story. Formal events of this sort do not demand nearly as much personal involvement on the part of the fieldworker; it is much easier to play the role of the detached observer and record spontaneous behavior, rather than actively stimulate informants to perform as one generally does in a home recording situation. The taping of formal events does require a certain degree of planning and protocol. The fieldworker must obtain permission to record the event from its sponsor and check out the physical layout and power supply situation beforehand. Equipment should be set up and tested on site well in advance of the actual performance time. Once the event starts, unnecessary movement and talking must be avoided; TV studio headset intercoms will be needed if multiple cameras and a video mixer are being used. Otherwise, shooting options can range from a single hand-held or tripod-mounted camera to two separate units used to record stage action and audience response. Battery-operated video recorders are well suited to document informal, small-scale activities taking place on the periphery of the main event, such as the impromptu picking and dancing sessions found at most fiddle contests and bluegrass festivals.

Video is still very new and its full potential remains to be explored. As portable video technology is increasingly refined, it will undoubtedly play a greater role in the collecting and study of folklore; even so, it will never be appropriate to all types of fieldwork. Media overkill is a constant danger, and older, more unobtrusive and less technically complicated collecting media, such as still photography, audio recording, even handwritten notes, may be better suited to the particular project at hand than portable video. The fieldworker needs to be aware of available options, in order to choose equipment accordingly, otherwise collecting tools may serve to hinder rather than enhance the information-gathering process. Portable video is no panacea; it has its virtues and flaws, but for the researcher interested in obtaining large quantities of audiovisual data at relatively low cost and gaining a deeper understanding of the ways in which participants perceive activities and events, portable video just might be the best available tool for the job.

NOTES

1. Information concerning currently available video recorders and accessories can be obtained free of charge from the following manufacturers:

Quasar Electronics Company
9401 W. Grand Avenue
Franklin Park, IL 60131

Sony Corporation of America
9 West 57th Street
New York, NY 10019

Panasonic Company
One Panasonic Way
Secaucus, NJ 07094

US JVC Corporation
58–75 Queens Midtown Expressway
Maspeth, NY 11328

Toshiba America, Inc.
280 Park Avenue
New York, NY 10017

For reviews of new equipment in the home-use video market, see: *Video* (Reese Publishing Co., 235 Park Ave. So., New York, NY 10003). For reviews of professional broadcast-quality equipment, see: *Broadcast Communications* (Globecom Publishing, Ltd., 4121 W. 83rd St., Suite 216, Prairie Village, KS 66208).

2. See Stephanie Krebs, "The Film Elicitation Technique," in *Principles of Visual Anthropology*, ed. Paul Hockings (The Hague: Mouton, 1974), pp. 283–302.

3. See Beryl L. Bellman and Bennetta Jules-Rosette, *A Paradigm for Looking* (Norwood, N.J.: Ablex, 1977).

Willard B. Moore

Folklore Research and Museums

When Joan Mondale decided in 1977 to decorate the Christmas tree in the vice-presidential mansion with original American crafts, she sought the help of Paul Smith, director of the Museum of Contemporary Crafts in New York. Through Smith, Mondale found Beatrice Coaxum, a black traditional basket-maker from Mount Pleasant, South Carolina, and obtained some of her sweet grass and palmetto leaf baskets. Then Coaxum was invited to the capital by the Mondales, visited the Smithsonian's Renwick Gallery, and was astonished to find there baskets from Angola which closely resembled her own. Though she knew that her family's craft had been traced to West Africa, she was nevertheless stunned by the reality of a cultural diffusion.[1]

This news item illustrates the basic functions of a museum. By definition, museums are artificial environments that serve as collecting points for those materials, cultural and natural, which our society deems valuable, often irreplaceable. If they are collected with sufficient contextual documentation and properly conserved they are invaluable to the researcher in need of tangible cultural evidence. A museum is the logical place to find culturally related objects, arranged so that they can easily be appreciated and studied.

The resourceful folklorist, whether in search of an accurate sampling of regional basketry, reviewing a taxonomy of mountain herbs and medicinal plants, or hoping to bolster a study of occupational folklore with the recorded narratives of sailors and miners, can turn to a wide variety of museums. They extend from the small lighthouse museums on Maine's rocky coast to the comprehensive Bishop Museum in Honolulu. Museums recognized by the American Association of Museums as meeting specific museological standards are listed in the official museum *Directory* together with each museum's specialty area and research facilities.[2] Many museums are not listed, but they should not be ignored. They are often small museums whose collections, though unsophisticated, are in themselves a key to the past and to local ideals.[3]

The story of American museums and their concern with preserving historical, ethnological, and folklife materials begins with a stone farm house near Newburgh, New York, once George Washington's headquarters. In 1851, it was appropriately furnished and opened to the public as an historic site and museum.

Through the remaining decades of the nineteenth century several dramatic imperatives, both here and abroad, impelled scholars and a new breed of technicians toward the establishment of museums of various types and functions.

In Europe, the growth of nationalism led to certain political and artistic expectations from the peasantry, the *folk* of the new word *folklore,* coined in 1846. The turbulence in the arts called Romanticism reflected the yeoman farmer and the village artisan as the central figures in paintings and literature, and eventually they were further ennobled by the museum as well. The international expositions of the late nineteenth century were devoted in part to displays of folk arts from the mountains and villages of the new nation states. In 1891, the Swedish museum at Skansen first presented folk and regional culture in an open air setting. These restorations and recreations soon became known as folklife museums.[4]

In America, meanwhile, somewhat different urgencies sent anthropologists and linguists to "salvage" what remained of the already eroded indigenous Indian cultures. These fieldworkers managed to collect artifacts, descriptions of ritual and belief, and extensive language studies.[5] The materials were deposited in universities and eventually moved to what were to become the best-known research museums of today: the Museum of Natural History in New York, the Peabody Museum at Harvard, the Field Museum in Chicago, and the Lowie Museum in Berkeley, California.

While academicians scurried to document Indian culture, the United States government began to take an active interest in preserving other American cultural resources. With the passing of the Antiquities Act (1906) and the establishment of the National Park Service (1916) within the Department of the Interior, local and regional historic preservation groups, historic sites, arboreta, and museums began to receive technical, philosophical, and financial support from the federal level. The result of these early efforts was the flowering of American museums and the establishment of valuable land reserves during the 1920s.[6]

In addition, American philarthropists contributed enormously to museum development. At the same time that Henry Ford was bringing together the mills, laboratories, and homesteads for his Greenfield Village as a "living textbook of mechanical progress," an endowment from John D. Rockefeller made possible the restoration of Colonial Williamsburg to its eighteenth-century appearance. The du Ponts began the collection that was to become Winterthur; Phoebe Apperson Hearst's interest in collecting launched the University of California Anthropology Museum on Mount Parnassus in San Francisco in 1901; William Randolph Hearst donated the site for reconstruction of the lost village of New Salem, Illinois, in 1906; the Wells family began Old Sturbridge Village; and Eli Lilly, who sponsored libraries and extensive archeological exploration, initiated the restoration that later became the Conner Prairie Pioneer Settlement in Indiana. What was important then and remains so today is the principal emphasis on "exhaustive research prior to the restoration of the buildings and careful presentation of the cultural context of each historic site to the public."[7] With their affluence and influence these stewards of American culture collected only the best. Because of their elitist preferences, they provided us with abundant evidence about the social and artistic bents of middle and upper class life since Colonial times.

By contrast, unfortunately, the lives of ordinary Americans down through the decades have been sparsely documented. Though Bicentennial fervor and a newly awakened interest in roots has helped somewhat, state historical societies and their museums still tend to house an embarrassment of details about famous men but precious little about folk traditions. County museums, where they exist, often have fallen prey to the genealogy craze or the nostalgia of some previous peak era—logging years or the gold rush—forgetting that traditions persist through time into the present. Certainly one exciting exception to this trend is the study by Rhoda R. Gilman, Carolyn Gilman, and Deborah M. Stultz on *The Red River Trails: Oxcart Routes Between St. Paul and the Selkirk Settlement, 1820-1870.*[8]

Currently there are significant efforts, especially in the larger museums, to correct this skewed view of the past. Old Sturbridge Village, after spending years acquiring and organizing an extensive collection and a working eighteenth-century farm, has devoted the 1960s and 1970s to stabilizing and expanding its research programs. Old World Wisconsin is carefully collecting oral family histories and ethnic folkways for the interpretation of its farms. Iowa Living History Farms, near Des Moines, has accumulated extensive probate records and other primary documents for the interpretation of traditional farming life in that region. Folk cultural specialists are surveying the ethnic enclaves of California for the Oakland Museum's exhibits and community education programs.

As in previous times, a new generation of museum professionals is filling the ranks, bringing fresh ideas to museum work and challenging the policies and techniques of earlier years. Many have profited by experience as interns or volunteers in folklife museums; some have received advanced degrees from university folklore programs. With historical archeologists and cultural historians, they are looking for ways to bring the theoretical discussions about cultural context to the museum artifact and to the processes which mark its functions.

Another notable phenomenon of recent years is the emergence of museum organizations such as the Association for Living Historical Farms and Agricultural Museums and the growth of regional museum consortia under the A.A.M. The Pioneer America Society, which counts folklorists, cultural geographers, and historians among its members, is concerned with historic preservation and outdoor museums as well. These groups publish scholarly journals useful for folklife research and hold annual meetings.[9]

But what about the problems? Museums, like other media, are responsible for selecting and interpreting phenomena precisely. If museum research is sloppy or meager, the impression conveyed is inaccurate. But even when pains are taken in meticulous research, as at Williamsburg, the interpretation can be misunderstood and distorted into a cliché. A thousand "colonial style" gas stations and shopping centers are the result.[10]

Equally discouraging is the museum which decides that historical truths can be bought and sold and therefore manipulated for a profit. Thomas Schlereth summarizes these problems under some half-dozen "fallacies that we all face in the researching, interpreting and communication of the past."[11] Among these is the fallacy that history is money, that museums have the right to show and tell whatever sells. Another concerns "consensus"—the conscious or unconscious portrayal of the past as idyllic, tranquil, and without poverty, protest, or disorder of any kind.

What might seem the obvious answer to this dilemma of inaccuracies—the establishment of a museum under the jurisdiction of an accredited college or university—is not necessarily the best solution. Research in the college library is different from museum research. Acquisition budgets for museums have no counterpart in the IBM cost printout that crosses the college bursar's desk. Research in museums is often less visible than in academe and has more difficulty showing that it can earn its own way. Curators never receive tenure.

For these and other reasons government support at the state and federal level increased in the 1970s. Massive programs from the National Endowments for the Arts and for the Humanities, the National Museums Act, and the Institute for Museum Services (part of Health, Education and Welfare) were designed to provide advanced training for museum personnel to enhance public awareness of museums, to improve their programmatic offerings, and to expand research facilities and make them more accessible. Further support (and some control) is forthcoming from the Office of Archeology and Historic Preservation (a branch of the National Park Service). OAHP social and cultural impact surveys are a reasonable preventive against neglect or wholesale destruction of those resources outside formal museum walls—a burial mound, historic trail, or a tribal fishing area—sites which are directly related to culture maintenance. In 1978, researchers from the American Folklife Center and the National Park Service cooperated in an ethnographic survey of the Blue Ridge Parkway at the Virginia–North Carolina border. The results will improve the park's research base and bring authentic folk performers into the interpretive programs. During 1981 and 1982, the Library of Congress, on behalf of the American Folklife Center and the National Park Service, on behalf of the Secretary of the Interior, agreed to prepare a study of intangible elements of the country's cultural heritage called for by the National Historic Preservation Act Amendments of 1980, P.L. 96-515.[12]

The integrity of a museum depends upon its past and continued attention to the authenticity of its data and artifacts, the thoroughness with which it explores the ideas that produced the artifacts, and the honesty with which it interprets the whole. Given a museum's integrity, the folklore researcher's needs and ingenuity will determine how the museum is used. One may simply wish to experience the grounds and furnishings of an historic house or the home of a famous author, or attempt some sensate impression of what was described in an autobiography.

A problem-solving approach to museums can attack such questions as, How did people choose and render quilt designs? How does a forged door latch differ between 1790 and 1840? The estate inventory of a carpenter who died in 1867 lists certain tools with curious names. A museum may provide examples of the tools in this "folk taxonomy."[13]

Few museums contain the depth of research necessary for a functional or structural analysis. Still, if enough attention has been given to some elements—fireplace mantelpieces or hay rakes—and supporting documentation has been gathered also, then a study can be initiated.[14]

SOME MUSEUMS AND THEIR POTENTIAL RESEARCH USES

Folk architecture. When they cannot be preserved *in situ*, buildings of historic or cultural importance and structural integrity are often moved to outdoor museums and parks. There a community may restore one or more such buildings to their original state or to a later, and particularly interesting, period of use. Meanwhile, similarly important buildings may be adapted on their sites for use as dwellings or business offices. Green Bay, Wisconsin, for example, has a number of Franco-

American houses, circa 1840, on their original sites. Four restored buildings of the same style are available at nearby Heritage Hills State Park. Their structural integrity and the written documentation that has been collected with them would improve any survey of that area's folk architecture.

Maritime traditions. The San Francisco Maritime Museum is dedicated to the holistic interpretation of west coast sea life from the mid–nineteenth century to 1940. A square-rigged Cape-Horner, the last San Francisco Bay ferry, a logging schooner, and a paddle tug are among the vessels owned. The J. Porter Shaw library houses 225 taped interviews with seafaring men, photographs from 1884, and hundreds of charts, logs, and shipping records.

Occupational folklore. Located on a 150-year-old logging road, the Lumberman's Museum at Patten, Maine, presents an accurately restored logging camp, circa 1825, and extensive equipment. Models of lumbering operations and a large collection of photographs of the men who worked in the woods and on the rivers offer the folklorist an opportunity to supplement folksong and narrative research with material culture. The same techniques can be applied at the Iron Range Interpretative Center, Chisholm, Minnesota. Extensive tool collections and oral folk history have been gathered. Taped recollections of iron miners and their families are heard by visitors through headphones. A research library has been built and it, together with the Center's collectanea and contacts with ethnic communities on the Iron Range, form a superb basis for further folklore research.[15]

Folk art research in an art museum. During the Bicentennial, the Cleveland Museum of Art invited folklorist John Vlach to research a retrospective of Afro-American material culture for an exhibit. To document Herskovits's premise that African slave survivals are extant in New World black cultures, Vlach worked with curators on an exhibit of nine crafts. They were presented with photographs of type variants and visual contexts. During 1978–79, the exhibit traveled to major urban museums.[16]

Folk art and the ethnographic museum. In 1978, the Stony Brook Ethnographic Museum at the State University of New York, Stony Brook, mounted an exhibit based on current research of Colonial Long Island gravestones. Following the work done by James Deetz, museum staff and students photograph, measure, and take rubbings of stones in the Hudson Valley–New Jersey–Staten Island–Long Island region. The work is guided by the Department of Anthropology and the Long Island Studies Program. A photo archive and data retrieval system for gravestone research are planned. The museum publishes the Association for Gravestone Studies Newsletter.

The folk art museum. The Museum of International Folk Art in Santa Fe, New Mexico, has strong holdings in Hispano culture of the Southwest as well as acquisitions from other world cultures, particularly costumes, textiles, silver, and religious and ceremonial objects. Most artifacts date from 1850, a few are one hundred years older, and some from the Middle East and South America date from the 1550s. European and American scholars visit frequently. Dissertations on African textiles and Mixtec costumes have been completed.

The museum and American Indian culture. Indian museums vary widely from the St. Francis Mission of the Rosebud Sioux in South Dakota to the Museum of the American Indian in New York City. The staff of the Arizona State Museum, University of Arizona, Tucson, studies and collects artifacts of the Arizona Indians (Hopi, Navajo, Apache, Pima, and Papago), past and present, as well as certain

Indians in northern Mexico, particularly the Tarhahumera. The museum staff, closely connected with the university's Department of Anthropology, coordinates artifact loans to museums with similar interests, accommodates scholars from Europe and the United States, and offers twelve hours of museum training. As much as possible, they collect cultural data with artifacts. The museum staff is attempting to deal with the problem of purchasing ever-increasing amounts of Indian-made objects, a practice that creates social and economic imbalance within the culture.[17]

Museums, historiography and behavior. Mark Leone, a professor of historical archeology at the University of Maryland, is concerned with why Americans visist museums. What are their expectations? What lessons are learned? How does their amateur sense of history and tradition affect what they see? Leone's research begins with the Mormon Church and its museum program throughout the United States, the particular way in which Mormons view history and the past, and the effect of these factors on present-day behavior and spiritual expression.[18]

The museum and religious traditions. Religious and ethnic lore are among the subjects available at the Judah L. Magnes Memorial Museum, Berkeley, California. Publications include *Pioneer Jews of the California Mother Lode* and *Free To Choose: The Making of a Jewish Community in the American West*. Other museums of religious movements include Historic New Harmony, New Harmony, Indiana; the Bishop Hill Museum, Bishop Hill, Illinois.

Ethnic museums. In every major city ethnic groups have their own museums and cultural centers. Consult the telephone directory. Existence of an ethnic center or museum indicates an interested population of significant size. These museums vary widely in their holdings and research services, from the Norwegian-American Museum, Decorah, Iowa (whose collections were begun in 1877, thus predating even Skansen), to Chicago's Polish Museum of America with its 15,000-volume library and archive, and the new Barrio Viejo district in Tucson, Arizona, and the nearby historical site, El Tradito. The American Folklife Center's ethnic folk arts survey in Chicago in 1977 relied extensively upon ethnic museums for contacts in the wider community and for authentication of artifacts.[19]

Folk history and museums. The University of Idaho at Moscow will interpret the traditions of farming life at the Palouse Hills Farm Museum. The university has chosen to interpret a decade within recall of living informants so that the research base includes oral narratives, legends and memorates, and family histories on video and audio tape. Similar research is carried out at Des Moines's Living History Farms.

Traditional farming in museums. The leaders in this experiment are Old Sturbridge Village, Iowa Living History Farms, the Colonial Pennsylvania Plantation, the Plimoth Plantation, Georgia Agrirama, and the Jensen Museum of Man and His Daily Bread, Logan, Utah. Some are following the examples set by the Danish museum at Lejre and England's Butser Ancient Farm Project (Hampshire) and carry on experimental history research in agricultural techniques.[20]

Sports traditions in museums. Cooperstown Baseball Hall of Fame, the Newport, Rhode Island, Tennis Museum, and the Indianapolis Speedway Museum are all well known. The modest Hall of Fame of the Green Bay Packers in Wisconsin includes players' memorabilia as well as taped interviews of players and their families—the folk and the folk heroes. A traditional initiation ceremony for nominated players is held each winter and enhances team awareness of the depth of tradition.[21]

Folk medicine and plant collections. The folklorist who first visits an herbarium or botanical garden might later more thoroughly interview folk healers and more capably participate in herb gathering expeditions. Comparison of field specimens with an herbarium's holdings can clarify the identification of specimens and help formulate a folk taxonomy. Most universities have herbaria; the one at Cornell is probably the best.

Museums are in and of themselves unique phenomena. They can serve spiritual and ideological as well as intellectual functions, inspiring us to higher purpose by recovering and explaining the missing pieces of our cultural matrix. The Winterthur Museum's documentation of iconographic representation of the United States, from Indian Maid to Uncle Sam, for example, is a museological contribution to the interpretation of patriotic symbolism through vernacular art and folk images.[22]

But because every item of our lives cannot be preserved, we tend to be highly selective in our endeavors. The things we save and the manner in which we do so reflect cultural and social values as well as economic, religious, and political trends; every county, it seems, now wants its own pioneer village in which to entertain the bright memory of its first settlers. Our tastes and allowances are especially visible when it comes to salvaging the relics of a specific group. Consider, for example, that there are more Shaker museums in this country than there are Shakers!

It has been the purpose of this essay to provide some history of American museums, especially those related to folklore and folklife studies, to clarify their problems, and to make some suggestions to researchers about their relative usefulness for studying folk culture. The truth is, folklorists should consider exploring many special environments if research is to be thorough. Museums, though specific environments of highly variable quality, nevertheless harbor much useful data and offer bountiful hunting grounds for those in search of traditional American artifacts. Unless we are studying cultures which have disappeared, modern folklorists must go beyond museums into the field and study folklife at close range.

NOTES

1. "South Carolina Basket Craft Has Origins in West Africa," *The Minneapolis Tribune*, 24 September 1978, p. 28F.

2. *The Official Museum Directory*, published periodically under the auspices of the American Association of Museums, New York, is one of the best research sources for anyone interested in American museums, not all of which are mentioned in this summary article.

3. For a thorough review of American museums and their relationship to folklore scholarship, see Howard W. Marshall, "Folklife and the Rise of American Folk Museums," *Journal of American Folklore* 90 (1977): 391–413.

4. Further remarks on the development of folk museums and agricultural museums in this country can be found in Virginia Wolf Briscoe, "Living Historical

Farms," Association of Living Historical Farms and Agricultural Museums, *Proceedings of the Annual Meeting* (Haverford, Pennsylvania, 1976), pp. 11-17. Also see Harold K. Skramstad, "Interpreting Material Culture: A View from the Other Side of the Glass," in *Material Culture and the Study of American Life*, ed. Ian M. G. Quimby (New York: W. W. Norton & Co., 1978), pp. 175-200.

5. An excellent summary of this work can be found in Anthony F. C. Wallace et al., eds., *Perspectives on Anthropology*, A Special Publication of the American Anthropological Association, No. 10 (Washington, D.C.: American Anthropological Association, 1977). A brief summary appears in T. F. King et al., *Anthropology in Historic Preservation* (New York: The Academic Press, 1977), pp. 14-16.

6. King., p. 19.

7. Charles B. Hosmer, "The Broadening View of the Historical Preservation Movement," in *Material Culture and the Study of American Life*, p. 127. Also see Daniel J. Boorstin, "Past and Present in America: A Historian Visits Colonial Williamsburg," *Commentary* 25 (1958): 1-7.

8. Rhoda R. Gilman, Carolyn Gilman, and Deborah M. Stultz, *The Red River Trails: Oxcart Routes Between St. Paul and the Selkirk Settlement, 1820-1870* (St. Paul: Minnesota Historical Society Press, 1979).

9. The ALHFAM Annual *Proceedings* are available from G. T. Sharrer, Association for Living Historical Farms and Agricultural Museums, Smithsonian Institution, Washington, D.C. 20560. Information about the Pioneer America Society is available through the Department of Geography, University of Akron, Akron, Ohio. Each regional conference of the A.A.M. has its own publications. For example, see *Inside SEMAC* (Southeast Museums Conference), Arkansas Arts and Humanities, Continental Building—Suite 500, Little Rock, Arkansas 77201.

10. A lively discussion about this cliché is found in Ada Louise Huxtable, "Architecture for a Fast Food Culture," *New York Times Magazine*, 12 February 1978, pp. 23-25, 32, 36. The problems of accurate and realistic museum interpretation are discussed in Robert J. Morgan, "Fortress Louisbourg: A Canadian Approach to Historic Preservation," a paper read at the Western History Association Conference, Tulsa, Oklahoma, 1975. Fortress Louisbourg is a National Historic Park, Nova Scotia, Canada.

11. Thomas J. Schlereth, "Collecting Ideas and Artifacts," *Roundtable Reports* (Summer/Fall, 1978). The *Reports* are published by the Office of Museums Programs, Arts and Industries Building, Smithsonian Institution, Washington, D.C. 20560.

12. The National Endowment for the Arts inaugurated its Folk Arts Program in 1974. See *Anthropology in Historical Preservation*, pp. 8-10. Also see Linda C. Coe, comp., *Folklife and the Federal Government*, Publications of the American Folklife Center, No. 1 (Washington, D.C.: American Folklife Center, 1977). The cultural surveys by the American Folklife Center in conjunction with local groups have produced publications and museums exhibits. Information is available from the American Folklife Center, Library of Congress, Washington, D.C. 20540.

13. See James Deetz, *In Small Things Forgotten* (New York: Doubleday, Anchor, 1977), p. 10.

14. A conceptual treatment of these remarks can be found in Henry Glassie, *Folk Housing in Middle Virginia: A Structural Analysis of Historic Artifacts* (Knoxville: University of Tennessee Press, 1975), pp. 3-21.

15. A pilot study of folklore and folklife on the Iron Range was carried out by the Minnesota Folklife Center, in cooperation with the Iron Range Historical Society, during the summer of 1978.

16. See John Vlach, *The Afro-American Tradition in Decorative Arts* (Cleveland: The Cleveland Museum of Art, 1978). See also *Rainbows in the Sky: The Folk Art of Michigan in the Twentieth Century*, a catalogue of 40 contemporary Michigan folk artists and their work prepared by the Folk Arts Division, The Museum, Michigan State University, East Lansing, MI 48824.

17. See Nancy O. Lurie, "American Indians and Museums: A Love-Hate Relationship," *Old Northwest* 3 (1976): 235-51. A recent bibliography on the subject is M. F. King, "Museums and the American Indian," *Council for Museum Anthropology Newsletter* 2:2, San Diego Museum of Man, 1350 El Prado, Balboa Park, San Diego, California 92101.

18. Mark Leone, "The New Mormon Temple in Washington, D.C.," in *Historical Archeology: The Importance of Material Things*, ed. Leland Ferguson (Special Publication Series No. 2, Society for Historical Archeology, 1977), pp. 43-61.

19. See *A Report on the Chicago Ethnic Arts Project*, prepared by and available from the American Folklife Center, Library of Congress, Washington, D.C. 20540.

20. See Geoffrey Bibby, "An Experiment With Time," *Archeology* 29:3 (1976): 97-102.

21. "The Pack Is Finally Back Despite Loss to Vikings," *The Chicago Tribune*, 24 October 1978, Section 4, p. 3.

22. E. McClung Fleming, "Symbols of the United States: From Indian Queen to Uncle Sam," in *Frontiers of American Culture*, ed. Ray B. Browne, Richard H. Crowder, Virgil L. Lokke, William T. Stafford (Lafayette: Purdue University Studies, 1968), pp. 1-24. The abundance of folk art in the Winterthur collection is also revealed in Elaine Eff and Donald L. Fennimore, "Folk Art from the Henry Francis du Pont Winterthur Museum," *Antiques* (August 1977): 506-13. Further evidence of the research that can be done in a museum setting is *A Checklist of American Coverlet Weavers*, which gives autobiographical and technical information concerning more than 900 nineteenth-century coverlet weavers. The catalogue is available from the Abby Aldrich Rockefeller Folk Art Center, Drawer C., Williamsburg, Virgina 23185.

Francis A. de Caro

Studying American Folklore in Printed Sources

Scholars generally stress that folklore is *oral* in nature, defining it as a mode of communication different from writing or print. But the dividing line between the written word and folkloric speech is a fine one. Except in preliterate societies whose communication by means of words is exclusively or predominantly oral, printed and folkloric communication are likely to coexist; certainly they do in the United States. Folklore sometimes finds its way into print, while what has been born in print may pass into oral tradition. For example, a joke circulating in oral tradition may at one point be printed in a popular joke book, where people who have never *heard* the joke may come to enjoy it only through reading it. Some of them may start to *tell* it and their having read the joke will have had some effect on oral tradition. To cite less hypothetical examples, Chaucer drew upon traditional oral narratives for his written (later printed) *Canterbury Tales,* while variants of those narratives still circulate orally (whether or not as a result of print); and a ballad written by Mathew G. Lewis for his 1795 horror novel, *Ambrosio, or The Monk,* has been collected in American oral tradition. Recently a student of mine was doing fieldwork in New Orleans involving the local tradition of St. Joseph's Day altars. As he talked to one informant he began to realize that everything she was telling him was drawn from a newspaper article on the tradition which had appeared the day before![1]

Thus folklorists recognize the interdependence of oral and non-oral channels of communication. Though oral transmission may be the essence of folklore, a chapbook or a broadside or even a postcard or comic strip can often be a link in the chain of folklore dissemination. The "raw material" of folklore is generally collected from "the lips of the folk," that is, by observing the actual transmission of folklore in the field, or, at a step removed, from tapes stored in archives. But folklore can also be collected from printed sources, and the study of folklore in print is a necessary aspect of folkloristics.

Types of Useful Printed Sources

A person might need to use printed sources for a variety of reasons, but once the researcher has decided what to find in print (riddles in chapbooks, folklore of all kinds in advertisements, or depictions of rural folklife in any kind of printed source), the first problem resides in locating source material. Systematic research on folklore in print can be pursued more easily for some sources than for others.

Newspapers are prime sources of folklore in print, as are *magazines*. Representative examples from recent years in my own modest collection include articles on graffiti clipped from an airline in-flight magazine, a university alumni publication (a survey of jottings in library carrels), and the *New York Times* (an article on Copenhagen's public "scribble board");[2] in the areas of folk belief and curing, a "Dear Abby" column on cats' sucking the breath out of newborn infants and a newspaper article on groundhog beliefs;[3] newspaper stories on a New Mexico whittler and on "vanishing" Indiana stonecarvers;[4] a tale-telling session captured in a "Snuffy Smith" comic strip;[5] a *New York Times* front-page account of a "miracle" in Lebanon;[6] a *National Enquirer* piece on the psychology of fairy tales;[7] a photo essay on Southern place names;[8] a 1971 "Amy Vanderbilt's Etiquette" column containing one reader's letter on a folk rhyme and another's on folk speech.[9] Folklore in newspapers and magazines is apt to be somewhat fugitive, however, and to be found only by laboriously scanning the press every day or by poring over the back files of likely publications. Richard M. Dorson employed a clipping service to provide him with material for "Paul Bunyan in the News,"[10] but any clipping service has its limitations because the personnel look for certain key words and often miss relevant items which do not contain those words; and clipping services need rather narrowly conceived, concrete things to look for and what is folklore in the news might not be immediately apparent to them.

Local histories often contain an odd legend or two, either identified as such or not, or perhaps even an entire section such as "Myths and Legends of the Indians" in Lucian Lamar Knight's *Georgia's Landmarks, Memorials and Legends.*[11]

There is a wealth of other, generally ephemeral, *regional publications* which may recount, for example, traditions about New Orleans voodoo,[12] tell of local miracles in New Mexico,[13] explain a folk saint of Texas[14] or the folk symbols of Pennsylvania.[15] Often folklore and folk history are presented as "facts" in such publications. Raymond J. Martinez, for example, deals with oral traditions of how Marie Laveau operated as New Orleans's "voodoo queen" as though they were established historical facts. Modern ephemeral publications relevant to folklore have been collected by a few individual folklorists, but libraries have often ignored them and they are not easy to find in great numbers.

Asking students to collect folklore from local newspapers or to locate relevant local books or pamphlets not only teaches the students how close folklore is to their daily lives but also creates a larger collection of printed material to be archived and drawn upon for research.

Chapbooks and broadsides ("street literature") have been extensively studied in connection with folksong but not so far as other folklore genres are concerned. British street literature is older and far more extensive than the American and is often relevant to American folklore.[16] Fortunately, the older examples of this street literature have been extensively catalogued and the researcher need but look through the mountains of materials in library collections, aided by finding guides (though of course that may be a laborious task fraught with "bibliographical" problems).[17]

Popular collections of anecdotes and other narratives by anthologists such as Bennett Cerf and H. Allen Smith provide a wealth of material originally oral, much of it traditional. Cerf's *Try and Stop Me* uses a number of urban legends, including "The Phantom Hitchhiker" and several less well-known to folklorists.[18]

Joke books draw heavily upon oral tradition but have been little noticed by folklorists, with some notable exceptions of course, such as William Clements in his *Types of the Polack Joke*.[19] For joke books recourse may be had to one of the large collections of such publications (see below).

Comic strips have attracted the attention of folklorists because they often incorporate folk motifs, folktale plots, or structural patterns also found in oral narrative.[20] The same may be true of *cartoons*, which might also reflect folk speech. A Charles Addams cartoon in the *New Yorker* shows a pigpen next to a silk purse factory, disputing the proverb that you cannot make a silk purse out of a sow's ear.[21] The myriad comic strips and *comic books* published in America over the years are far from being well catalogued or easily accessible for research, though popular culture scholars have made a few tentative moves toward ordering this material.

Various *works by writers on the occult* incorporate folklore. Those who have attempted to prove that astronauts from other planets visited the earth in ancient times have cited various myths and legends as evidence. *Fate*, the most widely circulated American occult magazine, is full of supernatural personal experience narratives. A recent issue carries what seems to be an African legend (presented as a factual account) as well as a fascinating advertisement incorporating the motif of a "genie" in a bottle (motifs R181, F403.2.2.4).[22]

Postcards as a source of folklore have been largely neglected except for those which exhibit "tall tale" motifs.[23] Humorous postcards are probably the most relevant, but songs, legends, and folklife activities have all been depicted on cards.[24] For example, a recent series of "potty proverbs" on cards provides a printed source for the proverb parodies folklorists have occasionally noted (one card depicts a "necking" couple to illustrate "Familiarity breeds attempt"). Postcard collectors have begun to publish a steady stream of guides, catalogues, and histories useful to the folklorist, but the work of ordering this great mass of printed materials has really only just begun. Publicly held collections of postcards to which researchers might have access are few and my own scanty knowledge of folklore on postcards comes mostly from attending antique postcard shows in London, a world center for collectors.

Also useful are: *special interest publications*, such as those concerned with folk recreations like cockfighting;[25] *advertising*, which may incorporate many kinds of folklore: play on proverbs, allusions to folktales, utilization of folk costumes or folk figures;[26] *commercial catalogues*, such as those which indicate what musical instruments were available to traditional performers at a certain time;[27] *xerographic folklore*, which is discussed elsewhere in this volume (see Dundes, "Office Folklore," in Part I); popular *songsters* and *sheet music*;[28] collections of *photographs*, which may depict folklife activities;[29] popular *books of games* and play activities, such as Eliza Leslie's *The American Girl's Book* or the fascinating *Hints for Happy Hours*, in which the games are set within the fictional narrative of a family houseparty, and hence allow the folklorist even to see something of the social context and performance aspect of play in the printed text.[30]

Of course deciding what *is* folklore in printed sources can be a problem, especially for those who are just beginning the study of folklore. For example, legends may appear in newspapers as factual accounts, and one not familiar with the corpus of modern legendry or at least attuned to the "feel" of such legends may not realize what is being read. But a good folklore course or even some basic reading in the subject should give an idea of what to look for. Occasionally, however, even the professional folklorist may find it hard to determine what is or isn't folklore. Are the personal narratives of encounters with the supernatural that appear in *Fate* magazine the equivalents of similar narratives told orally? When are we dealing with an oral tradition in print, when with a popular printed tradition that may have little or no basis in the oral tradition however much it may "look like folklore"? And of course there is the fact, more or less recognized by folklorists for a long time, that folklore in print is, to some degree at least, folklore extracted from its fundamentally oral context. How then do we compensate for that factor in order to judge the place of that item of folklore in the larger realm of oral expression? How do we decide what the writer who cast the item into print added to or subtracted from the folklore originally encountered?

It should be noted that many sources *written but not printed* are also of interest to folklorists; in this category are diaries, journals, or even personal letters in private collections or in (non-folklore) archives.[31]

Contexts in Which Printed Sources Are Useful

Even the random "collecting" of items of folklore in print can be instructive. That is, one can learn about folklore in, say, the region where one lives, simply by carefully reading local newpapers and other publications or by going through back files. At the very least such reading may provide "leads" for fieldwork. The notation of items relevant to folklore encountered in everyday reading of other kinds is not irrelevant to the study of folklore; for example, instances of how words like "folklore," "myth," and "legend" are used by non-folklorists tell folklore scholars something about how the rest of the world views what folklorists study. Beyond this, one might wish to undertake a more systematic study of folklore in print for one of several reasons, including the following:

Locating folklore which predates systematic collecting. Scholarly, scientific interest in collecting and analyzing folklore does not really go back further than the early nineteenth century and even then such interest was relatively rare. Francis Lee Utley has written, "We may even generalize to the extent of saying that we know no . . . American folklore before the end of the nineteenth century,"[32] meaning that we possess examples of earlier folklore only in literary versions or in non-folklore works. Hence printed sources are necessary for anyone studying the folklore of pre–twentieth century America.

Folklore in current circulation may of course have great time depth, having passed through oral tradition for centuries. A recent joke might consist of a story found in Chaucer,[33] and countless American ballads can be traced to British broadsides of the eighteenth or other centuries.[34] Broadsides, literary works, chapbooks help the researcher to determine the origin, circulation, and variation of any given tradition. In some rather rare instances a printed "original" can even be traced, a fact which may have particular significance for the study of how folklore is transmitted and what happens to it in the course of transmission. For example, the ballad "The Last Fierce Charge" (Laws A17) can be traced to a poem by Virginia Francis Townsend.[35]

Folklore of a type which no longer circulates or which seems particularly important in the context of an earlier historical period may also be documented through printed works. One of my own projects, for example, has been the search

surveyed. Folklore's use in occult publications of many kinds is another possibility for investigation. The comics have barely been tapped; the same is true of postcards (Gotham Book Mart, 41 West 47th Street, New York, N.Y. 10036, publishes an annotated bibliography of major publications which they stock on the subject of postcards). Folklore publications should report on a regular basis on folklore items that appear in the press, as *Western Folklore* used to do. The files of clippings in folklore archives and those reprinted in *Western Folklore* over the years have seldom been analyzed or commented upon. Except in studying balladry, folklorists have made relatively little use of the wealth of street literature in British and American library collections, such as those of Harvard University, Essex Institute in Salem, the New York State Library, the American Antiquarian Society, the New York Public Library Rare Book Division, Lincoln's Inn, the British Museum, the National Library of Scotland, and the John G. White Collection in Cleveland, all institutions with extensive collections of broadsides, chapbooks, or both. Little use has been made of the joke books in such collections as the Schmulowitz Collection of Wit and Humor in the San Francisco Public Library and the Franklin J. Meine Collection at the University of Illinois.[56]

One of the best ways to obtain ideas about further possibilities, however, is to look at some of the best work that has been done in the past. Several of Richard Dorson's books stand as exemplars of the use of printed sources to assess an older level of American folklore, that which predates systematic collection. In *Jonathan Draws the Long Bow*, a study of New England oral narratives, he draws his material exclusively from printed sources and shows how a wealth of older regional folklore lies in print. For his later *American Folklore* he mines such sources as colonial travellers' accounts (for travellers' tales of New World marvels) and the popular almanacs of the nineteenth century (for frontier yarns). *America in Legend* utilizes similar sources to provide a particularly rich exposition of American folklore; in this book Dorson also makes very full use of printed materials to provide illustrations. Students of American humor have also tapped earlier printed sources, and such books as *Half Horse Half Alligator*, edited by Franklin J. Meine and Walter Blair, an anthology of many nineteenth-century pieces, provides an important overview of related folklore materials. Certainly we could obtain little idea of earlier American folk humor without such works.[57]

Three rather recent studies are particularly good in showing the close interdependence of print and oral tradition. In her unpublished dissertation Rayna D. Green studies the popular American images of the Indian (which might be called folk stereotypes) and shows how we cannot really separate folklore from popular printed sources, for they merge together, influence each other, and jointly contribute to American viewpoints. In *Poor Pearl, Poor Girl!* Anne B. Cohen deftly shows how folk ballads and newspaper stories relating to the same subject—in this case the "murdered-girl stereotype"—can be remarkably similar, sharing the same stereotypes and formulae. And Bruce Rosenberg's stimulating study of the Custer legend ties together folk motifs both ancient and widely diffused with the printed sources which, in the American context, both reflected the legend and created it.[58] All of these books are examples of studies which might inspire similar attempts in new directions.

NOTES

1. Folklorists have generally been more concerned with folklore that has gotten into print than with the influence of print upon folklore; however, articles dealing with some aspect of the effect of writing and print upon folklore include Albert B. Friedman, "Tasso among the Gondoliers," in *Folklore International: Essays in Traditional Literature, Belief, and Custom in Honor of Wayland Debs Hand*, ed. D. K. Wilgus (Hatboro, Pa.: Folklore Associates, 1967), pp. 55-66; W. Edson Richmond, "Some Effects of Scribal and Typographical Error on Oral Tradition," *Southern Folklore Quarterly* 15 (1951): 159-70; Louise Pound, " 'Monk' Lewis in Nebraska," *Southern Folklore Quarterly* 9 (1945): 107-10; Charles Haywood, "Negro Minstrelsy and Shakespearean Burlesque," in *Folklore and Society: Essays in Honor of Benj. A. Botkin*, ed. Bruce Jackson (Hatboro, Pa.: Folklore Associates, 1966), pp. 77-92; Thomas A. Burns, "Dr. Seuss' *How the Grinch Stole Christmas:* Its Recent Acceptance into American Popular Christmas Tradition," *New York Folklore* 2 (1976): 191-204; Tristram Potter Coffin, *The Book of Christmas Folklore* (New York: Seabury Press, 1973), pp. 87-92, 154-63.

2. My *TWA Ambassador* clipping is unfortunately not dated, a mistake no collector of folklore from the popular press should make; "Not Quite the News," *Johns Hopkins Magazine*, November 1976, pp. 45-48; John M. Lee, "Smorgasbord Graffiti," *New York Times*, 20 July 1968, p. 3.

3. *Portales* [N.M.] *News-Tribune*, 7 October 1969, p. 10; "Epic Study Nets Groundhog Lore," *Austin American-Statesman*, 28 January 1974, p. 11.

4. "Talented Whittler Helps Give Folklore of Southwest Program," *Portales* [N.M.] *News-Tribune*, 20 November 1969, p. 3; *Bloomington* [Ind.] *Herald-Telephone*, 29 April 1964, pp. 1-2.

5. *Portales* [N.M.] *News-Tribune*, 8 January 1970, p. 6.

6. "The Pope Canonizes a Lebanese Monk . . . as Pilgrims Report Miracles at Saint's Tomb," *New York Times*, 10 October 1977, pp. 1, 5.

7. "Psychiatrist Tells . . . What Your Favorite Fairy Tale Reveals about Your Personality," *National Enquirer*, 5 August 1975, p. 8.

8. "Southern Towns Pose Question—What's in a Name?" *Baton Rouge State-Times*, 4 June 1971, p. 18A.

9. *Baton Rouge State-Times*, 19 July 1971, p. 6B.

10. Richard M. Dorson, "Paul Bunyan in the News, 1939-1941," *Western Folklore* 15 (1956): 26-30, 179-93, 247-61.

11. Lucian Lamar Knight, *Georgia's Landmarks, Memorials and Legends* (Atlanta: Byrd Printing Co., 1913), pp. 441-80. For an example of a single legend in another history of the same state see Frances Letcher Mitchell, *Georgia's Land and People* (Atlanta: Franklin Printing and Publishing Co., 1900), pp. 11-12.

12. Raymond J. Martinez, *Mysterious Marie Laveau, Voodoo Queen* (New Orleans: Hope Publications, 1956).

13. Sr. Mary Philibert, *Did Vargas Win His Battle With a Banner?* (Albuquerque [?]: Howard N. Rose, n.d.); Sr. Mary Philibert, "Did a Yard-High Statue Stall an Army? (Albuquerque: Howard N. Rose, 1967).

14. *The Faith Healer of Los Olmos: Biography of Don Pedrito Jaramillo* (n.p.: Brooks County Historical Survey Committee, 1972).

15. Jacob and Jane Zook, *Hexology: The History and Meaning of Hex Signs* (Paradise, Pa.: The authors, 1962). For a survey of the folklore in a variety of books on a particular region, see B. J. Whiting, "Folklore in Recent Maine Books," *Southern Folklore Quarterly* 11 (1947): 149-57; 12 (1948): 211-23.

16. Malcolm Laws, *American Balladry from British Broadsides: A Guide for Students and Collectors of Traditional Song*, American Folklore Society Bibliographic and Special Series, no. 8 (Philadelphia: American Folklore Society, 1957)

indicates something of how much American narrative folksong derives from British broadsides. Recently D. K. Wilgus, "American Ballads in Ireland," in *Folklore Today: A Festschrift for Richard M. Dorson*, ed. Linda Dégh, Henry Glassie, and Felix J. Oinas (Bloomington: Indiana University Research Center for Language and Semiotic Studies, 1976), pp. 507-23, has discussed American folksongs in Ireland, including their appearance on Irish broadsides; American folklore may disseminate to the British Isles as well as vice versa.

17. Alan Dundes briefly mentions some of these in *The Study of Folklore* (Englewood Cliffs, N.J.: Prentice-Hall, 1965), pp. 400-401; in the same volume, see also the article to which Dundes's remarks are an introduction, Harry B. Weiss, "Something about Simple Simon," pp. 402-13; and Francis Lee Utley, "Folk Literature: An Operational Definition," p. 14.

18. Bennett Cerf, *Try and Stop Me: A Collection of Anecdotes and Stories, Mostly Humorous* (New York: Simon and Schuster, 1944), reprinted in *Bennett Cerf's Bumper Crop of Anecdotes and Stories, Mostly Humorous, About the Famous and Near Famous*, 2 vols. (Garden City: Garden City Books, n.d.), I: 630-52. Smith published a great number of relevant books, including *Buskin' with H. Allen Smith* (New York: Trident Press, 1968).

19. William M. Clements, *The Types of the Polack Joke*, Folklore Forum Bibliographic and Special Series, no. 3 (Bloomington, Ind.: Folklore Forum, 1969), p. 6.

20. See, for example, Grace Partridge Smith, "The Plight of the Folktale in the Comics," *Southern Folklore Quarterly* 16 (1952): 124-27; *Funk and Wagnall's Standard Dictionary of Folklore, Mythology and Legend*, s.v. "Comics," by B. A. Botkin; Paul G. Brewster, "Folklore Invades the Comic Strips," *Southern Folklore Quarterly* 14 (1950): 97-102; Rolf Wilhelm Brednich, "Comic Strips as a Subject of Folk Narrative Research," in *Folklore Today*, pp. 45-55; Stuart A. Gallacher, "The Ideal Hero of Antiquity and His Counterpart in the Comic Strips of Today," *Southern Folklore Quarterly* 11 (1947): 141-48.

21. *New Yorker*, 3 May 1952, p. 31.

22. Mike Onobogu, "The Angry Rainmaker," *Fate*, April 1978, pp. 64-67; the advertisement appears on pp. 88-89.

23. Roger L. Welsch, *Tall-Tale Postcards: A Pictorial History* (South Brunswick and New York: A. S. Barnes & Co., 1976).

24. G. Legman recently requested that folklorists send him any old postcards they had to illustrate a work on "unexpurgated" pictorial humor; see *Folklore Women's Communication* 14 (November 1978): 10-11.

25. As Gerald E. Parsons has suggested, in "Cockfighting: A Potential Field of Research," *New York Folklore Quarterly* 25 (1969): 265-88; see especially pp. 287-88. In commenting on a paper on cockfighting at the 1978 American Folklore Society meeting Wayland D. Hand suggested the *Police Gazette* as an important source of information on illegal folk activities.

26. At the Centenary Conference of the Folklore Society, Royal Holloway College, Egham, Surrey, England, Lutz Rohrich presented an extensive analysis of folklore in the advertising of several nations, "Folklore and Advertising," 19 July 1978; see also Barbara and Wolfgang Mieder, "Tradition and Innovation: Proverbs in Advertising," *Journal of Popular Culture* 11 (1977): 308-19; and Tom E. Sullenberger, "Ajax Meets the Jolly Green Giant: Some Observations on the Use of Folklore and Myth in American Mass Marketing," *Journal of American Folklore* 87 (1974): 53-65.

27. Such seems to have been one purpose of the Country Music Foundation in reprinting *The 1921 Gibson Catalog*, ed. William Ivey (Nashville, Tenn.: Country Music Foundation Press, 1973) and *The 1940 C. F. Martin Catalog*, ed. George Gruhn (Nashville, Tenn.: Country Music Foundation Press, 1973).

28. Judith McCulloh, "Indiana's Treasure Store Is a Wealth of Good Old Hoosier Lore," *Folklore Forum* 3 (1970): 135–37; see also Jan Harold Brunvand, *The Study of American Folklore: An Introduction*, 2d ed. (New York: W. W. Norton, 1978), pp. 155–56.

29. George François Mugnier, *Louisiana Images, 1880–1920: A Photographic Essay*, ed. John R. Kemp and Linda Orr King (Baton Rouge: Louisiana State University Press for the Louisiana State Museum, 1975), provides an example of a collection of photographs, only recently published, which contains many pictures illustrating Southern folklife.

30. Eliza Leslie, *The American Girl's Book; or, Occupation for Play Hours* (New York: R. Worthington, 1880); [Harriet E. Fourdrinier] *Hints for Happy Hours; or Amusements for All Ages* (Boston: Monroe & Francis, 1851[?]).

31. For example, a late nineteenth-century diary has been explored by Austin E. Fife, "Folkways of a Mormon Missionary in Virginia," *Southern Folklore Quarterly* 16 (1952): 92–123, and "Virginia Folkways from a Mormon Journal," *Western Folklore* 9 (1950): 348–58. The Butler Collection in the Louisiana State University Archives contains a number of examples of traditional tunes from a nineteenth-century Southern family (see Judy R. Dickey, "The Music of a Louisiana Plantation Family, 1814–1874," M.A. thesis, Louisiana State University, 1968). Recently Charles K. Wolfe located a manuscript autobiography of the late country music performer Alton Delmore, since published as *Truth Is Stranger Than Publicity*, ed. Charles K. Wolfe (Nashville, Tenn.: Country Music Foundation Press, 1977). And the value of "ballet books," manuscripts of songs kept by traditional singers, has long been recognized also (see Ruth Ann Musick, "The Old Album of William A. Larkin," *Journal of American Folklore* 60 (1947): 201–51.

32. Utley, "Folk Literature: An Operational Definition," p. 15.

33. James T. Bratcher and Nicolai von Kreisler, "The Popularity of the Miller's Tale," *Southern Folklore Quarterly* 35 (1971): 325–35.

34. See Laws, *American Balladry from British Broadsides*, especially pp. 31–62.

35. D. K. Wilgus, notes to "Native American Ballads," RCA Victor LPV-548.

36. Charles M. Skinner, *Myths and Legends of Our Own Land* (Philadelphia: J. B. Lippincott, 1896), passim.

37. For example, Laconica, "The Bridge of the White Canoe: A Legend of Amoskeag Falls," *Granite State Magazine* 5 (1908): 208–16.

38. D. Hamilton Hurd, comp., *History of Worcester County, Massachusetts with Biographical Sketches of Many of Its Pioneers and Prominent Men* (Philadelphia: J. W. Lewis & Co., 1889), pp. 1354–1355.

39. John D. McAdams, "The Tragedy of Lover's Leap," *Alton Evening Telegraph* (centennial edition), 15 January 1936, p. II-6 (reprinting material from the edition of 28 September 1836).

40. Charles Etienne Gayarré, *History of Louisiana*, 4 vols., 4th ed. (New Orleans: F. F. Hansell & Bros., 1903), I: 383–86.

41. Folk ideas are defined by Alan Dundes, "Folk Ideas as Units of Worldview," *Journal of American Folklore* 84 (1971): 95, as "traditional notions that a group of people have about the nature of man, of the world, and of man's life in the world."

42. Henry Nash Smith, *Virgin Land: The American West as Symbol and Myth* (Cambridge, Mass.: Harvard University Press, 1950); Richard Slotkin, *Regeneration through Violence: The Mythology of the American Frontier, 1600–1860* (Middletown, Conn.: Wesleyan University Press, 1973), esp. pp. 6ff. for comments on the role of print.

43. Rayna D. Green, "The Only Good Indian: The Image of the Indian in American Vernacular Culture" (Ph.D. diss., Indiana University, 1973), pp. 118–19.

44. Ibid., p. 118.

45. Bruce A. Rosenberg, *Custer and the Epic of Defeat* (University Park: Pennsylvania State University Press, 1974), and "Custer: The Legend of the Martyred Hero in America," *Journal of the Folklore Institute* 9 (1972): 110-32.

46. Leola Copeland, "Happenings on Royal Drive," *Corinth Journal,* 2 November 1977, p. 6. I am indebted for this information to Barbara B. Sims, who plans to publish this text in a folklore journal in the future.

47. George Dolan, "Surprise Party Caught Him in His Birthday Suit," *Fort Worth Star-Telegram,* 10 August 1978, p. 1A.

48. William Hugh Jansen, "The Surpriser Surprised: A Modern Legend," *Folklore Forum* 6 (1973): 1-24. Two of Jansen's twenty-eight variants were from printed sources, one a joke book, the other a "sort of 8 x 11 broadside" circulated in a university medical center.

49. [F. A. de Caro and Elliott L. Oring] "J.F.K. Is Alive: A Modern Legend," *Folklore Forum* 2 (1969): 54-55.

50. [F. A. de Caro and James Durham] "McCartney's Lyke-Wake," *Folklore Forum* 2 (1969): 167-68.

51. Henry Glassie's extensive bibliography in his *Pattern in the Material Folk Culture of the Eastern United States* (Philadelphia: University of Pennsylvania Press, 1968), pp. 243-316, indicates a number of such sources.

52. Larry Danielson, "The Ethnic Festival and Cultural Revivalism in a Small Midwestern Town" (Ph.D. diss., Indiana University, 1972); Rosan A. Jordan, "The Folklore and Ethnic Identity of a Mexican-American Woman" (Ph.D. diss., Indiana University, 1975), pp. 72, 257-59.

53. For examples of news and feature stories quoted by *Western Folklore* which demonstrate the "slants" I have noted, see 17 (1958): 63-64; 12 (1953): 57-60; 21 (1962): 281-82; 17 (1958): 61-62; 12 (1953): 140; 21 (1962): 113-15; 27 (1968): 53. See Tom Burns, "Folklore in the Mass Media: Television," *Folklore Forum* 2 (1969): 90-106, for a model for the systematic analysis of folklore in television which might be adapted to provide a model for the systematic study of folklore in printed media for the masses.

54. Richard A. Gould, "Indian and White Versions of 'The Burnt Ranch Massacre,' " *Journal of the Folklore Institute* 3 (1966): 30-42, compares one white printed account with several oral texts narrated by American Indians.

55. Richard M. Dorson, *Jonathan Draws the Long Bow: New England Popular Tales and Legends* (Cambridge, Mass.: Harvard University Press, 1946); Donald M. Hines, "Dust Devils in the Great Desert: A Study of the Impress of the Frontier in Traditional Humor and Exaggeration, in Folk Beliefs, and in the Traditional Speech Gleaned from Some Old-Time Weekly Newspapers from the Inland Empire of the Pacific Northwest" (Ph.D. diss., Indiana University, 1969).

56. William L. Ramirez, "Scowah—The Schmulowitz Collection of Wit and Humor," *Folklore and Folk Music Archivist* 6 (1963): 2-3; John T. Flanagan, "The Meine Library of Folklore and Humor," *New York Folklore Quarterly* 13 (1957): 114-26.

57. Walter Blair and Franklin J. Meine, eds., *Half Horse Half Alligator: The Growth of the Mike Fink Legend* (Chicago: University of Chicago Press, 1956); for other references see above and Bibliography.

58. Anne B. Cohen, *Poor Pearl, Poor Girl! The Murdered Girl Stereotype in Ballad and Newspaper* (Austin and London: University of Texas Press, 1973); for other references see above and Bibliography.

Sandra K. D. Stahl

Studying Folklore and American Literature

No standard methodology exists for studying folklore and American literature. Even though the less restrictive notion of what constitutes "literature" posed by Howard Mumford Jones (*Ideas in America*) and other literary historians now allows critics of American literature to consider works of history such as Cotton Mather's *Magnalia*, colonial sermons, scientific treatises and reports of experiments, journalistic humor, travel tales, or autobiographies *as literature*, still neither folklorists nor literary critics have devised a methodology for analyzing this much-expanded body of American literature in relation to American folklore and the theories and methods of American folkloristics. In fact, though folklorists and literary critics might recognize that folklore and literary theory can complement each other in the study of American literature, there is little agreement on why folklore and literature should be studied together in the first place.

From one perspective, literature is viewed as a potential record or source for folklore. Cotton Mather's *Magnalia Christi Americana* could be viewed as a great storehouse of colonial legends and memorates, for example, or Edward Eggleston's works might be used as a record of currency on numerous American proverbs.[1] In such cases, literature would seem to be at the service of the folklorist. More often, the folklorist is called upon to aid in the explication of folkloric allusions or usages in literary texts. Though such aid might be essential to the literary interpretation, usually the folkloric explanations simply constitute editorial gloss on the literary text, as in the observation that the title of Ken Kesey's *One Flew Over the Cuckoo's Nest* represents a line from a children's counting-out rhyme. In either case, each discipline maintains its established methodology and merely uses materials or research from the other discipline as a helpful but secondary source.

A number of researchers have attempted to bring the two interests together more directly. Primarily they have looked to literature that incorporates folkloric material in some way, and have asked how the author has used that folklore. The reverse could be done as well. One could study folklore that has been influenced by literature or other written sources; for example, in many versions, the native American ballad usually titled "The Jealous Lover" has attracted to itself two stanzas from a printed song text popular during the late 1800s, though the stanzas are not entirely appropriate to the plot of the ballad.[2] The greater interest has, however, always lain with literary texts and the role folklore has played in the creation and interpretation of literature. This particular relationship has generally been the assumed focus of any study of folklore and American literature.

In an article originally published in 1957 but reprinted more recently in his *American Folklore and the Historian*, Richard M. Dorson proposed a scheme for identifying folklore in American literature: researchers should seek biographical, corroborative, and internal evidence to prove that they have identified authentic folklore in an author's writing.[3] More recently Dorson responded to critics who charged his scheme with an overemphasis on identification of the folklore and neglect of the interpretation of the literature itself. "It is banal to say we must interpret as well as identify. I originally set forth my tripartite scheme for identifying folklore in American literature because critics were interpreting before identifying. Of course we need both endeavors."[4] The method adopted by most contemporary students of folklore and literature, then, is the identify-and-interpret formula. And much needs to be done yet in the way of careful identification and persuasive interpretation of folklore in literature. Still, this method applies to only one particular relationship between folklore and literature, and, further, it makes interpretation of literature the primary goal. It is in effect a special variety of literary criticism with attention to literary rather than folkloric texts.

A more comprehensive methodology for studying folklore and American literature would involve some of the other points at which folklore and literary criticism converge. The following discussion outlines fifteen areas of overlapping interest or obvious relationship between folklore and American literature. A basic assumption behind these analytic concerns in the study of folklore and American literature is that folklore and literature are in many respects similar, at least similar enough to be compared meaningfully, yet different enough to warrant the separate designations of "folklore" and "literature." Furthermore there is a collectively fostered implication that the study of folklore and American literature is after all neither a branch of literary studies nor a "school" of folklore research. Rather, studying the two together is truly an interdisciplinary activity, perhaps reflective of a new paradigm altogether.[5]

Ideally, a student of folklore and American literature would be familiar with theories, concepts, terminology, methodology, and actual materials of both folklore and literary studies. With both fields expanding rapidly, however, scholars do well simply to recognize a few parallel terms, analogous concepts, historically divergent traditions, and differing assumptions that might be integrated in a unified study of folklore and American literature. The first analytic concern, then, would be a comparison and contrast of the *basic concepts and assumptions* of each field. The concept of authorial "intention," for example, is implicit in Roger Abrahams's "rhetorical" approach to folklore, as it is in the works of his literary mentor, Kenneth Burke. This so-called intentional fallacy has been hotly debated in literary criticism by such critics as W. K. Wimsatt and Monroe C. Beardsley, who argue against the need for an assumed intention of the author in order to ascertain meaning.[6] Or, again, even general notions about the analytic tasks of the scholar are being questioned in different terms, from different directions, but with the same result in the two fields. Robert M. Adams, speaking on behalf of literary critics, suggests that all criticism is after all simply a matter of persuasion using generally accepted terms and procedures, while Elliott Oring suggests much the same thing in regard to the interpretation of function in the study of folklore.[7] A thorough study of folklore and American literature would have to strip away much of the jargon of the two fields and express basic concepts in plain language in an effort to recognize real similarities and differences.

One general concept shared by the two disciplines is so basic as to warrant a separate designation in this methodology—the concept of *genres*. The system of analytic categories established long ago in literary tradition was adapted to the study of "folk literature" in the early 1800s as scholars became interested in extending the study of literature into the realm of oral tales and folksongs. Thus the practice of grouping kinds of literary works into genres, usually on the basis of form, was continued as critics turned their attention to the literature of the new continent—American literature—and as they collected and published the "literature of the folk." Some critics, such as André Jolles, went so far as to posit a list of primary genres (*einfache Formen*) common to all folk literature and generatively basic to all complex literary forms.[8]

More recently, American scholars of both disciplines have come to regard genre designations as simply descriptive groupings, analytic categories at the service of the critic.[9] Despite the seemingly arbitrary nature of genres, there are as well the "real" genres recognized by the literary authors or performers of folklore. Dan Ben-Amos has named such groupings "ethnic genres" in folklore studies.[10] And one can easily see that such culture-specific genres call for recognition in literary studies as well—as, for example, in Hawthorne's well-known defense of his genre as a "romance" rather than a history or novel. Differences in what one or the other discipline understands by a particular genre designation are apparent too, as, for example, in the folklorist's label of "tale" attached to any oral version of an international magic tale or in the literary critic's use of the same term in naming the genre of such works as Irving's "Adventures of the German Student" (from *Tales of a Traveller*) or Poe's "Ligeia." In the study of folklore and American literature continuing attention must be given to both the general theory of genres and the relationship between recognized genres of either discipline, or shared genres, such as the ballad, the tale, the anecdote, or the epic.

A third analytic topic that could be addressed in the study of folklore and American literature is *composition*. How does the process of creating written literature differ from the process of oral composition? Both Poe's 1846 essay on "The Philosophy of Composition" and E. D. Hirsch's recent book of the same title reflect the interest American writers and critics have had in the practical questions of composing in the written medium. Oral composition, on the other hand, has interested students of American folklore only recently, primarily with the publication and subsequent application of the Parry-Lord theory of oral-formulaic composition.[11] The actual process of composition in either medium must, of course, remain a topic of theoretical concern; no one has yet devised a way of getting into the brain of the creative artist. One can more easily explore the closely related question of conscious revision on the part of the writer or the gradual process of remolding on the part of the oral poet or storyteller. For example, one can compare the extensive revising apparent in Fitzgerald's pencil drafts of *The Great Gatsby* with the oral "reworking" of a song by the folk composer Dorrance Wier. In Kenneth Eble's study of Fitzgerald, the critic aligns the rough draft and final version of a short scene in an effort to show the author's stylistic and thematic concerns at work at this level of composition.[12] Similarly, in Henry Glassie's study of Dorrance Wier's "Take That Night Train to Selma," the dropping and adding of verses, the changing of words, and the rearrangement of stanzas are recorded over a three-year period.[13] What is needed beyond such focused studies of individual artists is a comparative study of composition in the written and oral media represented by American literature and American folklore.

A related analytical contact between folklore and literature is the study of *style*. The notion of "style" is poorly defined in both disciplines. In folklore, the style of the ballad, for example, has received considerable attention since certain stylistic features—especially repetition in the form of "commonplaces," refrains, parallel dialogues—are essential to the description of the genre. Some ballad scholars contend that such features are not flexible, idiosyncratic elements of style but rather the necessary "building blocks" in the process of oral composition.[14] Much the same problem arises in the study of literary style: the more diligently a critic tries to define or describe the "style" of an author, the more likely it is that "style" will always prove to be an element of content, or an aspect of traditional technique— something that cannot be abstracted from the work nor described apart from the work. Bennison Gray, in an exhaustive study of the problem of style in literary studies, contends that there is no such thing as style.[15] Nevertheless, scholars limp along with a crutch manufactured from their own conventions and resolve to talk about "style" anyway. Richard M. Dorson describes the "oral styles" of seven American storytellers; John Ball discusses the "style" of the folktale generally; in literary scholarship, general and individual studies of style abound, and an entire journal and yearly bibliography are devoted to the subject of style.[16]

Because an interest in style is not about to fade away in either discipline, perhaps greater efforts should be made to integrate the methods for studying oral and written style whenever possible as well as to establish those elements of style that do separate the two kinds of literary discourse. One could, for instance, bring together the many studies of Mark Twain's literary style, the specialized study of the intentional misspelling or eye dialect tradition of the Southwest humorists, and folkloric studies of oral narrative style for an informed treatise on the variety of style traditions at work in any one of Twain's books. Or one might investigate further the general similarities and differences between oral stylistic features and those found in written literature. In my own preliminary study of this question, I found seven parallel stylistic features, though I am sure there are more.[17]

One feature that is usually assumed to be a part of literary style is that of "poetic language." As with the notion of "style" generally, the concept of poetic language and its presumed opposite—"ordinary language"—is very fuzzy. Scholars in either discipline have often referred to the requirements of "poetic language" in attempts to separate "literature"—oral or written—from nonliterary products that merely employ "ordinary language." So the question of *poetic vs. ordinary language* represents yet another approach one could take in the study of folklore and literature. Actually one finds that in practice the differences between "poetic" and "standard" or "ordinary" language simply represent subjective judgments; indeed, Stanley Fish contends that there is no "ordinary" language.[18] The conventional notion that literary prose is poetic while the language of everyday oral stories, for example, is "ordinary" is easily countered not only through Fish's argument but also through even a "subjective criticism" of oral texts. Consider, say, Melville's description of Turkey in "Bartleby the Scrivener":

Turkey was a short, pursy Englishman, of about my own age—that is, somewhere not far from sixty. In the morning, one might say, his face was of a fine florid hue, but after twelve o'clock, meridian—his dinner hour—it blazed like a grate full of Christmas coals; and continued blazing—but, as it were, with a gradual wane—till six o'clock. . . .

Now compare this description with the following description prefacing an oral true experience story:

This is Uncle Dewey. When he was younger, he was the biggest, fattest son-of-a-bitch you ever saw in you life—just *tight* fat, like a *durgible* [dirigible]. And I's scared to death of him, cause he was *big*, man; he had arms like an elephant's.[19]

Allowing for the differences in vocabulary between written and oral prose—written composition fosters innovative word choice while oral composition invites repetition and familiar vocabulary—we can argue that both descriptions are "poetic"; both make use of metaphor, hyperbole, internal rhyme or assonance, and other poetic features. On the other hand, parts of each passage are intended to approximate ordinary or casual speech. I think much could be gained simply by aligning American folklore and American literature as two similar creative activities that by definition involve the manipulation of language.

In a more general sense, such alignment of the two activities has already produced a standard approach to much American folklore, especially the ballads. Song texts and rewritten oral stories have been the subjects of numerous *folklore as literature* studies. In these studies, folklore is presented or evaluated as though it were written literature. Tunes of songs, gestures, and other features of performance are not discussed; rather, the words to the songs or texts of tales are scrutinized for their aesthetic merit—or lack of merit—generally as indicated in comparison with written literature. In Europe, the Grimms revised (improved) their German tales with each new edition of the collection; Percy and Scott rewrote many of the folk ballads they published. Written literature is the "touchstone" in such studies, then, and folklore is thus more highly valued if it has in fact been "improved" or "popularized" as Francis Lee Utley suggests in his definition of "folk literature."[20] Thus Joel Chandler Harris's *Uncle Remus: His Songs and Sayings* is considered a work of American literature, and parts of it are frequently anthologized in college-level literature textbooks, as are the words to well-known American folksongs such as "The Buffalo Skinners" or "John Henry" or "The Jam on Gerry's Rock." Aesthetic concerns have influenced folklore collectors as well as literary artists. Certainly there is but a fine line between the designations of "folklore" or "literature" in the "poetic" texts Dennis Tedlock presents as translations of Zuñi oral narratives or for that matter in the whole of Zora Neale Hurston's *Mules and Men*.[21] Further study will likely underscore the inevitable confusion that occurs when oral texts are written down—whether verbatim or not—and thus appear to be literature rather than folklore.

Similar to the problem of folklore as literature is the problem of *folklore in literature*. In either case, there is an assumption that the two entities—folklore and literature—are easily discernible, that one can recognize James Douglas Suggs's story about Aunt Carolyn Dye's fortune-telling as folklore and Charles W.

Chesnutt's story of the "Goophered Grapevine" in *The Conjure Woman* as literature.[22] Furthermore, in the study of folklore in literature, there is usually an additional assumption that the author uses the folklore intentionally, consciously, for specific effects. Scholars seek to explain the author's purpose in using the folklore; such criticism is the important "interpretation" portion of the identify-and-interpret formula. It is not enough simply to identify the "old songs" Jay sings to Rufus in James Agee's *A Death in the Family*. A critic must instead take Agee's cue and focus on *why* the boy wanted his father with him, *why* he wanted him to sing, *why* he specifically asked for "Froggy would a wooin go," knowing it was the longest, *why* Jay—the father—"always loved to sing." Certainly, as Daniel Barnes warns, critics cannot justify simple "influence" studies that focus on the author and the folklore only.[23] Rather, we need studies of American literature that offer interpretations informed by the critic's knowledge of folklore *and* the critic's keenest insights into literary creativity. Ronald Baker's study of folklore in the works of Rowland E. Robinson is a commendable effort as far as it goes; the next step would be to expand the final chapter—"The Contributions of Folklore to Robinson's Fiction"—and, in fact, to replace it with a clearly *interpretive* volume that evaluates the literary talents of the writer.[24] An author's writing does often exhibit samples of folklore, popular lore, biblical allusions, lines from Shakespeare; the critic's task is to identify the "source" for his own reference and then to interpret the literature, not as the author's effort to "preserve" a source, but as the author's effort to move his readers, to create a meaningful discourse, to express his own thoughts and feelings no matter how encrusted with traditional plots and imagery those ideas may be.

The temptation in such interpretation is to step away from folklore altogether. The critic builds an elaborate and impressive interpretation out of the large blocks of generalized "folk" patterns or "pagan" ideas—as does Daniel Hoffman, for example, in his excellent discussion of the role of pagan values in Hawthorne's *Scarlet Letter*.[25] The smaller bits and pieces of actual folklore—the beliefs, motifs, stories, or songs—are attended to as illustrations perhaps, but the larger patterns they embody are the materials of greatest use to the literary critic. Studies that rely upon scholarly abstractions of folk patterns, themes, or rituals entail a certain amount of risk. It is one thing to note Melville's accurate depiction of oral storytelling situations in *Moby-Dick* and quite another thing to identify the major theme of the novel as the "folk" motif of the quest. In the second instance, the risk involved is exactly that which Dorson cautioned against in his 1957 article on folklore and American literature.

The risk is intensified if one moves to the field of *myth criticism*, dominated as it is by abstractions of ritual pattern and pagan customs. The conventions of myth criticism allow a critic simply to corroborate perceived patterns in a work of literature through reference to scholarly abstractions of mythic patterns, such as those discussed in Sir James Frazer's *The Golden Bough* or Lord Raglan's *The Hero* or Arnold van Gennep's *Rites de passage*. The critic who hopes to persuade both folklorists and literary critics toward a particular interpretation of a work of literature must be prepared not only to support generalized patterns with illustrations of actual folkloric material but also to demonstrate how the generalized patterns are reflected in the literature. Somehow, the critic must improve upon both Victor West's *Folklore in the Writings of Mark Twain*, which is only minimally annotated, and James M. Cox's "Remarks on the Sad Initiation of

Huckleberry Finn," which brings myth and literature together but ignores the folklore that Twain himself could not escape in his "re-creation" of the mythic adventures of Huck Finn.[26] Most welcome would be studies that authenticate folklore and mythic patterns encountered in works of literature and that rely upon that information for insights in the critic's interpretation of the literature.

Much of the problem in bridging the gap between the "myth criticism" of the literary critic and the "identification of folklore in literature" of the folklorist stems from inconsistencies in the definitions and uses of *concepts of mythos, types, archetypes*, and *motifs* in the two disciplines. In a recent article surveying texts of the story of the sailor who goes inland carrying an oar until he reaches a place where no one recognizes the oar, William F. Hansen notes that the plot of the story—whether found in the *Odyssey*, in modern literary versions, or in collections of oral stories—is stable, though the theme or "meaning" of the story may vary.[27] Now a folklorist would likely assume there is a "tale-type" already identified for such a story—but there is no type listed in the index.[28] Literary critics following Aristotle and Northrop Frye would suggest that there is a stable *mythos*, or plot, but a varying *dianoia*, or theme, from one text to the next.[29] Literary interpretations would build upon archetypal patterns of the "quest" and the riddling question as well as the symbolism of the oar and the sea. Folklorists would scour the motif-index looking for an appropriate correlation, but none can be found according to Hansen.[30] Literary critics regard the folklorists' concern with specific plot descriptions (tale-types) or recurrent narrative elements (motifs) as nitpicking; folklorists accuse literary critics of jumping to hasty conclusions on the basis of overgeneralized patterns (archetypes, themes, or "myths"). Nevertheless, opportunities abound for overcoming these differences in language and academic convention. Critics can identify the examples of superstition and witchcraft in *Huckleberry Finn* and then analyze the effects of that folklore on the characters, plot, and meaning of the whole novel; they can identify Emerson's use of proverbs and go on to relate not only specific proverbs but also the rhetorical pattern of the proverb to Emerson's writing and poetry.

Perhaps the difference in focus between those interested in the recurrence of specific content (folklore) and those interested in larger patterns (literary archetypes) is nowhere more apparent than in studies of popular fiction. The *relationship between popular literature and folklore* tends to follow lines of simple traditionality (not necessarily oral) and structural pattern. For example, Joseph Arpad, in his study of nineteenth-century American humorists, found that the spectacular eye-gouging fight stories reported in mock-oral style in weekly newspapers were in fact circulated exclusively through print.[31] The tradition flourished as a journalistic convention rather than as folklore. Similarly, Constance Rourke records the floating tradition of the Yankee character on the popular stage of the same period.[32] And in a more recent study of popular fiction, John G. Cawelti has isolated "literary formulas" that function for contemporary writers as traditional genre structures have always functioned for oral storytellers.[33] Thus, from the "classical" detective stories of Poe to the "hard-boiled" detective novels of Dashiell Hammett, Raymond Chandler, or even Mickey Spillane, formulaic patterns are at work *almost* as though there were "epic laws" of popular fiction such as those posed by Axel Olrik for folk narrative.[34] Certainly the structures and heroes of America's popular fiction as well as the compositional patterns themselves might profitably be compared to those of oral stories.

Structure and narrative strategy, then, represent another common interest among students of folklore and American literature. "Art" literature as well as popular literature is often analyzed through structural schemes borrowed from studies of folk narrative, notably those of Vladimir Propp and Claude Lévi-Strauss. Though Robert Scholes, in his helpful book *Structuralism in Literature*, usually refers to English or Continental authors for his illustrations, he does comment briefly on the effect of "structuralist thinking" in the works of the American author John Barth.[35] Structuralism, especially the paradigmatic structuralism of Lévi-Strauss, can be viewed as a real, consciously employed poetics in Barth's writing, and we can assume that other strategy-conscious writers and poets could be discussed in structural terms as well. And of course there are works of American literature that can be compared structurally to folktales, legends, and myths with an aim toward explaining in part their universal appeal. Lord Raglan's biographical scheme could illuminate some aspects of the plot in Tennessee Williams's *Suddenly Last Summer* as could Propp's sequential patterning of narrative "functions" in regard to an episodic work such as Poe's short novel, *The Narrative of Arthur Gordon Pym*. And the mediation of opposites at the base of Lévi-Strauss's structural methodology would illuminate some of the deeper themes in such works as Melville's "Benito Cereno" or the Leatherstocking novels of James Fenimore Cooper in which light and dark, nature and civilization, male and female, health and frailty are some of the contrasting pairs that continually call for the reader's mediating response.

The response of the reader, or, in the case of folklore, the response of the audience, is an increasingly important part of contemporary critical theory. Recent folklore studies are perhaps closest to current American literary theory in their attention to concepts of *metanarration and oral literary criticism*, in their view of *folklore as performance*, and in their emphasis on the *role of the audience*. Parallel interests in *metafiction and subjective criticism, literature as process*, and the *reader as audience* show literary theory to be already tilling the common ground between folklore and literary criticism. It is when both folklore and literature are regarded as performances involving artists and audiences that the two fields that study such "performances" seem most effectively allied. Roger Abrahams, in an article appropriately titled "Folklore and Literature as Performance," suggests that "though the process of creativity is not essentially different in oral and written literatures, there are certain performance features which are very different and it is precisely these traits which tend to be emphasized by the folklorist or the critic in considering the relationship between folklore and literature."[36] The encouraging sign in current American literary theory is the tendency to reverse the usual imposition of a literary framework on studies of "oral literature" and to instead adopt the folkloric interest in audience and performance and apply these concepts to the study of literature. Needed now are more studies that incorporate these ideas on audience, performance, and process into the interpretation of storytelling, reading, listening, singing, and writing.

A final research topic that combines the fields of folklore and American literature is one we might term studies in *applied folklore and literature*. Few such studies exist though there have been abundant examples of applied folklore and literature itself; that is, neither folklorists nor literary critics have been particularly interested in studying the uses to which folklore and literature have been put outside of general academic research. Much could be done in assessing the uses educators find for folklore in the English classroom, for example. A number of English educators of secondary and even college-level students are speaking of the need to concentrate on the "oracy" (as Stephen Judy calls it) or "orality" (Father Ong's term) of students and its relationship to their literacy.[37] Some teachers are using oral narratives to teach concepts of story structure, theme, and plot.[38] Others use rewritten tales in readers that teach basic English skills.[39] A related use can be seen in the journalistic endeavors encouraged by the *Foxfire* concept.[40] Here folklore simply serves as appropriate subject matter to be explored through procedures that develop skills in descriptive writing, photography, video- and audio-recording, layout, and marketing.

While education may seem a commendable channel for the use of folklore and literature, a much more popular employment of folklore in a literary guise is as children's literature. Much more than authors generally, the authors of children's books who adapt folklore materials to their own use may be seen as consciously "applying" folklore in a literary framework. Many American authors retell international fairy tales for American children, and such books are often recognized for their sensitive stylization and illustrations. Occasionally American folktales or legends are adapted as children's literature—stories of Mike Fink, John Henry, or Paul Bunyan, stories of haunted places, or American Indian tales.[41] Inevitably some examples of "fakelore," as Richard Dorson has termed such literary creations, do creep into children's literature as well. As Dorson has suggested, even apart from the rewriting of oral stories, many of the Paul Bunyan tales have never circulated orally; they were created as literary products from the beginning.[42] Even more offensive to the folklorist are books such as Jeremiah Digges's and Harold W. Felton's *Bowleg Bill: The Seagoing Cowboy*, which is heralded as an American tall tale but is, of course, not a traditional story at all.[43] Nevertheless, such "fakelore" along with the more authentic adaptations of collected stories should be studied by students of folklore and literature. Without such constructive criticism by scholars who know both folklore and American literary tradition well, the lamentably bad examples of applied folklore and literature will multiply.

Studying folklore and American literature need not be limited to the identification of folklore and folklife references in the works of obscure regional writers or "folksy" poets. The study of folklore and American literature can involve the fiction of Melville as well as Robinson, the plays of Eugene O'Neill as well as Benjamin A. Baker, the poetry of Emerson as well as James Whitcomb Riley.[44] For serious students of folklore and American literature all of the ties that bind folklore and literature together represent lines along which their study can be developed into a revived and newly expanded area of the humanities.

NOTES

1. Jan Harold Brunvand, for example, compiles a specialized proverb survey using the works of Eggleston among others in *A Dictionary of Proverbs and Proverbial Phrases from Books Published by Indiana Authors before 1890* (Bloomington: Indiana University Press, 1961).

2. Phillips Barry discusses the borrowing of two stanzas from the British broadside "She Never Blamed Him" in "Fair Florella," *American Speech* 3 (1928): 441–47.

3. Richard M. Dorson, *American Folklore and the Historian* (Chicago: University of Chicago Press, 1971), pp. 186–203.

4. Richard M. Dorson, "Folklore and Literature," *Journal of the Folklore Institute* 13 (1976): 327.

5. Kuhn's concept of "paradigm" as a shared set of assumptions, methods, etc., is stretched a bit but applicable; Thomas S. Kuhn, *The Structure of Scientific Revolutions*, 2d ed. (Chicago: University of Chicago Press, 1970).

6. Compare Roger D. Abrahams, "Personal Power and Social Restraint in the Definition of Folklore," in *Toward New Perspectives in Folklore*, ed. Américo Paredes and Richard Bauman (Austin: University of Texas Press, 1972), pp. 16–30, with W. K. Wimsatt and Monroe C. Beardsley, "The Intentional Fallacy," in W. K. Wimsatt, *The Verbal Icon: Studies in the Meaning of Poetry* (Lexington: University of Kentucky Press, 1954), pp. 2–18.

7. Robert M. Adams, "The Sense of Verification: Pragmatic Commonplaces about Literary Criticism," in *Myth, Symbol, and Culture*, ed. Clifford Geertz (New York: W. W. Norton, 1971), pp. 203–14; Elliott Oring, "Three Functions of Folklore: Traditional Functionalism as Explanation in Folkloristics," *Journal of American Folklore* 89 (1976): 67–80.

8. André Jolles, *Einfache Formen* (Halle: Max Niemeyer, 1930). See also the discussion of the "relation of primitive genres (those of folk or oral literature) to those of a developed literature," in René Wellek and Austin Warren, *Theory of Literature* (New York: Harcourt, Brace & World, 1956), pp. 235–36.

9. See Sandra K. D. Stahl, "Narrative Genres: A Question of Academic Assumptions," *Fabula* 21 (1980): 82–87.

10. Dan Ben-Amos, "Analytic Categories and Ethnic Genres," in *Folklore Genres*, ed. Dan Ben-Amos (Austin: University of Texas Press, 1976), pp. 215–42.

11. Albert B. Lord, *The Singer of Tales* (New York: Atheneum, 1971; originally published in 1960). See also Carl Lindahl, "Recent Folkloric Approaches to Oral-Formulaic Theory," Folklore Preprints Series, vol. 6, no. 5, 1979, pp. 1–20.

12. Kenneth E. Eble, "The Craft of Revision: *The Great Gatsby*," *American Literature* 36 (1964): 315–26.

13. Henry Glassie, " 'Take That Night Train to Selma': An Excursion to the Outskirts of Scholarship," in *Folksongs and Their Makers*, by Henry Glassie, Edward D. Ives, and John F. Szwed (Bowling Green, Ohio: Bowling Green University Popular Press, 1971), pp. 1–68.

14. See, for example, David Buchan, *The Ballad and the Folk* (London: Routledge & Kegan Paul, 1972).

15. Bennison Gray, *Style: The Problem and Its Solution* (The Hague: Mouton, 1969).

16. See, respectively, Richard M. Dorson, "Oral Styles of American Folk Narrators," in his *Folklore: Selected Essays* (Bloomington: Indiana University Press, 1972), pp. 99–146; John Ball, "Style in the Folktale," *Folklore* 65 (1954): 170–72; and the journal *Style*, established in 1966.

17. Sandra K. D. Stahl, "Style in Oral and Written Narratives," *Southern Folklore Quarterly* 43 (1979): 39–62.

18. Stanley E. Fish, "How Ordinary Is Ordinary Language?" *New Literary History* 5 (1973): 41–54; cf. Jan Mukařovsky, "Standard Language and Poetic Language," in *A Prague School Reader on Esthetics, Literary Structure, and Style*, ed. Paul L. Garvin (Washington, D.C.: Georgetown University Press, 1964), pp. 17–30.

19. The oral storyteller is Larry B. Scheiber of Huntington, Indiana.

20. Francis Lee Utley, "Folk Literature: An Operational Definition," *Journal of American Folklore* 74 (1961): 193–206.

21. Dennis Tedlock, "On the Translation of Style in Oral Narrative," in *Toward New Perspectives in Folklore*, pp. 114–33; see also Sandra K. D. Stahl, "Zora Neale Hurston's *Mules and Men*: Ethnography or Literature?" *Southern Folklore Quarterly*, in press.

22. Suggs is the prolific black storyteller who told Richard M. Dorson some 175 stories; see Richard M. Dorson, *American Negro Folktales* (Greenwich, Conn.: Fawcett Publications, 1958, 1967).

23. See Daniel R. Barnes, "The Bosom Serpent: A Legend in American Literature and Culture," *Journal of American Folklore* 85 (1972): 111–22.

24. Ronald L. Baker, *Folklore in the Writings of Rowland E. Robinson* (Bowling Green, Ohio: Bowling Green University Popular Press, 1973).

25. See Daniel Hoffman, *Form and Fable in American Fiction* (New York: W. W. Norton, 1961), pp. 169–86.

26. Victor Royce West, *Folklore in the Works of Mark Twain* (Lincoln: University of Nebraska Press, 1930); James M. Cox, "Remarks on the Sad Initiation of Huckleberry Finn," in *Myth and Literature: Contemporary Theory and Practice*, ed. John B. Vickery (Lincoln: University of Nebraska Press, 1966), pp. 277–87.

27. William F. Hansen, "The Story of the Sailor Who Went Inland," in *Folklore Today: A Festschrift for Richard M. Dorson*, ed. Linda Dégh, Henry Glassie, and Felix J. Oinas (Bloomington: Indiana University RCLSS, 1976), pp. 221–30.

28. The index of tale-types intended here is *The Types of the Folktale*, by Antti Aarne and Stith Thompson (FF Communications No. 184) (Helsinki: Academia Scientiarum Fennica, 1964).

29. See Frye's discussion in his *Anatomy of Criticism* (New York: Atheneum, 1969), pp. 82–83, 111, passim.

30. Hansen, p. 229, note 2. The motif-index intended here is the *Motif-Index of Folk-Literature*, by Stith Thompson (Bloomington: Indiana University Press, 1955), 6 vols.

31. Joseph J. Arpad, "The Fight Story: Quotation and Originality in Native American Humor," *Journal of the Folklore Institute* 10 (1973): 141–72.

32. Constance Rourke, *American Humor: A Study of the National Character* (Garden City, N.Y.: Doubleday, 1931); see also Richard M. Dorson, *America in Legend* (New York: Pantheon Books, 1973), pp. 108–21.

33. John G. Cawelti, *Adventure, Mystery, and Romance: Formula Stories as Art and Popular Culture* (Chicago: University of Chicago Press, 1976).

34. Axel Olrik, "Epic Laws of Folk Literature," in *The Study of Folklore*, ed. Alan Dundes (Englewood Cliffs, N.J.: Prentice-Hall, 1965), pp. 129–41.

35. Robert Scholes, *Structuralism in Literature: An Introduction* (New Haven: Yale University Press, 1974), pp. 192–93. Scholes briefly surveys the structural theories of Lord Raglan, Propp, Lévi-Strauss, Brémond, and others.

36. Roger Abrahams, "Folklore and Literature as Performance," *Journal of the Folklore Institute* 9 (1972): 81–82.

37. See Stephen N. Judy, *The ABC's of Literacy: A Guide for Parents and Educators* (New York: Oxford University Press, 1980), p. 15, and Walter J. Ong, S.J., "Literacy and Orality in Our Times," *PMLA Profession* (1979): 1–7.

38. See Mark B. Stahl, "Using Traditional Oral Stories in the English Classroom," *The English Journal* 68:7 (1979): 33–36.

39. An example would be Vinal O. Binner's *American Folktales, I and II: A Structured Reader* (New York: Thomas Y. Crowell, 1967).

40. The *Foxfire* magazine and books are compiled by high school students in Rabun Gap, Georgia, but the concept of student folklore publication has been tried

elsewhere. See Eliot Wigginton, *Moments: The Foxfire Experience* (Kennebunk, Maine: Star Press, 1975).

41. Harold W. Felton, *Mike Fink, Best of the Keelboatmen* (New York: Dodd, Mead, 1960); Ezra Jack Keats, *John Henry: An American Legend* (New York: Pantheon, 1965); Glen Rounds, *Ol' Paul, the Mighty Logger* (New York: Holiday, 1949); Bruce and Nancy Roberts, *America's Most Haunted Places* (Garden City, N.Y.: Doubleday, 1976); Anne Rockwell, *The Dancing Stars: An Iroquois Legend* (New York: Thomas Y. Crowell, 1972).

42. See Dorson's discussion of the term "fakelore" and its application, *American Folklore and the Historian*, pp. 3–14.

43. Jeremiah Digges and Harold W. Felton, *Bowleg Bill: The Seagoing Cowboy* (Englewood Cliffs, N. J.: Prentice-Hall, 1957); Felton also wrote *Pecos Bill and the Mustang* in 1965.

44. Benjamin A. Baker wrote *A Glance at New York* in 1848, and thereafter wrote several other plays that presented the hero Mose, the Bowery b'hoy. See a general discussion in Richard M. Dorson, *America in Legend*, pp. 99–108.

Archie Green

Sound Recordings, Use and Challenge

Today, folklorists use tape recorders variously, both in the field and in the classroom, as extensions of their five senses. It has become unthinkable to collect without electronic equipment and concomitant skill, while our subject can hardly be taught without playing recorded examples of tale or song in traditional style. From time to time, individual scholars assist members of folk society in their documentary projects. By such deeds study may complement cultural advocacy, for presenting folk material to society at large is an act of complex and value-laden dimension. In these multiple uses—pedagogic and pragmatic—we face, consciously or not, the tension arising between rival institutional realms. Most folklorists owe their prime allegiance to the academy and its sister intellectual and public agencies. Hence, we perceive commerce as distant from or as debasing traditional life. Yet we turn constantly to industry for vital equipment. Jesse Walter Fewkes used an Edison machine in 1890 to collect Indian lore, and all his "grandchildren" continue such dependency.

More important than this symbiotic relationship with industry is our special need to account for the effect of recordings on folk tradition. Metaphorically, the disc (and the process it stands for) is a double-edged sword. It preserves an artistic text or tune in all its nuances; it also accelerates change in tradition. In the United States, for half a century, a low-keyed debate has occurred between two sets of folklorists: those who have perceived canned music and cheap records as corrosive agents, destroying the past, robbing people of deep treasures; and those who have welcomed discs as exciting documents of folklife, indeed, as instruments in folk culture's counter-hegemonic role.

To understand the ambivalence of folklorists when faced by sound captured mechanically, it is useful to know about the so-called race and hillbilly records. In the years immediately following World War I, disc sales plummeted in the face of the then-new competitive challenge of radio. Among several responses, phonograph company executives sought fresh material and novel markets. Ralph Peer of the General Phonograph Corporation (Okeh) helped open the fields of black and white folk and folklike music in the period 1920–24. The terms then used, "race" and "hillbilly," held pejorative overtones, and eventually gave way to inoffensive substitutes such as "blues," "soul," "country," or "western." These shifts in nomenclature need not be detailed, beyond noting that strain between urban and rural life, as well as between black and white people, will always qualify the response by intellectuals to folk music, however this expressive material is labeled.

One of the least explored areas in our discipline is the nexus of folk and non-folk culture. To examine how and when scholars or collectors, based in the academy or in the government bureau, accepted recorded folk music is to cast light on a crucial area of American cultural interaction. We have some data from Carl Sandburg and Lloyd Lewis in Chicago in the 1920s, where together with friends such as John Lomax, they met to swap songs. Lewis, a sophisticated journalist from rural Indiana, became an early fan of cowboy phonograph ballads, conscious of their pastoral value in compensating for overmechanized urban living. In Manhattan's Harlem, Carl Van Vechten and Abbe Niles made similar pioneer collections of jazz and blues, accepting both forms as folksong and as emblem of vitality in Negro life. About 1927, a few Ivy League students gathered race records, leading to an informal sales and auction literature. Charles Edward Smith's *Esquire* article "Collecting Hot" (February 1934) revealed arcane secrets to a wide audience then ready to accept the new French word "discography."

In this reach to folk music across lines of class and status, before and after World War II, Alan Lomax actively pushed and pulled a host of young "citybillies" to an appreciation of "earthy" commercial recordings. In 1939, Moses Asch, in New York, issued folksong records on a series of small labels. His audience was initially radical and urban. Asch understood the imperatives of previous enthusiasts like Lewis and Niles, and developed a format to weld their diverse tastes into a steady market. In time, Asch amassed the largest single catalogue of American folk music, assisted by dedicated friends such as Henry Cowell and Pete Seeger. The term "folksong revival" is inexact; if it is ever understood fully, it will be seen as riveted to the discovery and use of sound recordings in their plural modes: pure/slick, field/commercial, down home/uptown.

From the mid-1920s, some scholars—for example, Guy B. Johnson and Howard W. Odum in "John Henry" studies—transcribed songs or cited commercial records in their articles and books. Generally, sociologists and anthropologists used texts from discs in descriptive ethnographies or in papers on social problems, while literary specialists spun ballad histories or spelled out rhetorical problems. In 1928 Abbe Niles undertook serious reviews of recorded folksong for *Bookman*, but the first academic criticism of such material came later: Herbert Halpert (1936); Claude M. Simpson (1947); Charles Seeger (1948). The longest span of serious folk record commentary is that of D. K. Wilgus, beginning in 1955 in the *Kentucky Folklore Record*, and continuing to this day in other publications. Among recent scholars, Charles K. Wolfe has approached recordings with sophisticated tools, integrating technical discographical detail with broad historical analysis.[1] Two examples of magazines from England round out this overview of criticism: *Old Time Music* sets rigorous standards for collectors of Anglo-American music; *Blues Unlimited* treats Afro-American material. Enthusiasts in many countries publish similar magazines on American folk and folklike recordings.

Folklorists frame problems wherever data is gathered and interpreted—in the field, in quiet libraries, in institutional archives. The Archive of American Folk-Song, established in 1928 in the Library of Congress, became the Archive of Folk Song in 1956 and the Archive of Folk Culture in 1981. In 1963, the Recorded Sound

Section began to parallel the Archive's work. This Section is important to scholars for its immense holding of commercial records and related ephemeral literature. The Archive and the Section together house invaluable field recordings collected under the auspices of the WPA and other New Deal agencies. Since 1942, the Library has issued albums of field recordings with annotated brochures for public sale, and, in 1976, the Library undertook a special Bicentennial set of 15 LPs, *Folk Music in America*, edited by Richard Spottswood. This set drew equally upon field and commercial recordings as well as upon some non–English language material.

Several other archives complement federal endeavor. The John Edwards Memorial Foundation at UCLA specializes in American folk music disseminated commercially, and within this area it focuses on old-time material. The *JEMF Quarterly* has functioned as a bridge joining private collectors and academic scholars. The Archive of New Orleans Jazz at Tulane University, and the Rutgers University Institute of Jazz Studies both house folk blues. The Archives of Traditional Music at Indiana University accepts ethnic music from all over the world and uses this to complement Indiana's comprehensive graduate program in folklore and ethnomusicology. The Rodgers and Hammerstein Archives of Recorded Sound at the New York Public Library's Lincoln Center branch works closely with private collectors, and that large section of the recording industry based in Manhattan. Finally, The Country Music Foundation Library and Media Center in Nashville is sustained mainly out of business funds, and explores the intersection of folk and popular culture. This Center's handsome *Journal of Country Music*, modern in format, is open to a wide range of contributors. The handful of sound archives mentioned above does not exhaust the list for the United States.

In suggesting that scholars have placed their response to sound recordings between poles tagged as "corrosive agent" or "exciting document," we treat an age-old attack by guardians of cultivated taste upon people called "philistines" and their expression judged "uncultured." Historically, such charges have been directed against the broadside press, music hall, circus ring, minstrel stage, cinema screen, sports arena, and ubiquitous television. It is helpful to situate this assault broadly. Within modern industrial society, particular groups contend for power or resources and generate cultural emblems to name players (winners or losers) in the drama. It is an article of faith in our land that many Americans are identified by the records they enjoy.

Within this *Handbook*, other contributors detail differences at respective levels of culture: high, popular, folk, tribal. Here, I focus only on the use of recordings by folklorists to identify large configurations of value. When Charles Seeger initiated record reviewing for the *Journal of American Folklore* (1948), he judged traditional performing style as a positive norm and concert style as negative. We continue to use related terms for class and culture: "pure," "authentic," "field," versus "slick," "exhibitory," "commercial." Seeger was especially concerned with the acculturative road for folksongs and viewed specific performances captured in wax as journey milestones. In *Only a Miner*, I attempted to go beyond locating records in stylistic array. Selecting a dozen discs for case studies, I set specific songs within networks of history, literature, and aesthetics. It is possible, of course, to combine for given recordings all the modes of analysis now open to scholarship. Placing records across a spectrum from field to market helps pose framing questions. Such an arrangement, no matter how brief, must begin with notices of collecting before recording equipment reached the field.

Archeologist Charles Peabody heard Negro workers while wheeling and digging on a mound in Coahoma County, Mississippi, and reported this "ethnological material in song" in the *Journal of American Folklore* (1903). In 1918 at Hampton Institute, Natalie Curtis Burlin used wax cylinders by a college quartet as sources for folksong booklets, and included a 27-stanza "Hammerin' Song." A year later, Frank C. Brown collected similar cylinder pieces from black workers in North Carolina, while, in 1922, Bascom Lamar Lunsford recorded "Swannanoa Tunnel" for him. During 1927, Brunswick released in its hillbilly series "Roll On, John" by Buell Kazee and "Nine Pound Hammer" by Al Hopkins and the Bucklebusters. Also, in 1927, Okeh released two work chants by Texas Alexander, "Section Gang Blues" and "Levee Camp Moan." A year later, Mississippi John Hurt offered "Spike Driver Blues" on Okeh. Parallel in time to these tradition-based discs, Paul Robeson arranged "Water Boy" for Victor, giving many concert-record purchasers a sense of the power that pulsed in black work song.

After 1933, John and Alan Lomax deposited a number of field discs of work chants in the Library of Congress, one of which, Jimmie Strothers' "This Ol' Hammer," is now heard on the LC's set *Folk Music in America*. Aunt Molly Jackson's field version of "Roll On Buddy" represents railroad construction in Appalachia. Bill and Charlie Monroe's song of this same name—different in text and recorded in 1937 for Bluebird—subsequently became a bluegrass standard. Meanwhile, Huddie Ledbetter's "Take This Hammer," recorded with the Golden Gate Quartet for Victor in 1940 and solo for Asch in 1942, became a "revival" favorite, featured in concert by The Weavers and other popular "folk" trios. Merle Travis recorded "Nine Pound Hammer" for Capital in 1946; his coal-mine version, close to folk sources, was later covered by artists as diverse as Tennessee Ernie Ford, Johnny Cash, Flatt & Scruggs, John Prine, and The Byrds. All the work songs (hammering/drilling/digging/driving/wheeling) named here cluster thematically; however, the discs cited represent black and white singers, contrastive marketing campaigns, and appeals to widely different audiences. In listening today, we define Aunt Molly and Strothers as traditional, and arrange other performers at their sides by falling back on notions of integrity in folk style, or on the convergence of antiquity and modernity.

Not all folklorists who use electronic gear in the field or on the campus wish to pursue questions of metaphor or meaning. All can, however, benefit by a glimpse at the phonograph's origin. The phonautograph, a device to trace sound waves on lampblacked paper, dates to the mid–nineteenth century; the merging of separate techniques to record and reproduce sound dates to 1877. Charles Cros in France and Thomas Edison in the United States share honors for this groundbreaking linkage. Edison's first talking machine consisted of a rotating cylinder holding a wrap-around tinfoil sheet, a mouthpiece diaphragm attached to an embossing point, and a reproducing point attached to a second diaphragm for playback. Literally, the first stylus cut (stored) continuous sound waves into the foil. Edison named the phonograph, noting that it resulted from his quest for a Speaking Telegraph, an apparatus intended to repeat Morse symbols. The inventor understood his device as a utilitarian office machine, but did not anticipate its full entertainment potential. Nor could he foresee its complex role in altering cultural expression as well as communicative norms. He saw but dimly his little machine's challenge to cultural documentarians.

The word "phonograph" has served for a century to cover three integrated functions: physical recording, permanent storage, instant playback of sound. The overarching combination "sound recording" now extends beyond these triple functions to include a series of self-contained technologies: multi-track recording studios, LP and 45-rpm discs, home stereo systems, film tracks, videotapes, portable tape cassettes—all of which extend the achievement of 1877. In many contexts, the verb "to record" and the noun "record" merge to blur distinctions between process and object, between action and item. By extension, some bluesmen refer to songs of their own composition as "sides," applying the designation of the disc's physical side to their own imaginative creations.

Edison's phonograph was improved in the 1880s by the introduction of wax cylinders in place of tinfoil, and by competition from Emile Berliner's gramophone, which substituted flat discs for cylinders. Quite apart from the aural qualities of these discrete forms, it was easier to store discs than cylinders. During the 1890s, coin-operated phonographs and gramophones together were first used in penny arcades, saloons, and other places of revelry. At the turn of the century some adventurous teachers began to play records in the classroom and the major firms responded with special educational catalogs. We see, then, that improvement went hand in hand with the movement of the phonograph from office to arcade, school, and home parlor.

A few key dates help establish the chronology within which we identify the turn to recordings by folklorists. In 1891, John Philip Sousa produced for the Columbia Phonograph Company, in Washington, a set of popular records of the United States Marine Band. Early in 1901, Enrico Caruso, in Milan, recorded his first song, from the opera *Tosca*. Victor inaugurated in 1903 its prestigious Red Seal series of classical discs. Within this series, Alma Gluck's "Carry Me Back to Old Virginny" (1911) became the first Red Seal to sell a million copies, providing listeners with both a genteel vision of southern plantation life and an idealized view of folk society.

Earlier, in 1901, the Columbia catalogue had announced the already traditional "Arkansas Traveler" as "Descriptive of a native sitting in front of his hut scraping his fiddle and answering the interruptions of the stranger with witty sallies. Record is full of jokes and laughter." Victor, in 1903, recorded the Dinwiddie Colored Quartet singing four "genuine Jubilee and Camp Meeting Shouts sung as only negroes can sing them." The pieces were: "Down on the Old Camp Ground," "Gabriel's Trumpet," "Poor Mourner," "We'll Anchor Bye and Bye." In the contrast between Alma Gluck and the Dinwiddie Quartet, the commercial recording industry presented to consumers extreme differences both in performer's origin and presentational style. Although the Columbia artist for the "Arkansas Traveler" was unnamed, several other stars of this rural fiddle tune/dialogue were popular artists either who had come out of folk society or who had skill in interpreting folk style.

We lack commentary by folklorists who heard recorded versions of "Carry Me Back to Old Virginny," the "Arkansas Traveler," or the Dinwiddie selections, but we do know that ethnographers from the beginning were attracted to the phonograph's potential as an aid in field research. The earliest known list of Berliner discs for sale (1895) included three separate records, each titled "Three Melodies from the Ghost Dance." These songs, apparently sung by James and

Charles Mooney, resulted from the former's work with the Sioux tribes for the Bureau of American Ethnology, Smithsonian Institution.

To establish a benchmark for ethnographic field recording within the United States is to honor Jesse Walter Fewkes, from Harvard's Peabody Museum. In March 1890 he took an Edison machine to Calais, Maine, to record the language and music of Passamaquoddy Indians, planning this trip as a trial run for future use of the phonograph among southwestern tribes. Not only did Fewkes use the talking machine as a scientific tool, but he reported his findings both in the *Journal of American Folklore* and *Science*, where he likened his cylinders' contents to specimens in a naturalist's case.

The major collector of Native American music was Frances Densmore. For more than three decades (1907–41) she used sound equipment, producing some 2,500 cylinders from tribes throughout the continent. Few American folklorists have matched her achievement. Today, a selection of Densmore's field recordings is available on Library of Congress and Folkways labels. Before her retirement from the BAE, the federal government had made the transition from recording Indian material alone to recording English-language folksong as well.

Robert Winslow Gordon came to Library of Congress in 1928 trained as a Harvard literary scholar, but with a Yankee mechanic's infatuation with camera and phonograph. Before his start at the Archive of Folk-Song, he had already used cylinder machines in 1920 to record chanties in California. Gordon's pioneering work was terminated by the Depression, but was carried on and strengthened in the New Deal decade by father and son, John and Alan Lomax. The feature film *Leadbelly* (1976) opens with a portrait of the two collectors in a Louisiana prison recording the great black folksinger Huddie Ledbetter.

In the year 1925, the Bell Telephone Company and its affiliate Western Electric ended a half-century of acoustical recording methods by introducing the electric microphone. A similar leap forward took place between 1948 and 1952 with LP "albums," 45-rpm discs, and portable tape recorders. These new artifacts greatly expanded the options of folklorists as well as the audiences for traditional material. Some scholars moved temporarily into the sound industry, serving as consultants or as editors. Many young people, learning from discs, turned both to imitative performance and to the serious study of folklore. Entrepreneurs within regional or ethnic groups used inexpensive recording techniques which gave them a competitive toehold in the commercial music industry. We have yet to assay records as "survival tools," employed strategically or unconsciously within folk society. Fortunately, discographers such as Richard Spottswood and Pekka Gronow have turned to the study of "foreign-language" recordings in the United states.[2] We shall need their reports, and many more by others, to understand national acculturation drives and group resistance, as well as the clash and convergence of cultural norms.

By considering a few of the plural uses of recordings by folklorists, and in glimpsing the history of sound technology, we assert that the physical LP (or perforated film soundtrack, or magnetic tape reel) is at once a modern artifact and an aural document of tradition. Consequently, the sound recording becomes the perfect trap attracting those who differ conceptually. I use the symbol "trap" deliberately, for one can easily be caught by the sheer attraction of the disc as an object of intrinsic value, and the recording process as one of skilled competence alone. Ideally, each folklorist should learn to record in the field, and should have at hand a good collection of demonstration discs and tapes. But beyond skill and beyond possessions, it is highly important to understand that the sound recording, both as item and as process, is keyed to many of the problems which carriers of tradition face in everyday life.

A talent scout or recording engineer employed by the phonograph industry literally goes to the field (or brings the folk into the studio) to obtain products that can be sold across music store counters or on supermarket display racks. The folklorist goes to this same field to document complex cultural patterns and perhaps to test rival hypotheses about expressive life. What of the folksinger who performs for either the scout or the ethnographer? In some instances, the folksingers cling stubbornly to style and repertoire regardless of the battery of microphones before them. Such individuals may even perceive their role as that of a partisan resisting erosion of community. Frequently, however, folk performers welcome the recording process as opportunity for advancement. Figuratively, the disc offers a chance at the carousel's golden ring. Jimmie Rodgers' rise from brakeman to pop-cult hero and Gene Autry's from telegrapher to millionaire seem to be known to every rural or blue-collar singer. Louis Armstrong's rise from orphanage to national ambassador of good will and Mahalia Jackson's from domestic servant to honored guest at the White House are similarly known.

Scholars must accept the fact that the recording process gives members of folk society access to wealth and fame. We also know that the process, in commercial hands, flattens and distorts folk culture. At times, we soften this contradiction by distinguishing the roles of dominant figures in the music industry from that of proprietors of small specialty labels. Space does not permit a full roster of entrepreneurs dedicated to traditional values, but one among many, Chris Strachwitz of Arhoolie Records, can be mentioned. He has geared himself to "turn on" music (for example—blues, Cajun, hillbilly) and has pioneered in recent years by opening the rich field of Mexican-American music to wide audiences. Strachwitz usually identifies his offerings in terms of taste, but beyond his aesthetic standard, he functions to slow down America's assimilative process. Metaphorically, the recorders of folk music, whether from the Library of Congress or from private specialty labels, retard the flame under the national melting pot.

To discuss Thomas Edison and Chris Strachwitz in a single overview marks one progression in time and another in function. America's best known inventor, seeking a Speaking Telegraph, did not consciously create a tool for folklorists. Strachwitz, not formally trained in folklore, has used Edison's talking machine to produce more folk discs in a decade and a half than the Library of Congress in half a century. This fact is both tribute to local enthusiasm and challenge to national cultural strategies. Sound recording technology will continue to touch folk culture whether or not scholars are engaged or passive, sensitive or dull, self-employed or using public funds. We make disciplinary commitments voluntarily; we have a magnificent kit of tools at hand; our choices have deep consequences beyond our actions.

N O T E S

1. See Charles K. Wolfe, *The Grand Old Opry: The Early Years, 1925–1933* (London: Old Time Music, 1975).
2. See Pekka Gronow, *Studies in Scandinavian-American Discography* (Helsinki: Finnish Institute of Recorded Sound, 1977).

Sharon R. Sherman

Studying American Folkloric Films

Across America, folklorists have documented the rhythms, words, and movements of people dancing, narrating, singing, or engaging in some other aspect of folkloric creativity. This documentation has generally taken the form of texts, written descriptions, or, more recently, tape recordings and still photographs. Such records often become part of a scholarly published work or are placed in archives as resource materials for the student of American folklore to investigate. Because of the growing recognition that films offer a means of viewing folklore holistically,[1] many folklorists have begun using this medium to document and analyze American folklore, and the folkloric film has become part of our discipline.

Film is best used as a methodological tool when the emphasis is on performance, interaction, and communication, or the processes of folkloric expression. Situations such as dancing, play activities, festive events, and rituals, in which motion is a vital element, demand film as a means of gathering and presenting the data; and blues, work songs, occupational tales, children's games, religious practices, and the traditions of Cajuns, Afro-Americans, Jews, and cattlemen have already served as film topics.[2]

My own work, "The Folkloric Film: The Relevance of Film for Understanding Folkloric Events," offers suggestions for study from several perspectives.[3] In addition to the overt reasons for any film's existence, such as documentation of quiltmaking or curing ceremonies, film can also be used to analyze gestures, facial expressions, proxemics, and interactions, while theoretical biases may be communicated through the editing style and sound devices chosen by the filmmaker. For example, those who conceptualize folklore as texts or artifacts generally structure their films with narrations, interviews, and sound-over to bind together vignettes or montages of nonlinear visuals. Filmmakers who examine creative processes or interactional events tend also to focus on individual artists and performers, communities or regions, but most often they use sync-sound or the sound-over voices of the participants combined with a *cinéma vérité* or linear progression editing style. By comparing the content focus of some well-known films with the film techniques used, I will suggest a model for studying folkloric films and illustrate why certain approaches to filming are particularly successful.

FILMS DOCUMENTING TEXTS

Bill Ferris's *I Ain't Lying: Folktales from Mississippi* (1975) combines sync-sound, sound-over, and narration with a series of vignettes. Ferris begins with his star informant, James Thomas, telling a tale about a woman and a preacher. Also included are various tales such as one about John and Ole Miss (a variation on the John and Old Marster tales), religious tales, toasts, and the dozens. Ferris shifts from James Thomas to Shelby Brown, back to Thomas in a graveyard in Leland, and then to Mary Gordon on her porch. Scenes of the Rose Hill congregation with Reverend Isaac Thomas and of Brown and Thomas and a group of men in a bar follow. A harmonica instrumental provides space for Ferris to act as narrator and to comment on the folktales. These narrative portions are not intrusive because Ferris does not have the typical newscaster's voice, and he does not romanticize the visuals. The narration indicates the presence of the folklorist rather than an anonymous interpreter, and serves only as a means of identifying informants and linking diverse scenes shot in Leland and Rose Hill, Mississippi. Although the tales are told "in context," the film emphasizes types of tales; and because the scenes do not portray the sessions as events, no real sense of the function of storytelling in rural Mississippi is provided.

In her film *Say Old Man, Can You Play the Fiddle?* (1974), Bess Lomax Hawes focuses upon the repertoire and fiddling technique of the late Earl Collins, but pays little attention to his personality and interactions with other musicians. Akin to a taped interview or a series of cuts on a record, the film dissolves from one straightforward shot of Collins sitting on a couch playing a tune to another similar shot. In voice-over, Earl explains when he learned to play, when he likes to fiddle, and how his fiddle was made; conversations between Earl and Hawes, whose voice is heard off camera, are interspersed with the tune performances. At one point Earl's son, a guitarist, magically "jumps" into the scene at Earl's side, a surprise that results because all of the interactions and intervening comments between shots have been deleted. *Say Old Man* concludes with a printed roll-up of the tunes played. The filmic technique—a series of dissolves—indicates that the film's primary purpose is to present fiddle tunes as visual "texts."

PROCESS AND EVENT FILMS

Although films that examine texts are valuable as visual records, they leave unanswered questions about how and why folkloric traditions are generated. By contrast, a focus on process and event enables viewers to perceive folklore as human behavior.

Religious events form the subject of Ferris's *Two Black Churches* (1975). The first half of the film includes an oral sermon by Reverend Isaac Thomas, shots of church members Mary and Amanda Gordon quilting and singing a gospel song, and the McGowan Gospel Singers performing "We Are Marching." All in all, these introductory sequences do not work well together because no connective shots clarify relationships between the scenes. But once Ferris shifts to a service at St. James Church in New Haven, Connecticut (identified by a title), their purpose is understood: they represent Southern rural religious practices in contrast to Northern urban ones. Using a voice-over technique, Ferris presents Reverend Coward discussing how he was called to preach. As the service continues, Mrs. Coward "gets the spirit," Reverend Coward heals by laying on hands, the congregation sings, and church members embrace. This second half of the film is powerful; by focusing on all aspects of one church service, the film provides insight into the meaning and variety of religious experiences of a specific gathering of people. The first segment with its superficial overview of rural forms of black religious expression does not accomplish the contrast Ferris obviously sought, while the remarkable scenes in the second portion of *Two Black Churches* indicate the effectiveness of studying events through film.

One of the best-known event-oriented films is *Pizza Pizza Daddy-O* (1968), by Bess Lomax Hawes. It shows eight singing games played by twelve girls in a Los Angeles schoolyard. Hawes begins with random playground activities, then focuses on two girls playing and singing a hand clapping game, "Oh Susianna," as more girls join in. The film freeze-frames while the narrator explains that "games brought over from the British Isles" were blended with the Afro-American heritage of the participants. Obviously all taken from one session, the scenes in the film detail the interactions, gesturing and posturing, and dance patterns of the players, as well as the words of the games. One particularly revealing sequence begins with a girl leading the group in performing "Who Do They Talk About? The Mighty, Mighty Devil." Another girl complains that the leader doesn't know how to lead properly, an argument develops, and the game resumes with a new leader. In this segment, certain individuals stand out from the group and we learn something about their personalities and interactions by watching for them in later games.

The use of sync-sound and the focus on a single situation implies an event emphasis, yet both the narrator's commentary and the technique of cutting or dissolving from one game scene to another without showing all of the interactions occurring between games point toward textual analysis. The accompanying study guide provides comparative notes, describes the performance, lists bibliographic sources, and includes transcriptions of the songs. Hence, for folklorists interested in texts or performance or both, the film has much to offer.

My own film, *Tales of the Supernatural*, has certain content and structural similarities to *Pizza Pizza Daddy-O*. It focuses upon a group of children engaged in one event, and uses both sync-sound and narration. Yet rather than emphasizing the textual features, *Tales of the Supernatural* tests hypotheses about the functions of horror tales (generally classified as legends), and notes the relationship between function and tale transmission.

In the film, I am seated in front of a fireplace with seven teenagers, who tell eleven tales, including the well-known "Vanishing Hitchhiker" and "The Hook." The filmed storytelling event is intercut with stills of other storytelling situations, famous art works on supernatural themes, and a series of photos from well-known horror films. Over these stills I comment about when and where ghost stories are usually told, the pseudoscientific "proofs" offered by narrators, and the influence of mass media. Shifts from my interactions with the group to my narration serve to identify the folklorist's presence, and imply that both the research and the analysis will be presented simultaneously.

Through an event approach, *Tales of the Supernatural* examines the storytelling situation, focusing on the roles, kinesics, proxemics, remarks, reactions, and tensions of the participants, and demonstrates its major hypothesis—that the telling of such tales is a socially approved means of expressing a belief in the supernatural.

Filmmakers have recently expanded their focus upon the single event to examine the participation in several events by individuals in communities. For example, *Spend It All* (1970), Les Blank's first film on the Cajuns of the Louisiana Bayou, features the Balfa Brothers, Nathan Abshire, and Marc Savoy, well-known white Cajun musicians. The Cajuns are shown at a horse race, clam fishing, making shingles, preparing tobacco, and slaughtering a hog. In one sequence, as Savoy makes an accordion in his shop, he comments that living in New York would be like prison. Blank's romanticization of the virtues of rural life continues as another laments how today the dollar is too important. Blank deals mostly with familiar traditional activities, giving us shots of gravestone art, music performances, dancing, picnics, and food preparation. We see a man "treating by hand"—holding his finger in a woman's mouth—and in another scene, a man extracting his own tooth with pliers, while the band plays in the background. Dewey Balfa, shown driving a school bus, explains in voice-over that he also sells insurance and plays music on the weekends. The extremely well-recorded sync-sound music track holds the film together, but the individual scenes, though professional in quality, are only superficially connected.

Unlike *Spend It All,* in which the use of montage leads to overviews which detract from any in-depth understanding of the function of music for the performers and their audiences, Jill Godmilow's *The Popovich Brothers of South Chicago* (1978) focuses squarely on the importance of music and ethnic traditions for a Serbian-American urban community. Godmilow begins with a fiftieth anniversary party held for the Popovich brothers, members of a singing and performing family. She intersperses formal concerts with local Serbian gatherings to demonstrate the significance of the brothers' music. Newspaper clippings and interviews with Serbian-Americans point out how individuals maintain cultural identity within the multicultural milieu of Chicago. One girl addresses the camera to discuss how her Serbian heritage influenced her choice of a husband. Godmilow's film clearly indicates that Serbian-Americans work in and are part of "the mainstream," but are not part of "the melting pot." Many different Serbian-American events are shown, but music dominates the film. Interviews with the brothers and still photos of family members impress the audience with the link to Serbian culture felt by the third and fourth generations. While one brother's reaction to the death of another brother intimates that the Popovich brothers may not continue to perform, the close-knit relationships and the strength of music as a form of ethnicity demonstrate that the music will endure.

Many of the problems of conveying the community influence on individual creativity are solved when filmmakers narrow their content focus and follow one individual through a series of interactional events that structure their films. Such efforts are generally more successful in organization and overall comprehensiveness than community-oriented films because viewers have a stronger sense of the significance of a tradition when they can identify with those who generate it. Blank's *A Well Spent Life* (1971) is such an in-depth portrait of Mance Lipscomb. Mance begins his own story, in sync-sound. Born in 1875 near Navasota, Texas, he spent his early days as a sharecropper. "We were bound down. We couldn't do anything but take it." Mance plays guitar and sings "Big Boss Man," and then talks about dogs, the land, and black-white relationships. Landscape shots are intercut with close-ups of Mance singing. We see Elnora Lipscomb cooking a chicken and hear "She's Your Chicken, Save Me the Wing," and then see Mance eating at the table. Both Mance and Mrs. Lipscomb stress the success of their marriage. Mance is shown in various activities and he talks about how he no longer has to work. A record player with one of Mance's albums as well as a shot of a University of Chicago Folklore Society poster featuring Mance and Buell Kazee signify Mance's success as a performer.

Street scenes, a poker game, and Mance playing "Rock Me, Mama" in a local club indicate his relationship to the communitiy. An effective segment depicts children playing in the yard while Mance explains that he raised twenty-three children in all—those of his brothers and sisters, his own, and his grandchildren. He is then shown singing "Motherless Children" and playing bottleneck guitar with a pen knife. A baptism ceremony and a church service in which Mance assists the preacher are followed by Mance expressing his thoughts about religion. The film concludes with Mance playing "St. James Infirmary." By integrating visuals treating Mance Lipscomb's musical, personal, community, and professional life with his own statements, Blank succeeds in conveying the creative expressions and personality of an artistic individual.

In a similar vein, my most recent film, *Kathleen Ware, Quiltmaker* (1979), examines the process of folk creativity and the individual artist. Mrs. Ware lives on a busy stretch of highway that leads to the Oregon coast. A handmade sign advertises her profession and curious quilt enthusiasts stream through her living room as she goes about her daily activities. Sync-sound scenes of her interactions with customers and family members capture Mrs. Ware's personality and her role as quiltmaker, wife, mother, and grandmother.

The film opens as a prospective purchaser arrives. She looks at various quilt tops, chooses a lone star pattern, and places an order. The rationale for the selection of materials and colors indicates Mrs. Ware's own unique artistic sensibilities within the traditional structure of a folk craft. Sound-over comments by Mrs. Ware and her husband relate the Wares' outlook on life, and the importance of quiltmaking for the family. *Cinéma vérité* scenes of customers coming in and out, John Ware and the Ware children making a comforter, a family dinner, and John working in his vegetable garden are surrounded by the making of the lone star quilt, from cutting the fabric to the completed product. Thus, personality and process, rather than folk objects, are the central concerns of the film.

In his latest films, Ferris has also featured portraits of folk artists, and has related them to his interest in black folklore from the Mississippi Delta. In 1972, Ferris joined with Judy Peiser, a free-lance filmmaker, to form the Center for Southern Folklore. Their first cooperative sync-sound venture was *Ray Lum: Mule Trader* (1973); it was also Ferris's first film on a white Mississippian. Lum is shown at his home, his saddle shop, and his family auction in Vicksburg. The film combines the sound-over voice of Lum describing his experiences as a trader with sync-sound scenes of Lum's daily interactions and storytelling abilities. Most of the stories Lum tells are personal narratives, but two contain common motifs. The first involves treacherous gypsies (K 2261.1) who tried to trick Ray Lum in a horse trade but were outsmarted. The second is about a horse that drops dead shortly after a man trades for it (J 1455a). Other stories include the purchase of eight thousand horses at once and a tale about a horse so tall that no river was deep enough to drown him. Old photos depict the shift from horses to automobiles while Ray describes changes he's seen in his eighty-one years. As the yard fills with cars, Ray talks about why he began auctioneering, and the film cuts to the arena where Ray conducts the auction, as people talk and bid on livestock. The film ends with Ray in his store swapping stories. By following Ray Lum through one day, the filmmakers successfully capture the essence of Lum as a narrator and the occupational events which shape his stories.

The *cinéma vérité* technique of focusing on events and using the voices of those filmed was also employed by Ferris and Peiser for their portrait of a black performer, *Fannie Bell Chapman: Gospel Singer* (1975). Chapman is shown at her home in Centreville, Mississippi, with her husband and daughters, at a gospel gathering, and going from house to house on healing trips. She discusses her healing powers and her songs, which come to her from God through a "pillar of cloud." Both *Ray Lum* and *Fannie Bell Chapman* represent what folkloric filmmakers can accomplish by demonstrating how the networks of personal interactions and past experiences of performers combine to produce creativity within a tradition.

CONTENT, FOCUS, AND TECHNIQUE: SUMMARY

The most useful American folkloric films illustrate the dynamism of traditions and provide a sense of involvement for the audience by showing processes and events in their entirety. Such films depict a narrative event from beginning to end and so include the interactions of participants in the proper sequence. They document a musical event by filming audience reaction as well as the performance itself. Craft production films begin with the gathering of the materials, show the processes of creation, demonstrate the products' use, and concentrate on individual folk artists, to place folklore traditions in the full scope of their lives. Folkloric films must at least suggest the actual structure of social interactions and the processes of narrating, singing, dancing, playing, and of similar ceremonies and events, in order to present these subjects as fully as possible.

NOTES

1. An early suggestion for using films to study folklore as communicative processes was made by John Ball, "Style in the Folktale," *Folk-Lore* 65 (1954): 170–72. Robert A. Georges has stressed the necessity of viewing folklore holistically and has noted that sound film is the logical tool for an event approach to folklore; see Robert A. Georges, "Toward an Understanding of Storytelling Events," *Journal of American Folklore* 82 (1969): 313–28.

2. Karl G. Heider, *Films for Anthropological Teaching*, 6th ed., Special Publication of the American Anthropological Association, no. 9 (Washington, D.C.: American Anthropological Association, 1977); Bill Ferris and Judy Peiser, eds., *American Folklore Films and Videotapes: An Index* (Memphis: Center for Southern Folklore, 1976).

3. Sharon R. Sherman, "The Folkloric Film: The Relevance of Film for Understanding Folkloric Events" (Ph.D. diss., Indiana University, 1977).

Angela J. Maniak

Bibliographies and Indexes in American Folklore Research

Research in American folklore begins with a knowledge of the fundamental tools of the discipline: indexes and bibliographies. To gather texts, make comparisons, and draw conclusions, the folklorist must have a systematic method of locating and consulting published sources. Since no single comprehensive index covers the entire field of American folklore, the scholar or student must consult a combination of works to develop a working bibliography for a particular subject (see "American Folklore Bibliographies" section of the general Bibliography concluding this *Handbook*).

The first works to consult are those that identify the general subjects, themes, and genres of American folklore. Several books and articles survey these topics and give references to appropriate sources. Richard M. Dorson's "American Folklore Bibliography" lists a number of interpretive studies, arranged according to headings such as "historical," "regional," "occupational," "folklife and material culture," and "the Indian." The scope and variety of American folk culture are illustrated by the nature and content of the works listed under these headings.

Two book-length bibliographies of American folklore are also indispensable: Charles Haywood's *A Bibliography of North American Folklore and Folksong* and Cathleen and John Flanagan's *American Folklore: A Bibliography, 1950-1974*. Haywood's two-volume work contains references for all aspects of traditional life and includes listings from personal diaries and letters, travel books, and regional cookbooks as well as specialized books and articles. The bibliography is an impressive undertaking and serves as one of the major reference tools in American folklore, with entries arranged according to regional, ethnic, and occupational groups. Haywood also has sections on specific American heroes and wars. The work, however, is marred by several major flaws and should therefore be used with caution and attentiveness. First, Haywood is not selective in the material he includes. As a result, we find literary, historical, and popular sources mixed in with folklore. Since Haywood's scanty annotations do little to distinguish these works from one another, the researcher must exercise careful judgment in selecting from among these entries. Also, the bibliography contains an excessive number of misspellings and inaccurate or incomplete citations.

The Flanagans' bibliography is complementary to Haywood's, covering material published between 1950 and 1974. (Haywood's journal coverage stops in 1948.) The entries are classified by genre rather than folk group. The Flanagans discover some previously uncited material, but their entries lack annotations and cross-references. Unfortunately, the authors' focus on verbal folklore leads to the exclusion of the entire field of material culture.

Such general bibliographies are a good starting point and may lead the researcher to more specific areas of study within the field of American folklore. Depending upon whether a proposed study is descriptive or comparative and whether or not it is to be based on fieldwork, published sources are most often used with one of three distinct purposes in mind.

First, published sources provide background information for the folklorist who is doing fieldwork with an unfamiliar group. Entering the field totally ignorant of some specific details of a group's traditions can be disastrous. A fieldworker may wander aimlessly for days looking for unspecified supernatural beliefs, while asking for explanations of such terms as *mal de ojo* or *susto* within a Mexican-American community may elicit proverbs and stories, or perhaps the name of a *curandero*, a folk healer. Reviewing the published sources in the area of study often provides fieldworkers with the key terms and concepts that prove helpful in their interviewing. Also, interpretive and analytical studies provide a framework for the subject and help to focus the research as the folklorist collects more information.

Once the fieldwork is done, the scholar must refer to published sources for corroborative or comparative data. To draw valid conclusions regarding theme, style, or distribution, it is essential to compare texts to others of a different type or to texts collected from a different group. Making another field trip to do this is not always feasible, nor is it advisable. Printed sources, along with archival materials, can often provide the necessary body of comparative texts.

Sometimes a folklorist will discover a subject that has not before been studied as part of American folklore. In this case, print research may substitute for field collecting; that is, the folklorist may base the study entirely on published sources. Richard Dorson was inspired by the folkloric themes of the Davy Crockett stories and compiled *Davy Crockett, American Comic Legend*, a study based on texts drawn from published sources. Some other areas of folklore—for example, folklore in literature—are by nature confined to library research.

Most bibliographies and indexes of American folklore are arranged by genre, theme, folk group, or region. To compile a working bibliography on a subject, the researcher should approach the topic from as many of these perspectives as possible. Let us take as an example the study of themes in American traditional songs. What bibliographies might yield both general information and specific comparative texts and studies?

First, the general bibliographies of American folklore cited above include appropriate headings that will direct the scholar to the major works on the subject. After scanning these sources, the folklorist might then choose to compare the themes in a particular corpus of songs to themes in narrative texts, perhaps from other cultures. The primary indexes of narrative folklore are *The Types of the Folktale* and the *Motif-Index of Folk-Literature*. Representing the lifelong dedication of Antti Aarne and Stith Thompson to the classification of folklore, these works should be the first step in any search for comparative texts. Their tale types and motif numbers are the basis of subsequent classifications of American folklore. A valuable supplementary compilation is Ernest W. Baughman's *Type and Motif-Index of the Folktales of England and North America*. In studying American traditional songs, the folklorist may use this index to find similar motifs and themes in the narrative repetoire of several regions in the United States.

After gathering a corpus of themes and motifs, the researcher might concentrate on the genre, in this case investigating studies under the heading "Folksong and Ballad." Two major bibliographical guides are available in this area. *The British Traditional Ballad in North America* by Tristram P. Coffin is an index to the published editions of Child ballads collected from oral tradition in the United States. Besides listing sources of texts, Coffin also provides a summary of the story types for each ballad along with a discussion of the status of the ballad, concentrating especially on how it departs from the English and Scottish tradition. In *Native American Balladry*, Malcolm G. Laws, Jr., studies the themes and characteristics of American ballads and establishes a classification system and bibliographical syllabus. Laws's categories are based on either the ballad topic or the group to which it belongs (e.g., ballads about tragedies and disasters and lumberjack ballads). Under each heading, Laws provides a list of all titles in that class and references to both printed texts and Library of Congress recordings. Folksingers and styles of performance are the primary subjects of *Folksingers and Folksongs in America* by Ray M. Lawless. The book consists mainly of biographies of specific folksingers, but also includes an index of folksong titles and a well-annotated bibliography of American folksong collections. Finally, recent publications on traditional songs are listed in the "Americas" section of the "Current Bibliography and Discography" in each issue of the journal *Ethnomusicology*.

If a folklorist has a collection of ballads or songs from several ethnic and racial groups in the United States, the next research step might be to consult the bibliographies compiled on the basis of these groups.

The American Indian is the subject of the entire second volume of Haywood's bibliography, and the researcher will find many references to traditional Indian songs here. A supplementary work on the subject is Judith C. Ullom's *Folklore of the North American Indians*. In this work, the author categorizes collections and studies of folktales according to the major culture areas of the North American Indian. The book is well annotated but is confined largely to anthropological works and children's anthologies.

Negro spirituals, as well as other forms of black music, song, and narrative, are covered in *Mississippi Black Folklore* by William R. Ferris. Comparative texts from Afro-American groups throughout the New World will likely be found in Roger Abrahams and John Szwed's *Annotated Bibliography of Afro-American Folklore and Culture*.

The Mexican-American culture also has a rich ballad tradition, and so the folklorist might refer to a bibliography concentrating on this ethnic group. Particularly good is *An Annotated Bibliography of Chicano Folklore from the Southwestern United States*. This compilation is exemplary as a source of studies in American ethnic folklore, for its focus is on scholarship dealing with the syncretism of European and New World traditions. Many indexes of ethnic folklore can be misleading in their concentration on survivals of European traditions in the United States.

It may be that the collection of songs is not from an ethnic group but from some other group in American culture. Any distinct group is a potential source of its own folklore, as witnessed by some of the bibliographies that have been compiled. Religious groups, such as Mormons, have their own folkloric traditions that are covered in William A. Wilson's "A Bibliography of Studies in Mormon Folklore." Women have been identified as a folk group in at least one bibliography, "Women: A Selected Bibliography from the *Journal of American Folklore*, 1888-1973." Cowboys and badmen are two American folk character types notorious in all parts of the country, and accordingly have been made the subjects of bibliographies by a nonfolklorist, Ramon F. Adams.

American folklore is divided not only on the basis of groups but also on the basis of geographical regions. Because a great deal of work has been done in regional American folklore, a number of good bibliographies exist. An outstanding example of a comprehensive, accurate, and easy-to-use regional bibliography is Vance Randolph's *Ozark Folklore*. Randolph does an especially complete job by tapping many ephemeral sources (newspapers, church periodicals, pamphlets, and jokebooks) often left untouched by other scholars. This is a work compiled by not just a bibliographer but a seasoned collector. Randolph's annotations, as a result, are lively and insightful.

The work of another regional scholar is *The Guide to Life and Literature of the Southwest*. J. Frank Dobie organizes his materials around folkloric topics such as "Backwoods Life and Humor" and "Cowboy Songs and Other Ballads." A word of caution: not all entries are annotated, and Dobie has a tendency to include romanticized and popularized sources along with the more reputable folkloric studies.

Annual bibliographies and indexes are also important research aids. The most comprehensive and uninterrupted source of publications in American folklore is the bibliography published in the *Southern Folklore Quarterly* for each year between 1938 and 1972. The bibliography, currently compiled by Merle E. Simmons, is continued as part of the Indiana University Folklore Institute Monograph Series and is published yearly as a separate volume.

The American Folklore Society issued an "Annual Bibliography of Folklore" as a *Journal of American Folklore* supplement from 1955 to 1963 and as separately bound *Abstracts of Folklore Studies* from 1963 to 1975. The annual bibliography of the *Publications of the Modern Language Association* also includes a section on folklore, and *American Quarterly* annually publishes "Articles in American Studies," including citations of American folklore.

Some of the major cumulative indexes of American folklore publications are Tristram P. Coffin's *Analytical Index to the Journal of American Folklore*, Joan Ruman Perkal's *Western Folklore and California Folklore Quarterly: Twenty-five Year Index*, James T. Brachter's *Analytical Index to the Publications of the Texas Folklore Society*, and Alice Morrison Mordoh's "Analytical Index to the *Journal of the Folklore Institute*, Vols. 1-15." Most such indexes include a subject as well as an author and title index, and those just cited cross-list their published texts according to type and motif numbers.

Finally, unpublished dissertations and theses are chronologically inventoried in Alan Dundes's *Folklore Theses and Dissertations in the United States*.

By referring to some of the bibliographies cited above, the folklorist will find a number of pertinent sources, no matter what aspect of American folklore is under study. From the general bibliographies and indexes, the scholar may go to those based on genre, folk or ethnic group, or region. The published sources tapped in this way will not only complete an initial research project, but may also lead to the discovery of new subjects in the vast field of American folklore.

Carl Fleischhauer

Folklorists at Work: A Portfolio from the American Folklife Center

The photographs in this portfolio, all made during team projects conducted by the American Folklife Center at the Library of Congress, describe fieldwork. They show some of the phenomena that have attracted our researchers and offer evidence of their working methods. The photos not only portray field visits but also suggest the necessity of library or archive research or the labor of writing fieldnotes. Included as well are photographs of folklorists sharing their findings with the people from whom they have learned.

The positive character of this portfolio reflects both our society's attitude toward photographs as cheerful mementoes, and the fieldworker's impulse to make his visits pleasant occasions, even if he should harbor negative feelings toward those he visits. Finally, it is fair to say that the American Folklife Center's goal of increasing public understanding of folk culture is best served by photographs accentuating the positive.

Folklorist Gerri Johnson photographing Florence Cheek's dried apples, Wilkes County, North Carolina (Geraldine N. Johnson; BR8-5-20257/35A)

I traveled on the hills all day,
Until my feet are sore;
I rustled at the High Ore,
But I will not any more.

I rustled at the Cora,
And I rustled at the 'Sweat;
I traveled for the last six months,
And still I'm rustling yet.

For the sake of comparison we list below variant readings of the first stanza.[a]
They are from the singing of Kevin Shannon, a young Irish tenor who has
established in the Dublin Gulch area quite a reputation for his barroom renditions of old-time songs; from Professor Oscar A. Dingman, of the Montana
School of Mines, Butte, who picked up the song between his lectures, many
a forgotten year ago, and sang it to us in spite of his scruples about its inflam-
matory character; and from another Butte townsman (Mr. X), who has vivid
recollection of the events mentioned in the song.

[a] See "The Bohunk Scare," *Copper Camp,* pp. 133–137.
[b] The reader should also consult the variant in Emrich, *op. cit.,* p. 227.

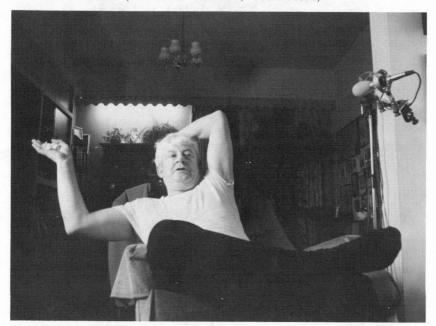

"Songs of the Butte Miner," by Wayland Hand et al.,
appeared in the January 1950 issue of *Western Folklore.* The article led a field team to Kevin Shannon, an
Irish-American raconteur and singer in Butte, Montana,
in 1979. (Michael S. Crummett; MT9-84599/8)

Retired rancher Alphonso Pasquale and fieldworker
Linda Gastañaga, Paradise Valley, Nevada (Carl
Fleischhauer; NV-4-19754/11)

Jessie Lee Smith and folklorist Beverly Robinson, Tifton, Georgia (Carl Fleischhauer; GA7-1-17607/33A)

Mr. and Mrs. Josh Easter of Surry County, North Carolina, peel apples for drying. Wally Macnow assists them as Terry Eiler and Bob Fulcher video-tape the process. The Center's field teams often include media professionals working side by side with folklorists. (Lyntha Scott Eiler; BR8-16-20543/26)

Folklorist Tony Hellenberg shares May wine, coffee, and pastry with Mr. and Mrs. Martin Schwarz in their north Chicago home. (Carl Fleischhauer; CH7-41253/31)

Folklorist Bill Lightfoot with Mr. and Mrs. Carlos Ross and their grandchildren, Turner County, Georgia (Carl Fleischhauer; GA7-4-17554/8)

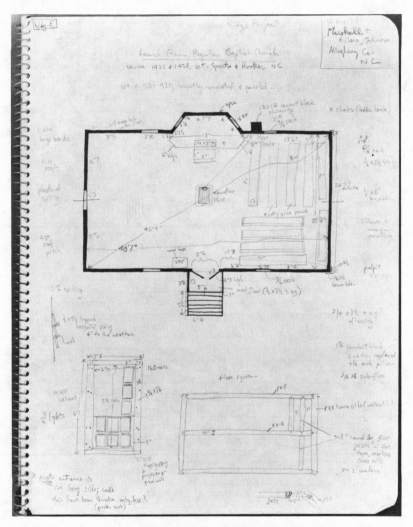

A page from folklorist Howard W. Marshall's fieldnotes: the floor plan of the Laurel Glen Regular Baptist
Church, Alleghany County, North Carolina

After completing fieldwork for a Folklife Center project in Chicago, folklorist Elizabeth Mathias returned to the city to lead a workship in documentation for members of the Italian community. (Carl Fleischhauer; CH7-4-18285/36A)

At a Baptist association meeting near Galax, Virginia, church deacon Leonard Bryan and folklorist Pat Mullen read an illustrated article in the *Washington Star* about Mullen's visit to Bryan's home a few days earlier. (Geraldine N. Johnson; BR8-2-20424/16)

PART IV PRESENTATION OF RESEARCH

Folklorists present the materials of folklore—which, if they are genuine, result from research in the field, the library, and the archives—through writing, teaching, lecturing, and consulting. In addition they may turn to museum exhibits, films, videotapes, audiotapes, and recordings to supplement written and verbal presentations. Their audiences range from students to academic colleagues to the general public. Addressing diverse audiences requires quite different modes of delivery and strategies of discourse, but throughout the many avenues of presentation, several issues recur, such as the balancing of educational and entertainment values and the question of protecting the confidentiality of informants.

The teaching of folklore displays a highly uneven pattern throughout the United States. A few centers for graduate study exist, a couple of hundred colleges offer introductory courses, the occasional high school may introduce a folklore unit, but the vast majority of college graduates do not know such a field of learning exists. Teaching folklore at the graduate, undergraduate, and secondary school levels calls for distinct and separate methods. Graduate programs introduce master's and doctoral candidates to the rigorous discipline of folklore studies. College courses acquaint students with the subject matter of a branch of knowledge previously unexamined by them. Should high schools begin to offer instruction in folklore and folklife, they ought to lay before their classes the outlines and principles of a subject that nicely complements history, English, and social studies. Although he did not realize he was teaching folklore to his high school journalism students in Georgia, Eliot Wigginton enjoyed great success in enlisting their attention for his *Foxfire* project when he set them interviewing their families and neighbors about old-time ways and customs. Students at all levels respond eagerly to folklore because they can immediately relate to a topic that deals with people in their daily lives and assigns a value to the cultural expression of ordinary folk. One problem with instruction in the schools proceeds from the lack of trained teachers who can distinguish folklore from fakelore. Much better that no course is offered than one which misleads and misinforms. Secondary school teachers may avail themselves of summer courses at the universities that offer graduate programs, and the appearance of this *Handbook* will hopefully provide a resource for mentors of American folklore courses.

Articles in this section by Ronald Baker and myself consider the teaching of folklore in colleges and graduate schools. Charles Camp in his essay on "Organizing a State Folklife Program" also comments on his role in assisting educators prepare school curricula in folklore. A new type of appointment is the short-term resident folklorist-in-the-schools, who acts as a resource person for the teachers and administrators.

Professors of folklore and state and federal folklorists are often called upon to address special audiences, and in this situation the difficulty of steering a path between the entertaining and the educational becomes acute. At one period I engaged in a good deal of this kind of speaking on the "creamed chicken and rubber peas circuit," and also held forth on a Sunday afternoon radio program. But increasingly I found my auditors wished to hear a performing storyteller and did not care about the fine points of folklore theories, and I withdrew from those activities.

In all these teaching and lecturing endeavors, at whatever level and to whatever audience, folklorists must present bona fide research, and refer to authentic and authoritative collections and studies.

Folklorists present the results of their research in articles, monographs, and books of field reports and theory. Several issues arise in connection with the publication of folklore: correlating the collection of texts with the interpreting of the collected materials; popularization, to which folklore readily lends itself, versus scholarly integrity; the always vexing question of how to handle obscenity, ethnic slurs, and similar sensitive matters. While these problems also concern the teacher, public lecturer, state folklorist, and indeed all those involved in the presentation of folk traditions, speakers and teachers may explain and defend their utterances, while writers on folklore commit themselves to irreversible print, and establish their reputations either as serious scholars or as panderers to popular taste and publishers' demands. The middle ground in folklore, as in other fields, is to strive for lively scholarship and intelligent popularization.

In my essay on "Preparing Research for Publication" I recount some of my pratfalls while learning the ropes about getting published. A key technical aid in any book of collected folklore is a well constructed index—indeed Stith Thompson's six volume *Motif-Index of Folk-Literature* is an open sesame to the world's folklore—and Michael E. Bell lucidly explains the process of preparing an index. Without such a finding tool folklorists cannot identify themes and variants scattered through the work. Indeed, after looking at the table of contents they may turn directly to the index of a collection they are examining. An indispensable resource for the researcher of oral folklore is the folklore archives in which collectors deposit manuscripts and tape recordings, and Joseph Hickerson, director of the Archive of Folk Culture in the Library of Congress, elucidates the mysteries of archive building. Equally indispensable for the researcher in material culture is the folk museum, a repository for artifacts of traditional life, and Ormond Loomis draws upon his curatorial experience in such museums to analyze their operation. Folk museum curators must consider not only the research potential of their holdings but also displays of their objects that will inform visitors about folk-cultural systems and lifestyles.

The development of visual technology is directly affecting the ways in which folklorists present their research. Film and videotape can serve both as means of recording ethnographic research data, and, in edited form, as modes of instruction supporting the lecturer's discussion. But showing a film or videotape in the classroom or lecture hall is one thing, and collaborating in a film production for eventual showing on public television is quite another, as George Carey makes very plain in his personal essay on that experience. Now the problem of balancing the claims of authenticity and popular appeal is compounded, and in addition is added a new concern, the possible effect of this media attention on the lives and expectations of the televised folk. Carey offers no simple solution to these puzzles. In my own involvement with a short film on an ethnic restaurant in Gary, I realized how the film crew and the contrived scene do tamper with the reality. We can of course argue that even the straightforward prose ethnographic report is skewed by the fieldworker's bias. At any rate the portable videocamera presently appears to be, as Richard Blaustein demonstrates in his essay, somewhat more adaptable than the motion picture camera to the folklorist's needs in the classroom as well as in the field. With the increasing prominence of film and videotape, a new type of scholarship evolves, in which the end product becomes not the article or the book but the reel and the cassette depicting a craft process, a church revival, and ethnic festival, a folk event of any kind in full dimension. Folklorists must judge these products with similar critical standards that they apply to published works, in terms of fidelity to the folk process and meaningful interpretation of the scene.

Finally, a question that enters into all the foregoing discussions receives direct attention, the place of the informants in the research enterprise. To what extent should or can their confidentiality be protected? Do folklorists even have a right to collect traditions and study people? The late William Jansen mulls over these ticklish matters.

A wholly new sector for the presentation of folklore research has opened up in the state and federal governments. Many states now have appointed state folklorists, while the American Folklife Center established in the Library of Congress by act of Congress in 1976 and the Folklife Unit in the Smithsonian Institution, which has sponsored the highly successful Festival of American Folklife annually since 1966, also engage the services of professional folklorists. The Maryland state folklorist, Charles Camp, outlines in this section an account of his exploratory efforts at defining his position, since no precedents exist to set models for such a role. One point of which he is convinced is the difference in approach between the academic folklorist and the state folklorist, who must do more than organize a state folk festival. He or she must establish connections with constituencies in the state (historical societies, labor unions, school boards), learn to cooperate with state agencies, and develop new, more intimate modes of talking about and demonstrating folklore. At the national level the problems of presenting folklore research become even more acute. The very success of the American Folklife Festival raised the question of whether this event had become an artificially induced spectacle. To counter this criticism, Ralph Rinzler, director of the Festival and the Smithsonian Folklife Program, and his staff incorporated into the festival events "presenters" who explained to the public the background of the performances, ethnographic films, articulate members of occupational groups who spoke about their work experiences, and symposia of folklore scholars open to the public. The American Folklife Center has responded to requests for regional field collecting and folklife surveys, sponsored conferences, and mounted folklife exhibits. Both the Center, under the direction of Alan Jabbour, and the Smithsonian's Folklife Unit, headed by Ralph Rinzler, are experimenting with ways in which to present folklife materials to the American people.

Whether at the state or federal level, the folklorists who face the public and depend upon tax dollars for the renewal of their positions must to some extent bowdlerize their materials. Scholars themselves have bowed to the Victorian taboos that limit or prohibit discussion of the bawdry that lies at the heart of much folklore. In her article on this subject Rayna Green considers the cultural complexities of obscene and scatological traditions, offensive to some in some situations, but never predictably, and sets forth the options open to folklorists who must make decisions, in classrooms, archives, publications, lecture halls, as to how to handle bawdry.

Implicit in this issue is an even larger one, the whole question of the relation of the informant to the collector. What is the degree of confidentiality, what is the share in the rewards, to which the informant is entitled, both on ethical and legal grounds? Conversely, to what extent do collectors record and tacitly approve ideas and expressions they find objectionable? Dealing with fellow human beings, the folklorist here walks through a potential minefield, as anthropologists have already discovered. William Jansen examines this delicate area and makes certain recommendations that most folklorists will agree with, based on cultural relativism and an appreciation of the contexts in which items are collected and presented. Tact and consideration are called for, but so are firmness and candor, for if we live in continual fear of giving offense, we should never seek to become folklorists.

Richard M. Dorson

Teaching Folklore to Graduate Students: The Introductory Proseminar

Introducing new graduate students to the discipline of folklore poses special problems, since they come to the subject from a variety of backgrounds, and since no teaching aids exist that concentrate on folklore methodology. History departments schedule an introductory graduate course in historiography, English departments offer a comparable course in bibliography, but the few folklore departments have not yet settled on their equivalent. Such a course should examine the skills that distinguish the folklorist from the practitioners of other disciplines. In my own teaching I have come up with a baker's dozen, each of which is the theme for a class lecture and in most cases a written report. I present the topics below in the order in which I assign them.[1]

Distinguishing Folklore from Fakelore

In my opening lecture I emphasize the looseness and lack of standards in the publications labeled folklore and the necessity for the student-scholar to draw sharp distinctions between authoritative and spurious works, between folklore proper and fakelore. A couple of minutes of handling a book of collected folklore can suffice to inform probing folklorists as to the general character of the goods they hold. Does the collection contain items of folklore as they were actually told, word for word, or are the tales or materials paraphrased? Are the tellers, singers, and carriers of the folklore—the informants—identified, and not just by names but with some personal details? And a crucial point, do comparative notes accompany the folklore texts, either as an introductory headnote (preferably) or in an appendix? Are other essential elements of the scholarly apparatus present: tables of motifs and tale types; a classified bibliography, hopefully with descriptive critical comments; a full subject index with a breakdown of key entries; an informative introduction describing the fieldwork methods? A few moments of thumbing through the pages will provide answers to these queries, and the folklorist can judge whether the book is a bona fide work worth serious attention, or one to be used cautiously, or to be disregarded. Large type size and dreamlike illustrations betray at a glance a children's edition of pseudo–fairy tales of dubious value for the serious student.

For this initial exercise I assign a volume in the Folktales of the World series, whose purpose is to present authoritative, properly annotated, national folktales to the scholarly and reading public.[2] Students can thus cut their critics' teeth on volumes equipped with scholarly aids, but they would still find opportunity aplenty to raise questions: about the principles of tale selection, to represent coverage of regions, genres, oral styles; about the faithfulness of the translation to the oral language of the original tongue; about the thoroughness of the documentation.

Fieldwork

In the second week I lecture on fieldwork methods and assign a collecting project of three jokes. I differentiate collecting from fieldwork since field research consumes one's full time and is devoted to a large objective, say, the ethnic folklore of a community, while collecting is piecemeal, limited, and interspersed in the round of regular activities. Nevertheless some experience collecting at home can serve as a prelude to forays into the field, and anybody can collect some jokes, the neglected but staple folk form of our time. For this report students must make contact with joke tellers, usually their peers or family, obtain a word-for-word text of the joke, through dictation or the use of a tape recorder, and provide an accompanying statement giving biographical information on the teller, details of the collecting situation, and interpretation of the humor from the points of view of the narrator, of the audience, and of the collector. Glosses should attempt to explain the point of the humor, in terms, say, of defiance of taboos or mores, release of aggression, or incongruity, surprise, or shock. Reports are to be divided into three categories: Text, Context, and Interpretation. At this stage, annotation is omitted. No student ever fails to complete this assignment, although questions arise as to what constitutes a joke. "Accept whatever your teller considers a joke," is the guideline, "and we can define joke more precisely in the exercise on terminology." Joke in our culture covers a wide spectrum of humorous narratives. Student collections reveal that the telescoped punchline comic story is being still further shortened to question-and-answer riddle jokes. Dirty jokes, violating our sexual and anal taboos, introduce the students to the obscene aspect of folklore, which they must accept if they intend to become full-fledged scholars in the discipline. Foreign students from African and Asian countries do encounter problems with this exercise, and express puzzlement at the nature of American humor.

Terminology

Every field of learning possesses its esoteric vocabulary, but folklore stands alone in sharing terms—folklore itself, fairy tale, legend, myth, custom, ritual—with the world at large, although the academic and popular senses diverge considerably. In addition, folkloristics possesses a lexicon of specialized terms denoting genres, concepts, and characters. For this exercise I distribute a sheet of "Folklore Terminology," listing about one hundred terms, divided into ten groups according to their cluster of associations—such as folk narrative forms, supernatural figures, folk medicine phrases. Students pick one of these terms and explore its uses by folklore scholars. I ask them to strive for a diversified selection, from the nineteenth and twentieth centuries, from popular and scholarly writings, from Europe and America, from different theoretical schools. To aid them they can consult, on reserve, the volumes of Laurits Bødker, *Folk Literature (Germanic)*, and Åke Hultkrantz, *General Ethnological Concepts*, which set forth variations in scholarly usage of folkloric terms. This assignment enables the student to perceive the fluidity and changing nuances of folklore's vocabulary, much as texts themselves vary from one tradition bearer to another. Also the consulting of the publications affords them an opportunity to read in the literature of folklore scholarship.

Bibliographical Expertise

In folkloristics the command of bibliographical aids, guides, and reference works requires special attention, since the field is so labyrinthine and amorphous, involving many—one might say all—languages and the whole spectrum of writing from the scholarly to the popular. Folklorists must learn to find their way through the maze by knowing what guideposts they may lean upon. The instructor might begin by invoking the great *vade mecum* of the folktale scholar, a five-volume work in German, the *Anmerkungen zu den Kinder- und Hausmärchen der Brüder Grimm*, compiled by Johannes Bolte and Georg Polívka (1913–31) as an exhaustive annotation of the variants to the Grimms' tales dispersed throughout Europe and carried to other continents. From this classic tool the lecturer can proceed to other classificatory systems for various genres indicating their virtues, flaws, and idiosyncrasies. The bibliographical exercise calls for selecting a topic, neither too broad nor too specialized—the evil eye, folk festivals, or industrial folklore would be suitable topics—and through the use of bibliographical aids choosing ten writings on the theme to evaluate. As with the terminology paper, the entries should represent a broad range of points of view, time periods, and cultural outlooks, and the student-critic should take into account these elements in formulating a fair scholarly assessment. This exercise should acquaint students with key reference works, enlighten them as to the diversity and disparity of sources at their disposal, and further sharpen their critical faculties.[3]

Library Uses

Because folklore is so much a child of circumstance when it comes to proper recognition and attention, library holdings on the subject may run heavily to fakelore or be widely dispersed throughout the library. The twenty-thousand-volume collection housed in the folklore section of the Indiana University Library brings together not only GR titles, identified as folklore in the Library of Congress classification system, but publications from other classifications as well that Stith Thompson succeeded in corraling. And still some substantial shelves of folkloric relevance will not be found in the Folklore section; witchcraft books, for example, are located under Religion. For the library exercise students have options of making reports on folklore shelvings (1) in the main library apart from the Folklore collection; (2) in special libraries in the university library system: e.g., the School of Music Library contains a number of ballad and folksong collections, the Fine Arts Library possesses some works on folk art, the Lilly Rare Books Library houses a special collection of ghostlore and occult books; and (3) in libraries outside the home university, such as public libraries, or libraries of other colleges and universities. Students appraise the holdings in terms of comprehensiveness and standards of selection, using as checklists the M.A. folklore examination reading list, the proseminar syllabus, and the chapter bibliographies in the course textbook, *Folklore and Folklife, An Introduction*. An immediate spot check, for instance, can determine whether a library holds Stith Thompson's six-volume

Motif-Index of Folk-Literature, or the volumes in the Folktales of the World series. The report then rates the library much as an instructor grades a paper. This exercise compels the folklore student to think about library resources and utility, and the advisability of developing one's own personal library of the most needful reference works, studies, and collections.

Use of Folklore Archives

Unlike historical archives of printed documents, folklore archives contain manuscripts, transcripts, tape and disc recordings of field-collected materials. These archives supplement the published collections and the individual folklorist's own fieldwork with the deposits of hundreds of collectors, and comprise an indispensable asset to the researcher. The great government-supported, professionally maintained European folklore archives, notably at Helsinki, Uppsala, and Dublin, set a high standard for the young archives being developed at some American universities. Every graduate student who becomes a folklore instructor should plan to establish an archive.

The special problems of accession, classification, retrieval, staffing, and research use of folklore archives should be brought to the attention of the graduate students. How does the archivist convert the raw collections into a systematically organized research facility? Invaluable aids in the process of classification are the extant indexes for various genres, such as Child for English and Scottish ballads, Taylor for riddles, Aarne-Thompson for tale types, Laws for native American ballads, Hand for folk beliefs, Brunvand for shaggy dog jokes, and Clements for Polack jokes. For the archives assignment the student can report on the holdings of a given topic or theme—say, college folksongs, Polish weddings, department store legends—in terms of extent, distribution, informant and contextual data, and accuracy of classification.

Annotation

In my view the hallmark of the folklorist lies in the ability to annotate a field-collected text. Conversely, the sign of the amateur, or even the impostor, is the text of an alleged folktale or other oral genre published naked of all comparative references. Proof of the traditional character of a tale, song, saying, or rhyme—proof that it is folklore—depends on the evidence presented in the accompanying note. Publishers often object to this scholarly apparatus, saying readers care only for the folklore itself, but the scholarly folklorist often finds the annotation more fascinating than the text. To get students on the track of preparing an annotation, a task difficult to explain in the abstract, I ask them to select from a Folktales of the World volume a tale with a well-documented note, and then to pursue the references in the note, in order to expand the note into essay form. They will consult the type and motif indexes, major reference works such as Bolte and Polívka, and collections containing variants of the tale in question. These procedures send the students to key volumes which they should examine early in their graduate careers, acquaint them with the intricacies of the folktale indexing systems, and lead them to publications from widely scattered sources in several languages. When they find a desired variant in an unfamiliar language, I suggest they enlist the aid of a foreign student on campus from that country. Also I recommend their xeroxing and assembling copies of variant texts to append to their reports. In their paper they should compare these variants in terms of stylistic qualities, cultural allusions, central motifs, and any other significant features. They are encouraged to single out for attention texts notable for literary or historical associations or delivery by a celebrated narrator. If information is available, the essay should comment on the geographical distribution of the tale, its functions in a given culture—didactic, symbolic, cathartic, wish-fulfilling. Also they should compare the given text with selected variants to determine its representative character, and finally an evaluation of the volume editor's note to rate its acccuracy, thoroughness, and success in distilling the reference material into a lucid and logical commentary. The seminar instructor must emphasize the need for an annotation to present a meaningful statement, a kind of mini-essay, and not resort to a string of arid citations. This exercise should afford neophyte folklorists a glimpse into the scaffolding of a comparative note, preparatory to constructing their own.

Material Culture Research

Chapters in *Folklore and Folklife, An Introduction* by Henry Glassie on "Folk Art," by Don Yoder on "Folk Costume," by Warren Roberts on "Folk Crafts" and "Folk Architecture," and by J. Geraint Jenkins on "The Use of Artifacts and Folk Art in the Folk Museum" can orient the student for the next exercise, which calls for a report on a folk artifact that the student personally observes and researches. This artifact may be identified in the museum (Indiana University possesses a Museum of Anthropology, Folklore and History containing objects from tribal and pioneer cultures) or among the possessions and heirlooms of the student's family. Any type of artifact is acceptable provided it derives from traditional manual techniques. Student reports have dealt with objects ranging from quilts to pottery to plows to statuary to colored Easter eggs. In the oral and written report the student must endeavor to (1) pinpoint the folk-cultural tradition and approximate period from which the object originates, and if possible discuss the style of the individual artisan, (2) describe the artifact's function, whether utilitarian, aesthetic, or magico-religious, or a combination of these, (3) explain the techniques and the learning process involved in the making of the product. Frequently basic information is hard to come by, and students find themselves scouring the library and the Human Relations Area Files for ethnographic clues. They come to perceive an analogy between documenting a handcrafted Appalachian chair and anno- tating an orally told Appalachian folktale. In connection with this project the seminar visits the museum for a guided tour.

Interdisciplinary Knowledge

The folklore scholar should acquire familiarity with the fields of anthropology, literature, and history. These skills begin to cross the line from techniques to theory, but the instructor can elucidate such technical matters as the identification of folklore in printed and literary sources, interviewing methods that combine oral history and folk tradition, and the diffusion of folklore between tribal and industrial societies. Such discussion, supplemented by the syllabus readings on these topics, opens the door to cross-disciplinary connections that a well-rounded folklorist must cultivate.

History of Folklore Studies

In each country folklore takes a different course. In European nations the discipline is well advanced, while the old peasant folk traditions recede. In Asia,

Africa, Latin America, the stuff of folklore far overshadows the scholarship. In the United States the discipline stands halfway between Europe and the other continents. Ideology and defensive nationalism give strong impetus to folkloristics in socialist countries and small proud states. At any rate students of folklore should recognize the diversity of concepts, theories, materials, institutions, and personalities they will confront in different parts of the world. A professor of folklore from Chile once astonished me by asking what my department did besides collect, study, and teach folklore, and when I in response inquired what else one could do, he declared, "Perform." By way of an exercise, the proseminar students can develop a paper on the national characteristics of folklore studies in a given country, using the foreword to the Folktales of the World volume as a springboard.

International Communications in Folklore

To keep abreast of the subject, and to facilitate one's research, a professional folklorist must cultivate the technique of international contacts and communications. Reading foreign folklore journals, attending international folklore congresses, corresponding with kindred spirits one meets there, conceiving collaborative projects, and visiting folklore archives and research institutes all contribute to this technique. Folklore studies especially depend for their successful prosecution on cooperative efforts, the classic example being *The Types of the Folktale*, initiated by the Finn Antti Aarne and twice expanded by the American Stith Thompson. This technique calls for a lecture rather than a report.

Folklore in the Mass Media

In the electronic age in which we live, the media of television, radio, films, mass circulation magazines, and newspapers engulf us and wash over every islet of traditional culture. But folklorists have learned that the mass and the folk cultures do not necessarily contend against each other but rather interpenetrate. The media assimilate and regurgitate folkloric items of all sorts, in advertisements, Sunday Supplement features, the columns of Ann Landers and Dear Abby, news stories that perpetuate urban legends, even articles about folklorists and folk festivals. At the outset of the course the instructor can announce this project, so that students may begin their clipping right away, with increasing confidence as they become more conversant with folklore matters. Noting folk items on TV, movies, and radio presents a problem but a summary description with details of the program may serve our purposes. After the collection is completed, by the semester's end, the student organizes it into categories based on theme or source, with interpretive notes appraising the relationship of a given item to field-collected folklore. This exercise alerts the student-folklorist to the omnipresence of folklore in the modern as in the tribal world, and to the issue that continually arises as a consequence: how to distinguish folk culture from popular culture.

If students can sustain this set of exercise-reports through the semester, they will perceive the range of technical skills demanded of them and practice each one. Also they are continually receiving feedback, unlike the one-research-paper seminar where all hinges on the final report. And they are getting a taste of the library, the archives, the field, and the museum, all arenas that the serious folklorist must cultivate.

NOTES

1. A syllabus provides readings and references on each theme. Richard M. Dorson, ed., *Folklore and Folklife, An Introduction* (Chicago: University of Chicago Press, 1972) is used for general reference.

2. The Folktales of the World Series is edited by Richard M. Dorson and published since 1963 by the University of Chicago Press. Volumes issued to date include Chile, China, Egypt, England, France, Germany, Greece, Hungary, Ireland, Israel, Japan, Mexico, Norway.

3. See the article in this *Handbook* by Angela Maniak on "Bibliographies and Indexes in American Folklore Research."

Ronald L. Baker

Teaching Folklore in American Colleges and Universities

Since the 1940s folklore courses have inched their way into college and university curricula in the United States and now are well established in most major universities and in many small colleges. The first survey of folklore studies in American colleges and universities, conducted in 1940, dealt mainly with graduate studies and found only 23 schools with folklore courses.[1] According to the most recent survey, conducted in 1977, the number of institutions offering folklore had grown to 404. Currently the most popular undergraduate folklore courses are "Introductory Folklore" and "American Folklore," with the genre courses in ballad and tale trailing behind. Folklore in literature, regional folklore, and ethnic folklore courses are the most popular of those recently introduced.[2] Three universities in the United States offer the B.A. degree in folklore, seven offer the M.A., and four offer the Ph.D. Indiana University alone in the United States confers all three degrees in folklore.[3]

Since relatively few American colleges and universities have folklore programs, and only a handful of these have departmental status, most folklore courses are taught in other departments, usually in English or occasionally foreign languages and literatures. Because folkloristics examines human beings within close-knit groups and borrows techniques and theories from the social sciences as well as from literature and language, folklore courses also are offered in social science departments, especially anthropology. Regardless of where it is housed, folklore, with its focus on informal human culture, makes fundamental contributions to the general education of American college students. By concentrating on formal culture and neglecting most of humanity, the conventional humanistic studies actually are not very humane. Although some contemporary ethnographic and sociological research overlaps with folklore research, most anthropologists still are concerned with non-Western cultures,[4] and most sociologists in their statistical studies are insensitive to the expressive and material traditions of close-knit urban and rural groups.

The most popular folklore courses, introductory and American, sometimes are combined in a single course. General concepts and major genres are introduced with American materials used as examples.[5] In the ideal situation, actually the most common one in practice, the two courses are separate since the organization and emphasis of each should be different. The introductory course should survey the methods and analytical approaches of folkloristics. Even when folklore is taught within another department to students not preparing for professional careers in folklore, the instructor should emphasize three areas: (1) the techniques of the folklorist (fieldwork, annotation, comparative analysis, and interpretation of data); (2) the mutual relationships of folklore, culture, literature, and the popular arts; and (3) the historical validity of tradition.

The introductory folklore course might be organized conceptually with stress on the international quality and universal functions of folklore. The common genre approach of many introductory folklore courses to some extent has been superseded by other orientations, especially theoretical, structural, functional, and contextual.[6] Although the contemporary aversion to genre and text and the concern with performance and process have been healthy for American folklore studies, the introductory teacher cannot dismiss the notion of genre entirely because both the folk and folklorists recognize different functional and formal qualities of the forms of folk tradition.[7] Still, a straightforward survey of the formal qualities of folklore genres from the simple to the complex neglects equally important contextual perspectives and misrepresents what folklore actually is: the dynamic process of sharing informal culture within close groups. Consequently, the generic approach should be balanced with other considerations. All the major theoretical approaches should be introduced to acquaint students with the intellectual development of the discipline and to allow them to evaluate each of the approaches.[8]

The functions of folklore in a particular culture may serve as the framework of an introductory course. Frequently, selected areas from the students' own folk groups are examined and related more broadly to the general functions of folklore. Robert J. Adams suggests that after introducing some basic concepts of folkloristics, outlining the main genres of tradition, discussing the modes of folklore transmission, and examining some stylistic and structural features of folklore, the instructor present units dealing with major folklore functions, including "Folklore in Education," "Folklore and the Economy," "Folklore and Entertainment," "Folklore as a Safety Valve," "Folklore and Protest," "Folklore as Validation and Sanction," and "Folklore and Cohesiveness." In preparation for class lectures and discussions, students are assigned specific collecting projects or exercises designed to emphasize the pervasive influence of folklore on their culture. For instance, the unit on "Folklore as Validation and Sanction" is preceded by assignments asking students to show how the biblical account of Christmas validates American Christmas rites and customs and to describe fully an incident in which a proverb was used to prove a point.[9] The main advantage of a functional approach is that in using traditions familiar to students it deals with living folklore within a specific social and physical context, not merely with survivals or texts in a book.

An excellent organizational plan for the introductory course, one that actually combines generic, functional, and contextual considerations, is suggested by Roger D. Abrahams in "The Complex Relations of Simple Forms."[10] Abrahams deals with genres, but not simply with the formal qualities or structure of texts. He compares and contrasts the entire performance context of folklore traditions, especially emphasizing the degree of participation between performer and audience. Consequently, folklore emerges as process rather than product. Since Abrahams is concerned equally with performer, text, and audience, his approach is not dogmatic but allows a natural and logical discussion of theories and functions within the framework of the performance context.

An American folklore course might be organized chronologically against a background of American cultural history with stress on the distinctive qualities of American folklore.[11] As this *Handbook* illustrates, American settings and experiences, American regional and ethnic folk groups, American industries and occupations, Canadian-American and Mexican-American border traditions, among other elements, all have contributed to an American folklore that is unique. The course might begin with the image of the new world in travelers' tales of the colonial period and then examine the transplantation and acculturation of European folk cultures in the new environment. The influence of the Native American on folk culture, especially on material culture and subsistence, should be emphasized. The remarkable providences and witchcraft of American Puritanism could form a large unit, with special attention paid to the distinction between Christian doctrine and folk belief. The folklore of other religious groups, notably the persisting traditional expressive and material culture of Quakers and Old Order Amish in Pennsylvania, should also be covered. The first third of the course could conclude with a discussion of the conflict between supernaturalism and reason that developed in the American Enlightenment, with Franklin as folk hero and bearer of Yankee wisdom.

The American folklore course should deal with the significant role of folklore in the emergence of American self-consciousness and national pride in the nineteenth century. A substantial unit might be devoted to the mutual influence of intellectual culture and folk culture on American Jacksonianism, Transcendentalism, and Romantic Nationalism. Slavery can be examined through Afro-American folktales, notably those of Old Master and John, and the roots of Afro-American folklore, especially hoodoo, spirituals, and blues, can be traced to the old plantations and perhaps beyond. Other units might deal with the westward movement and the frontiersman as a cultural hero, the development of American regional folklore, and the folklore of American occupational groups, including sailors, loggers, cowboys, miners, oil drillers, railroaders, and farmers.

In the American folklore course, as in the introductory course, the dynamic quality of folklore should be stressed. Changes in American culture have shaped American folklore in the twentieth century. The effects of changes in transportation, communications, industrialism, the economy, and demography on American folklore should be examined. The new immigrants, the urbanization of the farmer, and the migration of Afro-Americans have had an enormous impact on the folklore of American cities, which should be studied at length. The decline of folk crafts and subsequent depersonalization of work have significantly influenced American culture and personality in the twentieth century and might be discussed along with the impact of the Depression and several wars on American folklore. The folklore of factories and schools and the folklore of contemporary counter-cultures (i.e., druglore and protest lore) also might be considered. Throughout the American folklore course, the symbiosis of formal, mass, and folk cultures should be emphasized.

Since fieldwork gives students firsthand contact with living traditions within specific physical and social contexts, a collecting project probably should be required of all students in introductory and American folklore courses. Then general concepts about text, context, performance, and functions covered in class discussions can be illustrated and tested with the students' own field experiences. Students may concentrate on collecting a specific genre of expressive or material culture or on collecting the folklore of a folk group or individual. They may submit a number of variants of a specific item of folklore, or they may hand in a general collection. A large project may be due near the end of the semester, or shorter assignments related to classroom discussions required periodically throughout the semester. Students learn more about the context and functions of folklore if the assignments call for specific, in-depth fieldwork and analysis rather than for a general, shotgun approach without interpretation of the data.[12] In any case, the submission of texts alone is inadequate. Students should be required to report in detail the background and behavior of informants and the physical and social context of performance.[13]

Carefully selected and properly used, audiovisual teaching aids can greatly enrich the teaching of folklore. Slides for illustrating material culture and audiotapes and phonograph records for demonstrating verbal folklore and traditional music are as basic as blackboards and chalk in folklore classes. The best way of approximating folklore in context in the classroom, though, is with sound films or videotapes. Of course, the image of the folkloric event on film or tape is not the event itself. The camera operator selects, and the editor cuts, splices, and arranges, so the actual performance context is distorted. But since the live context cannot be transferred to the classroom, films and videotapes, much more than printed texts and audiotapes, can be used to emphasize and illustrate the folklore event. As Birdwhistell says, films and videotapes "give the student from other disciplines more dramatic and convincing insight into the dynamics of culture" and acquaint the student of traditional life with "basic storage techniques," while preparing both "for observation in a way heretofore impossible."[14]

Fortunately, some good folkloric films and videotapes are now available for both introductory and American folklore courses. One index lists over 1,800 films and videotapes dealing with American folklore alone.[15] Naturally, all of these do not meet the standards of folkloristics, so the folklore teacher must preview selected materials at least a couple of times before showing them. Visual communications produced by folklorists or ethnologists generally are the best choices,[16] but some documentary films, such as *The Holy Ghost People*, frequently shown in undergraduate folklore classes, also can be used to stress folklore in action and to show how various traditional genres—belief, ritual, tale, song, speech—intermingle within specific physical and social contexts.

In employing videotapes, Bell and Mastick suggest instant replay, so familiar on TV broadcasts of American sporting events, as an instructional aid to clarify points and to stimulate discussion.[17] Similarly, Birdwhistell recommends replaying films in slow motion:

> On slow motion viewing, many students become aware of things which the lecturer took for granted. As the student learns to appreciate the decelerated pattern, he often accelerates his viewing speed and becomes a more sensitive observer. Not only does he become a better spectator, but he often becomes aware of the relativity of time in patterned social interaction. One of the unexpected rewards of multiple reexamination of films is that many students for the first time get the idea that "natives" are human. In a film in which the cameraman inadvertently included a view of the audience to a native dance,

replaying even a small strip of this scene revealed that such audiences may argue, applaud, scoff, make love, or engage in any of the other everyday details of spectatorship. They were not merely ceremonial personages. No less important is the fact that for many students, it indicated that American audiences, who are often seemingly inattentive to our own ceremonials, are not without culture.[18]

Folklorists frequently use audiotapes and still photography from their own field research in their classrooms, and some are now using films and videotapes from their own fieldwork, too. In fact, anthropologist Felicitas D. Goodman films folklife with her classes always in mind and has found that students prefer the Super-8 ethnographic films of her own making to rented films "because," as one student said, "she puts herself into the films."[19] Most folklorists could use videotapes of their own field experiences in the classroom since videotaping is generally cheaper than filming and the equipment is fairly easy to use.[20] Whatever teaching aids are used, they are by no means substitutes for class preparation, lectures, and discussions. As Birdwhistell warns, "adequate use of audiovisual materials does not save time, but, rather, it makes severe demands on the serious teacher if he is to prepare properly for the presentation of such materials."[21]

Introductory and American folklore courses should be part of the liberal arts curriculum at every college and university. Francis Lee Utley argues that "every school worthy of its salt" should have at least five folklore courses. He recommends the development of a "folklife curriculum, with its eye on the social, the economic, the psychological, as well as the literary implications."[22] Although in principle Utley is right, his estimate of the minimum number of courses required in a folklore curriculum is conservative. Beyond the undergraduate introductory and American courses, the folklore curriculum should include advanced courses in folk music, regional folklore, ethnic folklore, folklore in literature, folklore in culture, traditional material culture, and the folklore of other national or cultural areas. In addition, at least a graduate proseminar and a graduate studies course, in which the topic changes from semester to semester, should be part of the folk curriculum.

Whenever it is virtually impossible to develop more than one or two basic folklore courses, whether in a community college, private college, or university, folklore can be smuggled into other courses. For example, if a folklorist teaches in an English department, folklore can be worked into language and composition courses as well as into literature. Units on folk speech, folk naming, and the ethnography of speaking fit into language and linguistics courses. Several articles dealing with the use of folklore in composition have appeared in English journals.[23] The students' own oral traditions furnish them with familiar source material for expository essays, encourage them to take their own language and culture seriously, and provide instructors with familiar examples of rhetorical strategies from the students' own language.

In nearly every literature course the mutual relations of oral and written literature can be examined. For instance, Winkelman describes how he worked folklore into a world literature survey at a small junior college for women.[24] Incorporating folklore into literature classes often offers insight into the sources and techniques of authors and into the meaning and functions of literary works. Folk literature also provides a bridge to written literature. Dealing mainly with the relationship of the folk ballad to literature, Utley demonstrates how "The Wife of

Usher's Well" can be used to teach tragedy in a literature class.[25] Brunvand advises folklorists in English departments that "the opening wedge" for new folklore courses "should be driven in at the softest spots of the [English] discipline's curriculum, that is as aids to studying literary history or linguistics. . . ."[26]

With its concern for informal culture—past or present, urban or rural—the study of folklore fills a vacuum in the liberal arts curriculum left by the more established disciplines. As Dorson has argued, though, folklore must have a power base as well as an intellectual base in order to develop as a professional discipline, and "the university department of folklore must be accounted the strongest power base for the discipline of folklore at present."[27] Although a folklore department is not an immediate reality at most American colleges and universities, something of a power base can be established with the development of a semiautonomous folk studies curriculum.[28]

Introductory and American courses are not simply means of developing folklore departments or folk studies programs. In most cases, they are taught for the general education of students, not for folklore majors; therefore, folklorists who teach these basic courses must make them challenging and meaningful, emphasizing concepts and relations rather than facts, covering selected areas in depth rather than superficially covering the whole subject. A single introductory or American folklore course constitutes the formal training in folklore for most students. While effectively taught basic folklore courses eventually might lead to folklore departments or programs at a few schools, at all schools they serve to transmit the insights of folklore studies into human culture, encouraging students to be more understanding of other cultures, and more reflective about their own.

Although most American folklorists teach in colleges and universities, folklorists are trained to be researchers, not teachers. The several programs offering advanced degrees in folklore provide instruction in field methods but not in teaching methods. Perchance a graduate student may serve an apprenticeship as a teaching assistant, but even then he or she is often turned loose to learn through trial and error. Since a discipline develops through research, American folklore programs should remain research-oriented; however, the discoveries of folklore research should be communicated not only to professionals who read scholarly books and journals and listen to papers at folklore meetings. Folklorists must share their understanding of human culture with educated laymen, and the college classroom is the best forum for the wide dissemination of folkloric ideas and subsequently the perpetuation of the discipline. Consequently, graduate folklore programs should offer at least an elective seminar in the teaching of folklore, folklorists should continue writing about teaching folklore, and the American Folklore Society should offer regular sessions on teaching folklore.

NOTES

1. Ralph Steele Boggs, "Folklore in University Curricula in the United States," *Southern Folklore Quarterly* 4 (1940): 93–109. Other surveys are: Richard M. Dorson, "The Growth of Folklore Courses," *Journal of American Folklore* 63

(1950): 354-59; MacEdward Leach, "Folklore in American Colleges and Universities," *Journal of American Folklore Supplement* (1958): 10-11; Donald M. Winkelman and Ray B. Browne, "Folklore Study in Universities," *Sing Out* 14 (1964): 47-49; and Ronald L. Baker, "Folklore Courses and Programs in American Colleges and Universities," *Journal of American Folklore* 84 (1971): 221-29.

2. Ronald L. Baker, "The Study of Folklore in American Colleges and Universities," *Journal of American Folklore* 91 (1978): 792-807.

3. The University of Pennsylvania, the University of California at Los Angeles, and the University of Texas at Austin offer both the M.A. and the Ph.D. in folklore. The University of California at Berkeley, the University of North Carolina, and Western Kentucky University grant the M.A. in folklore. Harvard University and Pitzer College at Claremont, California, offer the B.A. in folklore. Concentrations or minors in folklore are rapidly developing across the U.S. In 1977 well over 50 colleges and universities offered folklore concentrations, undergraduate as well as graduate.

4. Ward H. Goodenough, "Folklife Study and Social Change," in *American Folklife*, ed. Don Yoder (Austin: University of Texas Press, 1976), pp. 19-20. Some folklorists see folklore closely related to cultural anthropology in American academe, though. See, for example, Don Yoder, "Folklife Studies in American Scholarship," in *American Folklife*, p. 5.

5. A textbook organized by genres with Anglo-American examples is Jan Harold Brunvand, *The Study of American Folklore: An Introduction*, 2d rev. ed. (New York: W. W. Norton, 1978).

6. A textbook for an introductory course with a theoretical orientation is Alan Dundes, ed., *The Study of Folklore* (Englewood Cliffs, N.J.: Prentice-Hall, 1965). For an example of a structural approach in a college folklore class, see Bruce V. Roach, "Abuse and Disabuse: Structural Folklore and the College Classroom," *Journal of the Ohio Folklore Society* 2 (1973): 4-16. A textbook focusing on folklore as process rather than text is Barre Toelken, *The Dynamics of Folklore* (Boston: Houghton Mifflin, 1979).

7. See William Bascom, "The Forms of Folklore: Prose Narratives," *Journal of American Folklore* 78 (1965): 3-20.

8. An introductory textbook with a balance of theories and techniques and a wide coverage of folk genres is Richard M. Dorson, ed., *Folklore and Folklife, An Introduction* (Chicago: University of Chicago Press, 1972).

9. "A Functional Approach to Introductory Folklore," *Folklore Forum* 1 (1968): [2-4]. A detailed report on introducing beginning folklore students to the functional analysis of a specific item of folklore is Tom Burns, "Involving the Introductory Student in the Functional Analysis of the Material He Collects," in *Perspectives in Folklore and Education*, Folklore Forum Bibliographic and Special Series, no. 2, 1969, pp. 13-27.

10. In *Folklore Genres*, ed. Dan Ben-Amos (Austin: University of Texas Press, 1976), pp. 193-214.

11. For this approach I am indebted to the writings and lectures of Richard M. Dorson. Three of Dorson's books are especially useful in American folklore courses: *American Folklore* (Chicago: University of Chicago Press, 1959); *Buying the Wind: Regional Folklore in the United States* (Chicago: University of Chicago Press, 1964); and *America in Legend* (New York: Pantheon Books, 1973). Of course, there are other ways of organizing an American folklore course. Some are organized by genre, but these serve mainly as introductory courses with American examples. Some are organized by regions, but these present a limited view of American folk groups. Some stress American folk literature, but the materials and approach in these are more literary than folkloristic. Some deal with questions frequently asked about American folklore, but these emphasize methods and approaches.

12. Kenneth Laine Ketner and Michael Owen Jones, in "Folkloristic Research as a Pedagogical Tool in Introductory Courses," *New York Folklore* 1 (1975): 123–48, argue against collecting projects and interpretive papers and instead recommend research reports involving the "method of hypothesis," in which through observation and inquiry students determine whether their hypotheses are true or false.

13. A detailed collecting guide is Kenneth S. Goldstein, *A Guide for Field Workers in Folklore* (Hatboro, Pa.: Folklore Associates, 1964). For undergraduate classes, a more concise guide is MacEdward Leach and Henry Glassie, *A Guide for Collectors of Oral Traditions and Folk Culture Material in Pennsylvania* (Harrisburg, Pa.: The Pennsylvania Historical and Museum Commission, 1973).

14. Ray L. Birdwhistell, "The Use of Audio-Visual Teaching Aids," in *Resources for the Teaching of Anthropology*, ed. David G. Mandelbaum, Gabriel W. Lasker, and Ethel M. Albert. American Anthropological Association Memoir 95, 1963, pp. 60–61.

15. *American Folklore Films and Videotapes: An Index* (Memphis, Tenn.: Center for Southern Folklife, 1976).

16. The films on traditional music, crafts, religion, and tales produced by the Center for Southern Folklife (P.O. Box 4081, Memphis, Tenn. 38104), under the direction of Bill Ferris, are especially good. Ralph Rinzler, Bess Hawes, Bill Wiggins, and Carl Fleischhauer also have produced some useful folklore films. Indiana University folklorists have produced a film, *Jennie's*, dealing with urban folklore in the Calumet Region, Indiana, and a 58-minute color cassette videotape, *Joy Unspeakable: Pentecostalism in Southern Indiana*.

17. Carole O. Bell and Patricia A. Mastick, "Videotape: Hardware, History, and Applications," in *Saying Cheese: Studies in Folklore and Visual Communication*, ed. Steven Ohrn and Michael E. Bell. Folklore Forum Bibliographic and Special Series, no. 13, 1975, p. 83.

18. Birdwhistell, p. 58. In "Films for Finals," *Folklore Forum* 9 (1976): 9–17, Michael Owen Jones explains how a folklore course may be concluded with an analysis or review of a film.

19. "Films for the Classroom: The Home-Made on Super 8," in *Saying Cheese*, pp. 60–61.

20. See Bell and Mastick, p. 84. Richard March shares his experiences with the videotape machine in "How I Became 'The TV Man': Video Fieldwork in the Calumet Region," *Folklore Forum* 11 (1978): 254–64.

21. Birdwhistell, p. 56.

22. Francis Lee Utley, "The Academic Status of Folklore in the United States," *Journal of the Folklore Institute* 7 (1970): 113, 114.

23. Lee Haring and Ellen Foreman, "Folklore in the Freshman Writing Course," *College English* 37 (1975): 13–21; Andrew Badger, "Folklore: A Source for Composition," *College Composition and Communication* 26 (1975): 285–88; Ronald L. Baker, "Writing about Folklore: Folklore in the Freshman English Class," *Indiana English Journal* 11 (1976–77): 15–24.

24. Donald M. Winkelman, "Folklore in a Small College," *Kentucky Folklore Record* 7 (1961): 17–22.

25. Francis Lee Utley, "Oral Genres as a Bridge to Written Literature," in *Folklore Genres*, pp. 3–15.

26. Jan Harold Brunvand, "Crumbs for the Court Jester: Folklore in English Departments," in *Perspectives on Folklore and Education*, pp. 45–49.

27. Richard M. Dorson, *Folklore and Fakelore: Essays toward a Discipline of Folk Studies* (Cambridge, Mass.: Harvard University Press, 1976), p. 112.

28. See Richard M. Dorson's strategy for developing a semiautonomous Folk Studies Curriculum in "The Academic Future of Folklore," in *Folklore: Selected Essays* (Bloomington: Indiana University Press, 1972), pp. 295–304.

Richard M. Dorson

The Publication
of Research

Like other scholars in our publish-or-perish academic culture, folklorists must get their work into print, and they have an added incentive of doing so: one of their chief missions is to rescue oral traditions from oblivion. Younger folklore collectors regularly inquire about effective ways of finding publishing outlets from their seniors, none of whom seems to have set down experiences about getting published. I will retrace some of my own adventures with publishers, draw some morals therefrom, and then consider various models of folklore collections and studies, both admirable and otherwise, that indicate publishing trends. I here discuss only book publication.

My first book was published two years after I graduated from college, to the amazement of my professors and myself, and no one could have been more naive in the ways of publishing than that callow graduate student. It was *Davy Crockett, American Comic Legend*, and the idea for it came to me in my first job after college, at the Tuttle Publishing Company in Rutland, Vermont, where for fifteen dollars a week I wrote brochure and jacket copy for town histories and genealogies. The family of my Harvard classmate and friend Charles E. Tuttle operated both a small publishing business and a rare book business in Rutland. To the firm's directors I presented a plan for a book based on the Crockett almanacs issued between 1835 and 1856, which I had become acquainted with and fascinated by while doing my undergraduate honors thesis on frontier humor. One week at the American Antiquarian Society in Worcester enabled me to photostat choice anecdotes and woodcuts from their rare file of the almanacs. Back in Rutland, I engaged a typist at $7.50 a week to type the manuscript, while I wrote the introduction. Then I asked Howard Mumford Jones, one of my Harvard professors to write a foreword. Meanwhile Charles Tuttle's father, the bookseller, advised me not to publish with the small local Tuttle firm but to seek a major publisher. Accordingly I sent the manuscript off to Houghton Mifflin in Boston. During my senior year I had met one of their young editors, Paul Brooks, who had prepared for their company a volume of frontier humor, *Their Weight in Wildcats*, withholding his name in favor of the illustrator James Daugherty. (Brooks later became editor-in-chief of Houghton Mifflin.) My cover letter to him began "Bread cast upon the waters . . ." and I wrote that since he had shared my interest in frontier humor I was going to let him publish my book. At the end of two weeks I wrote again to find out why I had not heard from him. He soon replied saying he had pushed through the manuscript as fast as possible, that a small number of people would be very interested but not enough for sales that would justify publication, and so he was returning the manuscript.

I was flabbergasted. Publishers existed to publish books, I thought, and how could anybody not be interested in these comic-heroic tall tales about America's first superman? What was all this about sales? Well, there were other publishers, so I made the rounds: Little, Brown; Harcourt Brace; Macmillan. I went in off the street, asked to see an editor, was courteously received, and allowed—encouraged— to submit my manuscript. So imbued was I with the excitement of my material that even jaded editors responded to my enthusiasm. But all the publishers said no: not enough sales potential. For the first time I began to think about who buys books. Also I read the trade journal *Publishers Weekly* and learned that commercial houses practically never accepted unsolicited manuscripts.

After all these rejections by the big trade publishers Howard Mumford Jones put me in touch with a printer of fine books in New York, Joseph Blumenthal of the Spiral Press, who had decided to publish a select list of original Americana, under the imprint of Rockland Editions, to keep his press going in between print orders.[1] So in the fall of 1939 *Davy Crockett, American Comic Legend* saw the light of day, and I absorbed several key lessons. For one, the publishing world was divided roughly into commercial or trade publishers who sought books with large potential markets, and university or small presses who produced scholarly and specialized books. For another, Americans were highly resistant to book-buying, and needed much pressure from advertising, news publicity, movie versions, autograph parties, radio and TV interviews, and best-seller lists to part with cash for a book. With some astonishment I compared the vast sums annually expended on liquor and cosmetics with the paltry figure for books. The idea occurred to me of soliciting book orders from friends, but only one ever did buy the book, although many asked me to give them copies. A good friend from prep school, of considerable means, returned the five-dollar book to the press saying he had expected to receive it free. Apart from an award as one of the fifty best books typographically of the year, *Davy Crockett* gained little attention.[2]

Returning to graduate school at Harvard, I completed my doctoral dissertation in 1943 on "New England Popular Tales and Legends," using printed sources from the seventeenth to the twentieth centuries, and submitted it to Harvard University Press. The press accepted the work on its scholarly merits, but now I was to learn that acceptance did not guarantee publication. The reader, Howard Mumford Jones, recommended that the bulky typescript be considerably reduced. Authors hate to eliminate portions of their magnum opus, but they should recognize that no readers are as enamored of their creations as themselves, and that a friendly critic can suggest the needed amputations. After I had sliced the work in half, the director of the press informed me that production even of the truncated manuscript would strain their resources, and could I contribute funds? Here was another shocker, but I remembered Samuel Eliot Morison, Harvard's best-selling historian, saying in a seminar that an "indulgent mother" had put up the money to publish his first book, on his Federalist ancestor Harrison Gray Otis. Similarly my mother came through with one thousand dollars and in 1943 *Jonathan Draws the Long Bow* appeared. It received some prominent reviews and went into a second printing, and eventually the royalties recovered the subsidy. This practice of a university press soliciting funds from an author differs from the modus operandi of vanity presses, which print any book the author pays for, but still it places an unfair onus on the scholar. The current policy is for university presses to request authors of expensive or limited-appeal works to assist in the search for outside subsidies, but not to ask them for personal subsidies.

Taking a teaching position at Michigan State University in 1944, I undertook a field trip two years later to the Upper Peninsula of Michigan in quest of folk narratives and completed a manuscript the following year, which I titled *Bloodstoppers and Bearwalkers*. An acquaintance once remarked to me that he noticed a considerable difference in style between *Jonathan* and *Bloodstoppers*, the first being written in academic prose and the second in much freer idiom. In the interim between the two books I had begun writing occasional articles for the *American Mercury*, and came to perceive the chasm between writing to get published, in a learned journal, and writing to be read, in a commercial magazine. The academic style inculcated in graduate school stresses impersonality, jargon ("synchronic, diachronic"), obscurantism as a sign of profundity, and scorns the sound and feel and rhythm of words as vehicles of ideas. Smug in the thought that I had developed a readable style I turned again to the trade publishers. An editor and good friend at Viking Press shepherded *Bloodstoppers* through their board, but an outside reader objected to ethnic folklore as non-American and to variants as repetitious and boring. So once again the New York houses—Macmillan, Scribner's, Duell, Sloan and Pearce, Dutton's—said no, although expressing interest, and dallying with the idea that here might be another *Stars Fell on Alabama*. Each rejection fell like a triphammer on my heart, and the years passed. Finally I gave up on New York and turned the manuscript over to the newly founded Michigan State University Press: the press of my own teaching institution, established in part to promote state-based research. The first reader voted yes. The second reader, a female dietitian on the editorial board to represent the university's land-grant agricultural orientation, expressed disgust at the earthy contents. After nine months I received a rejection. Thoroughly despondent, on an impulse I sent *Bloodstoppers* to Harvard. In three months they accepted it and enclosed the letter of their reader—Howard Mumford Jones again, I later discovered—saying, "This is about the first manuscript I have ever read for Harvard that I had to force myself to put down." In 1952, after five years of looking for a home, *Bloodstoppers* reached print. Harvard advertised it handsomely, but the book did not do well, and was remaindered. In 1972 Harvard reissued it in paperback, and it has enjoyed five successive reprintings. In the twenty-year interval the market had changed, interest in ethnicity had mounted, and many more courses in folklore were being taught.

One last personal example involves a collection of Afro-American folktales I recorded in southern Michigan and offered directly to Harvard shortly after the publication of *Bloodstoppers*. They balked at my proposed title, "Old Marster Eats Crow," which some advisor considered beneath the press's dignity and smacking of Uncle Tomism, and we ended up with *Negro Folktales in Michigan*. (Harvard later published Bruce Jackson's collection of Afro-American prison folklore using the title *"Get Your Ass in the Water and Swim Like Me,"* when black rhetoric had become acceptable.) Sales of my third Harvard book proved modest, a couple of thousand copies, but eleven years later, in 1967, when Fawcett reissued it, with materials from another collection of mine, as a mass market paperback under the title *American Negro Folktales*, it took off like wildfire and has sold two hundred thousand copies, scholarly apparatus and all—headnotes, tables of tale types and motifs, and subject index. In 1968 the boom for black studies commenced, and "black" replaced Negro in the language.

The lessons here are clear enough on the unpredictability of markets and sales, the role played by outside readers, and the length of time it may take for books to find their audiences, if indeed they are destined ever to find them. My story could go on, but enough has been said to suggest the vagaries of the publishing world. My situation has come full circle, and where I once knocked on doors with manuscripts seeking contracts, now the contracts tumble in and I am always behind with the writing.

After glancing at some experiences of a folklorist with publishers, we may ask, how does a publisher look at folklorists? Fortunately we have available a splendid article on "Publishing Folklore" by Colin Franklin of the London house of Routledge and Kegan Paul which appeared in the journal of the (English) Folklore Society.[3] A devotee of folklore, Franklin developed a list in that area for Routledge, who fall somewhere between the sharp American division of the commercial and scholarly publishers. He wrote revealingly of the kinds of books about folklore he deplored, those he relished, and those he would like to see written. Chidingly he noted that folklorists withdrew from the pleasure of their subject, anxious to be scholars. They form a first puritanical law of scholarship something like this: "Don't make your book too agreeable or digestible, or it won't be accepted as serious scholarship." (I would add that scholars not only fear being readable, and ergo unscholarly, but also they have no idea how to be readable, since their graduate training and role models by and large encourage unreadability.) Franklin singled out for objection the writings that squeeze the juice from their material with endless categorization and an excessive "burden of detail," for instance in folklife studies that deal with the "shapes of handles and wheels and hammers, or local variations in the methods of cooking muffins." As for folklore books he particularly delighted in, he cited several memoirs of life in Britain before 1914, written without conscious artifice and with a sure sense for the traditional rhythms of that long ago world. One of his quoted passages comes from W. H. Barrett, small farmer and workingman in the Cambridgeshire Fens who has bequeathed us three extraordinary volumes of personal and autobiographical narratives. Comparable volumes of folk-memory from the American underclasses have not reached print. Franklin also suggested topics on which he would like to receive manuscripts, in such unconsidered areas as the folklore of men's clubs and board meetings, universities and public schools, law courts, parliament, cricket, and the testing of folk-medical beliefs. Shrewdly he remarked, "all of us are folk whose lore can be studied." We see here the publisher's mind at work with fertile ideas, and Franklin underscores the point that publishers look kindly on books they have shared in developing, if not actually initiated.

As my own experience as a folklore author suggests, and that of Colin Franklin as a folklore publisher reinforces, a constant tension exists between the demands of the marketplace and the demands of scholarship. Both commercial publishers and university presses are deeply concerned with sales, but the one looks for a print run of ten thousand on up and the other thinks of fifteen hundred. As a New York publisher visiting a university press remarked, "They do the same thing as us, only the decimal point is moved over." Committed to publishing works of scholarly merit, university presses can for the most part reach only limited markets, and depend on subsidies, grants, and university support to balance their budgets, but they are just as hungry as their brethren in New York for good sellers. We may distinguish two general models of folklore books, one for trade and one for scholarly outlets.

The profit-seeking publisher desires the widest possible geographical coverage and the broadest possible appeal for his folklore titles. In *A Treasury of American Folklore*, issued in 1944 by Crown Publishers in New York and distributed as a Book-of-the-Month-Club dividend, Benjamin A. Botkin hit on a highly successful book-merchandising formula: a hefty package at a bargain price of easy-to-read snippets of local-color, humor, nostalgia, human-interest pieces combed from all times and all places in the United States. Having established his market, he then applied the formula to large sections of the country: New England, the South, the West, the Mississippi Valley, and embraced cities in one treasury, and New York City in particular in another. In adopting such a model Botkin necessarily abandoned personal fieldwork. Printed sources can and should be utilized by folklorists, but only after being subjected to a rigorous sifting and scrutiny. The Botkin treasuries created a false conception of folklore as nostalgic and jolly, and a false model of how folklore should be presented. Others have followed this model, for example Duncan Emrich in *Folklore on the American Land*, which while borrowing from field sources lacks any philosophic purpose and too mixes a batter of sugar and spice and everything nice. To reach the most book buyers, this commercial model eschews complex analysis or the apparatus of scholarship. Some folklorists try to have it both ways, and seek to combine the national market with claims to scholarship. An example is *Folklore from the Working Folk of America*, pasted together from folklore journals by Tristram Coffin and Hennig Cohen and published by Doubleday. But the volume lacks any comparative notes, and its sources cannot justify its title because the basic fieldwork in occupational folklore remains to be done. To achieve national sellers some folklorists will compromise the integrity of their texts with composite tales or ballads spliced together to form more perfect versions than ever existed in reality. John and Alan Lomax have done this in some of their ballad collections, and joined the ideal songs with musical scores they have copyrighted, a clear admission they were adapting folk tunes to individual compositions. Richard Chase in *The Jack Tales* likewise constructed "improved" tales from the variants at his disposal for greater readability and literary power. These collectors indicate the sources they have used, so their works are superior to authors who rewrite folkstuff without giving credits to any source, on the premise that folklore belongs in the public domain and they can do with it what they will. But any alteration, editing, or tampering with the texts constitutes a breach of scholarship and cannot be tolerated. Also, with respect to publishability, we now recognize that oral texts can, when artistically rendered, prove far more readable and dramatic than texts rewritten to suit the tastes of a popularizer. Even if the mass-market writer does not alter texts, he selects them with a bias in favor of the "charming" qualities of folklore and against the coarse, obscene, racist, and sexist elements that characterize much oral tradition.

To turn to scholarly models of folklore publications, we note at once their limited geographical range. An exemplary field collection, covering the spectrum of the oral genres, rich in annotation, and with a sparkling introductory statement about the field experience, is Emelyn E. Gardner's *Folklore from the Schoharie*

Hills, New York, published by the University of Michigan Press. An exhaustive and valuable salvage of folk humor from printed sources is James R. Masterson's *Tall Tales from Arkansaw*, published by a small house in Boston, Allyn and Bacon. Vance Randolph, America's most active collector, confined his endeavors to the Ozarks, and issued his volumes through Columbia University Press, but even they balked at his offcolor stories.

These he had to separate out and assemble in a later, independent work which the University of Illinois Press released under the title *Pissing in the Snow*, with testimonials on the jacket's back cover from folklore scholars as to the research value of these dirty jokes. The University of Texas Press withheld their imprint in publishing *Urban Folklore from the Paperwork Empire* by Alan Dundes and Carl R. Pagter for the American Folklore Society in 1975, and refused to reprint the book, which contained some offcolor cartoons, but Indiana University Press acquired the rights and brought it back into print in 1978 with a new title, *Work Hard and You Shall Be Rewarded*. Folklore Associates, a small firm operating out of Hatboro, Pennsylvania, had to sell Roger Abrahams's *Deep Down in the Jungle: Negro Narrative Folklore from the Streets of Philadelphia* under the counter when it first came out in 1964, but by 1970 Aldine Press could place the revised edition openly on book counters. Thus do even the scholarly presses vacillate on the issue of obscenity.

We may distinguish two submodels of scholarly publishing of American folklore collections. The earliest recognized the need for the faithful printing of texts of folktales, folksongs, proverbs, riddles and other oral forms, with informants named and comparative notes and indexes provided. This battle was not won overnight, and Stith Thompson tells how the University of Chicago Press asked him to rewrite *Tales of the North American Indians*! Harvard University Press ultimately published the manuscript unaltered, in 1929. The most ambitious production following this model is the seven volumes of *The Frank C. Brown Collection of North Carolina Folklore*, undertaken by the Duke University Press from 1952 to 1964. Regional and institutional pride played a part in the consummation of this enterprise. Brown served for many years on the faculty of Duke University and collected all genres of folklore throughout the state, but died without preparing his hoard for print. A battery of specialists then organized and annotated the genres separately. An even more valiant undertaking, because the entire operation, from collecting through publishing, was conducted by one individual, is Harry M. Hyatt's *Hoodoo - Conjuration - Witchcraft - Rootwork* in five volumes, issued privately with the imprint of his family's foundation. An Episcopal clergyman, Hyatt single-handedly amassed an enormous amount of interview data on hoodooism, which he printed in exact transcript, leaving for others the task of interpretation. Had he not possessed the means to finance the publication, in all likelihood his invaluable materials would have lain buried in an archives.

In spite of these high-water marks for the older research model, a new generation of folklorists chafes at the presentation of uninterpreted collections; they have moved toward a newer model, in which the primary data is supplemented with ethnography and analysis. A forerunner of this new model appeared in Fanny Hardy Eckstorm and Mary Winslow Smyth's *Minstrelsy of Maine* (1927), a memorable pioneering effort which arranged the lumberjacks' songs in historical groupings and interspersed them with perceptive analytic essays on such matters as the replacement of sensational ballad stories by sensational newspaper stories, the passing of John Greenleaf Whittier's "Ballad of the Oysterman" into tradition, and the moot origin of "The Jam on Gerry's Rock." A trade publisher, Houghton Mifflin, considered this work of sufficient appeal to add to its list. In more recent years university presses sympathetic to folklore have responded to the updated model. The University of Texas Press, alerted to folklore through the presence on its faculty of J. Frank Dobie, Mody Boatright, and Américo Paredes, published the latter's *"With His Pistol in His Hand": A Border Ballad and Its Hero* in 1958, a study that went far beyond the enumeration of variants to assess the heroic qualities of a Mexican border hero, Gregorio Cortez, who defied the gringoes. The same press, which for a period published monographs of the American Folklore Society, also brought out Patrick B. Mullen's *I Heard the Old Fishermen Say* in 1978, another worthy example of the interpretive approach. Mullen set down local character anecdotes, buried treasure legends, and tall tales of fishing and the weather, narrated by Texas fishermen along the Gulf Coast, but he sandwiched these texts between extended analyses of their function, style, and relation to social reality. Yet the University of Texas Press regressed in its revised edition of William Owens's *Folk Songs of Texas* by limiting the contents to the hackneyed Anglo-American and Afro-American ballad traditions and failing to include Owens's fresh ethnic folksongs, and by eliminating the account of his field adventures—two lamentable steps backward.

In its series on Music in American Life, the University of Illinois Press has issued several titles that mark the new departure, notably Edward D. Ives's study of *Joe Scott: The Woodsman Songmaker*, released in 1978. Ives offers a candid account of his field and documentary research in Maine, and examines the history, structure, imagery, and layers of meaning in Scott's topical ballad compositions—a far cry from the simple reproductions of ballad texts in older collections.

Other examples could be produced of progressive presses recognizing the new research style. Indiana University Press is to be commended for publishing Austin and Alta Fife's *Saints of Sage and Saddle* (1956), with its historical treatment of Mormon legends, and Carla Bianco's *The Two Rosetos* (1974), placing interview transcripts and folklore texts of Italian-Americans within a perceptive analysis of ethnic folkways. The University of Chicago Press issued Jerome Mintz's *Legends of the Hasidim* (1968) in which legend texts of the Brooklyn Hasidic community share the volume with a detailed ethnographic report of the Rebbes and their courts. Scholarly folklorists may count in the 1980s on receptive and knowledgeable university presses for the publication of their research.

The question remains, is there no possible synthesis between the mass-market and the scholarly models? Can bona fide folklore research command a national audience? I would answer, only rarely. My own view is that a best-seller is not automatically suspect. Certain scholars have reached wide audiences while maintaining their standards. In history one thinks of Samuel Eliot Morison, Allan Nevins, Daniel Boorstin. If the quality of writing and thinking is meritorious, the work will find its audience. But because folklore is easily corrupted and does not enjoy the academic safeguards of more strongly entrenched disciplines, the folklorist must fight for standards, for notes, for variants, for indexes, for analysis and interpretation. But withal he can certainly, as Colin Franklin recommends, tell a story. The collector must explain his collection, but he need not end up a pedant.

NOTES

1. World War II terminated the series, and only one other title was published by Rockland Editions, *The Poems of Edward Taylor*, edited by Thomas H. Johnson.

2. In 1978 both Greenwood Press and Arno Press reprinted *Davy Crockett, American Comic Legend.*

3. "Publishing Folklore," *Folklore* 77 (1966): 184–204.

Michael Edward Bell

Indexing a Folklore Collection: Balance, Flexibility, and the Empathizing Indexer

Contemporary folklorists generally agree that the goals of folkloristics—diverse though they may be—are not consummated by compiling and publishing a collection of folklore. An unavoidable corollary of collecting folklore today is that the material obtained has potential value to other investigators only to the extent that they can identify and locate information contained in the collection. Retrieval of information thus becomes a major concern in conducting folkloristic analysis and interpretation. The central role occupied by indexes in this retrieval process is exemplified by the six volumes of the *Motif-Index of Folk-Literature*, a major reference tool for folklorists (and an index requiring its own index!). Speaking practically, it is no exaggeration to assert that the usefulness of a folklore collection hinges on the character of its index.

Accessibility measures the success of an index. The user is concerned primarily with being able to locate information in the collection and secondarily with the amount of time and effort this process requires. Rachel Baker's index to the two *Popular Beliefs and Superstitions* volumes of the *Frank C. Brown Collection of North Carolina Folklore* runs to nearly one hundred pages and is among the most complete and detailed of indexes, including several kinds of subheadings under many of the more inclusive retrieval terms—yet it still has weaknesses. A user interested in fish, for example, will find several references under the entry "fish," but he also will find different listings under "catfish," "codfish," "gar," and so on, with no cross references. To find all references to fish, then, the user must search the index for each specific variety in addition to the more general "fish" category. Other complex categories, such as "bird," evidence the same failing. A very strong point of Baker's index is the list of major categories in Hand's classification scheme and their inclusive numbers which is replicated at the bottom of each even-numbered page in the index, a thoughtful device allowing the user to apprehend immediately the context for any item in the index. For instance, one who locates "coral beads: 380" in the index can tell by glancing at the bottom of the page that the beads are associated with birth and childhood beliefs (1–479).

Baker's index generally fulfills the goal of locating information with only a minimum of tedious searching, but unfortunately other indexes do not work as well. Consulting "bad luck" in the index to *Kentucky Superstitions*, by Daniel and

Lucy Thomas, one finds almost four hundred references without further qualification. Indeed, this index contains no subheadings and only a handful of cross references for its relatively sparse major entries. One needs only to peruse the index to Emelyn Gardner's *Folklore from the Schoharie Hills, New York* to see how effectively subheadings and cross references can be utilized. The weakness of Gardner's index is found in the less than complete extraction of major retrieval terms. Of course, no extant index to a folklore collection embodies the ideal balance among retrieval terms, subheadings and qualifiers, and cross references.

Balance and flexibility form the core of the indexer's skill. The successful indexer, like the traditional storyteller, is a performer. He must know and play to his audience even on occasions when their tastes and aesthetic conventions conflict with his personal canons of correctness. This balancing act can be difficult, even distressing. Yet it is imperative that the indexer accept his role as a mediator between information and audience. As he spins his web connecting data and data user he must be understanding, sensitive, and empathic as well as knowledgeable and skillful.

Seven years ago I embarked on the arduous task of indexing Harry M. Hyatt's *Hoodoo - Conjuration - Witchcraft - Rootwork*, a published collection which is now complete in five volumes totalling nearly five thousand pages.[1] In the work space which innocently shielded me from feedback, I groped for a vicarious identification with my phantom audience. The strange hoodoo collection open on the desk before me seemed tangible then, locked in suspended animation. But along the way something happened: the audience and the collection began exchanging qualities. Now I see that the collection is dynamic, yet its structure is comprehensible. And the once-distant audience seems fixed and familiar. The indexing experience altered my views of both the collection and its potential users. Seeking knowledge and empathy, I have attemped to approach the balance required for a successful index.

Based on my experiences indexing the Hyatt collection, I see the indexing process as consisting of five stages: (1) assuming the role of indexer; (2) extracting from the collection; (3) sorting the extractions; (4) organizing the index; and (5) completing the index (or, better, maintaining the ongoing index). A general principle underlies the entire process: *Retain as much flexibility as possible* at each stage. Translated into practical terms, it is better to record too much rather than too little information during the initial stages of indexing. Combining or disregarding information later is much simpler than having to return to the collection for more detailed discriminations. I felt a persistent urge to "save time" by making extractions terse and concise, but eventually I learned to ignore the time-saver demon and his false economy. Some painful experiences taught me that, in the long run, it saves time to go through the collection only *once, but thoroughly.* The reality of this ideal increases with the size of the collection.

That flexibility and balance are important is obvious from the beginning, when a person becomes "the indexer" contemplating his task. He faces a "collection of folklore" which may be very specific (consisting entirely of Pennsylvania coal-miners' legends, for example) or extremely wide-ranging, perhaps almost to the point of seeming amorphous (such as the Brown collection from North Carolina). In the Hyatt collection, I confronted the nearly unedited transcriptions of interviews with over 1,600 amateur and professional root doctors recorded by Hyatt throughout the South during the late 1930s. The following example of a folk belief typifies the collection's contents:

4677. De bow an' a dirty sock—out de hat an' 'is dirty sock, lef' foot sock. An' git some Eve-an'-Adam [Adam-and-Eve], some *High John de Conkah*, some *love powdahs*, an' roll 'em to yuh. Make yore wishes as yuh roll 'em. Den yuh take it an' put it in yore pillah or in yore mattress, de woman; an' sleep on it an' he'll stay dere. [Norfolk, Va., (486), 517:3.][2]

Whatever the size and complexity of the collection, the indexer must realize that it will present inherent limitations he cannot circumvent. Information not collected or omitted from the collection obviously cannot be indexed, regardless of its potential value to scholars. In the Hyatt excerpt above, for instance, informant 486 will remain a number with no name. Although I can include informant numbers in the index, allowing its users to locate all individual contributions, I cannot supply names or other personal data not recorded by Hyatt. The indexer will become familiar with the collection's weaknesses (and strengths) as he plods through the pages, but first he must consider who will be using the collection.

The practical task during the first stage of indexing is matching the collection's contents to the needs and expectations of its users. What is important to them must be important to the indexer. To be a proper tool, the index will have to facilitate the interpretation and presentation of research by folklorists. Directly and indirectly, by interacting with folklorists and reading their works, he must seek answers to the following questions: How will folklorists use the information in this collection? What categories, classification schemes, typologies, indices, annotating conventions, and terminology impinge on the collected material? Ultimately the indexer will confront the perspectives, theories, and methods shared by folklorists. A knowledge of folklore's frames of reference and units of analysis, together with the inherent limitations of the collection, will allow the indexer to formulate a general working approach to his assignment.

During my first tentative struggles to grasp the contents of Hyatt's enormous collection, I found useful Wayland D. Hand's detailed classification of beliefs, based on seven categories of the human life cycle. Hand's system, which appears in the sixth and seventh volumes of the *Frank C. Brown Collection*, did not solve all of my terminological problems, but it did give me a practical understanding of the kinds of belief and practice, and associated terminology, familiar to folklorists. The above example from Hyatt would be classified under VI. Love, Courtship, Marriage, and, even more specifically, Flirtation, Jealousy, Discord, Loss of Sweetheart. At this stage, I began to recognize that the intended result—"he'll stay dere," in our example—was the key for organizing the hoodoo rituals which comprised the bulk of Hyatt's collection.

Having now at least a tentative plan for recognizing the significant units to be retrieved, the indexer embarks on the most tedious, laborious, and time-consuming phase of his work—pouring over the corpus item-by-item, line-by-line, word-by-word to extract the information which *may* appear in the completed index. Now his main concern is matching ideas and terminology. When his fortune is right (*and* he has taken stage one seriously) he will encounter information that is easily translatable into the language of folklorists. But fortune may smile only occasionally. The indexer undoubtedly will confront ideas and practices for which no generally accepted folkloristic terminology exists or, just as likely, he will encounter terms used by informants which shift from region to region, group to group, even person to person. I tried not to panic under such conditions.

Remembering the flexibility principle, I simply recorded the informant's term along with a description of how it was used and, on a separate slip, a *cross reference* containing a tentative but more general or widely used term. The informant's term would direct me to my tentative term, and vice versa. From the Hyatt transcription above, I recorded "to yuh," adding "sock and hatbow containing three ingredients are rolled *toward self.*" Then I made a cross reference containing the tentative phrase "toward self," being sure to note "see *to yuh.*"

While extracting, the indexer should be generous and inclusive, avoiding irreversible decisions as far as possible. My motto soon became: "That which is not extracted cannot be retrieved." Since no stage in the indexing process is completely separable from the others, each builds successively on previous ones and early exclusions can become greatly magnified later. It is especially important to keep options open if a large amount of the material in the collection is relatively new to or undocumented by folklorists. Procrastination, for once, will be rewarded. Even after I had gained hours of extracting experience, I made a point of recording more details than I planned to include in the actual index. For example, I summarized our transcription on a single extraction slip—using the intended result as the main heading and including page, item, volume, and informant number in addition to place of collection—as follows:

attraction *hand*—hold man   2670 (4677)
    ["he'll stay dere"]   III

roll 3 ingred's toward self in hatbow of man and dirty left sock of man: Eve-and-Adam, High John the Conker, "love powders"; wish while rolling ["make yore wishes"]; place in pillow or mattress of woman (woman sleeps on *hand*).

Norfolk (486)

One good method for preserving freedom of choice—the key to maintaining balance—is to record extracted terms on separate slips. Being relatively compact and stiff, 3x5 cards are ideal; but they also are expensive. (Libraries and offices are good places to salvage used-but-usable slips.) Having *one slip for each occurrence* of a potential entry allows the indexer the option of moving entries around, changing their order in a sequence, or collapsing or expanding categories as he sees fit. Although such maneuvers usually are unnecessary during stage two, this mobile capacity must be built in at the very moment extracting begins.

Each slip will record the *retrieval term*, a main entry word or phrase as it might appear in the completed index. Depending on the nature of the folklore collection and the indexer's perceptions of his audience, the retrieval term may be a genre of folklore, a tale-type or motif number, an informant's name or identifying code, a locale, an event or type of activity, or a label for a group of people. Other kinds of entries the indexer may extract as he transforms information into data include objects, actions, locations, directions and spatial attitudes, colors, numbers, amounts, and times. He will also index more abstract units, such as intention, belief, metaphor, and symbol, sometimes even translating an entire symbolic system or underlying theory into a word or phrase. This matching game embraces extremes ranging from a word-for-word correspondence between text and retrieval term (for example, "mattress" in the Hyatt transcription) to a wildly divergent situation where scores of words in the text describe a vague idea which must be subsumed under a single, subjective entry (such as "sympathetic magic" for summarizing the logic underlying the ritual in our example).

After I learned that the balancing fulcrum for assigning terms could shift, I proceeded with my labors under a minimum of anxiety, practically free of despair. I now understood that retrieval terms, even when complemented by cross references, often do not provide sufficient information for making final decisions regarding classification. I realized that recording the entry's *immediate context of use* may be extremely important when sorting and organizing begins: an entry in the index such as "sock" followed only by a long series of page (or item) numbers will frustrate many potential users of the index. I therefore extracted some connecting information, recording it on the same slip as the tentative retrieval term. My once simple "sock" slip became crowded with contextual data. Along with location of collection and page, item, volume, and informant number, the slip contained the following details:

> sock of man, dirty—left
>> rolling toward self w/ hatbow & 3 ingred's
>
>>> attraction *hand* (hold man)
>>> in woman's pillow or mattress

Even then I was uncertain exactly how this particular entry would appear in the completed index. But I was unconcerned, secure in the knowledge that I had enough contextual information on the slip to allow for several reasonable retrieval possibilities. For the moment I was content in learning how to recognize and record potentially significant connections. By the time I finished extracting and sorting I hoped to be able to make informed decisions regarding retrieval organization.

The indexer actually begins making *tentative* retrieval decisions while sorting extraction slips, an ongoing process accompanying extraction. Alphabetical sorting of extractions and cross references is not only a rehearsal for deciding on firm retrieval categories and terms, it also allows the indexer easy access to the material already extracted. A growing file of sorted extractions was a boon to my often frail memory. I saved time by not having to reinvent the category "toward self" or rediscover that "love powders" are a commercial product, and I could be more consistent in matching extracted ideas to retrievable terminology.

The sorting stage is an opportune time to practice empathy—even put it to a test. The indexer can make up a hypothetical problem requiring access to the collection and then attempt to locate the needed information using only the extraction file. By starting with relatively simple problems and gradually generating more complex demands, the empathizing indexer increases his awareness of the strengths and weaknesses of the evolving retrieval system. A better, more realistic test is to give interested folklorists access to the index-in-progress, while the indexer notes all exclamations (and causes) of delight and frustration in the attempt to locate data.

Above all, the indexer's decisions should be tentative and reversible at this stage, with reasonable options left open. The indexer later may have to retreat from what he once considered a hard-and-fast category. For example, had I decided to subsume "wishing" and similar formulations of intention under "incantation" while extracting, I would have lost for retrieval purposes all of the fine distinctions among commands, prayers, curses, and verbal charms, in addition to wishes.

Organizing the index is the decision-making time. Now the indexer must give up his hard-won flexibility and begin eliminating possible choices. But he can take solace in his farewell to procrastination because he knows that there will be no more expedient moment. He has extracted the entire collection; he has sorted the extractions; he has made many tentative decisions, returning to the files again and again. He knows the collection now better than ever before, probably more intimately than ever again. As he prepares for his final balancing act, the indexer accepts perfection as an *ideal*, aware that he will be unable to please every potential user of the index. He must strike a balance between too few discriminations (making the index too general) and too many discriminations (making the index unwieldy, too detailed for simple retrieval). The balance he seeks is qualitative as well: what kinds of immediate contextual data should he include in the completed index? Of course, cross references simplify his retrieval system, but cross referencing is a reductive process where information is traded for economy. In the Hyatt collection, for example, I could have decided to economize by not qualifying actions entered in the index (such as "rolling") with "toward self" but instead to direct users to the "toward self" entry where all actions performed in this manner are entered alphabetically.

Publisher's requirements also may direct decisions regarding the index's final form. A limitation on page length, for instance, will guide the indexer's choice between information and economy. He should attempt to recognize where redundance is built into his system and economize by tapping alternate retrieval paths: "sock, left" might simply refer users to "left sock" for all such entries. What great harm if the user has to search out two or three entries instead of one, especially if it means that the index is accepted by the publisher?

The index may not stand alone. An introduction may be necessary for guiding potential users, instructing them in how to find what they want in the indexer's labyrinthic masterpiece. He might even include supplemental, specialized indexes for retrieving information by informant, locale, genre, type number, and so on. In some cases the indexer may provide a great service to his audience by including a glossary of terminology, either native or academic or both.

The best indexes, after publication, do not remain static but are revised, updated, and improved. Even the printed index itself can be dynamic, reflecting ongoing changes in folklore collections and folklorists' conceptions, by allowing for periodic supplements to correct, amend, or illuminate various topics in the index. The indexer's extraction file should always be retained and made accessible to interested researchers, for it contains more connecting information than the streamlined and elegant printed version. An ideal storage system is the computer. Given sufficient funding and foresight, the index could be recorded simultaneously in manuscript form and on computer tape or cards.

Time and money are ubiquitous concerns: one always assumes that more of each will be used than allotted. The lone indexer offers more consistency, but time can be saved if money allows a number of workers. Consistency may be maintained if one person extracts while others sort, file, check back to the collection (alas, an inevitability), locate collateral references to aid the organizing process, and type manuscript drafts. When two or more people are extracting, however, it is mandatory that they remain in close consultation.

In many respects, a good indexer must be farsighted enough to focus on the *future* contributions of the task in hand, for the indexing process is inescapably tedious and usually devoid of notable excitement. To alleviate the boredom inherent in this repetitive work, it may be helpful to remember that the index will be an important key to unlocking information for other investigators embarking on folkloristic fieldwork, analysis, or presentation, but the indexer may also need to create smaller, more short-term goals. Each of the five stages described above can be conceived of as a destination to be reached, yet each stage can itself be approached as containing smaller objectives. During extraction, for instance, every page, section, or chapter completed is an achievement. I made up many games as I was indexing the Hyatt collection, turning work into play by competing with my own past performance on any given task. I often kept my interest alive in the face of impending ennui by attempting to accomplish some small objective faster, more elegantly, or with more precision than I had the previous week. The imaginative indexer can create a schedule of positive reinforcement to offset the delayed rewards of actually completing the index. Approached in this spirit, each problem becomes a riddle to be answered or a puzzle to be completed.

NOTES

1. Harry Middleton Hyatt, *Hoodoo - Conjuration - Witchcraft - Rootwork*, 5 vols. (Hannibal, Mo.: Western Publishing, Inc., 1970–78). The index is due to be published by G. K. Hall.
2. Hyatt, III, p. 2670.

Joseph C. Hickerson

Developing
a Folklore Archive

If we take the word "archive" to mean a collection of generally unpublished documents representing cultural activity, the folklore archive will refer to a gathering of such documents collected by and of interest to folklorists. In order for folklore field data to be useful to others, it is absolutely essential to place these data in a suitable facility, namely, a folklore archive. In fact, the moment a collecting project is contemplated, so should its archiving be planned.

Setting up a folklore archive involves several considerations, beginning with defining its scope and selecting a corresponding name. The scope may depend on the mission of a sponsoring organization (state institution, academic program, regional society), the interests of a director or contributors (specific genres, ethnic groups, regions), media representation (sound recordings, manuscripts, photographs), or the kind of collecting involved (student projects, oral history interviews, broad acquisitions policy). As a rule, an archive will develop as new media, genres, and interests are brought to bear upon it, and its initial name and stated purpose should allow for such development.

It is also important to consider the archive's affiliation with a larger organization. Each kind of affiliation will provide its own degree of independence, on the one hand, and kinds of support on the other. An archive belonging to a private individual or organization will allow freedom to control acquisitions and use, but will be difficult to fund and staff. Academic affiliation may assure student collectanea and archival assistants, but does not guarantee the preservation, cataloguing, and service facilities which a library or museum affiliation may provide. Sponsorship by a federal or state program can have the advantage of tapping a range of other agencies for assistance, while limiting the scope to a regional basis (although the national folk archive [Archive of Folk Culture] in the Library of Congress does admit a worldwide representation).

Of importance for a folklore archive at any stage of development is personnel. Whether they be full-time, part-time, student-assistant, or volunteer staff, it is crucial that an archive be provided with archivists. In addition, there needs to be one person who oversees the management and development of the archive and provides continuity as part-time workers come and go. All too often, folklore archives become vast collections of material largely unattended and unserviced except in a haphazard, episodic fashion. In planning for personnel, it is important to seek a variety of skills, including library, archival, and technical, in addition to the requisite folkloristic experience.

Equally germane is the archive's physical plant. The nature of the plant will partially depend on the types of collectanea gathered within it. Although an archive may initially specialize in a limited array of formats, it must be remembered that archives can encompass a variety of types of cultural representations, ranging from manuscripts (hand- or typewritten, including photocopies), unpublished sound recordings (cylinders, aluminum and acetate discs, magnetic wire, and tape), photographs (including slides), visual recordings (motion picture film, videotape), and microforms (microfilm, cards, and fiche), to ephemeral publications and extracts from published works. In addition, an archive should maintain a minimal reference collection of books, and journals (including photocopies of specific articles), and may include published sound recordings and a sampling of artifacts and other museum materials. Each of these formats necessitates different physical requirements for processing, storage, and servicing.

In the past, storage of folklore collectanea in an archive has followed either of two organizational principles: to facilitate retrieval and to maintain collection integrity. The first method presupposes that collections can be separated into individual items, each on its own sheet or card. The items are then filed as a catalogue would be, by genre, geographical location, title, informant, and the like. Minimal content lists and collection summaries can be maintained as well, but the emphasis here is almost entirely on text, rather than context. The second organizational method will place all parts of a collection together, maintaining its integrity and preserving its representation of context. Cataloguing is then a separate operation, independent of the actual arrangement of material. Of these two methods, I would strongly favor the second, because it enhances contextual analysis without sacrificing access through the use of catalogues, indexes, and duplicate copies of individual items arranged according to desired categories.

A third condition of storage is preservation, which has become increasingly important in recent years, particularly in older archives. In fact, the experience of the Library of Congress and other facilities has shown that this factor is not only primary but should be attended to from the outset in an archive's development. It is certainly easy to see that the best organized and most serviceable collection will become useless as manuscripts discolor or disintegrate, cylinders and discs become cracked and moldy, wires and tapes lose their fidelity through inadequate storage and use, and photographs fade away. The preservation of a collection will require serious consideration of storage facilities, servicing, and duplication.

In regard to storage, preservation is greatly enhanced by placing like materials together. This will maintain collection integrity insofar as format dictates; a collection will be broken up to place tapes in one area, manuscript pages in another, and slides in a third, while numbering, cataloguing, and a documentary file will tie them together as a unit. The types of containers, the storage units and rooms, the methods of shelving, and the physical environment (temperature, humidity, dust, mold) all play important roles in determining the permanency of collections. Technical assistance in these and other organizational matters can often be found through an affiliated or connected library or similar facility, and relevant national organizations.[1] In fact, it may be beneficial to store original copies in specialized sections of such a library. For example, the Archive of Folk

Culture utilizes the preservation copying facilities of the Library of Congress phonoduplication and photoduplication laboratories and places original copies in the storage facilities of the music, recorded sound, and other custodial divisions. The Archive maintains catalogue and servicing control and keeps duplicate reference copies and documentary files in most cases, without having to expend time and energy worrying about physical deterioration.

An archive should be in a position to control, at least in part, the condition and organization of its acquisitions. If the archive sponsors collecting projects, it can supply uniform materials and instructions to ensure a measure of compatibility between the collectanea and the archive's usual procedures for processing, cataloguing, and storage. In some cases, it may even request duplicate materials or logs to facilitate access and servicing. In any case, archive staff should be available to offer advice to potential donors on these matters.

Whether it is based on published statement or informal practice, an archive's acquisition policy delineates the kinds and formats of folklore it will acquire. The name itself may serve to define this policy, at least to the outsider. As I have urged before, both the name and purpose of an archive should avoid an implicit or explicit restrictive acquisition policy. For example, on too many occasions I found folklorists offering to edit spoken-word materials from their collections before donating them to the Library of Congress folk archive because of its antiquated, restrictive name, "Archive of Folk Song." Actually, editing of any sort should be avoided for it destroys contextual indicators which will be useful in the future. Ideally, an archive should acquire eclectically, rather than restrictively. As any long-time archivist will tell you, the "extraneous" material expunged from an early collection may be just what a current researcher is looking for.

Once a collection has been acquired, it must be processed and at least preliminarily catalogued before it can be considered more than dead storage. The first step in processing will be the identification of the collection and initiation of a simple processing log with such information as title of collection, when received, source, and kind of acquisition. The collection is then sorted into types of material (tapes, manuscripts, slides, etc.), maintaining maximum integrity within each type. Concordance sheets (for duplication projects) and general lists of contents should be made, if not supplied with the acquisition.

Preliminary cataloguing will begin with the title and brief description of the collection. An accession number is supplied to the collection; this number together with internal identifiers will serve to specify each page, recording, slide, and so on within the collection for cataloguing and retrieval purposes. In my judgment, numbering should be as simple as possible and avoid the prefixes, suffixes, and additional alpha-numeric codes which frequently serve to identify year or place of collection, personal or organizational names, and the like.

Once a collection has been logged, identified, and numbered, one or more cards are prepared indicating its identification number(s) and name, size of collection, and types of material (e.g., 3 cylinders, 5 12″ discs, 14 pp manuscripts, 16 slides, 10 5″ DT tapes at 7.5 ips), brief statement of contents (including names of principal collectors, locations, sponsoring institutions, genres, ethnic and language groups, informants), date of collection, date of accessioning, and type of acquisition.

After the basic collection card(s) is established, copies can be filed in (1) a shelflist (numerical file) and (2) one or more alphabetical card files by personal, place, and organizational names, ethnic and language groups, and genres. Vertical files

containing logs, concordances, fieldnotes, correspondence, and internal paperwork can then be filed by collection number. Duplicates of these lists and notes can
also be placed in a public service file for reader use, to avoid wear and tear on the
originals.

The more detailed a catalogue is, of course, the more accessible is the collection.
If time and staff permit, an item by item catalogue is extremely useful for many
types of research and has been a hallmark of European archives and the Archive of
Folk Culture in its earlier years. Item catalogues and indexes by geographical
locations, informants, title, genre, and such specialized classification schemes as
tale types and motifs still are extremely useful. There is presently a move afoot
among some folklore archivists at the Library of Congress and elsewhere to seek a
unified automated cataloguing system for folklore archives, with accompanying
classification schemes for all genres. Though it would be many years before such a
project saw fruition, it does signal the willingness to address the pressing problem
which most collectors face in dealing with their materials in a useful fashion. A few
specialized facilities have already embarked on modest computerized projects, but
their products may be of limited use to others and incompatible with each other.
Short of an already available comprehensive cataloguing scheme, archives can
certainly serve themselves and their clientele with a variety of item catalogues,
indexes, and finding aids based on existing folklore and related classification
schemes and local needs. Research projects by students and interns can locate and
index examples of certain genres, occupations, informants, and the like. Regional
archives may stress geographical location of collection items, while a folksong
archive might develop a title and first line index.

Although the use of folklore archives is treated elsewhere in this volume, I should
point out that from my experience, such collections are underused, and their use is
generally not encouraged. In spite of constraints of staff and time, archives should
provide at least minimal services to a variety of clientele, not just to folklorists and
their academic kin. With increasing demands for authentic folklore data from
authors, educators, presenters, and descendants of informants, the archive must be
prepared to make its materials available by a variety of means, including in-person
assistance (possibly by appointment), telephone responses, and correspondence.
The archive may have to charge for certain services, especially lengthy searches and
duplication. One way to ease the burden on archive staff would be to provide a list
of local persons who are familiar with the archive and are available for a fee to assist
individual researchers who cannot visit the plant.

A variety of specific factors will benefit archive users, including a knowledgeable
staff, adequate space and equipment, inquiry forms and worksheets for users to
delineate their needs, indexes and catalogues, working public files of lists and notes
which document the collections, service copies of collections and parts thereof
(particularly those which are frequently used and/or pose a preservation problem),
published guides to the collections and procedures, and a working reference
library. With these factors in operation, and willing staff with the ability to help
refine the needs of users, an archive can make a substantial contribution to the
researches of many users.

An archive's desire to serve the public and academic researcher will be tempered
by the need to restrict certain portions of collections. Such constraints may be
necessitated by deterioration of the collections, temporary provisions placed by
donors and informants, copyright protection of specific songs of recent prove-

nience, concern for "sensitive" materials (describing clandestine activities or containing slanderous remarks), and protection of "professional" informants (those who make all or part of their livelihood from performing).

Dealing with these problems can be simplified by the use of simple "release" or agreement forms which can be signed by informant and collector or archive, and which stress the cultural value of the material, while allowing for in-house servicing and duplication for personal research use and, if possible, scholarly nonprofit publication. In addition, it is also necessary to have a form in which a user agrees to make no further copies, to engender no monetary gain, and to otherwise assume responsibility for the use of the material. Although the imposing of restrictions on a collection can have negative connotations for the archivist and potential researcher, it is still possible and quite necessary to maintain a positive stance in handling these matters. In other words, access to restricted collections and the use of material for publication and sale are indeed possible, provided the requisite permissions are obtained.

Given staff and funds, the archive can play an active role in disseminating its holdings, through the publication of catalogues, indexes, and collectanea, in newspaper columns, journal articles, monographs, and sound recordings. Broadcasts and lectures are additional ways to promulgate archival information and solicit material. The archive can be utilized as a site for the training of interns and students in archival techniques. Many academic archives utilize student assistants (generally without archival training), but a few offer course units on archiving. The Library of Congress has had singular success with its intern program, giving students from many colleges and universities the folklore archival experience they desire.

As an archive is developing, it can share its experience with similar facilities through the Archiving Section of the American Folklore Society (AFS) and its newsletter,[2] archiving panels at AFS and regional meetings, and by exchange of published or in-house procedures and forms. A budding archive should at least make its presence known to the Archiving Section, as well as to the folk archive at the Library of Congress, which maintains files on most facilities and publishes directories and other aids on the subject.[3]

The Library of Congress has also been actively supportive of regional and specialized archives throughout the country, and in many cases has urged the exchange of materials between regional archives and the national collection. The reasons are twofold: to assure strong holdings in the regions themselves while maintaining a broad representation from all regions in the national folk archive, and to assure preservation of important materials, particularly in cases where regional facilities lack a preservation component.

To conclude with my original admonition: as fieldwork is a folklorist's basic tool, so is archiving, and a properly planned and operative folklore archive can be a useful and necessary adjunct to any folklore research.

NOTES

1. See especially various publications available from the American Library Association, 50 East Huron Street, Chicago, IL 60611; Association for Recorded

Sound Collections, P.O. Box 1643, Manassas, VA 22110; and Society of American Archivists, 330 South Wells Street, Chicago, IL 60606.

2. C/o Professor Richard Thill, UNO Folklore Archive, University of Nebraska at Omaha, Omaha, NE 68182.

3. Available lists include a directory of folklore archives and bibliographies on archiving, computers, and copyright. Requests for these and an inventory of other aids can be addressed to Archive of Folk Culture, Library of Congress, Washington, D.C. 20540.

Ormond H. Loomis

Organizing a Folklore Museum

Museums deal primarily with objects. They exist to care for and display tangible products of culture and of nature. The museum setting has specific public appeal because many people learn more from a three-dimensional exhibit than from a verbal description. For them seeing, and if possible, touching, smelling, tasting, and hearing, imparts understanding. When the object is a manifestation of traditional knowledge, as in the case of the folk artifact, it belongs in the folk museum, which exists to preserve craft processes, reconstruct cultural environments, and accentuate the humble, perhaps otherwise inconspicuous elements characteristic of regional life.

A folk musuem differs from other museums in its attention to the common man and its comparative approach in the interpretation of regional cultures. Originally the folk museum was intended for the study of peasant societies, to illustrate and preserve preindustrial ways of life. Beginning with Skansen, founded in 1891, the first folk museums were Scandinavian open-air facilities which expanded upon the period room exhibit technique to collect, restore, and display distinctive buildings and their entire contents. As this concept was exported, it was redefined and reapplied. In the United States, it has been combined with historical restoration, historic site interpretation, and local historiography to the point that folk character is often overlooked in American open-air museums.[1]

Although modern folk museums take a variety of forms, they usually divide into the holistic and specific. Holistic folk museums rely primarily on open-air exhibits for as complete a representation of the cultures treated as possible, whereas the specific emphasize particular facets of cultural expression. The Museum of International Folk Art in Santa Fe, New Mexico, is an example of the specific type. It deals only with decorative arts from non-elite traditions. A survey of holistic museums indicates that they limit themselves, too, according to their defined aims. Old Sturbridge Village near Sturbridge, Massachusetts, specializes in one regional culture portrayed at a particular historical time—rural, Yankee, New England at the beginning of industrialization. Old World Wisconsin in Eagle interprets several traditions within a broader temporal and geographic frame—the major ethnic groups which settled the state during the period from white settlement to the early twentieth century. Living Historical Farms in Des Moines, Iowa, presents an occcupational tradition spanning centuries—midwestern farming from the pioneers to a projected farm of the future.

Certain aims and problems are inherent in all museum work. In addition to the handling and exhibition of objects, each museum must concern itself with incorporation, funding, staffing, and housing, activities common to all formal organizations but shaped in this case by the peculiarities of museums. Recently, the study of museums has evolved into an area called museum science, or museology, a young field that has produced a substantial body of useful knowledge for those who want to establish a folk museum.

Throughout the history of museums, collection usually precedes creation. Most people seem to have a bit of the packrat in their nature, and museums frequently result from the institutionalization of their urge to amass. But establishing a museum involves more than building a collection of artifacts. In a museum artifacts must be cared for and made accessible to the public, and this kind of collection management generally exceeds what a collector can provide. Even assuming that a private collection can be well maintained and displayed, no real guarantee exists that heirs will continue these practices. The essential step in the creation of a museum, then, is the organization of a responsible group which will direct and support the acquisition and use of objects.

One of the best examples of the evolution of a museum can be found in the case of Old Sturbridge Village. This major folk museum grew out of the collections of two brothers, Albert B. and Joel Cheney Wells. According to the Wells' family history, A. B. began collecting in about 1926. He was on vacation in Vermont, and when rain prevented his scheduled golf game, his partner suggested they go antique hunting. Delighted by what he found, Albert developed a lasting fascination with the artifacts of everyday life: farm tools, common house furnishings, and the equipment and products of small industries. At about the same time, Joel Cheney formed an interest in clocks and paperweights, and began collecting them. Within less than ten years the collections were becoming a problem, especially for A. B. who was being squeezed out of his home by his treasures. He is said to have remarked that just inventorying the objects—required for his insurance—would take more than three years of full-time work.

The brothers founded the Wells Historical Museum in November of 1935, with A. B. as president. Soon help was employed to arrange, group, and describe objects. Space continued to be a problem, however, and George Burnham Wells, A. B.'s son, proposed developing a village site to house the museum. His idea led to the organization of the Quinabaug Village Corporation in 1938. It was this Village which, with the labor of architects, curators, two directors, and many others, plus organizational restructuring and redefinition, finally opened to the public in 1946 as Old Sturbridge Village, twenty years after the brothers began collecting and more than ten years after they decided to start a museum.[2]

Every museum has financial worries, so it is prudent to give thought to finances before starting out. Admission fees rarely cover expenses. The costs of housing and exhibiting objects can be sizeable, and to them one must add expenses incurred in the operation of any agency—office space and supplies, utilities, and a paid staff. Over time, pressures build to allocate money for research, conservation, security, lectures, and other professional refinements. Without the prospect of minimal financial support, organizing will prove futile. In the budget of a budding museum, membership fees, small donations, and in-kind goods and services figure significantly. Established museums are eligible for grants to support specific projects ranging from conservation to publication. Seasoned administrators, however, know that large donations constitute the most reliable source of income, and give the best return on time invested.

While community festivals and other evidences of a ground swell of regional pride indicate the potential for a folk museum, community organization is required for the museum to become a reality. In addition to interested individuals, existing groups such as ethnic heritage societies, labor organizations, local historical agencies, craft guilds, and businesses interested in tourism may lend support. If the idea is well received and commitment appears strong, the project can be formalized. This step requires the pooling of administrative ability, secretarial skills, legal advice, and business acumen. The most important element in the formation of a folk museum, however, is the judgment of a folklorist, who can emphasize folkloric themes and offer guidance based on knowledge of the successes and failures at other museums. This individual will also prove effective in explaining the project both to the public and to professionals.

Serious museums are set up with a written mandate or charter either as a nonprofit corporation or as an extension of such an organization. Incorporation varies slightly according to state law or sponsor's rules. The process is critical but not complicated. Museum organizers frequently debate bylaws, the choice of a name, and similar details, but these are commonplace matters. The statement of a museum's goals and purposes, on the other hand, explains its aims, defining it for all, and deserves lengthy consideration. Often during the formulative stage, the notion arises that a broad statement of purpose is best because it will allow flexibility and growth. The degree of truth in this idea must be weighed against the latitude for interpretation present in even the narrowest statement. Mystic Seaport, for instance, exists to preserve "our maritime heritage."[3] Limited though it sounds, this purpose required further qualification—concentration on the maritime heritage of New England—to make it operational. Despite its restrictions this museum, with extensive exhibit halls, an open-air village, numerous ships, and a ship restoration program, ranks as one of the largest folk museums in the United States. When drafting the charter it is important to remember that for accreditation, the museum is defined as "an organized and permanent non-profit institution, essentially educational or aesthetic in purpose, with professional staff, which owns and utilizes tangible objects, cares for them, and exhibits them to the public on some regular schedule."[4]

Staffing is a decisive factor in creating an effective museum. Over the phone, in guided tours, through exhibits, with prospective donors, the staff communicates what the museum is. They give the museum its personality. That roughly sixty-six to seventy-five percent of the budgets of established museums goes to salaries indicates the magnitude of the staff's contribution. Organization should be along clear, reasonable lines of authority, and fair, businesslike personnel practices should be established. The background of employees is equally important. With the development of museology as an area of study, it is now possible to find professionals with varying levels of experience and training to fill more responsible jobs, and in a folk museum, positions of leadership must be filled by people trained in both museology and folkloristics. Volunteers are a mixed blessing. While the value of their labor cannot be ignored, this labor has its costs. Their unbridled enthusiasm must be bridled, or at least supervised, and often the cost of supervision exceeds the value of the work or the generous spirit in which it is offered.

Even the smallest museum needs at least one employee to open display rooms at regular hours and provide information. Doing more than this business requires a larger staff. Many small museums function with only a secretary and a director. The board, or trustees, choose the director to represent them in running the museum. They give this individual the responsibility and authority to implement the policies and achieve the goals of the organization. For a small folk musuem, a generalist with training in folklore makes the best director, one who can put together exhibits, catalog artifacts, coordinate volunteers, and supervise an office. As a museum grows, the board will add positions for a general assistant and, if not provided by a parent organization, maintenance. Later, they may also hire a professional, traditionally called a curator, to manage collections. It is customary, in time, to add other professionals at the curatorial level, one to develop educational programs, another to produce exhibits. Further expansion creates a demand for a host of assistants and for specialists in business, conservation, public relations, registration, security, tours, and volunteer liaison.

Although museums sometimes begin in converted houses and civic buildings, these structures provide no more than a temporary home. Nor do open-air exhibit areas, if these are part of the folk museum, suit the noninterpretive agency business. The basic units of a museum building consist of exhibit halls, storage rooms, administrative offices, and restrooms, each designed with such factors as visitor access, security, climate control, and future expansion in mind. Growing museums always need extra exhibit, storage, and office areas. Facilities for technical museum work—audiovisual studio, conservation laboratory, graphics studio, library, and archive, shipping area and woodworking shop—and those for public use— auditorium, craft workroom, meeting room, snack shop, and souvenir shop—seem like amenities to budget-concious planners, but they greatly enhance the potential for service.

Educational Possibilities

Museums reach the public through educational programs. They have the same instructional methods available as exist for other educational institutions, and must plan to present coherent programs just as schools plan curricula. Publications, lectures, and workshops serve a museum well when it functions, as the folk museum often does, in the role of cultural center. Nevertheless, exhibits constitute the greatest, most distinctive educational asset of the museum.

Since the 1930s, exhibit creators, guided by the concept of thematic focus, have sought to relate all displays and objects in an exhibit to a unifying theme.[5] Accordingly, they achieve exegesis by means of labels written in outline form— topic headings in capitals, elaboration in lower case—and illustrate points with representative artifacts. The designers, using graphics to add emphasis and arranging furniture to subtly direct traffic, take care to ensure that visitors can appreciate the objects displayed. Before this approach gained popularity, displays usually consisted of shelves and cases strewn with objects with an occasional label giving a name or bit of an explanation. At best, exhibitors laid out specimens in a logical order to form a three-dimensional catalogue of a museum's better collections. Modern museums contain both types of exhibits, the thematic, and what is sometimes called the open storage, and these provide options for the folk museum with indoor galleries.

Folk museums pioneered the open-air exhibit mode. Through it a folk museum capitalizes on its most unique educational opportunity. Open-air exhibits consist of re-creations of entire cultural environments, usually homes, outbuildings, and small industries, built and furnished with a high percentage of authentic artifacts. Visitors who encounter these habitats are confronted with powerful comparisons between their own culture and those portrayed, and can see the shaping influences of geography and tradition. One seldom sees labels and other impersonal aids in this kind of exhibit because they would not have been found in the original site.

Decisions must be made regarding the best interpretive format for exhibits. Guided tours led by a trained guide or docent work well for both indoor and outdoor exhibits. Unfortunately, assembling and guiding groups not only requires considerable coordination, but the nature of groups limits the amount of information docents can relate about each point of interest. Interpreters stationed at critical points to explain exhibits as visitors pass by offer a popular alternative, especially at open-air museums. These guides frequently double as craftsmen or performers demonstrating traditional arts. As a third possibility, the museum's administration might utilize guidebooks and small portable tapes. Although these entail a high initial production cost, they compare favorably over time with a guide's salary; and more importantly, they provide a more controlled and authoritative source of information.[6]

The folk museum must step beyond exhibits to satisfy those with an active interest in folklife. Lectures, films, and performances can present broad topics, and expand on ideas glossed over in exhibits. Workshops and excursions, on the other hand, are suited to subjects that require personal instruction, since these activities necessarily limit participation. Publicity as well as an established schedule of related events helps remind the public of museum programs. Finally, major publications and recordings provide references which can be enjoyed in lieu of a museum visit.

Curatorial Work

In putting objects to a primarily educational purpose, museums use them in a way other than that originally intended. A nineteenth-century weaver never expected the coverlet he made for his granddaughter to be hung under bright lights on a museum wall where hundreds of tourists could examine it daily. To guarantee the educational value of an item, to ensure that coverlets and all other artifacts in a museum's collection do not become lost, damaged, stolen, or separated from their histories, the museum employees devote great effort to collection management.

Difficulties arise in limiting collecting. At times, people seem too eager to donate objects. Their reasons range from wanting a tax deduction to seeking to contribute to the education and enjoyment of others. But collections increase relentlessly unless checked, and as a result, every museum must establish guidelines for responsible collecting. It is not only ethically questionable for a museum to accept artifacts it will not use, but when storage space dwindles, thoughtless collecting will complicate acceptance of genuinely desirable items. Several ragged, unexhibitable coverlets occupy more room and require more attention than a few well preserved ones. For each prospective addition, thought must be given to whether the item relates to the aims of the museum, can be housed properly, fits potential exhibit plans, and justifies a donor's sacrifice. To avoid problems, donors must be advised of the intended uses of their gifts, and have them acknowledge full museum ownership in writing.

A donation or a purchase accepted into a museum, called an accession, must be registered, item by item, in a permanent log. Ideally, each item receives a unique registration number as soon after it enters the collection as possible. Perhaps a weaver's granddaughter presents her grandfather's loom and a coverlet he made. If she were the fifty-sixth donor to the museum in 1982, a registrar might assign numbers such as 82–56–1 to the loom, and 82–56–2 to the coverlet. Marked on the items and entered in the log next to a brief description, the numbers afford precise identification and make it possible to trace each object to its source. Professionals recommend that museum markings should be applied in a way which permits complete, undetectable removal. Documents regarding the items and their origin go into a file. Finally, a staff member distributes the accession within the museum and notes its disposition.[7]

Folk museums often generate models and reproductions of authentic artifacts either to use in presentations or as the result of demonstrations. Unless created by legitimate interpreters steeped in the folk aesthetic of a traditional culture there is no need to accession these new objects. Devise some means, however, to distinguish them from originals. To this end, curators at some folk museums designate copies with a permanent museum mark that serves as a trade mark as well as a registration symbol.

Cataloguing and registration are separate processes. Cataloguers accurately identify every object and place it within the system of categories and subcategories used to order collections.[8] In doing so, they commonly add a second, not necessarily unique, number to an object to indicate relationship to the full museum collection, for example, BL-cl-4, to designate a coverlet (Bed Linens—coverlet—fourth specimen in that category). A museum reproduction would be catalogued in a way that distinguishes it from genuine artifacts, e.g., BL-cl-rpro. As they work, cataloguers fill out a card for each item, naming it and giving a description, measurements, a sketch or photo, and significant background data. Later, after an object is stored, the card, placed in a separate file, can lead people to the object in the same way that a library catalogue card leads people to books. Well-organized storage in itself provides access to topical categories of the museum's collections, but it does not eliminate the need for cataloguing.

Questions frequently arise about cultural history and context for which no ready answer exists. A restorer may want to know the original color of a totem pole. An exhibit planner may want to know the placement of buildings, while an interpreter may want to know exactly how wool was dyed. The curatorial section usually assumes major research efforts since a certain amount of research goes into cataloguing, and accession records are commonly housed in this section. Moreover, the curators of collections usually have more experience and skill with research than other members of the museum staff.

Objects, the starting point for the museum, inevitably break, either as a result of accident or natural decay. Cautious handling, controlled climate storage, and other measures can lessen the amount of damage, but some destruction is unavoidable. When treatment is needed, it should be performed by a conservator. Strictly speaking, conservation tries only to arrest the rapid deterioration of objects. With their knowledge of basic materials and skills at treatment, conservators may also do types of preservation and restoration. They keep detailed notes of each step so that the original condition of an object and the work done can be recalled in case it must be reversed. Unfortunately, while reversibility is a goal in conservation, total reversibility is seldom possible, and unless significant improvement is expected, the best treatment is no treatment.[9]

Conclusion

In setting up a folk museum, problems arise that require specific solutions rather than general advice, but a problem that seems peculiar to one museum might well have been solved by another. Museum professionals willingly share their experiences with those who ask for help, and folklorists at national and regional folklife centers make it their job to assist budding folk museum groups. Despite its frustrations the labor of organization bestows abundant rewards, most important of which are the saving and sharing of the ways of life honored by the museum.

NOTES

1. For more background on folk museums see: Howard Wight Marshall, "Folklife and the Rise of the American Folk Museums," *Journal of American Folklore* 90 (1977): 391–413; and Don Yoder, "The Folklife Studies Movement," *Pennsylvania Folklife* 13 (1963): 43–56.

2. The history of Old Sturbridge Village must be pieced from a variety of sources. See Catherine Fennelly, *Life in an Old New England Country Village* (Sturbridge, Mass.: Old Sturbridge Village, 1969), pp. 4–12; Horace M. Mann, "Communication," *The Chronicle of the Early American Industries Association* 2 (1937): 8; "Quinabaug Village," *The Chronicle of the Early American Industries Association* 2 (1938): 46; "Two Brothers and Their Hobby," *New-England Galaxy* 7 (1966): 56–64; Charles Van Ravenswaay, *The Story of Old Sturbridge Village* (New York: Newcomer Society in North America, 1964), pp. 18–20; Alexander J. Wall, "A Village Anniversary," *New-England Galaxy* 8 (1967): 53–56; and Malcolm Watkins, "Old Sturbridge Village," *The Chronicle of Early American Industries* 3 (1946): 77.

3. Mystic Seaport, *Guide* (Mystic, Conn.: Mystic Seaport, Inc., 1976), p. 5.

4. Marilyn Hicks Fitzgerald, *Museum Accreditation: Professional Standards* (Washington, D.C.: American Association of Museums, 1973), p. 8.

5. See Neil Harris, "Museums, Merchandising, and Popular Taste: The Struggle for Influence," in *Material Culture and the Study of American Life*, ed. Ian M. G. Quimby (New York: W. W. Norton for the Henry Francis du Pont Winterthur Museum, 1978), pp. 140–74; and Armeta Neal, *Exhibits for the Small Museum* (Nashville: The American Association for State and Local History, 1976).

6. On methods of interpretation see: William T. Alderson and Shirley Payne Low, *Interpretation of Historical Sites* (Nashville: The American Association for State and Local History, 1975); Willard B. Moore, "Folklife Museums: Resource Sites for Teaching," *Indiana English Journal* 11 (1976–77): 3–10; and Freeman Tilden, *Interpreting Our Heritage* (Chapel Hill: The University of North Carolina Press, 1967).

7. The standard reference work is Dorothy H. Dudley and Irma Bezold, *Museum Registration Methods* (Washington, D.C.: The American Association of Museums, 1958).

8. For suggestions see: Robert G. Chenall, *Nomenclature for Museum Cataloging* (Nashville: The American Association for State and Local History, 1976); John W. Y. Higgs, *Folk Life Collection and Classification*, Handbook for Curators, Part C: Permanent Collections, Archaeology and Ethnology, Section 6 (London: Museums Association, 1963); and Holger Rasmussen, "Classification Systems of European Ethnological Material," *Ethnologia Europaea* 4 (1970): 73–77.

9. Per E. Guldbeck, *The Care of Historical Collections: A Conservation Handbook for the Nonspecialist* (Nashville: The American Association for State and Local History, 1972).

George Carey

Filming the Folk

Not long ago, I received a phone call from an educational film outfit in Virginia soliciting my help with a project they had in mind. The pleasant-sounding woman I talked with admitted with some embarrassment that their organization had recently received the outrageous sum of three hundred and thirty thousand dollars from HEW and the Office of Education to mount a one-half-hour pilot film on storytelling. She spoke at length about their aspirations and ideas, some of which would have made a seasoned folklorist blanch. She mentioned, for instance, the possibility of having a traditional raconteur tell a tale while a group of actors, in a kind of montage, pantomimed the story in the background. At that point it took a lot of diplomacy not to gag into the receiver. But as she rattled on, my dilemma became more and more acute. Either I could dismiss the whole thing as a bad dream which, God willing, would never reach the screen, or I could agree to help these people nurture a film which media and audiences, and also folklorists, would find palatable.

It strikes me that folklorists will face this same little scene and its attendant perplexity with increasing frequency over the next decade. Who among us is not aware of the incredible success of the Foxfire project or the recent *Roots* phenomenon as examples of the broadly based appeal folklore commands? And when you add to that the increase in grant funds over the years, I believe we are going to see more professional folklorists hustled out of their ivied cloisters to counsel in the slick world of media. From my perspective, the onus of this responsibility is one a folklorist should not take lightly or unadvisedly. Dealing with media people can be tricky business. My own viewpoint has been roughly shaped by experience, by assisting the public broadcasting system in producing a one-hour documentary entitled "The Folk Way." But let me begin at the beginning.

A million years ago, back in 1974, I held the post of Maryland State Folklorist, a position which fell under the auspices of the Maryland Arts Council. During my tenure there, the National Endowment for the Arts informed us that if we wished to apply, we were eligible for $25,000 to produce a film on some aspect of Maryland's folk culture. Anyone who has dealt with the NEA knows that they relinquish very little money without a dollar-for-dollar match from another organization. When we approached the Maryland Center for Public Broadcasting, they agreed to make the film and match the grant in what, around eleemosynary circles, is called "in-kind services." That meant they would provide the film crew, the transportation, the equipment, and the NEA funds would go for whatever else was necessary to mount such a project.

The NEA awarded the grant in February 1975. A month later I met with part of the film crew for the first time to map out our strategy. The Endowment placed few stipulations on us; they asked only that we deliver a final copy of the film to them within a year and that we restrict the subject matter to Maryland folklore or folklife. They cared little whether we did a fifteen-minute spot on fence building or a two-hour drama on a folk singer.

With those present at that initial encounter—Mike Styer, the producer, Steve Dubin, the director, and Chris Pogelak, the researcher/writer—I argued for a film that depicted Maryland's cultural diversity (its maritime and mountain elements, its agricultural traditions, its ethnicity) and I furnished a list of fifteen prospective individuals and groups to scout for their potential. It was clear from the start that, with the exception of Dubin, who had taken a ballad course of mine at the University of Maryland years before, no one at the meeting had anything but the usual misconceptions about folklore.

But if this media team knew little about my profession, I understood less about theirs. Mine, I confess, is a cultivated ignorance. I do not like and seldom watch TV, even public broadcasting which, I am told, carries excellent fare. Yet looking back, I would have benefited from a few hours spent watching public television to discover what sort of audience the network addresses in the majority of its features. When we came to edit the film, I found myself capitulating on certain issues simply because I had no rebuttal to their argument that this was not a film for folklorists but for public television viewers.

Three weeks after that initial meeting our scouting began. The four of us (a skeletal crew that would later swell to eight when filming started) visited twelve potential subjects "on location." Of these we filmed nine and used seven. We shot twenty-two hours of film for the one hour seen and we recorded close to forty hours of audiotape. As televised, the film showed short vignettes of a storyteller, a family of folksingers, a gunsmith, a Baltimore screen painter, a gathering of Mennonite quilters, a black gospel group, and a mountain couple.

Early on it was decided that I would participate in the film as an interpreter/ interviewer, briefly introducing each segment and, when feasible, talking with informants. The director, after witnessing my interview style during the scouts, felt that the film could show not only what the folk did, but how the folklorist found out what they did. Thus I became, as it were, a kind of poor man's Charles Kuralt.

An inexperienced one, at best. Kuralt over the years has developed a polished style that renders many of his media pieces downright moving. What I discovered right away was that interviewing before a television camera has little in common with conversing intimately in an informant's living room while the tape recorder turns. For one thing, there is absolutely no privacy. Seven crew members sit staring at you behind the glare of the lights. Suddenly a voice announces, "Roll sound, roll camera," then someone steps between you and the camera with one of those wooden snappers and cracks it. (I always thought those things were some sort of Hollywood cliché, but I later learned that they are the indispensable means of synchronizing sight and sound.) The interview begins.

Under the circumstances, it was difficult to rally much composure, though I continually marvelled at how unintimidated the informants seemed by the camera's presence. Since I constantly had to be thinking up my next question while a participant talked, instead of listening to their answers, the interviews seen in their raw form resembled essays in *non sequitur*. But many a halting scenario, I discovered, can be transformed miraculously on the cutting room floor, the place where ninety percent of the magic in this business takes place. Television, like film, has often been referred to as deceit masquerading as art. The Russian director Eisenstein explained it marvelously with a simple example. He said: "You go to Leningrad, and you film a girl taking a bath, if you're lucky. You then go to Moscow, and you film a keyhole; and then you splice the film together and the people think they're looking through a keyhole at a girl taking a bath."

If our deceit was not at all that blatant, it did tamper with reality. I quickly learned that directors dabble with delusion in the name of continuity and artistic impression. And our endeavor required this delusion from time to time simply because so many things occurred during the shoots that curtailed naturalness. Throughout the filming we worked with a single camera, and again and again the director called for retakes so that he might attain a different angle. This repetition proved a particular hardship for the singers, who had to repeat their songs as many as three times. On one occasion a participant's ignorance of sound recording methods almost aborted an entire sequence.

While arranging the shoot on the Crisfield waterfront, a bearded young sound crew member approached one of the old watermen and asked him to undo his trousers so that he might drop a cord down his pants leg. For a split second I feared for that young man's welfare when I saw the look he got, but nothing untoward occurred and they managed to get their man "wired for sound."

Obviously, some interviews proceeded more smoothly than others. The story-teller, Captain Alex Kellam, I knew well, and had heard his repertoire of tales countless times. I recognized his flair for the dramatic and understood how to draw it out. Consequently, that segment proved to be one of the best. By contrast, the screen painter, Richard Octivek, spoke little, and when he did it was in a high-pitched voice that recorded poorly. Yet with some astounding sorcery in the cutting room, we salvaged enough footage to include him. Edna and Paul Lewis, the mountain couple, provided arresting diversity: he terrified of being filmed, but very articulate when on camera; she constantly at ease and voluble and more than anxious to share her wisdom and folkways with anyone, on or off camera. One minor question and Edna could fill a role of tape.

We shot our last sequence in December. That left three months to edit the raw material into a one-hour production. I did not view the film until it had been shorn to a two-hour "rough cut." Generally, I liked what I saw, yet I was appalled by how much "good stuff" had been deleted. It was at this point that I faced a very rude awakening. I discovered that when retakes are impossible technical faults dictate what can and can't be used. What seems a feisty scene on location gets scrapped because the lighting "just wouldn't show up well on the home screen." Other poignant takes which sound fine to my untutored ear get trashed because "they won't broadcast well." Audio defects especially shaped much of our folksong presentations. Ola Belle Reed and her family, for instance, sang a wide variety of songs for us, but because of one sound aberration or another, we could use only her religious music, leaving the viewer with a distorted impression.

From the very beginning, we all agreed that the film's overriding theme should stress the continuity of tradition, but when we began to scrutinize isolated sections during the editing, we realized that this theme might be illustrated in several ways with different participants. Keith Castell, for one, could just as well have been filmed as a tall tale teller or a hunter steeped in the traditional lore of the western Maryland turkey shoot than as the gunsmith we depicted. Likewise, Edna Lewis might easily have been seen in detail as a traditional cook, rug hooker, quilter, herbal practitioner, or midwife, but we chose to show her as a self-sufficient woman whose uncluttered philosophy of life embraced the joys of simple living. Given the time and our chosen format of a number of short vignettes, we were unable to do what Bill Ferris has achieved so effectively in his films, namely, set the folk traditions against the baggage of day-to-day living. By showing only the exotic folk aspects as we did, the film led the audience to view these traditions as dominant in the informant's life when in fact they were sometimes insignificant.

When PBS aired the film locally in the spring of 1976, it received a rave review in the Baltimore *Sun*. Their TV critic, Bill Carter, called it "clean, professional and excellent—well above the standard for a locally based TV show" and then, citing what folklorists would later skewer as the romantic flaw in the film, Carter labelled the production "a kind of country hymn to the simple joys of simple living." This response, plus the fact that PBS in Washington didn't have to pay a nickel to use the film, destined its being aired nationally October 5, 1976. At the eight-to-nine time slot that night the TV viewer could sample either "Tony Orlando and Dawn," "Happy Days," "Laverne and Shirley," Merv Griffin, or "The Folk Way." To scare up an audience, I had a few friends over to the house to watch.

Since that evening I have shown and discussed the film with a succession of people. Most of them, I would say, identified with the "real' "down to earth" "ordinary" folk in the show. As one girl put it, "They're the kind you might see anywhere if you took the time to look." Folklore students were quick to uncover the weaknesses in our format. One black graduate student at Indiana University observed that the film lacked any participant under forty-five and that the emphasis was overbearingly rural. Even in the single urban segment, he pointed out, the Baltimore screen painter paints bucolic scenes. Others found the costume of the gunsmith objectionable, and rightly so. He appears garbed as a latter day Daniel Boone with leather clothing and coonskin cap. Ironically, those are the garments he frequently wears while working in his gunshop, but tell that to a folklorist.

Many viewers found the quilting scene disturbingly inaudible. When editing that footage back in Baltimore, we once more faced a technical problem. Though the camera work excelled, the whole sound track seemed muddled, in effect, a low indecipherable female chatter throughout. Our choice was obvious: either drop the entire section or play it *cinéma vérité*, which we did, assuming the sensitive person would recognize that this was what an actual quilting bee must be like.

One arresting comment came from, of all people, the then newly appointed director of the Arts Council. He confided he needed more proof that the storytelling session where Captain Kellam swaps yarns with other watermen on the liars' bench had not been staged. It both amused and puzzled me that this Brooklyn-reared man of the arts really thought we had sent down to central casting to secure the services of men like Alex Kellam and Dewey Landon and Steve Ward, all old residents of Chesapeake Bay whose banter and wit have spiced shoreside dialogues for generations.

Yet I must say, I reacted much more sensitively to the graduate student who inquired about the ethics of our enterprise. Had we, she wished to know, reimbursed any of the participants for their time? (We had—in funds commensurate with their salaries then or prior to retirement.) Had we thought about the matter of privacy? What, she persisted, had our intrusion done to the people and their traditions, given the insidious nature of media exposure? Had we perhaps taken something irretrievable from them? For these questions I had no easy answers. They were the very confusions that had haunted me since my earliest fieldwork, now simply magnified by television. It is only the fool as fieldworker who would not admit to an indulgence, however slight, in what we might call "cultural rip-off." And for any reasonable folklorist there is always a residue of guilt to allay in individual ways. Sometimes even the most well-intentioned designs backfire. A while ago folklorist Henry Glassie told me that he might send the proceeds from his book to his informants. Not long afterwards he discovered they had used the money to modernize their homes and thus destroy certain aspects of the traditional architecture he admired.

If I had no easy answers for that young graduate student, I certainly had things to confess. Yes, I admitted, as a deeply private man myself, I felt quite disturbed about encroaching on the lives of others even if I could justify my actions with the usual hackneyed reasons. Weren't we in fact preserving dying traditions? Weren't we educating the public about the subterreanean culture that lay beneath their line of sight? Still, I could tell her little about the subsequent effects of the film on the participants, though in fact some word had filtered back. According to producer Mike Styer, a week after the show was aired Richard Octivek called to say his screen painting business was booming. And by other word-of-mouth communication I heard that the annual Mennonite quilting bazaar in Westover had netted the church more money than ever.

The only participant I knew anything definite about was my longtime friend Alex Kellam. Because of the film he suddenly found himself thrust into the role of celebrity, coveted as a speaker by Rotary clubs and school groups, even lured to Washington to tell his yarns to the cronies of a Maryland congressman. But fortunately for Kellam, it is a role he thoroughly enjoys, one he has actually been rehearsing for years along the Crisfield waterfront. His recent remarks told me a lot: "George," he confided, the large sunburned hand on my shoulder, "you know, I didn't have any idea what I was going to do with myself when I retired; I didn't even know what this folklore thing was all about until you came along. But I'll tell you one thing, it sure has changed my life, and you're the man I'm grateful to."

And so the romantic folklorist rests his case. Some won, some lost, some undecided. Obviously, financial windfalls lead inevitably to change in folk tradition. Richard Octivek now paints for a larger clientele than his east Baltimore neighborhood, and for all I know the *Playboy* centerfold has replaced the mountain bungalow as subject matter for his screens. Nor is it hard to imagine that the traditional designs on the Mennonite quilts have given way to the dictates of wealthy ladies from Annapolis. The folk process may remain the same, but the folk product will never again be quite so pure. As for the effect on the traditions of the others, I cannot say; I never had the heart to go back and find out.

All this happened light years ago. In the interim, I have become somewhat of an aficionado of TV, probably because I am a little quicker on how it works. Though seldom realized, television has the potential to be, as Alistair Cooke has said, "an incomparable medium for touching people where they think and moving them where they feel . . . above all, a medium for entertaining instruction." Certainly I make no claims for "The Folk Way" as a match for "America," yet in our modest effort I think we did achieve a blend of enlightened entertainment. The constant rebroadcasting of the show attests to our success along those lines.

In my roles as folklorist/consultant there were admitted lapses. I see now that I should have been better informed about the media and how it works. I should have asked for a lot more money. Most of all, though, I should have been in on the editing from the start, not after twenty hours of raw footage had been discarded.

But all that is, of course, 20/20 hindsight, and the question that remains, one I get asked over and over, is, would I do it all again? All I can say is, when that lady from the Virginia film outfit made her proposal, would I help, chastened and wiser I told her: "Sure, count me in."

Richard Blaustein

Video in the Classroom and Community Outreach Projects

Portable video is still a very new medium and its potential for presenting folklore to students and the general public remains largely unexplored. Though an increasing number of professional folklorists and anthropologists have become interested in using video, no formalized methodology or set of guidelines for the novice to follow has yet emerged. While some folklorists are enthusiastic about the possibilities of video in their work, others have found it to be a temperamental and frustrating medium and have abandoned it in favor of simpler and more reliable types of equipment. Since portable video technology is new and rapidly developing, it is still far from being standardized or foolproof; the prospective user needs to be thoroughly aware of the quirks and limitations of any particular piece of equipment and make sure that it is properly handled and maintained. While most portable video recorders are almost deceptively easy to operate, they are nonetheless complicated, delicate devices with extremely low tolerance for rough treatment and haphazard maintenance. Bearing these precautions in mind, the beginner should not be discouraged from experimenting with what can be an exciting and effective teaching tool[1]—as long as it is treated with the care and respect it deserves.

The folklorist should consider using video in the classroom for a number of reasons, not the least of which is its convenience. Setting up a video deck and monitor is much less time-consuming and nerve-wracking than going through the rigamarole of threading film projectors, putting up screens, and pulling down shades. One can start and stop the videotape when necessary, instantly play back important sequences to emphasize major points, or even make notes on the blackboard while the tape is playing. These features make video a far more flexible classroom medium than film, much easier to integrate into lectures and discussions. As of yet there is no really satisfactory folklore videography to which the instructor can refer. Bill Ferris and Judy Peiser, *American Folklore Films & Videotapes: An Index*[2] includes only a limited and outdated selection of material from the Broadside Video Southern Appalachian Video Ethnography Series (SAVES) collection,[3] and the annual supplements they promised have yet to appear; a more comprehensive listing of folklore-related videotapes is to be found in *The Video Bluebook*,[4] included within an index of prerecorded videotapes dealing with a wide variety of scholarly and general subjects.

Though prerecorded videotapes (if they can be obtained) are valuable supplements to other types of classroom presentations, I personally feel that video is most effective when teachers and students make and show their own tapes. Using video in this way not only integrates student work with course material, but also serves to inspire beginning students to take an active interest in fieldwork as well as to build up a video library for use in subsequent classes. I experienced a particularly exciting illustration of the ability of video to bridge classroom and field experiences several years ago when one of my more enterprising students used portable video in studying a serpent-handling church in a nearby upper East Tennessee county. He showed his tapes in class, which inspired another student to arrange a showing for a group of local Protestant ministers of various denominations. Their responses and comments concerning the scriptural validity of the practice of serpent-handling were also videotaped. This project showed us how video could be used to generate a feedback process in which an initial recording elicits responses which are then incorporated into documentaries that now include several levels of information.[5]

More recently in a fieldwork class several students and I produced a videotape that documented the introduction of novice fieldworkers to the collection of folkloristic data through the video medium. The project involved the simultaneous use of two video systems, one to record and the other to play back. First the students viewed a tape of an elderly local farmer which I myself had recorded; their responses were videotaped by a graduate assistant. Then the students actually visited the farmer in his home, and their interaction with him was videotaped. Back in the classroom, they were able to see themselves in the field, which stimulated them to develop questions and research strategies for their next visit with him. After receiving instruction in the operation of the video equipment, they videotaped him once more, together with his family and neighbors, playing music, dancing, telling stories, and answering questions posed by the students. The students returned to the classroom where they reviewed their field tapes and discussed what they had learned from the experience. All the tapes, from classroom as well as field, were then edited into a thirty-minute program illustrating the highlights of this documenting process. (Though this resulted in an interesting documentary, I do not recommend it as an alternative to more conventional ways of teaching fieldwork methods. Assembling and testing the equipment each time proved to be extremely burdensome, even with the help of a graduate assistant, and in retrospect I feel that my students would have learned more had they been made to rely upon their own resources and initiative. Having students make their own tapes and then show them in class is much more effective and less artificial.)

Outside of the classroom, the ability of video to generate feedback can play an effective role in community enrichment and cultural consciousness-raising projects. For example, I began a study of the quilting tradition of a small East Tennessee farming community by showing a tape of a traditional weaver to members of a local women's club, then asking them to help produce a tape on their own quilting. Their response was enthusiastic, and they met with me to discuss the content of the program, following which several hours of videotape were shot, including life histories and recollections of changes that had affected the community's quilting tradition, as well as step-by-step documentation of the actual quilt-making process. This raw footage was then played back to the group and their responses and suggestions were incorporated into an edit outline. A thirty-minute tape was produced and shown back to them. While they were pleased with what they saw, it definitely seemed as though the process of being videotaped in itself attracted them every bit as much as the finished product. This project stimulated and increased their interest in quilting and they found themselves called upon to put on quilting displays at fairs and crafts festivals in the area.

The advent of portable video equipment and the burgeoning of cable television stations during the late sixties and early seventies sparked the development of community cable television projects in various parts of the United States. Fostered by then-existing local origination and public access policies established by the Federal Communications Commission, these projects, largely supported by federal and private grants, were based on the premise that this new technology would lead to decentralized, nonprofessional, community-oriented media systems capable of bypassing conventional mass communication systems and thereby negating their culturally homogenizing effects. While many of these community video projects have since fallen upon hard times, some did succeed in making it possible for members of various minority groups to learn how to operate video equipment and produce documentaries exploring their cultural roots. One such notable project is *Choctaw Swamp Cane Weaving*, an hour-long documentary produced by a young college-educated Choctaw woman named Dee Henry with the cooperation of the Communication Center in Louisville, Mississippi. Her tape featured an elderly member of the tribe who accompanied her demonstration of traditional basket making with comments and descriptions in the Choctaw language. Gwen Williams, a young black woman from Charleston, South Carolina, borrowed equipment from the Charleston Communication Center to record friends and family members at a home prayer and gospel-singing session, producing a tape which she called *Holy Ghost Prayer Meeting;* Phyllis Scalf, a native of upper East Tennessee and one of the original staff of Broadside Video in Johnson City, Tennessee, involved her family and neighbors in videotapes dealing with a variety of Southern Appalachian folk traditions, including a lively and detailed overview of the process of making apple butter. Though none of these tapes were of professional technical quality, they did show how the video documentary *process* could serve to foster an enhanced sense of cultural awareness.

Producing video programs coming up to professional broadcast standards is extremely time-consuming, technically demanding, and expensive, and thus far portable video has played a very limited role in presenting folklore and folklife to American television watchers. A documentary on Cajun Mardi Gras festivities in rural Louisiana produced by TVTV, an independent California-based video production company, was the first folklore-related program shot with portable video to reach a national viewing audience, but it was not favorably received by many folklorists because of the shallow and insensitive way in which the people and their customs were portrayed. At the present time, the only folklore-oriented videomakers to successfully break through the broadcast barriers have been Blaine Dunlap and Sol Korine, both of whom were actively involved in community and educational video projects before turning their sights toward public television. Working with the support of the National Endowment for the Arts and drawing upon the expertise of folklorist and country music historian Charles Wolfe, two of Dunlap and Korine's programs, *Showdown at the Hoedown*, an entertaining portrait of a fiddle contest held in Smithville, Tennessee, and *Raw Mash*, a demonstration of whiskey-making featuring folksinger and former moonshiner Hamper McBee, have appeared on PBS, and a third program dealing with the legendary Grand Ole Opry performer Uncle Dave Macon was broadcast nationally during 1980. (These programs are available on videocassette from the Center for Southern Folklore.)

At present Korine and Dunlap seemingly have little competition from other independent videomakers in the public television field,[6] and the community video idea, which was greeted with such enthusiasm during the early 1970s, has largely fallen by the wayside as a result of rising inflation and tightened budgets. Nevertheless, portable video has established a firm foothold in the home and educational marketplace. Despite inflation, costs are coming down and technical quality is dramatically improving, and it seems likely that we will see more folklorists using video in their research and classroom activities. It is encouraging to see that the Center for Southern Folklore has begun to distribute video programs on cassette; also, that the Archives of Appalachia at East Tennessee State University is currently working to set up a distribution system for the SAVES collection. Unfortunately, there has been all too little communication between producers of video documentaries dealing with folklore and folklife, and there is a great need for a really comprehensive folklore videography and tape exchange network to make prerecorded video material generally available for teaching and research purposes. Hopefully institutions like the Center for Southern Folklore and the American Folklife Center will take steps to meet this need in the not too distant future. Though a good deal of the glamor which surrounded portable video when it was first introduced in the late sixties has since evaporated, it has nonetheless demonstrated its value as a teaching and learning tool and will undoubtedly play an increasingly important role in presenting folklore to students and the general public.

NOTES

1. See Paul Hockings, "Educational Uses of Videotape," pp. 383–84; also Timothy Asch, "Using Film in Teaching Anthropology: One Pedagogical Approach," in *Principles of Visual Anthropology*, ed. Paul Hockings (The Hague: Mouton, 1974).

2. Available from the Center for Southern Folklore, 1216 Peabody Avenue, P.O. Box 4081, Memphis, Tennessee 38104.

3. This collection is now housed in the Archives of Appalachia, Sherrod Library, East Tennessee State University, Johnson City, Tennessee 37601.

4. Write to Esselte Publications, 600 Madison Avenue, New York, NY 10002 for further information.

5. See John Collier, Jr., *Visual Anthropology: Photography as a Research Method* (New York: Holt, Rinehart & Winston, 1967) for extended commentary on the use of photographs in interviews; also Stephanie Krebs, "The Film Elicitation Technique" in *Principles of Visual Anthropology*, pp. 283–302.

6. Since this article was first written, a number of folklorists and independent video producers in Florida, Kentucky, Indiana, and Mississippi have aired folklore-related programs on regional and national public TV. Also worthy of note is Appalshop's *Headwaters* series, which is shot on ¾" and dubbed to ½" VCR for local broadcast in Eastern Kentucky on commercial TV.

Charles Camp

Developing a State
Folklife Program

The sudden and unexpected blossoming of state folklife programs over the past eight years has brought about several important changes in the ways in which folklorists define their professional roles, scholarly interests, and sources of employment. In number alone these programs now represent a serious challenge to the traditional academic definition of the folkloristic enterprise. Since 1966, when Henry Glassie became Pennsylvania's (and the nation's) first state folklorist, over half the states have followed suit by establishing research and presentation programs in folk culture.[1] Fifteen of these programs sprang up between 1976 and 1979. While budgets for folklore research in these states vary greatly, depending upon the activities in which folklorists are engaged, most spend at least $40,000 per year for a folklorist's salary and essential equipment and supplies.

As impressive as these statistics may be, state governments in general are not exactly bullish on folklore. One of the many ironies of the trend is that its origins lie not in academe or a goundswell of public interest, but within the fine arts funding establishment—the National Endowment for the Arts and the fifty state arts councils. Beginning with Maryland and Tennessee in 1974, the NEA made available matching funds to state agencies interested in establishing folklorist positions or ongoing folklore research programs. Whether many of the states which subsequently created such positions would have done so without the NEA incentive is hard to say, but energetic arts administrators in several states have provided a necessary spark, especially where such public interest and political support have lagged. This odd alliance between arts agencies and public-sector folklorists is symbolized in the often cited and frequently abused term "folk art"—an expression used by arts administrators to justify the work of the folklorist and render more democratic the agencies they run, and by folklorists as a screen for the general study of folklore.

Arts administrators often consider the plural "folk arts" as the common man's versions of the fine arts. Thus a skilled woodcarver becomes a "folk da Vinci" and a badly rendered portrait is termed "folklike" in its crudeness or naiveté. The folklorist working in an arts agency may consequently be restricted in activity to those folk expressive forms which have a recognized fine arts counterpart (music, dance, painting, sculpture, architecture, and poetry). An arts agency, however, may reap political benefits from demonstrating interest or support of folk arts, since their practitioners and audience are seldom directly reached by the agency's fine arts programs and consequently represent a new and potentially supportive constituency. In such circumstances the folklorist must convert the political advantage his or her work represents into a broader province of activity and a greater say in policy matters. Having been given a voice the folklorist must use it to propose a less confining use of the term "folk art."

Of course, not all state folklife programs are attached to state arts councils and dependent upon NEA assistance. Some have followed the Pennsylvania model and have grown within historical agencies and museums. In Mississippi, South Carolina, and Virginia, folklorists have successfully worked with state media agencies as both administrative bases and project sources. Ellen Stekert established a state folklife program in Minnesota through the introduction of legislation to study and preserve Minnesota folklife, and to create a center for such work within the state historical society. Since the arts model is typical of the greater number of state folklore programs, however, and since it represents the setting for my own work during the past six years, most of my remarks will pertain to programs of this type. A brief history of the Maryland Folklife Program may illustrate some of the characteristics of state programs as a whole.

By 1974, when George Carey became Maryland's first state folklorist, a great deal of groundwork had been laid within the state government for the establishment of a folklore program. Carey had served as a member of a 1968 Study Commission on Maryland Folklife and written an "Introductory Guide to Maryland Folklore and Folklife"[2] which was bound with the commission's final report in 1970. The commission's recommendations for the creation of a central archive and grant program to be administered by a permanent commission and full-time folklife researcher were never fully implemented, but the body served an essential purpose in bringing before state legislators and the general public a view of folklore that suggested its deserved place within existing educational institutions and identified potential impact upon local tourism. The interest created by the commission was nourished by the Smithsonian Institution, when Maryland was chosen as featured state for the 1972 Festival of American Folklife. The politicking and consciousness-raising that took place at the festival were preceded by an unusually spirited year of lobbying, during which then-governors John Gilligan of Ohio and Marvin Mandel of Maryland actively competed on behalf of their states for the Smithsonian honor.

In much the same way as other states built upon their involvement in the Smithsonian festival, Maryland officials sought a way to extend the cultural and political benefits with an annual Maryland Folklife Festival.[3] Eighteen months later, the broad research and archive design proposed by the study commission and the more pragmatic objectives agreed upon by the legislators and the governor's staff came together, with the assistance of the NEA, in the creation of a state folklorist position at the Maryland Arts Council and the appointment of George Carey to fill the position. Carey was able to postpone the establishment of a state festival for a year while he began collecting information on Maryland storytellers, musicians, and craftspeople and speaking to school and civic groups about folklore. Carey summarized his experiences as a state folklorist in an issue of *Folklore Forum*, concluding that, "despite the difficulty of convincing arts councils in different states that folk arts provide a province worthy of recognition," the job of state folklorist "allows a folklorist a forum which is missing in the confinement of the academic community."[4]

When I took over the state folklorist position in February 1976, I did so with the understanding that I would direct the Maryland festival, but that there would be no other restrictions on the allocation of my time. During the first arts council meeting after my arrival I discovered that Carey had brought the members to an understanding of folklore which included oral and material culture, and simply bypassed the categories of folk, popular, and fine art that often entangle discussions with arts administrators. Consequently, I was spared the frequently serious obstacle to establishing a solid program—the definition of folklore within the context of the arts and the justification of research which does not pertain specifically to folk *art*.

One of the ways in which my approach to the state folklife program differed from Carey's was my view of it as a key link in a service network—not only a clearing-house for information, but also a place where educational materials could be produced, research reports prepared, and events organized.[5] Each of the projects since undertaken has been designed to meet the needs of a specific constituency (teachers, civic groups, union members, etc.), most often in response to a specific request. I began to refer to the sum of these individual projects as the Maryland Folklife Program in 1976 in order to draw attention to the services available to the public, thereby informing people interested in folklore that the Maryland Arts Council had something more to offer them than a free lecture on the subject. As other folklorists in Maryland have become involved in this work, I have come to consider the new title less a disguise for one folklorist working alone, and more an accurate title for a larger enterprise involving many.

State folklife programs must initially address a two-faceted problem inherent in the term "state folklorist" or any of its analogues. They must view a politically defined area (the state) as a distinct culture area, and then create research and presentation strategies appropriate to both the folkloric materials to be found within the state and the constituencies served. In states where a great deal of folklore research has not taken place, and there are many in this category, the problem is not easily solved. At a time when folklore training encourages specialization, it is difficult to determine how fieldwork time or program money, film or tape might be most widely used.

The matter of defining constituencies can be even more troublesome, since most folklorists are accustomed to seeing themselves primarily as educators and may feel more comfortable working with others who share a similar self-image or purpose. Within a state government, there is a natural tendency for other state employees to see the folklorist as a kind of scholar-in-residence, a conception which if en-couraged or acknowledged by the folklorist can greatly limit the range of what a state folklore program can accomplish. In other words, working as a folklorist in a state government is nothing like teaching within a college or university. Consequently, folklorists who attempt to transform a government position into a semi-academic occupation are certain to be misunderstood by fellow *workers* (not *colleagues*) as well as the public.

In a field with so few practical precedents, reasonable goals and a means for measuring the state folklorist's efforts are difficult to define. The objectives of most state folklore programs have something to do with furthering public awareness,

commit their time or resources to a cooperative venture until they are convinced the "outsider" offers something substantive. I spent much of my first year in Maryland trying to persuade the state department of education to place greater emphasis upon folklore studies in its curricula. After much agreement but little action, I contracted with six area folklorists to write syllabi for the courses we thought should be taught and then presented an eight-course curriculum to the department. Shortly thereafter, the education department contacted me to discuss long-range distribution of these materials and plans for future cooperation in curriculum development. The small amount of time and money invested in the preparation of these outlines has been more than offset by the improved relationship with the department of education and the sharp increase in the number of folklore courses taught in Maryland schools.

A second basic problem in developing a state folklife program is the uncritical reliance on conventional presentational models, such as festivals, concerts, exhibits, or lectures. State folklorists, for whom this problem is a particularly serious one, have yet to come to grips with the fact that the public's notion of folklore is virtually determined by the modes through which it is customarily presented. Thus folklore becomes what one sees and hears at folk festivals, and folk art is what one sees in museum exhibits using the term. To the extent that state folklorists make frequent use of festivals, exhibits, records, and other media as educational agents, it must be recognized that these media may provide less of an education and more of a definition than is intended. Limiting the investigation of folk music, for example, to the identification of performers for use in festivals or records denies an opportunity to experiment with performers and audiences—to probe assumptions about folk culture which shape the ways an audience hears or sees. All folklorists, of course, deal with these issues, but a folklorist whose primary constituency is the population of an entire state does not have an opportunity to augment and explain parts of a folk tradition inadequately conveyed in a concert performance or an exhibit photograph.

The evolution of the Maryland Folklife Festival may provide a case in point. The first two festivals in 1975 and 1976 featured a cross section of craftspeople and performers from throughout Maryland. The events were widely advertised, and each drew a large, mainly urban audience which related to the event as one of many mid-Atlantic summer folk festivals. In 1977 we began a regional festival plan that focused field research upon a single three- or four-county area per year. The regional festivals were not advertised outside the counties from which participants were selected. Craft demonstrations and music concerts were augmented by panel discussions, film screenings, and an exhibit of photographs of the region. Stages were lowered, then removed altogether, as were sound amplification systems, directional signs, and programs. Special tours were developed for school groups, and a curriculum guide was written to link festival presentations with general high school folklore courses. Festival performers visited many of the high schools in the area after the event.

Today the Maryland Folklife Festival no longer resembles its earlier incarnations. In many ways, the event is no longer a festival, at least in the eyes of many audience members. Few of the changes that have taken place are unique to the festival, but the sum of them reveals an event that is integrated with other folklife programs and serves as a sounding board for new ideas about folklore in the schools, field research technique, and changing public attitudes about folk culture.

The participants and audience are now neighbors, as the festival takes on a shape and character determined largely by the way the people respond to the image of themselves.

If there is a single strength which underlies today's state folklife programs, it is their opportunity and ability to experiment and change. In the future, these programs will succeed to the extent that they can build upon the academic legacy of American folkloristics and find new ways of extending this legacy to general audiences. Festivals, surveys, questionnaires, concerts, course outlines, films, and exhibitions are all valuable tools for the state folklorist, because each possesses in varying degrees some history of folkloristic application, but they do not add up to a complete state folklore program. With so little history behind us, we cannot identify an existing state program as a model for others to imitate, but in the sum of their experiments, successes, and failures state folklore programs hold one of the keys to the future of folklore research in America.

NOTES

1. States with folklore programs currently include Alabama, Alaska, Arizona, Arkansas, Colorado, Florida, Hawaii, Idaho, Indiana, Iowa, Kansas, Louisiana, Maine, Maryland, Michigan, Mississippi, Montana, Nebraska, New Hampshire, New Jersey, New York, North Carolina, North Dakota, Ohio, Pennsylvania, Rhode Island, Texas, Utah, Vermont, and Wyoming. For current information about states with state folklorists contact Folk Arts Program, National Endowment for the Arts, 2401 E Street N.W., Washington, D.C. 20506.

2. George Carey, "An Introductory Guide to Maryland Folklore and Folklife," Report of the Study Commission on Maryland Folklife, Part One, Bethesda, Maryland, 1970. Reprinted with additional material: George Carey, *Maryland Folklore and Folklife* (Cambridge, Maryland: Tidewater Publications, 1970).

3. Charles Camp, "Perspectives in Applied Folklore: American Folk Festivals and the Recent Maryland Experience," *Free State Folklore* 3 (1976-77): 4-15.

4. George Carey, "State Folklorists and State Arts Councils: The Maryland Pilot," *Folklore Forum* 9 (1976): 7.

5. Charles Camp, "State Folklorists and Folklife Programs: A Second Look," *Folklore Forum* 10 (1977): 26-29.

Rayna Green

Folk Is a Four-Letter Word: Dealing With Traditional ****in Fieldwork, Analysis, and Presentation

Obscenity occurs everywhere in traditional expression. Young, old, male, female, rich, poor, urban, and rural tradition-bearers use the bawdy in songs, stories, games, gestures, and artifacts. In some cultures, it may be highly visible; in others, quite submerged. It may be the inherent privilege of a certain class of person (e.g., old ladies, fishmongers, muleskinners) or the earned privilege of great artists, eccentrics, or deviants. The obscene may be understood as dirty but not shocking; shocking and funny; or funny but immoral, even while permissible in certain contexts. But common and permissible or not, since few folklorists can or will want to escape traditional bawdry, some knowledge of its special delights and problems is in order.

The mental notebooks of my first few months in graduate folklife studies (circa 1968) were filled with lists of past scholarly sins and omissions, especially of those which represented the follies of tender, Puritanical sensibility. My peers and I relished the X-rating of motifs in Thompson's *Index,* the omissions of bawdy materials in major collections like the *Frank C. Brown,*[1] and the Latinization, bowdlerization, and censorship that characterized published texts. We mocked the relegation of bawdy materials to the library's Delta collections, the Kinsey Institute, and "special access" sections of folklore archives and envied what tradition rumored to be the enormous collections of literary obscenity held in the Vatican. We sympathized with scholars like Vance Randolph, who had tried to publish bawdy materials along with his other Ozark collections, but failed because cowardly Victorian throwbacks in the publishing business played the villains in this melodrama.[2] While we cheered authors who had managed to sneak obscenity into print,[3] we still waited for a change in the basic refusal to publish filth.

In the sixties we had reason to believe scholarly Victorianism had begun to topple. Persuaded by a number of legal decisions in favor of bawdry and, no doubt, by the promise of great financial return on obscene literary investments, publishers began to risk more printing of bawdy works. "Folklore" in the form of limericks, rugby songs, and ethnic jokes began to appear in little paperbacks. Younger folklore scholars, as interested in popular materials and more liberal publishing standards as in changing disciplinary attitudes, began to hammer on the field's armor. Folklorist Frank Hoffmann insisted on making serious study of bawdry,[4] and Kenneth Goldstein and William Jansen wrote about the ethics of collecting and publishing such material.[5] The maverick scholar, expatriate, and neo-Freudian Gershon Legman published masses of traditional bawdry in his European-printed journals and huge two-part study, *The Rationale of the Dirty Joke*.[6] Alan Dundes promulgated Freudian folkloristic analysis, bringing the bawdry into print through an examination of traditional sexual materials.[7] And Roger Abrahams and Bruce Jackson successfully defied the theretofore sole passion in folkloristics for slave narratives and songs by publishing the (often) obscene lore of modern, urban, imprisoned, or street-dwelling blacks.[8] Even so, relatively little research broadened the discipline's restricted notions of who retained and transmitted bawdy traditions in America, and few presentational standards emerged. Printing those awful words still gave scholars and printers the shivers, and in print urban and lower-class black males, street people and prisoners, Caucasian fraternity boys, rugby players, and sorority girls appeared to be the sole repositories of obscene traditions.

Then in the 1970s a shift occurred, having to do with a change in both the social climate and the demography of folklore as a discipline. Large numbers of women came into the field. As I was persuading Vance Randolph to let me seek publication of his long-suppressed collection *Pissing in the Snow and Other Ozark Folktales*, previously available only on microfilm, even younger scholars like Robbie Johnson were presenting the extraordinary obscenities of a Texas madam to the shocked and delighted American Folklore Society.[9] Such events had two liberating effects on the discipline. They convinced folklorists that scholarly presses were ready to accept such material and that women, white mountaineers, and other quaint folk could and did do more than quilt, sing ballads, and weave baskets. In the 1970s, published articles, dissertations, and papers have presented the bawdy lore of all sorts of women (East Texas German grandmothers, southern and northern blacks, Serbians, Muslims, Sardinians),[10] and ballad-singing New England males such as Joe Scott and Larry Gorman have been allowed the occasional lewd slip of the tongue in their literary memorials.[11] But an integrated work that includes both bawdy and non-bawdy folklore and offers up a collection and analysis of a community or individual's repertoire has still to appear. Perhaps that lack has as much or more to do with the discipline's sturdy passion for genre analysis than with a reluctance to study traditional obscenity. I dream of a reissue of Randolph's Ozark materials with the obscene lore interwoven, chronologically, with the "clean" materials. And we all continue to wait for the major work on children's lore which portrays their folklore as it so often is—dirty.[12]

Certainly the 1970s broadened both the public and the scholarly vision of who maintains bawdy traditions, perhaps even of what roles the obscene plays in various cultures. But correct and noisy as professional folklorists were about previous failures, their acknowledgment of past omissions and mistreatment brought up new problems, ones perhaps even more profound than those which arose from their moral and aesthetic offense at obscenity's persistence. Still lacking is a standard, culturally unbiased word to describe such material as well as widely accepted ethical standards governing the research and presentation of bawdry. Thus, while New Age libertarianism demands full disclosure, New Age ethics demand careful attention to the results and impacts of disclosure. In short, readers cheering the account of battlements toppled in obscenity's name may yet be surprised to find this scholar suggesting that the villains of the piece may not be the conservative scholars and publishers, but those who wish to be in the vanguard. For such materials—dealing as they do with the most powerful and dangerous of social relations, biological functions, and cultural mores—may never be viewed as harmless, no matter how warmly we embrace cultural relativism in the field, in print, or in the classroom. Moreover, this particular form of "ethnographic dynamite"—often disarmingly humorous, even when hostile or seductive—opens a trap door for the scholar who takes its offering at face value. Perhaps a continued caution is best since a rush to focus on such material might produce yet another skewed portrait of the way obscenity exists and functions in tradition.

Field Research Encountering ****

Obviously, the surest way to collect bawdy folklore is to be part of the cultural contexts in which it appears most normally, or to be a natural or honorary member of a group of individuals who purvey the obscenity under scrutiny. If, like Roger Abrahams and Bruce Jackson, scholars live on the street or do political work in the prisons, and if they gain credibility through being there, being interested, and being "acceptable" in terms of gender and personality, they are more likely than the complete stranger to obtain a sense of traditional obscenity. If, like me, a scholar belongs to a family of bawdy female performers and is, by dint of being the right gender, "in training" for a starring role as a bawdy performer, that scholar will have guaranteed access to the material.[13] The researcher who is the wrong gender and asks the wrong questions of the wrong person at the wrong time or who thinks an informant's genuinely obscene tale is quite harmless can be in trouble, academically and personally. Consider, for example, the doubtless apocryphal story of the famous folklorist in search of urban folklore in a black neighborhood. On spying a young man in an upstairs window from his streetside strolling place, the folklorist shouts, "Hey, do you know any old stories?" "Fuck you, white motherfucker," the young man replies, and the folklorist happily writes in his notebook, "Chicago street cry."[14] A female graduate student who inquired into the possibilities of studying the "clean" hunting narrative traditions of a Texas male storyteller was subjected to the ritual, obligatory dude's initiation of rough-and-tumble narrative. She blushed, laughed, and received, post-initiation, the best treatment and material from the gentleman storyteller, and she recognized quickly enough that the embarrassment, seduction, testing of loyalty and durability under fire, and the welcomed banishment of prying scholars might often be the covert agenda of obscene narration. Best to treat both the material and the event as an entrance test which the scholar must pass in order to get the best of bawdy and non-bawdy traditions. In fact, scholars who deliberately set out to "collect" the obscene (e.g., "Say, I hear you know a lot of dirty songs") may find themselves misled, while those who look merely for songs may experience the delightful variety in an informant's and culture's repertoire.

After an encounter with bawdy material has taken place and the researcher expects (and desires) that more will be forthcoming, clear understandings between the scholar and informants ought to be the goal, especially if everyone is to feel happy about the end results. An explanation of the scholar's intent—to collect, analyze, archive, publish, and lecture on materials gathered in the field—is owed community members. Those who do not wish their bawdy traditions so exposed to the world can thus refuse to share them. The scholar can then make note of their existence in the community, but their absence from the collection. How much more honest it would be to find in a collection the admission that "so-and-so was willing to show me hundreds of obscene hand gestures, but refused to let me photograph them, draw pictures, or take notes, no matter how much I promised that no names and faces would be used in the book." Or how much better to find a preface stating that informants were assured of several options concerning the materials they told the scholar, and that some invoked the options and others refused at all to cooperate when they learned publication was the goal. Informants could then indicate certain preferences, whether to allow the use of real names or identifying descriptions, whether to deposit materials in archives or personal files, whether to restrict their use, whether to review the resulting manuscript, or whether to set special rules for children. The most willing informants can become the most outspoken enemy of the folklorist who exposes their "dirty mouth" to the world. Yet the fully involved informant, jointly bearing responsibility for the finished product along with the scholar, is likely to take pride in the finished work.

Fieldwork inevitably leads to analysis and the careful and caring field researcher must turn into the careful and caring analyst of culture. How sensitively and "correctly" that field researcher responds to the encounter with bawdy material determines much about how sensitively and "correctly" the material is presented. Misapprehensions about the nature of informants, the context, content, and meaning of bawdry or about where bawdy performers and performances stand—morally and aesthetically—in the culture will not benefit anyone, much less the scholar. What exactly constitutes a "dirty" performer and performance is the first act of analysis and the ethnocultural definitions best serve good scholarship. My grandmother was an acknowledged performer of tales, songs, and jokes, but she was the recognized mistress of bawdry. The traditional and inventive outrages for which she was justly quotable took place in an approved context—in the family circle and primarily in the female family circle. Males or outsiders were rarely present; in fact, some of her most memorable lines would not have taken place in "mixed" company. Once, for example, when Granny emerged from her bath, my sister commented that the hair on Granny's "privates" was getting sparse. "Why," she retorted, "grass don't grow on a race track!" Or, during a conversation in which several recently married young women debated whether a man's penis size affected sexual pleasure, she advised them that "it don't matter how deep the well or how long the rope, it's how you jiggle the bucket." She was a stellar performer acting in a revered, accepted performance tradition. Far from deviant, she was a pillar of the church and an accepted member of a farm community. Had she been willing, like another community woman of stained reputation, to open her "dirty mouth" to anyone who would hear, she too would have been a suspect "dirty mouth" to her social group. Some members of the community never heard nor would they have tolerated my grandmother's wicked art; and, of course, the thorough scholar would have troubled to find out who knew and sanctioned her material, who flocked to hear it, and who eschewed it—either as performers or audience—and who or what those people were to the community as a whole.

The scholar would also have troubled to find out what the material was called, by those who performed it, by those who listened to it, and by those who refused to perform it or listen. Generically and item by item, the determination of whether a song is dirty or naughty, lewd or wicked, blue or nasty is a major task. Are there clean versions of dirty songs and dirty versions of clean, even sacred, stories and do the dirty versions have names different from the clean ones? Are they all just called "songs"? Are there names for obscene events or sessions like "talking trash," "girl's talk," "men's talk," or "gross out," which can refer to obscene performance combined with scatological, repulsive, and disgusting narratives? Are there cover words for "dirty" such as "limerick," "rugby song," or "fraternity song"? Is the scatological, for example, equivalent to "dirty" or may there be a real variance in cultural interpretation between the two? In my Texas-Oklahoma youth, curses involving the Deity and the labeling of someone as a "Yankee" or "New Yorker" were obscene and profane. Sayings involving the word "shit" were not. A female relative's favorite and well-used expletive was "shit fire and save matches!" There were, in other words, boundaries, and the boundaries revealed as much as the open spaces. For example, my family members commonly described people as "piss ants," but I do not recall that the term "pissing" was permissible. It was all right to refer to genitalia and other centers of sexual attention or biological function by comic, bawdy names. Chore Girls, ChiChi's, tallywhackers, Peters, woolyboogers, and possibles abounded. But natural acts like defecation, menstruation, and urination could only be described by poetic avoidants (monthlies, flowers) or childhood baby talk (wee-wee, pee-pee, cucu, caca). Only female dogs could be called bitches without inviting physical retribution from someone close to the person so named. Words, moreover, had different meanings depending on who used them, when, and to whom. Men could refer to another man as a "son of a bitch" ("summich" in the vernacular), given both the right tone and degree of friendship (e.g., "come on over here, you ol' sorry summich, and have a drink"). Just because a word's cultural referent is vulgar does not mean the word is necessarily understood as vulgar. Context is all and rule violations must suit the cultural *chose de moment*. For example, the only vulgar tradition males in my family were permitted in female company was that of an elderly uncle's ritual farewell. Offering his hindparts to the assembled, anticipatory children, he would inquire if any of us wished to kiss him goodbye. In short, his one violation of the sacred rule of men's silence and cleanliness in mixed company did not contradict my cultivated opinion that men were artistically impoverished beings, incapable of delicious bawdry and vile performance.

Presentation of the ****

The main issue in field research, analysis, or public presentation is whether the scholar is prepared for the variations in the way material will be received and understood. Nothing guarantees a reception identical to the one an author or lecturer had in mind. In fact, the very reverse of what was intended is often the case, especially in the instance of bawdry, since it exhibits enormous variation in cultural definition and understanding. Those folklorists who have taught in public or private religious institutions will immediately recognize the problems, especially at the undergraduate level.

Three forums other than print for the presentation of bawdry—the classroom, the archive, and the lecture circuit—have been alluded to but not discussed, and much of traditional bawdry is and will be presented in these areas. They offer problems as difficult and serious as those of publication, though quite different. If guaranteed a homogeneous "audience" (readers, listeners, etc.), a scholar could try to fall inside those cultural boundaries, decide when to risk the unacceptable, or even defy acceptability and prepare for the consequences. But a homogeneous audience—even in a scholarly forum—is rare these days and presentation of the bawdy offers great possibility for misinterpretation. No matter how outrageous, an account of a basketmaker's material art cannot possibly infuriate an audience as much as an account of the same old, quaint folk craftsman's bawdy verbal art. What may seem harmless in private—told only to the researcher and the recorder—may be viewed as racist, sexist, obscene, and offensive when revealed to the public. Even other scholarly professionals may take offense if the forum for revelation is "wrong." I well recall the fallout from my invited lecture on the stereotypes of Indian women in which I recounted several mildly (or so I thought) bawdy songs and sayings—from whites—regarding Indian women. But the folklorists who sponsored the lecture were called to task by several students and a dean for their support of *my* obscene performance. The texts I quoted, the cultures that produced them, and the reasons for repeating them—to show that Indian women were often treated as obscenities by males—were lost in the furor over my public repetition of them.

Once having decided to take the field researcher's material or informants into the public eye, scholars face the possibility of a conflict between their perception and enactment of the rules governing the material and the sensibilities of the audience. Perhaps those library Delta collections, "masked" archival entries—privately maintained domains—guard the bawdy tradition from culturally inappropriate uses. Perhaps that privacy of tradition is culture's "plain brown wrapper," keeping things bawdy "under the counter" where they belong.

The classroom offers an especially touchy forum for presentation. Whether or not encouraged to do so by their professors, students inevitably collect bawdy materials, especially from their peers. While peer collection has its pitfalls in the potential for interracial/sexual/cultural conflict and misunderstanding, it will never present the problems of non-peer collecting. When and if students solicit (or accidentally intrude on) traditional obscenity from their relatives or from whatever "folk" they seek out, all scholarly hell can break loose for them and for whoever sent them to gather the material. The revelation in the classroom, either by professor or student, of bawdy materials has to be governed by the same tact that governs field research. Whether class time is set apart for discussion of traditional obscenity or not—and I would recommend that such time be spent—the obscene will appear in some way. Here as in the field the rules of voluntary revelation should apply, but—once put forward in the classroom—field rules of non-critical acceptance don't apply. Scholarly critical attempts to understand the material are essential. Since, however, there will inevitably be those awful classroom moments when males and females, majority and minority, older and younger, religious and non-religious students will fall into conflict over such material, *caveat professor!* The professor who assumes that every joke will be funny to everyone for the same reasons is as foolish as the professor who assumes that everyone likes a dirty joke and enjoys the graffiti on the library restroom walls.

I found myself, in the last few years of teaching, quite grateful for a women's folklore class where women's bawdy lore could be discussed *in camera*, as it were, and where I did not have to watch the tension that arose over the inevitable male presentation of a rugby song in a mixed class, or the equally inevitable female recitation of an "anti-male" joke. Believing, as I still do, that to avoid those recitations was irresponsible, I accepted the burden of cross-cultural, cross-gender conflict and therapy that had to follow its utterance. Any professor not prepared for this second burden should insist on confining recitations of this sort to written or *in camera* oral recitations which go no further than that professor's office. The daily folklore diary, kept so that a professor can be treated to a steady stream of postpubescent dirt, is the best steam valve I know of for the release of collected obcenities. Carefully chosen selections can then be presented to the class and suitable examples deposited in archives or the whole returned to the student.

The inevitable forum is print and it is printed bawdry that has caused the most visible obstruction. Publication is a more permanent and homogeneous form of presentation than the classroom. The scholar should be wary of the publisher too keen on publishing bawdy lore, the editor too anxious for low profile scholarship and high profile textual presentation. With obscene materials, be wary of the publisher who believes that paperback production is the "best" way to get the book to the public and that no outside readers need to be called in to comment and respond to the manuscript. The careful scholar will seek initial exposures of the material and analysis in scholarly journals, and will further gravitate toward a publisher who wants the analysis, the notes, the apparatus of scholarly work. Even the stuffiest and most boring of scholarly work will not deter the reader who is bent on reading the texts alone, but the choice of format, press, and medium of exposure does somewhat govern the public image of those texts. At the least, those choices will lend an air of impressive seriousness to the bawdy art found between the (tasteful, one hopes) covers of a published work.[15]

The "problem" of obscenity in folklore, then—in research, analysis, storage, public presentation in print, scholarly paper, or classroom lecture—persists as surely as the ambivalence of many toward obscenity. Thus, I have tried to deal with a number of presentational issues—ethical and editorial—inherent in the study of bawdy tradition. I wanted to set forth an ideal to be achieved through the sense of what is probable and possible. Yet the ideal remains a goal because, as the opening paragraphs stated, the issue of bawdry in traditional expression, in behavior, or in scholarly work raises more questions than answers, more problems than solutions. The main caveat is simple. It was and will be simpler to eschew study and publication of obscenity than it will be to deal honestly, ethically, and effectively with it in study or presentation. As traditional American folk wisdom warns us—"when in doubt, don't!"

NOTES

1. Stith Thompson, *The Types of the Folktale* (Helsinki: Suomalainen Tiedeakatemia, 1961); Thompson, *Motif-Index of Folk-Literature* (Bloomington: Indiana University Press, 1955-58); Newman I. White, ed. *The Frank C. Brown Collection of North Carolina Folklore* (Durham, N.C.: Duke University, 1952).

2. For the story of the volume's publication, see Rayna Green's Introduction to Vance Randolph, *Pissing in the Snow and Other Ozark Folktales* (Champaign-Urbana: University of Illinois Press, 1976).

3. Such as Allen Walker Read, *Lexical Evidence from Folk Epigraphy in Western North America: A Glossarial Study of the Low Element in the English Language* (Paris: privately printed, 1935) and Samuel Roth, *Anecdota Americana* (New York: Joseph Fliescher, 1934).

4. Frank Hoffmann, *An Analytical Survey of Traditional Anglo-American Erotica* (Bowling Green, Ohio: Bowling Green University Popular Press, 1973).

5. "Symposium on Obscenity," *Journal of American Folklore* 75 (1962).

6. Gershon Legman, *The Rationale of the Dirty Joke* (New York: Grove Press, 1968) and idem, *No Laughing Matter: Rationale of the Dirty Joke*, Second Series (Wharton, N.J.: Breaking Point, 1975), reprinted as *No Laughing Matter: An Analysis of Sexual Humor*, Vols. I and II (Bloomington: Indiana University Press, 1982). Recently, a new journal, *Maledicta*, follows much in the early steps of Legman with the publication and analysis, however eccentric, of multicultural obscene insults, names, and words.

7. Alan Dundes, *Analytic Essays in Folklore* (The Hague: Mouton, 1975). See especially those works which treat of psychoanalytic analyses.

8. Roger Abrahams, *Deep Down in the Jungle: Negro Narrative Folklore from the Streets of Philadelphia*, rev. ed. (Chicago: Aldine, 1970); Bruce Jackson, *"Get Your Ass in the Water and Swim Like Me"* (Cambridge, Mass.: Harvard University Press, 1974).

9. Robbie Davis Johnson, "Folklore and Women: A Social-Interactional Analysis of the Folklore of a Texas Madam," *Journal of American Folklore* 86 (1973): 211–24.

10. For example, Rayna Green, "Magnolias Grow in Dirt: The Bawdy Lore of Southern Women," *Southern Exposure: A Journal of the New South* 4, no. 4 (1977): 29–33; reprinted in *The Radical Teacher* 6 (1977): 26–30.

11. Edward Ives, *Joe Scott: The Woodsman Songmaker* (Urbana: University of Illinois Press, 1978).

12. Notable for its omission of children's obscenity is Peter and Iona Opie, *The Lore and Language of Schoolchildren* (Oxford: Clarendon Press, 1959). Such omissions are remedied to some extent in Mary and Herbert Knapp, *One Potato, Two Potato: The Secret Education of American Children* (New York: Norton, 1976) and to great extent, for post-pubescent children, in Ed Cray, *The Erotic Muse* (New York: Oak Publications, 1968).

13. See Green, "Magnolias," for an account of the training for bawdy female performers in the South.

14. Oral tradition, American folklorists, ca. early 1970s.

15. After long and careful conversations over details such as what the most tasteful dust cover for *Pissing in the Snow* would be, this writer and the University of Illinois editorial staff were gratified to note that many newspapers and journals still refused to print the title when they reviewed the book. Such reluctance lets one know that virtually no amount of caretaking may be sufficient in the matter of published obscenity.

Wm. Hugh Jansen

Ethics and the Folklorist

Few who attended the IXth International Congress of Anthropological and Ethnological Sciences held in Chicago in September 1973 will ever forget the flying teams of angry young African anthropologists who ran from session to session to deliver appropriately modified versions of a message that went something like this: "You, sir or madam, spent fifteen months studying my village, published two books about 'your' (spare the mark!) people, and never sent us so much as a copy of either book or helped us in any way to profit from what you learned."

Had there been young Eskimo, or Oglala, or South Pacific, or Chicano (or whatever) anthropologists in any noticeable numbers at this polysyllabically entitled congress, they could undoubtedly have formed similar flying teams to deliver the same angry message. Consider one Nathan whose manuscript autobiographical narrative afforded the basis of Charles C. Hughes's excellent book *Eskimo Boyhood*[1] and who neither knew his essay had been published nor had heard from Dr. Hughes in twenty years.[2] Nathan was "pleased" when he finally heard his autobiography had been published.

Illiteracy cannot be the reason why Nathan was not shown the book incorporating his manuscript. Such an explanation is frequently offered for the absence of communication between fieldworker and subject, and probably analphabetical cultures do not understand all the possibilities of non-oral communication. But even in the few cultures that survive there is usually some possibility of second-hand understanding of print. Américo Paredes says most aptly—and note the tenses—"it was one thing to publish ethnographies about Trobrianders or Kwakiutls half a century ago; it is another to study people who read what you write and are more than willing to talk back."[3] I'm not so certain that it is "another" thing; it's merely that accountability is more likely to be demanded!

I consider issues such as these to be the ethical concerns that confront folklorists. Other matters, such as courtroom squabbles about folksong copyrights, are, in my thinking, legalistic. Not that there is no ethical problem in copyrighting transcriptions of what are really folksongs. After all, whose financial interests are being protected when a collector copyrights in his name songs little different from those he has collected from a folksinger? It is a different matter, of course, if an arranger copyrights a sophisticated harmonic arrangement—the only ethical point at question in this situation is the honesty with which the label "folksong" can be attached to such an arrangement.

Ethics for the folklorist is responsibility—responsibility equally to a discipline, to sources or informants (even secondary and tertiary sources), and to the folklorist's intended audience. Folkloristics as a discipline has taken a long time to establish itself. What once seemed brawling, preposterous claims for its wide-reaching efficacy are now, however grudgingly, accorded a measure of tolerance and acceptance as a peer scholarly discipline by both the humanities and the social sciences.

As for responsibility to informants, I have always resented the very word, arguing that its usage implies a patronizing superiority in the user and suggests that individuals are being exploited as spies upon their own culture—a reason perhaps for less than total reliability in the *information* thus derived. Be this as it may, until a blander term is provided, the word *informant* prevails—although the folklorist may give it somewhat specialized denotation. And it is the folklorist's responsibility to informants that is of personal concern.

A perhaps cogent illustration is provided by an admirable little book. the Carawans' *Ain't You Got a Right to the Tree of Life?*[4] and a zealous fieldworker's reaction to it.[5] The volume conveys a hearty enthusiasm for the rich folk culture maintained despite economic hardships by the hardy, insouciant residents of John's Island. It is, of course, an enthusiasm intended to convince the non-islander of the values inherent in the island culture—inherent and now exposed to change. Carawan and his collaborators present in their volume "the strongest photograph to illustrate each text" and refrain "from caricaturing the pronunciation of Gullah dialect by distorted spellings."[6] Obviously their effort is to give to the members of a very different, even elite mainland culture a respectful and respectable representation of the life of John's Island. The cited researcher, drawing upon her own fieldwork on John's Island, writes, "the subjects . . . are insulted, aggrieved, and thoroughly disillusioned. . . . Their protest and hurt feelings were centered mainly around the pictures. . . . They feel sad that they were not allowed to be seen by the readers of the book in their Sunday finery [do I detect the same attitude in *Sunday finery* that makes *informant* suspect in my mind? Presumably the pejorative connotation of *finery* would be rejected by John's Islanders—or the term would not be used at all]. . . . It would be a thankless and impossible task to try to help them understand the importance or significance of the book; in their world it has none."[7] The last clause is not so irrelevant as it once seemed in the light of the Carawans' purpose. Instead, in these times when the products of folklore collection may become available to literate informants, it may point to a new ethical responsibility for the collector: to inculcate in informants an understanding that members of another culture will respect and admire the everday aspects of their culture at least as much as its Sunday formalities.

Clearly Carawan et al. have an ethical responsibility to represent their informants honestly and without deception (the two terms are not redundant, for in instances such as this the collector can be finically honest and at the same time unwittingly quite deceptive). Here folklorists are confronted with a dilemma: what pleases the informant may not instruct the student or scholar. Folklorists have an ethical responsibility to create a meaningful and understandable experience for their intended reading audience. They do *not* have a responsibility to make their informants look as pretty as possible, nor do they have a responsibility to portray those informants as those informants wish to be portrayed.

The folklorist must remember that a narrative in exact transcription and in print may create upon a habitual reader an effect very different from the one its recitation creates upon an experienced listener. There is no necessary relationship between proficient reading and practiced listening. A literate, experienced folk listener may not "hear" the narration behind a printed transcript, and an inexperienced listener who is a member of the literate elite may acquire the ability to "hear" the same narration. The situation is not unlike that arising from the different hearings that different readers give to a Shakespearian play. When transcribing tapes, a collector may discover that every sentence in a narrative begins with an indication of direct discourse, invariably including the word *say* in some inflected form—an anomaly unnoticed when the tale was performed. Not infrequently transcription reveals other strange solecisms—equally unnoted aurally. In a word or two, many transcriptions, unintentionally but quite actually, present to proficiently literate readers as an uneducated, ungrammatical person the very narrator who seemed to the proficient listener a peculiarly gifted speaker. It seems to me that there is an ethical problem here for the folklorist who has made a talented performer seem illiterate—a problem that I am glad to leave to others for solution. Interlinear texts may be the answer—or omnipresent parenthetical context reminders.

The folklorist's responsibility to the informant is much the same as that owed to the intended reading (listening? viewing?) audience—to present the informant in such a way as to create upon the folklorist's audience an impression similar (identical is probably impossible) to that which the informant creates upon an audience of his peers. The difficulty of achieving such an accurate portrayal cannot be overstated. Even Alan Lomax's superb sound films which use the everyday rhythms in various cultures to illustrate his kinemetric theories do not have the same effect on the outside viewer as the actual performance does upon the protagonist's cultural peers. The folklorist therefore has an ethical responsibility both to the performer and to the folklorist's audience to supply such context and to so explain the texture of the presented collection that the intended audience understands the effect the material has upon the folk who possess it.

In short, a folklorist's ethical duty is to be both honest and fully sensitive to his various responsibilities. Some of the most important issues that the folklorist must consider are confidentiality and its linked problems of slander, of obscenity, of sexism, and of racism. There could hardly be a list of more emotionally weighted words!

Confidentiality

The informant, no matter how whimsical his reasoning may be, has every right to remain anonymous or pseudonymous in any published rendition of his texts. In the case of a pseudonym, the collector might try to use an alias with the same ethnic overtones as the actual name—e.g., Patrick Di Carlo for Michael Florio, or Erik Olsen for Sven Hansen. This right to privacy extends to the informant's informant and even beyond. It is the folklorist's responsibility to ascertain the informant's wishes about confidentiality and to comply with them.

A "junk jeweler" who was also my neighbor once taught me some of his profession's argot and seemed terrified when I asked his permission to use my new knowledge in an article. Even if I didn't use his name, he feared the organization would find out what junk jeweler I knew and would put an end to his promising career. The article was never written, and the erstwhile neighbor went on to affluence in a more conventional line.

Certainly the real names of all informants should be known to the archivist, as should the correct ascription of their texts. For the sake of informants' desired anonymity, various devices such as coding, indices, and the like might be used, but I honestly doubt the necessity of such melodramatic resorts. And remember that words other than personal names may also betray identities: proper place names particularly in small communities; too-specific physical description (there's only one octogenarian in Monkey's Eyebrow, perhaps); identification of occupation (only one librarian, one visiting nurse, one male school teacher, etc.).

Slander

Sometimes it is not only the informants' wishes that collectors must consider, but their own fears of being sued for slander, libel, malice, embarrassment, or being endangered by criminal prosecution. These suits may be filed against the informant, or the collector, or the publishing medium—or all three. Two illustrations may serve here. In my own "Purpose and Function in Modern Local Legends of Kentucky,"[8] despite the constant reassurances of Mr. Fergus that I could publish without fear his and all other names in the collection, I finally, after much soul-searching, changed every proper name whether for animals, places, or people—even Mr. Fergus's—in the collection. I even changed descriptive words such as directions, in the hope that no one would recognize the charming little community of Williams Corners that I transported clear across Kentucky! While in my case no recriminations or threats of lawsuit followed, Leonard W. Roberts' monumental *Sang Branch Settlers*[9] was threatened with several lawsuits, even though the author had clearances both from his informants and from their sources—clearances that apparently eventually solved both ethical and legalistic questions. (It is probably worth noting that the legal actions against Dr. Roberts came from individuals who were neither his informants nor their sources, but did bear the family name of the *Settlers* and who felt their name was sullied by the book and the activities narrated therein.)

Other considerations also enter here. In the recording of legends and oral history, does fidelity to the discipline and the genre require the identification of living people with the commission of criminal acts? My answer is yes to the recording and to the storage in archives, but no to the publication, even as ascribed to an anonymous informant. Years ago, I recorded some colorful tales about a very proficient structural steelworker who dared not report to a security job lest his fingerprints reveal he had recently jumped bail, when faced with a murder indictment for a crime of passion. Although the statute of limitations—and perhaps the death of all concerned—may have intervened, the tales are unpublished, and it is better so.

Obscenity

Here, too, a bifocal perspective of ethical obligations to informant and to intended reader haunts the folklorist. Consider the very fact that obscenity has been indicated for centuries in print by a wild structure of blanks, dashes, initial letters, and cryptic symbols that challenged the reader's vocabulary and ingenuity. Consider, too, the mock-serious euphemisms of "blankety-blanks" appearing in both print and elite speech. Even the folk, influenced as they are by elite institutions and didacticism, are surprised by the appearance of words that are part of their own usage. Tale-teller Wilson Hughes[10] was shocked and only somewhat amused to find that the more elite of his neighbors used the euphemism, "Mr. Hughes's favorite word" when they felt constrained from using *damn!* Hughes admits to using the damn word quite frequently.

And how does this situation involve the folklorist with ethics? Above all, the folklorist must present the informant's language as it is naturally, while also indicating for the intended reader what elements of vocabulary and emphasis in that speech would seem in the informant's milieu obscene, very obscene, or not at all obscene. With such contextual and textual information folklorists will be meeting their ethical obligations to both reader and informant—and incidentally will probably be liberalizing and rationalizing their own and their readers' concepts of obscenity!

Sexism

It has already been said that the folklorist's ethical obligations do not include making folklore as pretty as possible or presenting informants as they wish to be seen in their Sunday finery. Those obligations also do not include apologizing for folklore. In varying degrees and by various standards folklore *is* sexist, but usually it is more sexist in the eyes of the beholder than in the eyes of the folk. Once more the crucial difference is supplying context. Two important points need to be made: male chauvinist pigdom is the conception of elite Western society; and the understanding of that pigdom varies wildly from one society to another. In the West, for example, Turkish culture is unanimously labeled as sexist, but its folklore rather unexpectedly is full of stories ridiculing henpecked husbands and extolling womanly wisdom—stories that in Western exoteric eyes support the charge of sexism and in Turkish esoteric eyes refute that charge. What we need to know is whether the popularity of Renaissance humor based on cuckoldry reflected a plethora or a paucity of cuckolds in real life!

Racism

Like sexism, racism is a form of folk discrimination or is so interpreted by an onlooker from a different or an elite culture, and of course by outside, exoteric standards much folklore is both sexist and racist. And again it behooves the collector to indicate how racist a particular narrative or belief is in its particular milieu. In our own complex society an interesting intracultural mesh is taking place among popular, elite, and folk cultures in regard to racism, one that seems to prove that frequently racism in the folk culture was not so very racist a generation or so ago. Wilson Hughes, who grew up in a society that considered *black man, nigger, negro, Jew, Yid, Kike* all fighting words, and therefore had sometimes to resort to ridiculous highfalutin euphemism, used to tell a number of tales employing black dialect, Yiddish dialect, stammering, the speech of the tongue-tied and the spastic. He laughs at himself as he admits that his black dialect was a hybrid of late blackface minstrelsy drawl and Uncle Remus vocabulary (Whuh's yo' all?), but he maintains that there was no malice in his dialect stories, that (some other informants have made similar statements) the very same stories could be (indeed are) told with no racial tones, that the use of dialect merely gave the narrator a chance to show his performing talents—and, besides, both Flip Wilson and

Myron Cohen tell dialect stories! Nevertheless, influenced by the changing attitudes and sensitivities of the elite and popular cultures around him, Wilson Hughes one day realized that he was no longer telling stories employing any kind of dialect or handicapped speech. He doesn't know when he first arrived at the decision to purge his repertoire of the "offensive" items. He doesn't remember even making the decision—just suddenly it was so.

Again, the ethical concerns of folklorists should be obvious. They should label discrimination when it exists. They should also, if possible, indicate whether it is recognized as discrimination by the performer and how that performer reacts to the alien-applied label of discrimination. However, the folklorist himself may be so much an integrated member of his intended audience that he does not recognize them as the aliens who will apply or accept the label. How far can the folklorist go in identifying with an informant's folk cultural criteria? How far can he go in escape from his own cultural criteria? How well will his intended reading audience perceive either process? That way surely, madness lies!

Conclusion

In brief, many of the ethical difficulties encountered by the folklorist could be alleviated if the superiority symbolized in the folklorist's usage of the term informant could be circumvented. There is a kind of pathos in one of Américo Paredes' examples that will make an adequate ending. He is speaking of the misunderstanding between Norwegian anthropologist Harald Eidheim and a Lappish informant: "To Eidheim, the Lapp is basically an informant: Making friends with him is a methodological tool—establishing rapport. But to the informant the ethnographer's friendship is real and of high value."[11]

But I do not want to leave the impression that this essay is a philippic against the word *informant*. I am attacking the attitude implied in the usage of the word, an attitude that may be a contributing cause for many of the ethical matters cited here. And I do not want to leave a negative or pessimistic impression. The ethical demands facing folklorists are complex, but not remarkably different from those facing various social sciences and the humanities. And I honestly believe that because of a concern with, and hopefully a sympathy for, contextual influences, folklorists have a greater chance to understand and solve these ethical-social problems than do social scientists or humanities scholars. If that belief is sound, opportunities for folklorists to contribute to crosscultural communication are impressive.

NOTES

1. Charles C. Hughes, *Eskimo Boyhood: An Autobiography in Psychosocial Perspective*, Studies in Anthropology, no. 8 (Lexington: University of Kentucky, 1974).

2. Thomas Johnston, "Review of *Eskimo Boyhood: An Autobiography in Psychosocial Perspective*, by Charles C. Hughes," *Tennessee Folklore Society Bulletin* 40 (1974): 158-60.

3. Américo Paredes, "On Ethnographic Work among Minority Groups: A Folklorist's Perspective," *New Scholar* 6 (1977): 2.

4. Guy Carawan, Candie Carawan, and Robert Yellin, *Ain't You Got a Right to the Tree of Life?* (New York: Simon & Shuster, 1966).

5. Mary Twining, "Field Notes on Reactions to *Ain't You Got a Right to the Tree of Life?*," *Journal of the Folklore Institute* 10 (1973): 214.

6. Carawan et al., p. 11.

7. Twining, pp. 214 and 216.

8. Wm. Hugh Jansen, in *Varia Folklorica*, ed. Alan Dundes (The Hague: Mouton Publishers, 1978).

9. Leonard Roberts, *Sang Branch Settlers: Folksongs and Tales of a Kentucky Mountain Family* (Austin: University of Texas Press, 1974).

10. Wm. Hugh Jansen, "A Narrator: His Repertoire in Memory and in Performance," in *Folk Narrative Research*, ed. Juha Pentikäinen and Tuula Juurikka (Helsinki: Suomalaisen Kirjallisuuden Seura, 1976), pp. 294–302.

11. Paredes, "On Ethnographic Work," p. 2.

Bibliography

AMERICAN FOLKLORE BIBLIOGRAPHIES

Aarne, Antti. *The Types of the Folktale: A Classification and Bibliography.* Translated and enlarged by Stith Thompson. 2d rev. ed. Helsinki: Suomalainen Tiedeakatemia, Academia Scientiarum Fennica, 1964.

Abrahams, Roger D., and Szwed, John. *Annotated Bibliography of Afro-American Folklore and Culture.* Philadelphia: Institute for the Study of Human Issues, 1978.

Adams, Ramon F. *The Rampaging Herd: A Bibliography of Books and Pamphlets on Men and Events in the Cattle Industry.* Norman: University of Oklahoma Press, 1959.

_____ . *Six-Guns and Saddle Leather: A Bibliography of Books and Pamphlets on Western Outlaws and Gunmen.* Norman: University of Oklahoma Press, 1954.

Baughman, Ernest W. *Type and Motif-Index of the Folktales of England and North America.* The Hague: Mouton, 1966.

Brachter, James T. *Analytical Index to the Publications of the Texas Folklore Society, Volumes 1-36.* Dallas: Southern Methodist University Press, 1973.

Bronner, Simon J. *A Critical Bibliography of American Folk Art.* FPG Monograph Series, 3. Bloomington: Folklore Publications Group, Indiana University, 1978.

Bronson, Bertrand Harris. *The Traditional Tunes of the Child Ballads.* 4 vols. Princeton, N.J.: Princeton University Press, 1959-72.

Child, F. J. *The English and Scottish Popular Ballads.* 5 vols. Boston: Houghton Mifflin, 1882-98.

Coffin, Tristram P. *An Analytical Index to the Journal of American Folklore, Volumes 1-70.* Philadelphia: American Folklore Society, 1958.

_____ . *The British Traditional Ballad in North America.* Philadelphia: American Folklore Society, 1950.

Dobie, J. Frank. *Guide to Life and Literature of the Southwest.* Dallas: Southern Methodist University Press, 1952.

Although each contributor was given an opportunity to update bibliographic entries in the spring of 1982, most of the items cited date from the original submission of the essays in 1979–80. —Ed.

Dorson, Richard M. "American Folklore Bibliography." *American Studies International* 16 (1977): 23–37.

Dundes, Alan. "North American Indian Folklore Studies." *Journal de la Société des Américanistes* 56 (1967): 53–79.

————, comp. *Folklore Theses and Dissertations in the United States.* Austin: University of Texas Press, 1976.

Ethnic Studies Bibliography. 2 vols. Pittsburgh: University Center for International Studies, 1975–76.

Ferris, Bill, and Peiser, Judy, eds. *American Folklore Films and Videotapes: An Index.* Memphis: Center for Southern Folklore, 1976.

Ferris, William R., Jr. *Mississippi Black Folklore: A Research Bibliography and Discography.* Hattiesburg: University and College Press of Mississippi, 1971.

Flanagan, Cathleen C., and Flanagan, John T. *American Folklore: A Bibliography, 1950–1974.* Metuchen, N.J.: The Scarecrow Press, 1977.

Haywood, Charles. *A Bibliography of North American Folklore and Folksong.* 2 vols. 2d rev. ed. New York: Dover Publications, 1961.

Heisley, Michael. *An Annotated Bibliography of Chicano Folklore From the Southwestern United States.* Los Angeles: Center for the Study of Comparative Folklore and Mythology, University of California, 1977.

Johnson, H. A. *Ethnic American Minorities: A Guide to Media and Materials.* New York: Bowker, 1976.

Laws, G. Malcolm, Jr. *Native American Balladry: A Descriptive Study and a Bibliographical Syllabus.* Philadelphia: American Folklore Society, 1964.

Lesser, Alexander. "Bibliography of American Folkore, 1915–1928." *Journal of American Folklore* 41 (1928): 1–60.

Loomis, Ormond. *Sources on Folk Museums and Living Historical Farms. Folklore Forum,* Bibliographic and Special Series, No. 16 (Bloomington, Ind.: The Folklore Forum, 1977).

Miller, W. C. *A Comprehensive Bibliography for the Study of American Minorities.* 2 vols. New York: New York University Press, 1976.

Mordoh, Alice Morrison. "Analytical Index to the *Journal of the Folklore Institute,* Vols. 1–15." *Journal of the Folklore Institute* 18 (1981): 157–273.

Perkal, Joan Ruman. *Western Folklore and California Folklore Quarterly: Twenty-five Year Index.* Berkeley: University of California Press, 1969.

Randolph, Vance. *Ozark Folklore: A Bibliography.* Bloomington: Indiana University Research Center for the Language Sciences, 1972.

Simmons, Merle E. *Folklore Bibliography for 1976.* Philadelphia: Institute for the Study of Human Issues, 1980. (One volume of annual series beginning in 1938 in *Southern Folklore Quarterly* and continuing as part of the Indiana University Folklore Monograph Series publications.)

Thompson, Stith. *Motif-Index of Folk-Literature.* Rev. ed. Bloomington: Indiana University Press, 1955.

Ullom, Judith C. *Folklore of the North American Indians: An Annotated Bibliography.* Washington, D.C.: Library of Congress, 1969.

Wasserman, P. *Ethnic Information Sources of the United States.* Detroit: Gale Research Co., 1976.

Wildhaber, Robert. "A Bibliographical Introduction to American Folklife." *New York Folklore Quarterly* 31 (1965): 259–302.

Wynar, L. R. *Encyclopedic Directory to Ethnic Newspapers and Periodicals in the United States.* Littleton, Colo.: Libraries Unlimited, Inc., 1972.

Wynar, L. R., and Buttlar, L. *Guide to Ethnic Museums, Libraries, and Archives in the United States.* Kent, Ohio: Program for the Study of Ethnic Publications, School of Library Science, 1978.

AMERICAN EXPERIENCES

Benedict, Ruth. *Zuni Mythology*. 2 vols. Columbia University Contributions to Anthropology. New York: Columbia University Press, 1935. An exhaustive study of cultural reflection and inversion in Southwestern folktales. The introduction can stand alone as a major essay on Native American folklore.

The Black Perspective in Music. New York: Foundation for Research in Afro-American Creative Arts. This journal, established in 1973 and published semiannually, is the only scholarly journal dedicated exclusively to the serious study of black music. Issues include articles, book reviews, discography, and special features that focus on African and Afro-American music and musicians.

Blair, Walter. *Native American Humor (1800–1900)*. New York: American Book Company, 1937. Repr. San Francisco: Chandler Pub. Co., 1960.

Boas, Franz. *Primitive Art*. Cambridge, Mass.: Harvard University Press, 1927. Repr. New York: Dover, 1955. An attempt to define the rules of North American Indian art from the perspective of Northwestern coastal tribes. Although more successful as a study of the latter, it has never been supplanted as a general guide to Native American art.

Boatright, Mody. *Folk Laughter on the American Frontier*. New York: Macmillan, 1949.

Clark, Thomas D. *Travels in the Old South*. 3 vols. Norman: University of Oklahoma Press, 1956–59. Describes autobiographical travelogues.

Dance, Daryl. *Shuckin' and Jivin': Folklore from Contemporary Black Americans*. Bloomington: Indiana University Press, 1978. Collection of black folklore from Virginia that is invaluable for comparative purposes.

de Lerma, Dominique-René. *Bibliography of Black Music*. 2 vols. Westport, Conn.: Greenwood Press, 1981. Vol. I, *Reference Materials*, is part of a new series and contains over 2,800 items arranged in 14 categories. Coverage is international and many of the major languages are represented. Vol. II, *Afro-American Idioms*, "provides access to a wide range of literature on the evolution, transition, and ultimate impact of Afro-American musical idioms." Coverage is international.

Dorson, Richard M. *America Begins*. New York: Pantheon Books, 1950. This anthology of early American writing offers a wide-ranging collection of seventeenth-century folkloristic materials complemented by some good notes on sources.

————. *America in Legend: Folklore from the Colonial Period to the Present*. New York: Pantheon Books, 1973. Section I, "The Colonial Period: The Religious Impulse," offers the most sophisticated integrative interpretation of colonial society from a folkloristic perspective yet published. Other sections cover American historical periods through the 1960s, including the "democratic," the "economic," and the "humane."

————. *American Folklore*. Chicago: University of Chicago Press, 1959. The chapter "Colonial Folklore," with its suggestive bibliographical accompaniment, is the best introduction to the folklore of the colonial period. Also includes chapters on "Regional" and "Immigrant" folklore.

————. *American Negro Folklore*. Greenwich, Conn.: Fawcett Publications, 1967. Conscientiously documented collection that is especially useful in comparative studies.

————. *Jonathan Draws the Long Bow*. Cambridge, Mass.: Harvard University Press, 1946. A fascinating collection of eighteenth-century tales and legends taken from a variety of printed sources. The notes are especially indicative of the wide variety of repositories for colonial folklore.

Du Bois, W.E.B. *The Souls of Black Folk*. Chicago: A. C. McClurg, 1903. Perhaps one of the most perceptive works treating Afro-American culture and thought.

Dundes, Alan. *The Morphology of North American Indian Folktales*. Folklore Fellows Communications, no. 195. Helsinki, 1964. A morphological approach to plot structure that concentrates on similarities among different Indian cultures, while suggesting some of the possibilities structuralist approaches might have for studying tribal differences.

————, comp. *Folklore Theses and Dissertations in the United States*. Austin: University of Texas Press, 1976. Much of the good work on American ethnic folklore appears in dissertations, which are listed here.

Ethnic Chronology Series, 31 vols. Dobbs Ferry, N.Y.: Oceana Publications, 1973–. At present there are 31 volumes in this series, each of which focuses on a different ethnic group.

Fry, Gladys-Marie. *Night Riders in Black Folk History*. Knoxville: University of Tennessee Press, 1975. Explores oral traditional history around the theme of post–Civil War intimidation of Southern freedmen.

Harvard Encyclopedia of American Ethnic Groups. Stephan Thernstrom, editor; Ann Orlov, managing editor; Oscar Handlin, consulting editor. Cambridge, Mass., & London: Belknap Press, 1980.

Hudson, Arthur Palmer, ed. *Humor of the Old Deep South*. New York: Macmillan, 1936.

Hultkrantz, Åke. *The North American Indian Orpheus Tradition*. Ethnographic Museum Publications, no. 2. Stockholm, 1957. A careful study of one motif that illustrates the strengths and possibilities of detailed comparative studies.

Hurston, Zora Neale. *Mules and Men*. New York: Harper & Row, 1970.

Hyatt, Harry M. *Hoodoo – Conjuration – Witchcraft – Rootwork: Beliefs Accepted by Many Negroes and White Persons These Being Orally Recorded among Blacks and Whites*. N.p.: Memoirs of the Alma Egan Hyatt Foundation, 1970-78. A five-volume collection of Afro-American folk beliefs and practices.

Jackson, Bruce, ed. *The Negro and His Folklore in Nineteenth-Century Periodicals*. Austin & London: Published for the American Folklore Society by the University of Texas Press, 1967.

Kittredge, George Lyman. *The Old Farmer and His Almanack*. Boston: W. Ware, 1904. Includes a variety of riddles, customs, anecdotes, folk cures, superstitions, farm lore, and tales from the almanac tradition of the late eighteenth century.

————. *Witchcraft in Old and New England*. Cambridge, Mass.: Harvard University Press, 1929. Pointing out the continuity of witchcraft beliefs between Europe and America, Kittredge catches the essence of American folklore.

Laws, G. Malcolm, Jr. *American Balladry from British Broadsides*. Philadelphia: American Folklore Society, 1957. A good place to begin for those interested in the colonial folksong tradition.

Levine, Lawrence W. *Black Culture and Black Consciousness: Afro-American Folk Thought from Slavery to Freedom*. New York: Oxford University Press, 1977. Best single analysis, given its comprehensive range of black American folklore.

Masterson, James R. "Travelers' Tales of Colonial Natural History." *Journal of American Folklore* 59 (1946): 51–71, 174–88. An impressive collection of materials that indicates the wealth of folklore available in the travel narratives and suggests that the American tall-tale tradition began in the travelers' tales of the colonial era.

Rosenberg, Bruce A. *Custer and the Epic of Defeat.* University Park: Pennsylvania State University Press, 1974. Provocative treatment of a national legend, especially significant for its being the only such major study by a folklorist.

Standifer, James A., and Reeder, Barbara. *Source Book of African and Afro-American Materials for Music Educators.* Washington, D.C.: Contemporary Music Project, 1972. The advantages provided by this volume are its ready-made activities and lists that educators can utilize. The work is divided into two sections (African Music and Afro-American Music), each with biblio-graphic references and discographic information. Lists of film strips, tapes, and films and appendixes with composers, performers, and musical analyses round out the presentation.

Szwed, John F., and Abrahams, Roger D. *Afro-American Folk Culture.* 2 vols. Philadelphia: Institute for the Study of Human Issues, 1978. This work is a treasure trove of useful information. Culled from forty-nine journals in six languages, it is current until 1973. The listing is not exhaustive, but the variety of subjects included more than compensates for any lacunae. Afro-American folklore from all parts of the Western Hemisphere is included and indexed (in both volumes) according to subjects and country. The combi-nation of these two features allows the reader to ascertain the depth of a particular subject in the research. Vol. I: North America. Vol. II: The West Indies, Central and South America.

Thompson, Stith. *Tales of the North American Indians.* Cambridge, Mass.: Harvard University Press, 1929. Repr. Bloomington: Indiana University Press, 1966. The classic example of the comparative method applied to archival texts of Indian tales.

Toelken, Barre. "The 'Pretty Languages' of Yellowman: Genre, Mode and Texture in Navaho Coyote Narratives," *Genre* 2 (1969): 211–35. A landmark study of the links between stylistic attributes of Navaho Coyote tales and the entire range of Navaho literary expression. It is also an important study of the relation of narrator, tales, and community context.

AMERICAN CULTURAL MYTHS

Barnett, Louise K. *The Ignoble Savage: American Literary Racism, 1790–1890.* Westport, Conn.: Greenwood Press, 1975. A study of Indian stereotypes in American literature of the nineteenth century.

Berkhofer, Robert F., Jr. *The White Man's Indian: Images of the American Indian from Columbus to the Present.* New York: Alfred A. Knopf, 1978. The most comprehensive discussion of the image of the Indian by a scholar well versed in sociology, history, and anthropology.

Cawelti, John G. *Apostles of the Self-Made Man.* Chicago: University of Chicago Press, 1965. Making heavy use of both popular and serious literature, Cawelti identifies various definitions of achievement and places them all against a background of cultural themes. Useful bibliographical essay accompanies each chapter.

Dippie, Brian W. *The Vanishing American: White Attitudes and U.S. Indian Policy.* Middletown, Conn.: Wesleyan University Press, 1981. A study of popular perceptions of the Indian as a "vanishing" race.

Garland Library of Narratives of North American Indian Captivities. 311 titles in 111 volumes selected and arranged by Wilcomb E. Washburn. New York: Garland Publishing, in progress. The most comprehensive collection of Indian captivity narratives.

Hassan, Ihab. *Radical Innocence: Studies in the Contemporary American Novel.* Princeton, N.J.: Princeton University Press, 1961. The self as hero and antihero in modern American literature viewed in terms of both destructive and constructive social tensions.

Lewis, R.W.B. *The American Adam: Innocence, Tragedy, and Tradition in the Nineteenth Century.* Chicago: University of Chicago Press, 1955. The classic study of the Adamic motif in American literature and thought from the early nineteenth century to the present.

Marx, Leo. *The Machine in the Garden: Technology and the Pastoral Ideal in America.* New York: Oxford University Press, 1964. The basic tension between nature and technological advance in literature and art.

Noble, David W. *The Eternal Adam and the New World Garden.* New York: Braziller, 1968. An intellectual historian's attempt to deal with what he takes to be the central myth in American fiction since 1830.

Parrington, Vernon Louis. *Main Currents in American Thought: An Interpretation of American Literature from the Beginnings to 1920.* New York: Harcourt, Brace, 1927-30, 1954, 1958. The classic presentation of the American cultural myth.

Pearce, Roy Harvey. *The Continuity of American Poetry.* Princeton, N.J.: Princeton University Press, 1961. A definitive account of the Adamic mode in American poetry that treats its development, expansion, and revision from the point of view of cultural history.

Rischin, Moses, ed. *The American Gospel of Success.* Chicago: Quadrangle, 1965. Covers a great variety of viewpoints from Cotton Mather through David Riesman with some stress on business and politics along with an interesting focus on ethnic and racial variations on the rags-to-riches myth.

Sheehan, Bernard W. *Savagism and Civility: Indians and Englishmen in Colonial Virginia.* New York: Cambridge University Press, 1980. A consideration of the "mythology" of "savagism": a study in intellectual history largely divorced from factual data.

Smith, Henry Nash. *Virgin Land: The American West as Symbol and Myth.* Cambridge, Mass.: Harvard University Press, 1950. Classic study of American cultural mythology; the West as symbol and myth in popular, belletristic, and serious fiction and prose writing from Jefferson to Frederick Jackson Turner.

Tebbel, John. *From Rags to Riches: Horatio Alger, Jr. and the American Dream.* New York: Macmillan, 1963. This work argues the central place of Horatio Alger in the national dream.

Turner, Frederick Jackson. *The Frontier in American History.* New York: H. Holt & Co., 1920.

Wyllie, Irvin G. *The Self-Made Man in America.* New Brunswick, N.J.: Rutgers University Press, 1954. Starting place for all treatments of success in American society. It responds to all the major interpretive problems and offers an extremely useful bibliography.

AMERICAN SETTINGS
(*See also* "Forms and Performers.")

Abrahams, Roger D. "Black Talking on the Streets." In *Explorations in the Ethnography of Speaking,* ed. Richard Bauman and Joel Sherzer, pp. 240-62. London: Cambridge University Press, 1974. Excellent delineation of urban Afro-Americans' public style of verbal performance, with careful descriptions of the terms blacks apply to their modes of street talk.

Adams, Charles C. *Boontling: An American Lingo.* Austin: University of Texas Press, 1971. A detailed study of a local language spoken extensively from about 1900 to 1920 in Boonville, a community in Northern California.

Bauman, Richard. "The La Have Island General Store: Sociability and Verbal Art in a Nova Scotia Community." *Journal of American Folklore* 85 (1972): 330–43. The "news, yarns, and arguments" exchanged at a general store are shown to be devices that create an aesthetically pleasing sense of sociability.

Bauman, Richard, and Abrahams, Roger D., eds. *"And Other Neighborly Names": Social Process and Cultural Image in Texas Folklore.* Austin: University of Texas Press, 1981.

Bendix, Reinhard. "Tradition and Modernity Reconsidered." *Comparative Studies in Society and History* 9 (1967): 292–346. Bendix convincingly argues against the concept of the folk/urban continuum and exposes the errors that result from abstractly considering "traditional society" and "modern society" to be bipolar opposites.

Berton, Pierre. *Hollywood's Canada: The Americanization of Our National Image.* Toronto: McClelland & Stewart, 1975. In spite of its bias, the book offers a vivid glimpse into a fascinating aspect of Canadian-American folkloric relations.

Boatright, Mody. "The Family Saga as a Form of Folklore." In *The Family Saga and Other Phases of American Folklore*, ed. Mody Boatright et al., pp. 1–19. Urbana: University of Illinois Press, 1958. Early discussion of stories as a genre of family folklore. Raises provocative questions about the defining characteristics of family stories.

Bossard, James H. S., and Boll, Eleanore S. *Ritual in Family Living: A Contemporary Study.* Philadelphia: University of Pennsylvania Press, 1950. Sociological approach to family ritual that is directly applicable to family folklore. Material gathered from autobiographies and interviews with college students.

Brandes, Stanley. "Family Misfortune Stories in American Folklore." *Journal of the Folklore Institute* 12 (1975): 5–17. Best discussion of a particular story type.

Brown, Lorin W., with Charles L. Briggs and Marta Weigle. *Hispano Folklife of New Mexico: The Lorin W. Brown Federal Writers' Project Manuscripts.* Albuquerque: University of New Mexico Press, 1978. Over one hundred documents describing many aspects of northern village life, with much lore presented in context. Also includes Brown's biography, a short history of the federal arts projects in New Mexico, and a selected bibliography of regional Hispano folklife.

Brunvand, Jan H. "As the Saints Go Marching By: Modern Jokelore Concerning Mormons." *Journal of American Folklore* 83 (1970): 53–60. One of the rare pieces that looks at Mormon folk humor. Much of the emphasis is on jokes used against the Mormon faithful by scoffers in and out of the church.

Carpenter, Inta Gale, ed. *Folklore in the Calumet Region.* New York: Arno Press, 1980. Reprinted from *Indiana Folklore* 10 (1977). Good collection of essays resulting from the work of a team of Indiana University folklorists in an urban region in northwest Indiana.

Christy, Jim, ed. *The New Refugees: American Voices in Canada.* Toronto: Peter Martin Associates, 1972. Of the many books that discuss the influx of American military dissenters into Canada in the 1960s and 1970s, this is perhaps the only one that is wholly composed of personal experience accounts.

Clements, William M. "The Rhetoric of the Radio Ministry." *Journal of American Folklore* 87 (1974): 318–27. An investigation of a folk religious performance that has been transferred from the context of the folk church to the mass media.

Collins, Camilla. "Bibliography of Urban Folklore." *Folklore Forum* 8 (1975): 57–125. Excellent source for those interested in urban industrial lore.

Cray, Ed. "Ethnic and Place Names as Derisive Adjectives." *Western Folklore* 21 (1962): 27-34.

Cutting-Baker, Holly, et al., eds. *Family Folklore*. Washington, D.C.: Smithsonian Institution, 1976. Collection of stories, photographs, and expressions collected from festival-goers at the Festival of American Folklife, 1974 and 1975.

Dargan, Mary Amanda. "Family Identity and the Social Use of Folklore: A South Carolina Family Tradition." M.A. thesis, Memorial University of Newfoundland, 1978. Excellent ethnographic study of the verbal arts and pastimes of an extended rural family.

Dorson, Richard M. *America in Legend: Folklore from the Colonial Period to the Present*. New York: Pantheon, 1973. The last section, pp. 253-310, deals with contemporary campus druglore and, read with Dorson's "The Folklore of Colleges," below, illustrates the dynamic quality of college folklore. It also presents a rich selection of the lore of regional heroes and occupations. Fully annotated, with the lore related to the temper of the times, this study provides an excellent starting point for occupational folklore study as well.

————. *Bloodstoppers and Bearwalkers: Folk Traditions of the Upper Peninsula*. Cambridge, Mass.: Harvard University Press, 1952. This regional folklore from Michigan cuts across ethnic, occupational, and generic boundaries. It includes the traditions of loggers, miners, and lakemen, with annotations pointing to other sources.

————. "The Folklore of Colleges." *American Mercury* 68 (1949): 671-77. The first comprehensive study of college folklore, this article is still one of the best introductions to the subject. It forms the basis of Dorson's treatment of college folklore in *American Folklore* (Chicago: University of Chicago Press, 1959), pp. 254-67.

Dundes, Alan, and Pagter, Carl R. *Work Hard and You Shall Be Rewarded: Urban Folklore from the Paperwork Empire*. Bloomington: Indiana University Press, 1978.

Fife, Austin E., and Fife, Alta S. *Saints of Sage and Saddle: Folklore among the Mormons*. Bloomington: Indiana University Press, 1956. Though dated, the Fifes' ground-breaking work is still the major key to Mormon lore. Links Mormon folklore to the principal events in Mormon history.

Funk and Wagnall's Standard Dictionary of Folklore, Mythology and Legend, s. v. "Micronesian Mythology," and "Polynesian Mythology," by Katharine Luomala. These two articles give concise summaries of the island cultures, the interrelationships of their lore, examples of their heroes and story cycles, along with indications of Western intrusions. Selective bibliographies are included.

Glassie, Henry. *Folk Housing in Middle Virginia*. Knoxville: University of Tennessee Press, 1975. A brilliant study that proceeds from meticulous analyses of regional folk houses to convincing observations on the evolution of the Western mind.

Glassie, Henry; Ives, Edward D.; and Szwed, John F. *Folksongs and their Makers*. Bowling Green, Ohio: Bowling Green University Popular Press, 1970. This collection brings together three essays on related topics, by Glassie, Ives, and Szwed.

Goodwin, Joseph P. "Relationships between Folklore and Dialectology." *Midwestern Journal of Language and Folklore* 3 (1977): 69-75. A review of the literature to date on folklore and linguistic geography.

Green, Archie. *Only a Miner: Studies in Recorded Coal-Mining Songs*. Urbana: University of Illinois Press, 1972. Green gives an assessment of Korson's contributions and explores the interrelationships of folklore, folksong, and the recording industry. Oriented to mining and mining lore, the extensive references, annotations, and bibliography constitute a fine introduction to mining folklore scholarship.

Gutman, Herbert G. "Work, Culture, and Society in Industrializing America, 1815-1919." *American Historical Review* 78 (1973): 531-88. An interesting discussion of the work ethic and its history in America. Gutman argues that the work ethic is not indigenous to this country and is based on the exploitation of the worker by management.

Hall, Max. "The Great Cabbage Hoax: A Case Study." *Journal of Personality and Social Psychology* 2 (1965): 563-69. A fruitless attempt to discover the origin of an item of paperwork folklore going back at least to the 1940s. See also Hall's article "26,911 Little Words," *The New Republic* 176 (April 23, 1977): 9-10.

Ives, Edward D. *Joe Scott: The Woodsman Songmaker*. Urbana: University of Illinois Press, 1978. A detailed biography of a single songmaker and a complete study of each of his extant songs.

————. *Larry Gorman: The Man Who Made the Songs*. Indiana University Folklore Monograph Series, No. 19. Bloomington: Indiana University Press, 1964. Ives traces the career of a composer of satirical folksongs and includes excellent ethnographic data on lumbering in Eastern Canada and Maine. The study illustrates the ease with which a working man could in his lifetime be a farmer, woodsman, and millworker. The annotations and bibliography constitute a rich cross section of lumbering folklore scholarship.

Jackson, George Pullen. *White and Negro Spirituals, Their Life Span and Kinship*. Locust Valley, N.Y.: J. J. Augustin, 1943. Presenting his case for the Euro-American origin of "Negro spirituals," the author discusses the development of American religious folksong in the context of American religious history.

Joannis, Claudette. *Les petits metiers des jardin publies*. Paris: Christine Bonneton, 1977. This is a history of the types of vendors, merchants, and buskers who have made their living in the public parks of Paris. The excellent illustrations offer insight into the continuity of the costumes and symbols of Parisian "park-folk." It is a model study that has no American counterpart.

Jones, Oakah L., Jr. *Los Paisanos: Spanish Settlers on the Northern Frontier of New Spain*. Norman: University of Oklahoma Press, 1979. Social history of the "ordinary" pioneers in Texas, Arizona, New Mexico, California, and northern Mexico before 1821. Includes summary accounts of folklore culture.

Korson, George. *Minstrels of the Mine Patch*. Philadelphia: University of Pennsylvania Press, 1938. Repr. Hatboro, Pa.: Folklore Associates, 1964. A collection of coal-mining songs from the anthracite region of Pennsylvania, including data on their origins and short biographies of well-known local songmakers.

Krase, Jerome. *Self and Community in the City*. Washington, D.C.: University Press of America, 1982. This theoretical case study offers an interdisciplinary analysis of neighborhood change and stability. The discussion of how city folk learn to evaluate the physical and social environment of neighborhoods and how their evaluations influence local activities has significant pertinency for urban folklore.

Lacourcière, Luc. *Oral Tradition: New England and French Canada*. Quebec: Archives de Folklore, Université Laval, 1972. Provides a survey of the special impact of French Canadian folklore on the traditions of one of the oldest border regions shared by Canada and the United States.

Lawless, Elaine. " 'What Did She Say?' An Application of Peirce's General Theory of Signs to Glossolalia in the Pentecostal Religion." *Folklore Forum* 13 (1980): 23-37. Linguistic study of a ritual language used in many American folk churches.

Leary, James P. "White Guys' Stories of the Night Street." *Journal of the Folklore Institute* 14 (1977): 59-71. Small-town white youth in southern Indiana use inflated personal experience stories to name, control, and celebrate their ambiguous existence.

Lee, Hector. *The Three Nephites: The Substance and Significance of the Legend in Folklore.* University of New Mexico Publications in Language and Literature, No. 2. Albuquerque: University of New Mexico Press, 1949. Based on 150 texts, Lee's work gives theological backgrounds for the legend, charts its distribution, compares it with other legends of eternal wanderers, and discusses its historical, sociological, and literary implications.

Liebow, Elliot. *Tally's Corner: A Study of Negro Streetcorner Men.* Boston: Little, Brown, 1967. The classic study of hanging out on the street as a lifestyle.

Limón, José E. "Agringado Joking in Texas-Mexican Society: Folklore and Differential Identity." *The New Scholar* 6 (1977): 33-50.

Lynch, Kevin. *The Image of the City.* Cambridge, Mass.: M.I.T. Press, 1960. This book sets forth the theory of the urban mental map and contains a particularly valuable section on fieldwork methods for image elicitation.

McDavid, Raven I., Jr. "Linguistic Geography and the Study of Folklore." *New York Folklore Quarterly* 14 (1958): 242-62. A good introduction to dialect study.

Marshall, Howard Wight, and Vlach, John Michael. "Toward a Folklife Approach to American Dialects." *American Speech* 48 (1973): 163-91. Demonstrates "the effectiveness of material culture traits as indexes of dialect change and development" by comparing the distribution of midwestern house and barn types to that of regional speech forms.

Miller, Ed. "The Use of Stereotypes in Inter-Ethnic Joking as a Means of Communication." *Folklore Annual* 7/8 (1977): 28-42.

Mintz, Jerome R. *Legends of the Hasidim: An Introduction to Hasidic Culture and Oral Tradition in the New World.* Chicago: University of Chicago Press, 1968. The oral narratives of a traditional Jewish group are presented with extensive ethnographic commentary.

National Film Board of Canada, Still Photography Division, Ottawa. *Between Friends / Entre Amis.* Toronto: McClelland & Stewart, 1976. Produced to honor the American Revolution Bicentennial, this is an eloquent compilation of works by thirty-two photographers who, in 1976, were commissioned to examine and interpret the Canada–United States border, "to document places in both countries where there is a sense of the border present in the daily lives of the people who live there."

Nicolaisen, W.F.H. "Folklore and Geography: Towards an Atlas of American Folk Culture." *New York Folklore Quarterly* 29 (1973): 3-20. A statement of the need for interdisciplinary regional studies by one of the organizers of SNACS.

Paredes, Américo. *A Texas-Mexican Cancionero.* Urbana: University of Illinois Press, 1976. A splendid work presenting songs of the Texas-Mexican border. Of particular comparative interest is the section devoted to thirty-four songs of border conflict, which, in addition to the song items themselves (pp. 46-109), includes an in-depth introduction, pp. 19-45.

————. *"With His Pistol in His Hand": A Border Ballad and Its Hero.* Austin: University of Texas Press, 1958. A detailed study of one ballad and its hero, set within a specific social and historical milieu.

Proshansky, Harold M.; Ittelson, William H.; and Rivlin, Leanne G., eds. *Environmental Pyschology: Man and His Physical Setting.* New York: Holt, Rinehart & Winston, 1970. This collection of readings is a fine introduction to a field that, in many areas, interfaces with the concerns of urban folklore.

Simmons, Ozzie. "The Mutual Images and Expectations of Anglo Americans and Mexican Americans," *Daedalus* 90 (1960): 286-99.

Sinclair, Upton. *The Jungle.* New York: New American Library, 1970. This well-known and influential novel describes conditions in the Chicago meat-packing industry around the turn of the century. The folklorist will be interested in the role of the union, politicians, and industrial accident stories.

Spicer, Edward H. *Cycles of Conquest: The Impact of Spain, Mexico, and the United States on the Indians of the Southwest, 1533-1960.* Tucson: University of Arizona Press, 1962. Good historical and anthropological reference.

———, ed. *Ethnic Medicine in the Southwest.* Tucson: University of Arizona Press, 1977. Papers on Black, Mexican-American, Yaqui, and lower-income Anglo folk medicine, with an introduction to "Southwestern Healing Traditions in the 1970s."

Stahl, Sandra K. D. "Cursing and its Euphemisms: Power, Irreverence, and the Unpardonable Sin." *Midwestern Journal of Language and Folklore* 3 (1977): 54-68. A discussion of the cultural significance of swearing and a classification of commonly used euphemisms.

Stocker, Terrance L.; Dutcher, Linda W.; Hargrove, Stephen M.; and Cook, Edwin A. "Social Analysis of Graffiti." *Journal of American Folklore* 85 (1972): 356-66. Analysis of social attitudes, homosexual content, and sex difference in college graffiti from Southern Illinois University, Carbondale; Western Kentucky University, Bowling Green; and the University of Missouri, Columbia.

Terkel, Studs. *Working.* New York: Pantheon, 1974. A valuable work for any occupational or factory folklorist. Although one can cavil at the book's anecdotal character, Terkel has managed to collect a wealth of material that is immediately useful for folklorists.

Thorp, N. Howard (Jack). *Songs of the Cowboys.* Edited by Austin and Alta Fife. New York: Clarkson N. Potter, 1966. In addition to the facsimile of Thorp's pioneer work, there are nearly three hundred pages of annotation, comment, and bibliography by the editors that provide entry to the extensive writing on the life and lore of the American cowboy.

Toelken, Barre. "The Folklore of Academe." In Jan H. Brunvand, *The Study of American Folklore: An Introduction,* 2d rev. ed., pp. 72-90. New York: W. W. Norton, 1978. A survey of genres and topics in high school and college folklore.

Vogt, Evon Z., and Albert, Ethel M., eds. *People of Rimrock: A Study of Values in Five Cultures.* Cambridge, Mass.: Harvard University Press, 1966. Summation of the 1949-55 Harvard "Comparative Study of Values in Five Cultures" Project. Navajo, Zuni, Spanish-American, Mormon, and Texas homesteader groups in western New Mexico were investigated from many perspectives, including their religious systems and expressive activities.

Whyte, William F. *Street Corner Society.* Chicago: University of Chicago Press, 1943. The social and political workings of Italian-American street gangs in an "eastern city's" slums; hanging out as a means of acquiring power.

Wilson, George P. "Folk Speech: Glossary, Salutations and Replies." In *The Frank C. Brown Collection of North Carolina Folklore,* vol. 1. Durham, N.C.: Duke University Press, 1952. Folk speech as part of a comprehensive statewide collection of folklore. Well annotated and interpreted.

Wilson, William A., ed. *Mormon Folklore*. Special issue of *Utah Historical Quarterly* 4 (1976). A collection of essays on themes in Mormon folklore, with special attention given to the way Mormon beliefs generate Mormon legends. Contains a survey, by the editor, of Mormon folklore scholarship and a bibliography of over 100 references to Mormon folklore studies.

Wilson, William A., and Poulsen, Richard C. "The Curse of Cain and Other Stories: Blacks in Mormon Folklore." *Sunstone* 5, no. 6 (November-December 1980): 9–13. Traces the development in legends and jokes of changing Mormon attitudes toward blacks. Focuses particularly on lore arising from the 1978 revelation granting lay priesthood to blacks.

Winks, Robin W., et al. *Four Fugitive Slave Narratives*. Reading, Mass.: Addison-Wesley Publishing Co., 1969. This is a sizeable compilation that includes a reprint of Benjamin Drew's *The North-Side of Slavery. The Refugee: or the Narratives of Fugitive Slaves in Canada, Related by Themselves*. Boston: J. P. Jewett, 1856.

Wolfenstein, Martha. *Children's Humor*. Glencoe, Ill.: Free Press, 1954. Repr. Bloomington: Indiana University Press, 1978. A psychological study of joking among children, including moron jokes, joking riddles, name-calling, and name-changing.

Zelinsky, Wilbur. *The Cultural Geography of the United States*. Englewood Cliffs, N.J.: Prentice-Hall, 1973. An excellent discussion of both regional theory and the major culture areas of America by a prominent cultural geographer.

AMERICAN ENTERTAINMENTS

Beezley, William. "Locker Rumors: Folklore and Football." *Journal of the Folklore Institute* 17 (1980): 196–221. An examination of the occupational code of professional football players and a treatment of the folktypes of coach and team joker shared by players.

Caillois, Roger. *Man and the Sacred*. Glencoe, Ill.: Free Press, 1959. *Man, Play and Games*. Glencoe, Ill.: Free Press, 1961. Caillois presents a comprehensive theory of festival based on an in-depth approach to the forms utilized and meanings expressed in festival.

Clark, Larry Dale. "The Toby Show: A Rural American Harlequinade." *Central States Speech Journal* 19 (1968): 91–96. Description and analysis of twentieth-century plays with a country-boy hero named Toby.

Coffin, Tristram. *The Illustrated Book of Baseball Folklore*. New York: Seabury Press, 1975. A comprehensive treatment of the occupational folklore of professional baseball players and baseball in journalism and literature.

Dorson, Richard M. *American Folklore*. Chicago: University of Chicago Press, 1959. The best survey. Includes good summary of his work on the powerful impact of folklore on popular culture before the Civil War.

———. "Mose the Far-Famed and World Renowned." *American Literature* 15 (1943): 288–300. Excellent study of Mose the Bowery Boy, a pre–Civil War urban folk hero of the stage, based on a New York volunteer fireman.

———. "The Yankee on the Stage—A Folk Hero of American Drama." *New England Quarterly* 13 (1940): 467–93. Important study of the stage Yankee.

Gmelch, George. "Magic in Professional Baseball." In *Games, Sport, and Power*, ed. Gregory P. Stone, pp. 128–37. New Brunswick, N.J.: Transaction Books, 1972. Based upon the Malinowskian hypothesis that magic occurs in situations marked by chance and uncertainty, the article compares the use of ritual, magic, and taboo by professional baseball players in batting, pitching, and fielding.

James, E. O. *Seasonal Feasts and Festivals*. New York: Barnes & Noble, 1963. A classic work describing calendrical festivals and drama in different historical periods and cultures.

Leach, Edmund. "Two Essays Concerning the Symbolic Representation of Time." In *Reader in Comparative Religion: An Anthropological Approach*, ed. William A. Lessa and Evon Z. Vogt, pp. 206–20. New York: Harper & Row, 1972. Exploration of the relationship between time and festival, including consideration of reversals and regeneration.

Metraux, G. S., ed. *Cultures, Festivals and Carnivals: The Major Traditions*. Special issue of *Festivals and Cultures* 3 (1976). An important collection of articles on contemporary festivals throughout the world demonstrating varied theoretical approaches.

Rourke, Constance. *American Humor: A Study of the National Character*. Garden City, N.Y.: Doubleday, 1931. Pioneering study dealing heavily with the role of folklore in American culture, including the popular stage.

Sper, Felix. *From Native Roots: A Panorama of Our Regional Drama*. Caldwell, Idaho: Caxton Printers, 1948. Good survey of plays set in fourteen American regions, including folk festivals and the use of folklore.

Sutton-Smith, Brian. "A Structural Grammar of Games and Sports." *International Review of Sports Sociology* 2 (1976): 117–35. Based upon Piaget's theories of the development of logic, Sutton-Smith analyzes the structural development of complexities of social interaction in games and sports.

Toll, Robert C. *Blacking Up: The Minstrel Show in Nineteenth-Century America*. New York: Oxford University Press, 1974. Comprehensive analysis of the form and content of minstrelsy, including uses of folklore by both white and black minstrels and a note on method.

Turner, Victor. "Liminal to Liminoid, in Play, Flow and Ritual." *Rice University Studies* 60 (1974): 53–92. Symbolic approach especially important for its distinctions between ritual and festival in preindustrial societies and related forms of expression in modern life.

Workman, Mark E. "Dramaturgical Aspects of Professional Wrestling Matches." *Folklore Forum* 10:1 (1977): 14–20. Explores the form and meaning of the professional wrestling match and examines the ambiguous perceptions of wrestling as a drama and contest.

Zug, Charles G., III. "Folklore and the Drama: The Carolina Playmakers and their 'Folk Plays.'" *Southern Folklore Quarterly* 32 (1968): 279–94. A good study of Frederick H. Koch's attempts to make drama from folklore.

AMERICAN FORMS AND PERFORMERS
(*See also* "Settings.")

Abrahams, Roger D. "The Complex Relations of Simple Forms." *Genre* 2 (1969): 104–28. How conversational genres relate to the larger spectrum of folkloric behavior.

————, ed. *A Singer and Her Songs: Almeda Riddle's Book of Ballads*. Baton Rouge: Louisiana State University Press, 1970. Contains extensive commentary by the singer on her aesthetic and her songs' sources and meaning.

Bauman, Richard, and Sherzer, Joel, eds. *Explorations in the Ethnography of Speaking*. London: Cambridge University Press, 1974. Articles consider different kinds of narratives as they are constructed in conversation. The volume consists of a number of case studies about speaking in various cultures.

Brendle, Thomas R., and Unger, Claude W. *Folk Medicine of the Pennsylvania Germans: The Non-Occult Cures*. New York: Augustus M. Kelley,

Publishers, 1970. Repr. Norristown, Pa.: Pennsylvania German Society, 1935. Classic work that not only provides a great many of the cures found in the Pennsylvania German tradition but also represents very well the "tradition attitude" of works on folk medicine. Closes with a very valuable annotated bibliography.

Clark, Margaret. *Health in the Mexican-American Culture: A Community Study*. Berkeley: University of California Press, 1959. Reprinted 1970. Intensive field study conducted in San Jose, California. Places folk medicine within its full cultural context and provides a very useful glossary and bibliography.

Cooper, Patricia, and Buferd, Norma. *The Quilters: Women and Domestic Art*. New York: Doubleday, 1977. Written as an art exhibition catalog, this volume is exceptional in that the authors spend a good deal of their time eliciting commentary from quilters. Suggestive for future research.

Dégh, Linda. *People of the Tobacco Belt: Four Lives*. Canadian Centre for Folk Culture Studies, Paper no. 13. Ottawa: National Museums of Canada, 1975. Investigates the life history as a narrative folklore genre. Four informants are interviewed, and the texts of their life histories are printed and analyzed by the author.

Dégh, Linda, and Vázsonyi, Andrew. "Legend and Belief." *Genre* 4 (1971): 281–304. Includes a description of the process of legend construction among a group of people in conversation.

Dorson, Richard M. *Bloodstoppers and Bearwalkers*. Cambridge, Mass.: Harvard University Press, 1952. In the section "Sagamen," Dorson presents a number of texts that easily fall into the category of personal experience stories. One of the first American publications to clearly identify such texts as folklore.

————. "Oral Styles of American Folk Narrators." In *Folklore: Selected Essays*, by Richard M. Dorson, pp. 99–146. Bloomington: Indiana University Press, 1972.

Dorson, Richard M., and Stahl, Sandra K. D., eds. "Stories of Personal Experiences." *Journal of the Folklore Institute* 14 (1977): 1–126. A special issue that grew out of a session on personal experience stories at the 1975 American Folklore Society meeting.

Evans, David. *Big Road Blues: Tradition and Creativity in the Folk Blues*. Berkeley: University of California Press, 1982. Study of how blues singers learn and compose folk blues within a local tradition, with an examination of the repertoires of two blues singers.

Fahey, John. *Charley Patton*. London: Studio Vista, 1970. Ethnomusicological study of the repertoire of a Mississippi folk blues singer.

Hand, Wayland D. *Magical Medicine: The Folkloric Component of Medicine in the Folk Belief, Custom, and Ritual of the Peoples of Europe and America*. Berkeley: University of California Press, 1980. Collection of twenty-three previously published articles on broad range of supernatural healing practices. Contains a bibliography and comparative annotations.

————, ed. *American Folk Medicine: A Symposium*. Berkeley & Los Angeles: University of California Press, 1976. Twenty-five papers dealing with a wide variety of ethnic and regional traditions, from many different points of view. Best single source for a comprehensive view of recent thought on folk medicine.

Hufford, David J. "Christian Religious Healing." *Journal of Operational Psychiatry* 8 (1977): 22–27. Example of the use of the study of one variety of folk medicine (plus popular and "official" healing beliefs and practices) to address specifically medical concerns.

Huizinga, Johan. *Homo Ludens: A Study of the Play-Element in Culture*. New York: Pantheon Books, 1939. The classic work.

Jones, Bessie, and Hawes, Bess Lomax. *Step It Down: Games, Plays, Songs, and Stories from the Afro-American Heritage*. New York: Harper & Row, 1972. Collection of children's game songs in the repertoire of Bessie Jones with her commentary and directions for steps and clapping.

Jones, Michael Owen. *The Hand-Made Object and Its Maker*. Berkeley & Los Angeles: University of California Press, 1975. First book-length treatment by a folklorist of a craftsman's biography. The theoretical discussion in the first and last chapters is most crucial, since insights expressed there are applicable to all examples of craftsmanship.

Kirshenblatt-Gimblett, Barbara. "Toward a Theory of Proverb Meaning." *Proverbium* 22 (1973): 821–27. A discussion of the multiple meanings of proverbs depending upon their situations of use.

———— , ed. *Speech Play: Research and Resources for Studying Linguistic Creativity*. Philadelphia: University of Pennsylvania Press, 1976. Contains an extremely useful bibliography, much of it concerned with children's folklore.

McCarl, Robert. "The Production Welder: Product, Process, and the Industrial Craftsman." *New York Folklore Quarterly* 30 (1974): 243–53. This article reminds us that crafts are not necessarily old-fashioned. Contemporary technology can and does provide the context for the development of modern craft traditions.

Mastick, Pat. "Dry Stone Walling." *Indiana Folklore* 9 (1976): 113–33. Both historical and ethnographic research are interwoven here. An Indiana dry stone waller gives his personal viewpoint on the subject while European and American antecedents of dry stone walling are discussed.

Opie, Iona, and Opie, Peter. *The Lore and Language of School Children*. Oxford: Clarendon Press, 1959. A rich sampling of children's folklore circulating in Britain after the second world war.

Robinson, John A. "Personal Narratives Reconsidered." *Journal of American Folklore* 94 (1981): 58–85. A linguistically based view of personal narratives in conversational contexts.

Stahl, Sandra K. D. "The Oral Personal Narrative in its Generic Context." *Fabula* 18 (1977): 18–39. Distinguishes the secular "personal narrative" from closely related narrative folklore categories.

Sutton-Smith, Brian. *The Folkgames of Children*. Austin: University of Texas Press, 1972. A useful survey of selected materials.

Wigginton, Eliot, ed. *The Foxfire Books*. Garden City, N.Y.: Anchor Books, 1972 and following years. Although these books contain the descriptive efforts of high school students, their finds often capture some primary data on craftsmen in North Georgia not yet available elsewhere. Informative photographs and sketches of craft processes.

Wolf, John Quincy. "Folksingers and the Re-creation of Folksong." *Western Folkore* 26 (1967): 101–11. Discussion of the handling of repertoire by Ozark ballad singers.

Wolfenstein, Martha. *Children's Humor*. Glencoe, Ill.: Free Press, 1954. Repr. Bloomington: Indiana University Press, 1978. A Freudian approach to children's verbal folklore, anticipating the current theoretical activity in this area.

Yerkovich, Sally. "Gossiping; or, the Creation of Fictional Lives, Being a Study of the Subject in an Urban American Setting Drawing upon Vignettes from Upper Middle Class Lives." Ph.D. dissertation, University of Pennsylvania, 1976. A processual and performance oriented account of gossiping as a form of expressive conversation.

Yoder, Don. "Folk Medicine." In *Folklore and Folklife, An Introduction*, ed. Richard M. Dorson, pp. 191–215. Chicago: University of Chicago Press, 1972. Excellent introduction to the subject in general, using the Pennsylvania German powwow tradition as a major example. Useful annotated reading list.

INTERPRETATION

Arewa, E. Ojo, and Dundes, Alan. "Proverbs and the Ethnography of Speaking Folklore." *American Anthropologist* 66 (1964): 70–85. Stresses the importance of context for the understanding of proverbs.

Bascom, William R., ed. *Frontiers of Folklore*. Boulder, Colo.: Westview Press, 1977. Six articles on recent theoretical concerns in American folkloristics.

Bauman, Richard, and Abrahams, Roger D., eds. *"And Other Neighborly Names": Social Process and Cultural Image in Texas Folklore*. Austin: University of Texas Press, 1981. Emphasis in this collection of essays is on the creative reaction to socially and culturally pluralistic situations.

Ben-Amos, Dan, ed. *Folklore Genres*. Austin: University of Texas Press, 1976,. A collection of papers by folklorists focusing on how the concept of genre may be approached from both the folkloristic and the native points of view; the editor's article and introduction spell out these alternative strategies.

Ben-Amos, Dan, and Goldstein, Kenneth, eds. *Folklore: Performance and Communication*. The Hague: Mouton, 1975. Essays drawing on the communication model for performance analysis, about half of which cover American traditional situations.

Burke, Kenneth. *Studies in Symbolic Action*. New York: Vintage Books, 1957. A classic approach to relationships between narrative and social conditions. Provides basis for interdisciplinary discussion by establishing a common vocabulary for literary scholars, folklorists, anthropologists, and sociologists.

Denisoff, R. Serge. *Great Day Coming: Folk Music and the American Left*. Urbana: University of Illinois Press, 1971.

Dorson, Richard M. *America in Legend*. New York: Pantheon, 1973. Makes the case that American folklore reflects and explains the American historical experience. Divides American history into four "lifestyles": religious, democratic, economic, and humane.

——— . *American Folklore and the Historian*. Chicago: University of Chicago Press, 1971.

——— . "The Debate over the Trustworthiness of Oral Traditional History." In *Folklore: Selected Essays*, by Richard M. Dorson, pp. 199–224. Bloomington: Indiana University Press, 1972. Discusses the historical use of oral materials.

Dundes, Alan. *The Morphology of North American Indian Folktales*. Folklore Fellows Communications, no. 195. Helsinki: 1964. Application of Pike's linguistic theories to folktale study to produce a "grammar" of tales, to compare them apart from content.

——— , ed. *Mother Wit from the Laughing Barrel: Readings in the Interpretation of Afro-American Folklore*. Englewood Cliffs, N.J.: Prentice-Hall, 1973. Brings together a wide variety of sources, primarily by black writers. Includes extensive headnotes by Dundes.

Fine, Gary Alan. "Small Groups and Culture Creation: The Idioculture of Little League Baseball Teams." *American Sociological Review* 44 (1979); 733–45. An interactionist analysis of the creation and usage of certain cultural forms among baseball teams.

Geertz, Clifford. *The Interpretation of Cultures*. New York: Basic Books, 1973. The first and last chapters are widely regarded as the classic descriptions of the doing of ethnography and the relating of the data to the larger systems of culture; the author, an anthropologist, draws on the range of expressive data as do folklorists.

Hareven, Tamara K., and Langenbach, Randolph. *Amoskeag: Life and Work in an American Factory-City*. New York: Pantheon Books, 1978. Interesting attempt to re-create the past through the use of oral interviews.

Hymes, Dell H. "Folklore's Nature and the Sun's Myth." *Journal of American Folklore* 88 (1975): 345-69. A concise but insightful discussion of five key notions central to folklore: genre, performance, tradition, situation, and creativity.

_____. *"In Vain I Tried to Tell You": Essays in Native American Ethnopoetics*. Philadelphia: University of Pennsylvania Press, 1981. Reprint of older essays as well as new ones.

Jacobs, Melville. *The Content and Style of an Oral Literature*. Viking Fund Publications in Anthropology, no. 26. New York: Viking, 1959. A collection of Clackamas Chinook narrative with scholarly introduction and notes that combine literary, folklore, and anthropological approaches to tales.

Kamenetsky, Christa. "Folktale and Ideology in the Third Reich." *Journal of American Folklore* 90 (1977): 168-78.

Levine, Lawrence W. *Black Culture and Black Consciousness: Afro-American Folk Thought from Slavery to Freedom*. New York: Oxford University Press, 1977. A good example of historical study based largely on folkloristic sources.

Montell, William Lynwood. *The Saga of Coe Ridge: A Study in Oral History*. Knoxville: University of Tennessee Press, 1970. Montell reconstructs the history of a small black community in Kentucky. Excellent example of the advantages of combining folklore and history in conducting historical research.

Oinas, Felix J., ed. *Folklore, Nationalism, and Politics*. Columbus, Ohio: Slavica Publishers, 1978. Wide range of articles reprinted from a special issue of the *Journal of the Folklore Institute*.

Paredes, Américo, and Bauman, Richard, eds. *Toward New Perspectives in Folklore*. Austin: University of Texas Press, 1972. A collection of papers illustrating the variety of ways folklorists have come to employ situational features and ethnographic laws of reference in presenting their data.

Sebeok, Thomas A., ed. *Style in Language*. Cambridge, Mass.: Technology Press of M.I.T., 1960. Attempt to establish an interdisciplinary perspective in stylistics. Dorson's essay discusses individual styles of folk narrators.

Truzzi, Marcello. "The 100% American Songbag: Conservative Folksongs in America." *Western Folklore* 28 (1969): 27-40.

Vansina, Jan. *Oral Tradition: A Study in Historical Methodology*. Chicago: Aldine Publishing Co., 1965. Discusses the historical use of oral materials.

Williams, John A. "Radicalism and Professionalism in Folklore Studies: A Comparative Perspective," and "Comments" by Richard M. Dorson. *Journal of the Folklore Institute* 11 (1975): 211-39.

METHODS

Allen, Barbara, and Montell, William Lynwood. *From Memory to History: Using Oral Sources in Local Historical Research*. Nashville: American Association for State and Local History, 1981.

American Folklife Center, Library of Congress. *Ethnic Recordings in America: A Neglected Heritage.* Washington, D.C.: American Folklife Center, forthcoming.

Baker, Ronald L. *Folklore in the Writings of Rowland E. Robinson.* Bowling Green, Ohio: Bowling Green University Popular Press, 1973. Identifies examples of folklore and folklife in the works of Vermont writer Rowland Robinson and discusses briefly the contributions of the folklore to his fiction. A fine model for identifying folklore in literature.

Bascom, William R., ed. *Frontiers of Folklore.* Boulder, Colo.: Westview Press, 1977. Six articles on recent theoretical concerns in American folkloristics, including a discussion by Ben-Amos of "context," Abrahams of "enactment," Dundes of "folk," and Scheub of "performances."

Bauman, Richard. *Verbal Art as Performance.* Rowley, Mass.: Newbury House, 1977. Outlines a general framework for the contextual study of folklore.

Bellman, Beryl L., and Jules-Rosette, Bennetta. *A Paradigm for Looking: Cross-Cultural Research with Visual Media.* Norwood, N.J.: Ablex, 1977.

Brunvand, Jan Harold. *Folklore: A Study and Research Guide.* New York: St. Martin's Press, 1976.

————. *A Guide for Collectors of Folklore in Utah.* Salt Lake City: University of Utah Press, 1971.

Carpenter, Inta Gale, ed. *Folklorists in the City: The Urban Field Experience.* *Folklore Forum* 11, no. 3 (1978). Personal accounts of fieldwork in the Calumet region of northwest Indiana.

Cohen, Anne B. *Poor Pearl, Poor Girl! The Murdered Girl Stereotype in Ballad and Newspaper.* American Folklore Society Memoir Series, vol. 58. Austin: Published for the American Folklore Society by the University of Texas Press, 1973. Important exploration of interrelationships between balladry and newspaper writing in nineteenth-century America.

Cohen, Norm. *Long Steel Rail: The Railroad in American Folksong.* Urbana: University of Illinois Press, 1981.

Collier, John, Jr. *Visual Anthropology: Photography as a Research Method.* New York: Holt, Rinehart & Winston, 1967. Conducting research with the aid of the still camera is Collier's major subject, but the last chapter is devoted to filmmaking as a fieldwork tool.

Cray, Ed. " 'Barbara Allen': Cheap Print and Reprint." In *Folklore International: Essays in Traditional Literature, Belief, and Custom in Honor of Wayland Debs Hand,* ed. D. K. Wilgus, pp. 41–50. Hatboro, Pa.: Folklore Associates, 1967. Points out interdependence of oral tradition and print in relation to a well-known Anglo-American ballad.

Deetz, James. *In Small Things Forgotten: The Archaeology of Early American Life.* Garden City: Anchor Press/Doubleday, 1977. An archaeologist's accessible, important presentation of the historical value of American artifacts.

Dorson, Richard M. *America in Legend.* New York: Pantheon Books, 1973; *American Folklore.* Chicago: University of Chicago Press, 1959; and *Jonathan Draws the Long Bow: New England Popular Tales and Legends.* Cambridge, Mass.: Harvard University Press, 1946. Excellent examples of how the folklore of earlier historical periods can be found in printed sources.

————. *American Folklore and the Historian.* Chicago: University of Chicago Press, 1971. Contains a number of essays valuable to students of folklore and American literature, including "Print and American Folktales" and a reprinting of the 1957 article on the "Identification of Folklore in American Literature."

———. "Paul Bunyan in the News, 1939-1941." *Western Folklore* 15 (1956): 26-39, 179-93, 247-61. Demonstrates the usefulness of newspaper clippings in keeping track of developments of interest to folklorists (in this case, American awareness of a "pseudo folk hero").

———. "The Use of Printed Sources." In *Folklore and Folklife, An Introduction*, ed. Richard M. Dorson. Chicago: University of Chicago Press, 1972. See especially on the question of how to distinguish the different relations that different items of folklore in print have to oral tradition.

Dundes, Alan. "Texture, Text and Context." *Southern Folklore Quarterly* 28 (1964): 251-65. Important early argument for the significance of situational context.

Glassie, Henry. *Folk Housing in Middle Virginia: A Structural Analysis of Historic Artifacts*. Knoxville: University of Tennessee Press, 1975. To join modern studies of artifacts and oral literature, this book extends structural methods of the kind normally used in folktale analysis into the realm of material culture; to interpret the historical architectural record of a small area, this book extends structural methods into time.

Goldstein, Kenneth S. *A Guide for Field Workers in Folklore*. Hatboro, Pa.: Folklore Associates for the American Folklore Society, 1964. Remains the fullest and best guide to folklore fieldwork, strongly informed by a contextual perspective.

Halpert, Herbert. "Folklore: Breadth Versus Depth." *Journal of American Folklore* 71 (1958): 97-103. Pioneering argument for "the collection of folklore in its proper context."

Heider, Karl G. *Ethnographic Film*. Austin: University of Texas Press, 1976. Heider develops a theoretical framework for analyzing and making ethnographic films. He presents a grid for judging the success of films according to their ethnographic attributes, provides a history of ethnographic films, and discusses the use of such films for teaching purposes.

Hoffman, Daniel. *Form and Fable in American Fiction*. New York: W. W. Norton, 1961. An interpretive study of Hawthorne, Melville, and Twain that draws upon both folklore and literary concepts of myth in the explication of classic American fiction.

Jackson, Bruce, ed. *The Negro and His Folklore in Nineteenth Century Periodicals*. Austin: Published for the American Folklore Society by the University of Texas Press, 1967. Important collection of articles (published 1838-1899) that include texts of Afro-American folklore or describe its performance.

Jenkins, J. Geraint. "The Use of Artifacts and Folk Art in the Folk Museum." In *Folklore and Folklife, An Introduction*, ed. Richard M. Dorson, pp. 497-516. Chicago: University of Chicago Press, 1972. A review of the folk museums of northern Europe and how folklife studies are integrated into the museums' work. The conceptual and practical uses of artifacts in museums are discussed and vivid examples given.

Jones, Michael Owen. *The Hand-Made Object and Its Maker*. Berkeley & Los Angeles: University of California Press, 1975. An intensive study of chair-makers in Kentucky; model folkloristic study of craft.

Laws, G. Malcolm, Jr. *American Balladry from British Broadsides: A Guide for Students and Collectors of Traditional Song*. American Folklore Society Bibliographic and Special Series, no. 8. Philadelphia: American Folklore Society, 1957. Standard catalogue to American folksongs derived from British broadsides; useful commentary also.

Leach, MacEdward, and Glassie, Henry. *A Guide for Collectors of Oral Traditions and Folk Cultural Material in Pennsylvania.* Harrisburg, Pa.: Pennsylvania Historical and Museum Commission, 1968. A guide for workers in Pennsylvania's Ethnic Culture Survey begun by Leach and completed and expanded by Glassie during his term as Pennsylvania state folklorist.

Lipton, Lenny. *Independent Filmmaking.* San Francisco: Straight Arrow Books, 1972. A basic handbook on the techniques of filmmaking.

List, George. "Fieldwork: Recording Traditional Music." In *Folklore and Folklife, An Introduction,* ed. Richard M. Dorson, pp. 445–54. Chicago: University of Chicago Press, 1972. Article on collecting folk music and songs.

Paredes, Américo. "On Ethnographic Work among Minority Groups: A Folklorist's Perspective." *The New Scholar* 6 (1977): 1–32. Argues for the need to know the language and the culture of the ethnic group being investigated.

Pentikäinen, Juha. "Depth Research." *Acta Ethnographica Academiae Scientiarum Hungaricae* 21 (1972): 127–51. Broadly comprehensive fieldwork-oriented framework for folklore research by a leading European folklorist.

Quimby, Ian M. G., ed. *Material Culture and the Study of American Life.* New York: W. W. Norton, 1978. The papers, presented by eleven noted authorities on material culture interpretation, some in museum environments, are carefully edited, illustrated, and well documented in footnotes and index.

Richardson, Robert D., Jr. *Myth and Literature in the American Renaissance.* Bloomington: Indiana University Press, 1978. Surveys the interest American writers of the 1800s exhibited in the process of mythical thought and myth formation. Suggests that American writers were experimenting with the application of mythic methods to the creation of literature.

Sherman, Sharon R. "The Folkloric Film: The Relevance of Film for Understanding Folkloric Events." Ph.D. dissertation, Indiana University, 1977. Concerns the use of film for folkloristic research and teaching. First scholarly work to provide definition, history, analysis, and suggestions for making folkloric films. Annotated filmography included.

Smith, Robert J. *The Art of the Festival.* University of Kansas Publications in Anthropology, #6. Lawrence: University of Kansas Libraries, 1975. Description and analysis of a regional Peruvian fiesta presented in a model adaptable to other festivals.

Stahl, Sandra K. D., ed. *Readings from the Journal of the Folklore Institute: Folklore and Literature.* Bloomington: Trickster Press, 1981. A collection of essays on various folklore and literature topics published in the *Journal* over the period 1964–75. Includes articles by Abrahams, Lüthi, Bruce Rosenberg, and others.

Tedlock, Dennis. *Finding the Center.* New York: Dial Press, 1972. A work that demonstrates a method of transcription and translation that maintains the poetic values of the original as nearly as possible.

Titon, Jeff Todd. *Early Downhome Blues: A Musical and Cultural Analysis.* Urbana: University of Illinois Press, 1977.

Vlach, John Michael. *The Afro-American Tradition in Decorative Arts.* Cleveland: Cleveland Museum of Art, 1978. A rich and intelligent survey of Afro-American folk art.

Welsch, Roger L. *Sod Walls: The Story of the Nebraska Sod House.* Broken Bow, Nebr.: Purcells, 1968. In providing an account of the sod house of the Plains, Welsch teaches how old photographs may be effectively used in artifactual research.

Wilgus, D. K., ed. "Commercialized Folk Music: Sources and Resources." *Western Folklore* 30 (1971): 171-246. Articles by Norm Cohen, Eugene Earle, Archie Green, Joseph C. Hickerson, Bill C. Malone, Guthrie T. Meade, D. K. Wilgus.

Wilgus, D. K., and Greenway, John, eds. "Hillbilly Issue." *Journal of American Folklore* 78 (1965): 195-287. Articles by Norm Cohen, Archie Green, Ed Kahn, Mayne Smith, D. K. Wilgus.

Yoder, Don, ed. *American Folklife*. Austin: University of Texas Press, 1976. Twelve folklife scholars write on a variety of topics in material and nonmaterial folk culture. The editor's chapter, "Folklife Studies in American Scholarship," and James Marston Fitch's "Uses of the Artistic Past" are especially appropriate to museum studies. Yoder's "The Folklife Studies Movement," *Pennsylvania Folklife* 13:3 (1963): 43-56, is a helpful companion reference.

PRESENTATION

Abrahams, Roger. *Deep Down in the Jungle: Negro Narrative Folklore from the Streets of Philadelphia*, rev. ed. Chicago: Aldine, 1970.

Altman, Terri, et al. "Folklore and Education: A Selected Annotated Bibliography of Periodical Literature." *Keystone Folklore* 22 (1978): 53-85. An annotated bibliography of articles dealing with the teaching of folklore in elementary and secondary schools as well as in colleges.

"Archiving Folklore." In *Four Symposia on Folklore*, ed. Stith Thompson, pp. 89-154. Bloomington: Indiana University Press, 1953. Discussions by leading European and American scholars on archiving techniques and problems.

Brunvand, Jan Harold. *On the Teaching of American Folklore*. New York: W. W. Norton, 1970. An instructor's manual for Brunvand's textbook, *The Study of American Folklore: An Introduction*. This booklet contains useful information on procedures, techniques, papers, projects, and exams in undergraduate folklore classes.

Burcaw, G. Ellis. *Introduction to Museum Work*. Nashville, Tenn.: American Association for State and Local History, 1975. Sketching the entire museum field, this work gives a good orientation to those with little knowledge of museums.

Burns, Tom. "Involving the Introductory Student of Folklore in the Functional Analysis of the Material He Collects." In *Perspectives on Folklore and Education*. Folklore Forum Bibliographic and Special Series, no. 2, pp. 13-27. Emphasizes that the student should be asked to analyze the material collected.

Camp, Charles. "Perspectives in Applied Folklore: American Folk Festivals and the Recent Maryland Experience." *Free State Folklore* 3 (1976-77): 4-15; and "State Folklorists and Folklife Programs: A Second Look." *Folklore Forum* 10:1 (1977): 26-29. Both articles discuss the relationship of specific projects to state folklore programs. The first is a response to Carey (1976), see below.

Carey, George. *Maryland Folklore and Folklife*. Cambridge, Md.: Tidewater Publishers, 1970. An expanded version of Carey's introduction to the report of the Commission on Maryland Folklife, widely used as a text in Maryland folklore courses.

————. "State Folklorists and State Arts Councils: The Maryland Pilot." *Folklore Forum* 9:1 (1976): 1-8. Carey's account of his term as Maryland state folklorist, including retrospective observations.

Ferris, Bill, and Peiser, Judy, eds. *American Folklore Films and Videotapes: An Index*. Memphis, Tenn.: Center for Southern Folklore, 1976. Contains 1,800 annotated entries, not all of which are directly related to folklore. Subject and distributor list.

Franklin, Colin. "Publishing Folklore." *Folklore* 77 (1966): 184-204. Revealing discussion of how a publisher views folklorists.

Green, Rayna. "Magnolias Grow in Dirt: The Bawdy Lore of Southern Women." *Southern Exposure: A Journal of the New South* 4 (1977): 29-33; reprinted in *The Radical Teacher* 6 (1977): 26-30.

Guthe, Carl E. *The Management of Small Museums*. 2d ed. Nashville, Tenn.: American Association for State and Local History, 1964.

Haring, Lee, and Foreman, Ellen. "Folklore in the Freshman Writing Course," *College English* 37 (1975): 13-21. Suggests using the students' own oral traditions in a college composition course to help students make "the crucial transition from oral fluency to power in writing."

Hockings, Paul. ed. *Principles of Visual Anthropology*. The Hague: Mouton, 1975. See especially Hockings's article, "Educational Uses of Videotape," Timothy Asch's "Using Film in Teaching Anthropology: One Pedagogical Approach," and Stephanie Krebs's "The Film Elicitation Technique."

Hoffmann, Frank. *Analytical Survey of Anglo-American Traditional Erotica*. Bowling Green, Ohio: Bowling Green University Popular Press, 1973.

Indiana University, Archives of Traditional Music. *A Catalog of Phonorecordings of Music and Oral Data Held by the Archives of Traditional Music*. Boston: G. K. Hall, 1975. Good example of a published card catalog, with indexes, from a large sound recording archive.

Ireland, Florence. *The Northeast Archives of Folklore and Oral History: A Brief Description and a Catalog of its Holdings, 1958-1972*. In *Northeast Folklore* 13 (1972). Orono, Maine: Northeast Folklore Society, 1973. Substantial listing, with introduction, of the holdings of an active regional folklore archives.

Jackson, Bruce. *"Get Your Ass in the Water and Swim Like Me": Narrative Poetry from Black Oral Tradition*. Cambridge, Mass.: Harvard University Press, 1974.

Jones, Suzi. *Oregon Folklore*. Eugene: University of Oregon and the Oregon Arts Commission, 1977. A model use of archival material by Oregon's state folklorists, and, by the author's account, a useful tool for educating teachers and the general public in folklore and its cultural contexts.

List, George. "Archiving." In *Folklore and Folklife, An Introduction*, ed. Richard M. Dorson, pp. 455-63. Chicago: University of Chicago Press, 1972. A succinct history and survey of folklore archiving in Europe and America.

————. "A Statement on Archiving." *Journal of the Folklore Institute* 6 (1969): 222-31. Some practical advice on preparing material for an archive.

Lloyd, Timothy Charles, ed. "An Introduction to Folklore for Arts Administrators." *Traditional Arts Program Publications in Folklore*, no. 1. Columbus, Ohio: Ohio Foundation on the Arts, 1978. Proceedings of a panel on folklore and arts administration.

Loomis, Ormond. *Sources on Folk Museums and Living Historical Farms*. Special issue of *Folklore Forum*, Bibliographic and Special Series, no. 16, 1977. This work can guide the reader to other books and articles written in English that relate to the field.

Randolph, Vance. *Pissing in the Snow and Other Ozark Folktales*. With an introduction by Rayna Green and notes by Frank A. Hoffmann. Urbana: University of Illinois Press, 1976.

Rasmussen, Holger, ed. *Dansk Folkemuseum and Frilandsmuseet, History and Activities.* Copenhagen: Nationalmuseet, 1966. One of the best works available on folk museums, it provides an illustration of the kinds of professional work done in such an agency.

Schlebecker, John T., and Peterson, Gale E. *Living Historical Farms Handbook.* Washington, D.C.: Smithsonian Institution Press, 1972. While specific to setting up working farm museums, it is the best guide available for starting an open-air museum in the United States.

"Symposium on Obscenity." *Journal of American Folklore* 85 (1962): 189-248. Examines three basic issues regarding traditional erotica: misconceptions, definitions, collecting techniques.

Toelken, Barre. *Instructor's Manual: The Dynamics of Folklore.* Boston: Houghton Mifflin, 1979. Designed for the teacher without much formal training in folklore who uses the author's introductory textbook. Suggests lecture and discussion topics and ideas for projects.

Contributors

Roger D. Abrahams is Alexander H. Kenan professor of humanities and anthropology at Scripps and Pitzer Colleges, Claremont, California.

Ronald L. Baker is chairperson and professor of English at Indiana State University. He is editor of the *Midwestern Journal of Language and Folklore*; author of *Hoosier Folk Legends* and coauthor of *Indiana Place Names*.

Richard Bauman, professor of anthropology and director of the Center for Intercultural Studies in Folklore and Ethnomusicology, the University of Texas, Austin, has published widely on American folklore, folklore theory and method, and the ethnography of speaking.

Michael Edward Bell is director of the Rhode Island Folklife Project.

Richard Blaustein, associate professor in the Department of Sociology/Anthropology of East Tennessee State University, Johnson City, has experimented with the use of portable video since the early 1970s.

Jan Harold Brunvand, professor of English at the University of Utah, is author of *The Study of American Folklore* and former editor of the *Journal of American Folklore*.

Charles Camp has served as Maryland state folklorist since 1976, and has published on folk architecture, music, cookery, and crafts.

George Carey is professor of English at the University of Massachusetts and author of *A Sailor's Songbag*.

Inta Gale Carpenter is associate director of special projects at the Folklore Institute, Indiana University.

Thomas D. Clark is emeritus professor of history at the University of Kentucky and author of *Frontier America, The Emerging South,* and *Indiana University: Midwestern Pioneer*.

William M. Clements is professor of English at Arkansas State University and coauthor of the forthcoming *Native American Folklore, 1879–1979: An Annotated Bibliography*.

Francis A. de Caro teaches in the Department of English, Louisiana State University, Baton Rouge.

Richard M. Dorson, who taught at Harvard and at Michigan State before becoming professor of folklore and history and director of the Folklore Institute at Indiana University in 1957, published more than a dozen books on various aspects of folklore. Professor Dorson died on 11 September 1981.

Alan Dundes is professor of anthropology and folklore at the University of California, Berkeley.

David Evans is professor of music and director of graduate degree programs in ethnomusicology at Memphis State University.

CARL FLEISCHHAUER is a folklife specialist at the American Folklife Center in the Library of Congress, with a special responsibility for documentary media.

HENRY GLASSIE is professor of folklore and American civilization at the University of Pennsylvania and author of *Pattern in the Material Folk Culture of the Eastern United States, Folk Housing in Middle Virginia,* and *Passing the Time in Ballymenone.*

ARCHIE GREEN is visiting professor of folklore in the Department of English at the University of Texas, Austin. He will retire in June 1982.

RAYNA GREEN, director of the Native American Science Resource Center at Dartmouth College, writes on Native American women; Native American science, medicine, and technology; and ethics and obscenity.

GILES GUNN, chairman of American studies and professor of religion and American studies, University of North Carolina, Chapel Hill, is author of *F. O. Matthiessen* and *The Interpretation of Otherness.*

JOSEPH C. HICKERSON, head of the Archive of Folk Culture at the Library of Congress, has served as folklore archivist at Indiana University and chairman of the Committee on Archiving of the American Folklore Society. He is currently secretary and bibliographer for the Society for Ethnomusicology.

DAVID J. HUFFORD, associate professor of behavioral science and director of the Center for Humanistic Medicine at the Pennsylvania State College of Medicine, is author of *The Terror That Comes in the Night* in addition to articles on a variety of aspects of folk belief.

EDWARD D. (SANDY) IVES is professor of folklore and director of the Northeast Archives of Folklore and Oral History in the Department of Anthropology, University of Maine.

ELAINE JAHNER is associate professor of literature and folklore at the University of Nebraska, Lincoln; she specializes in American Indian literatures and in critical theory.

WM. HUGH JANSEN's entire career was spent in the Department of English at the University of Kentucky. He was author of many articles on regional folklore and on the theory of folklore, and served as editor of the monograph series for the American Folklore Society. He died on 13 June 1979.

BARBARA KIRSHENBLATT-GIMBLETT is director of the Center for Performance Studies, New York University. She is author of *Image Before My Eyes: A Photographic History of Jewish Life in Poland, 1864–1939*; and editor of *Speech Play: Research and Resources for Studying Linguistic Creativity.*

ROBERT B. KLYMASZ is a Canadian folklorist living in Winnipeg, Manitoba, Canada.

AMY KOTKIN and STEVEN ZEITLIN are at the Smithsonian Institution, where they were founding members of the Family Folklore Program at the Festival of American Folklife.

JANET L. LANGLOIS is director of the Folklore Archive and assistant professor of English, Wayne State University, Detroit. PHILIP V. LARONGE has been assistant at the Folklore Archive since 1977.

GEORGE LANKFORD, currently associate professor at Arkansas College, maintains an ongoing interest in native American studies and particularly in the archeology and ethnohistory of the Southeastern United States.

JAMES P. LEARY, a native of northern Wisconsin, teaches folklore at the University of Kentucky and writes about rural and ethnic sociabilities in the upper midwest.

LAWRENCE W. LEVINE is professor of history at the University of California, Berkeley.

WILLIAM E. LIGHTFOOT studies southern folk culture and teaches courses in folklore and literature at Appalachian State University, Boone, North Carolina.

JOSÉ E. LIMÓN is associate professor in the Department of Anthropology, the University of Texas, Austin.

ORMOND H. LOOMIS is with the Florida Folklife Program, where his reponsibilities include education and outreach, developing exhibits, and consulting with local museums throughout the state.

ANGELA MANIAK, who holds an M.A. in folklore, is currently designing educational programs for the banking industry in Chicago.

DAVID W. MARCELL, provost and vice-president for academic affairs and professor of American studies at Skidmore College, is author of *Progress and Pragmatism*; *American Studies: A Guide to Research Sources*; and numerous articles.

JOHN H. MCDOWELL, associate professor of folklore at Indiana University, is author of *Children's Riddling*, co-winner of the Chicago Folklore Prize.

ROGER MITCHELL is professor of anthropology and folklore at the University of Wisconsin–Eau Claire.

WILLARD B. MOORE, formerly curator of education at Conner Prairie Pioneer Settlement and subsequently a consultant to museum and folklife programs in various parts of the United States, makes his home in Minneapolis.

BRUCE E. NICKERSON, since receiving his doctorate from Indiana University in 1976, has been teaching folklore courses at Northeastern University and developing training programs for businesses and industries in the greater Boston area.

ELIZABETH PETERSON is now working on her dissertation at Indiana University. She has served as folklife program administrator at the Florida Folklife Program.

WILLIAM D. PIERSON is chairman of the Department of History, Fisk University.

RICHARD A. REUSS received his doctoral degree at Indiana University in 1971 and has special interests in American folklore and folksongs and history of folklore studies.

W. EDSON RICHMOND, professor of English, comparative literature, and folklore at Indiana University, has published primarily in the area of balladry, with special attention to Scandinavian materials. He was elected to the Norwegian Academy of Sciences in 1977.

LEONARD ROBERTS is director of the Appalachian Study Center, Pikeville College, Pikeville, Kentucky, and author of *In the Pine: Selected Kentucky Folksongs*.

ADRIENNE LANIER SEWARD, a Ph.D. candidate in folklore, is currently assistant professor in the English Department at Colorado College, Colorado Springs.

SHARON R. SHERMAN earned her doctorate in folklore at Indiana University and is now an assistant professor in the Department of English and the Folklore and Ethnic Studies Program at the University of Oregon.

RONALD R. SMITH is assistant professor of folklore (ethnomusicology) at Indiana University, and has served as acting director, Archives of Traditional Music.

SANDRA K. D. STAHL is assistant professor of folklore at Indiana University. She is currently finishing a book on the interpretation of personal narratives and has published numerous articles.

BEVERLEY J. STOELTJE teaches in the department of English, the University of Texas, Austin.

ROBERT C. TOLL resides in Oakland, California. He is author of *Blacking Up: The Minstrel Show in Nineteenth-Century America*.

JOHN MICHAEL VLACH is associate professor of American civilization and anthropology and director of the Folklife Program at George Washington University, and author of several books and articles.

ROBERT H. WALKER, professor of American civilization at George Washington University, is author of *The Poet and the Gilded Age, Life in the Age of Enterprise, The Reform Spirit in America*, and *American Society*.

GERALD WARSHAVER holds a Ph.D. in folklore from Indiana University and specializes in the theory and practice of urban folklore and modern American cultural history.

WILCOMB E. WASHBURN is director of the Office of American Studies at the Smithsonian Institution.

MARTA WEIGLE, a folklorist with major interests in the Hispanic Southwest, New Deal patronage of all arts in New Mexico, and women in/and folklore-mythology, is associate professor of anthropology and English at the University of New Mexico.

D. K. WILGUS, professor of English and Anglo-American folksong and chairman of the Folklore and Mythology Program, University of California, Los Angeles, has conducted fieldwork in Kentucky, Arkansas, California, and Ireland.

WILLIAM A. WILSON is director of the Folklore Program at Utah State University and editor of *Western Folklore*.

SALLY YERKOVICH is a program officer for the Division of Special Programs, National Endowment for the Humanities.

Index